D1232961

# THE
# LITERATURE
# OF
# ANCIENT
# EGYPT

# THE
# LITERATURE
# OF
# ANCIENT
# EGYPT

## AN ANTHOLOGY OF STORIES, INSTRUCTIONS, STELAE, AUTOBIOGRAPHIES, AND POETRY

### THIRD EDITION

EDITED AND WITH AN INTRODUCTION BY

## WILLIAM KELLY SIMPSON

WITH TRANSLATIONS BY
ROBERT K. RITNER,
WILLIAM KELLY SIMPSON,
VINCENT A. TOBIN,
AND EDWARD F. WENTE, JR.

YALE UNIVERSITY PRESS/NEW HAVEN & LONDON

Published with assistance from
the William K. and Marilyn M. Simpson
Endowment for Egyptology at
Yale University.

Copyright © 2003 by Yale University.
All rights reserved.
This book may not be reproduced, in whole or in part, including illustrations, in any form
(beyond that copying permitted by Sections 107 and 108 of the U.S. Copyright Law and except
by reviewers for the public press), without written permission from the publishers.

Designed by Mary Valencia.
Set in Simoncini Garamond and Michelangelo
types by Keystone Typesetting, Inc.
Printed in the United States of America

ISBN: 978-0-300-09920-1

A catalogue record for this book is available from the
Library of Congress and the British Library.

The paper in this book meets the guidelines for permanence and durability of the Committee
on Production Guidelines for Book Longevity of the Council on Library Resources.

10   9   8   7   6   5

*To the memory of sages of our own time*
*who have made outstanding contributions*
*to the study and appreciation of the literature of ancient Egypt*

RAYMOND O. FAULKNER (1894–1982)

WOLFGANG HELCK (1914–1993)

GEORGES POSENER (1906–1988)

# CONTENTS

CONTENTS

# CONTENTS

# CONTENTS

*Illustrations follow page XIV*

# ABBREVIATIONS

ÄAbh    Ägyptologische Abhandlungen
ADAW    Abhandlungen der Deutschen Akademie der Wissenschaften
        zu Berlin, Philosophisch-historische Klasse
AEL     Miriam Lichtheim, *Ancient Egyptian Literature,* vol. 1: *The*
        *Old and Middle Kingdoms;* vol. 2: *The New Kingdom;* vol. 3:
        *The Late Period,* Berkeley, 1973, 1976, 1980
ÄF      *Ägyptologische Forschungen*
ANET    J. B. Pritchard, ed., *Ancient Near Eastern Texts,* 3d ed.,
        Princeton, 1969
ÄUAT    Ägypten und Altes Testament
BAR     James Henry Breasted, *Ancient Records of Egypt,* 5 vols., repr.
        London, 1988
BdE     Bibliothèque d'Etude IFAOC
BEHE    *Bibliothèque de l'Ecole des Hautes Etudes,* IVe section, Sci-
        ences historiques et philologiques
BES     *Bulletin Egyptological Seminar*
BIE     *Bulletin de l'Institut d'Egypte*
BIFAO   *Bulletin de l'Institut Français d'Archéologie Orientale*
BiOr    *Bibliotheca Orientalis*
BSEG    *Bulletin de la Société d'Egyptologie Genève*
BSFE    *Bulletin de la Société Française d'Egyptologie*

| | |
|---|---|
| CD | C. E. Crum, *A Coptic Dictionary,* Oxford, 1939 |
| CdE | *Chronique d'Égypte* |
| CNI | Carsten Niebuhr Institute, Copenhagen |
| CRIPEL | *Cahier de Recherches de l'Institut de Papyrologie et d'Egyptologie de Lille* |
| DAIK | *Deutsches Archäologisches Institut Kairo* |
| DE | *Discussions in Egyptology* |
| DFIFAO | *Documents de Fouilles de IFAO* |
| GM | *Göttinger Miszellen* |
| HÄB | Hildesheimer Ägyptologischge Beiträge |
| IFAO | l'Institut Français d'Archéologie Orientale, Cairo |
| JAOS | *Journal of the American Oriental Society* |
| JARCE | *Journal of the American Research Center in Egypt* |
| JEA | *Journal of Egyptian Archaeology* |
| JEOL | *Jaarbericht Ex Oriente Lux* |
| JESHO | *Journal of the Economic and Social History of the Orient* |
| JNES | *Journal of Near Eastern Studies* |
| JSSEA | *Journal of the Society of the Study of Egyptian Antiquities* |
| LÄ | W. Helck et al., eds., *Lexikon der Ägyptologie* I–VII, Wiesbaden, 1972–92 |
| MÄS | Münchner Ägyptologische Studien |
| MÄU | *Münchner Ägyptologische Untersuchungen* |
| MIFAO | *Mémoirs IFAO* |
| MIO | *Mitteilungen des Instituts für Orientforschung* |
| MDAIK | *Mitteilungen des Deutschen Archäologischen Institut, Abteilung Kairo* |
| OBO | Orbis Biblicus et Orientalis |
| OLA | Orientalia Lovaniensia Analecta |
| OLZ | *Orientalistische Literaturzeitung* |
| OMRO | *Oudheidkundige Mededelingen uit het Rijksmuseum van Oudheden te Leiden* |
| Or | *Orientalia* |
| RdE | *Revue d'Egyptologie* |
| RevEq | *Revue Egyptologique* |
| RSO | *Rivista degli Studi Orientali* |
| SAGA | *Studien zur Archäologie und Geschichte Altägyptens* |
| SÄK | *Studien zur Altägyptischen Kultur* |
| SAOC | Studies in Ancient Oriental Civilizations |

| | |
|---|---|
| *SBAW* | *Sitzungsberichte der Bayerischen Akademie der Wissenschaft, Phil.-hist. Abt.,* Munich |
| SSEA | Society for the Study of Egyptian Antiquities |
| *StudAeg* | *Studia Aegyptiaca,* Budapest |
| TUAT | Otto Kaiser, ed., Texte aus dem Umwelt des Alten Testament |
| *UGAÄ* | *Untersuchungen zur Geschichte und Altertumskunde Ägyptens* |
| Urk. | K. Sethe, ed., Urkunden |
| *VA* | *Varia Aegyptiaca,* San Antonio |
| *Wb.* | A. Erman and H. Grapow, *Wörterbuch der Aegyptischen Sprache* |
| *WdO* | *Die Welt des Orients* |
| *WZKM* | *Wiener Zeitschrift für die Kunde des Morgenlandes,* Vienna |
| *ZÄS* | *Zeitschrift für ägyptische Sprache und Altertumskunde* |
| *ZDMG* | *Zeitschrift der Deutschen Morgenländischen Gesellschaft* |
| *ZPE* | *Zeitschrift für Papyrologie und Epigraphik* |

1. Papyrus Chester Beatty I before unrolling. Courtesy Chester Beatty Library, Dublin.

2. Prince Khuenre, eldest son of King Mycerinus, as a scribe. Giza, Dynasty 4.
   Museum Expedition. Courtesy Museum of Fine Arts, Boston. Museum No. 13.3140.

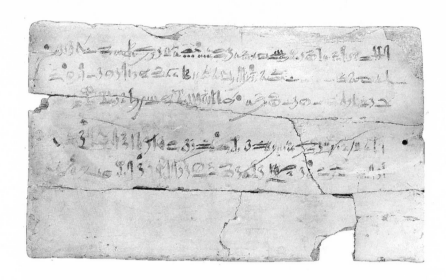

snnw.i ꜥnḫw psš.i m rmṯ, irw n.i ḳmdt n sḏm.tw.f
bw ꜥꜣ n [ꜥḥꜣ] n mꜣn.tw.f, ist ꜥḥꜣ tw ḥr mtwn, smḫ sf, nn
km n bw nfr n ḫm rḫ.f;r-sꜣ msyt pw, ḫꜣw ḫpr

sꜣḳ.tw r smdt rf tmt ḫpr, tmmt rdi ib m-sꜣ ḥr(y)t.s m tk[n]
im.sn [m] wꜥw.k, m mh ib.k m sn, m rḫ ḫnms, m sḫpr n.k ꜥḳ[w]

Oh you living images of me, my heirs among men, make for me a funeral oration which has
not been heard (before), a great deed of [battle] which has not been seen, for men fight in
the arena and the past is forgotten; goodness cannot profit one who does not know him
whom he should know. It was after supper and night had fallen . . . (Corresponding to *Pap.
Millingen* I, 9–11)

Be on your guard against all who are subordinate to you when there occurs something to
whose terrors no thought has been given; do not approach them [in] your solitude, trust no
brother, know no friend, make no intimates. (Corresponding to *Pap. Millingen I,* 3–5)

3. Reverse of wooden writing board, with parts of The Teaching of King Amenemhet I,
   transcription into hieroglyphic, transliteration in standard form, and translation.
   Courtesy The Brooklyn Museum, Gift of the Estate of Charles Edwin Wilbour.
   Museum No. 16.119.

4. Detail of scribe with papyrus roll, pen, and shell for black and red ink. From the tomb chapel of Nofer at Giza. Harvard University—Museum of Fine Arts Expedition. Courtesy Museum of Fine Arts, Boston. Museum No. 07.1002.

5. Front and back of a scribe's palette, Dynasty 13, with reed pens, inkwell, ink, and miscellaneous notations. Courtesy Museum of Fine Arts, Boston. Hay Collection, Gift of C. Granville Way. Museum No. 72.4295. Length 38 cm., width 5 cm.

6. Relief from a tomb wall at Sakkara, Dynasty 19, with figures of famous men of the
past. These include the sages Iyemhotep, Kaires, Khety, and Khakheperre-sonbe.
Photographs courtesy M. Z. Ghoneim and Henry G. Fischer.

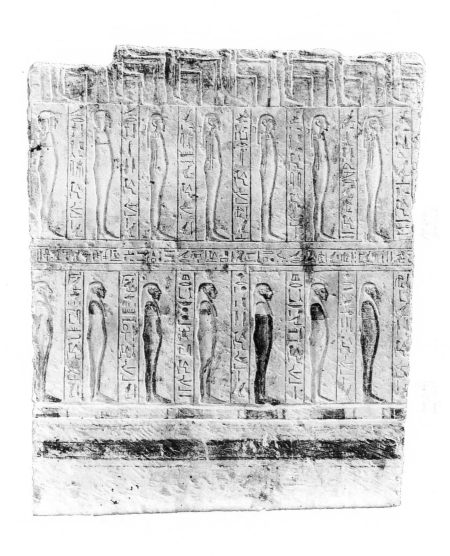

# INTRODUCTION

As for those learned scribes from the time of the successors of the gods, those who foretold the future, it has come to pass that their names will endure forever, although they are gone, having completed their lives, and although their offspring are forgotten. . . . They did not know how to leave heirs who were children who could pronounce their names, but they made heirs for themselves of the writings and books of instruction which they made. . . . Their mortuary servants are gone, and their memorial tablets covered with dust, their chapels forgotten. But their names are pronounced because of these books of theirs which they made. . . . More profitable is a book than a graven tablet, than a chapel-wall [?] well built. . . . A man has perished, and his corpse has become dust. . . . But writings cause him to be remembered in the mouth of the story-teller.

Is there any here like Hardedef? Is there another like Iyemhotep? There have been none among our kindred like Neferty and Khety, that foremost among them. I recall to you the names of Ptahemdjehuty and Khakheperre-sonbe. Is there another like Ptahhotep or Kaires?

Those sages who foretold the future, that which came forth from their mouths took place. . . . They are gone, their names are forgotten. But writings cause them to be remembered.

From *Papyrus Chester Beatty IV,* translated after A. H. Gardiner

1

We are reasonably familiar with the art and architecture of ancient Egypt, with the pyramids and sphinx, the great temples of Karnak, Luxor, Edfu, Dendereh, and the wall reliefs and paintings in the chapels of the mastabas of the Old Kingdom and in the tombs of the nobles of the New Kingdom at Thebes. The tomb equipment of Tutankhamun and the head of Queen Nefertiti are well known and can be appreciated through color photography. The visual aspects of Egypt of the pharaohs have now become part of our heritage.

Yet its no less remarkable literature is still relatively unknown except to specialists. The culture of Egypt was not expressed in epics or drama, nor did it produce authors to rival Homer or Virgil, Aeschylus, Sophocles, and Euripides, thinkers to match Plato and Aristotle, or lyric poets on a level with Sappho and Catullus. Yet the minute fraction of its literature which has survived deserves a wider audience, and the sages cited in the quotation above should not be entirely unfamiliar. The lack of easily available translations in English is partly responsible.[1]

When the Egyptian language was gradually deciphered in the first decades of the nineteenth century, the texts proved to be of an extremely heterogeneous nature. They included ledgers, inventories, payrolls, distribution lists of foodstuffs and equipment, and letters—all the usual components of a busy economy. Not unexpectedly, many of the inscriptions belong to the category of religious texts: hymns, prayers, rituals, and guidebooks to the underworld and the hereafter. On the temple walls are illustrated manuals of temple service and illustrated chronicles of the kings: their battles, conquests, and lists of tribute. In the tomb chapels of the officials are formulas relating to the provisioning of the funerary cult, a sort of perpetual care, and texts of a biographical nature relating their careers and describing in often stereotyped phrases their ethical probity. The texts from ancient Egypt include matters as diverse as the accounts of lawsuits, trials of thieves, medical and veterinary manuals, and magical spells against scorpions and other creatures.

Within the mass of material studied by several generations of Egyptologists there has emerged a series of compositions which can unquestionably be regarded as literature in our sense. The closest parallels are to be found in other parts of the ancient Near East in the literatures of Mesopotamia and the people of the Old Testament.[2] These compositions are narratives and tales, teachings (instructions), and poetry. Their identification, study, and analysis is a scholarly endeavor in its early stages, yet progressing rapidly; scholars of many countries are constantly contributing the results of their studies.[3]

For some of these texts a single, complete papyrus has survived.[4] For others a few poor copies can be eked out with the help of numerous fragmentary excerpts on potsherds and limestone flakes.[5] Still others lack the beginning or end, or both.[6] Not a few compositions are known by title or a few sentences only, and there remains the slim chance that luck or excavation will produce more of the text.

The compositions in the anthology at hand have been selected on the basis of literary merit or pretensions thereto, with a few additions. The selections from the pyramid texts, the hymns in honor of Senwosret III, the selections from the coffin texts, the Book of the Dead, and the great hymn to the sun of Akhenaten belong strictly speaking to the religious literature. Similarly, the poem of victory in the stela of Thutmose III has parallels in the historical texts and is not literary in itself. But the literary merit and interest of these selections warrant their inclusion. There are other literary texts which we would have wished to include and which may be added in future editions, notably The Plaintiff of Memphis (the tale of King Neferkare and the General), The Instruction of Ani, and The Satirical Letter of Hori to Amenemope, as well as several fragmentary compositions of various periods. Yet R. O. Faulkner, one of the first collaborators in this enterprise, remarked that Erman in his anthology cast his net far too wide.

The compositions have been arranged mainly by type rather than by date. The first section, the narratives and tales of the Middle Kingdom, consists of King Cheops and the Magicians, The Tale of the Eloquent Peasant, The Shipwrecked Sailor, and The Story of Sinuhe. These were probably set down in Dynasty 12 (1991–1786 B.C.), although the first relates events of the Old Kingdom and the foundation of Dynasty 5 (2494–2345 B.C.), and The Eloquent Peasant is set in Dynasty 9/10.

The second section comprises the narratives of the New Kingdom, Dynasties 18–20 (1554–1085 B.C.), which are known as the Late Egyptian Stories. This section is the work of Wente and incorporates many new ideas on his part. The tales included are The Quarrel of Apophis and Seknenre, The Capture of Joppa, The Tale of the Doomed Prince, The Tale of the Two Brothers, The Contendings of Horus and Seth, The Blinding of Truth by Falsehood, Astarte and the Insatiable Sea, A Ghost Story, and The Report of Wenamon. The last is a literary report relating events in the first years of Dynasty 21.

The third section, comprising wisdom or instruction literature and the lamentations and dialogues, encompasses a wide chronological range. The Maxims of Ptahhopet, The Teaching for King Merikare, The Teaching of King Amenemhet I to His Son Senwosret, The Man Who Was Weary of Life, The Admonitions of an Egyptian Sage, and The Prophecies of Neferty are presented in translations with notes by Tobin. The Teaching of Hardedef, The Teaching for Kagemni, The Lamentations of Khakheperre-sonbe, The Loyalist Instruction, and The Instruction of Amenemope, as well as The Instruction of a Man for His Son and The Instruction of Amennakhte, are the work of Simpson.

In the fourth section are selected texts from the religious literature translated by all four collaborators.

The fifth section includes the Cycle of Songs in Honor of Senwosret III, translated by Simpson, and the Love Poems and Song of the Harper, now translated by Tobin.

The sixth section includes several royal stelae translated by all four collaborators, only one of which was included in the earlier editions.

The seventh section is again a new inclusion consistings of "autobiographies" from stelae and tombs, since they exhibit marked literary features. The translators are Tobin and Simpson.

The eighth section includes the two texts added to the revised edition of 1973, again in translations by Simpson.

The ninth section is a most welcome addition on texts in demotic, translated by Ritner.

Of the genres included, the most comprehensive is *narrative*. The term includes a wide variety of elements, purposes, and aspects. The Sailor and Sinuhe are ostensibly straightforward tales. Both have been explained, however, as "lehrhafte Stücke," instructions or teachings in the guise of narratives, with the protagonists, the unnamed sailor and Sinuhe, as models for the man of the times, expressions of the cultural virtues of self-reliance, adaptation to new circumstances, and love of home.[7]

It is perhaps significant that there is no Egyptian term for narrative or story as such. A term *mdt nfrt* is usually rendered as *belles lettres* or fine speech. Otherwise, the terms for writings or sayings are employed. King Cheops and the Magicians is cast in the form of a cycle of stories, the recitation before the king of the marvels performed by the great magicians of the past, yet it concludes with a politically oriented folk tale of the birth of the first three kings of Dynasty 5. The narrative of the Peasant is a framework for an exhibition of eloquent speech in which injustice is denounced. In the Late Egyptian Stories the protagonists are frequently the gods, and the worlds of myth, religion, and folk history mingle.

The one genre for which the Egyptians had a specific term, *sboyet,* is the *instruction* or *teaching.* In almost every case these compositions begin with the heading, "the instruction which X made for Y." The practicality and pragmaticism of the advice given by Ptahhotep and the author of the Instruction for Kagemni are frequently contrasted with the piety expressed in the later Instruction of Amenemope. The two earlier instructions are set in the form of advice given to a son by the vizier. The two royal instructions, Merikare and Amenemhet, are of a different nature; they are political pieces cast in instruction form.

A third genre is *lamentation* and *dialogue,* of which The Lamentations of Khakheperre-sonbe, The Admonitions, and The Man Weary of Life are the main compositions. The Prophecies of Neferty was a popular text, to judge by the frequent Ramesside copies. Of similar nature are the nine speeches of the Peasant, although we have classified it under narrative.

As a last category one can isolate the *love poems* and *banquet songs.* The love songs have survived only from the New Kingdom, but it is likely that the lyric was represented in the classical literature also. There are traces of songs in the tomb reliefs of the Old Kingdom.

Recent study has singled out two not mutually exclusive aspects for special attention: a *literature of propaganda* and a *literature of pessimism.*[8] Under the former are grouped those compositions which have in common the theme of extolling the king or royal dynasty. The Loyalist Instruction is a prime example, and the theme is also developed in its most unadulterated form in the cycle of Hymns in Honor of Senwosret III. Three compositions relate to the beginning of Dynasty 12. The Prophecies of Neferty, although ostensibly set in Dynasty 4, foretell the dire straits of the land and the restoration of Egypt under a savior king, Amenemhet I. The same king's Instruction is an apologia for his life and a manifesto in favor of his son Senwosret I. The third composition is Sinuhe, a narrative beginning with the death of Amenemhet I and presenting a highly favorable view of his successor, Senwosret I. All three compositions were recopied extensively in Ramesside times.

The *literature of pessimism* comprises those compositions in which the land is described in great disorder, such as the just cited Prophecies of Neferty, the Lamentations, and the Admonitions. Here the theme is associated with the ideas of social and religious change. On a personal, psychological level The Man Who Was Weary of Life belongs to this category; it expresses most poignantly the man's distress and his necessary reorientation of values:

> To whom can I speak today?
> Brothers are evil,
> And the friends of today unlovable.
>
> To whom can I speak today?
> Gentleness has perished,
> And the violent man has come down on everyone.

Portions of the royal instructions and The Tale of the Eloquent Peasant reflect elements of the same pessimistic background.

With a few exceptions the texts in this anthology are translated from manuscripts written in hieratic in ink on papyrus.[9] Hieratic is the cursive form of hieroglyphic and bears roughly the same relation to the latter as our handwriting does to the type set in books or typewritten material. Texts are written horizontally from right to left or vertically, with the first column on the right. Papyrus is a vegetable precursor of paper which was rolled for safekeeping; over a period of years it becomes extremely brittle and is always subject to insect damage. Hence many of these texts have large sections missing as well as frequent damages within an otherwise well-preserved sheet. Use was also made of writing boards, wooden tablets coated with stucco to receive the ink. A very common writing material is the limestone flake (ostracon) or potsherd, and extensive texts written in ink have survived on these unlikely materials. Black ink and a reed pen were the scribe's mainstays; he also used red ink for contrast in headings, corrections, and account totals.

The problems of translation are considerable. The older stages of the language lack conjunctions and specific indications of tense. A sentence can be translated in several ways:

When the sun rises, the peasant ploughs his field.
The sun rises when the peasant ploughs his field.

The past, present, or future tense can be used in either part of this example, and the word "if" substituted for "when." Common sense indicates the first sentence of the pair is the correct translation. It is sometimes difficult to determine if a dependent clause between two main clauses belongs to the first or second main clause. Contrast:

> When the sun rose, the peasant ploughed his field. He saw a man approach . . .
> The sun rose. Now when the peasant ploughed his field, he saw a man approach. . . .

In poetry it is not always clear if a line belongs to the end of one stanza or the beginning of the next. The exact meaning of many words is still unknown and may remain so. Frequently, a translation is little more than an informed guess. In the Ramesside period certain texts were so carelessly copied that one has the distinct impression that the respective scribes did not understand them. In such cases it is hopeless for the modern scholar to be certain of the meaning or to make much sense out of the words and phrases garbled by the ancient copiest.

There is prose, poetry, and symmetrically structured speech, although the dividing line is not necessarily sharp.[10] A few texts are written in short lines, as is modern poetry. Yet the same composition may be found written continuously.[11] The latter is the usual practice. Only a few of the texts set as poetry in this volume were written in short lines in the manuscript. As studies in Egyptian metrics have progressed, one increasingly finds translations rendered in verse instead of prose. In New Kingdom texts large dots above the line serve as a sort of punctuation, and these help in ascertaining divisions. Red ink was used for headings, a device equivalent to our paragraphing. Some translators set these rubrics in small capitals. In our volume we have not used them except as a guide for paragraphing.

The translators have agreed that the use of archaic diction (e.g. *thou, thee, ye, shouldst, saith*) is artificial and distracting. They are indebted to several generations of scholars who have studied and translated the texts into English, French, and German in monographs, journal articles, and brief communications on specific words, sentences, or passages. For each composition the reader is referred to sources for bibliographies; the most recent articles are usually cited.

The volume is addressed to the general reader, the student, and the specialist. The student and specialist are advised, however, that free translations are often used for passages which are difficult or offer the possibility of alternative translations. The translation does not always reflect the final judgment of the translator; he cannot have consistently chosen the right alternative. In journal articles or monographs it is not uncommon to find a sentence discussed at length, with an equal number of pages devoted to the same passage several years later by another scholar. The translator of a text of some length for the general reader cannot burden it with extensive notes and investigations.

The few conventions used require identification. Brackets are employed for text which has been restored when there is a gap in the manuscript, and sometimes half brackets when the word or phrase is uncertain or imperfectly understood; three dots are used when the gap cannot be filled with any degree of certainty and represent an omission of indeterminate length: "Then the [wife] of the man ⌈wept⌉, and she said, [...]." Parentheses are used for phrases not in the original added as an aid to the reader; angle brackets are used for words which the copyist erroneously omitted: "His henchmen returned (to the house), and he went ⟨into⟩ the room." For convenience in reference the line or column numbers for many of the texts are provided in the margin. When the passage is set in prose a slash is used to indicate the change of line: "I went down to the shore / in the vicinity of the ship." The tag, "may he live, prosper, and be in health," frequently follows a royal name; following the usual custom, it is usually rendered in our texts as "l.p.h."

A word should be said on the language of the translations. In many cases the translator attempts to render an Egyptian sentence in such a way that its characteristics are retained in English. This often makes for a rather artificial diction, a kind of language not represented in everyday speech. Through this device the translator can indicate that the passive voice is used instead of the active, and so forth: "He was ferried across the river" is not as smooth a translation as "They ferried him across the river," yet the former may render the original more closely. Similarly, a passage is translated thus: "Now after many days had elapsed upon this and while they were (engaged) in their daily practice, presently the boy passed by them." The sentence is equivalent to "After some time, while they were busy with their daily affairs, the boy happened to come upon them." In the second version an attempt has been made to render the sense, in the first the Egyptian sequence of words. Another example is, "Is it while the son of the male is still living that the cattle are to be given to the stranger?" A smoother translation would be: "Is it customary to give the cattle to the stranger while the son of the man of the house is still alive?" The original, however, employs a verbal form which places emphasis on the clause, "while the son of the male is still living." The first of the two alternatives brings out this emphasis more closely. Our translations attempt to strike a compromise between these two poles. To opt consistently for the smoother translation results in a paraphrase and leads to an interpretative retelling. Yet to retain the artificiality of Egyptian phrasing in English makes for a clumsiness foreign to the Egyptian text itself.

A greatly expanded bibliography is included for those whom we hope to have interested in the study and appreciation of ancient Egyptian literature.

## NOTES

1. For many years the standard anthology for English readers has been A. Erman, *The Literature of the Ancient Egyptians,* trans. A. M. Blackman (London, 1927), a translation of Erman's *Die Literatur der Aegypter* (1923). A paperback reprint appeared under the title, A. Erman, *The Ancient Egyptians: A Sourcebook of Their Writings,* trans. A. M. Blackman, with new introduction by W. K. Simpson (New York, 1966). There is also Gaston Maspero, *Popular Stories of Ancient Egypt,* trans. A. S. Johns (New York, 1915, rpt. 1967) and Joseph Kaster, *Wings of the Falcon* (New York, 1968). The most reliable translations are those selections translated by John A. Wilson in James B. Pritchard, ed., *Ancient Near Eastern Texts Relating to the Old Testament* (Princeton, 1950 and subsequent editions), hereafter cited as *ANET.* Other than these anthologies and, of course, monographs and journal articles on individual texts, the reader has had to rely on the anthologies in French, German, and Italian. In many ways the most useful is G. Lefebvre, *Romans et contes égyptiens de l'époque pharaonique* (Paris, 1949). This includes the narratives but omits the instructions and poetry; Lefebvre's notes and introductions are extremely useful. Next there is E. Brunner-Traut, *Altägyptische Märchen* (Düsseldorf, 1963 and later editions). This includes all the narratives, a reconstruction of myths and fables, and also the demotic and Christian narratives; it omits the instructions and poetry. There is E. Bresciani, *Letteratura e poesia dell'antico Egitto* (Turin, 1969).

   After the first edition of the present work, there appeared the excellent three-volume anthology by Miriam Lichtheim, *Ancient Egyptian Literature:* vol. 1: *The Old and Middle Kingdoms;* vol. 2: *The New Kingdom;* and vol. 3: *The Late Period* (Berkeley, 1973, 1976, 1980); see also "Some Corrections to My Ancient Egyptian Literature I–III," *GM* 41 (1980): 67–74. Other anthologies of note include R. B. Parkinson, *Voices from Ancient Egypt: An Anthology of Middle Kingdom Writings* (London, 1991) and John L. Foster, *Echoes of Egyptian Voices: An Anthology of Ancient Egyptian Poetry* (Norman, Okla., 1992); K. A. Kitchen, *Poetry of Ancient Egypt* (Jonsered, 1999); and R. B. Parkinson, *The Tale of Sinuhe and Other Ancient Egyptian Poems* (Oxford, 1997).

2. See in particular the texts in Pritchard, *Ancient Near Eastern Texts;* and T. Eric Peet, *A Comparative Study of the Literatures of Egypt, Palestine, and Mesopotamia* (London, 1931).

3. Antonio Loprieno, ed., *Ancient Egyptian Literature: History and Forms* (Leiden, 1996), 39–58.

4. For example, The Shipwrecked Sailor, The Tale of Two Brothers, and The Contendings of Horus and Seth.

5. The Teaching of King Amenemhet I and The Prophecies of Neferty.

6. The beginning is missing for King Cheops and the Magicians, The Teaching for the Vizier Kagemni, and The Man Who Was Weary of Life. The end is missing for The Tale of the Doomed Prince and The Report of Wenamon.

7. E. Otto, in *ZÄS* 93 (1966): 100–11.

8. The pioneering and seminal work on literature as propaganda is Georges Posener, *Littérature et politique dans l'Egypte de la XIIᵉ dynastie* (Paris, 1956). Posener began a systematic catalogue of Egyptian literary compositions, even the fragmentary pieces, in a series of articles in *RdE* 6 (1951): 27–48; 7 (1950): 71–84; 8 (1951): 171–89; 9 (1952): 109–20; 10 (1955): 61–72; 11 (1957): 119–37; and 12 (1960): 75–82. An introduction to Egyptian literature (without translations) is Altenmüller et al., *Literatur* (zweite, verbesserte und erweiterte Auflage), in the series *Handbuch der Orientalistik* (ed. B. Spuler), Erste Abteilung: *Der Nahe und Mittlere Osten* (ed. B. Spuler), Erster Band *Ägyptologie* (Leiden, 1970). This comprises sections on many types of text not included in the present volume: religious and ritual texts, magical texts, medical, mathematical, and astronomical literature, historical annals, biographies. It presents fuller discussions and references than we have attempted in head notes to our texts. See also G. Posener, "Literature," in J. R. Harris, *The Legacy of Egypt,* 2nd ed. (Oxford, 1971), 220–56.

9. A lucid, informative, and highly interesting account of the subject is provided by Jaroslav Černý, *Paper and Books in Ancient Egypt* (London, 1952).

10. See general bibliography Burkard 1983; Fecht 1963, 1964, 1965, 1993; Lichtheim 1971; and Schenkel 1972; and Sinuhe bibliography Foster 1980, 1993.

11. See Amenemope bibliography Petersen 1966. Hardedef, p. 340.
The latter text with the various copies is studied by Wolfgang Helck, *Die Lehre des Djedefhor und Die Lehre eines Vaters an seinen Son* (Wiesbaden, 1984).

# I

## NARRATIVES AND TALES
## OF
## MIDDLE EGYPTIAN LITERATURE

# KING CHEOPS AND THE MAGICIANS

This cycle of stories about the marvels performed by the lector priests is cast in the form of a series of tales told at the court of Cheops by his sons. The name of the first son is missing together with most of his story. The second son, Khaefre, later became king and is known as the builder of the Second Pyramid at Giza. The third son, Bauefre, is known from other sources; a later text indicates that he may have also become king for a short time. The fourth son, Hardedef, is known as one of the sages of the past, and part of his instruction has survived.

The text derives from a single manuscript of which the beginning and conclusion are missing. The papyrus was inscribed in the Hyksos period before Dynasty 18, but the composition appears to belong to Dynasty 12; the events described are set in the Old Kingdom.

The last story is a prophecy of the end of Cheops's line through the birth of the three kings who founded Dynasty 5. The story of their actual birth is presented as a sort of annex. Elements of the miraculous royal birth are represented in later Egyptian and Near Eastern literature and even are reflected in the biblical accounts. The device of providing stories for the diversion of the king is also represented in The Prophecies of Neferty, The Admonitions, and The Eloquent Peasant, as well as several later compositions. The real substance of the composition is certainly the prophecy of the birth of the kings, and the other tales merely lead up to it. For bibliography and commentary on King

*Cheops and the Magicians (Papyrus Westcar), see Lefebvre,* Romans et contes, *70–90, and Erman,* The Ancient Egyptians *(New York, 1966), xxiv, lxviii–lxix, 36–49. The standard hieroglyphic text with photographs of the papyrus is now A. M. Blackman (ed. W. V. Davies),* The Story of King Kheops and the Magicians Transcribed from Papyrus Westcar *(Berlin Papyrus 3033) (Reading, Berks, 1988).*

W.K.S.

## [FIRST TALE: END OF THE MARVEL IN THE TIME OF KING DJOSER]

1,12      [... His Majesty] / the King of Upper and Lower Egypt, Khufu (Cheops), the vindicated, [said: Let there be given...], one hundred jugs of beer, an ox, [... to] the King of Upper and Lower Egypt, Djoser, the vindicated, [and may there be given...], a haunch of beef, [... to the lector priest...]. [For I] have seen an example of his wisdom. And [they] did according to [everything which His Majesty] commanded.[1]

## [SECOND TALE: THE MARVEL WHICH HAPPENED IN THE TIME OF KING NEBKA]

     The king's son Khaefre (Chephren) arose [to speak, and he said: I should like to relate to Your Majesty] another marvel, one which happened in the time of [your] father, [the King of Upper and Lower Egypt] Nebka,
1,20      the vindicated, as he proceeded to the temple of [Ptah,/Lord of] Ankh-towy.[2]

     Now when his Majesty went to [...], His Majesty made an [appeal? ... to] the chief [lector] Webaoner [...]. But the wife of Webaoner [... was
2,1      enamored / of a townsman. She caused to be brought(?)] to him a chest filled with garments [...], and he returned with [the] housemaid.[3] [Now

1. This is the conclusion of a tale of which the entire narrative section is missing. It concerns a marvel performed by a lector priest in the reign of Djoser, the builder of the Step Pyramid. Perhaps the lector was Iyemhotep himself. There is no way of knowing how much of the composition was lost at the beginning.
2. Nebka of Dynasty 3 is a predecessor of Cheops. Ankh-towy is a designation for Memphis or a part thereof.
3. Evidently the adulterous wife makes a present to the goodlooking townsman and he returns to thank her.

several] days [passed by ...]. There was a pavilion[4] [on the estate] of Webaoner. The townsman [said to the wife of Weba]oner: Is there a pavilion [...]? [Come], let us pass time in it. [Then said the wife of] Webaoner to the caretaker who [cared for the estate]: Let the pavilion be prepared, 
2,10     [...] and she spent the day there drinking / [with the townsman ... and] ʳrestingꜝ [...]. Now after [evening came ...] he [went to the Lake] and [the] housemaid [...].

[When day broke, and the second day came, the caretaker informed 
2,20     Webaoner of] this matter [...]. He gave it to his / [...] of the water. Then [he(?)] lit [a fire]. [Then Webaoner said]: Bring me [... my chest] of ebony and electrum [and he made ... and he opened ... and made] a crocodile [of wax ...] seven [fingers long ...]. He read out his [magic words 
3,1     saying ...]: [If anyone] comes [to bathe in my lake ...] the townsman. / Then he gave it to [the caretaker], and he said to him: After the townsman goes down to the pool, as is his daily fashion, you shall cast [the] crocodile after him. The [caretaker] went forth and he took the crocodile of wax with him.

Now the [wife] of Webaoner sent to the caretaker who was in charge of the [garden] saying: Let the pavilion which is in the garden be prepared for I have come to stay in it. The pavilion was prepared [with] every good thing. 
3,10     [They] (the wife and the maid servant?) went forth, and they (spent) / a pleasant day with the townsman. After night fell, the townsman returned as was his daily fashion, and the caretaker threw the crocodile of wax behind him into the water. [At once it grew] into a crocodile of seven cubits,[5] and it took hold of the townsman [...].

Webaoner tarried with His Majesty the King of Upper and Lower Egypt, Nebka, the vindicated, for seven days, all the while the townsman was in the [lake without] breathing. After the seventh day came, His Majesty the King of Upper and Lower Egypt, Nebka, the vindicated came forth, and the chief lector Webaoner placed himself in ⟨his⟩ presence and 
3,20     [he] said [to him]: May Your Majesty / come and see the marvel which has taken place in Your Majesty's time. [His Majesty went with] Webaoner. [He called out to the] crocodile and said: Bring back [the] townsman. [The crocodile] came [out of the water ...]. Then the [chief] lector [Webaoner] said: [Open up]! And he [opened up]. Then he placed [...]. Said

4. A sort of garden pavilion.
5. The cubit measures 20.6 inches, hence the crocodile was now about 12 feet long.

4,1    His Majesty the King of Upper and Lower Egypt, / Nebka, the vindicated: this crocodile is indeed ˹fearful˺! But Webaoner bent down, and he caught it and it became a crocodile of wax in his hand. The chief lector Webaoner told His Majesty the King of Upper and Lower Egypt, Nebka, the vindicated, about this affair which the townsman had in his house with his wife. And his Majesty said to the crocodile: Take what belongs to you! The crocodile then went down to the [depths] of the lake, and no one knew the place where he went with him.

His [Majesty the King of Upper] and Lower Egypt, Nebka, the vindicated, had the wife of Webaoner taken to a plot north of the capital, and he
4,10   set / fire to her [and threw her in] the river.

˹Such˺ is a marvel which happened [in] the time of your father, the King of Upper and Lower Egypt, Nebka, one which the chief lector Webaoner performed. His Majesty the King of Upper and Lower Egypt, Khufu, the vindicated, said: Let there be offered to the King of Upper and Lower Egypt, Nebka, the vindicated, one thousand loaves of bread, one hundred jugs of beer, an ox, and two cones of incense, and let there be offered to the chief lector Webaoner one large cake, one jug of beer, one joint of meat, and one cone of incense, for I have [seen] an example of his skill. And it was done according to all His Majesty commanded.

[THIRD TALE: THE MARVEL WHICH HAPPENED IN THE REIGN OF KING SNEFRU]

Bauefre arose to speak, and he said: Let me have [Your] Majesty hear a marvel which took place in the time of your (own) father King Snefru, the vindicated, [one] which the chief lector / Djadjaemonkh [made] and
4,20   which had not taken place [before] ... [Now His Majesty had searched out all the chambers] of the palace, l.p.h., to seek for him [some diversion ... and he said]: Hasten, bring me the chief [lector] and scribe, [... Djadjaem]onkh! He was brought to him immediately. [His Majesty] said to him: [I
5,1    have looked through the chambers of the] palace, l.p.h., to seek for myself / some refreshing matter, but I cannot find any. Djadjaemonkh said to him: Let Your Majesty proceed to the lake of the palace, l.p.h., and equip for yourself a boat with all the beauties who are in your palace chamber. The heart of Your Majesty shall be refreshed at the sight of their rowing as they row up and down. You can see the beautiful fish pools of your lake, and you can see its beautiful fields around it. Your heart will be refreshed at this.

⟨His Majesty said⟩: I will indeed fit out my rowing excursion. Let there be brought to me twenty oars made of ebony, fitted with gold, with the butts of sandalwood(?) fitted with electrum. Let there be brought to me twenty

5,10 women, / the most beautiful in form, with ⌜firm⌝ breasts, with hair well braided, not yet having opened up to give birth. Let there be brought to me twenty nets, and let these nets be given to these women when they have taken off their clothes. Then it was done according to all that His Majesty commanded, and they rowed up and down. The heart of His Majesty was pleased at the sight of their rowing.[6]

Now one of the strokes combed her tresses, and a fish-shaped charm of new turquoise fell in the water. She became silent and did not row, and her side of the boat became silent and did not row. His Majesty said: Are you

5,20 not rowing? And they said: Our stroke / is silent and does not row. Then [His] Majesty said to her: [Why] do [you] not row? She said: A fish-shaped charm of new [turquoise] fell into the water. And [His Majesty said to her]: Would you like one to replace [it]? But [she said]: I [prefer] my own [to a look-alike].[7] [His Majesty] said: [Let there be brought again] the [chief]

6,1 lector [Djadjaemonkh, and he was brought at once]. / His Majesty said: Djadjaemonkh, my brother,[8] I have done as you have said, and the heart of His Majesty was refreshed at the sight of their rowing. But a fish-shaped charm of new turquoise, belonging to one of the leaders, fell into the water. She was silent and did not row. And it came to pass that she ruined her side. I said to her: Why have you stopped rowing? She said to me: It is a fish-shaped charm of new turquoise which has fallen into the water. I said to her: Row! I will replace it! She said to me: I prefer my own to its look-alike. Then said the chief lector Djadjaemonkh his magic sayings. He placed one side of the water of the lake upon the other, and lying upon a potsherd he

6. Philippe Derchain, in *RdE* 21 (1969), 19–25, calls attention to the parallel of the maidens rowing and the goddess Hathor as a rower. The sense of the outing in his view is that of a sort of parody, with the king taking the place of the sun god Re navigating the heavens with the Hathors. The author of our tale would then have stressed the importance of the rulers of Dynasty 5 as the real adherents of Re, in distinction to Snefru as a ruler who merely parodied the god. See H. G. Fischer, in Jan Assmann, Erika Feucht, and Reinhard Grieshammer, eds., *Fragen an die altägyptische Literatur, Studien zum Gedenken an Eberhard Otto,* (Wiesbaden, 1977), 161–65.

7. Evidently a proverb with the sense that she wants the full account of the same thing. See Wm. Spiegelberg, in *ZÄS* 64 (1929): 90–91.

8. This familiar form of address places Snefru in a good light.

6,10 found the fish-shaped charm. Then he brought it back and it was given to its owner. Now as for the water, it was twelve cubits deep, and it amounted to twenty-four cubits after it was folded back. He said his magic sayings, and he brought back the water of the lake to its position. His Majesty passed a holiday with the entire palace, l.p.h. When he came forth, he rewarded the chief lector Djadjaemonkh with all good things.

Such is a marvel which took place in the time of your father, the King of Upper and Lower Egypt, Snefru, the vindicated, something done by the chief lector, scribe of the document, Djadjaemonkh. And His Majesty the King of Upper and Lower Egypt, Khufu, the vindicated, said: Let there be an offering made to His Majesty the King of Upper and Lower Egypt, 6,20 Snefru, the vindicated, / consisting of one thousand loaves of bread, one hundred jugs of beer, an ox, and two cones of incense, and let there be given a large cake, a jug of beer, and one cone of incense to the chief lector, scribe of the document, Djadjaemonkh. For I have seen an example of his skill. It was done according to all His Majesty commanded.

## [THE FOURTH TALE: A MARVEL IN THE TIME OF KING KHUFU HIMSELF]

The king's son Hardedef arose to speak, and he said: [You have heard examples of] the skill of those who have passed away, but there one cannot know truth from falsehood. [But there is with] Your Majesty, in your own time, one who is not known [to you ...]. His Majesty said: What is this, 7,1 Har[dedef, my son? Then said Har]dedef: There is a townsman / named Dedi. He lives in Ded-Snefru, the vindicated. He is a townsman of 110 years, and he eats 500 loaves, a shoulder of beef as meat, and as drink 100 jugs up to this day.[9] He knows how to reattach a head which has been cut off, and he knows how to make a lion go behind him, its tether on the ground. He knows the number of the ᴿshrinesᴸ of the enclosure of Thot. Now His Majesty the King of Upper and Lower Egypt, Khufu, the vindicated, had spent much time in seeking for himself these shrines of the enclosure of Thot to fashion for himself their likeness for his horizon. His Majesty said: You yourself, Hardedef, my son, you shall bring him to me. 7,10 Boats were prepared for the king's son, Hardedef, / and he sailed south to Ded-Snefru, the vindicated.

9. The Egyptians often wished for 110 years as an ideal life span.

After these boats were moored at the river bank, he went by land. He sat in a carrying chair of ebony, the poles made of *sesnedjem*-wood and sheathed in gold (leaf).[10] When he reached Dedi, the carrying chair was put down, and he proceeded to address him. It was lying down on a mat at the threshold of his house that he found him, a servant at his head massaging him and another wiping his feet. The king's son Hardedef said: Your condition is like a life before old age, although senility [has come], the time of mooring, burial, and interment. (Yet you) sleep until dawn, free from ailments, and there is no coughing in your throat. Greetings, / O honored one! It is to summon you on the business of my father, King Khufu, the vindicated, that I have come here, and that you may eat the delicacies of the king's giving, the food of those who are in his following, and that he may send you in good time to your fathers who are in the cemetery.

7,20

And this Dedi said: In peace, in peace, Hardedef, king's son, beloved by his father! May your father King Khufu, the vindicated, favor you! May he advance your station among the venerables. May your *Ka* contend with your enemy, and may your *Ba* learn the ways leading to the Portal of the One Who Clothes the Weary One.[11] Greetings, / O king's son!

8,1

The king's son Hardedef stretched out his hands to him and raised him up.[12] He went with him to the riverbank, giving him his arm. Dedi said. Let me have a *kakau*-boat that it may bring me (my) students and my writings. There were made to attend him two boats and their crews.

Dedi went northward in the barge in which the king's son Hardedef was. After he reached the capital, the king's son Hardedef entered to report to His Majesty the King of Upper and Lower Egypt, Khufu, the vindicated. The king's son Hardedef said: Sovereign, l.p.h., my lord, I have brought Dedi. His Majesty said: Hasten, bring him to me. His Majesty proceeded to the pillared hall / of the palace, l.p.h., and Dedi was ushered in to him. His Majesty said: What is this, Dedi, my not having seen you (before)? And Dedi said: It is (only) the one who is summoned who comes, Sovereign,

8,10

10. Nobles are sometimes shown in such carrying chairs in relief sculpture in the Old Kingdom. A carrying chair much like this one was found in the tomb of Snefru's queen Hetepheres, the mother of Cheops. The chair is now in the Cairo Museum, with a replica in the Museum of Fine Arts in Boston.

11. Formal greetings are exchanged on both sides. The *Ka* and *Ba* are spirits of the dead man and manifestations of his personality. The One Who Clothes the Weary One is the embalmer.

12. Again a signal favor in that a prince condescends to raise up a commoner.

l.p.h. I have been summoned and see I have come. His Majesty said: Is it true, the saying that you know how to reattach a head which has been cut off? Dedi said: Yes, I do know how, Sovereign, l.p.h., my lord. His Majesty said: Let there be brought to me a prisoner who is in confinement, that his punishment may be inflicted. And Dedi said: But not indeed to a man, Sovereign, l.p.h., my lord. For the doing of the like is not commanded unto the august cattle. So there was brought to him a goose, and its head was severed. Then the goose was placed on the western side of the pillared

8,20 court, and its head on the / eastern side of the pillared court. Dedi said his say of magic words. The goose arose and waddled and likewise its head. After the one (part) reached the other, the goose stood up and cackled. Next he caused a waterfowl to be brought to him, and the like was done with it. Then His Majesty caused that there be brought him an ox, and its head was felled to the ground. Dedi said his say of magic words, and the ox

9,1 stood up behind him with his tether fallen / to the ground. ⟨The scribe has obviously omitted the recovery of the ox and a paragraph dealing with the lion.⟩

Then King Khufu, the vindicated, said: Now as for the rumor that you know the number of the ⌐shrines⌐ of the enclosure of [Thot]? Dedi said: By your favor, I do not know their ⌐number⌐, Sovereign, l.p.h., my lord, but I do know the place where they are. His Majesty said: Where are they? And Dedi said: There is a chest for flint knives in a chamber called the Inventory in Heliopolis: in that chest.[13] [His Majesty said: Hasten, Bring it to me!] Dedi said: Sovereign, l.p.h., my lord, it is not I who can bring it to you. His Majesty said: Who then can bring it to me? Dedi said: It is the eldest of the three children who are in the womb of Reddedet; he will bring it to you. His Majesty said: I desire this indeed. But [as for] what you say, who is this Red-

9,10 dedet? Dedi said: She is the wife of a *wab*-priest of Re, Lord of Sakhbu, / giving birth to three children of Re, Lord of Sakhbu, of whom it is said that they shall exercise this magisterial office in the entire land. The eldest of them will be chief seer in Heliopolis.[14]

13. The sense of the arrangement or number of the secret chambers is entirely unclear. Possibly they were the architectural plan for a part of the pyramid complex of Cheops, as suggested by the text. In any case, the question of the chambers serves to introduce the matter of Reddedet. E. Hornung, in *ZÄS* 100 (1973): 33–35.

14. In Dynasty 5 a particular emphasis is placed on the sun god Re as the dynastic god. His chief place of worship was On (Greek Heliopolis); Re, Lord of Sakhbu, is a local variant. Sakhbu is in Lower Egyptian Nome II.

As for His Majesty, his heart became very sad at this, and Dedi said: What now is this mood, Sovereign, l.p.h., my lord? Is it because of the three children? I say: First your son, then his son, then one of them.[15] His Majesty said: When shall she give birth, Reddedet? She shall give birth in the month of Proyet on the fifteenth day. His Majesty said: Then the sandbanks of the Two Fishes Canal will be cut off, my servant, (otherwise) I myself could visit it and then I could see the temple of Re, Lord of Sakhbu. Dedi said: I shall cause there to be water four cubits deep on the sandbanks of the Two Fishes Canal. His Majesty proceeded to his palace, and His Majesty said: Let it be commanded to Dedi to (go to) the house of the king's son Harde-

9,20 def that he may dwell there / with him. Fix his rations at one thousand loaves of bread, one hundred jugs of beer, an ox, and one hundred bundles of greens. And one did according to all His Majesty had commanded.

## [THE BIRTH OF THE KINGS]

One of these days it happened that Reddedet took sick and it was with difficulty that she gave birth. The Majesty of Re, Lord of Sakhbu, said to Isis, Nephthys, Meskhenet, Heket, and Khnum:[16] May you proceed that you may deliver Reddedet of the three children who are in her womb; they who shall exercise this magisterial office in the entire land. For they shall build the shrines in your towns, they shall provision your altars, they shall renew your offering tables, and they shall increase your divine offerings.[17]

10,1 These goddesses proceeded, and they transformed themselves / into musicians, with Khnum accompanying them carrying the birthing-stool. When they reached the house of Rewosre, they found him standing with his apron untied.[18] They proffered to him their necklaces and (their) rattles. But he said to them: My ladies, see, there is a woman in labor, and her bearing is

15. Evidently an abbreviated version of history in which only the builders of the Giza pyramids, Chephren and Mycerinus, are considered as coming between Cheops and the first king of Dynasty 5, Weserkaf.
16. Four goddesses associated with childbirth and the ram god Khnum, regarded as the creator of man on a potter's wheel in one myth.
17. A graphic list of the usefulness of the kings to the gods.
18. Lit. "upside down." E. Staehelin, in *ZÄS* 96 (1970): 125–39, discusses this passage at length. In her view, Rewosre has his apron untied (unknotted) and hanging down as a sort of sympathetic parallel to the untied garments of his wife during childbirth; parallels in other cultures are cited.

difficult. They said to him: Let [us] see her, for we are knowledgeable about childbirth. So he said to them: Proceed! And they entered into the presence of Reddedet. Then they locked the room on her and on themselves. Isis placed herself in front of her, Nephthys behind her, and Hekert hastened the childbirth. Isis then said: Do not be strong (*wsr*) in her womb in this your
10,10 name of Wosref (*wsr rf*).[19] / This child slipped forth upon her hands as a child one cubit long, whose bones were firm, the covering of whose limbs was of gold, and whose headdress was of real[20] lapis lazuli. They washed him, his umbilical cord was cut, and he was placed upon a cushion on bricks. Then Meskhenet approached him, and she said: A king who will exercise the kingship in this entire land! Khnum caused his limbs to move.

Next Isis placed herself in front of her (Reddedet), Nephthys behind her, and Heket hastened the childbirth. Isis said: Do not kick (*sah*) in her womb in this your name of Sahure (*sāhu-Re*). And this child slipped out on her hands as a child one cubit long, whose bones were firm, the covering of whose limbs were ⟨of gold⟩, and whose headdress was of real lapis lazuli.
10,20 They washed him, his umbilical cord was cut, and he was placed / on a cushion on bricks. Then Meskhenet approached him and she said: A king who will exercise the kingship in this entire land! Khnum caused his limbs to move.

Then Isis placed herself before her, Nephthys behind her, and Heket hastened the childbirth. Isis said: Do not be dark (*kkw*) in her womb in this your name of Keku. And this child slipped forth upon her hands as a child one cubit long, whose bones were firm, the covering of whose limbs was of gold, and whose headdress was of real lapis lazuli. Then Meskhenet
11,1 approached him, / and she said: A king who will exercise the kingship in this entire land! Khnum caused his limbs to move. They washed him, his umbilical cord was cut, and he was placed on a cushion on bricks.

19. As each child is born, Isis makes a pronouncement involving a pun on the king's name. Weserkaf means "his Ka is strong"; Sahu-Re probably means "one whom Re has well endowed," but there is a pun on *sahu,* "to kick." In Neuserre Kakai there is a pun involving Kakai and Keku, "darkness." H. Altenmüller, in *Chronique d'Egypte* 45 (1970): 223–35, suggested that Reddedet is a pseudonym for Khentkaus, a queen of the end of Dynasty 4, and that she was the mother of the first three kings of Dynasty 5. He further suggests that she may have been the daughter of the same prince Hardedef who introduces the tale. Hence she and her sons would have been descendants of Cheops through a junior branch of the family.
20. As opposed to faience or glass with this color.

Now these goddesses came forth after they had delivered this Red-dedet of the three children, and they said: May you be pleased, Rewosre, for there have been born to you three children. And he said to them: My ladies, what can I do for you? Please give this corn to your birthing-stool bearer, and take it as a payment for ꜥmaking beerꜣ. And Khnum placed the sack on his back. So they proceeded to the place / from which they came. But Isis

11,10   said to these goddesses: What is this, that we are returning without performing a marvel for these children and can report to our father who sent us? So they fashioned three royal crowns, l.p.h., and they placed them in the corn. Then they caused the heavens to turn into a storm and rain, and they turned back to the house and said: Would you please put the corn here in a locked room until we can come back on our northward journey? So they placed the corn in a locked room.[21]

Reddedet cleansed herself in a purification of fourteen days, and she

11,20   said to her maidservant: Is the house / prepared? She replied: It is out-fitted with everything except for jars (for beer-making), for they have not been brought. Reddedet said: Why haven't the jars been brought? The servant replied: There is not anything here for ꜥ(beer-) makingꜣ, except for some corn of these musicians, which is in the room with their seal. So Reddedet said: Go and bring some of it, for Rewosre will give them its

12,1   equivalent when he returns. The servant went / and she opened the room. And she heard the sound of singing, music, dancing, and exultations—everything which is done for a king—in the room. She returned and she repeated everything that she had heard to Reddedet. So she (too) went around the room but could not find the place in which it was being done. Then she put her forehead to the bin and discovered it was being done in it. Then she placed (it) in a chest which was (in turn) placed in another sealed box tied with leather thongs, and she put it in a room with her stores and she sealed it off. When Rewosre came back, returning from the fields, Reddedet related this business to him, and his heart was more pleased than anything. They sat down and celebrated.

After some days had passed, Reddedet had an argument with the maid-servant, and she had her punished with a beating. So the maidservant said /

12,10   to the people who were in the house: Shall this be done to me? She has given birth to three kings, and I am going and I will tell it to His Majesty the

---

21. The goddesses leave magical tokens of the kingship for the children in the sack of grain. They invent the storm as an excuse to return.

King of Upper and Lower Egypt, Khufu, the vindicated! So she started out, and she came upon her eldest brother, on her mother's side, tying flax yarn on the threshing floor. He said to her: Where are you off to, little girl? And she told him about this business. Her brother said to her: Is this indeed something to be done, your coming to me thus? And am I to agree to [this] denunciation? Then he took a whip of flax to her, and he gave her a real beating. The maidservant ran to get herself a drink of water and a crocodile 12,20 caught her. Her brother went to tell it to Reddedet, / and he found her sitting with her head on her knee,[22] her heart very sad. He said to her: My lady, why are you so sad? She said: That little girl who grew up in this house, see, she has gone away saying: I am going and I will denounce. Then he put his head down and said: My lady, she stopped by, to tell me [...] that she might go off with me. And I gave her a sound beating, and she went to draw some water, and a crocodile caught her ...

(Here the papyrus breaks off.)

22. An attitude of mourning or sorrow.

# THE TALE OF THE ELOQUENT PEASANT

T his text, dating from the Middle Kingdom, combines the format of the short story with that of a poetic meditation on the need for justice. The narrative of the text is straightforward: a peasant, robbed of his goods, makes appeal to the Chief Steward of the crown. He makes nine separate petitions which constitute the poetic section of the composition. After his first appeal, the Chief Steward is so impressed with the eloquence of the peasant that, following the order of the king, he refuses to help the petitioner. The peasant is thus forced to return time and again, demonstrating each time his ability with rhetoric, and each time his words are recorded for the entertainment of the king. Eventually the peasant receives justice and, in recompense, is given the property of the rich man who had robbed him. The appeal of the text is not so much in its actual content as in the artistic manner in which that content is expressed, for it says nothing new or significant on its subject. The subject of the peasant's speeches is the Egyptian concept of Ma'at. This in itself presents a problem of translation: should we understand the peasant to be speaking about Ma'at, the personalized goddess and abstract concept of order and righteousness? Or is he speaking simply in terms of practical justice? For the purpose of the present translation, I have preferred to retain the Egyptian "Ma'at," as this term, I believe, conveys a better impression of the Egyptian original. The text has been published several times, but the most recent and most convenient edition is:

*R. B. Parkinson,* The Tale of the Eloquent Peasant, *(Oxford, 1991). It is this edition which I have used for the preparation of the present translation. However, for the convenience of readers who may wish to make comparison with other translations, I have retained the older system of line numbering. Other modern translations may be found in M. Lichtheim,* Ancient Egyptian Literature, *vol. 1 (Berkeley, 1973), 169–84, and R. B. Parkinson,* The Tale of Sinuhe and Other Ancient Egyptian Poems 1940–1640 BC *(Oxford, 1997), 54–88. The translation of R. O. Faulkner in the earlier edition of this book should also be noted as it shows a number of variations in the interpretation of various passages of the text.*

V.A.T.

R1        There was once a man whose name was Khunanup. He was a peasant of Sekhet-Hemat,[1] and he had a wife named Merit. Now this peasant said to his wife, "Behold, I am going down to Egypt in order to bring provisions from there for my children. Go and measure for me the barley which is in the storehouse, that which remains from last year's barley." (His wife did as

R5  he had requested),[2] and then he set out for her six measures of barley. / Then the peasant said to his wife, "Behold, (there are) twenty measures of barley as food (for you) and your children. Now make these six measures of barley into bread and beer for me as daily rations, that I may live on them."

        So the peasant then set out for Egypt, having loaded his donkeys with[3]

R10  reeds, herbs, / natron, salt, wood from [...] tyu,[4] staves of Ta-Menment,[5] /

R15  leopard skins, jackal hides, *nesha*-plants, *anu*-plants, *tenem*-plants, *kheprur*-

R20  plants, / *sahut, saskut, misut*-plants, *senet*-stones, *aba*-stones, / *ibsa*-plants,

R25  *inbi*-plants, pigeons, *naru*-birds, *weges*-birds, *tebu,* / *weben*-plants, *tebes*-

1. Field of Salt: the modern Wadi Natrun.
2. This sentence is not in the Egyptian, but one must assume that at this point the wife followed her husband's instructions, for what follows makes it evident that the peasant gave to his wife an amount of barley which he had taken from the total amount which she had measured.
3. Many of the items in the list which follows are unidentifiable, although the plants mentioned are probably medicinal.
4. An unidentified locality. Faulkner, in the previous edition of this book, suggests "[Hes]-tiu country."
5. Ta-Menment: "Cattle Country," the modern Farafra Oasis.

R30    plants, *gengent,* berries (?), and *inset*-seeds, a full / abundance of all the
R35    finest products of Sekhet-Hemat.

     The peasant continued on his way, traveling southward in the direction
Neni-nesut, and arrived at the district of Per-Fefi to the north of Medenit.[6]
There he encountered a man standing on the river bank whose name was
R40    Nemtynakhte. He was the son of a man / whose name was Isry, / and he was
a subordinate of the Chief Steward Rensi, the son of Meru. Then this
Nemtynakhte, when he had seen the peasant's donkeys which greatly delighted his heart, spoke saying, "Would that I had some kind of charm
endowed with power through which I might confiscate the possessions of
R45    this peasant!" Now the house of this Nemtynakhte was at the juncture / of
the beginning of a narrow path, one which was not broad enough to exceed
the width of a loincloth. One side of it was bounded by the water, and the
other side by the barley. Then Nemtynakhte said to his servant, "Go and
bring me a piece of clothing from my house." Immediately it was brought to
R50    him, and he stretched it out over the juncture of the beginning of the path, /
so that its fringe touched the water, and its hem the barley.

B1,1         Now the peasant was traveling along the public road, / and Nemtynakhte said, "Watch out, peasant! Do not tread on my clothing." Then
the peasant said, "I shall do what pleases you, for my path is good."[7] So he
B1,5    went toward the higher ground. Then Nemtynakhte said, / "Is my barley to
be a path for you?" Then the peasant said, "My path is good, but the bank is
steep, so my way (must be) through the barley, for you are obstructing the
road with your clothing. Will you not let us pass on the road?"

     He had just finished speaking these words, when one of the donkeys
B1,10    filled / his mouth with an ear of barley. Then Nemtynakhte said, "So now, I
shall confiscate your donkey, peasant, because he is eating my barley. Behold, he will tread grain because of his crime." But the peasant replied, "My
path is good, and only one (ear of barley) has been harmed. Could I buy

---

6. Neni-nesut is the Egyptian name of Herakleopolis in Middle Egypt, the capital of
Egypt during the Ninth and Tenth Dynasties, the time, presumably, when the story
takes place. The location of Per-Fefi is unknown, and Medenit refers to the twenty-
second nome of Upper Egypt.
7. "My path is good": The peasant perhaps means either that he wishes to cause no
inconvenience to anyone during his journey or that his general way and conduct of life
is good and in accordance with what is required by the values of religion and Ma'at. A
freer translation might render the line as "I am a peaceful man."

B1,15 back my donkey for its value, if you should seize him / for filling his mouth with an ear of barley? Moreover, I know the owner of this estate: it is the property of the Chief Steward Rensi, the son of Meru, and he curbs every thief in this entire district. Am I to be robbed on his estate?" Then Nem-

B1,20 tynakhte retorted, "Is there not a well-known proverb:/ 'A poor man's name is pronounced (only) for the sake of his master'?[8] I am speaking to you, and do you dare to invoke the Chief Steward?" Then he took for himself a switch of green tamarisk, beat his whole body with it, confiscated his donkeys, and drove them to his estate.

B1,25 Then the peasant / lamented exceedingly through grief for what had been done to him. But Nemtynakhte said, "Do not raise your voice, peasant! Behold, you will go to the domain of the Lord of Silence."[9] Then the peasant replied, "You whip me, you take away my property, and you even take the very lament out of my mouth. By the Lord of Silence, give me

B1,30 back / my property! Only then will I desist from my wailing which so disturbs you." So the peasant spent a period of ten days pleading with Nemtynakhte, but he paid no attention to it.

So the peasant made his way to Neni-nesut in order to petition the Chief Steward Rensi, the son of Meru. He met him just as he was coming

B1,35 out of the door / of his house to board his official barge. Then the peasant said, "I would like to be permitted to inform you about this situation of mine. There is good reason that a faithful assistant of yours should be charged to come (to me), so that I may send him back to you (to tell you)

B1,40 about it." Then the Chief Steward Rensi, the son of Meru, ordered / a faithful assistant of his to come to him,[10] and the peasant sent him back (to him) concerning the matter in its every detail.

Then the Chief Steward Rensi, the son of Meru, laid a charge against Nemtynakhte to the magistrates who were under his jurisdiction. They, however, said to him, "In all likelihood, this is one of his peasants who

B1,45 has gone over to someone other than him. / After all, this is the way they usually deal with peasants who go to the jurisdiction of someone else. Yes,

B1,50 this is the way they handle (such things). Is there any reason to punish Nemtynakhte on account of a few scraps of natron and a bit of salt? He will

8. I.e., a commoner has no value or rights except in relationship to his master.
9. The Lord of Silence is Osiris. Perhaps Nemtynakhte means this as a threat that he will kill the peasant if the latter does not keep quiet.
10. I.e., to the peasant.

be ordered to return it, and return it he will." / Then the Chief Steward Rensi, the son of Meru, kept silent, neither replying to the magistrates nor giving answer to the peasant.

1.

Then the peasant came to make petition to the Chief Steward Rensi, the son of Meru, saying: "O Chief Steward, my lord, greatest of the great, arbiter of everything, both that which is yet to be and that which (now) is:[11]

B1,55 If you descend to the Lake of / Ma'at,
You will sail thereon in the breeze.
The fabric of your sail will not be torn,
Nor will your boat be driven ashore.
There will be no damage to your mast,
Nor will your yards be broken.
You will not founder when you come to land,
Nor will the waves bear you away.

B1,60 You will not taste the perils / of the river,
Nor will you gaze upon the face of fear.
The swiftly swimming fish will come to you,
And you will catch (many) fatted fowl;
For you are a father to the orphan,
A husband to the widow,
A brother to her who has been cast out,
The clothing of him who has no mother.

B1,65 Permit me to exalt your name in / this land
In accordance with every good law:
A leader untainted by greed, a noble unpolluted by vice,
One who obliterates deceit, one who nurtures Ma'at,
One who answers the plea of him who raises his voice.
I shall speak and (surely) you will hearken:
Fulfill Ma'at, O exalted one,
Exalted even by those who are themselves exalted.

11. Here follows a series of nine appeals made by the peasant to the Chief Steward Rensi, much of which is written in poetry or poetic prose.

B1,70 Relieve / my distress, for lo, I am afflicted;
Take heed to me, for lo, I am in anguish."

Now the peasant spoke these words during the time of his Majesty, the King of Upper and Lower Egypt, Nebkaure the justified.[12] Then the Chief Steward Rensi, the son of Meru, went before his Majesty and said, B1,75 "My Lord, / I have found someone among the peasants who is exceedingly eloquent of speech. His property was stolen by a man who is in my service, and behold, he has come to petition me about it." Then his Majesty said, "As you desire to see me healthy, cause him to remain here, B1,80 without replying to anything which he says. And so that he may keep on / speaking, remain silent. Then let his words be brought to us in writing, that we may hear them. However, provide the means so that his wife and his children may live, for behold, one of these peasants comes to the city[13] only when there is nothing in his house. And furthermore, provide the means so that this peasant himself may live: you will see that food be supplied to him without letting him know that it is you who is giving it to him."

So there was apportioned to him ten loaves of bread and two jugs of B1,85 beer / every day. The one who supplied them was the Chief Steward Rensi, the son of Meru. He would give them to a friend of his, and he would give them to (the peasant). Then the Chief Steward Rensi, the son of Meru, wrote to the governor of Sekhet-Hemat about the issuing of provisions for the peasant's wife, three measures of barley every day.

2.

Then the peasant came to petition him a second time, saying, "O Chief Steward, my lord, greatest of the great, wealthiest of the wealthy, in you those who are great (know) one who is greater, and those who are wealthy B1,90 (know) / one who is wealthier:

O helm of heaven, support-beam of the earth,
O plumb line which carries the weight:
Helm, do not steer off course,

12. The Nebkaure mentioned here may be King Nebkaure Akhtoy who ruled from Neni-nesut (Herakleopolis) during Dynasties 9/10.
13. "To the city": lit. "to the land."

> Support-beam, do not list,
> Plumb line, do not vacillate.

A mighty lord should recover that which its owner has lost[14] and defend the desolate. What you require is (already) in your house, a jar of beer and
B1,95 three loaves of bread. What will it cost you to recompense / those who appeal to you? One who is mortal perishes along with those who are under him. Do you expect to live forever?[15]

> Surely these things are wrong:
> A balance which tilts,
> A plummet which errs,
> A precise and honest man who becomes a deceiver.
> Behold, Ma'at flees from you,
> Driven from her throne.
> Nobles perpetrate crimes,
> And rectitude of speech is overturned.
> Judges steal what has already been stolen,
> And he who can twist a matter in just the right way

B1, / Can make a mockery of it.
100 He who supplies the winds languishes on the ground,
> He who refreshes the nostrils (now) causes men to gasp.[16]
> The arbiter is (now) a thief,
> And he who should quell distress is one who creates its origin.
> The town is flooded (with wrong),[17]
> And he who should punish evil (now) perpetrates crimes."

Then the Chief Steward Rensi, the son of Meru, said: "Is your obstinacy greater than (the fear) that my servant might seize you?" But the peasant continued:

B1, "He who measures / the tax allotment embezzles for himself;
105 He who administers on behalf of another steals his goods;
> He who should rule in accordance with the laws condones thievery.

14. Lit. "that which is without its owner."
15. Lit. "Will you be a man of eternity?"
16. These two lines are a reference to Osiris as the giver of the winds and of breath. The reference is used as a symbol of the confusion of justice which the peasant laments.
17. Lit. "The town is in its flood."

Then who is there to redress evil?

He who should dispel crime commits transgressions?

One is meticulous in perversity,

And another gains respect because he commits crimes.

Do you see herein anything referring to yourself?

Punishment (now) is short, but iniquity is extensive.

Yet a good deed will bring its own reward,[18]

For there is a proverb:

B1, 'Do for one who may do for you,

110 That you may cause him thus to do.'[19]

This is like thanking him for what he will do,

It is like warding off something rather than attacking (it),

It is like entrusting something to a skilled artisan.

Would that (you might know) a moment of destruction,

Devastation in your vineyard,

Dearth among your birds,

Destruction among your water birds!

Let him who sees (now) become blind;

Let him who hears (now) become deaf,

For he who used to guide now guides but to confusion.

B1, / [...][20] Behold you are mighty and powerful,

115 Yet your hand is stretched out, your heart is greedy,

And compassion has passed far beyond you.

How destitute is the wretch whom you destroy!

You are like unto a messenger of Khenty![21]

B1, You exceed (even) the / Lady of Pestilence![22]

120 If it is not your concern, it is not her concern;

If something does not affect her, it does not affect you;

If you have not done something, she has not done it.

He who is well provided should be compassionate,

18. Lit. "A good deed will return to its place of yesterday."

19. Lit. "Do for the doer in order to cause him to do" (*ir n ir r rdit iri.f*).

20. The sense of the Egyptian here is virtually unintelligible. However, the peasant appears to be asking the Chief Steward what he would do if he were confronted with a certain difficult situation.

21. A crocodile deity.

22. The goddess Sekhmet.

For force belongs (only) to the desperate,
And theft is natural (only) for him who has nothing of his own;
That which is theft (when done) by the criminal
Is (only) a misdemeanor (when done by) him who is in want.
One cannot be wrathful with him on account of it,
For it is only a (means of) seeking (something) for himself.

B1,   You, however, are satisfied / with your bread
125   And contented with your beer;
      You abound in all manner of clothing.
      The gaze of the steersman is directed forward,
      But the ship drifts of its own will.
      The king is in the palace,
      And the tiller is in your hand,
      But evil is done all around you.
      Lengthy is my petition, and heavy is my lot.
      People will say, 'What business does that fellow have?'

B1,   Construct a refuge, keep your riverbank hale,
130   For behold, your abode reeks of crocodiles.
      Be meticulous with your tongue so as not to let it wander,
      For the power[23] which is in it is the abomination of a man.
      Do not utter falsehood; keep prudent the magistrates.
      The judges are an insatiable belly,[24]
      The speaking of falsehood is like (fine) herbs for them,
      For such poison is pleasant to their hearts.
B1,   You who know the affairs of / all men,
135   Can you ignore my plight?
      You who can extinguish the peril of all waters,
      Behold, I am on a voyage without a boat.
      You who are safe harbour for all who are drowning,
      Rescue one who has been shipwrecked.
      Deliver me from my plight, for you are mighty."

23. "Power": lit. "limb," "member."
24. "Insatiable belly": lit. "a basket of fat things," i.e., always ready to swallow rich
    bribes.

3.

B1,       Then the peasant came to petition him a third time, saying: / "Chief
140    Steward, my lord:
     You are Re, the lord of heaven, with your attendants;
     The provisions of all mankind are from you as from the flood.
     You are Hapy[25] who makes verdant the fields and revives the desert.
     Punisher of the thief, defender of the distressed,

B1,      Become not / a raging torrent against the supplicant.
145    Be vigilant against the approach of eternity,
     Cherish length of life, for, as is the saying,
     'To do Ma'at is the breath of the nostrils.'
     Inflict punishment on him who merits punishment,
     And none will resemble you in your integrity.
     Will the balance be off? Will the scale tilt to one side?

B1,      Will Thoth / be merciful, and then you do wrong?
150    You must show yourself the equal of these three;
     As these three are benign, so you must be benign.
     Neither answer good with evil,
     Nor put one thing in the place of another,
     For speech grows more (rapidly) than weeds
     To find the breath for its answer.[26]

B1,      Then wrong will pour forth / more (readily) than one spreads out
155    garments.
     This is my third attempt to make you act![27]

     You must steer your course by minding the sail;
     Ride the waves so as to do Ma'at.
     Be on guard, for you could run aground through the tiller rope,
     But the stability of the land is to do Ma'at.
     Do not utter falsehood, for you are noble;

B1,      Do not be petty, / for you are distinguished;

25. The god Hapy was the personification of the Nile flood and hence symbolic of the prosperity and well-being of Egypt.
26. I.e., be careful of what you say, for it is very easy to make a sudden wrong remark.
27. The peasant makes an aside reference to the fact that he is now trying for the third time to arouse the Chief Steward to action on his behalf. The Egyptian text has here the third person singular pronoun with the verb *iri,* but I emend it to the second person singular.

160 Do not utter falsehood, for you are a balance;
Do not go off course, for you are impartiality.
Behold, you are the sole one with the balance;
If it wavers, then you will waver.
Do not drift; steer your course; pull on the tiller rope.
Do not rob, but take action against the robber;

B1, / He is not truly great who is great (only) in greed.

165 Your tongue is the plummet,
Your heart is the weight,
And your two lips are its arms.
If you veil your face against brutality,
Who then will reprove evil?

Behold, you are a despicable scrubman,

B1, One so grasping as to abuse / a friend,

170 One who would abandon his friend in favor of a fawner,
One whose brother is he who comes and brings him (a bribe).
Behold, you are a ferryman who transports only him who has the fare,
An honest man whose honesty has been truncated.
Behold, you are the supervisor of a storehouse
Who does not permit a poor man to buy on credit.

B1, Behold, you are / a hawk to the commoners,

175 One who lives on the most worthless of the birds.
Behold, you are a butcher whose delight is slaughter,
And the mutilation thereof means nothing to him.
Behold, you are a poor shepherd of the flock, for you take no heed.[28]
Act, therefore, less like a gluttonous crocodile,
For there is no safety in any town of this entire land.

B1, / Hearer, you do not hear! Yet why do you not hear?

180 Have I today repulsed the marauder?
Does the crocodile recoil?
What profit is in it for you?
For the truth which was hidden has now been found,
And deceit is thrown backwards upon the earth.
Do not dispose tomorrow when it has not yet arrived,
For no one knows the evil thereof."

---

28. The meaning of this line is highly uncertain.

B1,185 Now the peasant had spoken this speech / to the Chief Steward Rensi, the son of Meru, at the entrance to the court. Then (Rensi) caused two attendants to set upon him with whips, and they thrashed his every limb. Then the peasant said, "The son of Meru is in error, for his face is blind to what he should see and deaf to what he should hear, and his heart neglects what has been brought to his attention.

> B1, Behold you are (like) a city / without a governor,
> 190 Like a people without a ruler,
> Like a ship on which there is no captain,
> (Like) a crowd without a leader.
> Behold, you are a constable who steals,
> A governor who takes bribes,
> A district administrator responsible for suppressing crime
> But who has become the archetype of the perpetrator."

4.

Then the peasant came to petition him a fourth time. He found him B1,195 / coming out from the gate of the temple of Herishef, and he said: "O gracious one! May Herishef be gracious to you, he from whose temple you have just come.

> Goodness is annihilated, for there is no fidelity to it,
> (No desire) to fling deceit backwards upon the earth.
> If the ferry has been beached, then how can one cross (the river)?
> Success is attained (only) in abomination.
> B1, To cross / the river on foot[29]—is this a feasible way to cross?
> 200 Such cannot be done![30]
> Who now can sleep peacefully until the dawn?
> Vanished (now) is walking during the night,
> Or even traveling by day,
> Or permitting a man to stand up for his own cause,
> Even though it be truly excellent.

29. "On foot": lit. "on sandals."
30. Lit.: "it does not exist" (Eg.: *nn*).

But behold, there is no gain for him who tells you these things,
For compassion has passed far beyond you.

B1,   How destitute is the wretch / whom you destroy!
205   Behold, you are a fisherman[31] who (fully) satisfies himself,
One who is determined to do what he desires,
One who harpoons hippopotami, shoots wild bulls,
Catches fish, and snares birds.
But he who is hasty of speech is not free from indiscreet talk,
And he who is light of heart is not serious of mind.

B1,   Be patient, so that you may learn Ma'at;
210   Control your own preference, so that the humble petitioner may gain.
There is no impetuous man who attains to excellence,
There is no impatient man to whom authority is given.


Let your eyes see! Let your heart be instructed!
Do not be tyrannical in your power,
That evil may not overtake you.

B1,   If you ignore one incident, it will become two.
215   It is the eater who tastes,
It is he who is questioned who answers,
And it is the sleeper who sees the dream.
As for the judge who merits punishment,
He is an archetype for him who does wrong.

Idiot! Behold, you are struck!

B1,   You know nothing! And behold, you are questioned!
220   You are an empty vessel! And behold, you are exposed![32]
Helmsman, do not let your ship veer off course;
Giver of life, do not let men die;
Provider, do not let men perish;
Sunshade, do not attract (the heat of) the sun;
Refuge, do not let the crocodile carry (me) off.

B1,225 This is the fourth time I appeal to you. / Must I spend all my time at it?"


31. The Egyptian term *mḥw* can also be used of a hunter of game.
32. Lit. "Pourer of water, behold you are entered." The meaning of this statement, however, is obscure, and I offer the above translation as a suggestion of its possible significance.


37

5.

Then the peasant came to petition him a fifth time, saying, "O Chief
Steward, my lord:

> The *khudu*-fisherman [...] kills the *iy*-fish,
> The spearer of fish harpoons the *aubeb*-fish,

B1,

> The *djabhu*-fisherman spears / the *paqer*-fish,

230

> And the *uha*-fisherman plunders the river.
> Behold, you are much the same as them.
> Do not deprive a pauper of his goods,
> One known to you as a lowly man.
> His possessions are the very breath of a pauper,
> And stealing them is (like) plugging his nose.
> You were appointed to judge complaints,

B1,

> To judge between two (disputants), and / to curb the thief when he steals.

235

> But behold, your actions are a support of the thief;
> Men trust you, but you have become a transgressor.
> You were appointed as a dam for the destitute
> That he might not drown,
> But behold, you are a torrent raging against him."

6.

B1,240

Then the peasant came / to petition him a sixth time, saying, "O Chief
Steward, my lord:

> He who fosters Ma'at diminishes falsehood (*grg*),
> And he who fosters goodness is a destroyer of evil (*bw*),
> As when satisfaction comes and ends hunger,
> As when clothing ends nakedness,

B1,

> As when the sky is calm after a / high wind and warms all who are cold,

245

> As when fire cooks what is raw,
> As when water quenches thirst.
> Look right before your face:
> The arbiter is a despoiler,
> He who should make peace (now) creates misery,

B1,

> / He who should create calm (now) causes trouble;

250

> But he who deceives diminishes Ma'at.

So fulfill (your duty) well,
That Ma'at may be neither defrauded nor made extreme.

If you receive something, share it with your companion,
For to devour (something) selfishly is a lack of righteousness.

B1, But my misery leads (only) to / my departing,[33]
255 My complaint brings (only) my dismissal.
No one knows what is in the heart.
Do not be idle, but attend to my accusation,
For if you destroy (something), who will restore it?
The sounding-pole is in your hand like an unused pole,
For by chance the water happens to be deep;
But if the boat should run aground, it will be ransacked,

B1, And its cargo cast onto the land / on every shore.
260
You are educated, you are intelligent, you are proficient—
But certainly not in order to steal—
But look at yourself! You make yourself just like everyone else!
Your deeds are perverse,
And the example for all men is now the deceiver of the entire land.
He who tends the garden of evil waters his field with corruption

B1, And cultivates his plot / with falsehood,
265 So as to irrigate iniquity for ever."


7.


Then the peasant came / to petition him a seventh time, saying, "O Chief Steward, my lord:

You are the rudder of the entire land,
And the land voyages in accordance with your guidance.
You are the equal of Thoth,
One who judges without discrimination.

B1, My lord, be patient,
270 That a man may entreat you / about his righteous cause.
Be not vexed, for it does not suit you.


33. I.e., I will leave here unsatisfied.

He who looks too far ahead will become disquieted,
So do not dwell on what has not yet befallen,
And do not rejoice about what has not yet happened.
Patience prolongs friendship,
But as for him who neglects a fault which has been committed,
There is no one who knows what is in his heart.
If law is subverted and integrity destroyed,

B1,     There is no poor man / who will be able to live,

275     For he will be cheated, and Ma'at will not support him.

Now my body was full, my heart was burdened,
And it has poured from my body of its own accord;
There was a break in the dam, its water gushed out,
And my mouth opened to speak.
Then I plied my sounding pole and drained off the flood (within me).
I have unburdened what was in my body,
I have washed my soiled linen.

B1,     / My harangue is (now) completed;

280     My misery is fully in your sight.
What (now) do you lack?
Your indolence will mislead you,
Your greed will deceive you,
And your cupidity will increase your foes.
But will you (ever again) encounter another peasant like myself?
As for one who is indolent, will a petitioner remain at the door of his house?

B1,     / There is no one who was silent whom you caused to speak,

285     There is no one who was sleeping whom you caused to wake,
There are none who were exhausted whom you have revived,
There is no one who was closemouthed whom you have opened,
There is no one who was ignorant whom you have made wise,
There is no one who was unlearned whom you have taught.
But magistrates are responsible for driving out evil;
They are masters of goodness;
They are artisans who bring into being that which exists,
(They are) responsible for joining the head which has been cut off."

8.

B1,290 / Then the peasant came to petition him an eighth time, saying, "O Chief Steward, my lord:

> Men flounder because of selfishness;
> The greedy man lacks success,
> For his (only) success is failure.
> You are greedy, but it (gains) you nothing;
> You steal, but it is no profit to you.
> Now, permit a man to stand up for his cause which is truly good.
> You have your provisions in your house, and your belly is full.
> Your grain is excessive and even overflows,

B1,
295
> / And what issues forth perishes on the earth.
> (You are) a rogue, a thief, an extortioner!
> Yet magistrates are commissioned to suppress evil,
> As safeguards against the aggressor;
> Magistrates are empowered to fight falsehood.

> It is not fear of you which causes me to petition you.
> You do not know my heart:
> A lowly man who turns again and again to make complaint to you,
> One who does not fear him to whom he makes his petition,

B1,
300
> / One whose equal will not be brought to you from any quarter (of town).

> You have a plantation in the country,
> You have a salary in the administration,
> You have provisions in the storehouse,
> The officials pay you, and still you steal.
> Are you an extortioner?
> Do men bring (bribes) to you
> And to the henchmen with you at the allotment of the farmlands?

> Perform Ma'at for the sake of the Lord of Ma'at,
> For the constancy of his Ma'at is absolute.

B1,
305
> / (You are) the pen, papyrus and palette of Thoth,
> So keep far from the doing of wrong.
> That goodness should be potent is excellent indeed,[34]

---

34. The text here has a wordplay on the Egyptian term *nfr: nfr nfrt nfr rf*.

For Ma'at will endure unto eternity
And go down to the grave with him who performs it.
He will be buried, and the earth will enfold him,
B1, / But his name will never vanish upon the earth,
310 For he will be remembered because of his goodness.
Such is the integrity of the decree of God:
It is a balance, and it does not tilt;
It is a scale, and it does not lean to the side.

Whether it is I or another who comes (before you),
You must acknowledge (him).
B1, / Do not give back (to him) the reply of a silent man.
315 Do not abuse one who himself has done no abuse.

But you show no compassion!
You are neither concerned nor perturbed!
You do not give me due recompense for this fine speech
Which comes from the mouth of Re himself.
B1, Speak Ma'at! Perform Ma'at!
320 For it is great, it is exalted, it is enduring,
Its integrity is evident,
And it will cause (you) to attain the state of veneration.

Can a balance tilt?
It is its scale-pans which bear things,
B1, And there must be no / exceeding the measure.
325 A criminal action does not reach safe harbor,
But he who is humble will reach land."

## 9.

B2,91 / Then the peasant came to petition him a ninth time, saying, "O Chief Steward, my lord:

Men's balance is their tongue;
It is the scale which determines what is lacking.
Inflict punishment on him to whom punishment is due,
So that men may conform to your integrity.
B2,95 / [...] As for falsehood, its deeds may flourish,
But Ma'at will turn herself to balance it.

Ma'at is the final end of falsehood,
And (falsehood) will diminish and be seen no more.
If falsehood walks, it goes astray;
It does not cross in the ferry, and it makes no headway.

B2, / As for him who prospers through it,
100 He will have no children, he will have no heirs upon earth.
As for him who sails with it, he does not reach land,
And his boat does not arrive at its mooring-place.

Do not be ponderous, but do not be frivolous;
Do not be tardy, but do not hurry;
B2, Do not be partial, and do not give in to / a whim;
105 Do not cover your face against one whom you know;
Do not blind your sight against one whom you have seen;
Do not spurn one who entreats you.
Turn away from this slothfulness,
And let your decision be pronounced.
Act on behalf of the one who has been active (in appealing) to you.
Do not listen to everyone,
But respond to a man in accordance with his righteous cause.

An idle man has no past;[35]
B2, / One who is deaf to Ma'at has no friend;
110 He who is grasping never has a joyful day.
He who suffers will become wretched,
And he who is wretched will become a plaintiff,
But an enemy may become a killer.

Behold, I appeal to you, but you do not hear it.
B2,115 I shall now depart and appeal about you to Anubis."

Then the Chief Steward Rensi, the son of Meru, had two attendants go
to bring him back. Then the peasant was frightened, for he assumed that
punishment would be inflicted upon him because of this speech which he
had made. Then the peasant said, "(Like) a thirsty man's approach to
120 water, (like) the reaching out of the mouth / of the child of a nursing woman
for milk, such is death for one who seeks (it), when he sees it coming, when
his death, long delayed, finally comes." Then the Chief Steward Rensi, the

35. I.e., has accomplished nothing.

43

son of Meru, said, "Have no fear, peasant. Behold, you will act in accordance with what is done on my part." Then the peasant swore an oath, saying, / "On my life! Shall I eat of your bread and drink of your beer forever?" Then the Chief Steward Rensi, the son of Meru, said, "Now wait here, and you will hear your appeals." Then he had someone read from a new scroll every petition word for word. [...]

/ Then the Chief Steward Rensi, the son of Meru, dispatched them to his Majesty, the King of Upper and Lower Egypt, Nebkaure the justified, and they were pleasing to his heart more than anything which was in this entire land. Then his majesty said, "Son of Meru, give the verdict yourself."

Then the Chief Steward Rensi, the son of Meru, caused to guards to go to [bring Nemtynakhte]. / He was brought in and a list was made [of his property ...] six servants, along with [...] his barley, his emmer, his donkeys, his pigs, and his flocks [...] of Nemtynakht [was given] to the peasant [...].

It has reached its conclusion [...]

*doesn't need to be a storm or star*
*we are chickens*
*we have no speech*

# THE SHIPWRECKED SAILOR

*NO NAMES*

*Pharaoh's not a god - they can be dealt with. He's an act of god, a force of nature*

T he narrative of the Shipwrecked Sailor is one of the most interesting, straightforward, and yet puzzling compositions of ancient Egyptian literature. The composition dates from somewhat later than 2000 B.C. in a single manuscript copy from not much later. Other roughly contemporary compositions are known from several manuscripts. The papyrus was found by the eminent Russian Egyptologist Wladimir Golénischeff in the Egyptian Collection in St. Petersburg, or else acquired by him. He published it in 1913, and it is now in the Hermitage Museum in St. Petersburg. It has been translated on many occasions, and every year there are at least one or two new studies and interpretations.

The basic situation involves the return of a trading, exploration, or military mission from the south and its arrival on the Nile at Elephantine at the southern border of Egypt proper at the first cataract on the Nile, the area of the new High Dam. The tale begins abruptly (one or more pages may have been missing at the beginning; see bibliography, Bolshakov 1993). A junior officer speaks to his superior, in which the former consoles his chief on what appears to be an unsuccessful mission and reassures the commander, who shows his anxiety about appearing at court before the king.

The junior officer then tells a story about his own experience when he traveled south and was shipwrecked on a desert isle (either on the Red Sea or the Nile). When he came to his senses, he was approached by the sole inhabitant

45

of the island, a large serpent. The serpent befriends the officer and relates its own misfortune when a shooting star fell and burnt his entire family of serpents. The serpent predicts that the sailor will be able to return to Egypt, gives him a cargo of trade goods, and bids him farewell when a boat appears. The sailor then returns to Egypt, is rewarded by the king, and hopes that his story has cheered the commander.

The commander, however, is still discouraged, and the story comes to an abrupt end, much as it begins, with the ironic and discouraging remark of the commander. Thus there are three levels: the situation of the return of the expedition, the story within a story of the sailor's experience, and the story within a story within a story of the serpent's misfortune.

Several features can be briefly mentioned. None of the protagonists is actually named, the commander, the retainer, nor the serpent. The island is also not named or located, but it is predicted by the serpent that it will disappear under the waves once the sailor leaves. Most scholars place the island off the coast of the Red Sea, but some maintain it must have been on the Nile in the south. The serpent calls himself the prince of Punt, a land which the Egyptians visited from the earliest times and is thought to lie in the south between the Nile and the Red Sea. A curious emphasis is placed on numbers, the height of the wave, the dimensions of the ship, the number of sailors, the length of the serpent's hood, the number of months of the sailor's stay, and so on. It is almost as if the tale is an allegory involving the movement of stars. Love of family and the return to Egypt is emphasized, paralleled by the cruel fate of the serpent's family. The resourcefulness of the Egyptian abroad is also a theme. All sorts of interpretations have been offered by scholars, but the precise message remains elusive. Is the serpent the god Re or a personification of Fate? Is the sailor a model of fortitude under adversity or a fool? Who is the fearful commander and why is he so afraid to report to the king? Do the talking serpent and the disappearing island characterize the narrative entirely as a fairy tale? Is the boat and crew which comes to get the sailor the same one which was wrecked with the loss of life to all its crew? These and other questions have found different answers as the study of the composition progresses. It is certainly a masterpiece of Egyptian literature and raises more questions than can be answered. It has been suggested that the sailor serves as a model for the man of the times as does Sinuhe (see bibliography, Otto 1966). For an extensive recent study, see bibliography, Burkard 1993.

W.K.S.

Then the able retainer spoke:
Be of good cheer, commander;
We have now reached home.
The mallet has been taken off, the mooring post driven in,
The bowline cast ashore.
Praise has been offered, and God has been thanked.
Every man embraces his comrade.
Our shipmates have returned safe
Without loss to our expedition.
After we reached the limits of Wawat,

10     We passed the island of Senmet.[1]
See us now, we are returning safely,
And we are reaching our land.

Listen now to me, commander,
I do not exaggerate.
Wash up, place water on your fingers    *water to the Chicken*
So you can reply when you are questioned,    *he thinks good not act of god*
So you can speak to the king with confidence,
So you can answer without stammering.    *Sailor's prediction*    *Sailor thinks it was him. It was*
The speech of a man can save him,    *Pharaoh's arrogance is evil*
And his words can cause indulgence for him.

20     Yet do only as you wish; for speaking to you is tiresome.    *Pharaoh hawling a name would be him as a god names can be reasoned with threatened or prayed to*

Now I shall tell you something similar
Which happened to me myself.
I went to the mining region for the Sovereign.
I went down to the Great Green[2]

1. A quarrying, mining, or military expedition has returned by Nile from the south, and its commander appears to be downcast at the prospect of facing the king after an unsuccessful mission. His chief aide tries to cheer him up. Wawat is northern Nubia, and Senmet the island of Biggeh, just south of Aswan in the First Cataract region. The mission took place on the Nile or in the eastern desert. The expression "our land" is probably not otherwise attested in Egyptian literature and may in fact have a patriotic nuance.

2. This expression has traditionally been regarded as the Red Sea. Recent scholarship, however, has attempted to show that the term must refer to the Nile itself. See Claude Vandersleyen, "En relisant le Naufragé," in S. Israelit-Groll, ed., *Studies in Egyptology Presented to Miriam Lichtheim,* vol. 2 (Jerusalem, 1990), 1019–24; *Wadj our: Un autre aspect de la vallée du Nil.* (Brussels, 1999). Here begins the story within a story.

In a ship 120 cubits long and 40 cubits wide.[3]
120 sailors were aboard from the best of Egypt.
Whether they looked at the sky or looked at the land,
30    Their hearts were braver than lions.

*For all their power their prediction didn't help*

They could tell a storm before it came
And a tempest before it happened.
But a storm came up while we were on the Great Green,
Before we could touch land,
And the wind picked up and howled.
A wave of 8 cubits was in it.
As for the mast, I grasped (lit. "struck") it.
Then the ship died, and of those who were in it
There did not remain a single one.
40    I was placed on an island by a wave of the Great Green,
And I spent 3 days alone, my heart as my companion.
I lay down within a shelter of wood,
And I embraced the shade.
Next I stretched my legs
To find what I could put in my mouth.

There I found figs and grapes
And all kinds of good vegetables.
Sycamore figs were there together with notched ones,
50    And cucumbers as if they were cultivated.
Fish were there with fowl.
There was nothing that was not in it.
Then I gorged myself, and I put (some) on the ground
Because of the abundance in my hands.
I removed the fire drill when I had lighted a fire,
And I made a burnt offering to the gods.

Next I heard the sound of thunder,
And I thought it was a wave of the Great Green.
60    The trees were shaking and the ground quaking.
When I uncovered my face,
I found it was a serpent about to come.

3. The cubit is about 20.6 inches or .523 meters. The ship is about 204 by 68 feet. In many instances a length of a ship three times the width is standard.

He was 30 cubits long,
And his beard (hood?) was larger than 2 cubits.
His body was covered with gold,
His eyebrows were of real lapis lazuli,
And he was coiled up in front.[4]

He opened his mouth toward me,
While I was on my belly in front of him.
He said to me:
Who has brought you, who has brought you, citizen,
70   Who has brought you?
If you delay in telling me
Who has brought you to this island,
I shall have you know yourself as ashes, *That's what Pharaoh could*
Turned into someone invisible.
He (text: "you") spoke to me, but I could not hear.
While I was before him,
I did not know myself.
Then he set me in his mouth
And took me off to his resting place.
He set me down without touching me.
80   I was intact without his taking anything from me.

He opened his mouth toward me,
While I was on my belly before him.
Then he said to me:
Who has brought you, who has brought you, citizen,
Who has brought you to this island of the Great Green,
The two sides of which are under water?
Then I answered him,
My arms bent before him.

I said to him:
90   It was I who came down to the mining country
On a mission of the Sovereign

---

4. E. Lucchesi in *ZÄS* 103 (1976): 148–49; Henry G. Fischer, in Jan Assmann, Erika Feucht, and Reinhard Grieshammer, eds., *Fragen an die ägyptische Literatur, Studien zum Gedanken an Eberhard Otto* (Wiesbaden, 1977), 155–58: a human-headed serpent.

In a ship 120 cubits long and 40 cubits wide.[5]
120 sailors were in it from the best of Egypt.
Whether they looked at the sky or looked at the land,
Their hearts were braver than lions.
They could tell a storm before it came,
Each one of them, his heart was braver,
100    And his arm more valiant than his companions.
There was no fool among them.

Then a storm came forth while we were on the Great Green,
Before we could set to land.
The wind picked up and kept on howling.
A wave of 8 cubits was in it.
As for the mast, I grasped onto it(?).
Then the ship died, and of those who were in it
Not a single one remained except for me.
See me now at your side.
Next I was placed on this island
110    By a wave of the Great Green.

Then he said to me:
Do not fear, do not fear, citizen,
Do not turn white, for you have reached me.
See, God has allowed you to live: *higher power*
He has brought you to this island of the spirit.[6]
There is not anything which is not in it.
It is filled with all fine things.
See, you shall spend month after month
Until you complete 4 months within this island.
120    A boat shall return from the Residence,
*good prediction*    Sailors in it whom you know.
You shall go with them to the Residence,
And you shall die in your town.[7]

---

5. This kind of repetition is frequent in all ancient literature.
6. An island of the *ka* or enchanted island.
7. Burial in a foreign land was abhorrent to the Egyptians, a theme developed in The Story of Sinuhe as well.

How joyful is one who relates what he has experienced
After painful matters have passed by.
I shall now relate to you something similar
Which took place on this island
When I was on it with my siblings,
Children among them.
We amounted to 75 serpents,
Including my children and my brothers and sisters.
Without my mentioning to you a little daughter
Brought to me through wisdom.[8]

130    Then a star fell, *higher power*
And because of it these went up in fire.[9]
It happened utterly.
But I was not with [them] when they burned;
I was not among them.
Then I died for them
When I found them as a single heap of corpses.[10]

If you would be brave, and your heart strong,
You will fill your arms with your children,
You will kiss your wife, you will see your house.
It is better than anything.
You will reach home where you were
Among your siblings!
I was stretched out on my belly,
I touched the ground in his presence.

But I (the sailor) say to you:
I shall relate your might to the Sovereign,
140    I shall have him learn of your greatness.
I shall have brought to you ladanum, oil,
Spice, balsam, and incense of the temples
With which every god is pleased.

8. Here begins the story within the story within the story.
9. M. Th. Derchain-Urtel, in *SAK* 1 (1974): 98–99. A meteor? In the historical text of
   Thutmose III from Gebel Barkal there is a description of a falling star.
10. Here the serpent's story ends. Like the sailor he was a sole survivor.

I shall tell what has happened to me
And what I have seen of your (text: "his") fame.
You will be thanked in the city
In the presence of the officials of the entire land.
I shall slaughter oxen for you as a burnt offering.
I will have the necks of fowl wringed for you.
I shall have barges brought to you
Laden with all the products of Egypt,
As should be done for a god who loves men
In a far-off land which men do not know.

Then he laughed at me for what I had said
In his opinion foolishly.
150   He said to me:
You do not have much myrrh,
Although you have become an owner of incense.
I am, sir, the Prince of Punt.
Myrrh belongs to me.
That oil which you said will be brought,
It is the main product of this island!

Now it shall happen
When you separate yourself from this place,
You will never see this island again,
Since it will be submerged under waves.

Then that boat returned, as he had predicted before.
I went and set myself on top of a tall tree,
And I recognized those who were in it.
Then I went to report it,
And I found him knowing it already.

He said to me:
In good health, in good health, citizen, off to your house.
You shall see your children.
Make a good reputation for me in your city.
160   This is my only request from you.

I placed myself upon my belly,
My arms bent in his presence.

He gave me a load of myrrh, oil, ladanum, spice,
Cinnamon, aromatics, eye-paint, giraffe tails,
Large cakes of incense, ivory tusks,
Hounds, apes, baboons, and all fine products.
Then I loaded them onto the boat,
And I was placed on my belly to thank him.

He said to me:
You shall reach the Residence in 2 months,
You shall fill your arms with your children.
You will become young again at home, until your burial.

170 Then I went down to the shore in the vicinity of this boat,
And I called out to the expeditionary force which was in the boat.
I gave praise upon the shore to the lord of this island,
And those who were in it likewise.

We sailed north to the Residence of the Sovereign,
And we reached the Residence in 2 months,
According to everything he had said.
Then I entered before the Sovereign
And I presented him with these gifts
Which I had brought from within this island.
Then he thanked me before the officials of the entire land.
I was appointed retainer, and granted 200 servants.

180 See me after I landed,
After I have seen what I experienced.
Listen to my [words]. It is good for men to hearken.
Then he (the commander) said to me:
Do not be so proper, friend.
What is the use of giving water to the fowl at daybreak
When it is to be killed in the morning?[11]
It has come from beginning to end as found in writing,
In the writing of the scribe, skilled with his fingers,
189 Ameny's son Amen-aa, may he live, prosper, and be in health.

11. These are the commander's only words. See M. Gilula, in J. Johnson and E. F. Wente, eds., *Studies in Honor of George R. Hughes,* SAOC 39 (1977): 75–82, and A. Spalinger, in *GM* 73 (1984): 91–95.

# THE STORY OF SINUHE

T he Story of Sinuhe was once regarded as a more or less factual account of the adventures of an Egyptian courtier copied from an inscription in his tomb. No trace of a real Sinuhe, however, has been found through tomb reliefs, statuary, or stelae. The story is a literary narrative—given its development, the psychology of the protagonist, the use of language, and the picture of the times in Syria and Palestine. Sinuhe is a resourceful man of his times, a prototype of the proper official at a time of rising prosperity in Egypt and its relations abroad. Impelled by some inner force he cannot explain to flee from the court, he makes his own way and recognizes later both the necessity to return to his king and the advantage of a traditional burial and funerary rites. The story begins with the death of the founder of Dynasty 12, Amenemhet I, and the report of his death made to the army headed by his son, coregent, and successor, Senwosret I. The treatment of the latter in the story is propagandistic.

With the exception of religious texts and various standard formulas, few other compositions are represented in as many copies or partial copies. Two papyri of Dynasties 12 and 13 provide a fairly complete text. In the Ramesside period in Dynasties 19 and 20 master scribes and their students copied the text in school on limestone flakes (ostraca). One of these has virtually the whole text inscribed on both sides of a large flake: J. W. B. Barns, The Ashmolean Ostracon of Sinuhe (Oxford, 1952). The chapter headings are not in the original text; they have been added as an aid to understanding the main divisions of the nar-

*rative and for reference. The standard text is now Roland Koch,* Die Erzählung des Sinuhe *(Brussels, 1990). See extensive bibliography under Sinuhe.*

W.K.S.

## INTRODUCTION

R, 1    The hereditary noble and commander, warden and district officer of the estates of the sovereign in the lands of the Asiatics,[1] this truly beloved royal acquaintance, the follower Sinuhe, said:

I was a follower who followed his lord, a servant of the king's harem and of the hereditary princess, greatest of praise, wife of [King] Senwosret in Khnumet-sut and daughter of [King] Amenemhet in Ka-nofru, Nofru, the possessor of an honored state.[2]

## DEATH OF AMENEMHET I AND SINUHE'S FLIGHT

Year 30, month 3 of Akhet, day 7. The God ascended to his horizon, the King of Upper and Lower Egypt, Sehetepibre. He penetrated the sky, being joined to the sun disk, the God's body being mixed with that of him who made him.[3]

The capital was silent, desires were weak, the Great Double Gate
10    was locked, / the court was with head upon knee,[4] and the nobles were mourning. Now His Majesty had dispatched an expeditionary force to the land of the Tjemehi with his eldest son as its leader, the good God, Senwosret. He had been sent to strike the foreign lands and to smite those who were among the Tjehenu people.[5] And now he was returning, having brought back captives of the Tjehenu people and all kinds of cattle without number. The Companions of the Palace sent to the Western Half to inform the king's son of the affairs which had taken place in the council chamber.

1. The inhabitants of Palestine and Syria are designated in this text as the Amu, the Setyu, and the Pedjtyu (bowmen); the first two terms are rendered as "Asiatics."
2. Sinuhe identifies himself here as an official of Queen Nofru, daughter of Amenemhet I, and wife of his son and successor, Senwosret I. Ka-nofru and Khnumet-sut are respectively the pyramid residence towns of these two first rulers of Dynasty 12.
3. A terse announcement of the death of Amenemhet I.
4. The position of mourners.
5. The Tjemehu and Tjehenu, people living to the west of Egypt, are Libyan tribes.

20      When the messengers found him upon the road / and reached him at dusk, he did not delay for a moment. The Falcon flew off with his followers without letting his expeditionary force know it.

Now [they had] written to the sons of the king who were in his follow-
B, 1     ing in this expeditionary force. When it was being read out / to one of them, I was standing by and I heard his voice, as he spoke, being in the vicinity of a conspiracy. My senses were disturbed, my arms spread out, and trembling came over every part (of me). I took myself off by bounds (?) to find for myself a place of concealment. I placed myself between two shrubs in order to separate the road from its traveler. I went south. I did not plan to reach the capital, for I anticipated riots might occur, and I would not be able to say "life" after him (the king). I crossed the (place called) The Two Truths in the vicinity of The Sycamore, and I landed at The Island of
10      Snefru. I waited at the edge of / the cultivation. I set forth at daybreak and I came upon a man standing in the middle of the road. He greeted me re-spectfully, for he was frightened. When the time of evening meal came, I arrived at the wharf of Negau. It was with the help of the west wind that I crossed over in a boat without a rudder. I passed by to the east of the Quarry, above the Mistress of the Red Mountain (that is, the opposite side of the river, beyond the cultivation, in the desert), and I gave a path to my feet northward (until) I touched the Walls of the Prince, which had been made to check the Asiatics and to crush the sand-travelers. I took a crouched position in the brush out of fear that the guard on duty on the
20      walls might see. I went / by night, and when day came, I had reached Peten. I alighted at the Island of Kem-wer. Thirst overcame me and it hastened me on; I was parched, my throat dry. And I said: This is the taste of death. But I raised up my heart and gathered together my limbs. I heard the sound of the lowing of cattle, and I looked upon Asiatics. Their bedouin chief recognized me, a man who had been in Egypt. He gave me water and boiled milk for me, and I went with him to his tribe, and what they did for me was good.[6]

One land gave me to (another) land. I set out for Byblos (near Beirut),
30      and I returned to Qedem. I spent / half a year there. It was Amusinenshi[7]

6. In this description of Sinuhe's precipitous flight he indicates that he intended to flee to the south but was set on a northern course through the drifting downstream of the rudderless boat. The places designated as The Two Truths, The Sycamore, and The Island of Snefru may lie in the pyramid area of Memphis. See H. Goedicke, in *JEA* 43 (1957): 77–85.

7. An Egyptianized version of an Amorite (West Semitic) name.

who brought me back: he was the chief of Upper Retenu.[8] He said to me: You will be well with me, for you will hear the speech of Egypt. He said this for he knew my reputation. He had heard of my intelligence, for the people of Egypt who were there with him bore witness to me. Then he said to me: Why have you come here? Has anything happened at the capital? Then I said to him: The King of Upper and Lower Egypt, Sehetepibre, has proceeded to the horizon, and no one knows what may happen because of this. But I then spoke equivocally:[9] When I returned from an expedition in the land of the Tjemehu, one announced (that) to me. My mind vacillated. My

40    heart was not in my body, and it brought / me to the ways of flight. (But) no one accused me, no one spat in my face. No reproach was heard, and my name was not heard in the mouth of the town crier. I do not know what brought me to this land. It was like the plan of a God.

## PRAISE OF SENWOSRET I

He said to me: How shall that land fare without him, that efficient God the awe of whom is throughout the foreign lands like Sakhmet in a year of pestilence?[10] I said to him so that I might answer him: To be certain, his son has entered the palace and has taken over the inheritance of his father. He is a God, indeed, without peer. No other came into being before him.[11] He is a master of knowledge, excellent in planning and efficient in commanding,

50    one by whose command one comes forth and goes down. / It was he who controlled the foreign lands while his father was in his palace. He reported to him what he (the father) decreed had come to happen. He is a champion who acts with his scimitar, a fighter without anyone like him when he is seen attacking the bowmen and engaging the fray. He is one who bends back the horn and renders hands powerless, so that his enemies cannot muster their ranks. He is vengeful when he cracks skulls, and no one can stand up to him. He steps wide when he annihilates the fugitive. There is no success for the one who shows his back to him. He is adamant at the moment of contact. He comes again and does not show his back. He is stalwart of heart

---

8. A designation for part of Palestine and Syria.
9. The equivocal statement seems to lie in the fact that the announcement was made to the king's son, not to Sinuhe himself.
10. Sakhmet is the lioness-headed goddess responsible for pestilence.
11. The following amounts to a hymn in praise of Senwosret I and is regarded as a propagandistic element of the text.

60 when he sees a crowd, and he does not allow cowardice around him. / He is eager when he falls upon the retinue, and he is joyful when he plunders the bow-people. As soon as he takes up his shield, he strikes down. He need not repeat the act of killing, for there is no one who can deflect his arrow nor one who can draw his bow. The bowmen retreat before him as if before the might of the great goddess. He fights on having forseen the outcome, and he takes no care for the remnants. But he is well-favored and very gentle; through love he takes. His city desires him more than herself, and they rejoice because of him more than for their god. Now that he is king, husbands and wives rejoice because of him. While still in the egg, he conquered, and his face was set to it from birth. It is he who has enriched those

70 born with him, / for he is one whom god has given. How joyful is this land now that he has reigned. He is one to extend borders. He has vanquished the southlands, and he will not even have to think about the northlands, for he was made to smite the Asiatics and crush the sandcrossers. Write to him, and let him know your name. Do not utter sedition against his Majesty, for he will do for you that which his father did and he will not fail to do good to a foreign land which is loyal to him.

## SINUHE IN PALESTINE

And then he said to me: Indeed, Egypt is fortunate, now that she knows that he flourishes. You are here, and you shall be with me, and what I shall do for you will be good. He placed me in front of his children, and he married me to (literally, moored me to) his eldest daughter. He allowed

80 me to pick from his country / the choicest part of what he owned on his border with another country.

It was a wonderful land called Yaa. There were cultivated figs in it and grapes, and more wine than water. Its honey was abundant, and its olive trees numerous. On its trees were all varieties of fruit. There were barley and emmer, and there was no end to all varieties of cattle.

That which fell to my lot as a favored one was great. He set me up as chief of a tribe of the finest in his land. I obtained rations as daily disbursements and wine as a daily requirement, cooked meat and roasted fowl,

90 beside the desert game. / They hunted for me and they set (food) down before me, in addition to the catch of my hunting dogs. They made for me many sweet things with milk in everything cooked. I spent many years while my offspring became strong men, each man managing his (own) tribe.

The messenger who came north and went south to the capital stayed with me, and I made all Egyptians stay. I gave water to the thirsty man, and I put the wanderer back on the road. I rescued the man who was robbed.

100   When the Asiatics began to stir and to oppose the authority of the chiefs of the foreign lands, I counseled their marches. This ruler / of Retenu had me spend many years as an officer of his troops. As to any land which I left, when I had made my attack it was driven off from its cultivation and wells. I had plundered its cattle and brought back its inhabitants, and their produce was taken. I killed the people in it by my strong arm, my bow, my maneuvers, and my efficient advice. It went well with me in his favor, for he loved me and he recognized my bravery. He placed me at the head of his offspring when he saw my arms grow so strong.

## THE COMBAT

110   There came a strong man of Retenu to challenge me / at my tent.[12] He was a champion without equal, and he had subdued all of it. He said that he would fight with me, for he thought to ruin me. He planned to plunder my cattle, at the urging of his tribe. But that chief consulted with me, and I said: I did not know him. I am not a confederate of his that I could stride about in his camp. Had it ever happened that I entered his women's rooms, or have I scaled his walls? It is ill will, for he sees me carrying out your affairs. I am like a bull of a grazing herd in the midst of another herd. The bull of the
120   kine attacks him,/ but the (Egyptian) bull prevails against him. Is a subject loved when he acts the master?

There is no foreign bowman who is an ally of a Delta man. What is it that can join a papyrus plant to a rock? Does a bull wish to fight? Then a champion bull will wish to retreat through fear of one who might equal him. But if his intention is to fight, let him say what he wants. Is God ignorant of what he has ordained, knowing (as he does) how the matter stands?

I spent the night stretching my bow and I shot my arrows. I gave an edge to my dagger, and I polished my weapons. When daybreak came,
130   Retenu had come. / It had urged on its tribes, and it had collected the lands of both its halves. It had intended this combat.

12. The following account of the fight with the champion of Retenu has frequently been compared to the David and Goliath duel, for which it may have served as a literary prototype. See G. Lanczkowski, in *MDAIK* 16 (1958): 214–18.

He (the strong man) came out to me where I was waiting, and I placed myself near him. Every heart burned for me, wives and husbands yelled. Every heart ached for me, saying: Is there another strong man who could fight against him? His shield, his axe, and his armful of javelins fell (to me). After I had escaped his weapons, I made his remaining arrows pass by me, and not one was left over. Then he let out a yell, for he thought to ruin me, and he approached me. I shot him, my arrow fixed in his neck. He

140 shouted and fell upon his nose. / I felled him with his (own) axe. I yelled my war cry over his back. Every Asiatic yelped. I gave praise to Montu,[13] while his adherents mourned for him. This ruler, Amusinenshi, took me in his arms, and he kissed me in my clasp.

I brought away his possessions, I seized his cattle. What he had thought to do to me I did to him. I took away what was in his tent. I stripped his camp, and it was abundant for me therein. I became rich in treasure, a great proprietor of cattle.

God acts in such a way to be merciful to one whom He had blamed, one whom He led astray to another land. For today His heart is appeased.

150 A fugitive fled / because of his situation, but my renown is in the capital. A wanderer wandered through hunger, but I give bread to my neighbor. Through nakedness a man departed from his land, but I have white clothes and fine linen. A man hurried for lack of someone to send, but I have many servants. My house is fine, and my dwelling place is wide. The thought of me is in the palace.

## SINUHE WISHES TO RETURN TO EGYPT

O God, whoever you are, who decreed this flight, may you be merciful and may you set me in the capital. Perhaps you will let me see the place where my desire lives. What can be more important than joining my dead

160 body to the land where / I was born? Come, help me! May a good solution come to pass. May God give me satisfaction. May He act similarly to better the end of one whom He had made miserable and be concerned about one whom He had shunted off to live in a foreign land. If today He is merciful, and He hearkens to the prayer of a man far off, may He change my region whence I roamed the earth for Him to the place from which He brought me.

13. The Egyptian god particularly associated with battle prowess.

May the King of Egypt be merciful to me, and may I live on his bounty. May I greet the mistress of the land who is in his palace, and may I attend to the errands of her children.

My body will be youthful again. For old age has come down on me and feebleness has hurried upon me. My eyes are heavy, and my arms are immobile. / My feet fail to proceed, and my senses are exhausted. I am near to passing on, when they shall send me to the cities of eternity. But may I still serve the Mistress-of-All that she may say something good for me to her children. May she pass eternity above me.[14]

Now this report was made to His Majesty, the King of Upper and Lower Egypt, Kheperkare,[15] who will be judged right, concerning this state in which I was. His Majesty sent to me with provisions of the royal bounty. He rejoiced the heart of this servant as might be done for a ruler of a foreign land. And the king's children who were in his palace had me hear their messages.

## THE ROYAL EDICT

Copy of the decree brought to this servant regarding his being brought back to Egypt: The Horus Life of Births, the Two Ladies Life of Births, the King of Upper and Lower Egypt, Kheperkare, Son of Re / Senwosret, living forever. The decree of the king to the follower Sinuhe: This decree of the king is brought to you to inform you that you have traversed the foreign countries and have come forth from Qedem to Retenu. By your heart's counsel to you, land has given you to land. What have you done that one should act against you? You have not blasphemed that one should reprove your words. You have not spoken in the council of the elders that one should reproach your speech. This idea of yours, it took over your senses, although there was nothing in my mind against you. This heaven of yours, which is in the palace, she is well and she flourishes today as in her former state in the kingship of the land, with her children in the audience hall. You shall pile up the treasures which they give you, and you shall live off their

14. It seems that the queen is here identified with the sky goddess; her image, surrounded with stars, is generally placed on the underside of the coffin or sarcophagus lid above the body. For old age, see the beginning of Ptahhotep.
15. Senwosret I.

190 bounty. Come back to Egypt, and you shall see the capital in which you were born. You shall kiss the ground at the Great Double Gate, and you shall associate with the Companions.

Today / old age has begun for you, and potency has left you. Think about the day of burial, the passing over to an honored state. The night will be appointed for you with oils and poultices from the arms of Tayet (goddess of weaving). A procession will be made for you on the day of interment, the anthropoid sarcophagus (overlaid) with gold [leaf], the head with lapis lazuli, and the sky above you as you are placed in the outer coffin and dragged by teams of oxen preceded by singers. The dance of the Muu will be performed at your tomb, and the necessary offerings will be invoked for you. They will slaughter at the entrance of your tomb chapel, your pillars to be set up in limestone as is done for the royal children. You shall not die in a foreign land, and Asiatics will not escort you. You shall not be placed in a ram's skin as they make your grave. All of this is too much for one who has roamed the earth. Take thought for your dead body and return.

## SINUHE'S REACTION AND HIS REPLY

200 It was while I was standing / in the midst of my tribe that this decree reached me; it was after I had prostrated myself and touched the ground that it was read to me. I spread it out (the dirt) over my chest. Then I went about my encampment rejoicing and saying: How could such a thing be done for a servant whose sense led him astray to the land of the barbarians? Indeed, (your) benevolence is excellent, O you who have saved me from death. Your *ka* will allow me to spend the end of my life with my body in the capital.

Copy of the reply to this decree. The servant of the palace Sinuhe says: In peace, in peace. This flight which this servant did in his ignorance is well known by your Ka, O good God, Lord of the Two Lands, whom Re loves and whom Montu, Lord of Thebes, favors, as well as Amun, Lord of the Thrones of the Two Lands, Sobek-Re, Lord of Sumenu, Horus, Hathor, all the gods of Egypt, Atum and his Ennead, Sopdu, Neferbau, Semseru, Horus the Easterner, the Mistress of Yemet, may she enfold your head, the council upon the flood waters, Min-Horus in the midst of the desert lands,
210 Wereret, the Mistress of / Punt, Nut, Haoreis-Re, and the gods who are the

Lords of the Beloved Land and the Islands of the Great Green.[16] They give life and prosperity to your nostrils; they grant you their bounty. They give you eternity without its end and everlastingness without its limit. Fear of you is repeated in the lowlands and in the highlands, for all that the sun disk encircles is conquered for you. Such is the prayer of this servant to his lord who has rescued him from the West.

Lord of perception, who perceives the people, may he perceive in the Majesty of the palace that this servant was afraid to speak. It is a serious matter to repeat. The great God, a likeness of Re, knows the mind of one who has inquired after him ⌐of his own accord⌐. For this servant is in the hands of someone who takes thought for him; I am set in his guidance. Your Majesty is the conquering Horus; your arms prevail over all lands. May now your Majesty command that there be brought Meki from Qedem, / Qhen-

220 tiuwash from out of Keshu, and Menus, those who set your authority over the lands of the Fenkhu.[17] They are rulers whose names are worthy and who have been brought up in your love. Not to mention Retenu, for it belongs to you even as your hounds. This flight which your servant made, it was not premeditated. It was not in my mind. I did not prepare it. I cannot say what separated me to this country. It was like a dream: as when a Delta man sees himself in Elephantine (Aswan) or a man of the marshlands in Nubia. Yet I was not afraid. No one chased me. I did not hear a word of censure. No one heard my name in the mouth of the town crier. Except that my body cringed, my feet scurried, and my senses overwhelmed me, with the God

230 who decreed this flight / drawing me on. I was not stubborn before. A man is modest when his homeland is known, for Re has placed the fear of you throughout the land and the dread of you in every foreign land. Whether I am in the capital or in this place, yours is everything which is covered by this horizon. The sun disk rises at your bidding, and the water of the river is drunk if you wish. The air of the heavens is breathed if you speak. Now that this servant has been sent for, this servant will hand over (his property) to his children, whom he has engendered in this place. May Your Majesty act as he wishes, for one lives by the air which you give. Re, Horus, and Hathor

16. The gods who make up this list are representative of the different parts of Egypt and the neighboring lands. See J. Yoyotte, in *Kêmi* 17 (1964): 69–73.
17. These three foreign rulers are thus commended by Sinuhe to the king. The Fenkhu are later known as the Phoenicians. But see Schneider in Sinuhe Bibliography.

love your noble nostrils; which Montu, Lord of Thebes, wishes that they live forever.

## SINUHE'S RETURN

I was allowed to spend a day in Yaa to transfer my goods to my chil-
240 dren. My eldest son was in charge of my tribe. / My tribe and all my possessions were in his hands, as well as all my serfs, my cattle, my fruit, and all my productive trees. This servant proceeded south. I halted at the Ways of Horus.[18] The commander in charge of the patrol there sent a message to the capital to give them notice. His Majesty had them send a capable overseer of field laborers of the royal estate and with him ships laden with presents of the royal bounty for the Asiatics who had come with me to lead me to the Ways of Horus. I called each one of them by name. Each servant was at his task. I started out and raised sail. (Dough) was kneaded and strained (for beer) beside me until I reached the wharf of Itjtowy.[19]

## SINUHE AT THE PALACE

When dawn came and it was morning, I was summoned. Ten men came and ten men went to usher me to the palace. I touched my forehead to the
250 ground between the sphinxes. / The royal children were standing in the gateway to meet me. The Companions who showed me into the pillared court set me on the way to the reception hall. I found His Majesty upon the Great Throne set in a recess (paneled) with fine gold. As I was stretched out on my belly, I lost consciousness in his presence. This God addressed me in a friendly way, and I was like a man caught by nightfall. My soul fled and my body shook. My heart was not in my body: I could not tell life from death.

His Majesty said to one of these Companions: Lift him up and let him speak to me. And His Majesty said: See, you have returned, now that you have roamed the foreign lands. Exile has ravaged you; you have grown old. Old age has caught up with you. The burial of your body is no small matter, for now you will not be escorted by the bowmen. Do not creep any more.
260 You did not speak / when your name was called out. You shall not fear

18. A frontier station on the border of Egypt.
19. The landing place of the capital, the residence city of the king.

punishment. It was with a timorous reply that I answered: What has my lord said to me? If I try to answer, there is no shortcoming on my part toward God. It is fear which is in my body, like that which brought to pass the fated flight. I am in your presence. Life belongs to you. May Your Majesty do as He wishes.

The royal children were then brought in, and His Majesty said to the queen: Here is Sinuhe, who has returned as an Asiatic whom the bedouin have raised. She let out a very great cry, and the royal children shouted all together. They said before His Majesty: It is not really he, O Sovereign, my lord. His Majesty said: It is he indeed.

Then they brought their *menyat*-necklaces, their rattles, and their *sistra* 270 with them, and they offered them to His Majesty. May your arms reach out / to something nice, O enduring king, (to) the ornaments of the Lady of Heaven. May the Golden One[20] give life to your nostrils, and may the Lady of the Stars be joined to you. The crown of Upper Egypt will go northward, and the crown of Lower Egypt will go southward that they may unite and come together at the word of Your Majesty, and the cobra goddess Wadjet will be placed on your forehead. As you have kept your subjects from evil, so may Re, Lord of the Two Lands, be compassionate toward you. Hail to you. And also to the Lady of All. Lay to rest your javelin, set aside your arrow. Give breath to the breathless. Give us this happy reward, this bedouin chief Simehyet,[21] the bowman born in Egypt. It was through fear of you that he took flight and through dread of you that he left the land. Yet there is no one whose face turns white at the sight of your face. The eye which has seen you will not be afraid.

280 His Majesty said: He shall not fear, / he shall not be afraid. He shall be a Companion among the nobles and he shall be placed in the midst of the courtiers. Proceed to the robing hall to wait upon him.

## SINUHE REINSTATED .

When I came from the robing hall, the royal children gave me their hands, and we went through the Great Double Gate. I was assigned to the house of a king's son. Fine things were in it, a cooling room in it, and

20. The goddess Hathor.
21. Si-mehyet, "son of the northwind," is a playful variant on Si-nuhe, "son of the sycamore."

representations of the horizon.[22] Valuables of the treasury were in it, vestments of royal linen were in every apartment, and first-grade myrrh of the
290 royal courtiers whom he loves. / Every domestic servant was about his prescribed task. Years were caused to pass from my body. I was dipilated, and my hair was combed out. A load was given to the desert, and clothes to the sand-dwellers. I was outfitted with fine linen and rubbed with the finest oil. I passed the night on a bed. I gave the sand to those who live on it and wood oil to those who rub themselves with it. A house of a ⌈plantation owner⌉, which had belonged to a Companion, was given to me. Many craftsmen were building it, and all its trees were planted anew. Meals were brought from the palace three and four times a day, in addition to what the
300 royal children gave. There was not a moment of interruption. /

A pyramid of stone was built for me in the midst of the pyramids. The overseers of stonecutters of the pyramids marked out its ground plan. The draftsman sketched in it, and the master sculptors carved in it. The overseers of works who were in the necropolis gave it their attention. Care was taken to supply all the equipment which is placed in a tomb chamber. *Ka*-servants were assigned to me, and a funerary estate was settled on me with fields attached, at (my) mooring place, as is done for a Companion of the first order. My statue was overlaid with gold leaf, its apron in electrum. It was His Majesty who ordered it to be done. There was no commoner for
310 whom the like had ever been done. So I remained in / the favor of the king until the day of mooring came.

Its beginning has come to its end, as it has been found in writing.

(The traditional colophon marks the end of the story.)

22. Perhaps wall frescoes.

# II

LATE EGYPTIAN STORIES

# THE QUARREL OF APOPHIS AND
# SEKNENRE

For nearly a century Asiatic Hyksos rulers and their vassals had dominated Egypt, controlling the Delta and Middle Egypt. This fragment of a Ramesside historical romance presents the origins of the conflict between Thebes in the south and the Hyksos King Apophis. At a time when Thebes was still tributary to the Hyksos, King Apophis, seeking to agitate the Theban ruler Seknenre, sends a fantastic complaint regarding hippopotamuses at Thebes creating so much noise that Hyksos citizens were unable to sleep.

How much history this story actually contains is debatable. The lost continuation of this tale may have provided more substantive immediate causes for the war that ensued. Examination of King Seknenre's mummy has revealed that his violent death resulted from wounds received from a Hyksos-type battle ax, suggesting that he died in battle against the Hyksos.

E.F.W.

1,1     It came to pass that the land of Egypt was in misery, as there was no Lord, l.p.h., (functioning) ⟨as⟩ a (proper) king of the time. It happened that[1] King Seknenre, l.p.h., was (but) Ruler, l.p.h., of the Southern City,[2] and

---

1. An alternative rendition is, "for there was no Lord, l.p.h., ⟨as⟩ (sole) king. A day came to pass that . . . ," see Wolfhart Westendorf, in *ZÄS* 79 (1954): 65–67.
2. I.e., Thebes.

misery was in the city of ⌈the Asiatics⌉,[3] while Prince Apophis, l.p.h., was in Avaris, and the entire land paid tribute to him, delivering their taxes in full as well as bringing all good produce of Egypt.

So King Apophis, l.p.h., adopted Seth for himself as lord, and he refused to serve any god that was in the entire land ex[cept] Seth. He built a temple of fine workmanship for eternity next to the House of King [Apo]phis, l.p.h., and he appeared [at break of] day in order to sacrifice [...] daily to Seth, while the officials [of the palace], l.p.h., carried garlands, exactly as is practiced ⟨in⟩ the temple of Pre-Harakhti.

1,5      Now as for / King A[pophis], l.p.h., it was his wish to s[end] an inflamatory message ⟨to⟩ King Seknenre, [l.p.h., the] Prince of the Southern City. And many days after this, King [Apophis, l.p.h.], had [the high official]s of his [⌈palace⌉] summoned, [and he proposed to them that a messenger should be] sent [to the Prince of the Southern City with] a complaint [... concerning the] river, [but he was unable to compose it himself. Thereupon his] scribes and wise men [...] and ⌈high⌉ officials [said, "O so]vereign, l.p.h., [our lord, demand that there be a withdrawal from the] lagoon of hippopotamuses [which is in the east (sector) of the City[4] because] they don't let [sleep come ⌈to us⌉ either in the daytime or at ni]ght, [for the noise of them is ⟨in⟩ our ears." And King Apophis, l.p.h., answered them saying, "I shall send a message] to the Prince of the [Southern Ci]ty [...] ⌈command⌉ [... that we may assess the power of the god

2,1 who is] / with him as protector. He does not rely upon any god that is in the [entire land] except Amon-Re, King of the Gods."

Now many days after this, King Apophis, l.p.h., sent to the Prince of the Southern City ⟨with⟩ the complaint that his scribes and wise men had concocted for him. And when the messenger of King [A]pophis, l.p.h., reached the Prince of the Southern City, he was taken into the presence of the Prince of the Southern City. Then One[5] said to the messenger of King Apophis, l.p.h., "Why have you been sent to the Southern City? Wherefore

2,5 have you come journeying here?" The messenger then / answered him, "It

---

3. The generally accepted emendation. The "city of the Asiatics" would thus be a designation of the Hyksos capital Avaris, located at Khatana-Kantir in the eastern Delta. The emendation to "city of the Asiatics," however, is by no means certain. Another possibility might be "city of Re-⟨At⟩um," referring to Heliopolis, the city of the sun god, see Donald B. Redford, in *Orientalia* 39 (1970): 50.
4. I.e., Thebes.
5. I.e., Seknenre.

is King Apophis, l.p.h., who has sent ⟨me⟩ to you in order to say, 'Let there be a w[ithdrawa]l from[6] the lagoon of hippopotamuses which is in the east (sector) of the City, because they don't let sleep come to me either in the daytime or at night,' for the noise of them is ⟨in⟩ his ears."

Then the Prince of the Southern City became stupefied for a long while, remaining unable to render [a reply] to the messenger of King Apophis, l.p.h. (Finally) the Prince of the Southern City said to him, "Is it through this (remark) that your Lord, l.p.h., would investigate matters regarding[7] [the lagoon of hippopotamuses which is in t]he east (sector) of the Southern City?" Then the messenger [answered him, "Implement the m]atters for which he sent me." [Then the Prince of the Southern City caused] th[e messenger of King Apophis, l.p.h.], to be taken care of [with] good [thing]s: meat, cakes, [.... The Prince of the Southern City said to him, "Go and tell] your [lord], 'As for whatever you will tell him, he[8] will do it,' so you shall tell [him." . . . Then the messenger of King] Apophis, l.p.h., hastened to journey to where / his Lord, l.p.h., was.

3,1

So the Prince of the Southern City had his high officials summoned, as well as every ranking soldier of his, and he repeated to them every issue concerning which King Apophis, l.p.h., had sent to him. Then they were uniformly silent for a long while, being unable to answer him, be it good or bad.

Then King Apophis, l.p.h., sent to . . .

(The remainder of the story is lost.)

6. Lit. "let one withdraw from," possibly a means of expressing that activity at the lagoon should be terminated.
7. Or simply, "hear words concerning."
8. The text has "I" referring to Seknenre. The meaning of the passage is that whatever Apophis will tell his messenger or Seknenre, Seknenre will do it.

# THE CAPTURE OF JOPPA

T he great pharaoh Menkheperre Thutmose III of Dynasty 18 had probably secured the vassalage of the Prince of Joppa during his initial campaign into Syro-Palestine. Subsequently Joppa, modern Jaffa, on the
coast of southern Palestine, rebelled against Egyptian domination. The story
*The Capture of Joppa* concerns the subjugation of the rebellious town by
Djehuty, a prominent general and garrison commander under Thutmose III.
Although the beginning of this fantastic story is lost, it can be surmised that the
two contenders had met outside the town unarmed to discuss the situation.
With the soldiers reduced to drunkenness, Djehuty offers to deliver himself and
his family to the Prince of Joppa as part of his stratagem for recapturing Joppa.
The introduction of baskets concealing soldiers into the town is reminiscent of
the story of the Trojan horse and the tale of Ali Baba and his forty thieves. There
is another fragmentary Ramesside story about Thutmose III's military activity
published by Giuseppe Botti, "A Fragment of the Story of a Military Expedition
of Tuthmosis III to Syria," JEA 41 (1955): 64–71.

E.F.W.

1,1     [...] 220+ Maryan-warriors[1] [...] them ⌜like⌝ baskets [... replied] to Djehuty, "Let him be [given] 100+ [soldiers][2] ⟨from⟩ the garrison of Pharaoh, l.p.h." [...] their faces.[3]

      Now after a time they were intoxicated, and Djehuty said to [the Rebel of Joppa, "I shall deliver] myself along with (my) wife and children ⟨unto⟩

1,5     your city for yourself personally. Let the / gro[oms] drive in [the chariot horses a]nd have fodder [giv]en to them; otherwise an Apir may pass by [and steal one of] them."[4] So the chariot horses were secured and given fodder. And [... the great baton of] King Menkheperre, l.p.h., and someone came and made report to Djehuty.

      Now [when the Rebel of Jo]ppa said to Djehuty, "It is my wish to see the great baton of King Menkheperre, l.p.h. [There is a woman here] by the name of Tiutnofre.[5] By the *Ka* of King Menkheperre, l.p.h., she shall be yours today / [if you will be so] kind as to bring it ⟨to⟩ me," he acquiesced and brought the baton of King Menkheperre, l.[p.h., concealed in] his apron. And he stood straight up and said, "Look at me, O Rebel of [Joppa! Here is] King Menkheperre, l.p.h., the fierce lion, Sakhmet's son, to whom Amon has given his [strength." And he] lifted his hand and smote upon the

2,1     Rebel of Joppa's temple so that he fell / [sprawling] before him. And he put him in manacles [...] the leather. And he [said], "⌜Let⌝ [there be brought to me] a clamp of copper. [We shall make a] restraint for this Rebel of Joppa." So the clamp of copper of four *nemset*-weight was attached to his feet.

      And he caused the two hundred baskets, which he had had fabricated,

2,5     to be brought and caused two hundred soldiers to descend / into them. And their arms were filled ⟨with⟩ ropes and manacles, and they were sealed shut. And they were given their sandals along with their carrying-poles ⌜and . . .⌝,[6] and every fine soldier was assigned to carry them, totaling five hundred men. They were told, "As soon as you enter the city, you shall

---

1. These, the elite Indo-Aryan chariot warriors associated with the Hurrian movement into Syro-Palestine, apparently lent their support to the Prince of Joppa.
2. Or, "loaves."
3. Or, "before them."
4. Assuming that Apir describes an adventurer without specific ethnic or political ties.
5. Meaning, "The beautiful one is yours." Presumably the king's baton accompanied the division of the army under Djehuty's command, symbolizing the king's presence in military undertakings in which he did not actually take part.
6. The word *itll* is of undetermined meaning, see James E. Hoch, *Semitic Words in Egyptian Texts of the New Kingdom and Third Intermediate Period* (Princeton, 1994), 43.

release your companions and seize hold of all persons who are in the city
2,10 and put them in rope-bonds / straightaway."

And someone came out to tell the charioteer of the Rebel of Joppa,
"Thus says your lord, 'Go tell your mistress, "Be of good cheer! It is ⟨to⟩ us
that Seth has delivered Djehuty along with his wife and his children. Here
are the first fruits of their servitude," so ⟨you⟩ shall say to her regarding
these two hundred baskets,'" which were (actually) filled with men and
manacles and ropes.

Then he went in advance of them in order to impart the good news to
his mistress saying, "We have captured Djehuty!" And the defenses of the
3,1 city were opened up for the arrival of the soldiers, / and they entered
the town [and] released their companions. And they captured [the] townspeople, both young and old, and put them in rope-bonds and manacles
3,5 straightaway. So the energetic arm / of Pharaoh, l.p.h., captured the town.

In the evening Djehuty sent a message to Egypt to King Menkheperre,
l.p.h., his lord, saying, "Be of good cheer! Amon, your good father, has
3,10 delivered to you the Rebel of [Jo]ppa and all his people as well as his / city.
Send men to take them away captive that you may fill the Estate of your
father Amon-Re, King of the Gods, with male and female slaves, who have
fallen beneath your feet forever and ever."

Thus it concludes happily.

# THE TALE OF THE DOOMED PRINCE

A lthough written in the simple and rather monotonous style character-
istic of stories of the New Kingdom, this tale, as far as it is preserved,
captures the reader's interest in its narration of the adventures of a
young Egyptian crown prince. Like The Story of Sinuhe, the theme is that of the
Egyptian abroad, but in this later story little attention is given to providing local
color. Rather the emphasis is upon plot. The reader, who has initially been informed of the boy's true identity and the three possible fates that may ultimately
prevail over him, seeks to learn how the youth will finally reveal his royal background to the foreigners among whom he lives and to see how Fate operates.

This story is illustrative of a certain degree of flexibility in the Egyptian
concept of predestination. Unfortunately, the conclusion of the tale is lost, so
that the reader's whetted appetite remains unsatisfied. A happy conclusion
would, however, conform to the fairy-tale nature of the story, and the hero's good
qualities and piety toward his god point to a resolution in which the sun god acts
as the ultimate arbitrator of his destiny. Although the manuscript is from early
Dynasty 19, the story was probably composed in late Dynasty 18, see Wolfgang
Helck, "Die Erzählung vom Verwunschenen Prinzen," in Jürgen Osing and
Günter Dreyer, eds., Form und Mass: Beiträge zur Literatur, Sprache und
Kunst des alten Ägypten, Festschrift . . . Fecht, (Wiesbaden, 1987), 218–25.

E.F.W.

4,1       Once upon a time there was a king, so the story goes, to whom no son had ever been born. [But when His Majesty, l.p.h., re]quested a son for himself from the gods of his time, they ordered a birth to be granted him, and he went to bed with his wife that night. Now when she [had become] pregnant and had completed the months of childbearing, a son was born.

      Presently the Hathors[1] came to determine a fate for him and said, "He shall die through a crocodile, or a snake, or even a dog." So the people who
4,5  were in the boy's company heard and reported it / to His Majesty, l.p.h. Thereupon His Majesty, l.p.h., became very much saddened. Then His Majesty, l.p.h., had [a] stone [house] built [for him] upon the desert, supplied with personnel and with all good things of the palace, l.p.h., so that the boy did not (have to) venture outside.

      Now when the boy had grown older, he went up onto his roof and espied a greyhound following a grown-up who was walking along the road. He said to his servant, who was beside him, "What's that walking behind the grown-up who is coming along [the] road?" And he told him, "It's a greyhound." And the boy said to him, "Have one like it brought to me."
4,10 Thereupon the servant went and reported it / to His Majesty, l.p.h. Then His Majesty, l.p.h., said, "Let a young springer be taken to him [because of] his heart's ⌜disquiet⌝." So they ⟨had⟩ a greyhound taken to him.

      Now after the days had elapsed for the boy to mature in all his body, he sent word to his father, saying, "What's the point of my staying put here? For look, I am committed to Fate. Let me be released so that I may act according to my desire until God does what is his will."

5,1       Then a chariot was harnessed for him, equipped [with] / all sorts of weapons, and [a servant was put in] his following for an escort. He was ferried over to the eastern bank and told, "Now you may set out as you wish," [while] his greyhound was (still) with him. He went northward over the desert, following his inclination and living on every sort of desert game.

      Presently he reached the Prince of Nahrin.[2] Now none had been born to the Prince of Nahrin except a daughter. There had been built for her a

---

1. According to popular religious belief in the New Kingdom, there were seven such Hathor goddesses who determined the fate of a child at birth; see below, The Tale of the Two Brothers, 9,8–9.
2. The land of the Mitannian kingdom, located east of the bend of the Euphrates River. Since this kingdom fell toward the end of Dynasty 18, the action of the story took place at a time in this dynasty when Syrian princes still owed their allegiance to Mitanni.

5,5 house whose window / was seventy cubits distant from the ground. He sent for all the sons of all the princes of the land of Khor (Syria) and told them, "As for the one who will reach my daughter's window, she shall be a wife for him."

Now after many days had elapsed and while they were (engaged) in their daily routine, presently the boy passed by them. They took the boy to their house, cleansed him, gave fodder to his team, did every sort of thing 5,10 for the boy, salving him and bandaging his feet, and / gave food to his escort. They said to him by way of conversation, "Where have you come from, you handsome youth?" He told them, "I am the son of a chariot warrior of the land of Egypt. My mother died, and my father took for himself another wife, a stepmother. She came to despise me, and [I] left her presence in flight." And they embraced him and kissed him over [all his] body.

[Now after many days had elapsed], he said to the boys, "What's this you are engaged in, [boys?" And they told him, "It's been three] whole 6,1 [month]s now that we have been spending / time here [leaping up, for the one who] will reach [the] window of the daughter of the Prince of Nahrin, [he will] give her to him for [a wife." He] said to them, "If my feet were [not] hurting me so,[3] I would proceed to leap up with you." They proceeded to leap up according to their daily routine, while the boy stood by at a distance watching, and the eyes of the daughter of the Prince of Nahrin were upon him.

6,5 Now after ⟨many days⟩ had elapsed, / the boy came in order to leap up along with the children of the princes. He leapt up and reached the window of the daughter of the Prince of Nahrin. She kissed him and embraced him over all his body. Then someone went in order to impart the news to her father and told him, "Somebody has reached the window of your daughter." Then the prince inquired about him, saying, "The son of which of the princes?" And he was told, "A chariot warrior's son.[4] It was from his stepmother's presence that he came in flight from the land of Egypt." 6,10 Thereupon / the Prince of Nahrin became very much angered. He said, "Is it to this Egyptian fugitive that I should give my daughter? Send him away!"

3. Or alternatively, "If I could but enchant my feet," since the restoration of a negative is far from certain and the determinative of the verb favors "enchant."

4. According to E. Cruz-Uribe, in *ZÄS* 113 (1986): 19, the Prince of Nahrin misunderstood the word for "chariot warrior" as "vagrant" and thus violently reacted to the Egyptian prince's achievement in reaching the daughter's window.

Someone came to tell him, "Now depart to where you came from!" But the daughter took hold of him and swore by God, saying, "By Pre-Harakhti, if he is taken away from me, I shall neither eat nor drink but shall die right away." Then the messenger went and reported to her father every ⟨word⟩ she had said, and her ⟨father⟩ sent men to slay him / right where he was. But the daughter said to ⟨them⟩, "By Pre, if he is slain, as soon as the sun sets, I shall be dead. I won't stay alive an hour longer than he."

6,15

Then [someone went] to tell this to her father. And / [her father had] the [youth] and his daughter [brought be]fore him. The youth [came before] him, and his worth impressed the prince. He embraced him and kissed him over all his body, and he said to him, "Tell me your background. See, you are (now) a son to me." And he told him, "I am the son of a chariot warrior of the land of Egypt. My mother died, and my father took for himself another wife. She came to despise me, and I left her presence in flight." Then he gave him his daughter for a wife and / gave him house and fields as well as cattle and all sorts of good things.

7,1

7,5

Now after ⟨many days⟩ had elapsed, the youth told his wife, "I am committed to three fates: crocodile, snake, and dog." Then she said to him, "Have the dog which follows you killed." And he told her, "ᴙWhat a demandᴙ! I won't let my dog, which I reared when it was a puppy, be killed." And she began watching over her husband very carefully, not letting him venture outside alone.

Now from the day that the boy had come from the land of Egypt in order to travel about, the crocodile had been / his fate [...]. It appeared [from the midst of] the lake opposite him in the town in which the youth was living with [his wife]. However, a water spirit[5] was in it. The water spirit would not let the crocodile emerge, nor would the crocodile let the water spirit emerge to stroll about. As soon as the sun rose, [they would be] engaged ᴙthereᴙ in fighting each other every single day over a period of two whole months.

7,10

Now after some days had elapsed, the youth sat down and made holiday in his house. And after the end of the evening breeze the youth lay down upon his bed, and sleep took possession of his body. Then / his wife filled one [bowl with wine and] another bowl with beer. Presently a [snake] emerged [from its] hole to bite the youth, but his wife was sitting beside

8,1

---

5. The word here and throughout translated "water spirit" is literally "strong one" and could also be rendered as "giant" or "demon."

him without falling asleep. The [bowls were thus standing] accessible to the snake, and it imbibed and became intoxicated. Then it reclined turning upside down. Thereupon [his wife had] it [chopped] to pieces with her hatchet. She then awoke her husband [...] / him, and she told him, "See, your god has delivered one of your fates into your hand. He will watch over [you henceforth." Then he] made an offering to Pre, praising him and extolling his power daily.

8,5

Now af[ter some days had elapsed], the youth went out to stroll about for recreation on his property. [His wife] did not go out [with him], but his dog was following him. Then his dog took on (the power of) speech, [saying, "I am your fate." Thereupon] he ran before it. Presently he reached the lake and descended into the [water in flight before the] / dog. And so the crocodile [seized h]im and carried him off to where the water spirit was, [but he had left. The] crocodile told the youth, "I am your fate that has been made to come in pursuit of you, but [it is two whole months] now that I have been fighting with the water spirit. Now see, I shall let you go. If my [opponent returns to engage me] to fight, [come] and lend me your support ⟨in order to⟩ kill the water spirit.[6] Now if you see the [...] see the crocodile."

8,10

Now after dawn and the next day had come about, the [water spirit] returned [...].

(The remainder of the tale is lost.)

6. Or possibly rather, "and boast of me in order that ⟨I⟩ might kill the water spirit." John W. B. Barns, discussing the conclusion of the tale in *JEA* 58 (1972): 162–63, suggests restoring "Kill the water-spirit! Now if you regard the [water-spirit, you shall regard] the crocodile." The restoration of "(I will let you go) if you[r dog will come] to fight [on my behalf, and] you shout on my behalf (i.e., to the dog): 'Kill the giant!'" proposed by Donald B. Redford, in Sarah Israelit-Groll, ed., *Studies in Egyptology Presented to Miriam Lichtheim,* vol. 2 (Jerusalem, 1990), 828, seems unlikely, see Péter Hubai, in *Studia Aegyptiaca* 14 (Budapest, 1992), 292–93. An imaginative reconstruction of the conclusion of the tale is found in the children's book by Lise Manniche, *The Prince Who Knew His Fate: An Ancient Egyptian Tale Translated from Hieroglyphs and Illustrated* (New York, 1981).

# THE TALE OF THE TWO BROTHERS

A lthough this story, fully preserved on Papyrus d'Orbiney of the reign of Seti II, may have been written simply for entertainment as a sort of fairy tale, it draws richly upon mythological and folkloristic themes. The first part, treating the filial-like relationship of two peasant brothers, Anubis and Bata, and its disruption by the elder brother's seductive and prevaricating wife, conforms to reality. After the sun god places a barrier between the two protagonists, Bata, the younger brother, emasculates himself; and Anubis, regretting his ill-founded suspicions and grieving for his upright brother, kills his wife for her treachery.

The second part of the tale makes liberal use of the supernatural and miraculous. Now living abroad in the Valley of the Cedar, the still impotent Bata is given a wife by the gods, but she is brought away to Pharaoh, who makes her Chief Lady. No longer attached to Bata, she is responsible for effecting his death; but Anubis journeys to the Valley of the Cedar, where he restores Bata to life and potency. Transforming into a bull, Bata carries Anubis back to Egypt and appears as a marvel at the palace, where Bata confronts his wife. She induces Pharaoh to have the bull sacrificed, but drops of its blood produce two Persea trees as a further transformation of Bata. Again confronted by Bata, she has the trees cut down, but a splinter enters her mouth, impregnating her.

The tersely worded conclusion of the story illustrates the "Bull of His Mother" principle in the theology of pharaonic kingship, whereby the female *element is both mother and spouse in the royal succession. The woman bears a son, who is really Bata, and Pharaoh, naturally believing the son to be his own, appoints him crown prince. When Pharaoh dies, Bata accedes as king and appoints his elder brother crown prince. After thirty years of rule, Bata dies to be succeeded by his elder brother Anubis. The story has been discussed in detail by Susan Tower Hollis,* The Ancient Egyptian "Tale of Two Brothers": The Oldest Fairy Tale in the World, *(Norman, 1990).*

E.F.W.

1,1  Once upon a time there were two brothers, so the story goes, having the same mother and the same father. Anubis was the name of the elder, and Bata was the name of the younger. Now as for Anubis, he [possessed] a house and had a wife, [and] his younger brother was just like a son to him, so that it was he (Anubis) who made clothes for him while he (Bata) followed after his cattle to the fields, since it was he who had to plow. It was he who reaped for him, and it was [he] who did for him every chore that was in the fields. Indeed, his younger brother [was] a perfect man: there was none like him in the entire land, for a god's virility was in him.

1,5  Now many days after this,[1] his younger brother / [was tending] his cattle according to his daily habit, and he would [quit work] for his house each evening laden [with] all sorts of field vegetables, [with] milk, with wood, and [with] every [good produce of] the fields; he would place them before his [elder brother] while he was sitting with his wife, and he would drink and eat, and [he would leave to spend the night in] his stable among his cattle [daily].

  Now after dawn and the next day had come about, [he would bring foods] which were cooked and would place them before his elder brother, [and he would] give him bread for the fields, and he would drive his cattle to let them graze in the fields while he followed behind his cattle. [And th]ey [would] tell him, "The herbage of such and such a place is good."

2,1  And he would listen to all that they said and take them to the place / with

---

1. This and similar expressions marking the passage of time occur throughout the story as conventionalized formulas that are not always to be taken literally. In fact, this paragraph and the following one are not really part of the narrative proper but serve to provide the necessary background for the action of the story that begins following the statement about the increase in the size of the herd. See E. F. Wente, in *JNES* 21 (1962): 308–10.

good herbage which they were desiring so that the cattle which were in his charge became exceedingly fine, and they multiplied their offspring very much.

At plowing time his [elder] brother told him, "Have a team [of oxen] made ready for us for plowing, for the soil has emerged so that it is just right for plowing. Also, you are to come to the field with seed because we shall 2,5 start plowing tomorrow,"[2] so he said to him. Then his / younger brother made all preparations that his elder brother had told him to [make]. And after dawn [and the next] day had come about, they went to the field carrying their [seed] and started [to] plow with [their hearts] very pleased with their project as [they] began working.

Now many [days] after this, while they were in the field, they needed seed. So he sent his younger brother, saying, "Go quickly and fetch us seed from the village." His younger brother found his elder brother's wife seated 3,1 plaiting her hair.[3] He told her, "Get up and give me seed / so that I may hurry off to the field, because it's for me that my elder brother is waiting. Don't cause a delay." Then she told him, "Go, open the granary and fetch for yourself what you want. Don't make ⟨me⟩ leave my hairdressing unfinished."

Then the youth entered his stable and fetched a large vessel, since it was his wish to take a lot of seed. He loaded himself with barley and emmer and came out carrying it. Then she asked him, "How much is what is on your 3,5 shoulder?" And he told her, "It is / three sacks of emmer and two sacks of barley, totaling five, that are on my shoulder," so he said to her. Then she [spoke with] him, saying, "There is [great] virility in you, for I have been observing your exertions daily," for it was her wish to know him through sexual intimacy. She got up, seized hold of him, and said to him, "Come, let's spend an hour lying together. Such is to your advantage: I will then make you fine clothes."

Then the youth became like an Upper Egyptian panther in ⌜furious⌝ rage over the wicked proposition she had made to him, and she became exceedingly fearful. He had words with her, saying, "Now look, you are just like a mother to me, and your husband is just like a father to me, for he who

2. In ancient Egypt the sowing of the seed for cereal crops was performed simultaneously with the plowing of the soil.
3. As the text stands, the translation should be, "His younger brother found the wife of his elder brother while one was sitting plaiting her hair."

4,1 is older than I it is who has brought me up. What means / this great offense ⟨you⟩ have said to me? Don't say it to me again! But I will tell it to no one, nor will I let it escape my mouth to anybody." He picked up his load and went off to the field. Then he reached his elder brother, and they started to work ⟨at⟩ their project. Afterward, at evening time, his elder brother quit work for his house, while his younger brother was (still) tending his cattle and [would] load himself with all produce of the field and

4,5 bring back his cattle / before him to let them spend the night ⟨in⟩ their stable, which was in the village.[4]

Now the wife of his elder brother was fearful ⟨because of⟩ the proposition she had made. So she got some fat and bandages and pretended to be an assaulted woman in order to tell her husband, "It's your young brother who has assaulted ⟨me⟩." Her husband quit work in the evening according to his daily habit. He reached his house and found his wife lying down, pretending to be sick. She did not pour water upon his hands as usual, nor had she lit up for his arrival, so that his house was in darkness as she lay vomiting.[5] Her husband said to her, "Who has quarreled with you?" She

5,1 said to him, "No one has quarreled with me except your / young brother. When he returned to take seed to you, he found me sitting alone and said to me, 'Come, let's spend an hour lying together. You shall loosen your plaits,'[6] so he said to me, but I refused to obey him. 'Isn't it so that I am your mother, and that your elder brother is just like a father to you?' so I said to him. And he became afraid and assaulted ⟨me⟩ to prevent me from making a disclosure to you. Now if you let him live, I shall pass away. See, when he returns, don't [let him live any longer], because I curse this wicked proposition which he would have carried out yesterday."[7]

4. This sentence, which is also not part of the narrative proper, serves to explain how Anubis would customarily return home before Bata, thus setting the stage for the episode at the barn door.

5. E. Rowińska and J. K. Winnicki, in *GM* 134 (1993): 85–89, argue that the verb here means "spitting," expressing contempt of Bata, rather than "vomiting," although in the Israel Stela, line 20, the same verb refers to disgorging after the manner of a crocodile.

6. On this passage and its sexual connotation, see E. Graefe, in *SAK* 7 (1979): 53–61, and P. Derchain, in *SAK* 7: 62–63.

7. Or, "I am suffering from this wicked proposition which he would have carried out yesterday," but the determinative of the verb favors "curse." The term "yesterday" is used because day was over at sunset, even though the Egyptian day began at dawn.

5,5  Then his elder brother became / like an Upper Egyptian panther, and he sharpened his spear and put it in his hand. His elder ⟨brother⟩ then stood behind the door ⟨of⟩ his stable in order to kill his younger brother as he was returning in the evening to let his cattle enter the stable. Now when the sun set, he loaded himself ⟨with⟩ all sorts of field vegetables according to his daily habit, and returned. The lead cow entered the stable and said to her herdsman, "Look, your elder brother is standing in wait for you holding his spear to kill you. You must get away from him." He heard what his lead 6,1 cow said, and / the next one entered and said the same. He looked under the door of his stable and saw his elder brother's feet as he was standing behind the door with his spear in his hand. He set his load onto the ground and hastened to run off in flight, and his elder brother went in pursuit of him, carrying his spear.

6,5  Then his younger brother prayed to Pre-Harakhti, / saying, "My good lord, it is you who distinguishes wrong from right." Thereupon Pre heard all his petitions, and Pre caused a great (gulf of) water to come between him and his elder ⟨brother⟩, infested with crocodiles, so that one of them came to be on one side and the other on the other (side). His elder brother struck twice upon (the back of) his hand because he had failed to kill him. Then his younger brother called to him on the (other) side, saying, "Wait there until 7,1 dawn. As soon as the sun disk rises, I shall / contend with you in his presence, and he will deliver the culprit to the just, for I shall nevermore be with you, nor shall I be in a place where you are. I shall go to the Valley of the Cedar."

  Now after dawn and the next day had come about, Pre-Harakhti arose, and they looked at each other. Then the youth had words with his elder brother, saying, "What's the meaning of your coming in pursuit of me in order to kill ⟨me⟩ unjustly without having heard what I have to say? For I'm 7,5 still your young brother; and / you are just like a father to me, and your wife is just like a mother to me, isn't it so? When you sent ⟨me⟩ to fetch us seed, your wife said to me, 'Come, let's spend an hour lying together.' But see, it has been distorted for you into something otherwise." Then he informed him about all that had transpired between him and his wife. He swore by Pre-Harakhti, saying, "As for your ⟨coming⟩ to kill me unjustly, carrying your spear, (it was) because of a sexually aroused slut!" He got a reed knife, cut off his phallus, and threw it into the water. The catfish swallowed ⟨it⟩, 8,1 and he / grew weak and became feeble. His elder brother became very grieved and stood weeping for him aloud. He could not cross over to where his younger brother was because of the crocodiles.

84

Then his younger brother called to him, saying, "If you have recalled a grievance, can't you recall a kindness or something that I have done for you? Now go to your home and take care of your cattle, for I shall not stay in a place where you are. I shall go off to the Valley of the Cedar. Now what you shall do on my behalf is to come and take care of me if ⟨you⟩ find out that something has happened to me ⟨after⟩ I extract my heart and put it on top of the blossom of the cedar tree. And if the cedar tree is cut down and 8,5 falls to the ground, / you are to come to search for it. Even if you spend seven years searching for it, don't let your heart become discouraged, for if you do find it and put it into a bowl of cool water, then I will become alive in order that ⟨I⟩ may avenge the wrong done to me. Now you shall ascertain whether something ⟨has happened⟩ to me if a jar of beer is delivered to you in your hand and produces froth. Don't delay upon seeing that this comes to pass with you."

Then he went off to the Valley of the Cedar, and his elder brother went off to his home, his hands placed upon his head and his (body) smeared with dirt. Presently he reached his home, and he killed his wife, cast her ⟨to⟩ the dogs, and sat down in mourning over his younger brother.

Now many days after this, his younger brother was in the Valley of the Cedar with no one with him as he spent all day hunting desert game. He returned in the evening to sleep under the cedar tree on top of whose 9,1 blossom his heart was. And / many days after this, he built for himself a country villa with his (own) hands ⟨in⟩ the Valley of the Cedar, filled with all sorts of good things, with the intention of establishing a household for himself.

Presently he went out from his country villa and encountered the Ennead[8] as they were walking (along) governing the entire land. The Ennead spoke in unison, saying to him, "Oh, Bata, Bull of the Ennead, are you alone here having abandoned your town before the face of the wife of Anubis, 9,5 your elder brother? / See, ⟨he⟩ has killed his wife, and thus you will be avenged upon him ⟨for⟩ all wrong done against you." And they felt very sorry for him. Pre-Harakhti told Khnum,[9] "Please fashion a (marriageable) woman for Bata so that he does not (have to) live alone." Thereupon Khnum made for him a house companion who was more beautiful in her body than any woman in the entire land, for ⟨the seed of⟩ every god was in

8. The company of the major gods.
9. A creator god represented as shaping man on a potter's wheel.

85

her. Then the seven Hathors[10] came ⟨to⟩ see her and said with one voice, "It is [by] an (executioner's) blade that she shall die."

So he coveted her intensely while she was dwelling in his house and
10,1 he spent all day / hunting desert game, bringing (it) back and putting (it) down before her. He told her, "Don't go outside lest the sea carry you away, for I will be unable to rescue you from it, because I am a female like you and my heart lies on top of the blossom of the cedar tree. But if another finds it, I shall fight with him." Then he revealed to her all his inmost thoughts.

Now many days after this, while Bata went to hunt according to his
10,5 daily habit, / the maiden[11] went out to stroll under the cedar tree which was next to her house. Then she beheld the sea surging up behind her, and she hastened to flee from it and entered her house. So the sea called to the cedar tree, saying, "Seize hold of her for me," and the cedar tree removed a tress from her hair. Then the sea brought it to Egypt and deposited it in the place of the launderers of Pharaoh, l.p.h. So the scent of the tress of hair turned up in the clothes of Pharaoh, l.p.h., and the king wrangled with the laun-derers of Pharaoh, l.p.h., saying, "Scent of ointment is in the clothes of
11,1 Pharaoh, l.p.h.!" The king got to wrangling with them daily, but / they didn't know what to do. The chief launderer of Pharaoh, l.p.h., went to the bank, very worried as a consequence of the daily wranglings with him. Then ⟨he⟩ stopped short and stood on the seashore opposite the tress of hair that was in the water. He had someone go down, and it was brought to him. ⟨Its⟩ scent was found exceedingly fragrant, and he took it away to Pharaoh, l.p.h.

Then the learned scribes of Pharaoh, l.p.h., were brought. They told
11,5 Pharaoh, l.p.h., "As for this tress of hair, / it belongs to a daughter of Pre-Harakhti in whom is the seed of every god. Now it is tribute to you ⟨from⟩ another country. Send envoys forth to every foreign country to search for her. As for the envoy who will go to the Valley of the Cedar, have many men go along with ⟨him⟩ to fetch her." Then His Majesty, l.p.h., said, "What you have said is very, very good." And (they) were sent off.

Now many days after this, the men who had gone abroad returned to render report to His Majesty, l.p.h., whereas those who had gone to the Valley of the Cedar failed to return, for Bata had killed them, leaving (only) one of them to render report to His Majesty, l.p.h. So His Majesty, l.p.h.,
12,1 sent forth many soldiers as well as chariotry in order to bring her back, / a

10. The goddesses who determine an individual's fate; see The Doomed Prince, n. 1.
11. Bata's wife is still a virgin.

woman being among them through whom all sorts of beautiful feminine adornments were presented to her (Bata's wife). The woman returned to Egypt with her, and there was jubilation for her in the entire land. His Majesty, l.p.h., loved her very much and appointed her to (the rank of) Chief Lady. Then he spoke with her in order to have her divulge the nature of her husband, but she said to His Majesty, l.p.h., "Have the cedar tree cut down and chopped up." The king sent / soldiers carrying their tools to cut down the cedar tree, and they reached the cedar tree. They cut off the blossom upon which Bata's heart was, and he fell dead that very instant.

12,5

Now after dawn and the next day had come about and the cedar tree had been cut down, Anubis, Bata's elder brother, entered his house, and he sat down and washed his hands. He was handed a jar of beer, and it produced froth. Another of wine was handed him, and it turned bad. Then he took his / staff and his sandals as well as his clothes and his weapons, and he hastened to journey to the Valley of the Cedar. He entered the country villa of his younger brother and found his younger brother lying dead upon his bed. He wept when ⟨he⟩ saw ⟨his⟩ younger brother lying in death, and he went to search for his younger brother's heart beneath the cedar tree under which his younger brother slept in the evening. / He spent three years searching for it without finding it. Now when he had commenced the fourth year, his heart desired to return to Egypt, and he said, "I shall depart tomorrow," so he said in his heart.

13,1

13,5

Now after dawn and the next day had come about, he began walking under the cedar tree and spent all day searching for it. He quit in the evening. He spent time to search for it again, and he found a (cedar) cone.[12] He left for home with it: it was indeed his younger brother's heart. And he fetched a bowl of cool water, dropped it into it, and sat down according to his daily ⟨habit⟩.

After night had fallen, / his heart absorbed the water, and Bata shuddered over all his body and began looking at his elder brother while his heart was (still) in the bowl. Anubis, his elder brother, took the bowl of cool water in which his younger brother's heart was and ⟨had⟩ him drink it. His heart assumed its (proper) position, and he became as he used to be. So they embraced each other and conversed with one another. Then Bata said to his / elder brother, "Look, I shall transform (myself) into a large bull that

14,1

14,5

12. Because of a cedar cone's similarity to a bunch of grapes, the Egyptian uses the word "grapes."

has every beautiful color and whose sort is unparalleled, and you shall sit upon ⟨my⟩ back. By the time the sun rises, we shall be where my wife is that ⟨I⟩ may avenge myself. And you shall take me to where the king[13] is, for every sort of good thing shall be done for you and you shall be rewarded with silver and gold for taking me to Pharaoh, l.p.h., because I shall become a great marvel, and there shall be jubilation for me in the entire land. And (then) you shall depart to your village."

15,1     Now after dawn / and the next day had come about, Bata transformed (himself) into the form which he had mentioned to his elder brother. Then Anubis, his elder brother, sat down upon his back. At dawn he arrived at the place where the king was, and His Majesty, l.p.h, was informed about him. He saw him and became very joyful over him. He made a grand oblation for him, saying, "It is a great marvel that has come to pass." And
15,5    there was jubilation for him in the entire land. Then / his weight was made up in silver and gold for his elder brother,[14] who (again) settled down in his village. The king gave him much personnel and many goods, for Pharaoh, l.p.h., loved him very much, more than anybody else in the entire land.

    Now many days after this, he (the bull) entered the kitchen and stood in the place where the Lady was, and he began speaking with her, saying, "See, I'm still alive!" She asked him, "Who indeed are you?" And he told her, "I am Bata. I realize that when you caused the cedar tree to be chopped up for Pharaoh, l.p.h., it was on account of me, to keep me from staying alive.
16,1    See, / I'm still alive, but as a bull." The Lady became very fearful because of the declaration her husband had made to her. Then he left the kitchen.

    His Majesty, l.p.h., sat down and made holiday with her. She poured (drinks) for His Majesty, l.p.h., so that the king was very happy with her. Then she said to His Majesty, l.p.h., "Swear to me by God as follows, 'As for what ⟨she⟩ will say, I shall grant it to her.'" And he heard all that she said,
16,5    "Let me eat of the liver of this bull, / for he will never amount to anything," so she said speaking to him. The king became very vexed over what she had said, and Pharaoh, l.p.h., felt very sorry for him.

    Now after dawn and the next day had come about, the king proclaimed a grand oblation as an offering up of the bull, and he sent a chief royal butler of His Majesty, l.p.h., to sacrifice the bull. Thereupon he was sacri-

13. Here and following, the Egyptian uses the term "One" in reference to the king.
14. That is, the elder brother was rewarded with an amount of silver and gold equivalent to the weight of the bull.

ficed. While he was upon the men's shoulders, he twitched in his neck and shed two drops of blood beside the two doorposts of His Majesty, l.p.h., one chancing on one side of the great portal of Pharaoh, l.p.h., and the 17,1 other on the other side. They grew into / two large Persea trees, each of which was exquisite. Then someone went to tell His Majesty, l.p.h., "Two large Persea trees have grown this night as a great marvel for His Majesty, l.p.h., beside the great portal of His Majesty, l.p.h." And there was jubilation for them in the entire land, and the king presented an offering to them.

Now many days after this, His Majesty, l.p.h., appeared at the audience window of lapis lazuli with a wreath of all sorts of flowers on ⟨his⟩ neck, 17,5 and he ⟨mounted⟩ a chariot of electrum / and came out from the palace, l.p.h., to inspect the Persea trees. Then the Lady came out in a chariot following Pharaoh, l.p.h. His Majesty, l.p.h., sat down under one Persea tree, ⟨and the Lady under the other. And Bata⟩ spoke with his wife, "Ha, you liar! I am Bata. I'm alive in spite of you. I realize that when you had ⟨the cedar tree⟩ cut down for Pharaoh, l.p.h., it was on account of me. I transformed ⟨myself⟩ into a bull, and you had me killed."

Now many days after this, the Lady stood pouring (drinks) for His Majesty, l.p.h., so that the king was happy with her. She told His Majesty, l.p.h., "Swear to me by God as follows, 'As for what the Lady will say to me, 18,1 I shall grant it to her,' so you shall say." And he heard / all that she said. She said, "Have these two Persea trees cut down and made into fine furniture." So the king heard all that she said. After [a] little while His Majesty, l.p.h., sent skilled craftsmen, and the Persea trees of Pharaoh, l.p.h., were cut down. The queen, the Lady, watched this, and then a splin- 18,5 ter flew up and entered the Lady's mouth. / She swallowed ⟨it⟩ and became pregnant in the completion of a brief moment, and the king made out of them (the Persea trees) whatever was her desire.

Now many days after this, she bore a son, and someone went to tell His Majesty, l.p.h., "A son has been born to you." Then he was brought, and nurse and maids were assigned to him. And there was jubilation ⟨for him⟩ in the entire land. The king sat down and made holiday, and they began to nurture him.[15] His Majesty, l.p.h., loved him very much from that moment, 19,1 and he appointed him / Viceroy of Kush. And many days after this, His Majesty, l.p.h., made him crown prince of the entire land.

15. The verb translated "nurture" refers basically to the physical act of nursing a child but its semantic range also included child-rearing in an extended sense.

Now many days after this, when he had completed many [years] as crown prince in ⟨the⟩ entire land, His Majesty, l.p.h., flew up to the sky.[16] Then the king[17] said, "Have my high officials of His Majesty, l.p.h., brought

19,5 to me that I may inform them regarding everything / that has happened to me." His wife [was] then brought to him, and he contended with her in their presence.[18] An affirmative (decision) was reached among them.[19] His elder brother was brought to him, and he made him crown prince in the entire land. He ⟨spent⟩ thirty years as king of Egypt. He departed from life, and his elder brother succeeded him on the day of death.

Thus it concludes happily and successfully.

16. A common expression used to refer to the death of the king, see above, The Story of Sinuhe, R 6.
17. I.e., Bata, the new king.
18. That is, Bata litigated with his wife. The expression cannot mean that Bata judged his wife, as is evident from the use of the same locution in Two Brothers 6,9–7,1.
19. The implication is the condemnation of Bata's unfaithful wife, whose death by execution had been fated by the seven Hathors.

# THE CONTENDINGS OF HORUS
# AND SETH

T his, the longest of the New Kingdom stories, is perhaps the one with the least literary merit, for there is very little in the way of suspense to maintain the reader's interest throughout the narrative. It is the theme of Horus's superiority over his rival Seth in contending for the throne, previously occupied by Horus's father Osiris, that serves to bind together an episodically constructed tale, whose narrative style is especially monotonous. The section in which Isis harpoons the two rivals who had transformed themselves into hippopotamuses appears independently in two Ramesside papyri that are calendars of lucky and unlucky days. Some of the episodes, such as the homosexual encounter between the two protagonists, are alluded to in earlier religious literature of the Old and Middle Kingdoms.

The Contendings is best appreciated in terms of the function of the mythically oriented short story during the New Kingdom. This particular story, preserved to us on a papyrus of the reign of Ramesses V, contains some other compositions of literary worth, so that it would seem that the papyrus may have been used by its owner for the purpose of entertaining himself and others. The behavior of some of the great gods is at points so shocking that it is hard to imagine that no humor was intended. Yet at the same time the story provides the reader with basic mythical concepts. Such a dichotomy between coarse humor, even about the gods, and seriousness in religion characterized the Ramesside age.

*Although in the resolution of the story Horus is awarded his father's king-ship, Seth is not totally defeated, for he is given a place in the scheme of things as an assistant to the sun god. It might be inferred that contention was a necessary prerequisite for the proper functioning of the kingship to bring about harmony in society. The tale concludes with a brief hymn in praise of Horus's ascendancy to the throne.*

*The Contendings is translated and treated extensively in Michèle Broze,* Mythe et roman en Égypte ancienne: Les Aventures d'Horus et Seth dans le Papyrus Chester Beatty I, *(Brussels, 1996).*

E.F.W.

1,1     [There came to pass] the adjudication of Horus and Seth, mysterious in (their) forms and mightiest of the princes and magnates who had ever come into being. Now it was a young [god] that was seated[1] in the presence of the Universal Lord, claiming the office of his father Osiris, beautiful in (his) appearances, the [son of Pt]ah, who illumines [the west with] his [shee]n, while Thoth was presenting the sound Eye to the great prince who is in Heliopolis. Then said Shu, the son of Re, in the presence of [Atum], the great [prince] who is in Heliopolis, "Justice is a possessor of power.

1,5     [Administer] it by saying, 'Award the office to [Horus].' " / Then said Thoth to the [Ennead], "That's correct a million times!" Thereupon Isis[2] let out a loud [cr]y rejoicing exce[edingly, and she stood be]fore the Universal [Lord] and said, "North wind, (go) to the west! Impart the good news to Onnophris,[3] l.p.h.!" Then said Shu, the son [of Re], "[The] one who presents the sound Eye[4] is loyal to the Ennead."

    [State]ment by the Universal Lord, "What's the meaning of your ex-ercising authority alone by yourselves?" [Onuris][5] then said, "He (Horus) shall [assum]e the cartouche of Horus, and the White Crown shall be [placed] upon his head." And so the Universal Lord was silent a long [whi]le, [being] furious [at] this Ennead. Then Seth, the son of Nut, said,

1. Referring to Harpocrates, the child Horus, frequently represented in late bronzes as a squatting infant with his finger in his mouth.
2. Isis and Osiris are the parents of Horus.
3. A designation of Osiris meaning: He who is continually beneficent.
4. Referring to Thoth. Alternatively this sentence can be translated, "[To] present the sound Eye seems right to the Ennead."
5. The restoration of this name is uncertain.

1,10   "Have him dismissed outside / with me, and you will, I assure you, see my hands prevail ⟨over⟩ his hands [in the pre]sence of the Ennead, since there is not known [any] other method of dispossessing him." Thoth then said to him, "Shouldn't we ascertain who is the imposter? Is the office of Osiris to be awarded to Seth even while his son Horus is still about?"

2,1         Pre-Harakhti became exceedingly furious, for it was Pre's wish / to award the office to Seth, great in virility, the son of Nut. Onuris let out a loud cry before the face of the Ennead, saying, "What are we going to do?" Then Atum, the great prince who is in Heliopolis, said, "Let Banebdjede, the great living god, be [summon]ed that he may judge between the two youths." Banebdjede, the great god who resides in Sehêl,[6] and Ptah-Tatenen were brought before Atum, who told them, "Judge between the two youths.

2,5   Stop them from being engaged so in quarreling every day." Thereupon / Banebdjede, the great living god, answered what he had said, "Let's not exercise (our) authority ignorantly. Have a letter sent to Neith the Great, the God's Mother. As for what she will say, we shall do it."

        The Ennead then said to Banebdjede, the great living god, "They have been adjudged already in the primeval time in the 'One are the Truths' court." Then the Ennead said to Thoth in the presence of the Universal Lord, "Please draw up a letter to Neith the Great, the God's Mother, in the name of the Universal Lord, the Bull who resides in Heliopolis." Thoth said, "I'll do so; yes, I'll do so, I'll do so!" Then he sat down to draw up the letter and wrote:

2,10   "The King of Upper and Lower Egypt, / Re-Atum, beloved of Thoth; the Lord of the Two Lands, the Heliopolitan; the solar disk that illumines the Two Lands with its sheen; the Nile mighty in flooding; Re-Harakhti (while Neith the Great, the God's Mother, who illumined the first face, is alive, healthy, and rejuvenated); the living manifestation of the Universal Lord, the Bull in Heliopolis, being the good King of Egypt. To wit: I, your humble servant, spend all night on Osiris's behalf inquiring about the Two Lands each day, while Sobek endures forever. What are we going to do with

3,1   these two individuals, who for eighty years now have been in court, but / no one has been able to judge between the two? Please write us what we should do."

        Then Neith the Great, the God's Mother, sent a letter to the Ennead, saying, "Award the office of Osiris to his son Horus. Don't commit such

---

6. An island in the area of the First Cataract.

93

blatant acts of injustice which are improper, or I shall become so furious that the sky touches the ground. And let the Universal Lord, the Bull who resides in Heliopolis, be told, 'Enrich Seth in his possessions. Give him

3,5 Anath and Astarte, your two daughters, and / install Horus in the position of his father Osiris.' "

And so the letter of Neith the Great, the God's Mother, reached this Ennead as they were sitting in the "Horus with the Projecting Horns" court, and the letter was delivered into Thoth's hand. Then Thoth read it out in the presence of the Universal Lord and the entire Ennead, and they declared unanimously, "This goddess is correct." Then the Universal Lord became furious at Horus and told him, "You are despicable in your person, and this office is too much for you, you lad, the odor of whose mouth is bad."[7]

Onuris became furious to the nth degree and so did the entire Ennead constituting the Council of the Thirty, l.p.h. Bebon,[8] the god, got right up

3,10 and / told Pre-Harakhti, "Your shrine is vacant!" Pre-Harakhti took offense at the insult which was said to him and lay down on his back very much saddened. And so the Ennead went outside and let out a loud cry before the face of Bebon, the god. They told him, "Get out! This offense that you have committed is exceedingly great!" And they departed to their

4,1 tents. And so the great god spent a day / lying on his back in his pavilion very much saddened and alone by himself.

After a long while Hathor, Lady of the Southern Sycamore, came and stood before her father, the Universal Lord, and she exposed her private parts before his very eyes. Thereupon the great god laughed at her. Then he got up and sat down with the Great Ennead. He said to Horus and Seth, "Speak for yourselves!" Then Seth, great in virility, the son of Nut, said, "As for me, I am Seth, greatest in virility among ⟨the⟩ Ennead, for I slay

4,5 the / opponent of Pre[9] daily while I am at the prow of the Barque of Millions, whereas not any (other) god is able to do this. I should receive the office of Osiris." Then they said, "Seth, the son of Nut, is correct." Onuris and Thoth then let out a loud cry, saying, "Is the office to be awarded to a maternal uncle even while a bodily son is still about?" Then said Baneb-

---

7. Referring to the bad breath of a young infant.

8. A disruptive god, in the form of a monkey or a dog.

9. The reference is to Seth's beneficial role as daily vanquisher of Apopis, the snake monster that embodied chaos.

djede, the great living god, "Is the office to be awarded to the lad even while Seth, his elder brother,[10] is still about?"

The Ennead let out a loud cry before the face of the Universal Lord and said to him, "What's the meaning of the words you spoke which are unfit to be heard?"[11] Then said Horus, son of Isis, "It's no good, this cheating me 4,10 in the presence of / the Ennead and depriving me of the office of my father Osiris." Thereupon Isis became furious at the Ennead and took an oath by god in the presence of the Ennead as follows, "By my mother Neith, the goddess, and by Ptah-Tatenen, with lofty plumes, who curbs the horns of gods, these matters should be submitted before Atum, the great prince who is in Heliopolis, and also (before) Khepri, who is in his barque." And the Ennead said to her, "Don't be angry! The rights will be given to the one who is in the right. All that you've said will be done."

5,1 Seth, the son / of Nut, became furious at the Ennead because they had said these words to Isis the Great, the God's Mother. So Seth said to them, "I shall take my scepter of 4,500 *nemset*-weight and kill one of you a day." And then Seth took an oath by the Universal Lord, saying, "I shall not contend in court as long as Isis is in it." Pre-Harakhti then told them, "You shall ferry across to the Island in the Middle and decide between them 5,5 there, and tell Nemty, the ferryman, not to ferry / any woman across resembling Isis." And so the Ennead ferried across to the Island in the Middle and sat down and ate bread.

Then Isis, having transformed herself into an old woman who walked with a stoop and (wearing) a small golden signet ring on her hand, came and approached Nemty, the ferryman, as he was sitting near his boat. She said to him, "It's in order that you might ferry ⟨me⟩ across to the Island in the Middle that I've come to you. For I've come with this bowlful of flour for 5,10 the young lad, / because for five days now he has been tending some cattle[12] on the Island in the Middle and is hungry." He said to her, "I've been told not to ferry any woman across." But she said to him, "It's with reference to Isis that you've been told this which you've (just) said." He asked her, "What will you give me that you may be ferried across to the Island in the Middle?" And Isis answered him, "I will give you this cake." Then he said

10. Through fusion of myths Seth is both the brother of Horus and his uncle.
11. The words of the Universal Lord have been omitted from the story, possibly for the very reason that they were not fit to be heard or written.
12. Lit. "after some cattle," but through paronomasia the word for cattle could also mean "office."

to her, "What good will it be to me, your cake? Is it in exchange for your cake that I should ferry you across to the Island in the Middle even though I was told not to ferry any woman across?" / Then she said to him, "I will give you the golden signet ring which is on ⟨my⟩ hand." He told her, "Hand over the golden signet ring!" and she gave it to him. Then he ferried her across to the Island in the Middle.

6,1

Now as she was walking under the trees, she looked and saw the Ennead sitting eating bread in the presence of the Universal Lord in his pavilion. Seth looked and saw her when she had come closer from afar. Then she conjured by means of her magic and transformed herself / into a maiden whose body was beautiful and whose like did not exist in the entire land. Thereupon he desired her most lecherously.

6,5

Seth got up from sitting eating bread with the Great Ennead and went to meet her, for no one had seen her except himself. Then he stood behind a sycamore tree, and he called her and said to her, "I'm here with you, beautiful maiden." And she said to him, "⌈Reflect⌉, my great lord. As for me, I was the wife of a cattleman to whom I bore a son. My husband died, and the lad started tending his father's cattle. / But then a stranger came and settled down in my stable. He said thus speaking to my son, 'I shall beat you, confiscate your father's cattle, and evict you,' said he speaking to him. Now it is my wish to have you be a champion for him." Thereupon Seth said to her, "Are the cattle to be given to the stranger even while the man's son is still about?"

6,10

And so Isis transformed herself into a kite, flew up, and perched on top of an acacia tree. She called Seth and said to him, "Be ashamed[13] of yourself! It's your own mouth that has said it. It's your own cleverness / that has judged you. What more do you want?" And so he became ashamed and went to where Pre-Harakhti was, (still) ashamed. Then Pre-Harakhti said to him, "What more do you want?" Seth answered him, "That wicked woman came back to me. She has tricked me again, having transformed herself into a beautiful maiden before my eyes. She said to me, 'As for me, I was the wife of a cattleman, who is dead. I bore him a son, who tended / some of his father's cattle. A stranger took lodging at my stable with my son, and I gave him food. Now many days after this, the vagabond said to my son, "I shall beat you and confiscate your father's cattle, and they will become mine," said he in speaking to my son.' So she said to me."

7,1

7,5

13. On the verb *ṯm*, "be ashamed," see Michael V. Fox, *The Song of Songs and the Ancient Egyptian Love Songs* (Madison, 1985), p. 60.

Then Pre-Harakhti said to him, "And what did you say to her?" And Seth told him, "I said to her, 'Are the cattle to be given to the stranger even while the man's son is still about?' so I said / to her. 'The vagabond's face should be struck with a rod, and he should be evicted and your son put in his father's position,' so I said to her." Thereupon Pre-Harakhti said to him, "Now look here, it's you yourself that has judged yourself. What more do you want?" So Seth said to him, "Have Nemty, the ferryman, brought and severe punishment inflicted upon him, saying, 'Why did you let her ferry across?' so it shall be said to him." Then Nemty, the ferryman, was brought before the Ennead, and the forepart of his feet removed. So / Nemty abjured gold even to this day in the presence of the Great Ennead, saying, "Gold shall be for me an abomination unto my city!"[14] Then the Ennead ferried across to the western bank and sat down on the mountain.

Now ⟨afterward⟩ at evening time Pre-Harakhti and Atum,[15] Lord of the Two Lands, the Heliopolitan, wrote to the Ennead, saying, "What are you doing still sitting there? As for the two youths, you will be having them finish out their lifetime in court! When my letter reaches you, you shall place the White Crown upon the head of Horus, son of Isis, and appoint him to the position of his father / Osiris."

Thereupon Seth became terribly enraged. And so the Ennead said to Seth, "Why have you become so enraged? Isn't it in accordance with what Atum, Lord of the Two Lands, the Heliopolitan, and Pre-Harakhti have said that action should be taken?" Then the White Crown was placed upon the head of Horus, son of Isis. Seth, being angry, let out a loud cry before the face of this Ennead, saying, "Is the office being awarded to my young brother even while I, who am his elder brother, am still about?" Then he took an oath as follows, "The White Crown shall be removed from the head of Horus, son of Isis, and he shall be thrown into the water so that I can contend with him for the office of Ruler." Pre-Harakhti acquiesced.

Thereupon Seth said to Horus, "Come, let's both transform ourselves into hippopotamuses and submerge in / the deep waters in the midst of the sea. Now as for the one who shall emerge within the span of three whole months, the office shall not be awarded him." Then they both submerged. And so Isis sat down and wept, saying, "Seth has killed Horus, my son!"

14. Apparently gold was taboo in Nemty's town of Djufyet, located just north of Assiut.
15. Pre-Harakhti and Atum were the morning and evening forms of the same god, as is evident in the lines following, where the first person singular pronoun is used.

Then she fetched a skein of yarn. She fashioned a line, took a *deben*-weight's (worth) of copper, cast it into a harpoon, tied the line to it, and

9,1   hurled it into the water at the spot where Horus and Seth had submerged. / Then the barb bit into the body of her son Horus. So Horus let out a loud cry, saying, "Help me, mother Isis, my mother! Appeal to your barb to let go of me! I am Horus, son of Isis!" Thereupon Isis let out a loud cry and told ⟨her⟩ barb, "Let go of him! See, that's my son Horus, my child." So her barb let go of him.

Then she hurled it back again into the water, and it bit into the body of Seth. So Seth let out a loud cry, saying, "What have I done against you,

9,5   my sister Isis? / Appeal to your barb to let go of me! I am your maternal brother, Isis." Then she felt very compassionate toward him. Thereupon Seth called to her, saying, "Do you love the stranger even more than ⟨your⟩ maternal brother Seth?" So Isis appealed to her barb, saying, "Let go of him! See, it's Isis's maternal brother whom you have bitten into." Then the barb let go of him.

Horus, son of Isis, became furious at his mother Isis and came out with his face as fierce as an Upper Egyptian panther's, holding his cleaver of sixteen *deben*-weight in his hand. He removed the head of his mother Isis,

9,10  put it in his arms, and ascended the mountain. Then Isis / transformed herself into a statue of flint which had no head. Pre-Harakhti said to Thoth, "What is she who has come having no head?" So Thoth told Pre-Harakhti, "My good lord, that's Isis the Great, the God's Mother, whose head Horus,

10,1  her son, has removed." Thereupon / Pre-Harakhti let out a loud cry and said to the Ennead, "Let's go and inflict severe punishment upon him." Then the Ennead ascended those mountains in order to search for Horus, son of Isis.

Now as for Horus, he was lying under a *shenusha*-tree in the oasis land. Seth found him, seized hold of him, threw him down upon his back on the mountain, removed his two eyes from their sockets, and buried them on the

10,5  mountain so as to illumine the earth. His two eyeballs became two bulbs / which grew into lotuses. Seth came away and told Pre-Harakhti falsely, "I didn't find Horus," although he had found him.

Then Hathor, Mistress of the Southern Sycamore, set out, and she found Horus lying weeping in the desert. She captured a gazelle and milked it. She said to Horus, "Open your eyes that I may put this milk in." So he opened his eyes and she put the milk in, putting (some) in the right one and putting (some) in the left one. She told him, "Open your eyes!" He opened his eyes, and she looked at them; she found that they were healed.

10,10       Then she / went to tell Pre-Harakhti, "I found Horus after Seth had deprived him of his eyes, but I have restored him (to health). See, he's back." Then said the Ennead, "Let Horus and Seth be summoned so that they may be judged." Then they were brought before the Ennead. The Universal Lord said before the Great Ennead to Horus and Seth, "Go and

11,1       pay heed to what I tell you: You shall eat and / drink so that we may have (some) peace. Stop quarreling so each day on end!" Then Seth told Horus, "Come, let's make holiday in my house." And Horus answered him, "I'll do so; yes, I'll do so, I'll do so."

      Now afterward at evening time, bed was prepared for them, and together they lay down. During the night Seth caused his phallus to become stiff and inserted it between Horus's thighs. Horus then placed his hands

11,5       between his thighs and caught Seth's semen. Then Horus / went to tell his mother Isis, "Help me, Isis, my mother, come and see what Seth has done to me." And he opened his hands and let her see Seth's semen. She let out a loud cry, took up her knife, cut off his hands, threw them into the water, and restored for him hands that were equivalent. Then she got some fragrant ointment and applied it to Horus's phallus. She caused it to become stiff and inserted it into a pot, and he caused his semen to flow down into it.

      Isis at morning time went carrying Horus's semen to the garden of

11,10   Seth, and she said to Seth's gardener, "What sort of vegetable / does Seth eat here in your company?" And the gardener answered her, "He doesn't eat any vegetable here in my company except lettuce."[16] And Isis put Horus's semen on it. Seth returned according to his daily habit and ate the lettuce, which he regularly ate. Thereupon he became pregnant with Horus's semen.

12,1       So Seth went to tell / Horus, "Come, let's go that I may contend with you in court." Horus said to him, "I'll do so; yes, I'll do so, I'll do so."

      Then they both went to court and stood in the presence of the Great Ennead. They were told, "Speak for yourselves!" Then Seth said, "Let me be awarded the office of Ruler, l.p.h., for as to Horus, the one who is standing (at law), I have performed a man's work against him." The Ennead then let out a loud cry, and they spewed and spat at Horus's face. Horus

---

16. Lettuce, being associated with the ithyphallic god Min, was regarded as an aphrodisiac.

12,5   laughed at them. Then Horus took / an oath by god as follows, "All that Seth has said is false. Let Seth's semen be summoned that we may see from where it answers, and my own be summoned that we may see from where it answers."

Then Thoth, lord of script and scribe of truth for the Ennead, laid his hand on Horus's shoulder and said, "Come out, you semen of Seth!" And it answered him from the water in the interior of the ⌜marsh⌝.[17] Then Thoth laid his hand on Seth's shoulder and said, "Come out, you semen of Horus!"

12,10   It said to him, "Where shall I come from?" Thoth said to it, "Come / out from his ear." Thereupon it said to him, "Am I, who am divine fluid, to come out merely from his ear?" Then Thoth said to it, "Come out from the top of his head." And it emerged as a golden solar disk upon Seth's head. Seth became exceedingly furious and extended his hand to seize the golden

13,1   solar disk, but Thoth took it away / from him and placed it as a crown upon his (own) head. Then the Ennead said, "Horus is right; Seth is wrong."

Seth became exceedingly furious and let out a loud cry when they said, "Horus is right; Seth is wrong." And so Seth took a great oath by god as follows, "He shall not be awarded the office until he has been dismissed outside with me and we build for ourselves some ships of stone and race

13,5   each other. Now as for the one who prevails over his rival, / he shall be awarded the office of Ruler, l.p.h." Then Horus built for himself a ship of cedar, plastered it over with gypsum, and launched it into the water at evening time without anybody who was in the entire land noticing this. Seth saw Horus's ship and thought it was of stone. And he went to the mountain, cut off a mountain top, and built for himself a ship of stone of 138 cubits. Then they embarked upon their ships in the presence of the Ennead, and Seth's ship sank in the water. So Seth transformed himself into a hippo-

13,10   potamus / and scuttled Horus's ship. Horus then picked up his harpoon and hurled it at Seth's body. Then the Ennead told him, "Don't hurl it at him!"

He gathered in the tackle, stowed it in his ship, and sailed downstream to Saïs in order to tell Neith the Great, the God's Mother, "Let me be

14,1   judged with Seth since it is eighty years now that we have been in court / and no one has been able to judge between us, nor has he yet been vindicated against me. But it is a thousand times now that I have been in the right against him each day, and yet he disregards all that the Ennead has said. I

17. Or possibly, "cucumber bed."

contended with him in the "Path of the Truths" court, and I was vindicated against him. I contended with him in the "Horus with the Projecting
Horns" court, and I was vindicated against him. I contended with him in
the "Field of Rushes" court, and I was vindicated against him. I contended
with him in the "Pool of the Field" court, and I was vindicated against him.
And the Ennead told Shu, the son of Re, 'Horus, son of Isis, is correct in all
that he has said.'"

14,5       / Statement which Thoth made to the Universal Lord, "Have a letter
sent to Osiris so that he may judge between the two youths." Then said Shu,
the son of Re, "What Thoth has told the Ennead is correct a million times."
The Universal Lord then said to Thoth, "Sit down and draw up a letter to
Osiris that we may hear what he has to say." Thoth sat down to fill out a
letter to Osiris as follows:

    "Bull, the lion who hunts for himself; Two Ladies, protecting the gods
and subduing the Two Lands; Horus of Gold, who invented humankind in
the primeval time; King of Upper and Lower Egypt, Bull residing in Heliopolis, l.p.h.; Son of Ptah, beneficial to the Two Banks, appearing as father
of his Ennead while he feeds on gold and every precious glaze: (In) life,
prosperity and health! Please write us what we should do with Horus and
Seth so that we do not exercise (our) authority ignorantly."

14,10       Now ⟨many days⟩ after this, the / letter reached the King, son of Re,
Great in Bounty and Lord of Sustenance. He let out a loud cry when the
letter was read out in his presence. Then he answered it very very quickly
(writing) to where the Universal Lord was together with the Ennead, saying, "Why should my son Horus be cheated when it was I who made you
mighty and it was I who created barley and emmer to sustain the gods as
well as the cattle[18] after the gods, whereas not any god or any goddess was
competent enough to do it?"

15,1       So / Osiris's letter reached the place where Pre-Harakhti was, sitting
together with the Ennead on the White Mound in Xois. It was read out in
his and the Ennead's presence, and Pre-Harakhti said, "Please answer for
me the letter very quickly to Osiris and tell him in the letter, 'If you had not
come into being and if you had not been born, barley and emmer would
exist anyway!'"

    The letter of the Universal Lord reached Osiris, and it was read out in
his presence. Then he wrote to Pre-Harakhti again as follows, "Very good is

18. Referring to mankind, see Papyrus Westcar 8,17.

all that you have done, O you who invented the Ennead as an accomplishment, yet justice has been allowed to sink down within the netherworld.

15,5 Please look at the situation also on your part. As for / the land in which I am, it is filled with savage-faced messengers who do not fear any god or goddess. I have but to send them forth, and they will bring back the heart of whoever commits misdeeds and they will be here with me. What's the meaning of my being here at rest in the west while you are all outside? Who is there among you[19] who is mightier than I? But see, you have invented injustice as an accomplishment. When Ptah the Great, South of his Wall, Lord of Ankhtowy, created the sky, isn't it so that he told the stars which are in it, 'Every night you shall set in the west in the place where King Osiris is'? (And he told me), 'Now after (the manner of) the gods, so patricians and commoners shall also go to rest in the place where you are,' so he said to me."

Now ⟨many days⟩ after this, Osiris's letter reached the place where the Universal Lord was together with the Ennead. Thoth received the letter

15,10 and read it out in the presence of Pre-Harakhti / and the Ennead. They said, "The Great in Bounty and Lord of Sustenance, l.p.h., is doubly correct in all that he has said." Then Seth said, "Let us be taken to the Island in the Middle so that I may contend with him." He then went to the Island in the Middle, and Horus was vindicated against him.

Then Atum, Lord of the Two Lands, the Heliopolitan, sent to Isis, saying, "Bring Seth restrained with manacles." Isis then brought Seth restrained with manacles, as a prisoner. Atum said to him, "Why are you preventing yourselves from being judged? Would you usurp for yourself the office of Horus?" Seth answered him, "On the contrary, my good lord.

16,1 Let Horus, son of Isis, be summoned and awarded the office of / his father Osiris."

Then Horus, son of Isis, was brought, and the White Crown was set upon his head and he was installed in the position of his father Osiris. He was told, "You are a good King of Egypt! You are good lord, l.p.h., of every land unto all eternity!" Thereupon Isis let out a loud shout to her son Horus, saying, "You are a good King! My heart is in joy; you have brightened earth with your sheen!"

The Ptah the Great, South of his Wall, Lord of Ankhtowy, said, "What

---

19. The papyrus actually employs the third person plural pronoun in this sentence and
the next.

shall be done for Seth now that Horus has been installed in the position of his father Osiris?" Pre-Harakhti replied, "Let me be given Seth, the son of Nut, that he may dwell with me, being a son to me, and he shall thunder in the sky and be feared."

16,5     Then someone / went to tell Pre-Harakhti, "Horus, son of Isis, has arisen as Ruler, l.p.h." Thereupon Pre-Harakhti rejoiced exceedingly and said to the Ennead, "You shall shout to the world in jubilation for Horus, son of Isis!" Then Isis said,

> "Horus has arisen as Ruler, l.p.h.
> The Ennead is in festivity;
> Heaven is in joy.
> They have donned wreaths
> Now that they have seen Horus, son of Isis,
> Arisen as great Ruler, l.p.h., of Egypt.
> As for the Ennead, their hearts are content;
> The entire land is in exultation
> Now that they have seen Horus, son of Isis,
> Assigned the office of his father Osiris, lord of Busiris."

Thus it concludes successfully in Thebes, the seat of Tebi.[20]

20. A designation of the sun god, unless in error for "the place of Truth."

# THE BLINDING OF TRUTH BY
# FALSEHOOD

I n Egyptian texts and iconography the concept of Truth is regularly personified as the goddess Maat, the daughter of Re. In this allegorical tale,
however, Truth is conceived of as a male who was blinded at his brother
Falsehood's behest because of circumstances, not quite clear, involving Truth's
treatment of a dagger that belonged to Falsehood. The theme of sibling rivalry is
reminiscent of the Horus and Seth feud and The Tale of the Two Brothers. In
none of these myths or stories is the antagonist totally annihilated, but rather a
resolution is effected so that a harmonious situation is achieved with the elimi-
nation of further strife. Such a resolution of conflicting opposites is typically
Egyptian and reflects the application of the principle of Maat, which embraces
the concepts of balance and harmony as well as truth. One's appreciation of this
short story would be enhanced if its beginning were preserved. The conclusion
and juridical aspects of the dispute are discussed by A. Théodoridès, in RdE 21
(1969): 85–105.

E.F.W.

1,5       [... / and ... ] went [... the Ennea]d [... : ... a dagger of which the
Moun]tain of E[l forms the blade, of which the ʿwoodsʾ of Coptos form
2,1       the haft], of which the / god's tomb forms the scabbard, and of which [the

herds of] Kal form the belt.[1] Then Falsehood said to the Ennead, "Let [Tru]th [be brought] and blinded ⟨in⟩ both his eyes and assigned to be doorkeeper of my house." [The] Ennead then did according to all that he said.

2,5   Now many days after this, Falsehood raised his eyes to have a look, and he observed / the exemplariness of Truth, his elder brother. Falsehood said to Truth's two servants, "Now ab[duct] your master and [cast] him [to] a vicious lion that has many lionesses [as mate]s, and ˹they˺ shall [devour him." So they] abducted him. Now as they were going up carrying him,

3,1   Truth [told his servant]s, "Don't abduct [me, but] put [someone] / else [in place of me ... One of you go to town] and find me a bit of ˹bread˺ [..." So the servant] went that he might tell Falsehood, "When [we] left [him ..., a lion] came out from the ... and ˹devoured˺ him in the ..."[2]

3,5   Now [many days] after this, (the lady) N.[3] / came out [of] her house [with her retinue], ˹clad˺ [..., and they s]aw him (Truth) [lying under a thicke]t and (saw) [how handsome he] was, there being none like [him in the] entire land. Then [they] went [to where] (the lady) N. was and [said,

4,1   "Co]me [along with] us so that [you can s]ee / [the blind man] left lying under the thicket. He should be fetched and assigned to be doorkeeper of our house." (The lady) N. said ⟨to⟩ her,[4] "You shall go to (fetch) him that I may see him." And she went and fetched him. [Then] (the lady) N. saw him, and [sh]e desired him intensely when she saw [how handsome] he was in all his ˹body˺. He went to bed with her that night and had sexual intercourse

4,5   with her. / So she became pregnant that very night with a baby boy.

Now many days after this, she gave birth to a son whose like did not exist in this [entire] land, [for he was] big in [...] a [...], being [in] the

5,1   nature [of] a young god. He was sent to / school and mastered writing very well, and he practiced all the arts of war so that he (even) surpassed his older (school)mates who were at school with him. His (school)mates said to

1. Falsehood had apparently lent a fantastic dagger, constructed of materials from the places mentioned, to Truth, who had either damaged or mislaid it. Although the location of the Mountain of El is unknown, Kal is well-known as an Egyptian province in the Sudan.
2. The restorations are uncertain.
3. The name of the lady is lost in all its occurrences. Possibly it was a personified concept such as Greed.
4. One of the lady's maidservants.

him, "Whose son are you? You don't have a father!" And they would revile him and mock him, "You don't really have a father!"

5,5     So the / boy said to his mother, "What's my father's name that ⟨I⟩ may tell it to my (school)mates? For if they speak with me, 'Where is your father?' they keep saying to me and mocking me." His mother said to him, "Do you see that blind man who is sitting next to the door? He's your
6,1     father," / so she said answering him. Then he said to her, "The members of your family ought to be gathered together and made to summon a crocodile."[5]

And the boy brought his father and had him sit down on a chair supporting him, and he placed a footstool under his feet. And he put food
6,5     before him and let him eat and / drink. The boy said to his father, "Who was it that blinded you so that ⟨I⟩ may avenge you?" And he answered him, "It was my younger brother who blinded me." And he told him all that had happened to him.

7,1     He set out ⟨to⟩ avenge / his father and took (along) ten loaves, a staff, a pair of sandals, a waterskin, and a sword. And he fetched an ox of very beautiful appearance and went ⟨to⟩ where Falsehood's herdsman was. He said to him, "Now take for yourself these ten loaves as well as this staff,
7,5     this / waterskin, this sword, and this pair of sandals, and keep watch over this ox for me until I return from town."

Now many days after this, his ox completed many months in the charge
8,1     of Falsehood's herdsman. Then Falsehood / went to the fields to inspect his cattle, and he saw that that ox belonging to the boy was exceedingly beautiful in appearance. He said to his herdsman, "Give me that ox that ⟨I⟩ may eat it." But the herdsman told him, "It isn't mine, so I won't be able to give it to you." Then Falsehood said to him, "See, all my cattle are in your charge. Give one of them to its owner."

8,5     The boy learned / that Falsehood had appropriated his ox, and he came to where Falsehood's herdsman was and said to him, "Where is my ox? I don't see it among your cattle." Then the herdsman said to him, "All
9,1     the cattle are at your disposition. Take / for yourself the one you want." The boy then said to him, "Is there an ox as large as my own ox? If it should stand on The Island of Amon, the tip of its tail would be lying ⟨upon⟩ the papyrus marshes, while one of its horns would be on the western mountain

5. The boy is suggesting that relatives should have his mother killed as punishment for her immoral conduct.

and the other on the eastern mountain, and the Great River would be its
9,5 resting place,[6] while sixty calves are born to it / daily."

The herdsman said to him, "Is there an ox as large as the one you've
described?" So the boy seized hold of him and took him off ⟨to⟩ where
10,1 Falsehood was. And he took / Falsehood to the tribunal before the Ennead.
⟨They⟩ said to the boy, "[What you have said] is false. We've [ne]ver seen an
ox as large as the one you've described." The boy then [said to the Ennea]d,
"Is there a dagger as large as the one you described, of which the Mountain
of El forms the blade, of which the ʳwoodsᴵ of Coptos form the haft, of
which the god's tomb forms the scabbard, and of which the herds of Kal
form the belt?"

10,5 / Then ⟨he⟩ told the Ennead, "Judge between Truth and Falsehood. I
am his (Truth's) son. It is in order to avenge him that I have come." Then
Falsehood took an oath by the Lord, l.p.h., saying, "By [Amon] and by the
Ruler, l.p.h., if Truth be found alive, I shall be blinded ⟨in⟩ both my eyes
11,1 and assigned [to be door]keeper in the [house of Truth]." Then / the boy
[took the Ennead to where his father was],[7] and he was found (still) alive.
So [severe punishment] was inflicted [upon Falsehood]. He [was] smitten
with a hundred blows and five open wounds, blinded ⟨in⟩ [both his eyes,
and assigned to be doorkeepe]r [in] the house of Truth. And he [...].

[And so] the boy av[enged] h[is father], and (the dispute between)
11,5 Truth and Falsehood was settled / [...] the [...].

[Thus it] concludes [happily and successfully].

6. "The Island of Amon" is Diospolis Inferior, modern Tell el-Balamun, in the far north-
central Delta, and the Papyrus Marshes, the biblical Yam-sûph, "Sea of Reeds," is a
swampy area near Lake Manzalah. The Great River is the main course of the Nile
River.
7. The restoration here follows Lichtheim, *AEL,* vol. 2, 213, rather than Théodoridès, in
*RdE* 21 (1969): 104–5.

# ASTARTE AND THE INSATIABLE SEA

W ith the establishment of an Asiatic empire during the Eighteenth Dynasty, certain western Asiatic deities were introduced into Egypt, where they were worshipped in cult. This poorly preserved legend, recorded on a papyrus probably of the reign of Amenhotep II, is included in the collection of Late Egyptian stories because of its treatment of a theme found elsewhere in ancient Near Eastern literature. It is likely that this story of a conflict between the gods and the sea is an adaptation of a Ugaritic tale of the fight between Baal and the sea god Yam (see Theodore H. Gaster, in BiOr 9 (1952): 82–85) although Wolfgang Helck, "Zur Herkunft der Erzählung des sog. 'Astartepapyrus,'" in Manfred Görg, ed., Fontes atque Pontes: Eine Festgabe für Hellmut Brunner (Wiesbaden, 1983), 215–23, suggests that the Egyptian text was inspired by the Hurrian "Song of Ullikummi." Aside from the presence of the Semitic goddess Astarte and the use of Semitic Yam for the hostile sea god, the Egyptian god Seth is the well-attested equivalent of Baal. In the lost conclusion of what was once a long tale, Seth probably prevailed over the greedy Sea. The fragmentary first page of the papyrus, containing an encomium of Amenhotep II, has recently been identified. See P. Collombert and L. Coulon, "Les dieux contre la mer: Le début du ⟨papyrus d'Astarte⟩ (pBN 202), BIFAO 100 (2001): 193–242.

E.F.W.

1,x+1 [...] / his two oxen. I will adore you [...]-men. I will adore the [...]. I will adore the Sky [in] her ⌐dwelling⌐ place [...] the Earth [...] the Sky.[1]

Now af[ter[2] ...] the Earth, the Earth became satisfied[3] [...] in order that I might [un]cover her [... Then] they proceeded to bend down as if

1,x+5 ⌐impelled⌐[4] [...]. / Thereupon [each] one embraced [the other. Now] after ⌐seven⌐ days the Sky [...]ed [...] and descended upon [...] the Sea, and [... the Ear]th gave birth to[5] [...] the four regions of the [Earth[6] ...] in its midst as if ⌐suspended⌐ [...] his throne of Ruler, l.p.h.,[7] and he [...]ed and delivered unto him tribute [...] in court. Thereupon Ernutet[8] delivered

1, [the tribute to the Sea which was due him] / as Ruler, l.p.h. [One of the

x+10 gods said, "... the] Sky. Now look, tribute is being brought to him [...] him [...]; otherwise he will take us away cap[tive ...] our own for [..." Then] Ernutet [delivered] his tribute consisting of silver, gold, lapis lazuli, [and turquoise which filled] the boxes.

Thereupon they said to the Ennead, "⌐Let⌐ [...] the tribute for the Sea in order that he may investigate for us [all] matters [pertaining to the

2,x+1 Earth],[9] (for) protection is by his hand. Will he [...]? [...] / since they are fearful of [... the tribu]te for the Sea. Give [... th]e tribute for the S[ea ...] bad."

And Ernutet took a [...] Astarte. Thereupon [⌐Ernutet⌐] said [to one of the] birds, "Hear what I have to say. You are not to depart [...] another.

2,x+5 Hurry up and go to Astarte [... flying to] / her house and cry out beneath [the window of the room where] she sleeps and tell her, 'If it should be that [you are awake, then hear my voice; but] if it should be that you are asleep, I will awa[ken you. The Ennead has to send tribute to the] Sea as Ruler over the [Earth and as Ruler over] the Sky. Please come before them right

---

1. Reading so rather than Gardiner's "Ptah."
2. Or, "at [the time of]."
3. Or, "rested."
4. See James E. Hoch, *Semitic Words in Egyptian Texts of the New Kingdom and Third Intermediate Period* (Princeton, 1994), 288–89.
5. In Egyptian both the word for earth and the word for the earth god Geb are masculine. Since the concept of mother earth is alien to Egyptian thought, this sentence probably reflects western Asiatic influence if the verb is taken in its basic meaning.
6. Or, "the four banks of the [Sea]."
7. The Sea is the Ruler.
8. The harvest goddess.
9. Or render simply, "that he may hear for us [all] words [of the Earth]."

2,     [away.'" ... ⌜Asia⌝tics⌝. And Asta[rte] / [...] the daughter of Ptah. Now
x+10   [... tribute] for the Sea, the [... "Please] go yourself carrying the tribute for
       [the Sea ...]."

       Then Astarte proceeded to weep [..., and] its Ruler, l.p.h., was silent.
2,     [... / said], "Lift up your eyes [...]; lift up your eyes and you shall [...
x+15   out]side." [So he] lifted up [his eyes ...] the [...], and she [⌜began to⌝] sing,
       making sport of him [... Then the Sea] saw Astarte as she was sitting on the
       shore of the sea. He said to her, "Where have you come from, you daughter
       of Ptah, you furious and tempestuous goddess? Did you wear through your
       sandals that are ⟨on⟩ your feet and did ⟨you⟩ tear your garments that are on
       you while you were transiting heaven and earth?"

3,1    Thereupon / [Astarte] said to him, ["..." Then the Sea said to her,
       "Tell Ptah in the presence of the Enne]ad, 'If they give me your [daugh-
       ter, ...] them. What would I, on my part, do against them?'" And Astarte
       heard what the Sea told her, and she hastened to go before the Ennead
       to [the] place where they were gathered. The great ones saw her and got
       up to meet her, and the lesser ones saw her and lay down on their bel-
       lies. Her throne was given to her, and she sat down. And the [tribute for
4,1    the Sea] was presented to her.[10] / [...] earth [...] the beads [...]. And the
       beads [...].

       The messenger of Ptah went to tell these matters to Ptah and Nut.[11]
       Then Nut proceeded to untie the beads which were on her neck. Lo, she
5,1    put ⟨them⟩ upon the balance / [...] Astarte, "O my [...]. This means [a
       dispu]te with the Ennead. Therefore he shall send and request [...] the
       signet ring of Geb [... to fill] the balance with it."[12] Then [...] him to-
10,1   gether with [...]s [...] my basket of [...] ⌜her⌝. And he [... / ...]s of the
       Sea [...] through the portals [...] portals. There came forth [...] ⌜servants⌝
       of the [...]. "If they come again [...], he [... the Se]a, and he shall ⌜go⌝
15,1   to cover the earth and the mountains and / [...] his [... come] to fight with
       him ⌜inasmuch as⌝ [...] sat himself down calmly. He won't come to fight
       with us." So Seth sat down [...].

10. Perhaps in turn to be presented to her future husband, the Sea, as a dowry.
11. The sky goddess, unless Nut in this sentence and the next is in error for Ernutet.
12. The individual gods of the Ennead seem to be divesting themselves of their jewelry
    to satisfy the Sea's appetite for more tribute. The remainder of the tale is extremely
    fragmentary.

[...] "ᒿYouᒿ shall [protect] ᒿmeᒿ together with your [...]."
And the Sea ᒿleftᒿ [...].
And he [...].
The seven [...] him [...] together with the Sky and [...].

(The manuscript of the story is lost beyond this point.)

# A GHOST STORY

This Egyptian ghost story, incompletely preserved on a number of Ramesside ostraca, most of which are sherds from two large pottery vessels, lacks the spooky quality that moderns associate with this genre of literature. Death for the deceased Egyptian who had undergone the rites of beatification was an extension of life, and as the practice of festal banqueting in tomb chapels indicates, rapport between the living and the dead was by no means always a gloomy affair. The living could communicate with the dead by means of letters, and in the Teaching of Amenemhet the dead king is conceived of as imparting advice to his son and successor. Egyptian ghosts were not so much eerie beings as personalities to whom the living reacted pragmatically.

Although the High Priest Khonsemhab was probably a fictitious character, the setting of the story in the Theban necropolis was familiar to its readers who lived and worked in western Thebes. We may assume that the story concluded with the successful completion of the spirit's tomb under Khonsemhab's direction.

For the basic publication, translation, and treatment of this story the reader is referred to Jürgen von Beckerath, in ZÄS 119 (1992): 90–107, where it is argued that the ostraca were copied in the early Ramesside period from an original papyrus that was paginated. Fragments of another ghost story have been published by Georges Posener, in RdE 12 (1960): 75–82.

E.F.W.

II,1    [... according to] his habit [...] after the way [he] had done [... He[1] ferried] across and reached his house. He caused [offerings to be] prepared, [saying, "I will provide him[2] with] all sorts of good things ⌐when⌐ I

II,5    go to the west side." He went up onto the roof / [of his house and invoked] the gods of the sky and the gods of the land, southern, northern, western and eastern, and ⟨the⟩ gods of the necropolis, saying to them, "Send me that august spirit." And so he came and said to him, "I am your [... who must go to rest] at nightfall next to his tomb."

Then the High Priest of Amon Khonsemhab [said to him, "Please tell me your name], ⟨your⟩ father's [name], and your mother's name that ⟨I⟩ may offer to them and do for them whatever has to be done [for those who are in their position]." [The] august [spirit] then said to him, "Nēbusemekh is

II,10   my name, Ankhmen is / my father's [name], and Iotiemshas is my mother's name."

Then the High Priest of Amon-Re, King of the Gods, Khons[emhab said to] him, "Tell me what you want and I will have it done for you. And I will have a sepulcher prepared [anew] for you and have a coffin of gold and *zizyphus*-wood made for you, and you shall [⌐rest therein⌐], and I will have done for you all that is done for one who is in [your position." The august spirit then] said to him, "No one can be overheated [who] is exposed in the wintry wind, hungry without food, [...]. It is not my desire to overflow like

II,15   the inundation,[3] / not [...], not see[ing ...] my [⌐tomb⌐], I would not reach it. [There have been] made [to me promises ...]."

Now after ⟨he⟩ had finished speaking [..., the High Priest of Amon-Re, King of the Gods], Khonsemhab, sat down and wept beside him ⌐with a face (full) of tears⌐.[4] [And he addressed] the spirit, saying, ["How badly you

III,1   fare] / without eating or drinking, without growing old / or becoming young, without seeing sunlight or inhaling northerly breezes. Darkness is in [your] sight each day. You do not get up early to leave."

III,5   Then the spirit said to him, / "When I was alive upon earth, I was overseer of the treasury of King ⟨Mentu⟩hotep,[5] l.p.h., and I was lieutenant

1. I.e., Khonsemhab.
2. I.e., the spirit.
3. Perhaps meaning, "to be as effusive as the inundation."
4. Or, "in the face of the . . .s."
5. Emending Rahotep to Mentuhotep, to be identified with the great Mentuhotep II of Dynasty 11, whose tomb and mortuary complex is located at Deir el-Bahri in western Thebes.

of the army, having been at the head of men and nigh to the gods. I went to rest[6] in Year 14, during the summer months, of the King of Upper and Lower Egypt, Men⟨tu⟩hotep, l.p.h. He gave me my four canopic jars and my sarcophagus of alabaster, and he had done for me all that is done for one in my position. He laid me to rest in my tomb with its shaft of ten cubits.

III,10  See, the ground beneath has ⸢deteriorated⸣ / and dropped away. The wind blows (there) and ⸢seizes a tongue⸣.[7] Now as for your having promised me, 'I shall have a sepulcher prepared anew for you,' I have it four times (already) that it will be done in accordance with them.[8] But what am I to make of the promises you also have (just) made to me so that all these things[9] may succeed in being executed?"[10]

Then the High Priest of Amon-Re, King of the Gods, Khonsemhab, said to him, "Please express to me a fine commission such as is fit to be done for you,[11] and I will surely have it done for you. Or I will (simply) have

III,15  five men (servants) and / five maidservants, totaling ten, devoted to you in order to pour libation water for you, and I will (have) a sack of emmer delivered daily to be offered to you. And also the overseer of offerings will pour libation water for you."

Then the spirit of Nēbusemekh said to him, "Of what use are the things you would do? Unless a tree is exposed to sunlight, it does not sprout foliage.[12] (But) stone never proceeds to age; it crumbles (only) through [...]."[13]

IV,  [... King] / ⟨Neb⟩hep⟨et⟩re,[14] l.p.h., ⸢there⸣ [... The High Priest of]
x+1  Amon-Re, King of the Gods, [commissioned] three men, each one [...]. And he ferried across and went up [... The men searched for the tomb] near the holy temple of King [Neb]hepetre, l.p.h., [the Son of Re, Mentuhotep],
IV,  l.p.h. And they [found ...] / in it, it being twenty-five cubits distant along
x+5  the king's causeway at Deir el-Bahri.[15]

6. I.e., died.
7. An obscure passage, the last clause of which perhaps refers to the howling of the wind in the subterranean portion of the tomb.
8. "Them" perhaps refers to previous promises to have a new resting place prepared.
9. Emending *nn m mdwt* to *nn n mdwt, n* becoming *m* by assimilation.
10. Lit. "succeed to advancing." The idea is that the promises should be realized.
11. Emending *n.i* here and following to *n.k.*
12. Or, "Isn't a tree grown through sunlight? Doesn't it sprout foliage?" Cf. G. Posener, in *ZÄS* 99 (1973): 132, n. 54, for another interpretation.
13. Following this obscure passage is a long lacuna.
14. The prenomen of Mentuhotep II.
15. Taking *dsrt* for "Deir el-Bahri"?

Then they went back down ⟨to⟩ the riverbank, and they [returned to] the High [Priest] of Amon-Re, King of the Gods, Khonsemhab, and found him officiating in the god's house of the temple of Amon-[Re, King of the Gods]. He said to them, "Hopefully you've returned having found[16] the excellent place for making the name [of that spirit] called [Nēbusemekh] endure unto eternity." Then the three of them said to ⟨him⟩ with one voice, "We have found the excellent place for [making the name of that august spirit endure]." And so they sat down in his presence and made holiday. His
IV,   heart became joyful when they told [him ... until] / the sun came up from
x+10  the horizon. Then he summoned the deputy of the estate of Amon Menkau [and informed him] about his project.

He returned in the evening to sleep in Nē,[17] and he [...].
(The conclusion of the story is lost.)

16. Emending *gm.i* to *gm.tn*.
17. I.e., the city of Thebes, located east of the Karnak temple of Amon. In the continuation Khonsemhab possibly saw the spirit again in a dream.

# THE REPORT OF WENAMON

The Report of Wenamon is preserved on a papyrus of Dynasty 21 or 22. From the manner in which the text is inscribed on the papyrus it would appear to be an official document, perhaps one where the writer made a conscious effort to transform what may have originally been rough entries in a diary into a polished account that has literary merit. But despite the format of the papyrus, it can also be argued that the report is fundamentally a literary work, to a large extent fictitious, though with some historical underpinnings.

The dating of the report has traditionally been to Year 5 of the Renaissance era, which corresponded to Year 23 of Ramesses XI, the last pharaoh of Dynasty 20, but there is now good reason to believe that the Year 5 of the report is of the joint rule of Herihor in the south and Smendes in the north after the death of Ramesses XI. Although Herihor and Smendes did assume royal titles in certain inscriptions, their joint kingship was subordinated to that of the god Amon-Re. The weakening of the older pharaonic concept of kingship possibly relates to the Libyan tribal background of Dynasty 21. At any rate, the report clearly reflects the decline of Egypt's prestige abroad following the collapse of the New Kingdom empire. The reader will find the article by Arno Egberts in ZÄS 125 (1998): 93–108, especially illuminating in its reassessment of the literary and historical aspects of Wenamon's report.

E.F.W.

116

1,1       Year 5, fourth month of the third season, day 16, day on which Wenamon, the Elder of the Portal of the Temple of Amon, [Lord of the Thrones]
of the Two Lands, departed to obtain lumber for the great and noble riverine barge of Amon-Re, King of the Gods, [the name of which is A]mon-
Userhat.[1] On the day when I arrived at Tanis, at the place [where Smen]des
and Tanetamon are,[2] I gave them the rescripts from Amon-Re, King of
1,5    the Gods, and they / had them read out in their presence. They said, "Will
do, will do according to what Amon-Re, King of the Gods, our [lord], has
said." I stayed from the fourth month of the third season in Tanis. Smendes
and Tanetamon sent me off with the ship captain Mengebet,[3] and I went
down to the great Syrian sea in the first month of the third season, day 1.

       I reached Dor, a Tjeker town;[4] and Beder, its prince, had fifty loaves,
1,10   one amphora of wine, / and one ox haunch brought to me. A man of my
freighter absconded, stealing a golden [vessel worth] five *deben,* four silver
jars worth twenty *deben,* and a purse containing eleven *deben* of silver.
[Total of what] he [stole]: five *deben* of gold and thirty-one *deben* of silver.[5]

       I got up that morning, and I went to where the prince was and said to
him, "I have been robbed in your harbor. Now not only are you the prince
of this land, but you are also its investigator. Search for my money! Indeed,
1,15   as for this money, it belongs to Amon-Re, / King of the Gods, the lord of the
lands; it belongs to Smendes; it belongs to Herihor, my lord, and the other
magnates of Egypt. It belongs to you; it belongs to Weret; it belongs to
Mekmer;[6] and it belongs to Tjekerbaal, the Prince of Byblos."

       And he said to me, "Are you serious, or are you ⌜joking⌝? See here, I
cannot understand this allegation you have made to me. If it were a thief
belonging to my land who boarded your freighter and stole your money, I
1,20   would repay it to you from my own storehouse until / your thief, whatever
his name, has been found. Actualy, as for the thief who has robbed you, he

1. The great barge of Amon, "Mighty of Prow," used in river processions during major
   Theban feasts.
2. Tanis, located in the northeast portion of the Delta, was governed by Smendes and his
   wife Tanetamon.
3. The captain is a Levantine.
4. Dor, a port town on the north coast of Palestine, was controlled by the Tjeker, one of
   the Sea Peoples related to the Philistines.
5. The value of this money to pay for the lumber was equivalent to 1.2 lb. troy of gold
   and 7.5 lb. troy of silver.
6. These two individuals may have been princes of Tyre and Sidon.

belongs to you and he belongs to your freighter. Spend a few days here by me that I may search for him."

So I spent nine days moored in his harbor, and I went to him and said to him, "Look here, you haven't found my money. Please [send] me [off] with the ship captains and those who go to sea." But he said to me, "Quiet! [If you wish to] find [your money], hear [my words and do what] I tell you, but

1,25 don't / [...] the place where you will be. You shall take possession [of] their [...]s and be compensated like [... until] they set out to search for their thief who [has robbed you ...] the harbor. Now [you shall proceed in this manner."⁷ Then I reached] Tyre.

I left Tyre at crack of dawn [...] Tjekerbaal, the Prince of Byblos,

1,30 [...] / a freighter. I found thirty *deben* of silver in it, and I seized possession of it. [I said to the ship's owners,⁸ "I have seized possession of] your money. It shall remain in my possession [un]til you have found [my money or the thief] who stole it. I have not robbed you, but I shall hold on to it. But as for you, [you shall ...] me to [...]."

So they went off, and I celebrated my triumph [in a] tent on the seashore in the harbor of Byblos. [I found a hiding place for] Amon-of-the-Road⁹ and placed his possessions within it. The Prince of Byblos sent word

1,35 to me, saying, "G[et out of / my] harbor!" And I sent word (back) to him, saying, "Where should [I go? ...] ⌜I⌝ go [...]. If [you can locate a ship] to transport me, let me be taken back to Egypt." I spent twenty-nine days in his har[bor while] he daily [spent] time sending word to me, saying, "Get out of my harbor!"

Now when he offered to his gods, the god took possession of a page¹⁰ (from the circle) of his pages and put him in an ecstatic state. He¹¹ told him,

1,40 "Bring [the] god up! Bring the envoy who is carrying him! / It is Amon who sent him forth. It is he who had him come." For when the ecstatic

---

7. The tenor of Beder's poorly preserved speech seems to be that Wenamon should exercise restraint in the hope that the money will be recovered, but apparently Wenamon impatiently left for Tyre.
8. Those whose money Wenamon confiscated were Tjeker.
9. The name of the idol that accompanied Wenamon to protect him on his trade mission.
10. Lit. "big boy" or "adolescent." Despite the orthography, others have proposed instead a Semitic word for "seer," see James E. Hoch, *Semitic Words in Egyptian Texts of the New Kingdom and Third Intermediate Period* (Princeton, 1994), 86–87.
11. I.e., the ecstatic individual speaking to the prince.

became ecstatic that night, I had located a freighter headed for Egypt and had (already) loaded all my possessions into it but, so as to prevent another eye from seeing the god, I was waiting for darkness to fall that I might put him aboard.

The harbor master came to me, saying, "Stay until tomorrow, so the prince says." And I said to him, "Are[12] you the one who daily has spent time coming to me to say, 'Get out of my harbor!'? Are you now telling me to stay 1,45 tonight / so that the freighter I located might first depart and you might then return and say, 'Move on!'?" And he went and told it to the prince, and the prince sent word to the captain of the freighter, saying, "Stay until tomorrow, so the prince says."

When morning came, he sent (for me) and brought me up while the god was resting in the tent where he was on the seashore. I found him sitting in his upper chamber, with his back turned toward a window, while behind his 1,50 head were breaking the waves of the great Syrian sea. / I said to him, "Amon be merciful!" And he said to me, "How long has it been until today since you came from where Amon is?" I answered him, "Five whole months ago." He said to me, "Now are you being truthful? Where is the rescript from Amon which is in your charge? Where is the letter from the High Priest of Amon which is in your charge?" And I answered him, "I gave them to Smendes and Tanetamon." He became very irritated and said to me, "Now look, you have neither rescripts nor letters in your charge. Where is the ship for (transporting) cedar which Smendes gave you? Where is / its 1,55 Syrian crew? When he entrusted you to that barbarian ship captain, was it to have him murder you and have you thrown into the sea? (If so), from whom then would the god have been sought? And you too, from whom would you also have been sought?" so he said to me.

I said to him, "Isn't it an Egyptian ship and thus an Egyptian crew that sail under Smendes? Does he have Syrian crews?" And he said to me, "Aren't there twenty cargo ships here in my harbor which are in commerce 2,1 with Smendes? As for that Sidon, / the other (port) which you passed, aren't there another fifty freighters there which are in commerce with Werkerer and are hauling to his (commercial) house?"[13]

---

12. Throughout my previous translation of this report *nn* was interpreted as a negative. However, more recent consideration of the use of *nn* in Wenamon has convinced me that *nn* throughout this text is a writing of the interrogative *in*.

13. Perhaps with the nuance of drawing in profit to his commercial house.

I was dumbfounded at this great moment, and he reacted, saying to me, "On what sort of business have you come?" And I answered him, "It is in quest of lumber for the great and noble barge of Amon-Re, King of the Gods, that I have come. What your father did and / what your father's father did, you will also do," so I said to him. And he said to me, "They did in fact supply it. You have but to pay me for supplying it, and I will supply it. Indeed my (forebears) carried out this commission, but only after Pharaoh, l.p.h., had sent six freighters loaded with Egyptian products, and they were emptied into their warehouses. You, what have you brought me in my turn?"

He had a journal roll of his forefathers brought and had it read out in my presence. A thousand *deben* of silver and miscellaneous items were found (entered) in his (journal) roll. / And he said to me, "As for the Ruler of Egypt, is he the lord of what is mine, and I his servant as well? (If so), would he have been needing to send silver and gold in order to say, 'Carry out the commission from Amon!'? Or was it rather a gift that used to be presented to my father? As for me in my turn, am I your servant? Or am I a servant of the one who sent you? I have but to let out a shout to the Lebanon so that as soon as the heavens open up, the logs will be deposited here on the seashore.[14] Give / me the sails you brought to take your freighters carrying your logs back to ⟨Egypt⟩. Give me the ropes you brought [to lash the cedar]s which I am to fell in order to make them for you [...] which I am to make for you ⟨for⟩ the sails of your freighters, or the yards will become too heavy and break and you will perish ⟨in⟩ the midst of the sea. Look here, it was only after he had placed Seth beside him that Amon could thunder in the sky. Now it is all the lands that Amon / has founded, but he founded them only after he had initially founded the land of Egypt, whence you have come. Thus not only was it from there that technology went forth to get to where I am, but also it was from there that learning went forth to get to where I am. What's (the point of) these foolish journeys that you have had to make?"

But I said to him, "That's wrong! They are not foolish journeys that I'm involved in. There is not any ship upon the river which doesn't belong to Amon. His is the sea, and his is the Lebanon, which you claim is yours. It is for Amon-Userhat, the lord of every ship, that he maintains / a growing-

14. For a different interpretation of Tjekerbaal's speech up to this point, see Jean Winand, in *GM* 138 (1994): 95–108.

tract (there). Indeed it was Amon-Re, King of the Gods, who told Herihor, my lord, to send me forth, and he had me come bringing this great god. But see, you have made this great god spend these twenty-nine days moored in your harbor, without your knowing whether he, who has been there, was present or not. You stand ready to haggle over the Lebanon with Amon, its lord. As for your mentioning that the former kings used to send silver and gold, if they had had life and health, they would not have sent such

2,30  products. / It was instead of life and health for your fathers that they sent such products. Now as for Amon-Re, King of the Gods, it is he who is the lord of life and health, and it is he who was the lord of your fathers. They spent their lifetimes offering to Amon. You too, you are a servant of Amon. If you say, 'Will do, will do so for Amon,' and accomplish his commission, you shall live, prosper, and be healthy and be beneficial for your entire land and your people. Don't covet for yourself anything belonging to Amon-Re, ⟨King⟩ of the Gods. Truly, a lion covets his own possessions. Have your

2,35  scribe brought to me / that I may send him to Smendes and Tanetamon, the planners Amon has installed in the north of his land, and they will cause whatever is (necessary) to be brought. I will send him to them with the words, 'Have it brought until I go (back) south, and (then) I shall remit to you whatever deficit is still due you,'[15] so I said to him.

He put my letter in his messenger's hand; and he loaded aboard the keel, the bow piece, the stern piece, along with four other hewn timbers, totaling seven, and sent them to Egypt. His messenger, who had gone to Egypt, returned to me in Syria in the first month of the second season,

2,40  Smendes and Tanetamon having sent along / four bowls and one *kakmen*-vessel of gold, five bowls of silver, ten articles of clothing of byssus, ten ⌜coverlets⌝ of fine thin linen, five hundred mats of smooth linen, five hundred ox hides, five hundred ropes, twenty sacks of lentils, and thirty baskets of fish, while she sent me (personally) five articles of clothing of fine thin linen, five ⌜coverlets⌝ of fine thin linen, one sack of lentils, and five baskets of fish. So the prince rejoiced, and he detailed three hundred men and three hundred oxen and assigned supervisors in charge of them to have them fell the timbers. They felled them, and they lay there throughout the winter.

In the third month of the third season they were hauled to the seashore,

2,45  and the prince went out and attended to them. He sent word to me, /

15. Wenamon is asking for an advance from the Tanite rulers, which he promises to pay back as soon as he returns to Thebes.

saying, "Come!" Now when I stepped into his presence, the shadow of his lotus fan fell upon me, and Penamon, a cupbearer whom he had,[16] interposed, saying, "The shadow of Pharaoh, l.p.h., your lord, has fallen upon you." And he[17] became angry at him, saying, "Leave him be!" I presented (myself) to him, and he reacted, saying to me, "Observe that the commission which my fathers carried out previously, I have carried it out, although you in turn have not done for me what your fathers used to do for me.[18] See, the last of your lumber has arrived and is stacked. Do as I desire and come

2,50    to load it aboard. But should they not give it to you, / don't come (simply) to observe the terror of the sea. If you should observe the terror of the sea, you would have to face my own. Truly, I have not done to you what was done to Khaemwase's[19] envoys when they had spent seventeen years in this land, and they died right at their post." And he said to his cupbearer, "Take him, let him see their tomb in which they lie."

But I said to him, "Don't make me see it! As for Khaemwase, they were humans whom he sent to you as envoys, and he was a human himself. You don't have one of his envoys (now before you) that you should say, 'Go and

2,55    see your fellow men.' Can't you be so joyful / as to have a stela [made] for yourself and say on it, 'Amon-Re, King of the Gods, sent to me Amon-of-the-Road, his envoy, l.p.h., and Wenamon, his human envoy, in quest of lumber for the great and noble barge of Amon-Re, King of the Gods. I felled it; I loaded it aboard. I provided it ⟨with⟩ my own freighters and my own crews. I let them reach Egypt to request for me fifty years of life from Amon in excess of my fate.'[20] And it may chance after another day that an envoy comes from the land of Egypt, who is acquainted with writing, and he reads your name on the stela; (then) you will receive water of the

2,60    West like the gods who are / there."

He said to me, "That's quite a wordy bit of advice you have given me." And I said to him, "As for the many things you have told me, if I arrive home to where the High Priest of Amon is and he sees your commission, it is your commission which will draw in profit to you."

I went off to the seashore to where the timbers were stacked and

16. The cupbearer's name indicates that he was an Egyptian.
17. I.e., Tjekerbaal.
18. Assuming that Tjekerbaal had previously received payment under Ramesses XI; most translators have understood "for me" to mean "for mine."
19. Khaemwase was probably the pharaoh Ramesses XI.
20. An indication that a person's fate could be altered through prayer to a god.

watched eleven freighters coming in from the sea belonging to the Tjeker, (who were) saying, "Apprehend him! Put no freighters at his disposal (headed) for the land of Egypt." So I sat down and wept. The letter scribe

2,65 of the prince came out to me / and said to me, "What's up?" And I said to him, "Can't you see the migratory birds that have (already) gone down twice to Egypt? Look at them journeying (north) to the cool region.[21] How long am I to be abandoned here? For can't you see those who have come again to apprehend me?"

He went and told it to the prince, and the prince started to weep because of the words which were said to him, for they were bitter. He sent out to me his letter scribe, bringing me two amphoras of wine and one sheep, and he had Tanetnē, an Egyptian songstress who was with him, brought to me, saying, "Sing for him! Don't let his mind be preoccupied

2,70 with concern." And he sent word to me, / saying, "Eat and drink, don't let your mind be preoccupied with concern. You will hear whatever I have to say tomorrow."

When morning came, he had his assembly summoned, and he stood in their midst and asked the Tjeker, "What's (the purpose of) your journeys?" And they answered him, "It's in pursuit of those blasted freighters which you are sending to Egypt with our rivals that we have come." He said to them, "I cannot apprehend the envoy of Amon within my land. Let me send him off, and (then) you set out in pursuit of him in order to apprehend him."

So he put me aboard and sent me off from there at the harbor of the

2,75 sea. The wind wafted me to the land of / Alasiya,[22] and the townsmen came out against me to kill me. So I jostled my way through them to where Hatiba, the princess of the town, was. I met her when she had left one house of hers and was about to enter her other one. I saluted her and asked the people who were standing near her, "Is there no one among you who understands Egyptian?" And one of them replied, "I understand (it)." So I said to him, "Tell my lady I used to hear as far away as Nē,[23] at the place where Amon is, that although in every town injustice is practiced, in the land of Alasiya justice is practiced. Is it here (too) that injustice is being practiced every day?"

21. Located north of Egypt, see A. Egberts, in *JEA* 77 (1991): 62–67.
22. I.e., Cyprus.
23. Nē, meaning "the City," was the popular designation of Thebes.

2,80    She said, "Now what do you mean by / saying this?" And I answered her, "If the sea rages and the wind wafts me to the land where you are, will you let them take charge over me to kill me although I am an envoy of Amon? Now look, as for me, they will be searching for me until whatever day.[24] Regarding this crew of the Prince of Byblos whom they are seeking to kill, won't its lord in turn find ten crews belonging to you and kill them too?"

So she had the people summoned, and they were arraigned.[25] And she said to me, "Sleep well!"

(The remainder of the report is lost.)

24. I.e., incessantly.
25. Or simply, "reprimanded."

# III

## INSTRUCTIONS,
## LAMENTATIONS,
## AND DIALOGUES

# THE INSTRUCTION OF HARDEDEF
## (FIRST PART)

H ardedef was one of the noted sages of the past, and his teachings were famous in antiquity. The beginning is preserved on several ostraca of the Ramesside period. First identified through an ostracon in Munich by Emma Brunner-Traut, the introduction has been studied with several parallels by Posener in RdE 9 (1952): 109–20. The text with the various copies has been treated by Wolfgang Helck, Die Lehre des Djedefhor und Die Lehre eines Vaters an seinen Sohn (Wiesbaden, 1984). The beginning is worth including as the "earliest" instruction preserved. A passage from it is cited by Ptahhotep, and the ideas have a long tradition in subsequent literature.

W.K.S.

I. The beginning of the instruction which the hereditary prince and count, the king's son Hardedef made for his son whom he raised up, named Auibre. He says: Reprove yourself in your (own) eyes, take care that another man does not reprove you. If you would be excellent, establish a household and acquire for yourself a caring wife; that a male child will be born to you.

II. May you build a house for your son, for [I] have built for you the place where you are. Equip your house in the necropolis and make excellent your place in the West. Accept (this maxim), for death is bitter for us. Accept (this maxim), for life is exalted for us. The house of death is for life.

III. Seek for yourself a field holding which becomes inundated [ . . .] for writing. To till, to fish, and (to) hunt.

# THE MAXIMS OF PTAHHOTEP

T his text, one of the undisputed masterpieces of ancient Egyptian literature, dates possibly from as early as the late Sixth Dynasty of the Old
Kingdom. Some scholarly opinions, however, prefer to see it as a Middle
Kingdom composition dating from the Twelfth Dynasty. Although it was not
intended to be a complete compendium of Old Kingdom thought and morality,
it does nevertheless present a very good picture of the general attitudes and
outlook of that period. The text was composed under the guise of an elderly
vizier who was on the verge of retirement and desirous of handing his position
on to his son who also bore the name Ptahhotep. In general, the text appears as
a handbook of etiquette and proper conduct and is obviously addressed to
members of the nobility and upper classes. The major purpose of the text was a
very practical and pragmatic one, for it provides guidelines of conduct designed
to aid the reader or hearer in getting ahead in life and in being successful, both
personally and financially. At the same time, the text also has a certain moral
value with its stress on Ma'at and the doing of what is right. It is also extremely
optimistic in its general outlook, i.e., if one behaves in the right and proper
fashion, all will be well. Due to the extreme difficulty of this text, modern
translations of it show very wide variations in the interpretation of certain
passages. There are four copies of the text in existence, only one of which,
Papyrus Prisse in the Bibliothèque Nationale in Paris, is complete. This version
is the earliest of the four, being a copy produced during the Middle Kingdom.

*Being the earliest, it is in all likelihood the most faithful reproduction of the original. The other copies show considerable variations from Papyrus Prisse, this being due perhaps to the fact that they were emended to make them more understandable to the Egyptians of the New Kingdom. In the following translation, I have for the most part followed the text of Papyrus Prisse, although in several instances I have inserted, where it seemed appropriate, lines from one of the other extant versions. There are several publications of the text, but the one which I have used in producing the following translation is that of Z. Žába,* Les Maximes de Ptahhotep *(Prague, 1956). The text has been translated several times, but those most easily accessible to the majority of readers will be that of Miriam Lichtheim* (Ancient Egyptian Literature, *vol. 1, [Berkeley, 1973], 61–80) and that of R. O. Faulkner in the earlier edition (1973) of this book. The edition of Žába also contains a French translation as well as translations of the other versions of the text.*

V.A.T.

4,1 The beginning of the Instruction written by the hereditary noble, the prince, the father of the god,[1] the beloved of the god, the judge of the six law courts, the arbiter who causes contentment throughout the entire land, the mayor of the city, the vizier Ptahhotep, under the Majesty of the King of Upper and Lower Egypt, Isesi who lives for ever and eternity. The mayor of the city, the vizier Ptahhotep says:

"My Sovereign Lord:
Old age has arrived, infirmity has descended,
4,3 Misery has drawn nigh, and weakness increases.
One must take a nap like a child every day,
The eyes are blurred, the ears are deaf,
And vigor wanes because of weariness.
The mouth is silent and no longer speaks;
5,1 The memory is gone and cannot recall (even) yesterday.
The bones ache through frailty,
Pleasure has become repulsive, and all taste has vanished.
What old age does to men is totally despicable.
The nose becomes plugged and cannot breathe;
Even standing and sitting are a bother.

1. Father of the god: a priestly title designating a court official of significant rank.

130

5,3 Permit your humble servant to appoint a staff of old age.[2]
Let my son be allowed to succeed to my position.[3]
To that end I will instruct him in the decisions of the judges,
The wisdom of those who have lived in earlier ages,
Those who hearkened to the gods.[4]
So may the same be done for you;
May discord be banished from the people,
And may the Two Banks[5] serve you."

Then the Majesty of the god said:

5,5 "Before you retire, teach him / about what has been said in the past;
Then he will be an example to the children of the nobles,
When understanding and precision have entered into him.
Instruct him, for no one is born wise."

The beginning of the wise maxims spoken by the Hereditary Noble, the Prince, the father of the god, the beloved of the god, the eldest son of the king, / of his very body, the judge of the six law courts, the arbiter who causes contentment throughout the entire land, the mayor of the city, the Vizier Ptahhotep, to teach the ignorant about knowledge and about the principles of good conduct, things such as are profitable to him who will listen, but a source of sorrow to him who disregards them. Thus he spoke to his son, Ptahhotep the younger:

5,7

1. "Do not be haughty because of your knowledge,

5,9 But take counsel / with the unlearned man as well as with the learned,
For no one has ever attained perfection of competence,
And there is no craftsman who has acquired (full) mastery.
Good advice is rarer than emeralds,
But yet it may be found even among women at the grindstones.

2. If you come up against an aggressive adversary (in court),

5,11 One who has influence and is more excellent than you,
Lower your arms and bend your back,
For if you stand up to him, he will not give in to you.

---

2. "Staff of old age": one who will assist the writer in carrying out his duties.
3. This line does not appear in Papyrus Prisse, but it provides an excellent explication of the previous line.
4. Or as an alternative reading: "those (who were) the servants of your ancestors."
5. I.e., the two banks of the Nile.

You should disparage his belligerent speech
By not opposing him in his vehemence.
The result will be that he will be called boorish,

5,13     And your control of temper will have equaled / his babble.

3. If you come up against an aggressive adversary,
Your equal, one who is of your own social standing,
You will prove yourself more upright than he by remaining silent,
While he speaks vengefully.
The deliberation by the judges will be somber,
But your name will be vindicated in the decision of the magistrates.

6,1     4. If you come up against an aggressive adversary,
A man of low standing, one who is not your equal,
Do not assail him in accordance with his lowly estate.
Leave him be, and he will confound himself.
Do not answer him in order to vent your frustration;
Do not alleviate your anger at the expense of your adversary.

6,3     Wretched is he / who persecutes one who is inept.
Things will turn out in accordance with your will,
And you will defeat him through the censure of the magistrates.

5. If you are a ruler responsible for the concerns of the populace,
Search for every opportunity to do good,
So that there may be no shortcoming in your actions.

6,5     Great is Ma'at, and its foundation is firmly established;
It has not been shaken since the time of Osiris,
And he who violates the laws must be punished.
In the eyes of the covetous man it goes unnoticed
That wealth can be lost through dishonesty,
And that wrongdoing does not result in success.

6,7     He[6] says, / 'I will procure (wealth) for myself.'
He does not say, 'I will procure (wealth) through my diligence.'
But in the long run it is Ma'at which endures,
And an (honest) man may state: 'This is my ancestral property.'

6. Do not stir up fear in people,
Or God will punish in equal measure.

6. I.e., the covetous man.

A man may determine to live thereby,[7]
But he will (eventually) be lacking in bread for his mouth.

6,9    A man may decide to become / rich,
And he may say, 'I will snatch for myself whatever I see.'
A man may decide to cheat another,
But he will end up by giving (his gains) to a total stranger.
It is not what men devise that comes to pass,
But what God determines comes to pass.
Live, therefore, contentedly,
And let what they[8] give come of its own accord.

6,11    7. If you should be one of those sitting (as guests)
At the table of someone who is greater than you,
Accept what he serves when it is placed in front of you.
Look only at what is right in front of you,
And do not stare at him constantly,[9]
For to force yourself upon him is an irritation to his spirit.
Do not speak to him until he invites you (to do so),
For one never knows what may be annoying.
You should speak only when he addresses you,
And (then) what you say will be of interest.
You should laugh only when he laughs,
And (this) will be very pleasant to his heart.[10]

7,2    As for a nobleman when he is at the table,[11]
His demeanor is determined by his mood.[12]
He will be generous to the one whom he favors,
For such is the way once night has come.
It is his mood which prompts him to be generous;[13]
A nobleman may give, but an (ordinary) man should not presume upon
him.

7. I.e., by causing others to fear him.
8. I.e., the gods.
9. "Constantly": lit. "with many glances," perhaps with the intention of trying to attract
the attention of the host.
10. These two lines are not in Papyrus Prisse, but they complement the present context.
11. "At the table": lit. "behind his food."
12. "Determined by his mood": lit. "according as his *ka* commands."
13. Lit.: "It is the *ka* which stretches out his hands."

7,3 The eating of bread is under / the governance of God,[14]
And it is only a churl who complains about it.

8. If you are a man entrusted with responsibility,
One whom one nobleman sends to another,
Be meticulous in your duty when he sends you,
And deliver his message exactly as he dictates it.
Resist (doing) anything offensive by (making) a comment
Which could cause one nobleman to be annoyed with the other.
Observe the truth; do not surpass it,[15]
Although one should not repeat an angry speech.
Do not speak against any person, be he great or small,

7,5 For this serves only to arouse the temper.[16]

9. If you engage in agriculture, and (your) field prospers,
And God causes it to increase under your hand,
Do not talk (about it) incessantly around your neighborhood,
For it is important that one should practice the discretion appropriate to
the prudent man.[17]
It is the man of integrity who is the possessor of (true) wealth,
And in the court he conquers like a crocodile.[18]
Do not praise him who has no children,
Neither speak ill nor boast about it,
For it is common that a father may be in misery,
And as for a mother who has given birth, another may be happier than
she.

7,7 It is the lone man / of whom God takes care,
And the head of a family may pray for someone to succeed him.[19]

14. These lines are probably not intended as any kind of profound statement. The
writer's meaning appears to be something like, "Be satisfied if you are invited to eat,
and don't complain if you are not given the royal treatment."
15. I.e., say only what you were told to say, nothing more.
16. "This serves only to arouse the temper": lit. "This is an abomination of the *ka.*"
17. The meaning of these lines seems to be something like this: If your harvest is
especially prosperous, do not boast about it to your less fortunate neighbors, for a
man should be discreet enough to show respect for the feelings of those who have
been less fortunate.
18. The comparison of the upright man to a crocodile is a positive comment: he is
protected by his own integrity as surely as a crocodile can defend himself.
19. The meaning of these lines is not absolutely clear, but the writer seems here to be

10. If you are humble and the servant of a well-to-do man,
Let all your behavior be flawless before God.
If you should learn that he was once of low estate,
Do not be disdainful toward him
Because you have learned about his past.
Respect him in accordance with what he has made of himself,
For wealth does not come of its own accord,
But it is the ordinance of the gods for one whom they favor.
As for his possessions, he has gathered them himself,
But it is God who has made him respectable
7,9     And watches over him even when he sleeps.

11. Follow your heart as long as you live,
And do not work beyond what is allocated (to you).
Do not waste the time of following the heart,
For wasting time is an annoyance of the spirit.
Do not lose the hours of daylight
Beyond (what is necessary for) keeping your household in order.
When wealth has been amassed, follow your heart,
For wealth brings no advantage when it is a burden.

12. If you are a well-to-do man
7,11    And beget a son who pleases / God:[20]
If he is upright and follows your disposition,
If he listens to your teachings,
If his conduct is worthy within your household,[21]
And if he manages your property well,
Then do every good thing for him,
For he is your son, begotten of your very being;
Do not withhold your love from him.[22]
But one's offspring may cause grief;

---

warning his reader not to regard childlessness as either a disgrace or a blessing, for
the childless man may sometimes be more fortunate than the one who has a large
family.

20. The expression "who pleases God" means here probably no more than "who behaves in a decent manner."
21. These two lines are not in Papyrus Prisse, but they fit the context admirably.
22. Lit. "Do not separate your heart from him."

If he goes wrong and disregards your counsel,
If he does not do as you instruct him[23]
But disobeys everything said (to him),
If his mouth prattles on with vile talk,
Then reject him, for he is not your son,
And for certain he was not born to you.[24]
Punish him for all his talk,
For he who has extended his arm against you is hateful to the gods.

8,1 Surely evil was fated for him from the womb,
For he whom the gods guide is one who cannot err,
And he whom they leave stranded is unable to cross the river.

13. If you are in the audience chamber,
8,3 Stand and sit / in accordance with your position
Which was given to you on the first day.
Do not exceed (your duty), for it will result in your being turned back.
Be attentive to him who enters bearing a report,
For he who has been summoned has complete freedom.
8,5 The audience chamber / tends toward strict etiquette,
And all its affairs follow (specific) rules of conduct.
It is God who promotes one's position,
And that men should force their way is not done.

14. If you are with the people,
Gain for yourself supporters who are trustworthy.
8,7 One who is trustworthy / is one who will not spread talk around the
community;
He will himself become an official
And a man of means due to his (good) performance.
As for your good reputation, you should not talk about it;
8,9 Provide for your body, but turn your attention / toward the people,[25]
And men will boast on your behalf without you being aware of it.
But as for him whose heart obeys his stomach,
He invites scorn for himself instead of respect.
His heart is morose and his body wretched.

23. This line is not in Papyrus Prisse.
24. These two lines are lacking in Papyrus Prisse.
25. "Turn your attention toward the people": lit. "your face toward the people."

8,11     Great of heart are those whom God has established,
But he who listens to his stomach is his own worst enemy.[26]

15. State your business without concealing (anything),
Proffer your opinion in the council of your lord.
If he can speak fluently and easily,[27]
It will not be difficult for an agent to give his account,

8,13     And no one will answer, 'What does he know of it?'
Even an official whose property has fared poorly,
If he thinks about reproaching him concerning it,
Will be silent saying (only), 'I have no comment.'[28]

16. If you are a leader,

9,1     Take responsibility in / the matters entrusted to you,
And you will accomplish things of note.
But think on the days which are still to come,
Lest some misdeed should arise to destroy your favorable position,

9,3     For an occasion of hatred is (like) the entrance of a crocodile.

17. If you are a man of authority,
Be patient when you are listening to the words of a petitioner;
Do not dismiss him until he has completely unburdened himself

9,5     Of what he had planned / to say to you.
A man who has been wronged desires to express his frustrations
Even more than the accomplishment of the (justice) for which he came;
But concerning him who dismisses petitions
Men say, 'Why ever did he reject it?'

9,7     Not everything about which he has petitioned will be done,
But a sympathetic hearing is a means of calming the heart.

18. If you desire that friendship should endure
In a house which you enter

9,9     As a lord, as a brother, or as / a friend:
In any place which you enter,
Avoid approaching the women,
For there is nothing good in any situation where such is done.

26. "His own worst enemy": lit. "belongs to the enemy."
27. "If he speaks fluently and easily": lit. "if his mouth overflows when he speaks."
28. Lit. "I have spoken."

It is never prudent to become overly familiar with them,[29]

9,11    For countless men have thus been diverted / from their own best interests.

One may be deceived by an exquisite body,[30]
But then it (suddenly) turns to misery.[31]
(All it takes is) a trifling moment like a dream,
And one comes to destruction through having known them.
Pricking the jealousy of a rival is a nasty piece of business;

9,13    A man may perish because of so doing, if the heart / becomes ensnared.[32]
As for him who is ruined through becoming embroiled with them,
No venture will ever be successful in his hand.

19. If you desire that your way of life be blameless,
Keep yourself far from every evil.
Guard yourself against the blemish of greediness,

10,1    For it is a grave affliction of an incurable disease,
And those who fall into it cannot recover.
It creates dissention among fathers, mothers,

10,3    And maternal brothers;
It embitters beloved friends;
It alienates a trustworthy man from his lord;[33]
It isolates a wife from her husband.
It is an embracing of every evil;
It is a combining of everything which is hateful.
That man will endure who is meticulous in uprightness
And who walks in accordance with his proper station;[34]

10,5    He will make a testament thereby;
But for the greedy there will be no tomb.

20. Do not be selfish in the division (of an estate)
By lusting for more than your rightful share.

---

29. "To become too familiar with them": lit. "to reveal them."
30. "A delicate body": lit. "a body of faïence."
31. These two lines are not in Papyrus Prisse, but their suitability to the context virtually demand their inclusion at this point.
32. The sense of these lines is very obscure, and any translation can only be regarded as tentative.
33. These two lines are absent from Papyrus Prisse.
34. Lit. "in accordance with his stride."

Do not be selfish with respect to your relatives,

10,7 For greater is the claim of / the good-natured man than that of the assertive.

He who forsakes his relatives is (truly) poor,

For he lacks the compassion to respond to their entreaties.[35]

Even a little of what one yearns for

Can calm a distressed man.

21. If you are well-to-do and establish your household,

10,9 Be gracious to your wife in accordance with what is fair.

Feed her well, put clothes on her back;

Ointment is the balm for her body.

Rejoice her heart all the days of your life,

For she is a profitable field for her lord.

Do not condemn her,

10,11 But keep her far away from power; control her,

For her eye is quick and sharp.[36] Watch her (carefully),

For thus you will cause her to remain long in your house.

If you are too strict with her, there will be tears.

She offers sexual favors in return for her upkeep,

And what she asks is that her desire be fulfilled.

11,1 22. Gratify your friends with what has come into your possession,[37]

For what has come to you is a boon from God.

As for him who fails to gratify his friends,

People will say that he is a selfish individual.

No one knows what will come to pass when he considers tomorrow,

11,3 And the righteous individual is he by whom men are sustained.

If deeds deserving of praise are done,

One's friends say, 'Well done!'

One cannot bring satisfaction to an (entire) town,

But one can bring happiness (to) friends when there is need.

35. The interpretation of these lines is made difficult due both to the obscurity of the meaning of the expressions involved and to the grammatical structure. I offer here a suggestion as to their possible significance.

36. "Quick and sharp": lit. "her storm."

37. I.e., share your material good fortune with your friends.

11,5    23. Do not repeat slander,
And do not listen to it,
For it is but the prattling of a churlish man.
Repeat only what is seen, not what is heard,
Or forget it and say nothing at all,

11,7    For he who is listening to you[38] can discern / what is trustworthy.
When taxation[39] is ordered and is carried out,
There arises against the tax collector (the same) resentment as against the
decree itself.
Slander is like a nightmare;
Divorce yourself from it.

11,9    24. If you are a man / of trust,
One who sits in the council of his lord,
Direct your attention toward excellence.
Your silence will be more profitable than babbling,
So speak only when you know that you are qualified (to do so).

11,11   It is (only) the proficient who should speak in council,
For speech is more difficult than any craft,
And only the competent can endow it with authority.

25. If you are influential, you should establish respect for yourself
Through knowledge and through courtesy in speech.

11,13   Do not be domineering / except in official matters,
For the aggressive man meets with trouble.
Do not be arrogant, lest you[40] be brought low;
Do not be silent, but yet be cautious of causing offence

12,2    When you answer a speech angrily.

---

38. Lit. "he who is in front of you."

39. The sense of these two lines is very obscure. The term *t3wt*, rendered here as "taxation," can mean "theft," "gathering up," "seizure," etc. The fact that such is actually ordered, however, seems to imply some kind of official seizure, and hence my suggestion of rendering *t3wt* as "taxation." The sense of the passage within the context, however, is still unclear. Perhaps the author is suggesting that the one who repeats slander, although he is not actually responsible for the deed under discussion, is resented as much as the tax collector who is doing no more than carrying out his duty the law.

40. The text has the third person singular pronoun here, but the second person is obviously more appropriate.

Turn away your face and control yourself,
For the flames of the quick-tempered spread quickly;
But the affable man, when offended, treads carefully.

12,4   One who is dour throughout the whole day
Will never have a happy moment,
And he who is frivolous throughout the whole day
Will never establish a household for himself.
He who aims for full control
Is like the one who guides the helm at the time of landing,
But another moors (the boat);

12,6   But he who obeys his heart will keep (everything) in order.[41]

26. Do not attempt to upstage an important official;[42]
Do not irritate one who is laden (with responsibility),
For it may happen that he will be annoyed at the one who opposes him,
While his mood[43] will be lightened by one who is loyal to him.

12,8   He / and the god[44] are the ones who bestow favors,
And what he wishes is what should be done for him.
His face will be kindly toward you even after anger,
And (your) well-being depends upon his mood.
There is hostility with an enemy,
But it is good will which increases favor.

27. Inform an official of what is beneficial to him,
12,10  And see to it that he is accepted by the people.
Cause his wisdom to be recognized by his lord,
And there will be abundance for you from his generosity.
A person of good disposition[45] is for your good,
For your back will be clothed by it.

12,12  His approval[46] will be upon you / for the support of your household
Under your noble master to whom you are loyal.
Support him thus,

41. The meaning of these last four lines is extremely obscure.
42. Lit. "Do not oppose yourself (i.e., set yourself in opposition) at the moment of a great one."
43. Lit. "his *ka.*"
44. By the term "the god" the writer may mean the king.
45. Or, "a (certain) amount of favor."
46. "Approval": lit. "acceptance."

And he will also provide excellent support for you.
Moreover, affection for you will endure
In the hearts[47] of those who respect you.
Behold, he who is gracious to listen is highly esteemed.[48]

13,1    28. If you should function as a noble official of the court,
Appointed to settle disputes among the populace,
Nurture (in yourself) ignorance of partiality.[49]
When you speak, do not incline toward one side.

13,3    Be careful lest / someone voice his opinion
(To) the magistrates: 'He turns the matter upside down.'
Then your action will turn into censure (of yourself).

29. If you feel merciful concerning a misdeed which has happened

13,5    And feel favorable toward someone / because of his honesty,
Pass over it and do not recall it,
Since he was silent before you from the very first.[50]

30. If you are wealthy after having been destitute,

13,7    And have amassed riches / after poverty
In a town where people know about you,
Do not boast of what has come to you in the past,
And do not be too confident in your possessions
Which have come to you as gifts of the god.[51]

13,9    (Thus) you will not lag / behind another like you
To whom the same thing has happened.[52]

31. Bow respectfully to him who is superior to you,
Your senior from the royal palace;

47. Lit. "in the bellies."
48. "Highly esteemed": lit. "a *ka*." The term *ka* in this text appears to have a very wide range of meanings, denoting in general a person of highly positive character.
49. This line is unintelligible. I offer this translation as a tentative suggestion.
50. The significance of this particular maxim is uncertain. I take it to mean that, if a judge is inclined to be merciful to a wrongdoer because he has been honest in admitting his wrong, then the judge should pardon him, especially if he does not try to defend himself.
51. The god: i.e., the king.
52. The place of these last two lines within this maxim is not totally clear, but it appears that the author is warning one who has gained wealth after poverty that he should not be overly confident lest he relax his diligence and let another surpass him.

Then your household will be firm in its possessions,

13,11 And your rewards (will come) / at their proper time.

But wretched is he who opposes a superior,

For one enjoys life (only) during the time when he is kindly disposed,

And the arm bared to salute him will not break.

14,1 Do not despoil / the house of neighbors,

Do not steal the property of one who is close to you,

Lest he complain against you until you be brought to trial.

A plaintiff is lacking in compassion,[53]

14,3 And if he learns of it, he will prosecute.

Wretched is he who stirs up adversity in his own neighborhood.

32. Do not fornicate with an effeminate boy.

14,5 Be well assured that / such debasement will only arouse his lust,[54]

And (the desire) which is in his body will not be cooled.

Let darkness never come for the performance of such lewdness,

So that he may be quiet after he has satisfied his desire.

14,7 33. If you are investigating / the character of a colleague,

Do not make inquiry of someone who is close to him.

Conduct your business with him alone

Until you are no more ambiguous about his personality.

After a while you will become familiar with him.

14,9 Examine his heart / at the time of speaking (with him).

If he talks too freely about what he has seen,[55]

Or if he does something at which you are taken aback,

Nevertheless, be amiable with him and remain silent.

Do not turn your face away (from him),

But be cautious about revealing anything to him.

14,11 Do not / answer him with an act of hostility,

Do not withdraw from him, and do not assail him.

He will eventually get what he deserves,[56]

For there is no escape for anyone from him who has determined his fate.

53. "Compassion": lit. "heart."
54. Lit. "will be water on his heart," i.e., will stimulate his desires all the more.
55. Lit. "if what he has seen goes out from him."
56. Lit. "His time (of reckoning) will not fail to come."

34. Be generous as long as you live,

14,13    For what goes out from the storehouse does not go back in,

And men are eager for bread which is freely given.

He whose stomach is empty is an accuser,

And (such) an opponent becomes a bringer of woe;

15,2    Do not make of him a friend.

Compassion is a man's monument

Throughout the years which follow his tenure of office.

35. Acknowledge your assistants when you have wealth,

And do not be of mean disposition toward your friends.

15,4    Such is (like) a riverbank which floods; it is greater / than one's wealth.

The property of one man may (pass) to another,

But the integrity of a gentleman is always beneficial to him,

And a good character will be his monument.

36. Punish soundly and reprimand thoroughly,

For the restraint of evil will reinforce morality.

15,6    As for a court case which is not concerned with criminal action,

Let him who has the complaint act as prosecutor.[57]

37. If you take to wife one who is silly and frivolous,[58]

Of light-hearted disposition, and known to her townsmen,

She may continue in her ways[59] when at any moment it strikes her fancy.

Do not send her away, but allow her to eat (from your table).[60]

15,8    A light-hearted woman / (at least) provides amusement.[61]

38. If you give heed to these things which I have spoken to you,

All your affairs will be successful.

---

57. The meaning of these two lines is somewhat ambiguous, but it appears that the writer is advising one who is a judge to avoid involvement in civil disputes until an actual complaint is laid.

58. The meaning of the Egyptian term *špnt*, translated here as "frivolous," is totally unknown. Its translation here as "frivolous" is a guess based on the context of the passage.

59. The Egyptian phrase *iw.s m hpwy* presents no obvious solution, and several translations have been suggested by various scholars.

60. I.e., continue to support her as your wife.

61. "Amusement": suggested translation of the unknown term *ꜥk??*.

If their truth is effected,[62] this will be (proof of) their worth,
And the remembrance of them will continue on in the speech of men
Because of the goodness of their precepts.
Men will cling to every word,
And they will never perish in this land for ever.
They have been recorded and spoken for good,
And noblemen will utter decrees in accordance with them.

15,11 This (treatise) is a means of teaching a man to speak to / posterity.
Let him who would be a recognized authority[63] give heed to it.
It is good to speak to posterity,
And it is the duty of posterity to give heed to it.[64]
If a noble action is done by one who is in authority,
He will be of good reputation for ever,
And all his wisdom will be for everlasting.
The learned man takes care for his *ba*

15,13 By assuring that it will be content with him / on earth.
The learned man can be recognized by what he has learned,
And the nobleman by his good actions;
His heart controls his tongue,

16,1 And precise are / his lips when he speaks.
His eyes see,
And his ears are pleased through hearing of the repute of his son
Who acts in accordance with Ma'at and who is free from falsehood.

39. Hearing is beneficial to a son who willingly hears,
For when what is heard takes root in[65] the hearer,

16,4 He who has heard will become / one (worthy himself of being) heard.
It is good to hear and it is good to speak,
But he who can hear possesses what is advantageous.
Hearing is beneficial to the hearer;
Hearing is better than everything,
For (through it) good affection comes into being.

---

62. The writer means, I suspect, the truth or Ma'at inherent in the maxims which he has
   laid down and which he hopes his hearers will put into effect.
63. "A respected authority": lit. "a master who is heard" or "a master of hearing."
64. This line is a free rendition of the Egyptian *ntf sḏm.f st* ("It belongs to it [posterity] to
   hear it.")
65. "Takes root in": lit. "enters into."

16,6 How good it is / that a son should accept what his father says,
For ripe old age will come upon him thereby.
He who listens is favored of God,
But he who is hated of God does not listen.

16,8 It is the heart which causes / its possessor to be
One who hears or who does not hear.
The 'life, prosperity, and health' of a man are his heart.
A hearer is one who gives heed to what is said,
And he who is willing to listen is one who does what has been said.

16,10 How good it is when a son heeds / his father,
And how joyful is he by whom it may be said:
'My son is pleasing, for he is skilled in obedience.'
As for him who heeds what is said to him, he will be self-sufficient

16,12 And respected by / his father;
He will be remembered in the mouths of the living,
Both those who are on the earth and those who will be.

40. If a nobleman takes to heart what is said by his father,

16,14 Never will fail / any endeavor of his.
Educate your son as a listener,
One who will be esteemed in the hearts of the nobles,
One who guides his speech in accordance with what is said to him,

17,2 One who acknowledges him who is to be obeyed.
It is such a son who is superior and whose actions are distinguished,
But error is ingrained into him who does not listen.
The education of a wise man (leads) to his success,

17,4 But as for the fool, he will labor (in vain).

41. As for the fool who will not listen,
He never accomplishes anything,
For he discerns knowledge in ignorance

17,6 And something beneficial in that which is baneful.
He does everything that is loathsome,
So that men are furious with him day after day.
He thrives on that whereby others die,
And the falsification of speech is his food and drink.

17,8 His disposition is known to the authorities;
(He is) a picture of living death day after day.

Men disregard his stupid deeds
Because of the many griefs which fall upon him every day.

17,10  42. A son who listens is a (true) follower of Horus,
For his fortune is good because he has listened.
He will attain ripe old age and will be honored,
And he will speak likewise to his own children,

17,12  Handing on / the instruction of his father,
For every man teaches according as he acts.
He will converse in the presence of (his) children,
And they in turn will speak to their children.

18,1  Build (their) character, do not instill (in them) anything offensive.
Strengthen Ma'at, and your children will live.
As for the first one who succumbs to evil,
Men will gossip about what they have seen,

18,4  For such is the way of the world;
And they will gossip about what they hear,
For such also is the way of the world.
Take heed of everyone, and try to keep people quiet;[66]

18,7  Wealth does not amount to much / otherwise.[67]

43. Do not say something and then go back on it;[68]
Do not put one thing in the place of another.
Beware of relaxing self-restraint (?) within yourself;
Give way to the speech of a wise man,

18,10  And listen well, if you wish / to be secure
In the speech of those who hear when you speak.
(First) attain to the status of an expert,
And then you will be able to speak with complete success,
And your every undertaking will be in order.

45. Suppress your impulses and control your mouth,

18,13  And then your advice will be (welcomed) by the officials.

---

66. I.e., try avoid letting people have anything to talk about.
67. The meaning of these last six lines is somewhat obscure, and I have taken certain liberties in the translation in order to convey what I believe is the actual sense of the text.
68. Lit. "Do not take a word; do not bring it back."

Be totally precise to your master;
Behave so that men may say to him, 'He is the son of so-and-so,'[69]
And that those who hear it may say,
'Fortunate is he who begat him.'

19,2 Be painstaking / all the time that you are speaking,
So that you may say things of importance.
Then the officials who are listening will say:
'How excellent are the words of his mouth!'

45. Behave so that your master may say of you,

19,4 'How well he was brought up by / his father
By whom he was begotten of his body.
(Surely) he spoke to him while he was still completely within the womb,
For what he has accomplished is more than what he was told.'
Behold, a good son who is given by God
Is one who exceeds what was told him by his master.
He will perform Ma'at,

19,6 For his heart will have controlled his actions.

As you now take over my position, your body being firm and hale,[70]
And the king being pleased with all that has come to pass,
May you enjoy (many) years of life.
What I have accomplished on earth is not insignificant;
I enjoyed one hundred and ten years of life

19,8 Given to me by / the king
And honors surpassing those of my predecessors.
(All of this came to pass) because of my doing Ma'at for the king until
(I reached) the state of veneration."

It has been transcribed from beginning to end as it was found in writing.

---

69. I.e., conduct yourself and your responsibilities in such a way so as to gain recognition.
70. These closing lines are addressed by the old vizier to his son who is now succeeding to his post.

# THE TEACHING
# FOR THE VIZIER KAGEMNI

T*he last part of this text is preserved in the Papyrus Prisse, which also contains the main text of the Maxims of Ptahhotep. The author was evidently the father of Kagemni, and it has been conjectured that he was the sage Kaires cited in the passage about the writers of the past in Papyrus Chester Beatty IV (see quotation at beginning of our introduction). The text has been translated and studied by A. H. Gardiner, in JEA 32 (1946): 71–74, to which additional comments were made by W. Federn, in JEA 36 (1950): 48–50. See also A. Scharff, in ZÄS 77 (1941–42): 13–21; G. Posener, in RdE 6 (1951): 32–33; J. Yoyotte, in BSFE 11 (1952): 67–72; A. H. Gardiner, in JEA 37 (1951): 109–10; and E. Edel, MIO 1 (1953): 210–26. Translated also in Erman,* The Ancient Egyptians, *xxvi, 66–67, and in Battiscombe Gunn,* The Instruction of Ptah-hotep and the Instruction for Ke'gemni: The Oldest Books in the World *(London, 1918). The instruction is similar to that of Ptahhotep to the extent that it is preserved.*

W.K.S.

I, 1      ... the submissive man prospers, the moderate man is praised, the tent is open for the silent man, and the place of the contented man is wide.[1]

1. Federn: the sense seems to be, "He is influential." Gardiner: untrammeled freedom of personal movement seems to be involved, not influence over others.

Do not talk (freely), for the flint knives are sharp against the one who strays from the road; ⸢there is no hastening, except indeed against his misdeed⸣.[2]

I,5  If you sit with a crowd, abstain from the food you desire, for controlling your desire is (only for) a brief moment. Gluttony is despicable, / and one points one's finger at it. A cup of water quenches thirst, and a mouthful of ⸢rushes⸣ makes the heart strong. Take a (single) good thing instead of dainties, and a little bit instead of much. Base is one whose gut is greedy when the (meal)time has passed by. He should not be mindful of those who eat voraciously at home.

I,10  If you sit down with a glutton, eat when his satiety has passed. If you drink with a drunkard, accept (only) when his desire is satisfied.[3] Do not be quarrelsome about meat in the company of a greedy man. / Accept what he gives you; do not reject it. Then matters will be pleasant. No words can get the better of the man who is free from reproach at meals, being meek to the degree of ⸢complaisance⸣. The harsh man is kinder to him than his own mother.[4] All mankind are his servants.

II,1  So let your (good) name go forth, / while you are silent in your speech, and you will be summoned.[5] Yet do not be proud by virtue of (your) strength among your contemporaries. Take care not to be ⸢opprobrious⸣. One does not know what will happen nor what God does when He punishes.

II,10  Then the vizier had his children summoned, after he had comprehended the manner of mankind. And he ended up by saying to them: As to all that is written in / this papyrus roll, heed it just as I have said it to you; do not go beyond what has been ordained. And they placed themselves on their bellies, and they read it out just as it was written. And it was more beautiful in their hearts than anything in this entire land. So they proceeded to live accordingly.

2. Federn: "Talk not! Ready are knives against the refractory, without proceeding, except for his fault"; i.e. they always lie in wait for him, but strike only when he commits himself.

3. Federn and others similarly: If you sit with a glutton, eat, and his surfeit will have passed. If you drink with a drunkard, accept, and he will feel satisfied.

4. On these passages, see J. W. B. Barns, in *JEA* 58 (1972): 159–60.

5. You will be called in order to be promoted or honored.

Then His Majesty the King of Upper and Lower Egypt, Huni, died and His Majesty the King of Upper and Lower Egypt, Snefru, was exalted as an excellent king in this entire land. Kagemni was then made overseer of the residence town and vizier.

It has come ⟨its beginning to its end, as it was found in writing⟩.

# THE TEACHING FOR KING MERIKARE

T*he text known as* The Teaching for King Merikare *continues the tradition of the instructional literature which had emerged earlier, perhaps as early as the Old Kingdom, and which is best exemplified by* The Maxims of Ptahhotep. *Like the text of Ptahhotep, that of Merikare is presented in a situation where the holder of an office prepares to hand over his duties to his son and successor, taking the opportunity to provide advice on the execution of the duties of the office. In the case of Ptahhotep, the speaker was the retiring vizier; in the case of Merikare, the speaker is an older king—probably of the family of Khety (Akhtoy)—of the Herakleopolitan line, who is addressing his successor, Merikare. It is highly unlikely that the text was in fact the work of this alleged Khety, but it may have been written during the reign of Merikare as a means of justifying his kingship and policies, or it may have been composed at some later point during the Middle Kingdom.*

*The time frame in which the text is set is the First Intermediate Period, between the Old Kingdom and the Middle Kingdom. The north of Egypt was ruled by Herakleopolis while Thebes in the south was commencing its rise to power under the early rulers of the Intef family. The contents of the text reflect the unstable conditions of the time and give a portrait of a monarch who is trying to maintain order and who realizes the need for caution and diplomacy in ruling. There is in this text little of the high optimism of the Old Kingdom, and there is a strong stress on the actual sense of responsibility of the monarch as opposed to his privileges. The work climaxes with a statement of the supreme power of the creator deity, an indication that the Egyptian theological mind was becoming more sophisticated and less reliant on the diversified mythological imagery of the past.*

*The main source for this text is a papyrus in St. Petersburg (No. 1116A). This papyrus, copied during the second half of the Eighteenth Dynasty, is marked by a number of textual corruptions and scribal errors, and the beginning of the text is badly fragmented. However, some restorations can be made on the basis of other manuscripts, namely, Papyrus Moscow 4658 and Papyrus Carls-berg 6. Original publication of the text: W. Golénischeff,* Les papyrus hiéra-tique nos. 1115, 1116A et 1116B de l'Ermitage impérial à St-Petersburg *(St. Petersburg, 1916). For a good modern edition, see W. Helck,* Die Lehre für König Merikare, *(Wiesbaden, 1988). For other modern translations see M. Lichtheim,* Ancient Egyptian Literature, *vol. 1 (Berkeley, 1973), 97–109, and R. B. Parkinson,* The Tale of Sinuhe and Other Ancient Egyptian Poems 1940–1640 BC *(Oxford, 1997), 212–34. The translation of R. O. Faulkner in the earlier edition of this book should also be noted, as it shows a number of variations in the interpretation of various passages of the text.*

V.A.T.

1    [The beginning of the Instruction made by the King of Upper and Lower Egypt, Khet]y, for his son, Merikare.

[...]
Be not indulgent in the matter of (any) crime which (you) have discovered;
Rather you should punish [...]
[...] their [...] in every detail,
For this is the start of [rebellion].
[...] which has been caused
When dissentious men are numerous.
5  / [...] with their plots against you.
[...]
As for someone who makes a report [...]
After your decision has been made concerning [...]
[...] biased.
[...]
[...]
He will make half of it as an allotment.

10    The one shall [... his] lord / [...]
He [...] division [with] my followers.
[...] say the same [...] many in your sight.
You will go astray on the path [...]
[Be not indulgent] toward him,
But you should rather kill [...] those who follow him in this,
For you know his supporters who are loyal to him.

If you find [...] of a city,
And he is the head of a family,
You should provide for him,
And then you will not [...] he [...] your many myriads.
Do not destroy a man as a matter of course,
Neither [...]
15    / He [...] the Great Mansions
[...] bread [...]
[...] his [...] he [...] his [...] of the family.
Be careful that [you] do not [...]
[...] those who guard the living for us.
When a month has passed [...]
[...] he [...] himself.
He will speak, he will ponder, he will remember:
"A man who is indeed mighty on earth in the limbs of his body!"
[Punish] those men who fall away,
But be gracious to him, when your heart is satisfied.
[...] everyone says, "He is reborn!"
20    (Thus) they become men who are/ content.

[...] your [...] like a god.
If you find someone who did not have many supporters,
And whom the townspeople did not know,
But whose many partisans are now a multitude
And respect him for his possessions and for his cleverness,
One who has gained (men's) confidence
And has ingratiated himself in the sight of his dependents,
And who persists as a troublemaker and a spreader of talk,
Get rid of him, and slay his children,
Obliterate his name, and destroy his supporters,
Banish (all) memory of him and of the partisans who respect him.

25   / A seditious man is liable to incite the citizens
And create two groups of malcontents among the youth.
If, therefore, you find that there is such a one among the citizens,
[A ...] whose actions challenge you,
Denounce him before the officials and get rid of him,
For he is indeed a rebel.
One who disseminates talk is a disrupter of the city.
Restrain the masses, and drive the violence out of them,
For there will be no quelling of dissent
On the part of rogues whose fathers (also) created dissent.

A single dissenter can disrupt the (entire) army,
So let his end occur in the (same) confusion which he had brought about.
If the masses become inflamed, let them be put in the workhouse,
But be merciful [to ...] when you punish,
30   / For you will thus cause [the ...] to be joyful.
Show yourself upright before God,
And then people will say, even in your absence,
That you administer punishment in due measure.
A good temperament means serenity for a man,
But the malice of the angry-hearted is (his) torment.

Be proficient in speech, so that you may be strong,
For the strength of a king is his tongue.
Words are mightier than any struggle,
And no one can outsmart him who is skilled of heart,
[But you will sit secure] upon the throne.
The wise man is a bulwark (even) for officials,
And those who are aware of his knowledge dare not assail him.
No evil happens in his presence,
But Ma'at comes to him refined,
Like the counsels of what was said by (our) ancestors.

35   / Emulate your fathers and your forefathers,
And [attain] success through knowledge.
Behold, their words endure in writing;
Open and read (them),
So that you may emulate their knowledge.
One who is proficient will become knowledgeable.

Do no evil; clemency is good.
Make your memory endure through (men's) love for you.
Prosper the [people] whom the city shelters,
And they will praise God for (your) generosity.
Guard [your good name],
Give thanks for your blessings,
And pray [to the gods] for your health.

Show due respect to the nobles, support your people,
Fortify your borders and your buffer zones,
For it is expedient to work for the future.
The life of him who takes forethought will be held in (high) esteem,
But he who is overly confident will suffer.
40    Make men loyal to you / through your good disposition.
Despicable is he who forcefully binds the land to himself [...],
A fool is he who covets that which belongs to others.
(One's) earthly life is transient and does not endure,
Fortunate is he who is (well) remembered because of it.
Do not countless men belong to the Lord of the Two Lands?
And is there a man (of them) who will live forever?
The man who walked in accordance with Ma'at shall depart,
Just as he whose life was pleasure filled will die.

Promote your officials that they may fulfill your decrees,
For he whose house is wealthy will not take sides (against you),
And he who wants for nothing is a wealthy man.[1]
A poor man does not speak honestly,
And he who says "Would that I had!" cannot be upright.
He will be partial toward him who is generous to him
And biased toward the one who pays him.
Great is the ruler whose officials are themselves great,
45    Mighty is / the king who has a (loyal) entourage,
And wealthy is he who is rich in officials.
Speak Ma'at within your palace,
So that the officials who are over the land may respect you,

---

1. I.e., he who lacks nothing is already sufficiently rich and will, therefore, have no
  reason to take sides against the monarch. Keeping one's nobles well provided was one
  way to ensure loyalty.

For an upright heart is becoming to a lord;
It is the front of a house which creates respect for the back.

Observe Ma'at, that you may endure long upon the earth.
Console him who weeps, and oppress not the widow.
Do not expel a man from the property of his father,
And do not demote the officials from their positions.

Beware of punishing unjustly;
Do no harm, for it will not benefit you.
Punish by means of flogging and imprisonment,
For thus will this land be kept in good order,
Except for the rebel who has contrived his plots.
But God is aware of the rebel,
50  / And God will smite his evil with blood;
But the merciful man [will prolong] the length of his days.

Do not execute a man of whose abilities you are aware,
One with whom you were educated,[2]
Who was reared as if destined [...] before God,
And who walked freely in the place of secrets.[3]
The *ba* will return to the place which it knows,
And it will not wander from its familiar ways;[4]
All magic rituals will be unable to oppose it,
And it will make its way to those who offer it water.

As for the (divine) tribunal which judges sinners,
You know that they are not indulgent
On that day of judging the offender,
In that hour of performing their duty,
And base is he who is found guilty despite his wisdom.
Be not confident in length of years,
55  / For they regard a lifetime as but an hour.
A man will survive after death,
His deeds will be set out beside him as (his) reward,[5]

2. Lit. "one with whom you used to chant (i.e., recite) the writings."
3. I.e., one who had free access to the palace.
4. Lit. "from its ways of yesterday."
5. Lit. "His deeds will be placed beside him in a heap."

And existence in the beyond is for eternity.
A fool is he who does what offends them;
But as for him who reaches them having done no wrong,
He will exist there like a god,
Walking proudly like the Lords of eternity.
Marshall your troops so that the Residence may respect you;
Increase your supporters in the military.
Behold, your cities are filled with new generations;
For these twenty years, the youth have been at ease,
Following their heart,
And the military goes forth in strength.
Those who are recruited enlist voluntarily
Like young men trained [and strengthened].
It is (our) ancestry which fights on our behalf,
60 / And I was raised up from it on my succession.
Elevate your officials, promote your fighters;
Bestow wealth upon the young men of your followers,
Provide them with possessions, confer fields upon them,
And endow them with cattle.

Make no distinction between a well-born man and a commoner,
But take a man into your service because of his deeds.
Let every occupation be carried on
[...] for the Lord of might.
Keep guard over your border, and strengthen your forts,
For troops are profitable to their lord.
Erect [many] monuments for God,
For this is a means of giving life to the name of him who constructs them,
And a man should do what is beneficial for his *ba*.

Perform the monthly priestly service, don white sandals;
Enrich the temple, be discreet concerning the mysteries;
65 Enter / into the holy place, eat bread in the house of the god;
Replenish the offerings, multiply the sacrificial loaves;
Increase the daily offerings, for such is beneficial to him who does it.
Strengthen your monuments as far as is within your power,
For even a single day can contribute toward eternity,
An hour can embellish the future,
And God recognizes him who works for him.

Let your images be sent to distant foreign lands,
(Even ones) which will not acknowledge them,
For he who lacks knowledge of the affairs of the enemy will suffer.[6]

But enemies will not be calm within Egypt,
For troops will fight troops,
As (our) ancestors foretold,
70 And Egypt will fight/ in the necropolis,
Destroying the tombs with havoc time and again.
I did the same, and the same will happen (again),
As is done by him who likewise transgresses against God.
Do not be too stern with the southern territory,
For you know what the Residence advises about it.
It has happened (in the past),
Just as such things may happen (again).
There was no attack on their part, even as they maintained,
But yet I advanced upon This right to its southern border at Tawer,[7]
And I seized it like a flood.
(Even King) Meryibre, justified, had not done such.
Be lenient on account of this toward the territory under your control.
[Leave things as they are], and renew the treaties.
75 / There is no honest intent which lets itself be hidden,
And it is expedient to work for the future.

You are on good terms with the southern territory,
Which comes to you bearing gifts and tribute.
The same thing was done for me by (their) ancestors.
But if someone has no grain, can he give it?
For your part, be gracious to those who are humble before you,
And be satisfied with your (own) bread and beer.
Granite comes to you without interruption,
So do not destroy the monuments of another.

6. The meaning of these last lines is somewhat obscure, but the sense seems to be that
the ruler is advised to make contacts with foreign lands, even if these contacts are not
recognized. At least this will be a means of ensuring that one has some knowledge of
what is happening in potentially hostile lands.
7. The town of This was the capital of the eighth nome of Upper Egypt and was situated
not far from Abydos. Tawer appears to have been to the south of This, although its
exact location is uncertain.

Quarry stones at Tura,[8]
And do not construct your tomb through wanton destruction,
For as you do, so it will be done to you.[9]
Behold, you can be contented,[10]
80 / You can slumber and sleep securely because of your strength.
Follow your heart as a result of my accomplishments,
For there is no foe within your border.

It came to pass that I arose as lord of (my) city,
One whose heart was heavy because of the Delta
(From) Hutshenu to Sembaq,[11]
Whose southern boundary was at Two Fishes Canal.
I brought peace to the entire west as far as the area of the lake;[12]
(Now) it serves (me) of its own accord and produces *meru*-wood,[13]
One may now see the juniper wood which they give us.
The east abounds with foreigners, and their taxes [pour in].
The Middle Island[14] has returned (to us) and every man within it.
85 The temples say: "O Great One, (all) men revere you."

Behold, the land which they had destroyed has been established as nomes,
And all the great cities [have been rebuilt].
What had been governed by one man is now under the control of ten;
Officials are appointed, taxes are levied,
And every responsibility is clearly understood.
When free men are granted a plot of land,
They serve you like a single company;
Such ensures that no one among them will be discontent.

The Nile flood will cause you no worry by failing to come,
And the revenues of the Delta are in your hand.

8. Tura was an important quarry for limestone and was situated about eight miles south of the site of modern Cairo. The king is advised to quarry his own building materials as opposed to plundering them from the monuments of his predecessors. Granite, on the other hand, comes from the south in the area not under the king's control.
9. Lit. "That which is done will be that which will be done."
10. Lit. "Behold, the king is a possessor of joy."
11. The location of these sites is uncertain.
12. Possibly a reference to the Fayyum Oasis.
13. Possibly cedar or cypress.
14. I.e., the central Delta.

Behold, the mooring post which I have made in the east is secure,
From Hebenu[15] to the Way of Horus,[16]
Well settled with towns and full of people,
90    The choicest of the entire land, to drive back / any attacks against them.
May I see a brave man who will emulate this,
One who will for his own sake add even more to what I have done.
I would be worried by an heir who is ineffective.

But as concerns the foreigners, let this be said:
The vile Asiatic is miserable because of the place wherein he is,[17]
Shortage of water, lack of many trees,
And the paths thereof difficult because of the mountains.
He has never settled in one place,
But plagued by want, he wanders the deserts on foot.
He has been fighting ever since the time of Horus.[18]
He neither conquers nor can he be conquered.
He does not announce the day of fighting,
But is like a thief whom society has expelled.

95    However, as I live / and shall be what I am,
These foreigners were like a sealed fortress
Which I had surrounded and besieged.
I caused the Delta to strike them,
I captured their people and seized their cattle
To the point that the Asiatics detested Egypt.
Do not distress your heart on his account,
For the Asiatic is only a crocodile on its riverbank,

15. Hebenu: possibly the capital of the sixteenth nome of Upper Egypt, although some would prefer to see it as a site in the Delta.
16. The Way of Horus was the road leading to Syria-Palestine and commenced at the border fortress of Sile in the northeast Delta.
17. This description of the Asiatics and their conditions reflects the Egyptian hostility to the bedouins of the east who were a serious threat to Egypt's eastern border. (A similar abhorrence for them is seen in The Prophecies of Neferty.) The writer here castigates virtually everything about the Asiatics, their character, their abode, the harshness of their life, and their general demeanor.
18. The time of Horus was the mythological period when the gods governed Egypt directly. The point here is that throughout all historical time the Asiatics have been a cause of disorder.

Which attacks on a lonely road
But does not invade the area of a crowded town.

Unite Medenit[19] to its [nome],
Take possession of its adjacent territory as far as Kem-Wer,[20]
For behold, it is a lifeline[21] against the foreigners.
100   / Its walls are a defence, its soldiers are numerous,
And the serfs within it adept at carrying weapons,
As are the free citizens within it.
As for the region of Djedsut,[22] it totals ten thousand men,
Both serfs and free citizens exempt from taxation.
Officials have been in it ever since it was the Residence;
Well established are its borders, and mighty are its garrisons.
Many northerners irrigate it as far as the borders of the Delta,
Taxed with grain after the fashion of free citizens.
For him who achieves (all) this, it will be means of surpassing me.
Behold, it is the gateway to the Delta,
105   And they have formed a protection[23] as far as / Neni-nesut.[24]
Well-populated cities mean satisfaction,
But beware of being surrounded by the supporters of a foe.
Vigilance prolongs one's years.

Equip your border against the lands to the south,
For they are aliens who take up the panoply of war.
Construct buildings in the Delta,
For a man's name will not be demeaned by what he has accomplished,
And a securely founded town will not be destroyed;
So build mansions for your image.

An enemy loves anguish, and his actions are despicable.
King Khety, justified, stipulated in his teaching:
110   / "He who is inactive against brutality is (as) one who destroys the altars;

19. Medenit: the twenty-second nome of Upper Egypt, situated about twenty miles to the north of Herakleopolis.
20. Kem-Wer: capital of the tenth nome of Lower Egypt, situated near the apex of the Delta.
21. Lit. "navel-string."
22. Memphis.
23. Lit. "a dyke."
24. Herakleopolis.

And God will attack him who rebels against the temple."
It will come upon him even as he has done.
He will be smug with what he contrived to grab for himself,
But none will be faithful to him on the day of reckoning.
Protect the altars and revere God;
Do not say, "This is a bore," neither abate your efforts.
But as for him who revolts against you, this is (like) a destruction of heaven,
(Like) destroying a hundred years of monuments.
If an enemy is prudent, he will not destroy them,
In hope that his action may be affirmed by another who comes after him;[25]
115     But there is no one who does not have an / enemy.

The (ruler) of the two banks is intelligent;
The king, the lord of courtiers, will not act foolishly.
He was wise even at his coming forth from the womb,
And God has made him preeminent over the land above countless others.
The kingship is an excellent office;
It has no son, it has no brother, who can make its monuments endure,
Though each man ennobles his successor,
And each man acts on behalf of him who preceded him
In hope that his action may be affirmed by another who comes after him.

Behold, a dreadful incident occurred in my time:[26]
120     / The nome of This was laid desolate.
Indeed, it did not happen through anything I had done,
And I learned of it only after it had been committed.
Behold my abomination! What I did is all too plain!
Verily, destruction is detestable.
It is pointless for a man to repair what he has destroyed
Or to rebuild what he has torn down.
Beware of such!

25. This line is found in the Egyptian but makes little sense in the context. Moreover, it is repeated in line 118 of the text. It appears likely that a copyist inserted this verse at this point and that it should be removed.
26. The four lines following are generally accepted as a reference to the plundering of the Abydos cemeteries and the sites of This by the Herakleopolitan army without authorization. The king who is writing (or dictating) the document recognizes the evil of this action and disclaims all responsibility for it.

Affliction will be requited in kind,
And every deed committed has its consequence.

One generation of mortals follows another,
But God, the all-knowing, has concealed himself.
There is none who can resist the might of the Lord of the Hand,[27]
125    For it is he who can restrain (all) / that the eyes can see.
God must be revered, He (who moves) upon His (unchanging) path,[28]
(Whose images) are made of costly stone and fashioned from copper.
As one flood is followed by another,
And there is no river which lets itself be hidden,
But will break the dyke in which it had sheltered itself,
So also the *ba* goes to the place which it knows,
And turns not back to its former path.[29]
Enrich your mansion of the West,
Embellish your dwelling of the necropolis
With uprightness and with the observance of Ma'at,
For in this (men's) hearts are confident.
The character of him who is upright of heart
Is more acceptable than the (sacrificial) ox of him who does wrong.
Act on behalf of God—and He will do likewise for you—
130    With offerings / such as enhance the altars and with inscriptions.
This is an assurance of your name,
And God takes note of him who acts on His behalf.

Shepherd the people, the cattle of God,
For it is for their sake that He created heaven and earth.
He stilled the raging of the waters,
And created the winds so that their nostrils might live.
They are His images who came forth from His body,
And it is for their sake that He rises in the sky.
For them He created plants and cattle, fowl and fish to sustain them.

27. The expression "Lord of the Hand" probably refers to Re-Atum, the creator god who began the creative process by his act of masturbation.
28. Lit. "God is revered upon his path." The suggestion that this line is no more than a reference to the carrying of the cult statues in procession appears as somewhat mundane, i.e., an exhortation to observe the proper rituals.
29. I.e., the course of human life is inevitably directed toward the point where the *ba* must leave the body and cannot return again to normal life on earth.

He slew His enemies and destroyed (even) His own children,
Because they contrived to make rebellion.[30]
For their sake He creates the daylight,
And voyages (across the sky) to observe them.
135    He has erected for Himself / a shrine around them,
And when they weep, He hearkens.
For them He has made rulers from the egg,[31]
Leaders to raise up the backs of the weak.
He has ordained for them magic
As weapons to fend off the impact of what may come to pass;
(It is He) who watches over them by night as by day.
He has slain the rebellious among them,
As if a man would smite his son for the sake of his brother.
And God knows every name.

Make no detraction from my discourse,
For it establishes all the precepts of kingship.
Instruct yourself, so that you may rise up as a man,
And then you will equal me, and none will indict you.

140    Do not slay even / one man who is close to you,
For you have favored him, and God knows him.
He is one of those who prosper upon the earth,
For those who serve the king are (as) gods.
Implant love for yourself in the entire land,
For a good disposition means being remembered,
Even after years are past and gone.
May you be called "Destroyer of the Time of Evil"
By those who are among the descendants of the house of Khety,
And may they pray, "Let him return this (very) day!"

Behold, I have told you the best of my thoughts;
May you conduct yourself in accordance with what is laid out before you.[32]

30. A reference to the myth of the destruction of mankind.
31. I.e., the Egyptian kingship is regarded here as a divinely created institution, and the kings are seen as appointed to rule from even before the time of their birth.
32. The St. Petersburg manuscript ends with a long colophon stating that the text was transcribed from an older version by a scribe named Khaemwaset who made the copy for his own use and for the use of his brother Mahu.

# THE TEACHING OF KING AMENEMHET I
# FOR HIS SON SENWOSRET

T his text is highly unusual in that it is based on a theme which was a virtual contradiction of the Egyptian concept of the divinity of the monarch. The whole tenor and atmosphere of the text is dependent upon its account of the assassination of Amenemhet I, and hence its general nature is pervaded with pessimism and with a realization of the less than secure position of the monarch. The main advice given to the new king is that he must constantly be on his guard against treachery, have no intimate friends, and put his trust in no man—a far cry from the positive and optimistic world of the Old Kingdom monarchy. The setting of the work is in the Twelfth Dynasty, in the thirtieth year of Amenemhet I, and it is likely that its composition dates from some time shortly thereafter, i.e., during the reign of his successor, Senwosret I. The text is presented as an address given by Amenemhet I, after his assassination, to Senwosret, presumably in a dream or vision, although this is nowhere specifically stated. There is a theory that Amenemhet had been assassinated in the thirtieth year of his reign, and the throne was passed to his son Senwosret, who had also been his coregent. (This is the first known occurrence of a coregency in Egyptian history.) The succession of Senwosret to the throne was probably not accomplished without some internal troubles, as is attested by The Story of Sinuhe. However, opinions on the assassination of Amenemhet and on the coregency differ. Some would suggest that there was an unsuccessful assassination attempt on Amenemhet during year 20/21 which, leaving him *disabled, led to a coregency with Senwosret. Other scholars would question whether or not there was ever a coregency. The actual composition, written mainly as a piece of political propaganda, probably dates from the reign of Senwosret, and its author may have been a scribe by the name of Akhtoy or Khety.*

*The popularity of the work in antiquity is attested by the fact that numerous copies of at least parts of it have been found. The chief source of the text is Papyrus Millingen, dating from the Eighteenth Dynasty. This papyrus is now lost, but a copy of the text contained on it was made by A. Peyron in 1843. The third page of Papyrus Millingen has been largely destroyed, and hence the latter third of the work is supplied from Papyrus Sallier II, from various ostraca, and from a writing board in the Brooklyn Museum. The line numbers of the following translation are those of Papyrus Millingen.*

*For the earliest publication of the text, see F. Ll. Griffith, "The Millingen Papyrus," ZÄS 34 (1896): 35–51. There have been several other editions, the most recent being W. Helck,* Der Text der "Lehre Amenemhets I. für Seinen Sohn," *(Wiesbaden, 1969; 1986). It is this edition which has been used in the preparation of the following translation. For other contemporary translations of the text, the reader may wish to consult Miriam Lichtheim,* Ancient Egyptian Literature, *vol. 1 (Berkeley, 1973), 135–39, and R. B. Parkinson,* The Tale of Sinuhe and Other Ancient Egyptian Poems, 1940–1640 BC *(Oxford, 1997), 166–99. The latter translation also includes a good number of useful notes. There is also the translation by R. O. Faulkner in the earlier edition of this book. For a study of the text, see H. Goedicke,* Studies in the Instruction of King Amenemhet I for His Son *(San Antonio, 1988). The "propaganda" aspect of the text has been examined by C. A. Thériault, "The Instruction of Amenemhet as Propaganda,"* JARCE 30 (1993): 151–60.

V.A.T.

1,1  The beginning of the Instruction given by his Majesty the King of Upper and Lower Egypt, Sehetep-ib-Re (l.h.p.!), Son of Re, Amenemhet, justified, when he spoke revealing truth to his son, the Lord of all. He said:

You who have risen as a god,[1]
Give heed to what I shall say to you,

---

1. The formula "risen as a god" seems to imply that Senwosret has only recently assumed the position of monarch.

So that you may reign over the land, rule the shores (of the Nile),
And bring about an abundance of what is good and beneficial.

Maintain your vigilance against those who should be subordinate to you,
But who turn out not to be so,
Men in whose loyalty one can place no trust;
Do not let yourself be alone with them.

Put no trust in a brother,
Acknowledge no one as a friend,
1,5     Do not raise up for yourself / intimate companions,
For nothing is to be gained from them.

When you lie down at night, let your own heart be watchful over you,
For no man has any to defend him on the day of anguish.
I was generous to the pauper, I sustained the orphan,
I caused him who had nothing to become at length like a man of means.
But it was one who ate my bread who conspired (against me),
One to whom I had given my support devised dread deeds thereby,
Those clad in my fine linen behaved toward me like worthless louts,
And those anointed with my myrrh made my way slippery before me.[2]

Oh you my living images, you who share mortality with me,
Make mourning for me, mourning such as has never been heard,
For the burden of (that) struggle was such as had never been seen.
When one fights on the field of struggle[3] with the past forgotten,
Excellence is of no avail to him who knows not what he should know.[4]

It was after supper, when darkness had fallen,
And I had decided to take an hour of relaxation;
I was lying on my bed, for I was tired,
2,1     And I started / to drift off to sleep.[5]

---

2. Lit. "poured water under me."
3. Or, "in the arena."
4. Or, "Excellence is of no avail to him who knows not him whom he should know." I.e.,
   No matter how excellent and skilled a monarch may be, it will be useless to him if he is
   unable to recognize the characters of those around him.
5. Lit. "My heart began to follow my sleep."

Weapons (intended for) my protection were raised against me,
While I acted like a snake of the desert.
I woke up to the fighting, pulled myself together,
And found that it was a skirmish of the palace guard.

If I could have quickly taken weapons in my hand,
I would have made the cowards retreat in turmoil.
But no one is strong at night, and none can fight by himself;
No successful result can come about without an ally.

2,5 / And so ruin occurred while I was without you,
When the courtiers had not yet heard that I would hand over (the throne) to you,
When I had not yet sat down with you so as to confirm your succession;
For I was not ready for it, I did not expect it;
My heart had not conceived of indolence of the part of the servants.

Had women ever organized the troops?
Are revolutionaries ever educated right within the palace?
Is the flood let loose so that it may destroy the land?
Are people ruined through their own actions?
Misfortune had never come near to me since my birth,
And there has never arisen one equal to me in doing deeds of valour.

2,10 / I subdued (the land) as far as Yebu,[6]
And turned my course back to the Delta.
I stood on the borders of the land and perused its interior;
I fulfilled the supremacy of power by the manifestation of my might.

I was one who increased the grain,
(For I was) favored by Nepri;[7]
Hapy[8] gave me honor on every field,
3,1 So that none hungered during my years, / none thirsted therein.
Men took their ease through what I had done
And recounted legends about me,
For I ordered everything in its proper place.

6. Elephantine, modern Aswan.
7. Nepri: god of the grain.
8. Hapy: god of the Nile flood.

I subdued lions, I captured crocodiles,
I enslaved the men of Nubia, took prisoner the Medjay,[9]
And I forced the Asiatic tribes to cower away like dogs.

I have raised for myself a palace adorned with gold,
Its portals of lapis lazuli, its walls of silver,
3,5    / Its doors of copper with bolts of bronze.
It has been built for eternity
And constructed (to endure) throughout all ages.
This I know, for I was its lord, its lord for all time.[10]

Verily, mobs are (now) in the streets;
The wise man says "Yes," while the ignorant says "No,"
For he who is devoid of your guidance knows nothing.

Senwosret, my son,
As my feet depart (this life), my only concern is for you,
And my eyes are fixed upon you.
May those who were born in a happier time
Give you praises in the presence of all the people.

Behold, I have established the foundation,[11]
So that I might ensure the outcome for you.
I have accomplished what was in my heart,
3,10    For you / wear the white crown, the privilege of the god's progeny.
What has been determined will come to its proper pass,
According as I have begun it for you.

I have entered into the Barque of Re;[12]
Succeed to your kingship which was created of old;
In all that I have accomplished, there is none who can do the same.
Erect your monuments, and make your throne distinguished;

9. The Medjay: a Nubian people to the southeast of Egypt, later employed as mercenaries and police in Egypt.
10. The meaning of the final verses of the text is highly uncertain. Papyrus Millingen is badly damaged and the other sources unreliable.
11. Lit. "I have made the beginning."
12. Or, "There is rejoicing in the Barque of Re."

Strive [...]

[...][13] in the presence of his majesty (l.p.h.!).

(The text) has been well transcribed, from its beginning to its end, as it was found in writing.[14]

13. The text here is so corrupt as to yield no acceptable meaning.
14. Several different versions of a colophon exist. What is given here is more or less standard for Egyptian texts.

# THE LOYALIST INSTRUCTION FROM THE SEHETEPIBRE STELA

T*he composition which Georges Posener has designated The Loyalist Instruction is known, mainly through his efforts, from two papyri, a tablet, and over twenty ostraca with fragments of the text. These are Ramesside copies except for the tablet (early Dynasty 18), the Louvre papyrus (second half of Dynasty 18), and the stela of Sehetepibre (Dynasty 12). Posener has hazarded the guess that the sage Ptahemdjehuty, known from the list of authors in Papyrus Chester Beatty IV, was the author.*

*The text comprises two sections, the first admonishing the author's children to respect and obey the king, and the second outlining the nature of the people. An abridged version of the first part is represented in the stela of Sehetepibre, a high official of Senwosret III and Amenemhet III of Dynasty 12. This is the oldest copy of a part of the text, and it is translated here, following Kuentz and Posener, since it is the only consecutive text available.*

*For the composition, consult Posener,* Littérature et politique *(Paris, 1956), 117–24, and* L'Enseignement Loyaliste, Sagesse Égyptienne du Moyen Empire *(Geneva, 1976); C. Kuentz, "Deux versions d'un panégyrique royal,"* Studies Presented to F. Ll. Griffith *(London, 1932), 97–110; Erman,* The Ancient Egyptians *(New York, 1966), xxviii, 84–85.*

W.K.S.

II,8     The beginning of the teaching which he made for his children:

I have something important to say; I shall have you hear it, and I shall
II,10   let you know it: the design for eternity, a way / of life as it should be and of
passing a lifetime at peace.

Adore the king, Nymaatre,[1] living forever, in your innermost parts.
Place His Majesty in friendly fashion in your thoughts.

He is Perception, which is in (all) hearts, and his eyes pierce through
every being.

He is Re, by whose rays one sees, for he is one who illuminates the Two
Lands more than the sun disk.

He is one who makes (the land) green, even more than a high inundation: he has filled the Two Lands with victory and life.

Nostrils are cool when he starts to rage, but when he sets in peace, one
can breathe the air (again).

He gives nourishment to those in his circle, and he feeds the one who
II,15   adheres to / his path.

The king is *Ka.*[2]

His utterance is Abundance.

The one whom he brought up is one who will be somebody.

He is Khnum[3] for all limbs,

The Begetter of the begotten.

He is Bastet,[4] who protects the Two Lands.

The one who praises him will be protected by his arm.

He is Sakhmet[5] against those who disobey his orders, and the one with
whom he disagrees will be laden with sorrows.

Fight on behalf of his name;[6] be obeisant to his life. Be free and clear of
any instance of negligence.

---

1. The praenomen of Amenemhet III (1842–1797 B.C.), in whose reign the stela was
erected. The original composition probably lacked the name of the king.
2. Erman, "Vital Force."
3. The creator god who fashioned mankind on a potter's wheel.
4. The goddess represented with a cat's head.
5. The fierce goddess of pestilence, with a lioness's head.
6. Posener points out that this phrase, at the end of the first part of the instruction,
corresponds with the phrase, "fight on behalf of the people," in the second part.

The one whom the king loves shall be a well-provided spirit; there is no tomb for anyone who rebels against His Majesty, and his corpse shall be cast to the waters.

II,20    Do this, and your body will flourish, / and you will find it (excellent) for eternity.

# THE INSTRUCTION OF A MAN
# FOR HIS SON (FIRST SECTION)

This instruction for Everyman, although known for some time, was first studied in detail by H. Goedicke in ZÄS 94 (1967): 62–71 and K. A. Kitchen in Oriens Antiquus 8 (1969): 189–208. The text with various copies is studied by Wolfgang Helck, Die Lehre des Djedefhor und Die Lehre eines Vaters an seinen Sohn (Wiesbaden, 1984). For a comprehensive new edition, translation, and study, utilizing 150 sources, mostly very fragmentary, see Hans-W. Fischer-Elfert, Die Lehre eines Mannes für seinen Sohn—Eine Etappe auf dem "Gottesweg" des loyalen und solidarischen Beamten der frühen 12. Dynastie, ÄAbh. 60, with plate vol. (Wiesbaden, 1998). The composition belongs to the loyalist tradition of literature; the author extols the virtue of the king and the concrete advantages to be gained through loyalty to him. Other loyalist compositions are The Loyalist Instruction from the Sehetepibre Stela and the Cycle of Songs in Honor of Senwosret III, with both of which The Instruction of a Man for His Son has points of contact in language and ideas.

W.K.S.

## [TITLE AND INTRODUCTION]

The beginning of the instruction which a man made for his son, as he says:

Listen to my voice. Do not neglect my words, do not be indifferent about what I shall say to you.

### 1.

Exhibit a (good) character without transgressing, for laziness on the part of a wise man should not come to pass.

A silent, just man, well disposed, who bends the arm, one who carries out what is said.

There is no valorous man who speaks in front of a strong man.

There is no brave man who extols(?) advice.

He who has access to (good) discourse is open to what is heard.

There is no ⟨winnower⟩ who converses with him.

Explain discourse without infringing thereby.

A reproach injures the one who speaks it.

### 2.

Do not turn your mind away from God, adore the king, love him as adherents.

He will make fortunate as his mind determines.

Whom he neglects is as one who will not come to port.

He is greater than a million men to one whom he has favored.

The king is a restraining dyke.[1]

He has surrounded the great ones before him.

To whom he loves he gives attention, taking care in speaking to seek him.

### 3.

Has a day of Renenwetet[2] ever gone astray?

Or is a day of a lifetime ever ⟨added⟩?

Or is any subtracted?

1. Compare the similar image in the Cycle of Songs in Honor of Senwosret III (II, 12).
2. "Fortune."

Meskhenet[3] is as she once was.

What he has decreed for him is not destroyed; very great is his punishment.

Great is the favor of God, and great is his might, for I have seen (its) renown.

His fate shall not overtake him.

4.

He educates the ignorant to wisdom, and those who are unloved become as those who are loved.

He causes the lesser folk to emulate the great, the last become as the first.

He who was lacking possessions is (now) the possessor of riches.

He who had only a little land is now the possessor of tenants.

He brings to land him who had no successful landing.

He who was homeless is now the possessor of a dwelling.

He teaches the mute to speak and causes the ears of the deaf to open.

5.

All of this is within a lifetime, without Renenwetet, without Meskhenet set against it, without breath placed to his nostrils.

What is more important to you than that it should be in the councils of your god that you should spend your lifetime?[4]

6.

Adore the King of Upper Egypt and honor the King of Lower Egypt, for it is an office pertaining to God.

Show his might. Rejoice in his decree.

Do not question what he wishes.

Whoever refrains from speaking his name shall be an honored one.[5]

When he is [...], success is given to him.

Whoever opens up his heart to him is ...

But he prepares the execution block (for) ...

3. "Destiny."
4. Following a reading hazarded by Fairman (Kitchen 1969, 196, n.60).
5. For the taboo on speaking the king's name in vain, see Fischer-Elfert 1998, 88.

# THE MAN WHO WAS WEARY OF LIFE

T his Middle Kingdom text, preserved on Papyrus Berlin 3024, has often been interpreted as a debate between a man and his ba on the subject of suicide. I offer here the suggestion that the text is of a somewhat different nature. What is presented in this text is not a debate, but a psychological picture of a man depressed by the evil of life to the point of feeling unable to arrive at any acceptance of the innate goodness of existence. His inner self is, as it were, unable to be integrated and at peace. His dilemma is presented in what appears to be a dramatic monologue which illustrates his sudden changes of mood, his wavering between hope and despair, and an almost heroic effort to find strength to cope with life. It is not so much life itself which wearies the speaker as it is his own efforts to arrive at a means of coping with life's difficulties. This text presents the earliest insights into the complexities of the human psychological structure. The translation offered here attempts to follow the Egyptian text as closely as possible, but I have taken a few liberties in order to bring out what I feel is the authentic meaning of the original. For the Egyptian text of this document, see R. O. Faulkner, "The Man Who Was Tired of Life," JEA 42 (1956): 21–40. The work of H. Goedicke cited below also reproduces the hieratic text and a hieroglyphic transliteration. For alternate translations the reader may wish to consult M. Lichtheim, Ancient Egyptian Literature, vol. 1 (Berkeley, 1973), 163–69, J. L. Foster, Echoes of Egyptian Voices (Nor-

*man, 1992), 11–18, and R. B. Parkinson,* The Tale of Sinuhe and Other Ancient Egyptian Poems 1940–1640 BC *(Oxford 1997), 151–65. Useful studies and interpretations of the text may be found in H. Goedicke,* The Report about the Dispute of a Man with His Ba (Papyrus Berlin 3024) *(Baltimore, 1970); O. Renaud, "Le dialogue du Désesperé avec son Ame: Une interpretation littéraire," (Geneva, 1991); and V. A. Tobin, "A Re-Assessment of the Lebensmüde,"* BiOr *48 (1991): 342–63. The latter article contains a translation of the text by the present author, and that translation, with considerable modifications, has been reproduced here with the kind permission of the editors of* BiOr.

V.A.T.

*The beginning of the manuscript has been lost, although there remain of it a few fragments which, as is obvious from the context, constitute the conclusion of a speech by the man's* ba.

[...] your [...] in order to speak [...] for their decision is unbiased [...] bribery, for their decision is unbiased.

I opened my mouth in response to my *ba,* answering what he had said:

5  "This is become too onerous for me today; my *ba* is not in accord with me. This is even worse than opposing me; it is like forsaking me!

But my *ba* shall not depart![1] He must stand now as my defense in this.
(I shall restrain him)[2] in my body as with a net of rope.
10  Never shall he succeed in fleeing on the day of anguish.

But behold! My *ba* would deceive me, but I heed him not,
While I am impelled toward a death whose time has not yet come.
He flings me on the fire to torment me [...]

1. The speaker's mood suddenly changes from despair to a determination that his *ba* cannot desert him.
2. The text here is unintelligible. The context suggests, however, that the man is determined that his *ba* will not desert him. Hence, it seems reasonable to suggest that he here voices his intention to force his *ba* to remain with him. The imagery of a net of rope, i.e., a fowler's net, is appropriate to the portrayal of the *ba* in the form of a bird.

15  And yet he shall be within me on the day of anguish;
He shall stand (with me) in the West[3] as one who perfects my happiness.
Though he would now depart, yet shall he return.[4]

My *ba* is senseless in disparaging the agony in life
And impels me to death before my time.
20  / And yet the West will be pleasant for me, for there is no sorrow there.[5]
Such is the course of life, and even trees must fall.
So trample down my illusions, for my distress is endless!

Thoth will judge me, he who satisfies the gods,
25  Khons will defend me, / he who records the truth.
Re will hear my words, he who guides the sun barque,
Isdes will defend me in the sacred hall,
For my longing is too intense to bring me any joy,
30  / And only the gods will purge my innermost pain."

What my *ba* said to me:

"Are you not a man? At least you are alive!
So what do you gain by pondering on your life like the owner of a tomb,
One who speaks to him who passes by about his life on earth?[6]
35  Indeed, you are just drifting; you are not / in control of yourself,
And any rogue could say, 'I shall guide you.'
You are, in effect, dead, although your name still lives.
The beyond is the place of rest, the desire of the heart;

---

3. "In the West": lit. "on that side."
4. These lines present a picture not of one who is contemplating suicide, but of one who is rather attempting to bolster his own inner confidence so as to avoid despair.
5. "There is no sorrow there": lit. "Is it misery?" A rhetorical question implying a negative response.
6. The *ba* here is—perhaps mockingly, but certainly in a very unsympathetic manner—comparing the speaker to a wealthy man who has died and who speaks, by means of his tomb autobiography, to those who pass by his burial place.

The West is the (final) landing place,[7]
But your journey (has not yet reached its end)."[8]

*The following passage is obviously spoken not by the* ba, *but by the man.*

"If my *ba,* my stubborn brother, will listen to me,
40    / And if his desire is in full accord with me, he will flourish;
For I shall cause him to reach the West
Like one who is in his pyramid
Which stands above his grave in the sight of his descendants.
I shall build a shelter over your corpse,
45    That you may be the envy of any other *ba* / who is exhausted.
I shall build a shelter, one which will be perfectly cool,
That you may be the envy of any other *ba* who is too hot.
I shall drink water at the pool and gather provisions,
That you may be the envy of any other *ba* who is hungry.[9]

50    But if you compel / me to death in this way,
You will not find a place whereon to rest in the West.
Let your heart be calm, my *ba,* my brother,
Until I have an heir who will make offerings and officiate at my tomb
55    On the day of burial and complete my resting place / in the necropolis."

My *ba* opened his mouth to me in answer to what I had said:

"If you are obsessed with burial, it will cause only sadness of heart,
For it brings tears to grieve a man.
It will bear a man away (untimely) from his home
And bring him to a tomb in the desert.
60    Never again will it be possible for you to go up and see / the sunlight.
Even those who built with stones of granite,

7. The *ba* here is attempting to recall to the man the very real distinction between earthly life and the life after death. There appears here to be a very pragmatic suggestion that life on earth must be lived as it is, and that the afterlife can be attained only when the proper time has come.
8. This suggested restoration appears to make sense in the context, for the *ba* is attempting to convince the man that the end of life has not yet arrived.
9. The speaker is here not addressing his *ba* as a separate entity. He is rather musing upon the joys and the peace which he will know in death. He addresses his *ba* only as a symbol of addressing himself.

Who constructed magnificent pyramids,
Perfecting them with excellent skill,
So that the builders might become gods,[10]
Now their offering stones are empty,
And they are like those who die on the riverbank with no survivors.
65   / The flood carries off some, and likewise the sun (takes) others,
And now only the fish are curious about them at the edge of the river.
For your own sake, listen to me!
Behold, it is good when men listen.
Seek happy days and forget your care.

There was a peasant who farmed his plot of land.
70   He loaded his harvest / into a boat and towed it,
For his time of taxation had come.
He saw the approach of the darkness of a storm from the north,
So he kept watch over the boat.
The sun disappeared, and then came out again,
But meanwhile his wife and children had perished
75   On a lake / infested at night by crocodiles.
Finally he sat down and cried aloud, saying,
'I weep not for the mother,
For it is not within her power to go out from the West
For another life on earth.
I grieve for her children who were crushed in infancy,
80   And who saw the face of the crocodile / without ever having lived.'[11]

There was (another) peasant who asked for something to eat,
But his wife said to him, 'It will soon be suppertime.'[12]

---

10. This reference to the builders of the pyramids having become gods is essentially negative, i.e., even the builders of such great monuments had to die, a reminder that death is inevitable and that there is no profit in dwelling on it.

11. The two parables which the *ba* speaks at this point are extremely difficult to translate and interpret, and their relevance to the problem under discussion in the text is not immediately evident. In the case of the first parable, its meaning may be seen in the figure of the peasant who, while taking care of the grain stored in his boat, was neglectful of greater joys, i.e., his wife and children. Their untimely death was a loss which could not be reversed. The *ba* is possibly warning the man to forget about his misery and look to the real source of happiness, life itself.

12. The exact meaning of the wife's words (*iw r msyt*) is not clear. However, it is evident

He went outside to sulk (?) for a while
And then forced himself to come back to his house;
But he was like a completely different man.
His wife was civil (?) with him, but he would not listen to her.
85    He was moody (?) / and his family was disrupted (?).”

I opened my mouth to my *ba* in answer to what he had said:[13]

1.

“Behold, my very being[14] is loathsome,
Behold, more than the dung of vultures
On summer days when the sky is hot.

Behold, my very being is loathsome,
Behold, more than a catch of fish
90    / On a day of fishing when the sky is hot.

Behold, my very being is loathsome,
Behold, more than the stench of ducks
Or reed-coverts where waterfowl lodge.

Behold, my very being is loathsome,
Behold, more than the smell of fishermen
95    / Or the marshes where they fish.

Behold, my very being is loathsome,
Behold, more than the stench of the crocodiles
Which lurk on that shore which breeds them.

---

that she is offering her reason for refusing to serve her husband at that particular moment.

13. Here follows the heart of the monologue, a series of four poems in which the man expresses his own misery, the wretchedness of his society, the desirability of death, and the peace of the West. There is no real indication here that the man has actually decided in favor of suicide, but rather a firm conviction that true peace and contentment cannot be found in this world.

14. The Egyptian text reads literally “my name.” The term “name” (*rn*), however, refers to the totality of the character, personality, and being of the individual. Hence I prefer to translate freely in order to arrive at the real meaning of the Egyptian text.

Behold, my very being is loathsome,
Behold, more than a woman
Of whom lies are told to her husband.

Behold, my very being is loathsome,
100  / Behold, more than a vigorous youth
Of whom it is said, 'He is despised by his father.'[15]

Behold, my very being is loathsome,
Behold, like a king's land
Which contrives mutiny as soon as he turns his back.

2.

Whom can I trust today?[16]
One's brothers have become evil,
And friends of today have no compassion.

105  Whom can I trust today?
Hearts are greedy,
And every man steals his neighbor's goods.

(Whom can I trust today?)[17]
Compassion has perished,
And violence attacks everyone.

Whom can I trust today?
(Men) are pleased with the evil
Which everywhere throws goodness underfoot.

110  Whom can I trust / today?
Though a man be woeful through ill fortune,
His evil plight causes all to mock him.

15. Or: "He is part of what he should hate"; perhaps a reference to homosexuality.
16. The text reads literally, "To whom shall I speak today?" To speak to someone, however, implies the ability to put one's trust in that individual.
17. This line is not in the text at this point, but the lacuna allows sufficient room for such a restoration, and the context makes it obvious.

Whom can I trust today?
Men plunder,
And everyone robs his comrade.

Whom can I trust today?
A reprobate is my closest friend,
115 And the companion with whom I associated has become / a foe.

Whom can I trust today?
There is no remembrance of the past,
And men now do not treat one in accordance with one's deeds.

Whom can I trust today?
One's brothers have become evil,
And one turns to strangers for integrity.

Whom can I trust today?
People are indifferent,
120 And every man is sullen to / his comrades.

Whom can I trust today?
Hearts have become greedy,
And no man has a heart which can be trusted.

Whom can I trust today?
There are no righteous men,
And the land is abandoned over to the lawless.

Whom can I trust today?
There is emptiness in faithful friends,
125 And one must turn to strangers for / comfort.

Whom can I trust today?
None are contented,
And he with whom one walked is now no more.

Whom can I trust today?
I am laden down with sorrow,
And there is none to comfort me.

Whom can I trust today?
Evil runs rampant throughout the land,
130 / Endless, endless evil.

3.

Death is before me today
(Like) the healing of a sick man,
Like going outside after illness.

Death is before me today
Like the fragrance of myrrh,
Like sitting under the sails on a windy day.

Death is before me today
135     / Like the fragrance of the lotus,
Like tottering at the verge of drunkenness.

Death is before me today
Like the course of the Nile,
As when men return home from a campaign.

Death is before me today
Like the clearing of the sky,
140     As when a man understands / what had been unknown to him.

Death is before me today
Like a man's yearning to see his home
After passing many years in exile.

4.

But surely, he who is yonder[18] will be a living god,
Having purged away the evil which had afflicted him.

Surely, he who is yonder will be one who stands in the sun barque,
145     Having made the necessary offerings / to the temples.

Surely, he who is yonder will be one who knows all things,
Who will not be prevented from standing in the presence
of Re when he speaks."

18. I.e., in the Western Land, the realm of the blessed dead.

What my *ba* said to me:

"Lay your complaining aside, my companion and my brother.
150    Make offerings on the altar / and struggle for your life,
Just as you have declared.
Love me here (and now),[19] and forget about the West.
Continue indeed in your desire to reach the West,
But only when your body is buried in the earth.
I shall alight after you have become weary,[20]
And we shall make our dwelling place together."

155    So it has been transcribed from its beginning to its end as it was
found in writing.

19. I.e., appreciate your life in this world.
20. I.e., after your body sleeps in death.

# THE ADMONITIONS OF AN
# EGYPTIAN SAGE

T his text, also known as *The Admonitions of Ipuwer*, is preserved in only a single copy on *Papyrus Leiden 344*. The papyrus itself dates from the Nineteenth Dynasty, but the text is a copy of an older document. The date of its composition is highly uncertain, and various suggestions have been made as to the time of its writing. A. H. Gardiner had dated it to the Twelfth Dynasty and had seen it as a reflection of the chaos which he claims pervaded Egypt during the First Intermediate Period. The text is unlikely to have been that early, and a more probable, and more widely accepted, dating would place it at some point during the late Middle Kingdom.

The text presents many difficulties in translation and interpretation, some of which are probably due to errors by the scribe who transcribed it. Moreover, both the beginning and the ending of the text have been lost. Due to the large loss at the beginning of the text, possibly forty or fifty verses, we have no way of knowing the exact setting in which the speech of Ipuwer was purported to have been made. The final conclusion of the work is also unknown, although one may presume that there must have been some kind of summation speech either by the king or by Ipuwer himself.

The text may be said to fall into the general category of "national calamity" literature, a format based on a reflection of the postulated upheaval which took place during the First Intermediate Period. In all likelihood, however, this *setting is used here as a literary device in order to present a treatise describing the dramatic contrast between a situation of order and one of disorder, Ma'at as opposed to Isfet. The text is aristocratic in nature, and one of its main complaints is that the lower classes have usurped the place and prerogatives of the wealthy nobility. Ipuwer is portrayed as addressing a king whose name is not known, although it may have been mentioned in the lost beginning of the text. As the text unfolds, Ipuwer, in somewhat repetitive language, describes the lawless and chaotic situation within Egypt, the rich made poor and the poor made wealthy, the lack of food and other necessities, the absence of social stability, and the total uncertainty as to anyone's future or safety. He urges the monarch to try to establish order again in the land and to observe the traditional rituals of the religion in order to obtain the help and support of the gods.*

*For the first published version of this text see A. H. Gardiner,* The Admonitions of an Egyptian Sage, from a Hieratic Papyrus in Leiden *(Leipzig, 1909). For a more recent publication see W. Helck,* Die "Admonitions" Pap. Leiden I 344 recto *(Wiesbaden, 1995). This edition also contains a German translation. It is this latter edition which has been used in the preparation of the present translation. Other translations of the text exist, among which is that of R. O. Faulkner in JEA 51 (1965): 53–62 and reproduced with a few minor changes in the earlier edition of this book. Miriam Lichtheim's translation in* Ancient Egyptian Literature, *vol. 1 (Berkeley, 1973), 149–63 follows Faulkner's interpretation quite closely, although some differences may be noted. A more recent translation is offered by R. B. Parkinson in his book* The Tale of Sinuhe and Other Ancient Egyptian Poems, 1940–1640 BC *(Oxford, 1997), 166–99. The latter translation also includes a good number of useful notes.*

V.A.T.

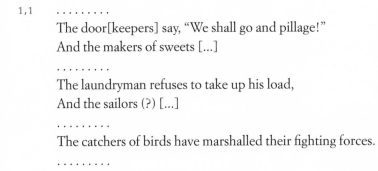

1,1 . . . . . . . . .

The door[keepers] say, "We shall go and pillage!"
And the makers of sweets [...]

. . . . . . . . .

The laundryman refuses to take up his load,
And the sailors (?) [...]

. . . . . . . . .

The catchers of birds have marshalled their fighting forces.

. . . . . . . . .

[The men of] the Delta marshes bear shields,
1,5    And the brewers of beer/ [...]

[Verily, (every) face goes white with fear]

. . . . . . . . .

[Verily, every man] is distressed, for a man sees his son as his foe,
And rancor [is everywhere.]

[Verily, (every) face goes white with fear]

. . . . . . . . .

[And one man incites] another: "Come, take control of the mob."

[Verily ...]

. . . . . . . . .

[Verily, (every) face goes white with fear],
[For now is fulfilled] what was fated for us[1]
In the time of Horus,[2] in the age [of the Ennead.]
[Verily ...]

[Verily, (every) face goes white with fear],
A man of integrity goes mourning for what has happened in the land,
But [a man of depravity] goes about [in glee].

[Verily ...]
[And] foreigners have overrun the whole of Egypt.[3]

Verily, (every) face goes white with fear,
1,10    . . . . . . . .

. . . . . . . .

[Verily ...]
For what men of old foretold has come to [fulfillment].

[Verily, (every) face goes white with fear]

. . . . . . . . .

[Verily], there are none who can escape [...]

. . . . . . . . .

1. The Egyptian text has "for you," but "for us" seems more appropriate to the context.
2. Or, "in the time of Re."
3. Lit. "foreigners have become Egyptians in every place."

[Verily, (every) face goes white with fear],

2,1 [For citizens bow] / their heads to the earth, subject to marauding bands,
And a man goes out to plough bearing his shield.

Verily, the common man says:
"[My heart] is in agony [because of the condition of the land],"
But one who is sly can become wealthy.

Verily, (every) face goes white with fear,
For archers are arrayed in order, evil is everywhere,
And men are not what they used to be.[4]

Verily, thieves [plunder] everywhere,
And the servant pilfers whatever he finds.

Verily, the Nile overflows, but no one tills the earth on account of it,
And all men say, "We know not what will happen throughout the land."

Verily, the women are barren, and none conceive,
Khnum does not shape men because of the condition of the land.

Verily, paupers have become men of affluence,

2,5 And he who could not provide / sandals for himself is (now) the
possessor of wealth.

Verily, faithful servants, their hearts have become surly,
And the magistrates do not satisfy their people when they [cry out].

Verily, [the heart] is horrified,
For affliction pervades the land,
Blood is everywhere;
There is no end of death,
And the death-shroud summons,
Though one's time has not yet come.[5]

Verily, countless corpses are entombed in the river;
The waters are a tomb, and the place of embalming is the river.

Verily, the nobles are in lamentation, while paupers are in glee,
And every city says, "Let us drive out the mighty from our midst."

4. Lit. "There is no man of yesterday."
5. Lit. "although there is not (yet) the approach to it."

Verily, the people are like ibises, for filth pervades the land,
And there are none at all in our time whose garments are white.

Verily, the land whirls like the movement of a potter's wheel,
The thief is a possessor of wealth, and [he who was wealthy] is a robber.

Verily, the road to the tomb lies open;
Even the cattle are driven off, and the peasant says:
"How appalling! What shall I do?"

2,10   / Verily, the river is blood, but one drinks from it;
One may turn away from people, yet one will thirst for water.

Verily, the portals, columns, and walls have been burned,
But the halls of the palace (l.p.h.!) are established and strong.

Verily, the ship of the Southerners is shattered,
The cities are ravaged, and Upper Egypt has become a desolate plateau.

Verily, the crocodiles belch (?) from the fish they have seized,
As men go freely to them,
For this is the utter destruction of the land.

[Verily], men say, "Do not tread here, for behold, it is a net."
But behold, men fall into the trap like fish,
For, in (his) dismay, the terror-stricken does not notice it.

Verily, the people are diminished in number,
And he who buries his brother in the earth is everywhere;
A wise man speaks, but then [he flees] without [delay].

Verily, the son of one whose name is known lacks recognition,
And the child of his wife becomes the son of his maidservant.

3,1    Verily, the desert pervades the land,
The nomes are annihilated, and foreign aliens have come into Egypt.

Verily, [Asiatics] have arrived [in the land],
And in truth there are no Egyptians anywhere.

Verily, gold, lapis lazuli, silver, turquoise, carnelian, amethysts,
Emeralds (?), and [all precious stones] adorn the necks of maidservants,
Noble looking ladies are throughout the (whole) land,
But the housewives sigh, "If only we had something to eat!"

192

Verily, [life] is abhorrent to the hearts of the noble women,
For their bodies are wretched because of (their) ragged clothes,
And their hearts languish when they give one another greeting.

3,5   Verily, / ebony caskets are destroyed,
And the costly aromatic wood from the beds is smashed,
[...] their [...]

Verily, builders arrive, but they depart as (mere) farm hands,
And those who (once sailed) in the royal barque are now harnessed (to it).

Verily, none indeed voyage north to Byblos today.
What then are we to do for cedar trees for our mummies?
For the priests are entombed in the wood of such trees,
And the nobles even as far as Keftiu⁶ are embalmed with the oil thereof.
But these things arrive (here) no longer.
Gold too is no more,
And the materials for all workmanship have been depleted.
Even the [contents] of the royal palace (l.p.h.!) have been despoiled.
How significant it is when the men of the oases come with their goods,
3,10   Rugs, [pelts], fresh *redmet*-plants, / and bird [oil] to sell for profit(?).⁷

Verily, Elephantine and Thinis [which is in Coptos] of Upper Egypt
No longer pay tax because of conflict.
Vanished now are grain, charcoal, blue dye, *maa*-wood, *nut*-wood, and brushwood,
The works of the artisans, the bitter [gourd, *he*]*mit,* (those things which are) the revenue of the palace.
Of what use is a treasury without its income?
Indeed the heart of a king is content (only) when his tribute comes to him.
Moreover, all the foreigners claim:
"This is *our* water! These are *our* crops!"
And what can we do about it?
Things have fallen into ruin.

6. The name Keftiu is usually taken as a reference to the island of Crete.
7. I.e., goods are in such short supply that even peasants selling their produce are welcome.

Verily, rejoicing is perished and no longer arises;
It is grief which pervades the land, mingled with lamentation.

Verily, every worthless man is (now) one of note,
4,1   And those who were / Egyptians [have become] aliens and are cast out.

Verily, everyone's hair has become thin,
And no one can tell an honorable man from one who is worthless.

Verily, deafness has set in with regard to complaints,
There is no honesty of speech in this time of complaints,
And there is no end of complaints.

Verily, old and young say, "I would rather be dead,"
And even little children say, "No one should have given me life."

Verily, the children of the nobles are smashed against the walls,
And suckling children are thrown out onto the desert.

Verily, (bodies) which were in the tombs are cast out onto the desert,
And the skills of the embalmers are undone.

4,5   Verily, / vanished are those things which were seen yesterday,
And the land is remnants of its own weakness like the trimmings of flax.

Verily, the entire Delta, there is nothing protected therein,
And Lower Egypt relies on roads freely traveled (by all).
What can be done?
There is no means of [escape] in any place,
And men cry out, "Down with the sanctuary!"
Behold, it is under the control of the impious as of the pious,[8]
And nomads are (now) experts in the professions of the Delta.

Verily, citizens are consigned to (work) the millstones,
And those who were once clothed with fine linen are unjustly beaten.
Those who (once) did not see the daylight can now go out with no
restraint;

8. Or, "Behold, (everything) is under the control of the unskilled as of the skilled." The
exact meaning of the passage is uncertain, but the writer is pointing out that the
institutions and traditions of Egypt have fallen into the hands of men unable to deal
with or respect them.

As for those who (once) were in the beds of their husbands,
4,10    / Let them (now) sleep on the ground.
[Those who used] to say, "It is too heavy for me"
About a package of myrrh
Are (now) laden down under vessels filled with grain
And are no longer accustomed to (be carried in) litters.
As for the butler, he no longer exists,
And there is no cure for this.
Noble ladies bewail their lot like maidservants;
Musicians are at the looms in the place of weaving,
While their lays to Meret[9] are laments,
And the tellers of tales are at the millstones.

Verily, all maidservants are mean-mouthed,
But let the mistress speak, and it vexes the servants.

Verily, trees are hewn down and the branches knocked off,
And the servants of (a man's) house have driven him out.

5,1    Men will both say and hear,
"Food is lacking for numerous children,
And there is no sustenance from [the different grains].
What would it taste like now?"

Verily, the nobles perish from hunger,
And men follow those who once themselves were followers,
For the arm of the violent is protection and succor.

Verily, the unruly man says,
"If I knew where God is, I would serve him."

Verily, Ma'at pervades the land, at least in name,
But what men do is lawlessness, establishing themselves upon it.

Verily, (one must) be quick to fight for what belongs to him,
5,5    / Or he will be robbed and all his property seized.

Verily, even all the animals, their hearts weep,
And the cattle lament the condition of the land.

---

9. The goddess of song.

Verily, the children of the nobles are smashed against the walls,
Suckling children are thrown out onto the desert,
And Khnum groans because he is weary.

Verily, horror commits murder,
The fearful man prevents those who would act against your foes,
And only a remnant are unharmed and safe, only a few.

Is it by stalking the crocodile and destroying it?
Is it by slaughtering the lion and roasting it on the fire?
Is it by sprinkling water for Ptah and bringing [offerings]?
Why do you give to him?
For it does not reach him.
It is only trouble that you offer him.

5,10   Verily, servants [rule ...] / throughout the land,
The strong man issues (orders) to everyone,
And a man strikes his maternal brother.
What are these things which have come to pass?
I can cry only "Destruction!"

Verily, the roads are avoided and the paths are ambushed,
Men crouch in the bushes until the arrival of a traveler at night
In order to seize his burden and to take what he is carrying;
He is attacked with blows of a cudgel and foully murdered.

Verily, vanished are those things which were seen yesterday,
And the land is remnants of its own weakness like the trimmings of flax.
The peasants wander about aimlessly because of the desolation,
And goldsmiths [are employed on the canals].
If only this were the end of men!
6,1   No more conceiving!/No more giving birth!
Then the land would be hushed from (its) discord,
And (its) turmoil would be no more.

Verily, [men feed] on wild plants and wash them down with water,
For they can find neither fruit, nor herbs, nor fowl;
They seize the [slops] from the mouths of the pigs.
No one is cheerful, for all have succumbed to hunger.

Verily, grain is depleted everywhere,
And men are deprived of clothing, perfume, and oil.
Everyone says, "There is nothing left."
The warehouse is bare and its attendant stretched out on the earth.

6,5 All joy is lacking to my heart; I am / totally undone!
If only I had uttered my words at the (proper) time,
For it would have rescued me from the suffering into which I have fallen.

Verily, the sacred chamber, its writings are stolen,
And the place of secrets, which was therein, is disclosed.

Verily, the sacred spells have been exposed,
Incantations and rituals have been invalidated
Through being known by the people.

Verily, the offices are opened and their records pillaged;
Men who once were serfs have (now) become owners of serfs.

Verily, scribes are murdered, and their writings are stolen;
How evil is my plight through the misery of our time.

Verily, the scribes of the land registry, their records are destroyed,
And the grain of Egypt is up for grabs.

6,10 Verily, the decrees / of the council chamber are tossed aside;
Moreover, men walk on them in public,
And the rabble smash them in the streets.

Verily, the pauper has acquired the rank of the Ennead,
And the business of the House of the Thirty is laid bare.

Verily, the great council chamber is open to all,
Paupers come and go in the great palaces.

Verily, the children of the nobles are cast into the streets;
The wise man says "Yes!" while the fool says "No!"
And he who understands nothing of it (finds it) pleasing in his sight.

Verily, (bodies) which were in the tombs are cast out onto the desert,
And the skills of the embalmers are undone.

7,1 / Behold now, a fire has blazed up to the height,
And its flame goes forth against the land.

Behold now, deeds are done which have never before occurred,
For the king has been overthrown by the rabble.

Behold, he who was buried as a falcon (now) sleeps on a bier,
And what the pyramid once held hidden will (now) be wanting.

Behold now, the land begins to lose the kingship
At the hands of a few men who ignore tradition.

Behold now, there arises rebellion
Against the mighty Uraeus of Re who contents the Two Lands.

Behold, the secret of the land, whose limits are unknown, is laid bare,
And the Residence could fall at any moment.

7,5    Behold, Egypt has begun to / pour water,[10]
And he who once irrigated the land has carried off the mighty in misery.[11]

Behold, the Serpent has been wrenched from its lair,
And the secrets of the Kings of Upper and Lower Egypt are laid bare.

Behold, the Residence is fearful because of want,
And everyone will arouse strife with no opposition.

Behold, the land is fettered by mobs,
And as for the brave man, the craven seizes his property.

Behold, the serpent devours (?) the dead,
And he who could not make a coffin for himself
Is (now) the owner of a tomb.

Behold, those who (once) owned tombs
Are thrown out onto the desert plateau,
While he who could not make a grave for himself
Is (now) the owner of a treasury.

Behold now what men have become:
He who could not build for himself a (single) chamber
Is now the owner of a mansion.

10. I.e., a funerary ritual, used here as a symbol of the demise of Egyptian culture.
11. I.e., the ordinary peasant farmer has overthrown the rulers.

Behold, the judges of the land are driven away throughout the land,
7,10   And those who once herded bulls are (now) in the / royal palace.

Behold, noble ladies (now sleep) on the floor,[12]
And princes are in the workhouse.

[Behold, ...]
While he who did not have a floor on which to sleep
Is (now) the owner of a bed.

Behold, he who once owned wealth (now) spends the night in thirst,
While he who (once) begged dregs for himself has overflowing bowls.

Behold, those who (once) owned robes are in rags,
While he who could not weave for himself is the owner of fine linen.

Behold, he who could not build a boat for himself
Is (now) the owner of a fleet,
While their (former) owner can (only) gaze at them,
For they no longer belong to him.

Behold, he who had no shelter is (now) the owner of a shelter,
While those who (once) had shelters are in the blast of the tempest.

Behold, he who could not play the lyre is skilled on the harp,
And he who could not sing for himself now praises Meret.

Behold, those who once owned bronze vessels,
Not one of them has garlanded jars.

8,1    Behold, he who once slept / wifeless through poverty
Can now find noble women,
And he who was inconspicuous
(Now) stands in a position of importance.

Behold, he who had nothing is (now) the owner of wealth,
And the official favors him.

Behold, the poor of the land have become the wealthy,
And he who owned property (now) has nothing.

12. Lit. "on boards."

Behold, cupbearers have become the masters of butlers,
And he who was a messenger (now) sends someone else.

Behold, he who did not have a loaf is (now) the owner of a storehouse,
But his storeroom is stocked with the property of another.

Behold, he who had lost his hair and was lacking in oil
Has become the owner of jars of sweet myrrh.

Behold, she who had no box is now the owner of a chest,
8,5     / And she who used to look at her face in the water (now) owns a mirror.

Behold [...]

Behold, a man is contented when he eats his food,
So consume what you have with joyful heart
While there is still nothing preventing you.
It is pleasant for a man to eat his food,
And God ordains it for the one whom he has favored.

. . . . . . . . .[13]

[Behold now, he who did not know] his god (now) makes offering to him
With incense belonging to another whom he does not even know.

[Behold], noble ladies, highborn and possessors of wealth,
(Now) sell their children in exchange for provisions.

Behold now, a [lowly] man [takes] a noble woman as (his) wife,
And her father supports him so that he may not kill him.

Behold, the children of magistrates are in [rags],
8,10    And [the calves] / of their cattle [are surrendered] to robbers.

Behold, the serfs slaughter cattle,
And the poor [have become robber]s.

Behold, he who did not slaughter for himself (now) slaughters bulls,
And he who did not know how to carve (now) sees all [choice meats].

Behold, the serfs slaughter geese
which are given to the gods instead of oxen.

13. The scribe left a considerable space blank at this point, possibly sufficient for a full
    verse.

Behold, maidservants [...] make offerings of ducks,[14]
And noble women [...].

Behold, noble women flee in one single flight,
Their [hearts] failing through fear of death.

[Behold], the chiefs of the land flee;
They have no function through lack of one to back them.

9,1   [Behold], / those who (once) owned beds (sleep) on the ground,
While he who spent the night in squalor
Is (now) one who spreads a leather mat for himself.

Behold, noble ladies have fallen upon hunger,
While serfs are satisfied with what had been made ready for them.

Behold, no function is in its (proper) place,
Like a herd wandering aimlessly without its herdsman.

Behold, the cattle wander off with no one to collect them,
And every man takes for himself the one branded with his name.

Behold, a man can be slain in the presence of his (own) brother,
And he deserts him in order to save himself.

Behold, he who did not have a pair (of oxen)
Is (now) the owner of a herd,
And he who could not find oxen for ploughing
Is (now) the owner of cattle.

Behold, he who had no grain is (now) the owner of a granary,
9,5   / And he who used to borrow grain (now) lends it out.

Behold, he who had no dependents is (now) the master of serfs,
And he who was a [director] is (now) one who conducts his own affairs.

Behold, the mighty of the land,
The condition of the people is not recounted to them,
For everything has been destroyed.

Behold, all the artisans no longer work,
For the enemies of the land have ruined its artisans.

14. Or, "pigs."

[Behold, he who reported the harvest (now) knows nothing of it,
While he who did not plough [for himself is (now) rich in grain.
The harvest] is carried out, but is not reported;
As for the scribe, his hands [are idle] at his post.

Destroy [...]
[...] his [...] in his time.
A man regards [his brother as] his enemy,
And the weak man brings coolness [...]
[...] in the office is fearful.

9,10   No / [...]
The wretched [...]
The land does not brighten because of it.

Destroy[ed ...] their food [is seized] from them.
The pauper begs [...] the messenger,
But no [...] time.
He is seized while burdened with his property,
And he is robbed [...],
Men [pass] by his door.
[The *wab*-priest sits] outside the wall
In the office of the rooms containing falcons and ram[s],
[A vigil without dawn].
As for the commoner, he is watchful,

10,1   / So that the day may dawn on him without his fearing it.
Men flee (as if driven) by the wind.
Those who once worked with fine linen in a house,
(Now) all they make are tents like the nomads.
No longer are commissions carried out by servants on the business of
their masters,
For there is no readiness on their part (to do so).
Even though there are five men, (yet) they (all) say:
"Take care of that yourself! You know that we have just come back!"

The Delta weeps, for the royal storehouse is up for grabs by everyone,
And the entire royal palace (l.p.h.!) lacks its income.
To it are due grain and barley, fowl and fish;

10,5   To it are due white fabric and fine linen, bronze and / oil;

To it are due carpets and mats, [...]-blossoms and sheaves,
Every fine work which should arrive (expertly) fashioned.
If there is dearth of these in the royal palace (l.p.h.!),
Then no one can be free from the lack of them.

Destroy the enemies of the noble Residence, glorious in (its) nobles,
Who [...] in it like [...]
. . . . . . . . .
For the ruler of the city must go about without his escort.

Des[troy the enemies of the noble Residence], glorious [in ...]
. . . . . . . . .

[Destroy the enemies of] that noble Residence, abundant in laws,
. . . . . . . . .
. . . . . . . . .
. . . . . . . . .

10,10  [Destroy the enemies of] / that noble [Residence ...]
For [...] its [...]

Destroy the enemies of that [noble] Residence, [...]
For none can stand [...]

Destroy the enemies of that noble [Residence], abounding in offices,
For verily [...]

Remember the anointing [of ...]
One who suffers due to the sickness of his body.
Give respect to [...]
[...] because of his god.
He will guard his mouth [...]
[...] (and) his offspring will witness the rising of the (Nile) flood.

11,1  Remember [to reple]nish the shrine, to make offering of incense,
And to pour a libation from a vessel at dawn.

Remember (to bring) fat *ro*-geese, *terep*-geese, and *set*-geese
And to sacrifice sacred offerings to the gods.

Remember to chew natron and to prepare white bread,
(As is done) by a man on the day of the anointing of the head.

Remember to set up flagpoles and to carve offering tables,
As the priest purifies the sanctuaries,
The house of the god is plastered (as white) as milk,
The fragrance of the Horizon is made sweet,
And offerings of bread are presented.

Remember to observe the ordinances, rightly to assign the dates,
11,5 And to expel him who is initiated / as a priest despite physical impurity,
For this is undertaking it wrongly,
This is malevolence of heart.

[Remember] the day which precedes eternity,
The months which are numbered and the years which are known.

Remember to slaughter oxen,
[...] from the best which you have on record.

Remember to go forth and seek [the god] who summons you,
To place a *ro*-goose on the fire [...],
To open the jar, and [to make offering on] the bank of the Nile flood.

[Remember ...]
[...] of women
. . . . . . . . .
[...] clothing.

11,10 / [...] to offer praise,
. . . . . . . . .
[...] to content you.
[... through] lack of people.
Come, [...]
[...] of Re who commands [...]
[...] while revering him, the one who journeys to the West,
To weaken [... those who are] by the gods.

Behold, why does (God) even consider creating (men),
When the peaceful man is not distinguished from the aggressive?
12,1 Let him but bring coolness upon their passion, / and men will say:
"He is the shepherd of all mankind, and there is no evil in his heart."
Small is his herd,
But he has had to spend the (entire) day to herd them

Because of the fire in their hearts.
Would that he had perceived their nature in the first generation!
Then he would have smitten (their) sinfulness
And extended his arm against it;
He would have destroyed herds of them and their heirs.
Yet men desire to procreate,
And so sorrow has come to be, and misery on every side.
Such is the way it is, and never will it end,
As long as the gods exist in the midst of it all
And the seed issues forth from the wives of men.
None may be found upon the (right) way,
But only struggle has come forth.
12,5 / The chastiser of crimes is the one who devises them,
And there are no pilots on watch.

Where is (God) today? Does he indeed sleep?
Behold, his power is no more seen.
Though we have been afflicted,
Yet did I not find you?
You did not call to me in vain.

"Resistance against these things means (only) discouragement."
These words are now on the mouth of everyone,
For today those who fear these things (are more) than millions of men,
And no defenders against (our) enemies can be seen.
[... the tumult] in his outer hall
Has entered into the temple [...].
The south[erners weep] for him [...]
[Behold him!] He is the one who acts so that his words are contradicted.
How often the land [...]
12,10 / Has not the land fallen? [...]
The statues are burned, and their workshops are destroyed.
[Every man] is on his guard,
For he sees the day of [calamity now established].
The Universal Lord, who has made for himself a division between heaven
and earth,
Has become fearful for every man.
If he does not act in our defense, who then will,

If you refuse to save?[15]
Authority, perception, and Ma'at are with you,
But it is confusion which you have permitted throughout the land
Along with the noise of tumult.
Behold, one man strikes out at another,
For men transgress against what you have decreed.
If three men set out on a journey, only two arrive,[16]
For the many kill the few.
Is there indeed a shepherd who desires death?
Then you may command that such be done.

13,1 There is (now) a destruction of affection,
For one man hates the other.
Now there is a reduction in (men's) persons everywhere,
And it is you who have behaved so that this might come to pass,
For you have spoken falsehood.
The land is (now) a bitter weed which destroys mankind,
And none can be certain of life.
Through all these years there is conflict,
And a man can be murdered on the roof of his own house.
Let him be vigilant in his gatehouse,
And if he is strong, he may save himself.
This is life!

Men devise crimes (even) against a commoner:
He travels on the road until he sees the ambush;[17]
13,5 The road is blocked, / and he stops in fear.
What he has with him is seized,
And he is attacked with blows of a cudgel and cruelly murdered.
Would that you might taste even a little of such misery!
Then you would say, "[Keep silent no longer]!"
. . . . . . . . .

15. The meaning of this section is generally obscure due partially to the lacunae and also
   to the difficulties of the text itself. However, these lines appear to be addressed to the
   king as an appeal for help.
16. Lit. "they are found as two men."
17. Lit. "until he sees the flood." The term "flood" here appears to be used metaphorically.

[... his ...] as a guard on the wall,
As well as [...]

. . . . . . . . .

[...] hotter than the body.
The years when speech was uttered [...]

. . . . . . . . .

[Verily, it is] good when ships sail southward [...],

. . . . . . . . .

13,10　[And no robbers] plunder them.

Verily, it is good[...]

. . . . . . . . .

[Verily], it is good when the net is pulled in,
And men tie up the birds [in] the evening.

Verily, it is good when [...] honors for them,
When the roads are open to travel.

Verily, it is good when men's hands construct pyramids,
When pools are dug, and orchards planted with trees worthy of the gods.

Verily, it is good when men drink deep,
When they drink strong liquor, and their hearts rejoice.

Verily, it is good when shouts of joy are in (men's) mouths,
When the lords of the estates stand

14,1　Watching the rejoicing / in their houses,
Dressed in fine linen,
Their foreheads anointed, and secure for the future.

Verily, it is good when beds are prepared,
When the headrests of the nobles are well secured,
When all men's wants are satisfied by a couch in the shade,
And a door is shut (to protect) him who used to sleep in the bushes.

Verily, it is good when fine linen is laid out on New Year's Day,
[...] on the bank,
When fine linen is laid out, and cloaks (spread) on the ground,
When the keeper of the clo[aks ...]

. . . . . . . . .

14,5    / [...] trees,
      And the common folk are [...]
       . . . . . . . . .[18]

*The King answers Ipuwer.*

14,10   [...] / they [...] acts of robbery
      [...] while sailing southwards.
      The [Delta] is confined [...]
      [... in] their midst like Asiatics.
       . . . . . . . . .

      But men ignore their schemes,
      And so bring about their own doom,
      And none can be found who will arise
      And defend themselves against the [Libyans] and Asiatics.
      Each man fights only for his sister and protects himself.
      Are Nubians (the threat)? Then we shall protect ourselves,
      For the warriors are numerous to drive back the foreign bowmen.
      Is it Libyans? Then we shall route them,
      For the Medjay are friendly with Egypt.[19]

      But how? For every man slays his (own) brother,
15,1     And the troops / we recruited for ourselves have become foreigners
      And have turned to pillaging.
      The outcome of that will be to let the Asiatics realize the condition of the land.
      But all the foreigners are still held in awe of it,
      And what the peoples have experienced (is enough to) say:
      "Egypt will not be subjected to the desert;
      She will be victorious because of her walls."

      But (this will be) said of you in later years:
      "[...] destroyed itself."

18. A very large lacuna occurs at this point in the text. In what is missing, the speaker, Ipuwer, concluded his speech, and the monarch commenced his reply. The verses following are the continuation of the king's speech.
19. The Medjay were Nubians employed as mercenaries and police in Egypt. The sense of what the king says is that, with the help of the Medjay, the Egyptians will be able to defeat any Libyan invaders.

It is a time [...] their [...] will give life to his children.
There will be [...]
What has been brought to pass is that there will not be [...]
15,5   / [...] said.
The troops [...]

*Five lines have been lost at this point in the text.*

15,11   [...] make sandals for yourselves

. . . . . . . . .

bonds [...] resin,
Lotus leaves, reeds, [...]
[...] in excess of the provisions [...]

*Ipuwer again resumes his speech.*

What Ipuwer said when he answered the majesty of the Lord of All:

You have deceived the whole populace!
It seems that (your) heart prefers to ignore (the troubles).
Have you done what will make them happy?
Have you given life to the people?
16,1   They cover / their faces in fear of the morning!

Once there was a man who had grown old and was approaching death,
And his son was a child still without understanding.
He began to defend [...]
But he could not open [his] mouth [to] speak to you,
And you robbed him even in the agony of death.
Weep [...]

*Eight lines are lost here.*

16,12   [...] after you,
The land will be [...]
[...] on every side.
If men call to [...]
The peo[ple of the land] weep [because of] their [enemies]
Who have entered the funerary temples
And burned the images.
[Destroyed are ...]

And the bodies of the mummies [are carried off].

17,1 How evil [...]

[...] of the Director of Works

. . . . . . . . .

*The rest of the text is lost.*

# THE LAMENTATIONS OF
## KHAKHEPERRE-SONBE

T*he author of our lamentations is included in the list of the authors of old, the great sages of the past, in Papyrus Chester Beatty IV. Our text recalls The Admonitions of Ipuwer, The Prophecies of Neferty, and The Man Who Was Weary of Life. In common with the first two, it describes the plight of a disorganized land in a time of troubles. Like the third, it has a discourse with the man's other self. If it were not that The Lamentations is a dialogue with the heart and The Man Weary of Life a dialogue with the soul (ba), one might suspect that The Lamentations represents a reworking of the lost beginning of the latter.*

*The text is written on both sides of a writing board of Dynasty 18 in the British Museum (EA 5645). It was probably composed in the Middle Kingdom or the Second Intermediate Period. The board is covered with a network of string over which stucco has been washed to form the writing surface, and it is pierced for suspension from a wall or hook.*

*The last line in the text is complete but lacks any indication that it represents the end of the composition. Perhaps the composition was continued on another tablet. See R. B. Parkinson, "The Text of* Khakheperreseneb: *New Readings of EA 5645, and an Unpublished Ostracon," JEA 83 (1997): 55–68; "Khakheper-*reseneb *and Traditional Belles Lettres," in P. D. Manuelian, ed.,* Studies in Honor of William Kelly Simpson *(Boston, 1996), pp. 647–54. See bibliography.*

W.K.S.

## RECTO

1  The gathering together of sayings, the culling of phrases, the search for words by an inquisitive mind, which the *wab*-priest of Heliopolis, Seny's
2  son Khakheperre-sonbe, who is called Ankhu, wrote./

He said: Would that I had unknown speeches, erudite phrases in new language which has not yet been used, free from (the usual) repetitions, not
3  the phrases of past speech / which (our) forefathers spoke. I shall drain myself for something in it in giving free rein to all I shall say. For indeed whatever has been said has been repeated, while what has (once) been said has been said. There should be no boasting about the literature of the men
4  of former times / or what their descendants discovered!

5  / The speaker has not (yet) spoken. One who will speak now speaks. What another has found will be said. Not a tale of telling after the fact: they
6  did it before. Not yet a story for future telling. / Such is seeking disaster. It is falsehood. And there is no one who shall recall such a man's name to the people.

I have said these things just as I have seen, beginning with the first gen-
7  eration down to / those who shall come afterward, when they (too) shall imitate the past.

Would that I might know what others did not know, even what has not
8  yet been repeated, that I might speak and my heart answer me, / that I might enlighten my grief to it, and that I might thrust onto it the weight which is on my back, (and speak) thoughts about what afflicts me, that I might
9  express to it what I suffer through it, / that I might speak, Yea, about my feelings!

10  / I am thinking about what has happened,[1] the things that have come to pass throughout the land. Changes are taking place. It is not like last year; one year is more troublesome than the next. The land is in chaos, has become my destruction, has been made into a state of unrest.

11  / Justice has been cast out, and evil is inside the shrine. The designs of the gods are disturbed, and their perquisites are passed over. The land is in
12  dire state. Mourning is everywhere. / Towns and districts are in lamentation. All alike are grief stricken. The back is turned on anything of worth; the tranquil are distressed. Troubles occur daily, and the face shrinks from what is about to happen.

1. Here begins the parallel text of the ostracon.

13     I will say my say about it, for my limbs are heavy laden. I am distressed in my heart, and it is painful to hide my thoughts about it. Although another heart would break, a stout heart in a difficult situation is the companion of its master.

14     O would that I had a heart / that knew how to suffer. Then I might alight, and I would load it with phrases of misery, and I might drive off to it my suffering.

## VERSO

1     He said to his heart: Come now, my heart, that I may converse with you and you may answer me my sayings, that you may interpret for me that which is throughout the land, for those who were radiant (in white garments) have been cast down.

2     I am thinking about what has taken place. Misery is ushered in / today. By the morning the strangers have (still) not passed away. Everyone is silent about it. The entire land is in a serious plight, and there is nobody free from wrong: all people alike do it. Hearts are dejected. The one who gives com-

3     mands / is (now) one to whom commands are given, and the hearts of both are quieted.

One rises to these things daily, and hearts have not thrust them aside. Yesterday's state is like today's, because of the passing by of many things.

4     The countenance is perplexed. There is no man wise enough to know it, / and there is no man angry enough to speak out. Every day one wakes to suffering.

Long and burdensome is my suffering. There is no strength for the wretched to rescue him from one stronger than him. Silence about what is

5     heard is painful. It is miserable to have to give an answer / to the ignorant. To oppose a speech makes for disaffection. The heart cannot accept truth. A reply to a speech is insufferable. All a man wants is his own talk. Everyone is based in crookedness. Precision in speech is abandoned.

6     I speak to you, / my heart, that you may answer me. Yet a heart which is appealed to cannot be silent. The needs of a servant are like those of a master. Plentiful (now) are the things which weigh upon you.[2]

2. The tablet ends here and perhaps the text as well.

# THE PROPHECIES OF NEFERTY

T he sole complete copy of this text is preserved on Papyrus St. Petersburg 1116B and dates from the Eighteenth Dynasty, although smaller portions have been found on ostraca and two writing tablets. The original text was written purportedly during the reign or after the death of Amenemhet I of the Twelfth Dynasty as a propaganda document justifying his seizing of the throne from the Mentuhotep family. To view this text solely as political propaganda, however, is to do it an injustice. Its contents are an elegant poetic lament over the disasters which had befallen Egypt during the First Intermediate Period, and its literary value far outweighs its propaganda purposes. The setting of the text is the court of King Snefru, "the first king of the Fourth Dynasty of the Old Kingdom," to which the lector-priest Neferty is summoned to entertain the king with his eloquent speech. At the request of the king, Neferty proceeds to foretell the future of Egypt and launches into a lament over the evils which are to come. His prophecy concludes with the "propaganda" element of the text, the foretelling of the rise of Amenemhet I, who will restore Ma'at (order) and dispel the chaos and turmoil which had troubled Egypt. The text has been published by W. Golénischeff (Les papyrus hiératiques nos. 1115, 1116A et 1116B de l'Ermitage impérial à St-Petersburg [St. Petersburg, 1916]) and by Helck (Die Prophezeiung des Nfr.tj, 2nd ed. [Wiesbaden, 1992]). It is the latter edition which has been used for the preparation on this translation. For studies of the

*text, see E. Blumenthal, "Die Prophezeiung des Neferty," ZÄS 109 (1982): 1–
27, and H. Goedicke,* The Protocol of Neferty *(Baltimore, 1977).*

V.A.T.

Now it came to pass that the King of Upper and Lower Egypt, Snefru,
justified, was a mighty ruler over this entire land. On one of those days, the
Court of the Residence made a solemn entrance into the Great House
(l.p.h.!)[1] to pay their homage. Then they took their departure after they had
paid homage according to their daily custom. Then his Majesty said to the
seal-bearer who was attending him, "Go! Bring to me the Court of the
Residence which has just departed after paying homage this morning." So
they were brought to him / immediately and they again prostrated themselves before his Majesty.

Then his Majesty said to them, "My loyal subjects, behold, I have had
you brought here in order to have you search out for me a son of yours who
is wise, a brother of yours who is outstanding, a friend of yours who has
done a noble deed, one who will speak to me a few fine words and elegant
phrases so that my Majesty may be pleased by listening to them."

Then they again prostrated themselves before his Majesty, and they
said to his Majesty, "Our sovereign Lord, there is a famous lector-priest of
Bastet, / whose name is Neferty. He is a citizen strong of arm, a scribe of
outstanding skill, and a rich man whose wealth is greater than that of any of
his peers. Let him be brought to attend your Majesty." Then his Majesty
said, "Go! Bring him to me." So he was brought to the king immediately,
and he prostrated himself before his Majesty.

Then his Majesty said, "Come now, Neferty my friend, speak to me a
few fine words and elegant phrases so that my Majesty may be pleased by
listening to them." Then the lector-priest Neferty asked, "About what has
come to pass, or about what will come to pass, my sovereign Lord?" /
And his Majesty answered, "About what will come to pass, for today has
(already) occurred and is past and gone." Then he stretched his hand
toward a box of writing materials, took a scroll and palette, and proceeded

1. This formula, traditionally used after references to the king and to the royal house,
   reflects the solemnity of Egyptian royal protocol but can be clumsy in translation.
   Hence, it will be omitted in the following rendition, although readers should understand that it occurs frequently in the original text.

to record the sayings of the lector-priest Neferty, the wise man of the east, the servant of Bastet in her glory,[2] the son of the nome of On.[3]

20 He pondered on what would come to pass in the land and foretold the misery of the east when the Asiatics would invade in their might, terrorizing the hearts of the farmers, and seizing the oxen at the plough./ And he said:

> "Arise, oh my heart!
> Weep for this land wherein you were born!
> Falsehood is as the flood,
> And behold, evil is spoken with impunity.
> Behold, nobles are deposed in the land where you were born.
> Become not weary, though it be before your very eyes,
> Mark well what is before you.
> Behold, nobles no longer guide this land,
> And what is done is such as should not be done.
> The day dawns amidst falsehood,
> And the land is totally ravaged.
> Not a trace remains—not even a fingernail—due to its (evil) fate.
> The land perishes, and there is no one who cares for it.
> There is no one who speaks out,
> No one who makes lament.
>
> In what (dread state) is this land!
25 > The sun is obscured / and gives no light that men may see.
> Men cannot live when stormclouds hover,
> And all are stunned in its absence.
> I shall speak (only) what is before my face;
> I shall not foretell what will not come to pass.
>
> The river of Egypt is empty,
> And the waters may be crossed on foot.
> Men search for water that the ships may sail,
> But the watercourse has become a river bank.
> The river bank will be where now the water is,
> And the water will be where the bank is now.

2. Lit. "in her rising."

3. On was the Egyptian name for the site later called Heliopolis by the Greeks, the site of the sanctuary of Re (or Re-Atum), not far from Memphis.

South wind will clash with north wind,
And the sky will not be of a single breeze.
Foreign birds will breed in the Delta marshes,
Having made their nests beside the people,
30   / For men have let them approach through laxness.

Perished and gone are those joyful places,
The fish ponds where dwell fish-eating birds,
(Ponds) alive with fish and fowl.
All joy has been driven out,
And the land is plunged into anguish
By those voracious Asiatics who rove throughout the land.

Foes have appeared in the east,
Asiatics have entered Egypt.
We have no (border) fortress, for foreigners now hold it,
And there is no one to heed who the plunderers are.
One may expect attack by night;
The fortress will be breached and sleep driven from all eyes.
35   / I (too) have slept, but (now) I am awake.[4]

Desert beasts will drink at the river of Egypt,
They will rest on its shores,
For there will be no one to frighten them.
The land is in turmoil, and no one knows the outcome.
What will come to pass is concealed in my words,
But sight and hearing are dead.
Only silence abounds.[5]

I shall show you the land in distress,
For incredible things have come to pass.[6]
Men will take up weapons of war,

4. These lines (VII.g-i) are very obscure. The sense here suggested is a description of sudden attacks by the Asiatic invaders. The speaker further states that he himself has been sleeping, i.e., unaware of the dangers, but now at last he has seen the truth of the situation.
5. The sense of these last two lines is that although the words of the speaker hold the truth about the future, men refuse to accept what he is saying.
6. Lit. "that which has not happened (before) has happened (now)"; or, "what should not happen has happened."

40    And the land will live in / turmoil.
They will make arrows from copper,
They will seek blood as food.
They will laugh gleefully over suffering,
And none will weep at death.
None will lie awake fasting at the time of death,
For each man's heart cares for himself alone.
None will make mourning today,
For hearts have completely turned from it.
A man will sit and turn his back,
While one murders another.
I shall show you a son who has become foe,
A brother who has become an enemy,
45    And a son / who kills his father.

Every mouth is full of 'Take pity on me,'
But all goodness has been driven away.
The land perishes, for its fate has been ordained,
Its produce has been laid waste
And its harvest made desolate.
All that has been accomplished is now undone.
A man's property is taken away
And given to one who is a stranger.
I shall show you a nobleman with nothing, a foreigner prosperous.
The one who was slothful now is filled,
But he who was diligent has nothing.
Men will give alms grudgingly to silence a mouth which begs.
One answers a (man's) remark by a hand which lashes out with a stick.
Instead of speaking, one kills him,
For speech strikes the heart like fire,
50    And none can endure what issues forth from the mouth.

The land is destitute, although its rulers are numerous;
It is ruined, but its taxes are immense.
Sparse is the grain, but great is the measure,
For it is distributed as if it were abundant.

As for Re, he has withdrawn himself from men.
He will rise at the appointed time,

But none will know when noon has come.
None will behold his shadow,
None will rejoice when he is seen.
No longer will the eyes stream with water,
For he will be in the sky only like the moon.
(And yet) his times of night will never stray,
And his rays will surely be in (our) sight as in times of old.

I shall show you the land in turmoil.
He who was weak of arm is (now) a possessor of might,
55 And men / honor those who once were obliged to show respect.[7]
I shall show you lowly men in exalted positions,
He who (once) followed obediently now goes his own way.[8]
Men will live amidst the tombs,
The pauper will gain wealth;
The noble woman (will toil) in order to subsist;
The beggar will eat bread, and slaves will be exalted.
The Nome of On shall be no more on earth,[9]
The birthplace of all the gods.

But then there shall come a king from the south.
His name will be Ameny, justified.
He will be the son of a woman of Ta-Sety,[10]
An offspring of the royal house of Nekhen.[11]
He shall receive the White Crown,
He shall wear the Red Crown;
60 / He shall unite the Two Powers,

7. Lit. "One salutes him who (once) saluted."
8. Lit. "He who walked behind is one who turns his body."
9. The prophesied end of the Nome of On, i.e., Heliopolis, signifies the total destruction of the Egyptian religious tradition.
10. The name Ta-Sety refers usually to Nubia but seems here to designate the southernmost part of Upper Egypt. The line appears to be a deliberate statement of political propaganda, stating that after the fall of On, symbolic of the northern kingship, the true Egyptian kingship will emerge from the south. The new Theban kingship of the Twelfth Dynasty is in this way given a solid foundation in prophesy.
11. This reference to the royal house of Nekhen is an attempt to connect Amenemhet I with the most ancient Egyptian kingship and thus to justify his tenure of the throne. Nekhen is in the second nome of Upper Egypt.

He shall satisfy the Two Lords with that which they desire,[12]
For the field-encircler will be in his grasp,
The oar in his control.
/The people of his time will rejoice,
For this son of a man will establish his name for ever and eternity.

But those who fall into evil,
Those who raise the cry of rebellion,
They have lowered their voices through dread of him.
The Asiatics will fall before his sword,
The Libyans will fall before his fire;
Rebels will fall before his wrath,
65 And enemies will fall through / awe of him,
For the uraeus on his brow will subdue his enemies for him.
He will found Inbu-Heqa,[13]
So that never will Asiatics be permitted to come down to Egypt.
They will seek water in the manner of beggars
So that their herds may drink.
Then Ma'at will return to her throne,
And Chaos (*Isfet*) will be driven off.
Joyful will he be who will see (these things),
He who will serve the king.
The wise man will pour water for me (at my tomb)
When he sees my prophecies fulfilled."

It has been well transcribed.

12. The Two Powers and the Two Lords refer to Horus and Seth as protecting deities of Upper and Lower Egypt. "That which they desire" is a unified Egypt, free from internal strife.
13. A border fortress, whose name means "Walls of the Ruler," constructed by Amenemhet I as a protection for the eastern Delta against Asiatic invaders.

# THE INSTRUCTION OF AMUNNAKHTE

T he author of this instruction was a scribe of the House-of-Life, an institution which amounted to the school and library in the New Kingdom and later. The language of the text indicates its composition in
Dynasty 18, and the manuscripts do not postdate the Ramesside period. Posener
recognized and edited the text in RdE 10 (1955): 61–72, and this translation
follows his interpretation in most respects. He has suggested the possibility that
much of the missing continuation of the text is to be identified in the portions of
an instruction preserved on the verso of Papyrus Chester Beatty IV, a hypothesis
which he indicates can only be proved if a new text provides a passage connecting the two sections. The text and its author have been studied by Susanne
Bickel and Bernard Mathieu, "L'Écrivain Amennakht et son Enseignement,"
BIFAO 93 (1993): 31–51.

W.K.S.

(1) The beginning of the teaching instruction, the utterances for the
way of life, (2) which the scribe Amunnakhte made (for) his apprentice
Hor-Min. He says: Are you a man who hears (3) a speech to distinguish
what is good from what is bad? Pay then attention and hearken to (4) my
sayings. Do not neglect what I say. It is very fine to encounter a man able
(5) in every work. Make your heart become like a great restraining dyke,

while the flood (6) is turbulent at its side. Accept my words in all their import. Do not refuse (7) to keep them. Cast your eyes on every profession, (8) and everything done in writing, and you will be instructed in the affairs (to see) that they are (9) excellent, the utterances which I say to you. Do not neglect these (wonderful) sayings. (10) A long report is not in its (proper) place. Make your heart patient (11) in its haste. Speak out (only) after you are called. (12) May you become a scribe and frequent the House-of-Life. Become like a chest of writings.[ . . .]

# THE INSTRUCTION OF AMENEMOPE

T his major text was first made available for study in 1923 through the publication of a magnificent, virtually complete manuscript in the British Museum (B.M. 10474). The text is written in short lines like poetry, and the sections are consecutively numbered from chapter 1 to 30. Portions of the text are also known from writing boards in the Turin Museum, the Pushkin Museum in Moscow, and the Louvre, an ostracon in Cairo, and a fragmentary papyrus in Stockholm. A recent study is Irene Grumach, Untersuchungen zur Lebenslehre des Amenope (Munich, 1972), of which limited use has been made. Bibliographical information about this important text can be followed through the articles by B. J. Peterson in JEA 52 (1966): 120–28, and R. J. Williams in JEA 47 (1961): 100–106, the latter a convincing refutation of the suggestion that the text is a translation of a Semitic original. There are indeed close parallels between verses in Amenemope and the Book of Proverbs, especially Proverbs 22:17, 24:22. For the most part, however, the concepts presented in Amenemope are present in earlier Egyptian instruction literature and must be viewed in that context. The contrast between the intemperate, hot-headed man and the tranquil, truly silent man is one of the main themes of the text. The present consensus places the date of composition in the New Kingdom, although the manuscripts in the main do not predate Dynasty 21. The author of the instruction was a resident of Akhmim in the Panopolite nome north of Abydos. A recent treatment with a lengthy introduction, translation, and extensive *notes is provided by Pascal Vernus,* Sagesses de l'Égypte pharaonique, *2001, 299–346.*

W.K.S.

## (INTRODUCTION)

1,1   The beginning of the instruction about life,
      The guide[1] for well-being,
All the principles of official procedure,
      The duties of the courtiers;
To know how to refute the accusation[2] of one who made it,
      And to send back a reply to the one who wrote;[3]
To set one straight on the paths of life,
      And make him prosper on earth;
To let his heart settle down in its chapel,[4]
1,10   As one who steers him clear of evil;[5]
To save him from the talk of others,
      As one who is respected in the speech of men.
Written by the superintendent of the land, experienced in his office,[6]
      The offspring of a scribe of the Beloved Land,
The superintendent of produce, who fixes the grain measure,
      Who sets the grain tax amount for his lord,
Who registers the islands which appear as new land over the cartouche of His Majesty,[7]
      And sets up the land mark at the boundary of the arable land,
2,1   Who protects the king by his tax rolls,
      And makes the Register of the Black Land.[8]

---

1. Lit. "testimony."
2. Perhaps only, "to return an answer."
3. Or, "to the one who sent him."
4. Griffith notes that the heart is shown in a kind of shrine or chapel in amulets of the New Kingdom; perhaps the idea of self-composure is intended.
5. The metaphors of sailing and rowing are frequent in the text.
6. Here begins an extended description of the offices and duties of Amenemope.
7. When the annual inundation of the lands subsided, the newly formed islands in the Nile were immediately designated as royal property.
8. The usual name for Egypt.

The scribe who places the divine offerings for all the gods,
  The donor of land grants to the people,
The superintendent of grain who administers the food offerings,
  Who supplies the storerooms with grain.
A truly silent man in Tjeni in the Ta-wer nome,
  One whose verdict is "acquitted" in Ipu,
The owner of a pyramid tomb on the west of Senut,
2,10   As well as the owner of a memorial chapel in Abydos,
Amenemope, the son of Kanakht,
  Whose verdict is "acquitted" in the Ta-wer nome.[9]
For his son, the youngest of his children,[10]
  The least of his family,
Initiate of the mysteries of Min-Kamutef,
  Libation pourer of Wennofre;[11]
Who inducts Horus upon the throne of his father,
  His stolist in his august chapel,
  [...] secret [...]
3,1   The seer of the Mother of God,
The inspector of the black cattle of the terrace of Min,
  Who protects Min in his chapel,
Horemmaakheru is his true name,
  A child of an official of Ipu,
The son of the sistrum player of Shu and Tefnut,
  The chief singer of Horus, the lady Tawosret.


## HE SAYS: CHAPTER 1


Give your ears and hear what is said,
3,10   Give your mind over to their interpretation:


9. Tjeni in the Ta-wer nome (Abydos) was the great temple and cult site of the god Osiris, where many royal and private memorial buildings were dedicated. Ipu and Senut are in the Panopolite nome to the north of Abydos, the area of modern Akhmim, of which the patron god was Min-Kamutef.
10. As in other instructions, the addressee is the man's son, in this case Hor-em-maakheru, whose name means "Horus is vindicated," the son of Amenemope and Tawosret.
11. Min-Bull-of-his-Mother, the god of Akhmim; Wennofre is an epithet of Osiris.

It is profitable to put them in your heart,[12]
    But woe to him that neglects them!
Let them rest in the shrine of your insides
    That they may act as a lock in your heart;
Now when there comes a storm of words,
    They will be a mooring post on your tongue.
If you spend a lifetime with these things in your heart,
    You will find it good fortune;
4,1    You will discover my words to be a treasure house of life,
    And your body will flourish upon earth.

## CHAPTER 2

Beware of stealing from a miserable man
    And of raging against the cripple.
Do not stretch out your hand to strike an old man,
    Nor snip at the words of an elder.
Don't let yourself be sent on a fraudulent business,
    Nor desire the carrying out of it;[13]
4,10    Do not get tired because of being interfered with,[14]
    Nor return an answer on your own.[15]
The evildoer, throw him ⟨in⟩ the canal,[16]
    And ⌐he will bring back its slime⌐.
The north wind comes down and ends his appointed hour,
    It is joined to the tempest;
The clouds are high, the crocodiles are nasty,
    O hot-headed man, what are you like?
He cries out, and his voice (reaches) heaven.
    O Moon, make his crime manifest!

12. Possibly, "profitable is he who places it in your heart."
13. Or, "nor desire (the company of) the one who does it."
14. Or, "do not revile someone you have hurt," or "do not act the part of a tired one (be downcast) toward the one you deceive."
15. Do not plead your own case in person?
16. Or, "the shore abandons him."

5,1   Row that we may ferry evil away,
     For we will not act according to his (evil) nature;[17]
  Lift him up, give him your hand,
     And leave him ⟨in⟩ the hands of God;[18]
  Fill his gut with your own food
     That he may be sated and ashamed.
  Something else of value in the heart of God
     Is to stop and think before speaking.


## CHAPTER 3


5,10   Do not get into a quarrel with the argumentative man
     Nor incite him with words;
  Proceed cautiously before an opponent,
     And give way to an adversary;
  Sleep on it before speaking,
     For a storm come forth like fire in hay is
  The hot-headed man in his appointed time.
     May you be restrained before him;
  Leave him to himself,
     And God will know how to answer him.
  If you spend your life with these things in your heart,
     Your children shall observe them.


5,20                   ## CHAPTER 4


6,1   The hot-headed man in the temple
     Is like a tree grown in an enclosed space;
  In a moment is its loss of foliage.
     It reaches its end in the carpentry shop;
  It is floated away far from its place,
     Or fire is its funeral pyre.


17. Not act like one of his kind.
18. Or, "the hands of God will abandon him."

The truly temperate man sets himself apart,
 He is like a tree grown in a sunlit field,
But it becomes verdant, it doubles its yield,
6,10  It stands before its owner;
 Its fruit is something sweet, its shade is pleasant,
  And it reaches its end in a grove.[19]

## CHAPTER 5

Do not take by violence the shares of the temple,
 Do not be grasping, and you will find abundance;
Do not take away a temple servant
 In order to do something profitable for another man.
Do not say today is the same as tomorrow,
 Or how will matters come to pass?
7,1 When tomorrow comes, today is past;
 The deep waters become a sandbank.[20]
Crocodiles are uncovered, the hippopotamuses are on dry land,
 And the fishes gasping for air;
The wolves are fat, the wild fowl in festival,
 And the nets are ⸢drained⸣.
Every temperate man in the temple says,
 "Great is the benevolence of Re."
Adhere to the silent man, you will find life,
7,10  And your body shall flourish upon earth.

## CHAPTER 6

Do not displace the surveyor's marker on the boundaries of the arable
land,
 Nor alter the position of the measuring line;
Do not be covetous for a single cubit of land,
 Nor encroach upon the boundaries of a widow.

---

19. The parable of the two trees has been frequently discussed. See Georges Posener, in
 *ZÄS* 99 (1972): 129–35.
20. Possibly meaning that the time for action is now past.

One who transgresses the furrow shortens a lifetime,
>One who seizes it for fields
And acquires[21] by deceptive attestations,
>Will be lassoed by the might of the Moon.

8,1  To one who has done this on earth, pay attention,
>For he is an oppressor of the feeble;
He is an enemy worthy of your overthrowing;
>Life is taken from his eye;
His household is hostile to the community,
>His storerooms are broken into,
His property is taken away from his children,
>And his possessions are given to someone else.

8,10  Take care not to topple over the boundary marks of the fields,
>Not fearing that you will be brought to court;[22]
Man propitiates God by the might of the Lord
>When he sets straight the boundaries of the arable land.
Desire, then, to make yourself prosper,
>And take care for the Lord of All;[23]
Do not trample on the furrow of someone else,
>Their good order will be profitable for you.[24]
So plough the fields, and you will find whatever you need,
>And receive the bread from your own threshing floor:
Better is a bushel which God gives you

8,20  >Than five thousand deceitfully gotten;

9,1  They do not spend a day in the storehouse or warehouse,
>They are ⌜no use for dough for beer⌝;
Their stay in the granary is short-lived,
>When morning comes they will have vanished.
Better, then, is poverty in the hand of God
>Than riches in the storehouse;
Better is bread when the mind is at ease
>Than riches with anxiety.

21. Or, "if he is caught . . ."
22. Or, "lest fear carry you off."
23. Osiris? See Goedicke, in *JARCE* 7 (1968): 16–17.
24. Griffith: "It is good for thee to be sound concerning them."

## CHAPTER 7

9,10    Do not set your heart upon seeking riches,
> For there is no one who can ignore Destiny and Fortune;[25]

Do not set your thoughts on superficial matters:
> For every man there is his appointed time.

Do not exert yourself to seek out excess
> And your allotment will prosper for you;[26]

If riches come to you by thievery
> They will not spend the night with you;

As soon as day breaks they will not be in your household;
> Although their places can be seen, they are not there.

9,20    When the earth opens up its mouth, it levels him and swallows him up,

10,1        They will plunge in the deep;

They will make for themselves a great hole which suits them.
> And they will sink themselves in the underworld;[27]

Or they will make themselves wings like geese,
> And fly up to the sky.

Do not be pleased with yourself (because of) riches acquired through robbery,
> Neither be sorry about poverty.

As for an officer who commands one who goes in front of him,
> His company leaves him;

10,10  The boat of the covetous is abandoned ⟨in⟩ the mud,
> While the skiff of the truly temperate man ⌐sails on⌐.

When he rises you shall offer to the Aten,
> Saying, "Grant me prosperity and health."

And he will give you your necessities for life,
> And you will be safe from fear.

## CHAPTER 8

Set your deeds throughout the world
> That everyone may greet you;

25. Shay and Ernutet: deities of Destiny and Fortune.
26. Or, "your own property is good enough for you."
27. John Ruffle, in *JEA 50* (1964): 177–78.

They make rejoicing for the Uraeus,

10,20      And spit against the Apophis.

Keep your tongue safe from words of detraction,

11,1      And you will be the loved one of the people,[28]

Then you will find your (proper) place within the temple

     And your offerings among the bread deliveries of your lord;

You will be revered, when you are concealed ⟨in⟩ your grave,

     And be safe from the might of God.

Do not accuse a man,[29]

     When the circumstance of (his) escape is unknown.

Whether you hear something good or bad,

     Put it outside, until he has been heard;

11,10  Set a good report on your tongue,

     While the bad thing is concealed inside you.


## CHAPTER 9

Do not fraternize with the hot-tempered man,

     Nor approach him to converse.

Safeguard your tongue from talking back to your superior,

     And take care not to offend him.

Do not allow him to cast words only to entrap you,[30]

     And be not too free[31] in your replies;

With a man of your own station discuss the reply;

11,20      And take care of ⌜speaking thoughtlessly⌝;

12,1  When a man's heart is upset, words travel faster

     Than wind over water.

He is ruined and created by his tongue,[32]

     When he speaks slander;

He makes an answer deserving of a beating,

     For his freight is damaged.


28. Or, "that you may do what people love."

29. "Summon up a crime."

30. Lit. "lasso."

31. *ntfi,* a word used of unharnessing horses and untying captives.

32. He makes and breaks reputations.

He sails among all the world,[33]
    But his cargo is false words;
He acts the ferryman in twisting words:[34]
12,10      He goes forth and comes back arguing.
But whether he eats or whether he drinks inside,
    His accusation (waits for him) outside.
The day when his evil deed is brought to court
    Is a disaster for his children.
Even Khnum will straightway come against him, even Khnum will
straightway come against him,[35]
    The potter of the ill-tempered man,
[...]
It is to knead and bake the hearts that he moulds
    He is like a wolf cub in the farmyard,
And he turns one eye to the other (squinting),
13,1      For he sets families to argue.
He goes before all the winds like clouds,
    He changes his hue in the sun;
He crocks his tail like a baby crocodile,
    He curls himself up to inflict harm,
His lips are sweet, but his tongue is bitter,
    And fire burns inside him.
Do not fly up to join that man
    Not fearing you will be brought to account.


10,13                    CHAPTER 10


Do not address an intemperate man in your (unrighteousness)[36]
    Nor destroy your own mind;
Do not say to him, "May you be praised," not meaning it
    When there is fear within you.


33. The Stockholm fragment begins here. See Peterson, in *JEA* 52 (1966): 120–28.
34. The ferryman goes back and forth.
35. Peterson, in *JEA* 52 (1966): 125.
36. Or, "in forcing yourself."

Do not converse falsely with a man,
  For it is the abomination of God.
Do not separate your mind from your tongue,[37]
  All your plans will succeed.[38]
You will be important before others,[39]
14, 1   While you will be secure in the hand of God.
God hates one who falsifies words,
  His great abomination is duplicity.


## CHAPTER 11


Do not covet the property of the dependent[40]
    Nor hunger for his bread;
The property of a dependent is an obstruction to the throat,
    It makes the gullet throw it back.[41]
It is by false oaths that he has brought himself up,
10,14   While his heart slips back inside him.
It is through the "disaffected" that "effectiveness" is "weakened,"[42]
    And then evil will topple good.
If you are ⌐at a loss¬ before your superior,
    And are confused in your speeches,
Your flatterings are turned back with curses,
    And your prostrations by beatings.
Whoever fills the mouth with too much bread swallows it
and spits up,
    So you emptied of your good.[43]


37. Say what you really mean (Lange).
38. Or, "all your good plans will come to pass."
39. Lit. "It will happen that you will be weighty in the presence of other men."
40. Here ends the fragmentary duplicate text in Stockholm.
41. Perhaps meaning that the limited property of a poor man is barely enough to keep
    him alive, like moisture in his throat. The connection with the next verses is unclear
    to me.
42. Or perhaps, "do not let disaffection wear away success."
43. Lit. "O filler of the mouth, with a large bite of bread, you swallow it, you vomit it,
    you are emptied. . . ."

To the examination of a dependent pay attention

15,1       While the staves touch him,

And while all his people are fettered with manacles:

      Who is to have the execution?[44]

When you are too free[45] before your superior,

      Then you are in bad favor with your subordinates.

So steer away from a dependent on the road,

      That you may see him but keep clear of his property.

## CHAPTER 12

Do not covet the property of an official,

10,15       And do not fill (your) mouth with too much food arrogantly;

If he sets you to manage his property,

      Respect his, and yours will prosper.

Do not deal with the intemperate man,

      Nor associate yourself to a disloyal party.

If you are sent to transport straw,

      Abstain from profiting thereby,

If a man is detected in a dishonest transaction,

      Never again will he be employed.

## CHAPTER 13

15,20 Do not lead a man astray (with) reed pen on papyrus:

      It is the abomination of God.

16,1 Do not witness a false statement,

      Nor remove a man (from the list) by your order;

Do not reckon with someone who has nothing,

      Nor make your pen be false.

If you find a large debt[46] against a poor man,

      Make it into three parts;

44. Griffith: "and where(?) is the executioner?"
45. See n. 31, above.
46. Arrears, default, debit balance.

Release two of them and let one remain:
> You will find it a path of life;

16, You will pass the night in sound sleep; in the morning
9–10 > You will find it like good news.

Better it is to be praised as one loved by men
> Than wealth in the storehouse;

Better is bread when the mind is at ease
> Than riches with troubles.

## CHAPTER 14

Do not ingratiate yourself with a person,
> Nor exert yourself to seek out his hand,

If he says to you, "take a bribe,"
> There is no need to respect him.

16,20 Do not be afraid of him, nor bend down your head,
> Nor turn aside your gaze.

Address him with your words and say to him greetings;

17,1 > When he stops, your chance will come;

Do not repel him at his ⌐first approach⌐,
> Another time he will be apprehended.

## CHAPTER 15

Do well, and you will attain influence.
> Do not dip your reed against a transgressor.

The beak of the Ibis is the finger of the scribe;[47]
> Take care not to disturb it;

The Ape (Thot) dwells (in) the temple of Khmun,[48]

17,10 > While his eye travels around the Two Lands;

If he sees one who cheats with his finger (that is, a false scribe),
> He takes away his provisions by the flood.

47. The Ibis here is Thot, patron god of the scribe.
48. Hermopolis, the town of Thot.

As for a scribe who cheats with his finger,
    His son shall not be enrolled.
If you spend your life with these things in your heart,
    Your children shall observe them.


## CHAPTER 16


Do not tilt the scale nor falsify the weights,
    Nor diminish the fractions of the grain measures;
17,20  Do not wish for the grain measures of the fields
    To cast aside those of the treasury.[49]
The Ape sits by the balance,
18,1      While his heart is the plummet.
Who is a god as great as Thot,
    The one who discovered these things,[50] in order to create them?
Do not get for yourself short weights;
    They are plentiful, yea, an army by the might of God.
If you see someone cheating,
    At a distance you must pass him by.
Do not be avaricious for copper,
    And abjure fine clothes;
18,10  What good is one cloaked in fine linen,[51]
    When he cheats before God.
When jewels are heaped upon gold,[52]
    At daybreak they turn to lead.


## CHAPTER 17


Beware of tampering[53] with the grain measure
    To falsify its fractions;


49. Do not use different measures to your own benefit?
50. Hieroglyphs?
51. Černý, *Hieratic Inscriptions from the Tomb of Tut'ankhamūn*, p. 8.
52. Following Grumach.
53. Following Grumach.

Do not act wrongfully through force,[54]
  Cause it not to be empty inside,
May you have it measured exactly as it arrived,
18,20  Your hand stretching out with precision.
Make not for yourself a measure of two capacities,[55]
  For then it is toward the depths that you will go.
The measure is the eye of Re,
19,1  Its abomination is the thief.
As for a grain measurer who multiplies and subtracts,
  His eye will seal up against him.
Do not receive the harvest tax of a cultivator,
  Nor set a papyrus against him to harm him.
Do not enter into collusion with the grain measurer,
  Nor defraud the share of the Residence,
More important is the threshing floor for barley
  Than swearing by the Great Throne.


19,10        CHAPTER 18


Do not go to bed fearing tomorrow,
  For when day breaks how will tomorrow be?
Man knows not what tomorrow will be!
God is success,
  While man is failure.
The words which men say pass on one side,
  The things which God does pass on another side.
Do not say, "⌐I am⌐ without fault,"
  Nor try to seek out trouble.
19,20 Fault is the business of God,
  It is sealed with his finger.
There is no success in the hand of God,
  Nor is there failure before Him;
20,1 If one turns himself about to seek out success,
  In a moment He destroys him.


54. Interpreted variously, and possibly a corrupt text.
55. So Griffith. A measure which can be read two ways?

Be strong in your heart, make your mind firm,
 Do not steer with your tongue;
The tongue of a man is the steering oar of a boat,
 But the Lord of All is its pilot.


## CHAPTER 19

Do not enter the council chamber in the presence of a magistrate
 And then falsify your speech.

20,10 Do not go up and down with your accusation
 When your witnesses stand readied.
Do not ⌐overstate¬ ⟨through⟩ oaths in the name of your lord,
 (Through) pleas (in) the place of interrogation.
Tell the truth before the magistrate,
 Lest he gain power over your body;
If you petition before him the next day,
 He will concur with all you say;
He will present your case ⟨in⟩ court before the Council of the Thirty,
 And it will be ⌐decided¬ another time as well.


20,20        ## CHAPTER 20

Do not defraud a person in the law court
 Nor put aside the just man.
21,1 Do not pay attention to garments of white.
 Nor scorn one in rags.
Take not the bribe of the strong man,
 Nor repress the weak for him.
As for the just man who bears the greatness of God,[56]
 He will render himself as he wishes.
The strength of one like him
 Saves a poor wretch from his beatings.
Do not make for yourself false ⌐enrollment¬ lists,
21,10  For they are punishable offenses (deserving) death;

56. H. Goedicke, in *RdE* 46 (1995): 99–102.

They are serious oaths which promote respect;
    And they are to be investigated by a reporter.
Do not falsify the oracles[57] on a papyrus
    And (thereby) alter the designs of God.
Do not arrogate to yourself the might of God
    As if Destiny and Fortune did not exist.[58]
Hand property over to its (rightful) owners,
    And seek out life for yourself;
Let not your heart build in their house,[59]
21,20    For then your neck will be on the execution block.

## CHAPTER 21

22,1    Do not say, find for me[60] a strong patron,
    For a man in your town has afflicted me.[61]
Do not say, find for me[62] an active intecessor,
    For one who hates (me) has afflicted me.[63]
Indeed, you cannot know the plans of God;
    You cannot perceive tomorrow.
Sit yourself at the hands of God:
    Your tranquility will overthrow them (the adversaries).
As for a crocodile deprived of ⸢his tongue⸣,
22,10    His significance is negligible.[64]
Empty not your soul to everybody
    And do not diminish thereby your importance;
Do not pour out your words to others,
    Nor fraternize with one who is too rash.

57. G. Posener, in *ZÄS 90* (1963): 99.
58. See n. 25, above.
59. Meaning: "do not build within another's property"?
60. So Lichtheim.
61. So Lichtheim.
62. So Lichtheim.
63. So Lichtheim.
64. G. Posener, in *Festschrift für Siegfried Schott zu seinem 70. Geburtstag,* ed. W. Helck (Wiesbaden, 1968), 106–11.

Better is a man whose report is inside him
  Than one who tells it to disadvantage.
One cannot run to attain perfection;
  One cannot create (only) to destroy it.


## CHAPTER 22

22,20 Do not provoke your adversary,
   And do not ⟨let⟩ him say his innermost thoughts;
 Do not fly up to greet him
23,1   When you cannot see ⌐how he acts⌐.
 May you first comprehend his accusation
   Be calm and your chance will come.
 Leave it to him and he will empty his soul;
   ⌐Sleep knows how to find him out⌐;[65]
 Touch his feet,[66] do not disrespect him;
   Fear him, do not underestimate him.
 Indeed, you cannot know the plans of God,
   You cannot perceive tomorrow.
23,10 Sit yourself at the hands of God;
   Your tranquility will overthrow them.


## CHAPTER 23

Do not eat a meal in the presence of a magistrate,
  Nor set to speaking first.
If you are sated, pretend to chew,
  Enjoy yourself with your saliva.
Look at the cup in front of you,
  And let it suffice your need.
Even as a noble is important in his office,
23,20  So he is like the abundance of a flooded well.[67]


65. Griffith: "Know how to sleep and he will be comprehended."
66. Meaning?
67. "He is abundant like a well from which one draws water."

## CHAPTER 24

24,1 Do not listen to the proposition of an official indoors,
    And then repeat it to another outside.[68]
Do not allow your discussions to be brought outside
    Lest your heart be grieved.
The heart of a man is the beak of God,
    So take care not to slight it;
A man who stands ⟨at⟩ the side of an official
    Should not have his name known (in the street).

## CHAPTER 25

Do not laugh at a blind man nor taunt a dwarf,
24,10     Neither interfere with the condition of a cripple;
Do not taunt a man who is in the hand of God,
    Nor scowl at him if he errs.
Man is clay and straw,
    And God is his potter;
He overthrows and He builds daily,[69]
    He impoverishes a thousand if He wishes.
But He makes a thousand into officials
    When He is in His hour of life.
How fortunate is he who reaches the West,
24,20     When he is safe in the hand of God.

## CHAPTER 26

Do not sit in the beer hall
25,1     Nor join someone greater than you,
Whether he be low or high in his station,
    An old man or a youth;

68. The Turin text supplies a duplicate from here to the end of the second paragraph of chap. 26 (line 25,9).
69. The creative and destructive powers of God are also stressed in chap. 18. See also n. 32, above, for the association of ideas.

But take as a friend for yourself someone compatible:
>    Re is helpful though he is far away.
When you see someone greater than you outside,
>    Follow him, respect (him).
And give a hand to an old man filled with beer:
>    Respect him as his children would.[70]

25,10    The strong arm is not ⌐weakened⌐ when it is uncovered,
>    The back is not broken when one bends it;
A man is not denigrated when he speaks sweet words,
>    More so than a rich man whose words are straw.
A pilot who sees into the distance
>    Will not let his ship capsize.

## CHAPTER 27

Do not reproach someone greater than you,
>    For he has seen the Sun before you;
Do not let yourself be reported to the Aten when he rises,

25,20    With the words, "Again a young man has reproached an elder."
Very painful in the sight of Re

26,1    Is a young man who reproaches an elder.
Let him beat you with your hands folded,
>    Let him reproach you while you keep quiet.
Then when you come before him in the morning
>    He will give you bread freely.
As for bread, the dog of his master
>    Barks to the one who gives it.

## CHAPTER 28

Do not identify a widow if you have caught her in the fields,

26,10    Nor fail to give way if she is accused.
Do not turn a stranger away ⟨from⟩ your oil jar
>    Double it (more than) for your (own) family.

---

70. The Turin text duplicate ends here.

God loves him who cares for the poor,
>   More than him who respects the wealthy.

## CHAPTER 29

Do not turn people away from crossing the river
>   When you have room in (your) ferryboat;
If an oar is given you in the midst of the deep waters,
>   So bend back your hands ⟨to⟩ take it up.

26,20 It is not an abomination in the hand of God
27,1 >   If the crew does not agree.
Do not acquire a ferryboat on the river,
>   And then attempt to seek out its fares;
Take the fare from the man of means,
>   But (also) accept the destitute (without charge).

## CHAPTER 30

Mark for yourself these thirty chapters:
>   They please, they instruct,
They are the foremost of all books;
27,10 >   They teach the ignorant.
If they are read before an ignorant man,
>   He will be purified (of his ignorance) through them.
Fill yourself with them; put them in your mind
>   And get men to interpret them.
As for a scribe who is experienced in his position,
>   He will find himself worthy of being a courtier.
>                 [Colophon]
It is finished.
28,1 By the writing of Senu, son of the god's father Pamiu.

# IV

## FROM THE RELIGIOUS LITERATURE

# SELECTIONS FROM THE PYRAMID TEXTS

T he Pyramid Texts, found in the last royal pyramid of the Fifth and those of the Sixth Dynasties, constitute the oldest collection of Egyptian religious and mythological texts, consisting of mortuary rituals which had developed over a period of centuries. The general theme of these texts is the burial and rebirth of the deceased king, and the texts themselves are rich in the varied mythological traditions of the Old Kingdom. The texts were constructed from a number of originally separate mythological strains and were used during and after the burial rituals of the king. Although the Pyramid Texts were not intended to be a systematic exposition of Egyptian myth and theology, they can nevertheless serve as a basis for the reconstruction of Old Kingdom religious thought. A careful study of these texts will reveal the ingenuous manner in which the Egyptian myth-makers were able to combine religious speculation and the royal political ideology which had developed around the kingship. There are many references and expressions in the Pyramid Texts which make little sense to the modern reader, but their mystery can to an extent be overcome by realizing the symbolic value of such mythic expression. Despite the obscurity of some passages, the religious and poetic genius of many of these texts is very much in evidence. The hieroglyphic texts are available in Kurt Sethe, Die altägyptischen Pyramidentexte, vols. 1–4 (Leipzig, 1908–22; repr. Hildesheim, 1960). The oldest selection of texts, those from the pyramid of Unis, may be found in A. Piankoff, The Pyramid of Unas (Princeton, 1968). A translation *of the full corpus of the Pyramid Texts is available in R. O. Faulkner,* The Ancient Egyptian Pyramid Texts *(Oxford, 1969). A number of useful studies of various aspects of the Pyramid Texts are also available: R. Anthes, "Egyptian Theology in the Third Millennium B.C.,"* JNES *18 (1959): 169–212; J. G. Griffiths,* The Conflict of Horus and Seth *(Liverpool, 1960); V. A. Tobin, "Myth and Politics in the Old Kingdom of Egypt,"* BiOr *49, no. 5/6 (1991): 605–36.*

*Thanks are due to Dr. James Allen of the Metropolitan Museum of Art, New York, for some useful suggestions on the translation of the Pyramid Texts. With regard to the Egyptian terms* ba, akh, *and* ka, *I have preferred to leave them in their original rather than to translate them by English terms which may not render their exact meaning. Finally, in several passages I have preferred a slightly freer translation in order to produce a smoother English rendition.*

V.A.T.

## UTTERANCE 214: A SPELL FOR ASCENSION

136 Hail, Unis![1] Take heed of the lake! (*these words to be spoken four times*)
The messengers of your *ka* have come for you,
The messengers of your father have come for you,
The messengers of Re have come for you.

137 Follow behind your sun, that you may purify yourself.
Your bones are the divine falcons and the uraei which are in the sky.
You will abide at the side of the god,
You will entrust your house to your son whom you have begotten.
As for anyone who speaks evil against the name of Unis when you go out,
138 Geb[2] will degrade him to the lowest place in his city.
He will retreat and be weary,
But you will purify yourself in the celestial waters.

---

1. The name of the deceased king varies in the Pyramid Texts according to the owner of the tomb in which the texts were inscribed.
2. Geb was the primeval god who personified the earth. A member of the Heliopolitan Ennead, he was descended from the creator deity, Re-Atum, through Shu and Tefnut, the brother/sister twin deities who had been begotten by Re-Atum. In Egyptian myth, Geb was paired with his sister Nut, goddess of the sky.

You shall come down upon the bands of bronze on the arms of Horus
In his name of "He who is in the *Henu*-barque."

139 (All) mankind shall acclaim you,
For the stars which know not destruction have exalted you.
Get yourself up to the place where your father abides,
To the place where Geb abides,
And he will give you the uraeus which is on the brow of Horus.
Through it you will become an *akh*,
Through it you will become mighty,
Through it you will be preeminent among the Westerners.

## UTTERANCE 217: THE DECEASED ASCENDS TO RE-ATUM

152 O Re-Atum, this Unis has come to you as an *akh* who knows not
destruction.
As Lord of the destiny of the ends of the earth.[3]
Your son has come to you, this Unis has come to you.
You will travel the firmament, united in the darkness,
And you will rise on the horizon, in the place where you are radiant.

153 O Seth and Nephthys,[4] go and declare to the gods of Upper Egypt and
their *akhu:*
"Behold! This Unis comes indeed as a spirit who knows not destruction.
Should he will that you die, then die you shall;
Should he will that you live, then live you shall."

154 O Re-Atum, this Unis has come to you as an *akh* who knows not
destruction,
As Lord of the destiny of the ends of the earth.
Your son has come to you, this Unis has come to you.

3. Lit. "Lord of the affairs of the place of the four pillars," the four pillars being the
cardinal points of the compass.
4. From Geb and Nut were born two pairs of twins: Osiris and Isis, and Seth and
Nephthys, each pair being also husband and wife. Although Nephthys remained a
positive symbol of royal power, Seth, through his jealousy of Osiris, became the god of
chaos and confusion.

You will travel the firmament, united in the darkness,
And you will rise on the horizon, in the place where you are radiant.

155 O Osiris and Isis, go and declare to the gods of Lower Egypt and their *akhu:*
"Behold! This Unis has come indeed as a spirit who knows not destruction.
Praiseworthy is he, Lord of the Nile flood.
Praise him, O spirits who are in the waters.
Whomever he wills to live, he indeed shall live;
Whomever he wills to die, he indeed shall die."

156 O Re-Atum, this Unis has come to you as an *akh* who knows not destruction,
As Lord of the destiny of the ends of the earth.
Your son has come to you, this Unis has come to you.
You will travel the firmament, united in the darkness,
And you will rise on the horizon, in the place where you are radiant.

157 O Thoth, go and declare to the western gods and their *akhu:*
"Behold! This Unis has come as an *akh* who knows not destruction.
One adorned as Anubis around his neck, ruler of the western height.
He will try the hearts, for he is powerful over the hearts.
Whomever wills to live, he indeed shall live;
Whomever he wills to die, he indeed shall die."

158 O Re-Atum, this Unis has come to you as an *akh* who knows not destruction,
As Lord of the destiny of the ends of the earth.
Your son has come to you, this Unis has come to you.
You will travel the firmament, united in the darkness,
And you will rise on the horizon, in the place where you are radiant.

159 O Horus, go and declare to the eastern *bau* and their *akhu:*
"Behold! This Unis has come as an *akh* who knows not destruction.
Whomever he wills to live, he indeed shall live;
Whomever he wills to die, he indeed shall die."

160 O Re-Atum, your son has come to you, Unis has come to you.
Cause him to ascend to you, and clasp him to yourself in your embrace.
For he is your son, the son of your body unto eternity.

## UTTERANCE 364: A SPELL FOR RESURRECTION

609    Hail, Osiris Teti! Stand up now!
Horus has come to install you among the gods.
Horus has set his love on you and has provided for you.
Horus has fastened his eye to you;
610    Horus has opened your eye for you that you might see with it.
The gods have raised your face for you, for they have set their love on you.
Isis and Nephthys have restored your strength,
And Horus is not distant from you, for you are his *ka,*
611    And your sight will be delighted by him.
Make haste and take to yourself the word of Horus to be at peace through it.
Hearken to Horus! Evil will never befall you,
For he has appointed the gods to attend you.

612    Hail, Osiris Teti! Awake now!
Geb has brought Horus to you that he may establish you.
Horus has found you, and has become an *akh* through you.
613    Horus has appointed the gods to approach you,
He has given them to you that they may brighten your face.
Horus has placed you in the forefront of the gods
And has ordained that you should claim your full supremacy.
Horus has bound himself to you and will never part from you.
614    Horus has given you life in this your name of 'Andjety.
Horus has given to you his mighty eye,
He has given it to you that you may be powerful,
And that all your enemies may fear you.
Horus has made you complete and whole with his eye in this its name of "Divine offering."

615    Horus has taken the gods captive on your behalf,
And they will not flee from you in the place whither you have gone.
Horus has assembled the gods for you,
And they will not flee from you in the place wherein you drowned.[5]

---

5. A reference to the deceased king as symbolized by Osiris, who, according to one tradition, met his death by drowning.

616  Nephthys has united for you all your limbs
In this her name of "Seshat,[6] Mistress of Builders."
She has restored them for you,
So that you are given to your mother Nut in her name of "Sarcophagus."
(Nut) has embraced you in her name of "Sarcophagus,"
And you have been carried to her in her name of "Tomb."

617  Horus has united your limbs for you, and he will not permit you to decay.
He has assembled you, and there will be no disorder within you.
Horus has established you; do not falter.

618  Hail, Osiris Teti! Raise your heart!
Be justly proud! Open your mouth!
Horus has protected you, and his protection of you shall not fail.

619  Hail, Osiris Teti! You are a powerful god, and there is no god like you.
Horus has given you his children that they may raise you on high.

620  He has given to you all the gods, that they may attend you,
And that you may rule over them.
Horus has carried you in his name of "*Henu*-barque,"
And he will exalt you in your name of "Sokar."

621  You shall live and travel every day;
You shall become an *akh* in your name of "Horizon from which Re
proceeds";
You shall be honored, You shall be mighty,
You shall be a *ba,* you shall be powerful unto ages of ages.

## UTTERANCE 412: A SPELL FOR RESURRECTION

721  The Great One has fallen upon his side,
He who is of Nedit[7] trembled;
But his head has been raised up by Re,

722  For he despises sleep and scorns languor.
O flesh of Teti,
Do not rot, do not putrefy, do not smell foul.

6. Seshat, a goddess of intelligence, knowledge, and architecture, is here understood as a
manifestation of Nephthys.
7. The term "Nedit" refers to the bank of a river. Here it is used as a designation of the
mythological location where Osiris was struck down by Seth.

Your foot will not go astray, your movements will not wander,
You will not tread upon the decay of Osiris.

723    You shall approach the sky like Orion,
And your *ba* will be watchful like Sothis.
You shall be a *ba,* for you are a *ba;*
You shall be honored, for you are honored.
Your *ba* shall stand amidst the gods as Horus of Iru.

724    Let awe for you well up in the hearts of the gods,
Like unto the Neith-crown on the head of the King of Lower Egypt,
Like unto the crown of Upper Egypt upon the head of her King,
Like unto the braids on the heads of the Bedouin.
You shall hold fast to the hands of the stars which know not destruction;

725    Your bones will never perish, your flesh will never decay.
O Teti, your limbs will not be far from you,
For you are indeed one of the gods.

Pe sails southward to you, Dep sails northward to you.[8]

726    The ritual mourner wails for you, officiating priests are robed for you.
"Come in peace!" (is said) to you, O Teti, by your father,
"Come in peace!" (is said) to you by Re.

727    The portals of heaven open to you, the gates of the Duat unfold to you,[9]
For you have descended as the jackal of Upper Egypt,
Even as Anubis who reclines upon his stomach,
Even as Wepiu[10] who is at the head of On.[11]

728    The Great Maiden who is at On has laid her hands upon you,
For you have no human mother to bear you,
For you have no human father to beget you.

729    Your mother is the Great Wild Cow of Nekheb,

8. Pe and Dep: archaic cities in the northwest Delta sacred to the serpent goddess Wadjit, protecting diety of Lower Egypt.

9. The Duat, the netherworld, had its significance not so much as a geographical location, but as a place where the deceased king ruled and from where he was reborn at dawn. The opening of the gates of the Duat for the king indicates the recognition of his authority and his ability to enter and to leave freely.

10. Wepiu: a jackal god with whom the dead king is sometimes identified in the Pyramid Texts.

11. On: Heliopolis, the ancient sanctuary of the creator solar deity Re-Atum, situated not far from Memphis, and the mythological center of the Heliopolitan Ennead.

She who wears the white royal head cloth,
She who wears the lofty plumes, she who is pendulous of breasts;
She will nurse you and never wean you.

730   Bestir yourself on your left side,
Place yourself on your right side,[12]
For your thrones among the gods are established,
And Re supports you with his shoulder.
Your odor is their odor,
Your sweat is the sweat of the Two Enneads.

731   You will appear in the royal headdress,
Your hand clutching the scepter,
And your fist grasping the mace.
Stand at the forefront of the Conclaves of Upper and Lower Egypt;
Arbitrate between the gods,

732   /For you are among those who surround Re,
Those who are before the morning star.
You will be born in your months as the moon,
Re will support you on the horizon,

733   And the stars which know not destruction will attend you.
Prepare yourself for the coming of Re,
So that you may be pure when you go forth to Re.
The heavens will not be without you unto eternity.

## UTTERANCE 422: TRANSFORMATION OF THE DECEASED INTO AN *AKH*

752   Hail, Pepi! Go forth, that you may become an *akh,*
That you may be mighty as a god, successor to Osiris.

753   You have your *ba* within your body,
You have your power around you;
You have your crown of Lower Egypt upon your head,
You have your crown of Upper Egypt upon your shoulder.
Your face is forward, and adoration of you precedes you.

754   The followers of the god are behind you,
The nobles of the god precede you,

12. The imagery here is that of the dead body gradually beginning to stir as life returns to it.

Proclaiming, "The god has come! The god has come!
This Pepi has come upon the throne of Osiris!
This *akh* has come, he who is in Nedit,
He who is mighty in the nome of Abydos."

755    Isis greets you, Nephthys cries out to you;
The *akhu* approach you and prostrate themselves;
They kiss the earth before your feet
Because of fear of you, O Pepi, in the cities of Sia.

756    Go forth into the presence of your mother Nut,
That she may grasp your hand,
That she may show you the road to the horizon, to the place where Re is.
The portals of heaven unfold for you,
The portals of the sky give way before you.

757    (There) you will find Re standing and waiting for you.
He will grasp your hand for you,
He will lead you to the two Conclaves of heaven,
He will secure you upon the throne of Osiris.

758    Hail, Pepi! The Eye of Horus has come to you that it may speak for you;
Your *ba* which is among the gods has come to you;
Your power which is among the *akhu* has come to you.
The son has protected the father; Horus has protected Osiris;
Horus has protected this Pepi from the hand of his enemies.

759    You shall stand firm, O Pepi, protected and equipped as a god,
Endowed with the essence of Osiris on the throne of Khenty-Imentyu.[13]
You will do what he was wont to do among the *akhu,* the stars which know
not destruction.

760    Your son will ascend your throne, endowed with your essence,
And will do what you were wont to do at the head of the living,
In accordance with the command of Re, the Great God.

761    He will cultivate barley, he will cultivate emmer,
And he will offer them to you.

762    Hail, Pepi!
All life and dominion has been given to you for eternity by Re.

13. Khenty-Imentyu: "He who is at the head of those in the West," a title of Osiris.

You will lay claim to your own, for you have taken the essence of a god.
You will be great in the West[14] with the gods who are at the head of the
Lake.

763    Hail, Pepi! Your *ba* will stand among the gods, among the *akhu,*
For the fear of you is upon their hearts.[15]
Hail, Pepi! Ascend, O Pepi, to your throne at the head of the living,
For the terror of you is upon their hearts.[16]

764    Your name shall live on earth,
Your name shall be eternal on earth.
You shall never perish,
Neither shall you be destroyed unto the ages of ages.

## UTTERANCE 473: THE DECEASED CROSSES THE RIVER OF HEAVEN

926    The ferries of heaven have been launched by the day-barque for Re,
So that Re may travel on them to Horakhty[17] on the horizon.
The ferries of heaven have been launched by the night-barque for
Horakhty,
So that Horakhty may travel on them to Re on the horizon.

927    The ferries of heaven have been brought down to Pepi by the day-barque,
So that Pepi may go forth on them to Re on the horizon.
The ferries of heaven have been brought down to Pepi by the night-
baruqe,
So that Pepi may go forth on them to Horakhty on the horizon.

928    Pepi will go forth on the east side of heaven where the gods are born,
And Pepi will be born as Horus, as He of the Horizon!

14. "In the West," lit. "there."
15. Lit. "For what is upon their hearts is fear of you."
16. Lit. "For what is upon their hearts is terror of you."
17. Horakhty was a very common designation of Horus meaning "Horus of the Horizon" or "Horus of the two Horizons." As a sun god Horus traversed the sky between
the eastern and western horizons, the title "Horakhty" thus indicating the transcen-
dent nature of the god. At an early stage, the ancient sun god, Re, was often syn-
cretized with Horus to produce Re-Horakhty.

929　Pepi is justified, and the *ka* of Pepi is justified.
　　Sothis is the sister of Pepi, and the morning star is the child of Pepi.

930　Pepi has found the *akhu* who are eloquent of speech,[18]
　　Sitting on the two banks of the Lake of Sehseh,
　　The drinking place of an *akh* eloquent of speech,
　　"Who are you?" say they to Pepi, say the *akhu* eloquent of speech.
　　This Pepi is an *akh* eloquent of speech.

931　"Then how did this happen to you?" say they to Pepi,
　　Say the *akhu* eloquent of speech,
　　"That you have come to this place which is more noble than every place?"

　　Pepi has come to this place which is more noble than any place,
932　For the ferries of heaven have been launched by the day-barque for Re,
　　So that Re may travel on them to Horakhty on the horizon.
　　The ferries of heaven have been launched by the night-barque for
　　Horakhty,
　　So that Horakhty may travel on them to Re on the horizon.

933　The ferries of heaven have been brought down to Pepi by the day-barque,
　　So that Pepi may go forth on them to Re on the horizon.
　　The ferries of heaven have been brought down to Pepi by the night-
　　barque,
　　So that Pepi may go forth on them to Horakhty on the horizon.

934　Pepi will go forth on the east side of heaven where the gods are born,
　　And Pepi will born as Horus, as He of the Horizon.

935　Pepi is justified, and the *ka* of Pepi is justified.
　　Give praise to this Pepi! Give praise to the *ka* of this Pepi!
　　Sothis is the sister of Pepi, and the morning star is the child of Pepi.

936　This Pepi will go with you,
　　This Pepi will stroll with you in the Field of Rushes,
　　He will moor as you moor in the Field of Turquoise.

937　This Pepi will eat what you eat, this Pepi will live on what you live on;
　　This Pepi will be clothed with that with which you are clothed;
　　This Pepi will be anointed with that with which you are anointed.

18. "Eloquent," lit. "provided," i.e., the spirits have full knowledge of the proper spells
　　and incantations which must be recited in order to ensure their happiness in the next
　　world.

Pepi will receive water with you from the Nursing Pool,
The drinking-place of an *akh* eloquent of speech.

938 This Pepi will sit at the head of the Great Conclave,
Pepi will control the *akh* eloquent of speech.
This Pepi will sit on the two banks of the Lake of Sehseh,
This Pepi will control the *akh* eloquent of speech.

## UTTERANCE 570: THE DEIFICATION OF THE DECEASED

1443 The face of heaven is brilliant,[19] the expanse of the sky is dazzling.
"The god is begotten," says heaven,
"On the arms of Shu and Tefnut and on my arms."[20]

1444 The Great One has risen, he whom the gods proclaim.

Hear now this decree which Pepi speaks to you.
Be informed concerning this Pepi:
Pepi is a great one and the son of a great one.
This Pepi is with you.
Take this Pepi to life and dominion forever with you.

1445 Hear now, O Kheprer, this decree which is spoken to you.
Be informed concerning this Pepi:
Pepi is a great one and the son of a great one.
This Pepi is with you; take this Pepi with you.

1446 Hear now, O Nu,[21] this decree which is spoken to you.
Be informed concerning this Pepi:
Pepi is a great one and the son of a great one.
This Pepi is with you; take this Pepi with you.

1447 Hear now, O Atum, this decree which is spoken to you.
Be informed concerning this Pepi:

19. Lit. "The face of heaven has been washed."
20. Shu and Tefnut were the twin male and female offspring of Re-Atum, begotten in the primeval age by a combination of masturbation and spitting. They functioned as gods of the air, Shu being the dry air and Tefnut the moist air.
21. Nu: the primeval waters out of which Re-Atum first arose to begin the process of creation.

For Pepi is a great one and the son of a great one.
This Pepi is with you; take this Pepi with you.

1448   O mighty one, son of Geb,
O powerful one, son of Osiris,
Hear now this decree which is spoken to you.
Be informed concerning this Pepi:
For Pepi is a great one and the son of a great one.
This Pepi is with you; take this Pepi with you.

1449   Ascend to this Pepi in your name of Re,
That you may banish the storm clouds of the sky until Horakhty has
appeared,
That he may hear his mighty deeds and his praise in the mouths of the two
Enneads.

1450   "How beautiful you are," says his mother;
"My heir," says Osiris.

This Pepi will not swallow the Eye of Horus,
Lest men say, "He will die because of it."
This Pepi will not swallow a limb of Osiris,
Lest the gods say, "He will die because of it."

1451   This Pepi will live on the offerings of his father Atum,
And you will protect him, O Nekhbet.[22]
You have protected Pepi, O Nekhbet,
Within the palace of the magistrate which is at On.

1452   You have entrusted him to one who is in his service,
So that this Pepi may be provided for.
He who is in his service has entrusted this Pepi to him who serves the
litter,[23]
So that Pepi may be provided for.

22. Nekhbet had been from earliest times the protector goddess of Upper Egypt. Her
cult was centered at Nekheb, modern day El-Kab. Her role in connection with the
monarch was frequently seen as a maternal one.
23. I.e., an attendant of the royal litter carrying the deceased king; or possibly Sepa, one
of the seven spirits who guarded Osiris.

1453  This Pepi has escaped his day of submission to death,
      As Seth also escaped his day of submission to death.
      This Pepi has escaped his fortnights of submission to death,
      As Seth also escaped his fortnights of submission to death.
      This Pepi has escaped his months of submission to death,
      As Seth also escaped his months of submission to death.
      This Pepi has escaped his year of submission to death,
      As Seth also escaped his year of submission to death.

1454  Sink not down, O arms of Pepi,
      You pillars which support Nut even as Shu,
      You metal bones of this Pepi,
      And you his limbs which know not destruction.

1455  This Pepi is the star which gives light to the sky;
      This Pepi has ascended to the god so that this Pepi may be protected.
      Heaven will never be without this Pepi,
      And the earth will never be without this Pepi.

1456  This Pepi will abide as a living being in your midst,
      O gods of the lower heaven, you stars which know not destruction,
      You who pass over the land of Libya, who support yourselves on your
      *djam*-scepters;
      This Pepi supports himself with you on a *was*-scepter and a *djam*-scepter.

1457  Pepi is your fourth,
      O gods of the lower heaven, you stars which know not destruction,
      You who pass over the land of Libya, who support yourselves on your
      *djam*-scepters;
      This Pepi supports himself with you on a *was*-scepter and a *djam*-scepter.

1458  Pepi is your third,
      O gods of the lower heaven, you stars which know not destruction,
      You who pass over the land of Libya, who support yourselves on your
      *djam*-scepters,
      This Pepi supports himself with you on a *was*-scepter and a *djam*-scepter
      By command of Horus, the heir and king of the gods.

1459  This Pepi is the one who has seized the White Crown,
      The one upon whom is the tie of the Red Crown;
      This Pepi is the uraeus which proceeded from Seth,

The uraeus which moves back and forth;
Restore Pepi to health; restore him to life.[24]

1460    This Pepi is the one of gore came from *Nwnw*.[25]
This Pepi is the Eye of Horus which was not eaten but spat out,
And he will not be eaten but will be spat out.

1461    Hear now this utterance which is spoken to you, O Re:
Your essence is in Pepi, O Re,
Your essence is given life in Pepi, O Re.

1462    The baboons have been killed by the ape,
And the ape has been killed by the baboons.

You, O trapper, and you, O potent male,[26]
You who belong to the primeval generation:
You will hasten, one to punishment and one to justification,

1463    You who were born when wrath had not yet come to be,
You who were born when dispute had not yet come to be,
You who were born when conflict had not yet come to be,
You who were born when strife had not yet come to be,
You who were born when the Eye of Horus had not yet been injured,
And when the testicles of Seth had not yet been torn away.

1464    This Pepi is the blood which came forth from Isis,
He is the blood which came forth from Nephthys.
He will gird up his loins,
And there is nothing the gods can do against him.
This Pepi is the successor of Re, and this Pepi can never die.

1465    Hear, O Geb, prince of all the gods, and endow him with his nature;
Hear, O Thoth, source of concord among the gods;
Horus will open (the way) for him, and Seth will be his defender;
This Pepi will rise on the eastern side of heaven,
Like Re who rises on the eastern side of heaven.

24. A variant text reads: "This Pepi moves back and forth."
25. *Nwnw:* meaning unknown.
26. This appears to be a reference to Seth and Horus, the hunter being Seth and the
youthful one Horus, his would-be victim.

## UTTERANCE 571: THE DECEASED IS THE ETERNAL SON OF ATUM

1466    The mother of Pepi has become pregnant with him who is in the lower heaven.
This Pepi has been begotten by his father Atum,
(At a time) when the sky had not yet come into being,
When the earth had not yet come into being,
When mankind had not yet come into being,
When the gods had not yet been born,
When death had not yet come into being.

1467    This Pepi will escape the day of submission to death,
Even as Seth escaped his day of submission to death.
This Pepi is on the road to your domain, O gods of the lower heaven,

1468    You who know not the assault of your enemies,
And this Pepi will not know the assault of his enemies.

O you who die not at the hands of a king,
This Pepi will not die at the hands of a king.
O you who die not through any form of death,
This Pepi will not die through any form of death.

1469    Pepi is a star which knows not destruction,
The offspring of the Great Heaven which is in the palace of Selket.
Re has received this Pepi to himself in the heavens,
And this Pepi shall live,
Even as he who sets in the west of the sky lives
When he rise in the east of the sky.

1470    He who is in his service has entrusted this Pepi to him who serves the litter,
That he may attend to this Pepi, for this Pepi is a star.
The protection of Re is upon this Pepi,
And the protection of Re cannot be removed from upon this Pepi.

1471    Horus has extended his two arms to him, even to this Pepi,
That he may entrust this Pepi to Shu who raises his arms to support the sky.
O Re, give your hand to this Pepi,
O Great God, give your staff to this Pepi,
So that he may live unto eternity.

# SELECTIONS FROM THE COFFIN TEXTS

F ollowing the collapse of the Old Kingdom, royal Pyramid Texts were gradually appropriated by commoners, and new spells were also composed for general use. There are over a thousand spells that make up the corpus of funerary texts known as the Coffin Texts, inscribed primarily on coffins of the Middle Kingdom. The two spells translated here have been selected because of their literary interest. Spell 148, pertaining to the myth of Horus's birth, is of dramatic nature and may actually have been performed in a religious ritual. Spell 162 is poetic in its treatment of the Four Winds and seems to have been adapted from the secular realm for funerary usage.

E.F.W.

## SPELL 148

To make a transformation into a falcon:

A thunderbolt claps. The gods become afraid. Isis awakes pregnant with the seed of her brother Osiris. The woman gets up in a hurry, her heart joyful over the seed of her brother Osiris. She says,

"O you gods, I am Isis, Osiris's sister, who wept for the father of the gods, Osiris, who settled the massacring of the Two Lands. His seed is within my womb. It is as son of the foremost of the Ennead who will rule this land, become heir to Geb, speak on his father's behalf, and slay Seth, the adversary of his father Osiris, that a god's form has congealed in the egg. Come, you gods, and make his protection within my womb. Know in your hearts that he is your lord, this god who is in his egg, blue in aspect, the lord of the gods. Large and beautiful are they, the barbs of the double plumes of lapis lazuli."

"Oho!" says Re-Atum, "may your heart be wise, O woman."

(*Atum to the gods*): "But how do you know that it is a god, the lord and heir of the Ennead, that you should act against him inside the egg?"

"I am Isis, more potent and august than the gods. A god is within my womb, who is the seed of Osiris."

Then Re-Atum said, "If you are pregnant, young woman, it means that you should conceal from the gods whom you are pregnant with and are giving birth to, that he is the seed of Osiris lest that enemy who slew his father should come and break the egg in its nonage[1]—the one[2] against whom the Great-of-Magic shall make protection."

"Hear this, O gods," says Isis, "which Re-Atum, lord of the Mansion of Sacred Images, has said. It is within my body that he has decreed for me my son's protection, and it is within this womb of mine that he has disposed an entourage around him, for he knows that he is Osiris's heir. So protection of the falcon that is in this my body has been set by Re-Atum, lord of the gods."

(*Isis to Horus*): "Pray, come forth on earth,[3] and I will give you praise and the retainers of your father Osiris shall serve you. I will make your name once you have reached the horizon, having passed over the battlements of the Mansion of Him-whose-name-is-hidden."

(*Isis describes her situation*): "Strength is leaving from within my flesh now that the critical moment has arrived within my flesh and the moment for him[4] to become vigorous has arrived. As soon as the Radiant One[5] journeys, he[6] will have taken his own place, seated at the head of the gods in the entourage of the Unfurler."[7]

1. I.e., prematurely.
2. I.e., Seth.
3. An expression for birth.
4. I.e., Horus.
5. The sun god.
6. Horus.
7. One who casts out the mooring rope from the prow of the solar barque. A variant has "helmsman."

(*Isis to Horus*): "Give the falcon-cry, my son Horus. Settle down in this land of your father Osiris in this your name of Falcon who is upon the battlements of the Mansion of Him-whose-name-is-hidden. I am asking that you be among the followers of Re of the horizon at the prow of the primeval barque forever and ever."

Isis goes down to the Unfurler, who has brought Horus, for Isis had asked that he should be the Unfurler as leader of Eternal Recurrence.

(*Isis to the gods*): "Look at Horus, you gods!"

"I am Horus, the (great) Falcon who is upon the battlements of the Mansion of Him-whose-name-is-hidden. My flight has reached the horizon, for I have overpassed the gods of the sky, making my position more prominent than (that of) the primordial gods—even the Contender-bird cannot equal my initial flight. My place is far away from Seth, the adversary of my father Osiris, for I have used the roads of the eternal recurrence of dawn-light and by my flight I have become elevated. There is no god who has achieved what I have achieved. I shall be savage against the adversary of my father Osiris, placed beneath my sandals, in this my name of Ademu. I am Horus, whom Isis bore and whose protection was made inside the egg. The fiery blast of your mouths shall not assail me, and what you might say against me cannot reach me. I am Horus, more distant of place than humans and gods. I am Horus son of Isis."

## SPELL 162

To gain control over the Four Winds of the sky:

By these maidens have I been given these winds.

North Wind is she who circulates about the Haunebut, stretches out her arms to the ends of the Two Lands, and subsides after she has brought her beloved's needs each day. North Wind is breath of life. It is in order that I may live through her that she has been given to me.

By these maidens have I been given these winds.

East Wind is she who opens the celestial window, releases the eastern breezes, and prepares a fair path for Re that he may ascend on it. May Re grasp my hand and set me in this rush-bearing field of his that I may graze in it after the manner of the Apis bull and gorge in it after the manner of Seth.[8]

---

8. This sentence seems to have been interpolated in converting a secular poem for funerary usage.

East Wind is breath of life. It is in order that I may live through her that she has been given to me.

By these maidens have I been given these winds.

West Wind is he, Ha's[9] brother and Iaau's[10] offspring, who lived as a single entity before duality existed in this world. West Wind is breath of life. It is in order that I may live through him that he has been given to me.

By these maidens have I been given these winds.

South Wind is he, South Wind as a Nubian of the South, who brings water and germinates life. South Wind is breath of life. It is in order that I may live through him that he has been given to me.

Hail to you, you Four Winds of the sky, bulls of the sky! I tell (each of) you your name and the name of the one who has given them to you. I know your genesis. You[11] came into being even before people were born and gods existed, before birds were snared and bulls lassoed, before the jaws of Matjeret, the great god's daughter, were bound up and the wish of the Ancient One, lord of heaven and earth, was fulfilled. It was from the Lord of Powers that I requested them, and it is he who has given them to me.

Come now yourself and journey with me that I might let you see the barque which you shall board and in which you shall sail. If I am rebuffed, it is I who will construct my barque myself that I might cross over in it to the boat basin. Then I will take possession there of a barque of a thousand cubits overall, and I will sail in it to the Stairway of Fire at the same time as Re, when he sails to the Stairway of Fire. My bread is lying outside Tjenet.[12]

9. A god of the western desert.
10. A god in the form of a bird, perhaps symbolizing desolation and renewal like the phoenix.
11. Some variants have "I."
12. An unknown locality.

# BOOK OF THE DEAD 125
## "THE NEGATIVE CONFESSION"

T he most famous of all Book of the Dead chapters, Spell 125 contains the celebrated protestation of innocence by the deceased before an underworld tribunal of forty-two gods, corresponding to the like-numbered nomes, or provinces, of Egypt. The duality of the "Two Truths" also reflects geographical, not ethical, considerations, as the goddesses correspond to the dual nature of the Egyptian kingdom, with two regions (Upper and Lower Egypt), royal titles, tutelary deities, insignia, etc. Although Spell 125 does not specifically mention the weighing of the heart before this tribunal and its overseer Osiris, god of the dead,[1] the accompanying vignette regularly depicts this psychostasis. The address by the deceased serves as a preamble to this pivotal event, purifying him from all misdeeds (literally, "things protected against/excluded") that he may in fact have done. Since the list of infractions includes seemingly unavoidable actions such as winking, impatience, aggressiveness, and wading in flowing water, as well as all forms of sexual activity, this "ethical code" is not absolute but reflects restrictions and abstinence preparatory for entrance into a sacred space and state.

1. Though surely indicated by "that day of the reckoning of characters in the presence of Wennefer" and by the placing of "the scale in its proper position in the Land of Silence."

*Following two declarations of innocence, the reciter defends his knowledge of religious mysteries in response to hostile questions posed by the constituent elements of the judgment hall itself. While cryptic, these responses detail ritual enactments of the mysteries of Osiris, slain by the severed leg of Seth, discovered in Phoenician Byblos, interred, shattered, and scattered. The concluding rubric provides instructions for utilizing Spell 125 in ritual mysticism by the living. Attested from the Eighteenth Dynasty onward, Spell 125 survives well into the Hellenistic period, when it appears in a Demotic funerary papyrus written in the reign of Nero and in Greek translation as an initiatory recitation for priestly induction.*

*The primary manuscripts appear in Charles Maystre,* Les déclarations d'innocence (Livre des Morts, chapitre 125), *Recherches d'archéologie, de philologie et d'histoire 8, Cairo, 1937; and Edouard Naville,* Das aegyptische Todtenbuch der XVIII. bis XX. Dynastie *(Berlin, 1886), 275–335 and plates CXXXIII–CXXXIX. Translations are found in J. A. Wilson, "The Protestation of Guiltlessness," in J. B. Pritchard, ed.,* Ancient Near Eastern Texts Relating to the Old Testament *(Princeton, 1969), 34–36; P. Barguet,* Le Livre des Morts des anciens Égyptiens, *LAPO 1 (Paris, 1967), 157–64; T. G. Allen,* The Book of the Dead or Going Forth by Day, *SAOC 37 (Chicago, 1974), 97–101; M. Lichtheim,* Ancient Egyptian Literature, II *(Berkeley, 1976), 124–32; E. Hornung,* Das Totenbuch der Aegypter *(Zurich, 1979), 233–45 and 491–93; R. O. Faulkner,* The Book of the Dead *(London, 1985), 29–34; and Gloria Rosati,* Libro dei Morti, *Testi del Vicino Oriente antico 1.2 (Brescia, 1991), 88–96. For the Demotic version, see Franz Lexa,* Das demotische Totenbuch der Pariser Nationalbibliothek *(Milan, 1977; repr. of Leipzig, 1910). For the Greek translation, see Reinhold Merkelbach, "Ein ägyptischer Priestereid,"* ZPE 2 (1968): 7–30; and Die Unschuldserklärungen und Berichten im ägyptischen Totenbuch, in der römischen Elegie und im antiken Rome *(Giessen, 1987). This translation was first prepared for W. W. Hallo and K. L. Younger, eds.,* The Context of Scripture, *vol. 2 (2000), 59–64, and appears courtesy of Brill Press.*

*The translation is derived from multiple manuscripts that display no standardized line numbering. Sections of text that are highlighted in the manuscripts by the use of red ink (rubrics) are here indicated by spellings in all capital letters. Minor variants are indicated by { }.*

R.K.R.

## WHAT IS SAID WHEN ARRIVING AT THIS HALL OF TWO TRUTHS, PURGING NN OF ALL MISDEEDS THAT HE HAS DONE AND SEEING THE FACES OF THE GODS.[2]

Recitation by NN: "Hail to you, great god, Lord of the Two Truths! I have come before you, my lord, just so that you might bring me so that I might see your beauty. I know you and I know your name and the names of the forty-two gods who are with you in this Hall of the Two Truths, who live on those who preserve evil, who swallow their blood on that day of the reckoning of characters in the presence of Wennefer.[3] Behold, The Two Daughters, His Two Eyes, {Lord} of Truth is your name. Behold, I have come before you bringing to you Truth, having repelled for you falsehood.

I have not committed wrongdoing against anyone.

I have not mistreated cattle.[4]

I have not done injustice in the place of Truth.

I do not know that which should not be.

I have not done evil.

I have not daily made labors in excess of what should be done for me.

My name has not reached the bark of the Governor (i.e., Re).[5]

I have not debased a god.[6]

I have not deprived an orphan.

I have not done that which the gods abominate.

I have not slandered a servant to his superior.

I have not caused pain.[7]

I have not caused weeping.

I have not killed.

I have not commanded to kill.

I have not made suffering for anyone.

I have not diminished the offering loaves in the temples.

I have not damaged the offering cakes of the gods.

2. Variants: "Spell for descending to the Hall of the Two Truths {and learning what is in it} by NN."

3. "The Perfect Being," an epithet of Osiris, now surviving as the surname Onofrio.

4. Common variant: "I have not mistreated associates."

5. Variant: "Governor of slaves."

6. Variant: "I have not debased a deed of the king in my time."

7. Common variant: "I have not caused hunger."

I have not stolen the cakes of the blessed dead.
I have not copulated.[8]
I have not been lascivious.[9]
I have not added to nor have I subtracted from the offering measure.
I have not subtracted from the aroura measure.[10]
I have not encroached upon fields.[11]
I have not added to the weight of the balance.
I have not tampered with the plummet of the scales.
I have not taken milk from the mouths of children.
I have not deprived the flocks of their pasturage.
I have not snared birds of the branches of the gods.
I have not trapped fish in their marshes.
I have not diverted water in its season.
I have not erected a dam against flowing water.
I have not extinguished a fire at its critical moment.
I have not neglected the days concerning their meat offerings.
I have not driven away the cattle of the god's property.
I have not stopped a god in his procession.
I am pure, I am pure, I am pure, I am pure!

My purity is the purity of that great phoenix that is in Heracleopolis, because I am indeed that nose of the Lord of breath, who vivifies all the subjects on that day of filling the Eye of Horus in Heliopolis in the second month of winter, last day, in the presence of the Lord of this land. I am one who has seen the filling of the Eye of Horus in Heliopolis. Evil shall not happen against me in this land or in this Hall of the Two Truths because I know the names of the gods who are in it, the followers of the great god.[12]

O Wide-of-Stride, who has come forth from Heliopolis, I have not committed wrongdoing.
O Embracer-of-Fire, who has come forth from Egyptian Babylon, I have not robbed.

8. Variant: "I have not copulated with a boy."
9. Variant: "I have not been lascivious in the sanctuary of my local god."
10. Variant: "I have not subtracted from the palm-measure (1/7 of a cubit)."
11. Variant: "I have not falsified the half-aroura of field."
12. Variant: "Then you (Osiris) will protect NN from these gods who are with you in the Hall of the Two Truths."

O Beaky,[13] who has come forth from Hermopolis, I have not been envious.

O Swallower-of-Shadows, who has come forth from the cavern, I have not stolen.

O Rough-of-Face, who has come forth from the Memphite necropolis, I have not killed people.

O Twin-Lions, who has come forth from heaven, I have not damaged the offering measure.

O He-Whose-Eyes-Are-Flint, who has come forth from Letopolis, I have not committed crookedness.

O Firey-One, who has come forth backwards, I have not stolen a god's property.

O Smasher-of-Bones, who has come forth from Heracleopolis, I have not told lies.

O Sender-of-Flames, who has come forth from Memphis, I have not seized food.

O Cavern-Dweller, who has come forth from the West, I have not been sullen.

O White-Toothed-One, who has come forth from the Faiyum, I have not transgressed.[14]

O Eater-of-Blood,[15] who has come forth from the slaughtering-block, I have not slain sacred cattle.

O Eater-of-Entrails, who has come forth from the Court of Thirty, I have not committed usury.[16]

O Lord-of-Truth, who has come forth from The Place of the Two Truths, I have not robbed bread-rations.

O Wanderer, who has come forth from Bubastis, I have not eaves-dropped.[17]

O Pale-One, who has come forth from Heliopolis, I have not blabbered.[18]

13. An epithet of Thoth, the long-beaked ibis.
14. Address to the crocodile Sobek. Variants conclude: "regarding the property of Osiris" or "against another."
15. Used to signify "cannibal" in Coptic.
16. Translated variously "extorted," "profiteered," or "practiced usury," the infraction (ḥnwy.t) is perhaps related to "greed" (ḥnt). Faulkner's "perjury" derives from the Demotic substitution: "I did not commit falsehood [ . . .]."
17. Variant concludes: "on another in his house."
18. Lit. "The speech/mouth of NN has not run on."

O Doubly-Evil-Viper, who has come forth from Busiris, I have not disputed except concerning my own property.

O *Wamemti*-Viper, who has come forth from the place of execution, I have not copulated with a man's wife.[19]

O He-Who-Sees-That-Which-He-Has-Brought-Away, who has come forth from the House of Min, I have not been lascivious.

O Chief-of-the-Nobles, who has come forth from Kom el-Hîsn, I have not caused terror.

O Wrecker, who has come forth from Xois, I have not transgressed.

O Disturber, who has come forth from the sanctuary, I have not been hot-tempered.[20]

O Child, who has come forth from the Heliopolitan Nome, I have not turned a deaf ear to words of truth.

O Proclaimer-of-Speech, who has come forth from Wensi, I have not made disturbance.

O Bastet, who has come forth from the shrine, I have not winked.[21]

O He-Whose-Face-Is-Behind-Him, who has come forth from the pit, I have not masturbated; I have not copulated with a catamite.[22]

O Hot-Footed-One, who has come forth from the dusk, I have not dissembled.[23]

O Dark-One, who has come forth from the darkness, I have not reviled.

O He-Who-Brings-Away-His-Offering, who has come forth from Sais, I have not been aggressive.[24]

O Lord-of-Faces, who has come forth from the Heroonopolite Nome, I have not been impatient.[25]

O Accuser, who has come forth from Wetenet, I have not transgressed my nature; I have not washed out a god.[26]

---

19. For this passage, see M. Heerma van Voss, "Drie Egyptische Goboden," in M. A. Beek, et al., eds., *Symbolae Biblicae et Mesopotamicae Francisco Mario Theodoro De Liagre Böhl Dedicatae* (Leiden 1973), 185–87.
20. Variant: "My speech has not been heated."
21. Variant adds: "at another."
22. For this passage, see Heerma van Voss 1973, 185–87.
23. Lit. "I have not swallowed my heart." In medical texts, "swallowing the heart" is a physiological designation for "fainting."
24. Elsewhere always a positive designation of a warrior: "champion."
25. Lit. "my heart has not been hasty."
26. Faulkner understands: "I have not washed out (the picture of) a god."

O Lord-of-Horns, who has come forth from Siut, I have not been verbose in matters.

O Nefertum, who has come forth from Memphis, I have not sinned; I have not done wrong.

O He-Who-Is-Not-Abandoned, who has come forth from Busiris, I have not reviled the king.

O He-Who-Has-Acted-According-to-His-Heart, who has come forth from Antaeopolis, I have not waded in water.[27]

O Surging-One, who has come forth from the Abyss, I have not raised my voice.

O Commander-of-the-Subjects, who has come forth from his shrine, I have not reviled a god.

O Provider-of-Goodness, who has come forth from the Harpoon Nome, I have not been puffed up.

O Nehebkau, who has come forth from Thebes, I have not made distinctions on my behalf.

O Serpent-Whose-Head-Is-Erect, who has come forth from the cavern, my possessions have not increased except by my own property.

O Serpent-Who-Has-Brought-Away-His-Portion, who has come forth from the Land of Silence, I have not debased the god in my town."

RECITATION BY NN:

"Hail to you, you gods.[28] I know you; I know your names. I shall not fall to your slaughter. You will not report my misdeed to this god in whose following you are. No fault of mine will come forth concerning you. You will speak Truth concerning me in the presence of the Lord of All, because I have done Truth in Egypt. I have not cursed a god. No fault of mine has come forth concerning a king who was in his reign.

Hail to you gods who are in this Hall of the Two Truths, who have no lies in their bodies, who live on Truth in Heliopolis, who swallow their putrifaction[29] in the presence of Horus who is in his Aten-disk. May you save me from Babai, who lives on the entrails of the great ones on that day of the great reckoning. Behold me; I have come before you without falsehood of mine, without guilt of mine, without evil of mine, without a witness against

27. Variant: "in flowing water."
28. Variant adds: "who are in this Hall of the Two Truths."
29. Variant: "who swallow/consume Truth."

me, without anyone against whom I have done anything.[30] As I live on Truth, so I consume Truth. I have done what people say and that on account of which the gods are pleased. I have contented the god with that which he loves.[31] I have given bread to the hungry, water to the thirsty, clothing to the naked, and a boat to the boatless. I have made divine offerings for the gods, invocation-offerings for the blessed dead. Save me, then. Protect me, then. You will not report against me in the presence of the great god. I am pure of mouth, pure of hands, one to whom 'Welcome!' is said at seeing him, because I have heard that speech[32] said by the Donkey and the Cat in the house of the One of the Gaping Mouth,[33] I being a witness before him[34] when he gave a shriek. I have seen the splitting of the persea tree within the Memphite necropolis.[35] I am one who provides assistance in the presence of the gods, who knows the requirements of their bodies. I have come here specifically to testify to Truth, to place the scale in its proper position in the Land of Silence. O he who is high upon his standard, Lord of the *atef*-crown, who has made his name as Lord of Breath,[36] may you save me from your messengers, who inflict bloody injury,[37] who create punishment, who are without compassion, because I have done Truth for the Lord of Truth, since I am pure, my front clean, my back cleansed, my middle as a pool of Truth. There is no limb of mine lacking in purity. As I have washed in the pool of the South, so I have rested in the city of the North, in the field of grasshoppers in which the crew of Re bathes in that second hour of night and third of day, which soothes the hearts of the gods when they pass by it by night or day."

"Let him come," so they say regarding me.

"Who are you?" so they say regarding me.

"What is your name?" so they say regarding me.

---

30. Variant: "for I have not done anything against him."
31. Variant: "the gods with that which they love."
32. Variant: "great word/speech."
33. A reference to the punishment of Seth in donkey form by the cat goddess Mafdet; see J. F. Borghouts, *Ancient Egyptian Magical Texts* (Leiden, 1978), 38, no. 59.
34. Variant: "He-Whose-Face-Is-Behind-Him being my witness."
35. A reference to Re's victory against Apep described in Book of the Dead 17.
36. Epithets of Osiris.
37. See R. K. Ritner, *The Mechanics of Ancient Egyptian Magical Practice,* SAOC 54 (Chicago, 1993), 170.

"I am the stalk of the papyrus plant, He-Who-is-in-the-Moringa-tree is my name."[38]

"By what have you passed?" so they say regarding me.

"By the city north of the moringa tree I passed."[39]

"What did you see there?"

"It was the calf and the thigh."

"What did you say to them?"

"I have seen rejoicing in the lands of the Phoenicians."

"What did they give to you?"

"It was a firebrand and a column of faience."

"What did you do with them?"

"I buried them on the bank of the lake of Two Truths in the evening meal rite."

"What did you find there on the bank of the Two Truths?"

"It was a scepter of flint, whose name is Breath-Giver."

"What did you do with the firebrand and column of faience after you had buried them?"

"I lamented over them. I dug them up. I extinguished the fire. I broke the column and threw it in the lake."

"Come, then, enter by this portal of the Hall of the Two Truths, since you know us."

"I shall not let you enter by me," so say the door-posts of this portal, "unless you have said my name."

" 'Plummet of Truthfulness' is your name."

"I shall not let you enter by me," so says the right door-leaf of this portal, "unless you have said my name."

" 'Scale-pan which bears Truth' is your name."

"I shall not let you enter by me," so says the left door-leaf of this portal, "unless you have said my name."

" 'Scale-pan of wine' is your name."

"I shall not let you enter by me," so says the threshold of this portal, "unless you have said my name."

" 'Ox of Geb' is your name."

38. Epithet of Osiris.

39. For the following Osirian mysteries, see Ritner 1993, 150, n. 678.

"I shall not open for you," so says the bolt of this portal, "unless you have said my name."

" 'Toe of his mother' is your name."

"I shall not open for you," so says the hasp of this portal, "unless you have said my name."

" 'Living Eye of Sobek, Lord of Bakhu' is your name."

"I shall not open for you, I shall not let you enter by me," so says the door-keeper of this portal, "unless you have said my name."

" 'Breast of Shu which he placed as protection for Osiris' is your name."

"We shall not let you pass by us," so say the cross-timbers of this portal, "unless you have said our name."

" 'Children of Renenutet' is your name."

"You know us. Pass, then, by us."

"You shall not tread upon me," so says the floor of this Hall of the Two Truths."

"Why, then, since I am pure?"

"Because we do not know the names of your feet with which you would tread upon us. Say it to me then."

" 'He who is inducted into the presence of Min' is the name of my right foot.

" 'Flower of Nephthys'[40] is the name of my left foot."

"Tread, then, upon us. You know us."

"I shall not announce you," so says the door-keeper of this hall, "unless you have said my name."

" 'He who perceives hearts, who examines bodies' is your name."

"To which god on duty shall I announce you, then?"

"Tell it to the Interpreter of the Two Lands."

"Who is the Interpreter of the Two Lands?"

"It is Thoth."

"Come," so says Thoth, "Why have you come?"

"I have come here expressly to report."

"What is your condition?"

"I am pure from all misdeeds. I excluded myself from the strife of those who are in their days. I am not among them."

"To whom, then, shall I announce you?"

40. Variant: "He who opens heaven for Hathor."

"To him whose roof is of fire, with its walls of living uraei, and the floor of whose house is in flood."

"Who is he?"

"He is Osiris."

"Proceed, then. Behold, you are announced. Your bread is the Eye of Horus; your beer is the Eye of Horus; your invocation offerings on earth are the Eye of Horus," so says he regarding me.

What should be done when being present in the Hall of Two Truths. A man should say this spell when pure and clean, dressed in clothing, shod in white sandals, painted with black eye-paint, anointed with the finest myrrh-oil, and having offered fresh meat, fowl, incense, bread, beer, and vegetables. Now make for yourself this image[41] in drawing upon pure ground with Nubian ochre, overlaid with soil on which neither pig nor goats have trod. As for the one for whom this book is done, he will flourish and his children will flourish. He will be a confidant of the king and his entourage. There shall be given to him a cake, a jug of beer, a loaf and a large portion of meat from upon the altar of the great god. He cannot be turned back from any portal of the West. He will be ushered in with the kings of Upper and Lower Egypt. He will be a follower of Osiris.[42] Truly effective, millions of times.

41. Presumably the corresponding vignette of the weighing of the heart.
42. Variant adds: "He goes forth in any transformation that he desires, being a living *ba*-spirit forever and ever."

# THE HYMN TO THE ATEN

I n the reign of Amen-hotep IV-Akhenaten of Dynasty 18 the royal family
espoused the worship of the sun disk, the Aten, and neglected the older
state and local gods, particularly Amen-Re. The king changed his name
from Amen-hotep (Amun is pleased) to Akhenaten (the effective form of the
Aten), and he constructed a new residence city at Amarna called Akhet-Aten,
the Horizon of the Aten, marked out by royal boundary stelae and filled with
temples, palaces, villas for the nobles, workshops for the artisans, and housing
for the laborers. Throughout Egypt the names of the old gods were systemati-
cally hacked out whenever they appeared in inscriptions on temple walls and
elsewhere. The movement was viewed as a reformation, a return to the royal
sun cult of the pyramid builders. It was later regarded as a heresy and did not
survive the king's reign. Akhenaten emphasized the international supremacy of
the sun disk and his relation to it as a son. In effect, he interposed himself
between the Aten and the people, with his worship directed to the Aten and the
people's attention focused upon him as the son and interpreter of the Aten.
Whether the system can be considered monotheism is debatable. The broad
outlook represented in these texts is a development of earlier Egyptian thought
with new elements. Noteworthy is the almost anthropological view of the races
of mankind differentiated in color and language. There are close parallels in
wording, thought, and sequence of ideas to the verses of Psalm 104. The text is
presented in hieroglyphic in N. de G. Davies, The Rock Tombs of el Amarna

*(London, 1908), pt. 6, pl. 27; this version derives from the tomb of Eye. For a lucid and interpretive account of the king's reign and times, consult Cyril Aldred,* Akhenaten, King of Egypt *(London, 1968). See Aten bibliography, especially Murnane 1995. I am indebted to Dr. James Allen for reading my translation and suggesting several significant improvements.*

W.K.S.

1 Worshipping (The Living One) Re-Horakhty who Rejoices in the Horizon) (In his Identity as the Light who is in the Aten) living forever and ever, the Living Aten, the Great One who is in Jubilee, Master of all that the Aten encircles, Master of Heaven, Master of the Earth, Master of the Per-Aten in Akhet-Aten;[1] and the King of Upper and Lower Egypt, the one Living on Maat, Lord of the Two Lands (Nefer-kheperu-Re Wa-en-Re), son of Re, living on Maat, Master of Regalia (Akhenaten), the long lived; and the Foremost Wife of the King, whom he loves, the Mistress of Two Lands (Nefer-nefru-Aten Nefertiti), living, well, and young forever and ever.

2 He says:

You rise in perfection on the horizon of the sky,
living Aten, who determines life.
Whenever you are risen upon the eastern horizon
you fill every land with your perfection.
You are appealing, great, sparkling, high over every land;
your rays embrace the lands as far as everything you
      have made.

3 Since you are Re, you reach as far as they do,
and you curb them for your beloved son.
Although you are far away, your rays are upon the land;
you are in their faces, yet your departure is not observed.

Whenever you set on the western horizon,
the land is in darkness in the manner of death.

1. Just as the king's name is inscribed in a pair of cartouches, so too the Aten is regarded as a king with cartouches for his names and is considered to celebrate the royal jubilee festivals. Re-Horakhty is the sun god Re united with Horus of the Horizon. The Per-Aten is the house (temple) of Aten in Akhet-Aten.

They sleep in a bedroom with heads under the covers,
and one eye cannot see another.
If all their possessions which are under their heads were
    stolen, they would not realize it.

4    Every lion comes out of his cave and all the serpents
    bite,
for darkness is a blanket.
The land is silent now, because He who makes them
is at rest on His horizon.

But when day breaks you are risen upon the horizon,
and you shine in the Aten in the daytime.
When you dispel darkness and you give forth your rays
the two lands are in a festival of light,
alert and standing on their feet,
now that you have raised them up.

5    Their bodies are clean, / and their clothes put on;
their arms are ⟨lifted⟩ in praise at your rising.

The entire land performs its work:
all the flocks are content with their fodder,
trees and plants grow,
birds fly up to their nests,
their wings ⟨extended⟩ in praise for your *Ka.*
All the kine prance on their feet;
everything which flies up and alights,

6    they live when you rise for them.
The barges sail upstream and downstream too,
for every way is open at your rising.
The fishes in the river leap before your face
when your rays are inside the sea.

You who places seed in woman
and makes sperm into man,
who brings to life the son in the womb of his mother,
who quiets him by ending his crying;

7    you nurse in the womb,
giving breath to nourish all that has been begotten.

When he comes down from the womb to breathe
    on the day he is born,
you open up his mouth ⌜completely⌝, and supply his
    needs.
When the fledgling in the egg speaks in the shell,
you give him air inside it to sustain him.
When you have granted him his allotted time to break out from the
    egg,
he comes out from the egg to cry out at his fulfillment,
and he goes upon his legs when he has come forth from it.

How plentiful it is, what you make,
although they are hidden from view,
sole god, without another beside you;
you create the earth as you wish,
when you were by yourself, ⟨before⟩
mankind, all cattle and kine,
all beings on land, who fare upon their feet,
and all beings in the air, who fly with their wings.

The lands of Khor and Kush[2]
and the land of Egypt:
you set every man in his place,
you allot their needs,
every one of them according to his diet,
and his lifetime is counted out.
Tongues are separate in speech,
and their characters / as well;
their skins are different,
for you differentiate the foreigners.
In the underworld you make a Nile
that you may bring it forth as you wish
to feed the populace,
since you make them for yourself, their utter master,
growing weary on their account, lord of every land.

8

9

2. Khor is Syro-Palestine in the northeast, and Kush is the Nubian region in the Sudan to
the south.

For them the Aten of the daytime arises,
great in awesomeness.

All distant lands,
you make them live,
for you set a Nile in the sky
that it may descend for them
10    and make waves upon the mountains like the sea
to irrigate the fields in their towns.
How functional are your designs,
Lord of eternity:
a Nile in the sky for the foreigners
and all creatures that go upon their feet,
a Nile coming back from the underworld for Egypt.[3]

Your rays give suck to every field:
when you rise they live,
and they grow for you.
You make the seasons
to bring into being all you make:
11    the Winter to cool them,
the Heat that you may be felt.
You have made a far-off heaven
in which to rise
in order to observe everything you make.
Yet you are alone,
rising in your manifestations as the Living Aten:
appearing, glistening, being afar, coming close;
you make millions of transformations of yourself.
Towns, harbors, fields, roadways, waterways:
every eye beholds you upon them,
for you are the Aten of the daytime on the face of the
        earth.

12    When you have gone
[no] eye can exist,
for you have created their sight

3. Egypt is essentially rainless and watered only by the Nile. Hence the rains of other
   lands are here regarded as a Nile in the sky.

so that you (yourself) are not seen
(except by your) sole [son] whom you have made.

You are in my heart,
and there is no other who knows you
except for your son (Nefer-kheperu-Re Wa-en-Re),[4]
for you have apprised him of your designs and your
      power.
The earth comes forth into existence by your hand,
and you make it.
When you rise, they live;
when you set, they die.
You are a lifespan in yourself;
one lives by you.

13    Eyes are / upon your perfection until you set:
all work is put down when you rest in the west.
You who rise and make everything grow
for the King and (for) everyone who hastens on foot,
because you founded the land
and you raised them for your son
who has come forth from your body,
the King of Upper and Lower Egypt, the one Living on
      Maat,
Lord of the Two Lands (Nefer-kheperu-Re Wa-en-Re),
son of Re, the one Living on Maat, Master of Regalia,
(Akhenaten), the long lived,
and the Foremost Wife of the King, whom he loves,
the Mistress of the Two Lands,
(Nefer-nefru-Aten Nefertiti),
living and young, forever and ever.

4. The king's praenomen. His exclusive relation to the Aten is stressed.

# PENITENTIAL HYMNS

T he three hieroglyphic inscriptions translated here were carved during the reign of Ramesses II on votive stelae placed in chapels associated with the necropolis workmen's village of Deir el-Medina in western Thebes. They are representative of numerous Ramesside texts expressing an individual's humility before a deity, who not only punishes the wrongdoer but also pardons the contrite sinner. Although personal piety is especially evident in the Ramesside period, brief antecedents are found on hieratic ostraca from the mortuary temple of Amenhotep II, published by Georges Posener in RdE 27 (1975): 195–210.

E.F.W.

## STELA OF NEBRE (BERLIN 20377)

1    Giving praise to Amon:
     I make to him adorations in his name.
     I give him praises to the height of the sky,
          To the breadth of the earth.
     I declare ⌜the greatness⌝ of his power
          To the one traveling north and the one traveling south.

Beware of him!
Herald him to son and daughter,
    To those senior and junior.
Declare him to generations (now) and generations still yet to come.
Declare him to fish in the deep,
    To fowl in the sky.
Herald him to him who knows him not and him who knows him.
Beware of him!

You are Amon, the lord of the silent one,
Who comes at the plea of the lowly one.
5     I called out to you when I was distressed,
And / you came and rescued me.
You give breath ⟨to⟩ him who is weak;
You rescue him who is in dire straits.
You are Amon-Re, Lord of Thebes,
Who rescues him who is in the abyss,
For you are one who is ⸢merciful⸣ when you are called upon.
You are the one who comes from afar.

Made by the draftsman of Amon in the Place of Truth,[1] Nebre, justified, son of the draftsman in the Place of Truth, Pay, [justified], in the name of his lord Amon, Lord of Thebes, who comes at the plea of the lowly one.

I made for him adorations in his name,
So great is his might.
I made to him supplications before him
In the presence of the entire land,
On behalf of the draftsman Nakhtamon, justified,
When he was lying ill and moribund,
Being ⟨in⟩ the power of Amon because of his cow.[2]
I found that the Lord of the Gods came as the north wind,
With a pleasant breeze before him.
He rescued the draftsman of Amon Nakhtamon, justified,
Son of the draftsman of Amon in the Place of Truth, Nebre, justified,
10    Born / of the lady of the house Pashed, justified.

1. Here designating Deir el-Medina.
2. Some sort of infraction involving a cow, either one belonging to Nakhtamon or to
   Amon's herd.

He says:

Just as a servant is wont to commit sin,

So the lord is wont to forgive.

The Lord of Thebes does not spend a whole day being angry;

If he becomes angry,

In an instant, it no longer lasts.

˹The wind˺ has turned around for us in mercy;

Amon has returned with his breeze.

As your *ka* endures, you will be gracious.

We are not backsliding ever again.

By the draftsman in the Place of Truth, Nebre, justified.

He says:

I shall make this stela in your name

And record for you this hymn in writing upon it,

Because you rescued for me the draftsman Nakhtamon.

15   ·/ So I said to you, and you hearkened to me.

Now see, I have done what I promised.

You are a lord who can be called upon,

Content with Maat, the Lord of Thebes.

Made by the draftsman Nebre and his son, the scribe Khay.

## STELA OF NEFERABU (TURIN N 50058)

1   Giving praise to the Peak of the West,[3]

Kissing the ground to her *ka*.

I give praise; hear my invocation!

For I am a righteous person upon earth.

Made by the servant in the Place of Truth, Neferabu, justified.

⟨I was⟩ an ignorant man and witless,

Not distinguishing good from bad.

I made the mistake of transgressing against the Peak,

So she chastised me,

5   I being in her hand / by night as by day,

---

3. The stela is dedicated to Mertseger, "She Who Loves Silence," depicted on the right side as a three-headed serpent. "Peak of the West," which was Mertseger's "good name" and embodiment in nature, was the mountain-head that dominated the Theban necropolis.

Sitting upon brick(s) like a woman in labor.
I called out to the wind, but it did not come to me.
I inclined[4] ⟨myself⟩ to the Peak of the West, great in strength,
And to every god and every goddess.

Now see, I shall tell senior(s) and junior(s) who are in the gang:
Beware of the Peak!
For a lion exists within her.
10  The / Peak strikes with the stroke of a fierce lion
When she is in pursuit of the one who has transgressed against her.

I called out to my mistress.
I found that she came to me as a pleasant breeze.
She forgave me after she had made me see her hand.
She turned round to me in mercy;
15  She made me forget the pangs / that were in my heart.[5]
Lo, the Peak of the West is merciful when she is called upon.
Said by Neferabu, justified.

He says:
See, may all ears that are alive upon earth hear:
Beware of the Peak of the West!

## STELA OF NEFERABU (BRITISH MUSEUM 589)

1  Giving praise to Ptah, Lord of Maat, King of the Two Lands,
Beautiful of Countenance, who is upon his great throne,
Unique god among the Ennead,
Beloved as King of the Two Lands.
That he may grant life, prosperity and health,
Proficiency, favors, and affection,
5  And that my eyes behold Amon / daily
Just as is done for a righteous person,
Who places Amon in his heart.
By the servant in the Place of Truth, Neferabu, justified.

---

4. In humility. Because the corner-sign in its hieratic form serves as a determinative, the verb must be *ḳnb,* with omitted *n.*
5. Before *mr* understand *n* as a writing of the plural definite article. The heartaches were probably mental rather than physical.

(*Reverse*):

1    Here begins the recital of the power of Ptah, South-of-his-Wall,
by the servant in the Place of Truth on the West of Thebes,
Neferabu, justified. He says:
I am a man who swore falsely by Ptah, Lord of Maat.
He caused me to see darkness by day.
I shall declare his power
To him who knows him not and him who knows him,
To juniors and seniors.
Beware of Ptah, Lord of Maat!

5    See, he does not overlook / anyone's misdeed.
Avoid uttering Ptah's name falsely.
Lo, he who utters it falsely; lo, he falls down.
He caused me to be like street dogs
When I was in his hand.
He caused people and gods to look on me,
Just like a man who has committed abomination against his lord.
Ptah, Lord of Maat, was correct toward me
When he chastised me.
May you be merciful to me that I may see your mercy!

10    By the servant in the Place of Truth / on the West of Thebes,
Neferabu, justified before the great god.

# THE BOOK OF THE HEAVENLY COW

T his composition, modernly entitled The Book of the Heavenly Cow, is
included because it contains possibly the oldest extended mythical narrative from ancient Egypt and because the text also provides information
regarding the practical use to which the myth was put. Although this myth is first
attested in New Kingdom royal tombs after the Amarna period, the first part,
treating the attempted destruction of mankind, is alluded to in The Teaching for
Merikare of the First Intermediate Period, and it is likely that the entire myth
was composed in the Middle Kingdom. Aside from the theme of the sun god's
ultimate compassion toward a rebellious mankind, whose annihilation he initially sponsored, the story explains how, as a result of humanity's fallen nature,
the universe as we know it came to be, with the sun, moon, and stars moving
across the sky, which the Egyptians depicted in an accompanying scene as a cow
uplifted by the god Shu and eight assisting deities. Embedded within the narrative are etiological statements (indicated in italics) that involve plays on words
contained in divine quotations that immediately precede each statement. Since
some of these etiologies are essential to the development of the narrative, they
must be considered as integral to the myth, not as later interpolations.

Unlike the Pyramid Texts, composed primarily for the king's afterlife, The
Heavenly Cow was a nonroyal composition whose narrative myth and the
directions for its use by nonroyalty were quite mechanically inscribed in New

289

*Kingdom royal tombs. By magical means a person could participate, especially after death, in the sun god's process of renewal.*

E.F.W.

1     Once it came to pass [under] the Majesty of Re, the self-generated god, that when he had been in the kingship over mankind and the gods combined, mankind proceeded to contrive a plot against the person of Re now that His Majesty, l.p.h., had grown old, his bones being of silver, his flesh of gold and his hair of genuine lapis lazuli. His Majesty became aware of the plot being contrived against him by mankind, and so His Majesty, l.p.h., said to those who were his retinue, "Please summon to me my Eye, Shu, Tefnut, Geb, and Nut as well as the fathers and mothers who were in my company when I was in Nun,[1] and also the god Nun, bringing his cour-

5     tiers / along with him. It is stealthily that you must bring them lest mankind see and they lose heart as you come back with them to the palace so that they may offer their sound advice. It is within Nun, at the place where I originated, that I shall return."

So these gods were brought [right away], and these gods were (positioned) on either side of him, touching the ground with their foreheads in His Majesty's presence, so that he might state his problem in the presence of the father of the eldest ones,[2] the maker of mankind and king of humanity. They then said unto His Majesty, "Speak to us so that we may learn about it." Then said Re to Nun, "O eldest god in whom I originated and you ancestral gods, see, mankind, who originated from my Eye,[3] has contrived a plot against me. Tell me what you would do about this, since I am seeking (a

10     solution). I cannot slay them until I have heard / what you might have to say about this."

The Majesty of Nun replied, "O my son Re, the god mightier than the one who produced you and greater than those who created you, stay put on your throne! The fear of you is great; your Eye shall proceed against those who conspire against you." The Majesty of Re said, "See, they have fled into the desert, their hearts fearful over what I might say to them." Then they said unto His Majesty, "Send out your Eye that it may smite them for you,

1. The primeval abyss.
2. The god Nun.
3. Through a play on words the Egyptians conceived of mankind (*rmṯ*) as being the tears (*rmyt*) that issued from the sun god's eye.

those who have conspired so wickedly. No eye is as capable as it to smite them for you. May it descend in the form of Hathor."

Then this goddess returned after she had slain mankind in the desert. The Majesty of this god said, "Welcome, Hathor! Have you accomplished that for which you set out?" This goddess replied, "As you live for me, I have overpowered mankind, and it was agreeable to my heart." The Majesty

15 of Re said, "I shall gain power over them ⸢as king⸣. / Hold off decimating them!" *And so Sakhmet came into being.*[4]

The nightly beer-mash for wading in their blood starting from Heracleopolis.[5] Re said, "Please summon to me speedy emissaries whose pace is as swift as a body's shadow." So these emissaries were brought immediately. Then said the Majesty of this god, "Run up to Elephantine and fetch me red ocher in quantity." So this red ocher was brought to him. The Majesty of this great god assigned the Side-locked One who is in Heliopolis[6] to pulverize this red ocher, while maidservants were engaged in grinding barley for beer. This red ocher was then added to that beer-mash so that (it) was just like human blood. Seven thousand *hebenet*-jars of beer were thus produced.

Then the Majesty of the King of Upper and Lower Egypt Re came

20 with these gods to inspect this beer—it was the eve / of the day when the goddess was to slay mankind during her[7] days of journeying south. The words spoken by the Majesty of Re, "How good it is! I shall preserve mankind from her." Then said Re, "Transport it please to the place where she said she would slay mankind."

The Majesty of the King of Upper and Lower Egypt Re got up early in the deep of night in order to have this intoxicating draught poured out. Then the fields became filled (to a height of) three palms with the liquid through the power of the Majesty of this god. This goddess set out in the morning, and she found these (fields) inundated. Her face became delighted thereat. So she proceeded to drink, and it was just fine in her

---

4. The statements in italics concerning origins are generally based on word play; in this instance the dangerous lioness goddess Sakhmet reflects word play on *sḫm,* "be powerful."

5. As Lichtheim notes in *AEL* 2, 199, n. 7, these words serve as an introduction to what follows.

6. The high priest of the sun god Re.

7. The text has "their," but surely the reference is to the annual southward journey of the goddess as the Eye of the sun god.

estimation. She returned so drunk that she had been unable to recognize mankind.

The Majesty of Re then said to this goddess, "Welcome, darling!" ⟨*And* 25 *so*⟩ *beautiful women came to be in Imau.*[8] The Majesty of Re then told / this goddess that intoxicating draughts shall be prepared for her on the seasonal feasts of the year; maidservants shall be held responsible for this. *And so the preparation of intoxicating draughts became the assignment of maidservants on the Feast of Hathor on the part of all people since the first day.* The Majesty of Re said to this goddess, "Has the heat of sickness[9] become painful?" *And so respect is bound to originate through pain.* Then said the Majesty of Re, "As I live for myself, my heart is too weary to remain with them, that I should slay them to the very last one. The reach of my arm[10] shall in no way diminish."

What the gods who were in his retinue said: "Don't withdraw in your weariness, for you (still) have power over what you desire." The Majesty of this god then said to the Majesty of Nun, "My body is weak for the first 30 time. I won't wait[11] until another gets to me." Then said the Majesty of Nun, "(My) son Shu, [your] eye / shall serve [your] father (Re) as his protection. (My) daughter Nut, you shall place him [upon your back]." Nut replied, "But how, my father Nun?" said Nut, "Don't [ᵣbe silly¹],[12] Nun." [*And so*] *Nut became* [*a cow*]. Then the Majesty of Re [placed] himself upon her back.

Thereupon these men [came ...], and they saw him on the back of this cow. Then these men said to him, "[ᵣ... have re]be[lled against you¹]. We have [come] so that we might overthrow your enemies, who complotted against those who created them." His Majesty proceeded to [his] palace [on the back] of this cow. He did [not] set off with them. So the land lay in darkness.

35 When it dawned in the early morning, these men / came out carrying bows and clubs [...], and they [found] a way of shooting at the enemies. The Majesty of this god said, "Your baseness be behind you, o slaughterers; may

---

8. A cult place of Hathor in the western Delta.

9. Possibly referring to fever.

10. Possibly meaning "generosity," "leniency."

11. Understanding *s3y.i*, the writing *i3y.i* being due to similarity of signs in hieratic.

12. Restoring a word related to *ihw*, "childish weakness," so as to yield *iht*, "cow," through word play.

your slaughtering be far removed [from ⌐me⌐]." *And so murderousness*[13] [*origina*]*ted among mankind.*

This god then said to Nut, "It is in order that I may be uplifted that I have placed myself on your back." "What's this?" asked Nut. *And so ⌐she⌐ came to be there in both the heavens.*[14] The Majesty of this god ⌐said⌐, "Stay far away from them! Lift me up! Look at me!"[15] *And so she became the sky.* Then the Majesty of [this] god was visible within her. She said, "If only you would provide me with a multitude!" [*And so ⌐the Milky Way⌐*] *came into being.*

His Majesty, l.p.h., said, "Peaceful is the field here." *And so the Field of Offerings came into being.* "I shall make vegetation grow / in it." *And so the Field of Rushes came into being.*[16] "I shall provide them with every-thing." *And so ⌐planets⌐ and stars ⟨came into being⟩.* Then Nut started trem-bling because of the height. So the Majesty of Re said, "If only I had millions supporting her!" *And so the Infinite Ones*[17] *came into being.*

The Majesty of Re said, "O my son Shu, place yourself under (my grand)daughter Nut and watch over for me the two groups of Infinite Ones there so that they may live in the twilight. Place her over your head and nurture her." *And so originated the (custom of) giving a nurse to a son or daughter. And so originated the (custom of) a father's placing a son on top of his head.*

This spell is to be recited over a (picture of) a cow at whose chest is (inscribed) "The Infinite Ones who are" and over whose back is (inscribed) "The Infinite Ones who are," / whose four ⌐hoofs⌐ are filled out in (black) paint and upon whose belly are a plurality of stars, issuing from its hind-quarters in front of its hind legs, while beneath its belly stands Shu, painted in yellow ocher, his arms under these stars, and inscribed with his name between them using the word "Shu" by itself. A barque, on which are a steering-oar and a shrine with a solar disk over it and Re in it, is in front of Shu next to his hand, while another version (of a barque) is behind him next to his (other) hand. Its udder is rendered in the middle of its left hind

40

45

13. I.e., the will to murder.
14. Or, without emending, "She is the one who came to be there in both the heavens." By "both the heavens" are meant the day and night skies.
15. Or possibly emending to, "Lift me up so I'm visible."
16. The two fields mentioned lay in the beyond for the benefit of the blessed dead.
17. Two groups of four Heh-gods, the Infinite Ones, assist Shu in supporting the celes-tial cow.

leg, its profile being drawn in paint in the middle of this hind leg with the following words (inscribed) outside in retrograde: "I am who I am. I will not let them take action." What is (inscribed) beneath the barque that 50 is in front is as follows: "You shall not grow / weary, my son," they (the signs) being in retrograde, and as follows: "Your condition is like that of one who lives forever," and as follows: "Your son is in me.[18] Life, prosperity and health be to this your nose!"

What is (inscribed) behind Shu next to his arm is as follows: "Watch over them!" What is behind him at his flank is (inscribed) in retrograde as follows: "It is right that they[19] should enter in when I retire each day." What is (inscribed) under the arm of the figure that is beneath the left hind leg and behind it is as follows: "Everything should be sealed." What is (inscribed) above his head, beneath this cow's hindquarters and what is between its hind legs is as follows: "As for him who shall go forth." What is (inscribed) 55 behind the two figures that are between its hind legs and above their heads: "The aged one is in ⌐Igeret¬.[20] Praise / is given, moreover, when he is ⌐introduced¬." What is (inscribed) over the heads of the two figures that are between its forelegs: "⟨He who adores⟩ ⌐rectitude¬, Hearer, Support of the Sky."[21]

The Majesty of this god then said to Thoth, "Please summon to me the Majesty of Geb saying, 'Come quickly at once!'" So the Majesty of Geb came, and the Majesty of this god said, "Take heed because of your snakes which are in you![22] See, they feared me when I was there. Also you have become acquainted with their magical power. Go now to the place where my father Nun is and tell him to keep watch over terrestrial and aquatic snakes. And also you are to draw up notices with respect to each mound for your snakes that are there, saying, 'Beware of disturbing anything!' They should know that I am here, for I am shining for them. Now as for their habitation, it is what will exist in this land forever. Moreover, guard 60 against those magicians / who know their spells, since (the god) Magic is himself therein. Now as for the one who ingests him, there I am. ⌐The guarding of me originated not through greatness; it originated even before

18. Or, "Your son am I."
19. Perhaps referring to the stars.
20. The realm of the dead.
21. Some discrepancies exist between the texts of these instructions and the inscriptions actually accompanying the picture of the cow.
22. I.e., in the earth, for Geb was the earth god.

me¹. I commend them²³ to your son Osiris. Keep watch over the youngest of them and cause the hearts of the oldest of them there to forget their magical power, they who act as they please against the whole world, using their magic which is in their bodies."

Then said the Majesty of this god, "Please summon Thoth to me." So he was brought immediately, and the Majesty of this god said to Thoth,
65 "Look, I am here in the sky in my abode. Since I / am going to produce the light of sunshine in the underworld and the Isle of the Twin *Bas*,²⁴ you shall do writing there and calm down ⌈for me⌉ those who are therein, beings of
70 our own making who fomented rebellion, ⌈namely⌉ the earth gods, / followers of this Irascible One.²⁵ You are to be in my place, my vicar. Thus you shall be called Thoth, the vicar of Re. Besides, I shall cause you to send out those who are greater than you." *And so the Ibis of Thoth came into being.* "Besides, I shall cause you to stretch out your hand in front of the primeval gods, who are greater than you; good is the ⌈gesture⌉ you shall make." *And so the Ibis-bird of Thoth came into being.* "Besides, I shall cause you to encompass both the heavens with your perfection and with your brightness." *And so the Moon of Thoth came into being.* "Besides, I shall cause you to drive back the Haunebut." *And so the Baboon of Thoth came into being. He is the one who then became vizier.* "Besides, as long as you are my vicar, the eyes of all who look at you are opened through you, and everyone²⁶ thanks you."

75 A man shall pronounce this text over himself, / rubbed down with olive oil and salve, while (holding) a censer containing incense in his hands. The backs of his ears should be cleansed with natron, and natron pellets should be in his mouth. As for his clothing, it should be two fresh linen garments after he has bathed himself in flowing water, and he should be shod with sandals of white leather. (The image of the goddess) Maat should be painted on his tongue in a scribe's fresh ink. If it is Thoth's intention to recite this for Re, he is to purify himself with a purification of nine days, and
80 human servitors should do / just the same.

As for one who recites this, if he carries out this procedure which is in this book, he increases his lifetime doublefold [...] of excess. His eyes will

23. The snakes.
24. Located in the underworld.
25. Probably the god Seth.
26. Or, "all that I have created."

be (of use) to him, and all his limbs will be (of use) to him. His steps will not go astray. It is said of him by people, "He is like Re on the day of his birth." His possessions cannot be diminished, nor can his gateway crumble. A successful method a million times!

Spell of ⌜this magical formulary⌝:[27]

When Nun was embraced by the Great One[28] himself, he told the gods who ascend in the east of the sky, "Give praise to the eldest god,[29] in whom / I originated! It is I who made the sky and set [it] in place in order to install the *ba*s[30] of the gods in it so that I am with them for the eternal recurrence (of time) produced through the years. My *ba* is Magic. It is (even) greater than this." Wind is the *ba* of Shu, and rain is the *ba* of Hehu.[31] Night is the *ba* of darkness, and Re is the *ba* of Nun. The ram of Mendes is the *ba* of Osiris, and crocodiles are the *ba*s of Sobek. The *ba* of each god (and each goddess) is in the snakes. The *ba* of Apopis is in the Eastern Mountain, whereas the *ba* of Re is in magic thoughout the whole world.

A man should say that he may make his protection through magic, "I am this pure Magic that is in the mouth and belly of Re. O gods, spirits, and the dead, keep away from me! I am Re, the radiant one."

You should say when you pass by in the evening at twilight, "Upon your face! You shall fall down, o enemy of Re! I am his *ba,* pure Magic," (and say), "O lord of Eternal Recurrence, who created Eternal Sameness, who makes the years of the gods to sweep by and in whom Re descends each day,[32] ⟨I⟩ am his god,[33] the ruler who created the one who created him and whom his fathers, the gods, love,[34] / while pure Magic is upon his head."[35]

27. Reading possibly *rȝ nʿ ftt tn* at the beginning of the hieratic version in Papyrus Turin 1982 (W. Pleyte and F. Rossi, *Papyrus de Turin,* 2 vols. [Leiden, 1869–76], Plate vol., pl. 84).

28. Re.

29. Nun.

30. The *ba* is a manifestation of power.

31. Hehu, whose name refers to the primordial flood waters, was one of the eight deities of the precreation chaos.

32. Variant: "in whom those who ascend descend each day."

33. The reciter identifying himself with Re. Or translate, "lord of his god," as an epithet of the god being addressed.

34. Or, "whom the fathers of the gods love."

35. Or simply "above him." Alternatively, this clause might be taken separately as a vocative, "O magician who is pure upon his head," heading the following impera-

Make a female figure, standing to the south of you, and draw a goddess upon her in the middle of her, and a snake standing erect upon its tail, with her hand upon its belly and its tail upon the ground. (Recite), "O you to whom Thoth gives praise while the dignity of heaven is upon you and toward whom Shu extends his arms, may you save me from those two great and mighty gods[36] who dwell in the east of the sky, who guard heaven and guard earth, and who are with enduring mysteries." Then they are bound to say, "How great he is when he goes forth to see Nun!"

Words recited after being purified on new crescent day and on half-month day in accordance with this ancient procedure. The one who recites this spell shall stay alive in the necropolis, and respect for him shall be greater than (for) those who are upon earth. If they ask, "What are your names?" (answer), "Eternal Recurrence and Eternal Sameness." Then they are bound to say, "[He is truly] a god," and to say, "He has reached us here by this route."

I know the name[37] of that god whose face is that of Arsaphes.[38] I am one to whom an amulet is affixed in the evening. I am Re / amid his Ennead, his entourage with magical power. I shall pass by uninjured, (for) I am one belonging to the flame, which is the *ba* of fire. I have no eradicators among men, gods, spirits, and the dead or in anything in this whole world.

Words spoken by these gods who have proceeded to life,[39] "The gods are to be informed so that their hands are at their faces and he is allowed to pass by upon the road." *And so the Flaming One came into being in the sky.*

As for any able scribe who knows the divine words that are in his mouth, he can ascend and descend within the sky. Those of the West cannot hold him back, nor can the saliva of his mouth become hot. His head cannot be removed by decapitation, nor does he (need to) bend his arms before the tribunal. He shall enter at the head of the spirits together with those who know the spells in the magical formulary. Not any crime that he may have committed upon earth can be reckoned. Moreover, his ⌜provi-

95

---

tives; but the divine determinative and previous mentions of "pure Magic" favor the first interpretation.

36. The two deities are probably Eternal Recurrence and Eternal Sameness.

37. Variant: "*ba.*"

38. The ram-headed god of Heracleopolis in whom the *ba*s of Re and Osiris are combined.

39. A euphemism for "have died."

sions[140] cannot be diminished, nor can a net be readied against him. Now as for the one whom you hand over[41] to any magistrate or to any spirit, it is he who must care for the one who has no food. His headcloth need not be taken off for the magistrates so that they regard him as leafy branches and as [...]. ... ⌈added to it.⌉ One shall not do anything harmful to him or ⌈retard⌉ [...].

(The text breaks off here.)

40. Or, "entrance"?
41. Or, "who hands you over."

# V

SONGS AND ROYAL HYMNS

# CYCLE OF SONGS IN HONOR OF
# SENWOSRET III

T his series of six songs, of which only the first four are well preserved, is part of the archive of papyri from Illahun. They were first published by F. Ll. Griffith, Hieratic Papyri from Kahun and Gurob (London, 1898), text, 1–3; pls. 1–3. The hieratic of the first four songs is reproduced in G. Möller, Hieratische Lesestücke (Leipzig, 1909), 1, pls. 4–5, and the hieroglyphic in K. Sethe, Ägyptische Lesestücke (Leipzig, 1924), 65–67. There is an analytical study and translation by Hermann Grapow: "Der Liederkranz zu Ehren Königs-Sesostris des Dritten aus Kahun," MIO 1 (1953): 189–209. More recently there is Hans Goedicke's valuable study with translations, "Remarks on the Hymns to Sesostris III," JARCE 7 (1968): 23–26. See also Jürgen Osing, "Zu zwei literarischen Werke des Mittleren Reiches," in J. Osing, ed., The Heritage of Ancient Egypt: Studies in Honor of Erik Iversen (Copenhagen, 1992), 101–20.

In the second, third, and fourth songs the lines after the first are indented, so that the first words are to be repeated at the beginning of the following verses. The first four are closely allied in subject matter and expression. Erman suggests that they were composed for the arrival of the king at a town south of Memphis. A related composition is The Loyalist Instruction studied by Georges Posener in his Littérature et politique, where these songs are also considered (127–30). Although they belong to religious (as opposed to secular) literature, the dividing line between the categories is not sharp. The songs embody ideas about the *nature of the kingship in the Middle Kingdom, and as examples of poetry they are of particular significance.*

W.K.S.

1.

I,1   The Horus Godlike of Transformations, the Two Ladies
      Godlike of Births, the Falcon of Gold Kheper, the King of
      Upper and Lower Egypt Khakaure, the Son of Re Sen-
      wosret who takes possession of the Two Lands as one
      vindicated:[1]

2     Salutations to you Khakaure, our Horus Godlike of
           Transformations,[2]
      Who has protected the land, and has extended its borders,[3]

3     Overwhelming the foreign lands with your crown,
      Enclosing the Two Lands with the deeds of your hands,

4     [Encompassing] the foreign lands with the strength of
           your arms,

5     Slaying the bowmen,[4] without striking a blow,
      Shooting an arrow, without drawing a bow.
      Terror of whom strikes the cave dwellers[5] in their land,

6     Fear of whom slays the nine bows.[6]
      Whose slaughtering causes thousands to die among the bar-
           barians,
      [And the enemies] who approach your borders.

1. The full five-part titulary of Senwosret III.
2. "Our" Horus is elsewhere unattested; the idea of "our king" is unusual but perhaps
   suits the context of a hymn addressed to the ruler by his people. Neteri-kheperu
   means "divine in respect to (his) transformations."
3. The song is set in the third person, lit. "one who protects the land, one who extends
   his borders." I have occasionally substituted "you" for "he" and "your" for "his" in
   accordance with English usage.
4. Foreigners from the north.
5. Probably Nubians in the south.
6. The traditional subjects or foes of the king, represented in statuary as bows beneath
   his feet. See E. Uphill, "The Nine Bows," *JEOL* 19 (1967): 393–420.

7    When shooting an arrow as Sekhmet does,[7]
        You fell thousands who know you not.

8    It is the tongue of your Majesty which restrains Nubia,
        It is your words which rout the Asiatics.

9    Unique divine being, youthful one, / [fighting] on your
            border,
        Not allowing your people to grow weary,

10    Letting men sleep until daybreak;
        Because your young troops were at their slumbers,
        And your heart was their protector,

11    Your commands have made your borders,
        And your word united the two river banks.

2.

II,1    How jubilant are [your gods],
        For you have made firm their offerings.

2    How jubilant are your citizens,
        For you have fixed their boundaries.

3    How jubilant are your fathers who came before,
        For you have increased their shares.

4    How jubilant are the Egyptians because of your might,
        For you have protected [their] traditions.

5    How jubilant are men with your counsel,
        For your might has won [their] /
           increase.

6    How jubilant are the two river banks in awe of you,
        For you have extended their portions.

7    How jubilant are your recruits,
        For you have brought them to manhood.

8    How jubilant are your honored old folk,
        For you have granted them youth.

9    How jubilant are the Two Lands because of your vigor,
        For you have protected their ramparts.

10    Its ⌜burden:⌝ Horus, who extends his border, may you re-
        peat eternity!

7. Sekhmet is the goddess of plague and warfare.

3.

11      How great is the Lord for his City!
        He is Re, and other rulers of men are insignificant.[8]

12      How great is the Lord for his City!
        Yea, he is a dam which holds back the river against
            its floodwaters.

13      How great is the Lord for his City!
        Yea, he is a cool place which lets every man sleep
            to daybreak.

14      How great is the Lord for his City!
        Yea, he is a rampart of walls of copper from Goshen.[9]

15      How great is the Lord for his City!
        Yea, he is a refuge ʿwhose bolt does not waver.ʾ

16      How great is the Lord for his City!
        Yea, he is a resting place which protects the fearful
            man from his enemy.

17      How great is the Lord for his City!
        Yea, he is a shade ʿinʾ the Inundation season, a cool
            place in Summer.

18      How great is the Lord for his City!
        Yea, he is a warm, dry corner in time of Winter.

19      How great is the Lord for his City!
        Yea, he is a mountain which wards off the stormwind
            at the time of tempest.

20      How great is the Lord for his City!
        Yea, he is Sekhmet against the enemies who tread
            upon [his] border.

8. This reading is owed to Goedicke; for "rulers," perhaps read "fathers."
9. The geographical term "Shesem" is used of the Sinai peninsula, a source for copper
   and turquoise. Through a later misreading the term comes to be represented in the
   Old Testament as Goshen, and I have therefore used it thus here.

4.

III, 1   He has come to us that he might take possession of the
       Southland,[10]
     in that the Double Crown be set upon his head.

2   He has come to us, he has tied together the Two Lands,
     in that he had joined the Sedge to the Bee.[11]

3   He has come to us, he has ruled the Egyptians,[12]
     in that he has placed the desert in his control.

4   He has come to us, he has protected the Two Lands,
     in that he has pacified the two banks of the river.

5   He has come to us, he has nourished the Egyptians,
     in that he has dispelled their poverty.

6   He has come to us, he has nourished the patricians,
     in that he has given breath to the throat of the
       populace.

7   He has come to us, he has trampled upon the foreign lands,
     in that he has beaten off the cave dwellers who know
       not the fear [of him].

8   He has come to us, he has [fought upon] his border,
     in that he has rescued one robbed [of his possessions].

9   He has come to us, his arms have [received] the honor
     Which his valor has brought us.

10   He has come to us, [he has seen to it that we have raised] our
     children
     And that we have buried our elders. . . .

10. The verse suggested to Erman that the songs were recited upon the triumphal entry
of the king to a city south of Memphis.
11. The sedge is the heraldic plant of the south, the bee emblematic of the north—hence
"to join Upper to Lower Egypt."
12. The people of Egypt, a term based on Kemet.

### 5.

1 . . . . . . . . .

2 May you love Khakaure,[13] who lives forever and ever . . .

3 ⌜He gives you nourishment,⌝ and rescues . . .

4 Our shepherd who knows how to give breath . . .

5 May you repay him with life and dominion millions [of times] . . .

### 6.

1 The praise of Khakaure, living forever and [ever] . . .

2 I raise sail on . . . . . .

3 Overlaid with electrum to . . . . . .

4 . . . the two river banks . . .

5 They have [lost] the way . . .

13. Or "may Khakaure love you," in which case the song is not addressed to the king. Indeed, the last two songs are probably not part of the cycle represented by the first four.

# THE LOVE SONGS
## AND THE SONG OF THE HARPER

T he love songs here translated date from the New Kingdom and were written in Late Egyptian. The songs were originally arranged in groups, the three major collections being found in Papyrus Harris 500 (British Museum 10060), Papyrus Turin 1996, and Papyrus Chester Beatty 1 (British Museum 10681). A few additional texts are also known from various hieratic ostraca. Alfred Hermann has listed a total of fifty-five individual songs plus a number of other fragments. The present translation, like the translation of W. K. Simpson in the earlier edition of this book, follows the numbering given by Hermann, although numbers 48 to 55 and the fragments have been omitted.

The love songs have seen a number of translations, many of which are listed in the general bibliography at the end of the book to which readers seeking other renditions are referred. I would mention here only the very interesting and useful work of Bernard Mathieu, La Poésie Amoureuse de l'Égypte Ancienne: Recherches sur un genre littéraire au Nouvel Empire (Cairo, 1996). This work contains the hieroglyphic text of the poems, a French translation, and a detailed grammatical analysis. In preparing this translation I have accepted certain of Mathieu's corrections and reconstructions while rejecting others.

Many of these texts are extremely difficult and their meanings are frequently very obscure. It is, therefore, likely that some of the passages are approximations of what the Egyptian text was intended to say, but I believe that the *following translation will at least convey the general spirit of what Egyptian love poetry essentially was. In a few cases I have taken certain liberties with the texts in order to create a more "romantic" English rendering, but for the most part I have attempted to provide a literal rendering of the Egyptian text. In referring to the object of their devotion, the Egyptians were accustomed to use the terms* sen *(brother) and* senet *(sister). In the following translations, I have preferred the use of the English terms "lover" and "beloved" as being more in keeping with the modern idiom.*

*The text of the Song of the Harper here translated was, for some unknown reason, inserted among the love poems of Papyrus Harris 500, between numbers 16 and 17. (So as not to break the unity of the love poems, I have placed it here at the very end.) An incomplete copy from the time of Akhenaten was also inscribed in the tomb of Paaten-em-heb at Saqqara. The text itself, the language of which is Middle Egyptian, claims to be from the tomb of an unidentified King Intef. A number of different Harper Songs are known, their themes being twofold: the sorrow associated with death, and the advice to enjoy the life of the present. The actual origin of Harper Songs is uncertain, but they do provide an interesting insight into the attitude of the ancient Egyptians toward the balance of life and death. For information on other treatments of this text, the reader is advised to consult the bibliography.*

V.A.T.

## THE LOVE SONGS OF PAPYRUS HARRIS 500[1]

1.

. . . . . . . . .

If I am not beside you, where will you set your desire?
If [you] do not embrace [me and seize] the moment,
[Whom will you] approach (for) pleasure?
But if you woo me to touch my breasts and my thighs,
[...]

---

1. The love songs of Papyrus Harris 500 are divided into three groups. At least one song at the beginning of the first group (nos. 1–8) and the title are missing. The second and third groups (nos. 9–16 and 17–19, respectively) have their titles preserved. The Song of the Harper is found between the second and third groups.

Would you depart because you have the urge to eat?
Are you a man who is devoted to his stomach?
Would [you depart] in your fine clothing,
While I am left with nothing but the bed sheets?

Would you leave me for the sake of drink² [...]?
Then take my breast, for its milk wells up for you.
More wondrous is a single day in your embrace [...]
Than a hundred thousand upon earth.

2.

Your love has merged completely with my body
As [... mingled] with water,
As a drug to which resin has been added,
As when milk is mixed with [water].

Make haste to see your beloved,
Like a horse in the open field,
Like a falcon [diving down] to its reeds,

For heaven has bestowed its love
Like the course of an arrow [...],
Like the swiftness of a falcon.

3.

(How) intoxicating are the plants of my garden!
[The lips] of my beloved are the bud of a lotus,
Her breasts are mandrakes,
And her arms are ornate [...].
Behold, her forehead is a snare of willow,
And I am a goose.
My [hands are in] her hair as a lure,
Held fast in the snare of willow.

2. Lit. "beer."

### 4.

My desire is not yet quenched by your love,
My wanton little jackal cub.
My lust for you I cannot forgo,
Though I be beaten and driven off
To dwell in the Delta marshes,
(Driven) to the land of Khor[3] with sticks and clubs,
To the land of Kush[4] with switches of palm,
To the high ground with rods,
Or to the low ground with branches.
I will pay no heed to their warnings
To abandon the one whom I desire.

### 5.

I am sailing downstream on the ferry,
(Guided) by the hand of the helmsman,
With my bundle of reeds on my shoulder.
I am bound for Ankh-Tawy,[5]
And I shall say to Ptah, the Lord of Ma'at,
"Grant me my beloved this night."

The river is wine,
Ptah is its reeds,
Sekhmet is its lotus leaf,
Iadet is its lotus bud,
Nefertum is its lotus flower.[6]

There is rejoicing as the land brightens in its[7] beauty;
Memphis is a bowl of mandrakes
Laid before the god who is beauteous of face.[8]

3. Syria-Palestine.
4. Nubia.
5. "Life of the Two Lands," a designation of the city of Memphis.
6. Ptah, Sekhmet, and Nefertum were the three deities who constituted the traditional Memphite divine triad. The connection of Iadet with Memphis is not very evident.
7. The suffix pronoun .st is feminine, but its translation as masculine appears more appropriate here.
8. The epithet "Beauteous of Face" was frequently applied to Ptah.

6.

I shall lie down in the house
And pretend to be ill.
Then my neighbors will drop in to see me,
And my beloved will come with them.
She will send the physicians away,
For (only) she understands my illness.

7.

The villa of my beloved:
The entrance to her (room) is at the heart of the house,
Her double doors are open,
Their bolt is unlatched,
And my beloved is angry.

If only I could be appointed as door keeper!
I would make her irate at me,
And so I would hear her voice when she is riled,
And I would make like a child in the face of her anger.

8.

I am sailing north on the Stream of the Ruler
And have entered the Stream of Pre.
I wish to go to prepare the pavilions
On the hill beside the canal.

I shall raise my sail to hasten unceasingly,
And my heart will remember Re.
Then I shall watch the entry of my lover,
As he approaches the park.

I shall stand beside you at the mouth of the canal,
So that you may carry off my heart to On of Re,
And I shall slip away with you
To the trees of the park.

I shall take (some leaves from) the trees of the park,
And these will be my fan.
I shall observe what my lover[9] does,
Though my gaze is fixed toward the garden.
My arms will be laden with persea boughs,
And my hair anointed with unguents.
I am the Noble One, Mistress of the Two Lands,
And I am [content].


The Beginning of the Songs of Pleasant Entertainment for Your Beloved,
the Chosen of your Heart, When She Comes from the Fields

9.[10]

My beloved, my cherished one,
My heart is in search of your love
And everything created for you.
I shall speak to you, that all I do may be open.

I have come to set my snare;
In my hand are my bird cage and my throw-stick.
All the birds of Punt[11] alight in Egypt, anointed with myrrh,
But the one who comes first seizes my lure.

His fragrance has come from Punt,
And his talons are covered with resin,
But my yearning is toward you.
Let us set him free together,
And I shall be alone with you.
I shall let you hear my voice
Lamenting over my (bird) anointed with myrrh.
How wonderful it would be if you were there with me
When I set my snare.
(How) pleasant it is for one who is cherished to go to the fields.


9. "My lover": lit. "he."
10. The following eight poems are recited by the lady.
11. Punt: a fabled area along the coast of Africa from where Egypt imported such goods
  as myrrh, incense, gold, ivory, and other luxury items.

10.

The cry of the goose calls out,
When he is trapped in the lure (set for) him.
(My) love for you restrains me,
And I know not how to undo it.

I shall gather up my nets,
But what shall I say to my mother
To whom I return every day
Burdened with my catch of birds?

I did not set my snare today,
For love of you has ensnared me.


11.

The goose soars up and alights;
It has plunged into the snare,
While many birds are circling around.
I hasten [away] but turn back again,
Held fast by love when I am alone.
My heart inclines toward your heart,
And I shall never be distant from your beauty.


12.

I shall go out [to seek my lover].
[I yearn] for your love,
And my heart stops within me.

To look at a sweet cake
Is like looking at salt;
Sweet pomegranate wine in my mouth
Is like the bitter gall of birds.

The breath of your nostrils
Is the sole thing which can revive my heart,
And I am determined that Amun will grant you to me
For ever and eternity.

13.

Oh beauteous youth, may my desire be fulfilled
[To become] the mistress of your house.
With your hands resting upon my breasts,
You have spread your love (over me).

I speak to my innermost heart
With the prayer that my lord may be with me this night.
I am like one who is in her tomb,
For are not you alone my health and my life?
[Your] touch [... brings] the joy of my well-being,
(The joy) of my heart seeking after you.

14.

The voice of the dove speaks, saying:
"The earth brightens;[12] whither are you going?"
Desist, bird, from prattling at me.

I found my lover on his bed,
And my heart was more than happy.
We said (to each other):
"Never shall I be parted (from you).
With my hand in yours,
I shall wander with you
Through all choice places."

He has chosen me as foremost of beauties,
And he will never wound my heart.

15.

I fix my gaze upon the outer door,
And behold, my lover comes to me.
My eyes are fixed upon the path, and my ears listen,
That I may throw myself into the arms of Pa-Mehy.[13]

12. I.e., the day dawns.
13. Lit. "That I may ambush Pa-Mehy." Pa-Mehy appears to be the name of the lover

I have set devotion to my lover as my only yearning,
My gaze directed only at him.

(But) my heart will not be still.
It has sent me a messenger swift of foot,
One which comes and goes,
To tell me that he has wronged me,
In brief, that he has found another,
And she is wondrous in his eyes.

But what of it!
Will the wiles of another drive me away?

16.

My heart recalled your love,
When only one side of my hair was arranged.
I went running off to seek you,
And see! I forgot all about my hair.

(But now) [...] I have adorned my hair,
So that I may be perfect at any time.[14]

The Beginning of the Songs of Entertainment

17.

(There are) blossoms of purslane (in my garden)![15]
My heart pursues you;
And I shall do for you whatever it demands.

That I may lie in your embrace
Is the (sole) prayer which shines in my eye.[16]

---

for whom the girl is waiting. See under S. Donadoni in love songs section of
bibliography.

14. The Song of the Harper is found at this point in Papyrus Harris 500. In order to
preserve the unity of the love songs, however, I have transferred it to the end.

15. The Egyptian term *mḫmḫ.wt* stands alone here without any connection to the following lines. The point of its use lies in the word play with the verb *mḫꜣ*, "to incline
toward" (here translated as "pursue") in the next line.

16. Lit. "which paints my eyes."

To gaze upon you brings brightness to my eyes
When I draw near to you to behold your love,
(For you are) the master of my heart.
How wondrous is this my hour!
May this hour extend for me into eternity.
Since I have slept with you,
You have exalted my heart.

Be there lamenting or be there rejoicing,
Do not abandon me!

18.

There are *sa'am* plants in (my garden),
And one becomes sublime in their presence.

I am your first beloved;
I belong to you like a plot of land
Which I have made to bloom
With flowers and every sweet herb.

Delightful is the canal there,
Dug by your hand to refresh us in the breeze,
A lovely place for strolling,
Your hand holding mine.
My body is aroused and my heart joyous,
As we wander together.

It is pomegranate wine for me to hear your voice,
And I live (only) to hear it.
If I gaze at you, with every glance
I am more refreshed than by eating and drinking.

19.

Thyme plants are in (my garden).
I shall remove your wreathes
When you come home drunk.
You will lie on your bed,

And I shall caress your feet.
The children in your [...][17]

### THE CAIRO LOVE SONGS[18]

#### 20.

My idol, my lotus,
[...] in the north wind [...]
It is sweet to go and approach [...]
The breeze [...]
[...] blooming [...]

My desire is to descend
And to bathe in your presence,
That I may let you look upon my beauty
In a tunic of finest royal linen
Besprinkled with perfume.

[...] I shall go down into the water with you,
And I shall come out to you bearing a red fish
Firmly held in my fingers,
And I shall lay it before you [...].
My beloved, come! Look upon me!

#### 21.

The love of my beloved is on yonder shore,
But the Nile would engulf my limbs,
For the waters are mighty at the time [of the flood],
And a crocodile lurks on the bank.

But I shall go down to the water
And plunge into the waves.
My heart is fearless on the flood,
And I have found that the crocodile is like a mouse
And the surface of the water like land to my legs.

17. The remainder of the text is too fragmented to yield any intelligible meaning.
18. The first poem, no. 20, is recited by the lady, and the others by her lover.

22.

It is her love which empowers me
And will be for me a spell against the water,
For I see my heart's beloved
Standing right before my face.

My beloved has come and my heart exults.
My arms open wide to embrace her,
And my heart is joyful within my breast[19]
Like a fish in its pond.

Oh night, you will be to me for eternity,
For my mistress has come to me.

23.

When I embrace her, her arms open wide before me ·
As if for one who (has returned) from Punt.
It is like a *misty* plant blooming in its fullness,
Whose perfume is that of laudanum.
Her lips open wide as I kiss her,
And I rejoice (even) without beer.

24.

What is the completion of preparing to make love?
Let Menqet be adorned there [...][20]
[...] her bed chamber.
Come, and I shall tell you.
Put fine linen on her body
While laying her bed with royal linen.
Be meticulous about white linen,
Adorn [...] her body,
Found like one sprinkled with perfume.

19. "Within my breast": lit. "in its (proper) place."
20. Translation highly uncertain. Menqet was the goddess of beer, and perhaps the text
    is suggesting that the bedchamber should be equipped with drink and other appro-
    priate items to add to the pleasure.

25.

Would that I were her Nubian maidservant
Who attends to her personal needs;[21]
[...] This would mean that the skin of her whole body
Would be exposed to me.

26.

Would that I were the launderer
Of my beloved's linen even for one month.
I would thrive by touching [the garments]
Which had been in contact with her body,
And it would be I who would wash out
The moringa oil from her clothing.
I would rub my limbs with her charms,
[I would be] joyful and jubilant,
And my body [would become] vigorous.

27.

Would that I were her signet ring
Which is upon her finger,
For I would see her love every day,
And it would be I who would touch her heart.

THE TURIN LOVE SONGS: SONGS OF THE ORCHARD[22]

28.

[The pomegranate tree says]:

My seeds are like her teeth,
My fruits are like her breasts;
[I am the first] of the trees of the orchard,
For I endure throughout every season.

21. Lit. "who is the attendant of her feet."
22. In each of the following three poems, the speaker is one of the trees of the garden.

All that is done by the beloved and her lover [I see],
When they are drunk on wine and pomegranate liquor,
And anointed with oil of moringa and balsam [...]

[Every last tree] except me vanishes from the field,
But I pass the (full) twelve months in the orchard.
When I begin to lose my bloom,
Last year's is (still) within me.

I am the first of my companions,
But I am regarded only as second.

If they do it again, I shall not be silent about them.
I shall tell it to her companion, and the deceit will be seen.
The beloved will be taught,
And she will no longer wrap her staff
With blossoming lotus [...], with lotus buds,
With sweet ointment [...], with strong beer, or with anything.

She will cause you to pass the day in pleasure,
In a shelter of reeds in a guarded place.

And now behold, it has finished aright.[23]
Come and entice him!
Cause him to pass the entire day enjoying[24] his hiding place.


29.

The sycamore fig has sent forth its voice;
Its leaves have come to say:

Cause [...] I have done [...] for my mistress,
For she is indeed a noble like myself.
Though you have no servants,
Yet I am your servant [brought from afar]
As a captive for my beloved.


23. I.e., what the pomegranate tree has spoken.
24. "Enjoying": the Egyptian reads literally "ruining" (*sjḏa*), but such makes little sense
within the context.

She caused me to be planted in her orchard,
But she gave me no [water when I needed] to drink,
Nor was my body filled with water from the waterskins.

They find me for pleasure,
[...] because of not drinking.
As my *ka* endures, my beloved,
Get yourself into my presence.

### 30.

The little sycamore which she planted with her own hand
Sends forth its voice to speak,
And the chatter which comes from its mouth
Is (like) a stream of honey.

It is beautiful, and its boughs are lovely;
It is verdant and flourishing,
Burdened down with notched figs
More crimson than red jasper.

Its leaves are like turquoise, and their hue like faience.
Its wood is like the tinge of feldspar,
And its resin is like the *besbes* draught.
It attracts him who is not under it,
For its shade is refreshing.

It put a message in the hand of a little girl,
The daughter of its orchard keeper,
And caused her to hasten to the beloved.

"Come and spend a moment among the girls,
For the countryside is at its best,
And there is a kiosk and a pavilion beneath me.
The gardeners will rejoice and revel like children
When they see you.

Have your servants sent on before you
Equipped with their utensils,
For I am drunk when hastening toward you
Without even taking a drink.

Give heed! Have them come bearing their equipment,
Bringing every kind of beer, all sorts of bread in abundance,
Vegetables, strong drink of yesterday and today,
And all kinds of fruit for enjoyment.

Come and pass the day in happiness,
Tomorrow, and the day after tomorrow,
Even for three days, sitting beneath my shade."

Her companion is on her right,
And she causes him to become drunk
While obeying what he says.
The beer house is riotous with drunkenness
All the while she is with her lover.

Her secret is safe with me,[25]
The beloved one in her adventures.[26]
I am discreet enough not to repeat what I have seen,
And I shall not say (even one) word.

## THE LOVE SONGS OF PAPYRUS CHESTER BEATTY I[27]

### The Beginning of the Poems of Great Delight

#### 31.
#### [FIRST STANZA]

My beloved is unrivaled,
There is none to equal her,
She is beautiful beyond all women.
Behold, she is like the star which appears
At the onset of a prosperous year.

---

25. Lit. "Her secret is beneath me." This translation of the line is uncertain and depends upon the reading of several hieroglyphs as a scribal error. However, the translation does fit the context.
26. Lit. "in her promenade."
27. In this collection of seven love songs, each poem, with the exception of the first, is designated by number: "First Stanza," "Second Stanza," etc. The first word and the last word of each stanza either repeats the number of that stanza or produces a word play based on that number. For example, in the second stanza, the term *senet*

Exquisite is her splendor,
Gleaning is her complexion,
Brilliant are her gazing eyes.
Sweet are her lips when they speak,
For she is not given to excessive speech.

High is her neck,
Resplendent are her breasts,
Of pure lapis lazuli is her hair.
Her arms surpass (even) gold,
Like lotus flowers are her fingers.

Her buttocks are soft, her waist is slender,
And her thighs extend her beauty.
(So) charming are her movements as she strolls on the earth
That she seizes my heart in her embrace.

She causes the necks of all men to turn to watch her,
And everyone rejoices who embraces her,
For he is first among (all) lovers.

When she goes outside, she is revealed
As that goddess without rival.

### 32.

#### SECOND STANZA

My lover enkindles my heart by his voice,
Causing yearning for him[28] to seize me.
Though he is the neighbor of my mother's house,
I am unable to go to him.

---

("second") is picked up in the word *sen* ("brother," "lover") which occurs at the
beginning and at the end. The fifth (*djut*) stanza begins with the word "praise" (*dua*)
and ends with the word "five" (*dju*). The poems are recited alternatively between the
lover and his beloved, the odd numbered songs assigned to the male, and the even
numbered ones to the lady. A modern version of this collection was produced by
Ezra Pound on the basis of earlier translations.

28. "Yearning for him": lit. "illness."

Wise is my mother in commanding me:
"Give up looking after such things!"

Behold, my heart is tormented when it remembers him,
For love of him takes hold of me.
Behold, he is senseless,
But yet I am exactly like him.

He knows nothing of my desire to embrace him
Or that he should contact my mother.
Oh my beloved! I have been fated for you
By the Golden Goddess of women.

Come to me, that I may see your beauty,
And my father and mother will be happy.
All my people will rejoice together because of you,
They will rejoice because of you, my beloved.

## 33.

### THIRD STANZA

My heart was unable to see her beauty[29]
While I was sitting within her house.

Then I met Mehy on a chariot
On the road with his lusty youths,
And I did not know if I could prevail before him,
Or if I could just pass casually by him.

But behold, the river is like a road,
And I do not know any place for my feet.
Oh my heart, you are not the brightest!
Why would you (think to) pass by Mehy?

Behold, if I pass in front of him,
I would tell him of my perplexity.
"Look! I am yours!" I would say to him,
And he would bellow out my name.

29. Or, "My heart was intent on seeing her beauty."

But (then) he would assign me
To the coterie[30] of the headman of his followers.

### 34.

#### FOURTH STANZA

My heart swiftly betakes itself to flight
Since I have remembered my love for you.

It does not permit me to walk like an ordinary person,
But leaps from its proper place.
It does not permit me to put on a dress,
Nor can I don my mantle.

I put no makeup on my eyes
Nor anoint myself in any way.
"Do not delay! Go straight to (his) house!"
So it says to me each time I think of him.

Do not create folly for me, my heart.
Why do you act like a fool?
Sit quietly, and your lover will come to you,
And many others as well.

Do not let people to say about me,
"She is a woman distraught by love."
Be strong each time you remember him;
Oh my heart, do not take flight!

### 35.

#### FIFTH STANZA

I worship the Golden Goddess,
I adore Her Majesty,
I exalt the Mistress of heaven,
I make praises for Hathor
And acclamation for my Mistress.

30. "Coterie": or perhaps "harem."

I appeal to her that she may hear my petitions,
That my Mistress may grant (my beloved) to me.
She has come of her own accord to see me;
A wonderful thing it is which has befallen me!

I am joyful, I exult, I have become sublime,
Since it was announced, "Ah! Behold! It is she!"
Behold, she has come, and the young men bow down
Through the extent of (their) love for her.

I shall sing praises to my Goddess,
That she may grant me my beloved as a boon.
It has been three days yesterday
Since (I made) my petitions in her name,
And it has been five days since she left me.

### 36.
#### SIXTH STANZA

I passed near his house
And found his door open,
My lover standing beside his mother,
And all his brothers and sisters with him.

Love for him seizes the hearts
Of all who pass by on the road.
Oh excellent youth! Without equal!
Outstanding in character!

He gazes at me whenever I pass by,
And I keep my joy to myself.
How with bliss is my heart delighted,
For my lover is in my sight.

Would that my mother knew my desire,
And that (the same desire) had now entered into her!
Golden Goddess! Oh establish him in her heart!
Then shall I hasten to my lover.

I shall kiss him in the presence of his family
And not be embarrassed by the people.
I shall rejoice because they are aware
That he has been intimate with me.

I shall celebrate festivals for my Goddess,
My heart leaps to burst forth (from my breast)
And to let me gaze upon my lover tonight.

How happy (I am) in thus passing by!

## 37.

### SEVENTH STANZA

It is seven days yesterday that I have not seen my beloved!
Affliction has spread throughout me,
My limbs have become heavy,
And I have forgotten my own body.

Even if the foremost physicians were to attend me,
My heart would not be soothed by their medicines.
As for the magicians, there are no resources in them,
And my affliction cannot be cured.

Only (if someone were to) say to me,
"Look! It is she!" would revive me,
For her name alone can refresh me.
The coming and going of her messengers
Is the one thing which can revive my heart.

More beneficial to me than all medicines is my beloved,
She is better than all medical skill.
My healing is her coming in to me;
(Let me but) see her, and then I will be healthy.

Let her open her eyes, and my body will be vigorous,
Let her speak, and I shall be firm.
When I embrace her, she banishes (all) ill from me.
But it has been seven days since she left me.

## THE CHESTER BEATTY CYCLE OF THREE SONGS

### 38.

Would that you might come in haste to (your) beloved
Like the messenger of the king,
When the heart of his master is eager for his messages,
And his desire is set upon hearing them.

The stables are totally at his disposal,
There are horses for him at the relay point,
The chariot is ready at its place,
And he has no rest on the journey.
He has arrived at the home of the beloved,
(And now) his heart rejoices.

### 39.

Would that you might come (to me) like the horse of a king,
The choicest of a thousand from all the steeds,
The boast of the stables.

It is given special treatment in its feeding,
And its master knows its stride.
If it hears the sound of the whip,
It knows no turning back,
And there is no captain in the chariotry
Who can master it.

How well the heart of (his) beloved knows
That he can never be distant from her!
Would that you might come in haste to (your) beloved
Like a gazelle bounding across the desert.
Its feet move swiftly, and its limbs are weary,
And fear is spread throughout its body,
For a hunter is in pursuit of it, and a dog with him,
Though they cannot see it for the dust.
It spies a place of rest [in the reeds]
And takes the river as a path.

You must make your way right up to her gateway
That your hand may be kissed four times,
For you are pursuing the affections of your beloved,
And it is the Golden Goddess who has destined her for you.

## THE NAKHT-SOBEK SONGS FROM PAPYRUS CHESTER BEATTY I

The Beginning of the Delightful Verses
Found in a Box of Manuscripts
Written by the Scribe Nakht-Sobek of the Necropolis

### 41.

Now you shall bring it[31] to the house of (your) beloved
And go as far as her portal.
Her chamber will be open (for you),
And her housemaid will have prepared it.

Provide her with songs and dances,
Wine and strong beer in her pavilion.
You will arouse her passions
And fulfill them during this night.

She will say to you,
"Take me into your embrace."
And when the dawn comes,
She will still be there.[32]

### 42.

Now you shall bring it to the chamber of (your) beloved,
Alone, no other (with you),[33]
And you will accomplish your desire in her [embrace].[34]

31. There is no indication as to what the pronoun "it" (*sw*) refers. Perhaps some magic spell or charm is indicated.
32. Lit. "It will be the same."
33. Or, "When she is alone and without another (with her)."
34. The meaning of the term *ḫg3i,* here translated as "embrace," is uncertain. It may in fact refer to a specific part of the female body.

The curtains will flutter,
And the sky will descend in a gale of wind.
(Hathor) will bring you her fragrance,
And its perfume will overwhelm and intoxicate
All those who are present.

It is the Golden Goddess
Who destines her for you as a boon
To let you fulfill the span of your life.

### 43.

How skilled is my beloved in throwing the snare,
Although a breeder of cattle did not beget her.
With her tresses she throws the snare at me,
With her eyes she entraps me,
With her necklace she binds me,
And with her signet ring she brands me.

### 44.

Although you say within your heart,
"After her! It is my lot to embrace her!"
As Amun lives, I have come to you
With my mantel on my shoulder.

### 45.

I found my lover at the canal
With his feet standing in the river.
He was setting up an offering table for the festival
Marked by (the drinking of) beer.
He brings a blush to my cheeks,
For his height is in perfect proportion to his breadth.

46.

As for what my beloved has done to me,
Shall I be silent about it?
To make me stand at the door of her house
While she went inside!
She did not tell me, "You are welcome to come in,"
And so she cheated me of my night.


47.

I passed by her house in the darkness,
I knocked, but no one opened to me.
Perhaps our doorkeeper was enjoying a good night's sleep!

Oh door bolt, I will open (you)!
Oh lock, you are my fate,
You are my guiding spirit,
And our ox will be butchered for you inside.
Oh lock, do not use your strength.

An ox will be sacrificed to the door bolt
A short-horned ox to the door pin,
A fatted goose to the doorposts,
And its fat to the key.

All the choice parts of our ox
Will be for the carpenter lad
That he may make for us
A door bolt of reeds and a lock of straw.

Then any time when the lover comes,
He will find her house open.
He will find the bed laid out with fine linen
And a beauteous maiden in it.

And the maiden will say to me,
"This lodging is for the son of the mayor of the city.

## The Song of the Harper

The song which is in the chapel of King Intef,[35] justified in front of the singer with the harp:

> Fortunate is this prince,
> For happy was his fate, and happy his ending.
>
> One generation passes away and the next remains,
> Ever since the time of those of old.
> The gods who existed before me rest (now) in their tombs,
> And the blessed nobles also are buried in their tombs.
> But as for these builders of tombs,
> Their places[36] are no more.
> What has become of them?
>
> I have heard the words of Imhotep and Hardedef,[37]
> Whose maxims are repeated intact as proverbs.
> But what of their places?
> Their walls are in ruins,
> And their places are no more,
> As if they had never existed.
>
> There is no one who returns from beyond
> That he may tell of their state,
> That he may tell of their lot,
> That he may set our hearts at ease
> Until we make our journey
> To the place where they have gone.
>
> So rejoice your heart!
> Absence of care is good for you;

35. The name "Intef" belonged to a number of kings in the Eleventh and Seventeenth Dynasties, but there is no indication as to which specific Intef is meant here.
36. The term "places" refers to the cult chapels of the individuals in question.
37. Imhotep was a famous Old Kingdom sage and the architect of the Step Pyramid of King Djoser of the Third Dynasty. There is, however, no known text written by him. Prince Hardedef was the son of King Cheops of the Fourth Dynasty. There exists a fragment of an Instruction which bears the name of Hardedef, although in all likelihood the work dates from the time of the Fifth Dynasty and is, therefore, pseudepigraphical.

Follow your heart as long as you live.
Put myrrh on your head,
Dress yourself in fine linen,
Anoint yourself with the exquisite oils
Which are only for the gods.[38]

Let your pleasures increase,
And let not your heart grow weary.
Follow your heart and your happiness,
Conduct your affairs on earth as your heart dictates,
For that day of mourning will (surely) come for you.
The Weary-Hearted[39] does not hear their lamentations,
And their weeping does not rescue a man's heart from the grave.

*Refrain:*
Enjoy pleasant times,
And do not weary thereof.
Behold, it is not given to any man to take his belongings with him,
Behold, there is no one departed who will return again.

38. Lit. "Anoint yourself with the true wonders which belong to a god."
39. "Weary-Hearted": a title of the god Osiris.

# VI

ROYAL STELAE

# THE SEMNA STELA

T*his boundary stela was placed at the southern "border" of the Second Cataract region in Nubia where the Middle Kingdom fortresses of
Semna and Kumma were erected on opposite banks of the river, partly
to control passage on the Nile northward to Nubia and Egypt proper. It is
of brown quartzite and an impressive 1.60 meters in height (Berlin Museum
1157). The statement of the king is a rare literary autobiographical exhortation
to his subjects. See bibliography, especially Eyre 1990. Beneath a winged sun
disk labeled twice Behdet (the Lower Egyptian locality sacred to Horus) are
twenty-one lines of text, of which the first two with the five-part titularly of
Senwosret III are in larger hieroglyphs.*

W.K.S.

(1) Live the Horus Divine of Manifestations, He of the Two Ladies Divine
of Manifestations, King of Upper and Lower Egypt Khakaure, granted life,
(2) Live the Falcon of Gold Manifestations, the Son of Re of his body,
beloved of him, lord of the Two Lands Senwosret (III), granted life, en-
durance, and dominion forever.

(3) Regnal Year 16, third month of Proyet. His Majesty's making the southern boundary at Heh (Semna).

(4) I have made my border, having gone (farther) south than my ancestors. I gave (5) more than what was entrusted to me. I am a king who speaks and accomplishes. (6) What my mind plans is what takes place through my action. One aggressive to seize, swift to (achieve) (7) success. One who does not sleep (with) a matter on his mind, but who takes thought for the humble and stands for (8) mercy. One who is not lenient to the enemy who attacks him. Who attacks when he is attacked, but who desists when (he) is desisted. (9) Who answers a matter according to what transpires in it. Because, as for desisting after attacking, it is strengthening (10) the heart of the enemy.

Aggression is bravery, and to retreat is vile. (11) One who is driven back from his border is a real coward. For the Nubian listens only to fall at a word. It is responding to (12) him which makes him retreat; but if one is aggressive against him, he shows his back. Retreating, he tends toward aggression. (13) Indeed, they are not men of worth. They are wretched, broken hearted.

(14) My Majesty has observed this, without prevarication, for I have carried off their women and I have brought away (15) their inhabitants, coming forth to their wells, driving away their cattle, cutting down their grain, (16) and setting fire therein.

As my (divine) father lives for me, I speak in truth, there is not therein a word of (17) boastfulness which came from my mouth. Now indeed as for any son of mine who shall maintain this boundary (18) which I have established, he is my son born to my Majesty, the model of a son, the protector of his (divine) father, (19) who causes the border of the one who begat him to flourish. But as for him who shall give it up and not fight (20) for it, indeed he is not my son, indeed he is not born to me. Moreover, indeed, my Majesty has caused the likeness of (21) my Majesty to be made upon this border which my Majesty made, so that you will maintain it and so that you will fight for it.

# THE NEFERHOTEP STELA

The stela of Neferhotep I of Dynasty 13, found and copied by Mariette at
Abydos, was apparently transported to the Boulaq Museum in Cairo
and then lost sight of. Its present location is unknown. Neferhotep I is
considered the twenty-second king of Dynasty 13 and credited with a reign of
eleven years in the Turin Royal Canon. The family is discussed in Michel
Dewachter, "Le roi Sahathor et la famille de Neferhotep I," RdE 28 (1976): 66–
73, and Labib Habachi, "New Light on the Neferhotep I Family, as Revealed by
Their Inscriptions in the Cataract Area," in W. K. Simpson and W. M. Davis,
eds., Studies in Ancient Egypt, the Aegean, and the Sudan: Essays . . . Dun-
ham (Boston, 1981), 77–81. Mariette's text was studied in detail and various
possible corrections were made by Pieper in 1929. The standard version is
Wolfgang Helck, Historisch-Biographische Texte der 2. Zwischenzeit und
Neue Texte der 18. Dynastie, 2nd rev. ed. (Wiesbaden, 1983), No. 32, 21–29.

Although the text is somewhat disjointed from our perspective, several
elements are clear. The king, apparently in the north at his Residence, desires to
fashion or refashion an image of Osiris for use in the religious drama enacted
each year at Abydos. He seeks out the plans and designs for this image in the
library and boasts of his personal success in this. He sends one of his officials
south to Abydos, and upon the official's return, the king himself apparently
journeys to Abydos to celebrate the ritual, which includes a procession and the
enactment of the drama in which actors attack the god's vessel and are driven

*off. The king boasts of his own supervision of the work on the divine image. The sequence of events is not entirely clear.*

W.K.S.

The round top stela has in its lunate the winged sun disk with uraei and the label: *Behdet, the great god, lord of the sky.* Beneath this is the king's titulary in equally large hieroglyphs: *The Horus: Founder of the Two Lands, King of Upper and Lower Egypt Kha-sekhem-Re, Son of Re Neferhotep, beloved of Osiris-Foremost-of-the-Westerners, Lord of Abydos, The Falcon of Gold: Lasting of Love, King of Upper and Lower Egypt Kha-sekhem-Re, Son of Re Neferhotep, beloved of Osiris-Foremost-of-the-Westerners, Lord of Abydos.*

Below the lunate are forty lines of text.

1      Regnal Year 2 under the Majesty of the Horus: Founder of the Two Lands, He of the Two Ladies: Revealing the Truth, Falcon of Gold: Lasting of Love, King of Upper and Lower Egypt Kha-sekhem-Re, Son of Re Neferhotep, born to the king's mother Kemi, granted life, stability, and dominion like Re forever.

The appearance of the king upon the Horus throne in the palace (called) Exalted of Beauty.

His Majesty said to the nobles and the Companions who were in his retinue, the scribes loyal to hieroglyphs and those who were in charge of all confidential matters: My heart wishes to see the primeval writings of Atum.[1] Unroll for me the Great Inventory. Let (me) know the god in his essence and the Ennead in its nature that (I) may offer to them divine offerings and offer breads upon the altars so that I might know the god in his forms, that I might fashion him according to his first time. For it is in order to effectuate their monuments upon earth and that they might grant me the inheritance of Geb,[2] being (precisely) all which the sun disk encompasses, that they have made me their protector. My office as head of the land has been given

5      ⟨to me⟩, / for he (the god) knows the rectitude of my wisdom. I gave more than was entrusted to me. It was because of their desire that one act according-ing to what they command that they gave (it) to me.

---

1. For a king searching the archives (Ramesses II), see Mahmud Abd el-Razik, *JEA* 60 (1974): 144; *JEA* 61 (1975): 125.
2. Geb is the earth god.

These Companions then said: What your *Ka* decrees is what will come to pass, Sovereign, Lord. May your Majesty proceed to the Libraries (houses of writings) that your Majesty may see all the hieroglyphic writings.

So his Majesty proceeded to the Library. Then his Majesty unrolled the writings together with these Companions. Thereupon his Majesty found the writings of the Temple of Osiris-Foremost-of-the-Westerners, Lord of Abydos.

Then his Majesty said to these Companions: My Majesty will protect my father, Osiris-Foremost-of-the-Westerners, Lord of Abydos, that I may fashion him together with his Ennead, as my Majesty has observed in his writings. It was as he issued from the womb of (the goddess) Nut that his form was made as King of Upper and Lower Egypt. I am his son, his protector, his seed who came forth as master of his Broad Hall, to whom Geb gave his inheritance about which the Ennead is content, I being in his great office which Re granted, an effective son who fashions him who fashioned him.

10 / I will say something important, and I will have you hear it,[3] that you may open the heart so that it might live thereon, for I will have you know a righteous life in the manner of one who endures on the earth, making monuments for Osiris and perpetuating the renown of Wenennefer. If this is done, it will be beneficial for the land and it shall be made effective for every land.

I am the one who is in the thoughts of his father Re, the lord of that which exists and that which does not exist, one whom the gods made effective (even) in the womb when he (I?) came forth designated as King of Upper and Lower Egypt, the crown of the south having being manifest on his (my?) head, as he (I?) ruled the entire Ennead.

Then these Companions said: As for those who are in [the sky], they grant what your heart desires, and what your Majesty decrees comes to pass. Then his Majesty had the Custodian of the Royal Property[4] who was in his retinue summoned to him, and he said to him: Journey southward together with a crew of sailors. Do not sleep night nor day until you reach Abydos. Cause Foremost-of-the-Westerners to proceed, for I will make his monuments as at the time of creation.

3. The same phrase in The Loyalist Instruction II, 8.
4. Note that in this "royal" stela the individual is not named, in contrast to the "private" stela of Iykhernofret.

Then these Companions said: How excellent is [what you have said, Sovereign], Lord, that you would make your [monuments] in Abydos for your father, Foremost-of-the-Westerners!

15     This official journeyed southward / according to that which his Majesty decreed for him. He arrived at [Abydos] at the appearance of [this god]. The Majesty of this god [proceeded] to the *neshmet*-barque "Mistress of Eternity" to [organize] his crossing and the river was greatly flooded with the scent of Punt.

They arrived at the Residence [...] and one went to report to his Majesty saying: This god has proceeded satisfactorily. His Majesty then proceeded [to] the god's barque, this [fleet] being equipped with the night-barque and transport boats, the king himself traveling at the front upon the canal to fraternize with this god and to cause divine offerings to be made to his father Foremost-of-the-Westerners: myrrh, wine, and divine products for Osiris-Foremost-of-the-Westerners in all his identities, which he set down for [this] god, pacifying the destroyers and turning back the rebel against the *neshmet*-barque.

Then the Majesty of this god was caused to appear, his Ennead assembled [in his company], while Wepwawet[5] was in front of him as he cleared the roads from his enemies. Then the Majesty of this god was caused to proceed to the shrine so that he came to rest in the workshop to fashion the beauties of his Majesty together with his Ennead, his altars being fashioned

20     with [bronze] and ornamented with every noble precious / stone of god's land.

Now [his Majesty] himself supervised their work [in silver], gold, and [copper], his Majesty being pure in the purification of the god in his [...] of Lord of the West. Now as for a stolist, scribe, or [craftsman] of the [workshop], who saw him at work [in] this temple [...]. Now as for his Majesty [who found] these writings himself, never had any scribe who was in his retinue found them! It was in confidence that the god placed these things in his heart like Osiris [Foremost-of-the-Westerners, Lord of Abydos].

For it was ordered [to him to be] while (still) in the egg. For he felled the rebels of your Majesty(?) that he might be praised day and night. For [he] grasped the enemies of your ship, annihilating the rebels in Ro-Poqer.[6]

5. Wepwawet is an important jackal-headed god connected with funerary rites, especially at Abydos. The name means "Opener of the Ways," and this function applies to the present context.

6. The site of the royal tombs of Dynasties 1 and 2 and the "tomb of Osiris" at Abydos.

He knows the gateways of the Netherworld and the gateways of the Fields of Reeds, his heart joyful with the calendrical offerings of the processions of every god on the *Wag*-festival, the Thoth-festival and an eternity of years therein.

> Your effective son, beside whom there is none like Horus,
>> As this son avenges his father.
> Your offspring who provisions your offering tables,
>> Who makes pleasant the scent of your temple.
> Uncover the Great Throne,
>> / Open the Great Shrines of him who made him.

25

He stands up as king, possessing an eternal time upon [earth], that he might [prosper] like the heavens, that he might be stable like the earth, that he might pass eternity like Neheb-kau[7] therein. May the hearts of your priests be joyful when they offer to his statues. [The hearts of those who praise you] are joyful, making acclamation to his [images], the King of Upper and Lower Egypt, Kha-sekhem-Re, Son of Re Neferhotep, living forever and ever, born to the king's mother Kemi, the vindicated.

Then his Majesty said: I will make recitations for you while driving off the rebels on the road of [Ro-Poqer. I will make] jubilation [for you and praise] on the road of god when you (the god) arrive at Abydos in joy. The magistrates will be in front of you. The enemies will be pacified for you and the arms of the evildoers brought low for you [...] in Abydos, in the evening of night offerings, you shall be vindicated in the Broad Hall, your subjects in exultation, your adherents in joy, since I have opposed the rebels against your Majesty, just as I have appeased the heart of [my father Osiris-Foremost-of-the-Westerners, Lord of Abydos], for god loves the one who loves him, in whose (your) heart is all that I do.

You make my memorials effective in your temple, and you let me be in / the following of your Majesty. [You] fulfill my [contract] (or: you strengthen my arm) in praise. Let there be given to me the arms of the priests in the procession at the great altar that they may remember me with a good remembrance, that they may respect those who pronounce my name, that they may rejoice in allowing me to live, that they may wish the giving of praise to me at the seasons of this shrine through that which a father transmits to his son when he becomes a *wab*-priest of this god, his

30

7. Alan H. Shorter, "The God Nehebkau," *JEA* 21 (1935): 41–48.

rod of old age, guarding the property of his inheritance. Then shall he be firm upon his throne.

Hear this. Repeat what I command. Indeed, one makes memorials by perpetuating the primeval times of the gods. Behold me having [you] learn, for I am before you. Be vigilant for the temple. Gaze at, pray, the memorials which I have made. I shall have ⟨you⟩ learn about eternity according to my desire—that I might seek out what is beneficial for the future in placing this matter in your hearts, it being about to happen within this place (Abydos).

35 God has accomplished it at my behest / to make effective my memorials in his temple, to fulfill my contracts in his house. His Majesty desires what I have done for him and he is rejoicing in what I ordained to be done. Vindication was awarded to him.

I am his son, his protector. He gives me the inheritance of one upon the earth. I am a king, great of strength, effective of utterance. He who defies me shall not live.[8] My opponent shall not draw breath. His name shall not be among the living. His *Ka* shall be bound before the nobles and he shall be (cast) out before this god as one who opposes what my Majesty commands, they who will not act according to this decree of my Majesty, they who will not raise me up to this noble god, they who will not be favorable to what I have done with his offerings, they [who will not] grant me praise at the festival of this shrine within this entire temple of this shrine and every office of Abydos.

Indeed, my Majesty has made these memorials for my father Osiris-
40 Foremost-of-the-Westerners, Lord of Abydos, / inasmuch as I love him more than all the gods.

He gives me a reward [for] these [monuments of mine (namely) a lifetime] of millions of years. The reward of the doer lies in what he has done: it is Maat in the opinion of god.

8. For threats and curses, see Scott Morschauser, *Threat Formulae in Ancient Egypt: A Study of the History, Structure and Use of Threats and Curses in Ancient Egypt* (Baltimore, 1991).

# THE KAMOSE TEXTS

T*he text of Kamose's "wars of liberation" is divided between two stelae set up at Karnak, the first extant in a few fragments and the second discovered in 1954 as the base for a statue of Ramses II. A larger section of the text of the first stela was first discovered on a writing board. The main* studies are: Labib Habachi, The Second Stela of Kamose and His Struggle against the Hyksos Ruler and His Capital *(Glückstadt, 1972); A. H. Gardiner,* "The Defeat of the Hyksos by Kamose: The Carnarvon Tablet No. 1," JEA 3 *(1916): 95–110; Wolfgang Helck,* Historisch-Biographische Texte der 2. Zwischenzeit und Neue Texte der 18. Dynastie, 2nd rev. ed. *(Wiesbaden, 1983), 82–98. A penetrating and careful analysis is presented by H. S. Smith and Alexandrina Smith,* "A Reconsideration of the Kamose Texts," ZÄS 103 *(1976): 48–76, to which the following translation is indebted in many instances. The narrative is frequently in the first person and exhibits marked literary aspects. There are several terms for Asiatics, the designation Aamu is translated as Asiatic and the term Setiu left untranslated. Several places are cited in the text and have been located, as far as possible, on the accompanying map.*

W.K.S.

## CARNARVON TABLET TEXT

Regnal Year 3 (of) the Horus: He who has appeared upon his throne; The Two Ladies: Repeating of Monuments; The Golden Falcon: He who contents the Two Lands; King of Upper and Lower Egypt [Wadj-kheper-Re Son of Re] Kamose the valiant, granted life, beloved of Amun-Re, Lord of the Thrones of the Two Lands like Re, forever and ever. The victorious King within Thebes, Kamose the valiant, given life forever, is the effective King. It is Re [who has placed him] as King, himself, to whom he has given victory in very truth.

His Majesty spoke in his palace to the council of officials which was in his following: To what effect do I perceive it, my might, while a ruler is in Avaris and another in Kush, I sitting joined with an Asiatic and a Nubian, each man having his (own) portion of this Egypt, sharing the land with me. There is no passing him as far as Memphis, the water of Egypt. He has possession of Hermopolis, and no man can rest, being deprived by the levies of the Setiu. I shall engage in battle with him and I shall slit his body, for my intention is to save Egypt, striking the Asiatics.

The officials of his council (then) spoke: Indeed, it is the water (the area of influence) of the Asiatics as far as Cusae. And (then) they drew in their tongues in unison: We are content with our (part of) Egypt. Elephantine is firmly in our control, and the middle section is with us as far as Cusae. The finest of the fields are ploughed for us, and our cattle graze in the Delta. Emmer is sent for our swine. Our cattle are not taken away, and [...] are not pillaged from the (encampments?). He possesses the land of the Asiatics, (but) we possess Egypt. Should one who acts against us come, then we shall act against him.

They (these words) were disturbing in the heart of His Majesty. As for your counsels [...]. Dividing the land with me is not tolerable for me. [...] the Asiatics (allied?) with him. I shall sail northwards to do battle with the Asiatics, and success will come to pass. If he intends to be at ease in ..., then his eyes will be about to weep, and the entire land [will say]: the ruler within Thebes, Kamose the valiant, is the protector of Egypt.

By the command of Amun, astute of counsel, I sailed north to my victory to drive back the Asiatics, my courageous army in front of me like a flame of fire, with the bowmen of the Medjai upland of our encampment (ready) to seek out the Setiu and to destroy their dwellings, the eastern

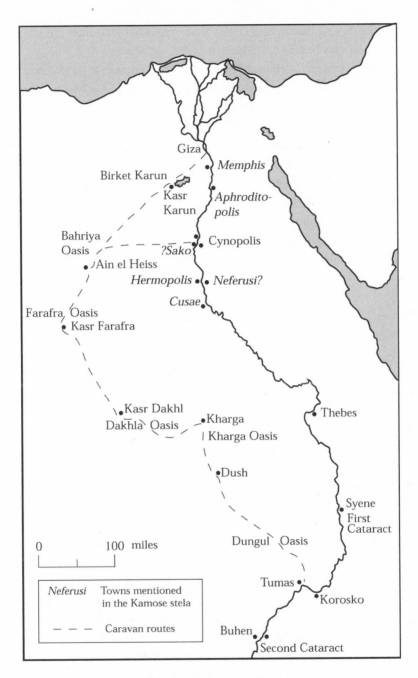

Giza

*Memphis*

Birket Karun

Kasr
Karun

*Aphrodito-
polis*

Bahriya
Oasis

?*Sako*

Cynopolis

●Ain el Heiss

*Hermopolis*

*Neferusi?*

Farafra Oasis

*Cusae*

●Kasr Farafra

●Kasr Dakhl

Dakhla Oasis

●Kharga

| Kharga Oasis

●Thebes

●Dush

Syene
First
Cataract

Dungul Oasis

Tumas ●

0          100 miles

Buhen

Korosko

| *Neferusi* | Towns mentioned
in the Kamose stela |
| - - - | Caravan routes |

Second Cataract

Map 1. Sites mentioned in the Kamose texts

desert lands and the western desert lands provided with their fat and my army being supplied with produce from their dwellings.

While I was on watch near Wahyt(?), I sent a mighty patrol of Medjai to confront Teti son of Pepi within Neferusy without letting him flee, and I confined the Asiatics who were defying Egypt, for he had made Neferusy as a nest for the Asiatics. It was with my heart at ease that I spent the night in my boat. When dawn came, I was upon him as if I were a falcon, and when the time of midday meal had come, I had driven him back and had destroyed his walls and had slain his people. I had his wife (women) go down to the shore. As lions are with their prey, so was my army with (their) servants, cattle, milk(?), fat and honey, in dividing up their property, their hearts joyful. The region of Nefer[usy] was in retreat, and it was not an important matter for us to enclose Tibasepa. Per-Shaq was in flight when I reached it, their chariot teams fled inside, the patrols ... being remembered(?) at the valley(?) ... their property. He ...

(End of text of the Carnarvon Tablet.)

## THE SECOND STELA

a miserable report within your town. You are driven back in the presence of your (own) army. Your speech is despicable in making me out to be (only) an official while you are a ruler, only to beg for yourself the chopping block by which you will fall. Your (own) miserable back is seen, while my army is at your (own) back. The women of Avaris will not conceive, for their hearts will not open within their bodies when the battle cry of my army is heard.

I moored at Per-djed-qen, my heart joyful. I made Apopi see a miserable moment, the prince of Retenu, weak in action, who planned brave deeds in his heart which did not come to pass for him.

I arrived at the southward-bound landing place, and I crossed over to them to address them. Having placed prow to stern, I set the fleet deployed one (ship) after another, with my forces flying over the river like a falcon, my (own) ship of gold at the front thereof like a falcon before them, setting the brave fleet to thrust as far as the desert edge, the remainder (of the fleet) behind it, as if a carrion bird were preying upon the region of Avaris.

I espied his women upon his palace looking out from their embrasures toward the shore, and their bodies did not move when they saw me. They looked out from their loopholes on their walls like young lizards within their burrows, saying: It is an attack.

See, I have come for I am fortunate. The rest is in my hand, and my cause will be effective. As Amun the valiant endures, I will not let you alone, I will not let you tread the ground without my being upon you. May your heart quake thereat, O miserable Asiatic. See, I am drinking the wine of your (own) vineyard which the Asiatics whom I have captured (have been forced to) press for me. I have destroyed your dwelling place, I have cut down your orchards. I have carried off(?) your women to the holds (of the ships) and I have seized the chariot teams. I have not spared a plank of the three hundred ships of new cedar filled with gold, lapis lazuli, silver, turquoise, and copper axes without number, aside from moringa oil, incense, unguents, honey, willow, *sesnedjem*-wood, *sepny*-wood, and all precious woods, and all fine products of Retenu. I took them away entirely. I did not leave anything of Avaris for it was emptied out, O unfortunate Asiatic. Let your heart quake thereat, O miserable Asiatic, who used to say: I am a lord without equal as far as Hermopolis, and as far as the Temple of Hathor.

My intention(?) is to control Avaris between the two rivers. I will leave them laid waste without people there. I destroyed their towns, I burned their abodes, being made into desolate mounds forever because of the destruction which they made within (this part of) Egypt, for they set themselves to hearken to the summons of the Asiatics, having betrayed Egypt, their mistress.

For it was on the upland way of the oasis that I captured his messenger going south to Kush with a written letter. I found on it saying in writing: From the ruler of Avaris, Aa-user-re. Son of Re Apopi, greetings to the son of the ruler of Kush: Why have you arisen as ruler without letting me know? Do you see what Egypt has done against me? The ruler who is in it, Kamose the valiant, given life, attacks me on my soil, although I have not attacked him in the manner of all he has done against you, for he chooses the two lands to afflict them, my land and yours, and he has devastated them. Come northward, do not blench, for he is here with me, and there is no one who can stand up to you in (this part of) Egypt. See, I will not give him a way until you arrive. Then we shall divide the towns of Egypt, and both our fine lands(?) shall be in joy.

Wadj-kheper-Re (Kamose), given life, who controls occasions: I have placed the deserts and the front of the land in my control, and the rivers likewise, and one cannot find any way of overthrowing me. I am not lazy with my army. The one north of me has not seized, for he was fearful of me while I fared north, before we had yet fought. Before I reached him, he saw my flame, and he had sent (a letter) as far as Kush to seek out his protection. But I captured it on the way. I did not let it arrive. Then I let it be taken back to him; it was placed upon the eastern desert at Tep-ihu (Aphroditopolis). My victory entered his heart and his limbs were devastated when his messenger recounted to him what I had done against the district of Cynopolis, which had been his property. While I was in Saka, I sent a powerful troop of bowmen which had been traveling overland to destroy Bahria Oasis to prevent any enemy to my rear. With strong heart and rejoicing I sailed south and I destroyed every enemy along the way.

How splendid was the southward journey of the ruler, l.p.h., with his army before him, for there were no losses, nor did any man have to inquire about his comrade, nor did their hearts weep. I moved into the district of No (Thebes) at the inundation season, every face shining, the land in abundance, the riverbank excited, and Thebes in festival! Wives and husbands came to see me, every woman embracing her companion, and there was no face in tears.

Incense for Amun in the sanctuary. Incense for Amun in the sanctuary at the place wherein it is said: Accept the offering, as he gives the scimitar to the Son of Amun, l.p.h., the enduring king, Wadj-kheper-Re, Son of Re Kamose the valiant, given life, who subdues the south and drives back the north, who takes possession of the land in victory, given life, stability, dominion, and joy together with his *ka,* like Re forever and ever.

The decree of His Majesty to the hereditary prince and count, confidant of the palace, overseer of the entire land, king's sealbearer, pupil of the two lands, commander, overseer of the magistrates, overseer of the treasury, strong of arm, Nesha: Let one set all that which My Majesty has accomplished in victory upon a stela, and let its place remain in Karnak in Thebes forever and ever.

Then he said before His Majesty: It is [according to what] my father, my lord, has decreed that I am acting, that my praise may endure before the king.

The overseer of the treasury, Neshi.[1]

---

1. This official is known from a much later lawsuit among his descendants, as first noted by Georges Posener, "Neshi du proces de Mes . . . ," *RdE* 16 (1964): 213–14.

# THE POETICAL STELA OF THUTMOSE III

T*hutmose III of the Eighteenth Dynasty was the greatest empire builder of Egypt's history, having conquered from the Sudan as far as Meso- potamia. The black granite stela (Cairo Museum 34010) which bears the present text was erected in the great temple of Amun-Re at Karnak to celebrate the numerous conquests of Thutmose. Although erected after the king's victories, the text is composed in the form of a prophecy spoken by the god Amun-Re promising Thutmose his support in the winning of universal domin- ion for Egypt. The text is divided into three sections: a prologue composed in a poetic prose style, the actual poem of victory, and a short epilogue also in poetic prose. The poem is a masterpiece of martial poetry which aptly reflects the military spirit of the victorious Egyptian army. The text was first published by P. Lacau (*Stèles du nouvel empire, *vol. 1, Catalogue général . . . du Musée du Caire (Cairo, 1909), 17–21 and pl. vii), and an edition may be found in A. de Buck,* Egyptian Reading Book, *(Leiden, 1948), 53–56. A number of other translations of the text are also available, including the one of R. O. Faulkner in the earlier editions of this book (pp. 285–88), although that translation omits the prologue and epilogue. Miriam Lichtheim also has a complete translation in* Ancient Egyptian Literature, *vol. 2 (Berkeley, 1976), 35–39.*

V.A.T.

## PROLOGUE

1    Thus speaks Amun-Re, Lord of the Thrones of the Two Lands:

Come to me and rejoice at the sight of my beauty,
My son, my defender, Men-Kheper-Re,[1] who lives to eternity.

I shall shine through love for you,
2    My heart / gladdened at your joyful entry into my temple.
My hands shall endow your person with protection and life,
For your comeliness is exceedingly pleasant to my breast.

3    I shall establish / you in my sanctuary and delight in you,
I shall give you dominion and victory over all foreign lands.
I shall establish your power and the awe of you in all the nations,

4    And the fear of you shall extend to / the four pillars of heaven.
I shall increase admiration for you in all flesh
And extend your majestic battle cry throughout the Nine Bows.[2]
The nobles of every foreign land will be united in your fist,

5    For I myself shall extend my arms to bind them for you.
I shall shackle the Nubian archers by ten thousands of thousands
And the men of the north by hundreds of thousands of captives.

6    I shall cause your foes to fall beneath your feet,
And you will trample upon the rebellious and traitors,
For I have assigned to you the earth in its length and its breadth,
And men of west and east are under your control.

7    You will trample down all foreign lands, your heart rejoicing,
For there will be none who can stand in your Majesty's presence.
Under my guidance you shall overwhelm them,

8    Having crossed the water of the great river which surrounds / Naharin[3]
In the victory and power which I have destined for you.
They shall hear your war cry and hide in their holes,
For I have deprived their nostrils of the breath of life,

9    Implanting the fear of your Majesty deep within their hearts.
My uraeus[4] upon your brow will destroy them,

1. Men-Kheper-Re, the prenomen of Thutmose III, was the name given to the king at the time of his succession to the throne. In its capacity as the *nisut-bity* name, it designated the function as ruler of Upper and Lower Egypt.
2. The designation "Nine Bows" signifies the traditional enemies of Egypt.
3. Naharin: Mesopotamia, the land bounded by the Tigris and Euphrates rivers.
4. The uraeus, the traditional emblem of royal power worn on the forehead of the king,

10   Making the savages easy prey / and consuming the islanders with its fire.
     It will behead the Asiatics, for they will have no protection,
     And your enemies will succumb to its strength.

11   I shall cause your victory to encompass all lands,
     My glittering uraeus will be your protector,
     And there will be none who can oppose you to the farthest reaches of
     heaven.
     (All men) will come weighed down beneath their tribute

12   And bowing to your Majesty as I have ordained.
     I shall cripple the opponents who come against you,
     For their courage will have burned away as their bodies quake with fear.


## POEM OF VICTORY

13   I have come to empower you to crush the rulers of Djahi:[5]
     I shall lay them low beneath your feet throughout their lands,
     I shall cause them to know[6] your Majesty as the lord of sunlight,
     And you will shine before them as my image.

14   I have come to empower you to crush the men of Asia:
     You will smash the heads of the nomads of Retjenu,[7]
     And I shall cause them to know your Majesty adorned in your royal
     insignia,
     When you raise up weapons of war in (your) chariot.

15   I have come to empower you to crush the eastern lands:
     You will tread down those who dwell in the regions of God's Land,[8]
     And I shall cause them to know your Majesty as a thunderbolt
     Which hurls its flame as fire as it makes its attack.

---

had the form of a serpent. It was a protective symbol of royal and divine power, and its
purpose was protection against the enemies of the king.

5. Djahi: the general area extending through Palestine, Syria, and northern Mespotamia.
6. "to know": lit. "to see." The sense of the text, however, is not that the foes of Egypt
   will simply see the king as expressed by the various images which follow in the text,
   but that they will actually experience him as such.
7. Retjenu: Syria-Palestine.
8. The expression "God's Land" was used to designate those lesser-known and somewhat exotic territories outside the traditional boundaries of Egypt. Its normal usage
   refers to the land of Punt (possibly Somaliland), but here it appears to be used of
   territories to the east.

16    I have come to empower you to crush the western lands:
Keftiu[9] and Isy[10] stand in awe of you;
I shall cause them to know your Majesty as a young bull,
Firm of heart, sharp of horn, whom none can hinder.

17    I have come to empower you to crush the heathen:
The lands of Mitanni[11] tremble through dread of you;
I shall cause them to know your Majesty as a crocodile,
The dread one of the river, whom none dare approach.

18    I have come to empower you to crush those who dwell on the islands:
Those who dwell in the midst of the sea shall succumb to your war cry;
I shall cause them to know your Majesty as the avenger
Who stands upon the back of his wild bull.[12]

19    I have come to empower you to crush the Libyans:
The islands of Utjentiu[13] belong to the strength of your might;
I shall cause them to know your Majesty as a hostile lion,
And you will render them carrion throughout their valleys.

20    I have come to empower you to crush the very ends of the earth:
All that the ocean encircles is enclosed within your grasp;
I shall cause them to know your Majesty as lord of the wings of Horus,
One who seizes with (only) his glance whatever he desires.

21    I have come to empower you to crush the leaders of the earth:
You will fetter the Bedouins as prisoners;
I shall cause them to know your Majesty as the Jackal of Upper Egypt,
The swift runner who traverses the Two Lands.

22    I have come to empower you to crush the bowmen:
Nubia as far as Shat[14] is in your possession;

9. Keftiu: the island of Crete, or possibly the general area of the Mediterranean.
10. Isy: possibly the island of Cyprus, although Cyprus is not to the west of Egypt.
11. The kingdom of Mitanni was situated between the Tigris and the Euphrates rivers. Its empire, which reached its height during the fifteenth century B.C., extended across Syria as far as the area of Palestine.
12. The imagery of these two lines is based on that of Horus, the avenger of Osiris, who defeats Seth (the wild bull). The Horus Thutmose is thus portrayed as the rightful conqueror of the foreigners who are the enemies of Egypt.
13. An unknown region.
14. A territory in Nubia.

I shall cause them to know your Majesty as your Two Brothers,[15]
Whose two hands I have joined for you in victory.


## EPILOGUE

23    (Behold) your Two Sisters:[16] I have placed them as a protection around
you,
And the arms of my Majesty are uplifted to disperse (all) evil.
I shall make firm your defense, my son, my chosen one, Horus,
Victorious Bull in Thebes, whom I have begotten from my very body,

24    Thutmose who lives to eternity, who performs for me everything which
my *ka* desires.
You have erected my temple as a structure enduring to eternity,
Wider and longer than it had previously been,

25    And its great portal (is named) "Men-Kheper-Re / celebrates the beauty
of Amun-Re."
Greater are your monuments than those of any ruler who has ever
existed;
I ordered you to construct them, and I am content with them.
I shall establish you upon the Horus throne of millions of years,
And you will rule the living forever.


15. The Two Brothers mentioned here are Horus and Seth, symbols of the dual kingship
of Upper and Lower Egypt.
16. Two Sisters: Isis and Nephthys, used here as symbols of the divinely given royal
power.

# THE ISRAEL STELA

ommonly referred to as the Israel Stela, this monumental text was
inscribed on the verso of a large freestanding stela of Amenhotep III
(Cairo Museum 34025) from western Thebes and on a more poorly
preserved stela at Karnak. As an encomium to Merenptah it dwells principally
upon the results of his victory over Libyans who had invaded Egypt from
the west and ensconced themselves in the Delta. While some translators have
treated the entire composition as a poem, I have restricted a poetic rendition to
the final section, asserting the king's dominance over Egypt's western Asiatic
neighbors, including Israel. At Karnak there is a pictorial counterpart to several
lines of this poem, discussed in articles by Frank J. Yurco and Anson F. Rainey,
who, however, disagree on which of the peoples depicted in the Karnak reliefs
are Israelites.

E.F.W.

1      Year 5, third month of the third season, day 3, under the Majesty of Re-
Harakhti, Mighty Bull, who rejoices over Maat; the King of Upper and
Lower Egypt, Baenre-miamon; the Son of Re, Merenptah-hetephimaat:
magnifying the strength and exalting the might of Re-Harakhti, Mighty
Bull, who has smitten the Nine Bows and set his name for all eternity, and

recounting his victories in all lands so as to cause every land combined to know and to cause perfection to be beheld in his valorous deeds.

The King of Upper and Lower Egypt, Baenre-miamon; the Son of Re, Merenptah-hetephimaat; the Bull, possessor of strength, who has slain his enemies, handsome upon the field of valor when his onslaught has succeeded; the Sun who has cleared away the storm cloud that had been over the Black Land[1] and who has caused Egypt to see the rays of the solar disk, who has removed a mountain of ore from the people's necks that he might give air to the folk who had been constrained, who has let (those of) Hikuptah[2] exult over their foes and caused Tatenen[3] to rejoice over his rebels, who has opened the portals of the Walled City[4] that had been barred and allowed its temples to receive their food offerings—the King of Upper and Lower Egypt, Baenre-miamon; the Son of Re, Merenptah-hetephimaat.

The Unique One, who fortified the hearts of myriads, at the sight of whom breath entered nostrils, who shattered the land of the Tjemeh during his lifetime and instilled perpetual dread / in the hearts of the Meshwesh. He caused Libyans to desist treading the Black Land, great terror being in their hearts because of Egypt. Their vanguard turned tail; their legs could not stand firm but ran. Their archers discarded their bows; their runners' hearts were weary with moving on. They unfastened their water-skins, flung to the ground; their haversacks were untied, thrown away. The vile enemy chief of Libya fled all alone in the deep of night, no feather on his head and his feet unshod. His wives were abducted in his very presence; the flour for his food provisions was taken away. He had no water from the water-skin to sustain him. His siblings' faces were fierce enough to slay him; they were fighting one another among his leaders. Their tents were set afire, reduced to ashes; all his goods were consumables for the troops.[5] When he reached his country, he was in laments; every survivor in his land was loath to receive him. "The chief whom an evil fate has shorn of the feather!" all those of his town were saying about him.

He is in the power of all the gods of Memphis. The lord of the Black

5

1. A term for Egypt, referring to the dark alluvial soil of the Nile Valley.
2. I.e., the people of Memphis.
3. An earth god, here synonymous with Ptah, the principal god of Memphis.
4. Memphis.
5. The Egyptian troops.

Land has anathematized his name. Meriy[6] is an abomination of the White-Walled City,[7] so also son after son in his family for eternity. Baenre-miamon will be in pursuit of his children; Merenptah-hetephimaat has been set upon him as fate. He is become proverbial / to Libya, one generation telling the next generation of his victories. "Never had this been done to us since (the time of) Pre,"[8] says every old man in telling his son.

It goes ill with Libyans! They have ceased living ⟨in⟩ the goodly habit of roaming about within the countryside. In one day their movement was curtailed; in a single year the Tjehenu (Libyans) were consumed. Seth has turned his back upon their chief; by his dictate their villages have been devastated. No longer is there work of carrying a load these days. It is advantageous to hide since one is safe in the cave.[9]

The great lord of the Black Land is powerful; might belongs to him. Who dares to fight being aware how freely he strides? Foolish and witless is he who would take him on. He cannot remain ignorant of tomorrow, the violator of his border. "As for the Black Land," so it is said, "since (the time of) the gods she is the sole daughter of Pre, and it is his son who is upon the throne of the sun god. No mind can devise a scheme for violating her people.[10] The eye of every god is in pursuit of her despoiler. It will put an end to her foes," so say those who gaze at their stars and all who predict[11] by observing the winds.

A great wonder has come to pass for Egypt: the one who attacked her was placed ⟨in⟩ her hand as a captive by the counsels of the divine king, vindicated against his adversaries in the presence of Pre. Meriy, the one who committed evil ⌜and subversion⌝ against every god who is in the Walled City, was judged / with him in Heliopolis, and the Ennead declared him guilty of his crimes.

The Universal Lord said, "Give the falchion to my son, who is straightforward, gracious, and kind, Baenre-miamon, the one who has cared for Hikuptah and defended Heliopolis, who has reopened the towns which had been shut tight. He has released many confined in each district. He has restored offerings to the temples and let incense be reintroduced before the

6. The name of the Libyan chief.
7. Memphis.
8. A Late Egyptian spelling of the name of the sun god Re.
9. Variant: "in their cave."
10. Or, "The heart of one who attacks her people cannot achieve success."
11. Lit. "all who know their spells."

god. He has let nobles regain their possessions and let private persons frequent their towns."

So the lords of Heliopolis said regarding their son, Merenptah-hetephimaat, "Grant him a lifetime like Re's that he may defend the one who is distressed because of any foreign country. Entrust the Black Land to him for a portion; allot it to him forever that he may protect its people."

See, only in the vicinity of the energetic one do people dwell at ease; only from the hands of the valiant one does breath of life come. Wealth is made to flow only to the just person; a cheat does not retain his ill-gotten gains. As for the one who accumulates possessions illicitly, they accrue to others, not his children. This was said ⟨of⟩[12] Meriy, the vile ignorant one, the Libyan enemy, who came to attack the Walls of the Sovereign,[13] the son of whose lord[14] appears in his place, the King of Upper and Lower Egypt, Baenre-miamon, the Son of Re, Merenptah-hetephimaat.

20     Ptah said regarding the Libyan enemy, "Collect all his crimes / to be turned back upon his head. Place him in the hand of Merenptah-hetephimaat that he may cause him to disgorge what he has swallowed like a crocodile."

See, it is the swift one who overtakes the swift one. The lord, conscious of his strength, was wanting to ensnare him. It is Amon who curbed him with his hand. It is to his *ka* in Southern Heliopolis[15] that he was delivered, (to) the King of Upper and Lower Egypt, Baenre-miamon, the Son of Re, Merenptah-hetephimaat.

Great joy has arisen in the Black Land, and shouts of jubilation come forth from the towns of Egypt. They are talking about the victories which Merenptah-hetephimaat achieved over the Tjehenu: How beloved he is, the victorious ruler! How exalted he is, the king among the gods! How distinguished he is, the lord of command! Oh, how pleasant it is to dwell at ease while people are babbling away! It is without any fear in people's hearts that one walks freely upon the road. Fortresses are left alone to themselves, and wells are open, ⌜accessible⌝ to messengers. The bastions of the enclosure wall are calm. It is the sunlight that (first) awakens their watchmen. Medjay-guards are recumbent in their slumber. Desert-trackers and

12. Or possibly, "This shall be said to."
13. The stronghold of Memphis.
14. Referring to Ptah as lord of Memphis, and Merenptah as his son.
15. Thebes. The *ka* of Amon is Merenptah.

Tjukten-rangers are in meadows they long for. Field cattle are left as freely roaming herds; no longer are herdsmen crossing the river's flood. No longer is there shouting aloud at night, "Stop! Come here, come here!" in the mouths of strangers.[16] It is with song that one goes and / comes. No longer is there wailing of people being in mourning. Towns are resettled once again. The one who sows his crop will consume it. Re has turned himself around to the Black Land. She is reborn[17] as befits her champion, the King of Upper and Lower Egypt, Baenre-miamon, the Son of Re, Merenptah-hetephimaat.

Princes[18] are prostrate saying, "Shalom!"
Not one lifts up his head among the Nine Bows.
Now that Tjehenu has come to ruin,
   Khatti is pacified;
   The Canaan has been plundered into every sort of woe:
      Askalon has been overcome;
      Gezer has been captured;
      Yanoam is made nonexistent.
      Israel is laid waste; his seed is no longer;
   Khor is become a widow because of Egypt.[19]
All lands combined, they are at peace.
Whoever roams about gets subdued
   by the King of Upper and Lower Egypt, Baenre-miamon;
   the Son of Re, Merenptah-hetephimaat,
   given life like Re every day.

16. Or possibly, "No longer is there shouting for aid (lit. a shout of summoning) at night; 'Help, help!' has ceased from the mouths of strangers."
17. I.e., reconstituted, reconstructed.
18. Variant: "All princes."
19. The Nine Bows denote the traditional subjects or foes of the pharaoh. Tjehenu is Libya; Khatti is the land of the Hittites. Within the region of Canaan (Palestine) were situated the city states of Askalon, Gezer, and Yanoam and the still unsettled tribe of Israel. Khor is a general term for Syro-Palestine.

# THE BENTRESH STELA
## (LOUVRE C 284)

*S*et, like the Demotic tale of Setna Khaemuas, during the illustrious reign of Ramses II, this pseudepigraphic tale of demonic possession is attested in two late sources from Thebes. The better-known exemplar, a black sandstone stela now in the Louvre in Paris, derives from a small Ptolemaic chapel that formerly stood beside the Khonsu temple at Karnak. The date of the Louvre stela is disputed, with suggestions ranging from Dynasty 25 to the Ptolemaic period. The second, still unpublished exemplar was discovered by the Oriental Institute's Epigraphic Survey at Luxor temple during its 1978–79 season. Once erected in monumental format, the Dynasty 30 text survives in some thirty-five stone blocks containing approximately one-fifth of the previously known version.

Though anachronistic, the Bentresh stela preserves historical memory of the diplomatic marriages of foreign princesses to the New Kingdom rulers Thutmose IV and Ramses II, whose royal titularies are mingled in the opening protocol. The figure of Neferure is surely derived from the latter's Hittite wife, accorded the Egyptian name Maat-Neferure, and the princess Bentresh appears to have a Semitic name, devised on the model of Bentanat, daughter of Ramses II. The central theme of the tale has some historical foundation as well, since the exchange of physicians and healing statues is well documented in the surviving diplomatic correspondence between Egypt and its eastern neighbors. One such exchange was even initiated by a request from the father of Maat-Neferure, *though for his sister rather than a younger daughter.*[1] *The exotic land of Bakhtan, perhaps to be identified with Bactria, is otherwise unknown.*

*The hostile manifestation of an "effective spirit" (akh) as a "ghost" is well attested in Egyptian writings, ranging from Old Kingdom private tomb curses to Hellenistic-era Demotic romances. The exploitation of disgruntled spirits underlies state execration rituals, in which the damned are placed in the power of forsaken spirits whose tomb offerings—and pleasant dispositions—have long since lapsed.*[2] *Medical texts (and private "letters to the dead") regularly attribute illness to ghostly possession, and the physician Thothemheb's diagnosis is both traditional and expressed precisely in standard medical phraseology. For Egyptian conceptions, it is significant that the possessing spirit, once dispelled by the protective image of Khonsu, is pacified by appropriate offerings and a party. The spirit is famished and in need of attention, but not inherently evil.*

*Styled as a formal state document with full titulary and royal encomium, the late text served as cultic propaganda for the healing shrine of the Theban lunar deity Khonsu and his portable image Khonsu-the-Authority. Khonsu is associated with specific illnesses by the New Kingdom, and in the Third Intermediate Period his temple issued "oracular amuletic decrees" protecting the bearer from a detailed list of maladies, including spirit possession of the type detailed below. The statue's name "Authority" refers to his ability to govern or control roaming spirits.*

R.K.R.

1  The Horus: "Strong Bull, whose crowns are pleasing"; (The Two Ladies): "He whose kingship endures like Atum"; the Golden Horus: "He whose arm is powerful, who repels the Nine Bows";[3] the King of Upper and Lower Egypt, Lord of the Two Lands, Usermaatre-setepenre, the bodily Son of Re,

1. The Hittite monarch Hattusili III, the father of Maatneferure, requested that an Egyptian doctor be sent to provide a drug enabling his elderly sister to become pregnant; see Elmar Edel, *Ägyptische Ärzte und ägyptische Medizin am hethitischen Königshof* (Göttingen, 1976), 67–70. Conversely, Amenhotep III was sent a healing statue of Ishtar of Nineveh.
2. See R. K. Ritner, *The Mechanics of Ancient Egyptian Magical Practice,* SAOC 54 (Chicago, 1993), 180–83.
3. The tale's author has conflated the initial "Horus," "Two Ladies," and "Golden Horus" throne names of Thutmose IV with the following "Nomen" and "Prenomen" of Rameses II.

Ramses-beloved-of-Amon, beloved of Amon-Re, Lord of the Thrones of the Two Lands, and of the entire Ennead of Thebes.

> The Good God, Son of Amon,
> Offspring of Horachty,
> The effective seed of the Lord of the Universe,
> Whom Kamutef has begotten,
> The King of the Black Land,
> The ruler of the Red Land,[4]
> The sovereign who seizes the Nine Bows,
> Who came forth from the womb with victories foretold for him,
> For whom heroism was decreed in the egg,
> The bull whose heart is firm as he treads the arena,
> The divine King who goes forth on the day of victory like Montu,
> He whose strength is great like the son of Nut.

Now His Majesty was in Mitanni in accordance with his customary annual ritual, while the princes of all foreign lands had come bowing in peace to the might of His Majesty from as far as the remote marshlands, with their gifts of gold, lapis lazuli, / turquoise and every manner of aromatic plant of God's Land on their backs, each one exceeding his fellow.

Then the prince of Bakhtan presented his gifts, and he placed his eldest daughter in front of them, paying homage to His Majesty and beseeching life from him. The woman was exceedingly beautiful in the estimation of His Majesty, beyond anything. Thus her titulary was set down as the Great Queen, Neferure. When His Majesty arrived in Egypt, then she did all that a queen does.

Regnal year 23,[5] month 2 of Summer, day 22 occurred. Now His Majesty was in Thebes the victorious, the mistress of cities, performing what is praiseworthy for his father, Amon-Re, Lord of the thrones of the Two Lands, in his beautiful festival of Luxor temple, his favorite place from earliest time. One came to say to His Majesty: "A messenger of the prince of Bakhtan has come with many gifts for the Queen." Then he was conducted

---

4. The royal hymn, employing six thematic couplets, here pairs the rulership of Egypt (the "Black Land") and the surrounding desert (the "Red Land").
5. Following an early suggestion by Erman, the text has been emended from "year 15" on the basis of the seventeen months' journey supposedly required for a journey between Egypt and Bakhtan (l. 17).

into the presence of His Majesty together with his gifts. He said, in paying homage to His Majesty: "Praise be to you, O Sun God of the Nine Bows! Behold, we live through you!" Then he spoke, kissing the ground before his Majesty, and again he said before His Majesty: "I have come to you, O sovereign, my lord, concerning Bentresh, the younger sister of Queen Neferure. A malady has pervaded her body. May Your Majesty send a wise man[6] to examine her!"

Then His Majesty said: "Bring to me the staff of the House of Life and the council / of the Residence!" They were ushered in to him at once. His Majesty said: "Behold, you have been summoned to hear this matter. Now, bring to me from among you one who is skilled in his mind, who can write with his fingers." So the royal scribe Thothemheb came before His Majesty, and His Majesty commanded that he go to Bakhtan with this messenger.

So the wise man arrived at Bakhtan and he found Bentresh in the condition of one who has a ghost. He found him to be an enemy with whom one could contend.[7] The prince of Bakhtan sent word again before His Majesty, saying: "O sovereign, my lord, may His Majesty command that a god be brought [to contend with this ghost."]

[The message reached] His Majesty in regnal year 26, the first month of Summer, during the festival of Amon, when His Majesty was in Thebes. Then His Majesty reported before Khonsu-in-Thebes-Neferhotep, saying: "My good lord, it is concerning the daughter of the prince of Bakhtan that I report before you." Then Khonsu-in-Thebes-Neferhotep was conducted to Khonsu-the-Authority, the great god who expels wandering spirits. Then His Majesty said before Khonsu-in-Thebes-Neferhotep: "My good lord, will you give your attention to Khonsu/-the-Authority, the great god who expels wandering spirits, to cause that he go to Bakhtan?" Very favorable response.[8] Then His Majesty said: "Place your magical protection with him, so that I might cause His Majesty to go to Bakhtan to save the daughter of the prince of Bakhtan." Very favorable response by Khonsu-in-Thebes-Neferhotep. Then he made magical protection for Khonsu-the-Authority-

10

15

---

6. Lit. "a knower of things."

7. The physician Thothemheb employs one of the three standard Egyptian medical diagnoses: "an illness with which I shall contend." The others include the optimistic "an illness that I shall treat" and the pessimistic "an illness not to be treated."

8. Lit. "Very great nodding of the head," a reference to the oracular gesture made by the portable statue of Khonsu-in-Thebes-Neferhotep.

in-Thebes four times.[9] His Majesty commanded that Khonsu-the-Authority-in-Thebes be made to proceed to the great bark with five transport boats, a chariot, and many horses of the West and East.

This god reached Bakhtan at the completion of one year and five months. Then the prince of Bakhtan together with his army and his officials came before Khonsu-the-Authority, and he placed himself upon his belly, saying: "As you have come to us, so may you be favorable to us, in accordance with the commands of the King of Upper and Lower Egypt, Usermaatre-setepenre!" Then this god went to the place where Bentresh was. Then he made magical protection for the daughter of the prince of Bakhtan, and she was well at once.

Then this ghost who was with her said before Khonsu-the-Authority-in-Thebes: "Welcome, O great god who expels wandering spirits! Bakhtan is your town; its people are your servants; I am your servant. / I shall go back to the place from which I came, in order to set your heart at rest concerning that for which you came. May Your Majesty issue a command to celebrate with me and the prince of Bakhtan!" Then this god nodded approval to his prophet, saying: "Let the prince of Bakhtan make a great offering in the presence of this ghost."

While these things were done, Khonsu-the-Authority-in-Thebes was with the ghost, while the prince of Bakhtan was waiting with his soldiers, being very greatly afraid. Then he made a great offering in the presence of Khonsu-the-Authority-in-Thebes and the ghost of the daughter of the prince of Bakhtan, celebrating for them. Then the ghost went away in peace to the place that he wished in accordance with the command of Khonsu-the-Authority-in-Thebes. The prince of Bakhtan was shouting for joy very fervently together with everyone who was in Bakhtan.

Then he schemed with his heart, saying: "I shall cause that this god be here in Bakhtan. I shall not allow him to go to Egypt." Then this god completed three years and nine months in Bakhtan. Thereafter, the prince of Bakhtan was sleeping on his bed, and he saw this god having come out of his shrine as a falcon of gold, flying up toward Egypt. / So he awoke in panic. Then he said to the prophet of Khonsu-the-Authority-in-Thebes: "This god, he was here with us, but he should go to Egypt. Let his chariot go to Egypt!" Then the prince of Bakhtan allowed this god to proceed to

9. A standard repetition in magico-religious ritual, once for each cardinal direction.

Egypt, giving to him very many gifts of everything good and very many soldiers and horses.

They arrived in peace in Thebes. Then Khonsu-in-Thebes-the-Authority-in-Thebes went to the temple of Khonsu-in-Thebes-Neferhotep, and he placed the gifts that the prince of Bakhtan gave to him, consisting of everything good, in the presence of Khonsu-in-Thebes-Neferhotep, without giving everything from it to his temple.[10] Khonsu-the-Authority-in-Thebes arrived at his temple in peace in regnal year 33, month 2 of Winter, day 19, of the King of Upper and Lower Egypt, Usermaatre-setepenre, who has attained the state of being given life like Re forever.

10. The traveling image of Khonsu retains a portion of the gifts for the support of his own shrine.

# THE VICTORY STELA OF PIYE
# (CAIRO JdE 48862+47086–47089)

T he Piye Victory Stela is justly famous as a unique work of royal historical propaganda. The legitimacy of Piye's rule is indicated not merely by expressions of divine approval, royal victory, and obsequious flattery, but by conscious attempts to present the Nubian ruler as truly Egyptian, while his Libyan opponents are debased and unclean outsiders who sport feathers, eat fish, and are uncircumcised. Like the Mahdi of the nineteenth century, Piye led an Egyptian campaign that was both military invasion and religious pilgrimage designed to "cleanse" a debased aristocracy. Piye's zeal in the cause of Amon is explicit, with a detailed "holiness code" for his soldiers and a military itinerary dependent upon the celebration of religious festivals. Composed in classical Middle Egyptian, the language of the stela also serves the theme of cultural revival, and the exceptional lapses into the common vernacular are intentionally placed in the speeches of vanquished Libyans. As implied in the concluding line, this literary revival was certainly the work of Nubian-allied Thebans who would have been familiar with local Ramesside monuments that stigmatized the ancestral Libyans as uncircumcised, feather-wearing barbarians.

The stela was discovered in 1862 within the temple of Gebel Barkal at the Nubian capital of Napata, and additional fragments were recovered in situ during excavations from 1915 to 1920. In the lunette, Piye stands before an enthroned Amon followed by his standing consort, Mut. Splayed on either side *of the central group, two registers of vanquished Libyan rulers make obeisance to the victorious king, while the upper righthand register illustrates the surrender of Namlot, ruler of Hermopolis, through the intervention of the royal wives. Though Namlot does not grovel like his confederates, his status is consciously inverted as the queen occupies the male position at the head of the register. Following afterward, Namlot adopts the standard position and gesture of a queen with raised sistrum, and, like a mere servant, he leads a horse on a tether.*

*For geographic terms in the stela, one should consult Farouk Gomaà,* Die libyschen Fürstentümer des Deltas *(Wiesbaden, 1974). This translation was first prepared for R. K. Ritner,* The Libyan Anarchy: Documents from Egypt's Third Intermediate Period *and appears courtesy of the Society of Biblical Literature.*

R.K.R.

1    Regnal year 21, first month of Inundation, under the Majesty of the King of Upper and Lower Egypt, Piye, beloved of Amon, living forever. The decree which My Majesty has spoken:

> "Hear what I have done in exceeding the ancestors.
> I am the king, the representation of god,
> the living image of Atum,
> who issued from the womb marked as ruler,
> who is feared by those greater than he,
> [whose father] knew and whose mother perceived
> even in the egg that he would be ruler,
> the good god, beloved of the gods,
> the Son of Re, who acts with his two arms,
> Piye, beloved of Amon."

One came to say to His Majesty: "The Chief of the West, the count and chief in Behbeit el-Hagar, Tefnakht, is in the (Harpoon)[1] nome, in the nome of Xois, in Hapi, in [...], in the marshy region of Kom el-Hisn, in Per-noub

---

1. Incompletely carved. For the geographic identification of this series of nomes, see J. Yoyotte, "Les principautés du Delta au temps de l'anarchie libyenne," in *Mélanges Maspero* I/4, MIFAO 66/4, 1961, 154. For the name of the Harpoon nome, see W. Helck, *Die altägyptische Gaue* (Wiesbaden, 1974), 153, and for the "Bull of the Desert" (Xoite) nome, see pp. 163–67.

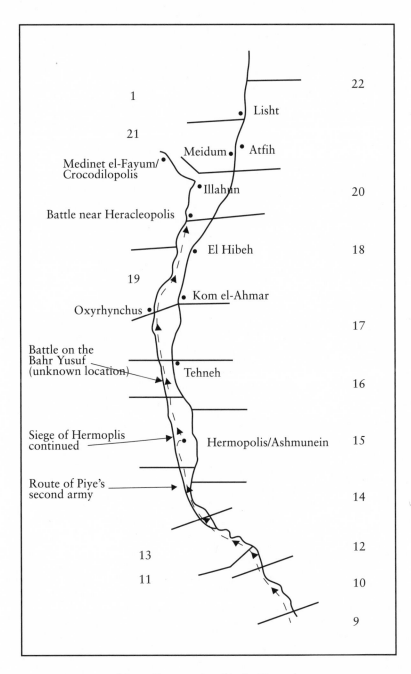

Map 2. Sites mentioned in the Piye stela

and in the nome of Memphis. He has seized the West even in its entirety, from the northern coastal marshes to Lisht, sailing southward with a sizable army, while the Two Lands are united behind him, and the counts and rulers of estates are as dogs at his heels.

No stronghold has closed [its doors in] the nomes of Upper Egypt: Meidum, the Fort of Osorkon I, Crocodilopolis (Medinet el-Faiyum), Oxyrhynchus (el-Bahnasa), and Takinash. Every city of the West has opened doors just through fear of him. When he turned about to the nomes of the East, then they opened to him likewise: The Mansion of the Phoenix, El-Hibeh, the Mansion of the King, and Aphroditopolis (Atfih).

5      Behold, [he is] / beleaguering Heracleopolis (Ihnasya el-Medina), and he has made himself an enclosing uroborous,[2] not allowing goers to go nor allowing entrants to enter, while fighting every day. In its full circuit he has measured it, with every count knowing his (assigned) wall, while he stations every man among the counts and rulers of estates to besiege his section."

Then [His Majesty] heard [this] defiantly, laughing and amused.

But these chiefs, counts and generals who were in their cities were sending word to His Majesty daily saying:

"Have you been silent so as to ignore Upper Egypt and the nomes of the Residence, while Tefnakht seizes what is before him, having found no resistance? Namlot, [ruler of Hermopolis], count of Hutweret, has thrown down the wall of Nefrusy. He has demolished his own city through fear of the one who would seize it for himself in order to beleaguer another city. Behold, he has gone to be a subordinate at his (Tefnakht's) heels, having shrugged off allegiance to His Majesty. He stands with him just like one of [his followers] in the nome of Oxyrhynchus, while he (Tefnakht) gives to him rewards as his desire dictates from among everything that he has found."

Then His Majesty sent word to the counts and generals who were in Egypt, the commander Pawerem, and the commander Lamersekny,[3] and every commander of His Majesty who was in Egypt:

2. Lit. "tail-in-mouth," designating a snake biting its tail, a symbolic enclosure both protective and hostile. For the religious context of this passage, see R. K. Ritner, "A Uterine Amulet in the Oriental Institute Collection," *JNES* 43 (1984): 219–20.

3. The names of Piye's commanders, Lemersekny and Pawerem, are often considered Libyan, but the latter is a late spelling of the purely Egyptian name and title *Pȝ-wr-mȝȝ.w;* see W. Erichsen, *Demotisches Glossar* (Copenhagen, 1954), 94; correcting D. M. Dixon, "The Origin of the Kingdom of Kush," *JEA* 50 (1964): 127, and

"Proceed in battle formation, engage in combat, encircle and beleaguer it! Capture its people, its herds, its ships upon the river! Do not allow the cultivators to go forth to the fields! Do not allow the plowmen to plow! Beleaguer the frontier of the Hare nome; fight against it every day!"

Then they did likewise.

Then His Majesty sent an army to Egypt, charging them forcefully:

10     "Do not attack at / night in the manner of a game. You should fight when there is sight. Announce battle to him from afar! If he should say: 'Wait for the troops and cavalry of another city,' then may you sit until his army comes. Fight when he says. If, further, his supporters are in another city, let one wait for them. The counts, these whom he has brought to support him, and the trusted Libyan troops, let one announce battle to them in advance, saying:

'O you whom we do not know how to address in mustering the troops! Yoke the best steeds of your stable! Line up in battle formation! Be informed that Amon is the god who sent us!'

When you arrive within Thebes before Karnak, you should enter into the water. Purify yourselves in the river! Clothe yourselves in the best linen! Lay down the bow, withdraw the arrow![4] Do not boast of greatness as a possessor of strength! The mighty has no strength in ignorance of him (Amon), for he makes the broken-armed strong-armed. (Thus) do multitudes turn tail to the few; one seizes a thousand men. Sprinkle yourselves with the water of his altars. You should kiss the ground before him and you should say to him: 'Give us passage, that we might fight in the shadow of your strong arm! The corps of recruits whom you have sent, let its onslaught occur while multitudes tremble before it.' "

Then they placed (themselves) on their bellies before His Majesty, (saying):

> "It is your name that will serve as our strong arm,
> your counsel that brings your army to port,
> with your bread in our bellies on every passage,

15     and your beer / quenching our thirst.

---

R. Caminos, "Another Hieratic Manuscript from the Library of Pwerem Son of Ḳiḳi (Pap. B.M. 10288)," *JEA* 58 (1972): 208.

4. A conscious paraphrase of a passage from the classical Middle Kingdom literary "Tale of Sinuhe" (B 274); see A. Gardiner, *JEA* 21 (1935): 220, n. 3. For other adaptations of classical passages, see Logan and Westenholz, *JARCE* 9 (1971–72): 111.

It is your valor that provides our strong arm,
so that one is terrified at the mention of your name.
No army profits whose commander is a coward.
Who is your equal there?
You are a mighty king, who acts with his two arms,
the master of the art of war."

They then went sailing northward and they arrived at Thebes; they did exactly as His Majesty had said. They then went sailing northward on the river, finding that numerous ships had come southward with soldiers, sailors, and troops of every valiant warrior of Lower Egypt equipped with weapons of warfare to fight against the army of His Majesty.

Then a great slaughter was made among them, in incalculable numbers. Their army and their ships were captured and brought away as captives to the place where His Majesty was. They then advanced to the frontier of Heracleopolis, announcing battle.

List of the counts and kings of Lower Egypt:

King Namlot and King Iuput,
Chief of the Ma, Sheshonq, of Busiris,
Great Chief of the Ma, Djedamoniuefankh, of Mendes,
and his eldest son, who was the general of Hermopolis Parva,
the army of Hereditary Prince Bakennefi
and his eldest son, the Chief of the Ma, Nesnaiu, in Hesebu,
every plume-wearing chief who was in Lower Egypt,
and King Osorkon (IV) who was in Bubastis and the district of
    Ranefer,
with every count and ruler of estates in the West, in the East, and the
    islands in between being united in a single alliance as subordinates
    at the heels of the Great Chief of the West, the ruler of estates of
20  Lower Egypt, the prophet of Neith, Lady of Sais, / the *setem*-priest
    of Ptah, Tefnakht.

They then went forth against them. Then they made a great slaughter among them, greater than anything, and their ships on the river were captured. The remnant then crossed over, landing on the West in the vicinity of Perpega.

As the land lightened and the morning dawned, the army of His Majesty crossed over against them, so that army joined battle with army.

Then they slew numerous men among them together with horses in incalculable numbers, with trembling occurring in the remnant so that they fled to Lower Egypt from a beating more severe and painful than anything.

List of the slaughter which was made among them.

Men: (...)⁵ persons. (Horses: ...)

King Namlot fled upstream to the South when he was told: "Hermopolis is faced with enemies from the troops of His Majesty, with its people and its herds captured."

Then he entered into Hermopolis while the troops of His Majesty were on the river and the bank of the Hare nome.

Then they heard it and surrounded the Hare nome on its four sides, without letting those who would go out go out nor letting those who would enter enter. They sent word explicitly to report to the Majesty of the King of Upper and Lower Egypt, Piye, beloved of Amon, given life, detailing every attack which they had made, detailing every victory of His Majesty.

Then His Majesty raged because of it like a panther: "Have they allowed a remnant to remain among the troops of Lower Egypt so as to let go an escapee among them to relate his campaign, not killing them to exterminate the last of them? As I live, as Re loves me, as my father Amon favors me, I shall go northward myself, that I might overturn / what he has done, that I might cause that he retreat from fighting for the course of eternity! After the rites of the New Year are performed, when I offer to my father Amon in his beautiful festival, when he makes his beautiful appearance of the New Year, let him send me in peace to behold Amon in the beautiful festival of the Opet feast, that I might convey his image in procession to Luxor temple in his beautiful festival of "The Night Feast of Opet" and the festival of "Abiding in Thebes" which Re devised for him in the primordial time, that I might convey him in procession to his house in order to rest on his throne on the day of ushering in the god in the third month of Inundation season, day 2, and that I might make Lower Egypt taste the taste of my fingers."

Then the troops who were there in Egypt heard the raging that His Majesty had made against them.

Then they fought against Oxyrhynchus of the Oxyrhynchite nome,

---

5. The engraver has left spaces blank for the insertion of battlefield tallies, but these were never added.

taking it like a burst of water and sending word before His Majesty, but his heart was not appeased because of it.

Then they fought against "The Peak, Great of Victories," finding it filled with troops comprising every valiant warrior of Lower Egypt.

Then a battering ram was employed against it, so that its walls were demolished and a great slaughter made among them in incalculable numbers, including the son of the Chief of the Ma, Tefnakht.

Then they sent word to His Majesty because of it, but his heart was not appeased regarding it.

Then they fought against Hutbenu, so that its interior was opened and the troops of His Majesty entered into it.

Then they sent word to His Majesty, but his heart was not appeased regarding it.

First month of Inundation season, day 9. His Majesty then came sailing northward to Thebes. At the feast of Opet, he celebrated the festival of Amon. His Majesty then went / sailing northward to the quay of the Hare nome. His Majesty came out of the cabin of the barge, the horses were yoked, the chariots were mounted, so that the grandeur of His Majesty extended to the hinterlands of the Asiatics, and every heart was quaking before him.

Then His Majesty burst forth to revile his army, raging at it like a panther: "Do they endure[6] while your combat is such that my business is delayed? It is the year for finalizing a conclusion, for placing fear of me in Lower Egypt, and for inflicting upon them a severe and painful defeat by striking."

He made for himself a camp at the southwest of Hermopolis, keeping a stranglehold on it daily. A talus was made to clothe the wall, and a platform was erected to elevate the archers when shooting and the slingers when slinging stones, slaying the people among them daily. Days passed, and Hermopolis became foul to the nose, deprived of its ability to breathe.

Then Hermopolis threw itself upon its belly, pleading before the King of Lower Egypt,[7] while messengers came and went bearing everything beautiful to behold: gold, every sort of precious gemstone, clothing by the

6. Lichtheim assumed an error for *mn-tn:* "Are you continuing to fight . . . " Grimal assumed an error for a bookroll determinative: "Is this the manner of your fighting?"
7. The Hermopolitans acknowledge Piye's legitimacy as ruler of Lower Egypt (*bỉ.ty*) and thus make supplication to his crown.

chest, and the diadem which had been on his brow, the uraeus which had inspired respect of him, without ceasing for numerous days, imploring his crown.

Then One (King Namlot) sent his wife, the royal wife and royal daughter, Nestanetmehu,[8] to implore the royal wives, the royal concubines, the royal daughters, and the royal sisters, and she threw herself upon her belly in the women's house before the royal women:

"Come to me, royal wives, royal daughters and royal sisters! May you appease Horus, Lord of the palace, whose wrath is great, whose vindication is grand! Cause / that he [...] me. Behold, he [...] [...] him. Behold, [...] ... [Speak (?)] to him, so that [he] might then turn about to the one who praises him. [...]"

[...] provision [...] [...] of life in [...] / [...] [...] they filled(?) with what was efficacious [...] praise him [...] the royal wives, the royal sisters [... They threw] themselves upon their bellies [before His Majesty ...] the royal wives [... Namlot,] ruler of Hutweret. [...] for his city (?), the ruler / [...] [...] as ruler [...] in the city (?) [...] [...] through lack of [...] / [...] to the place where [His] Majesty was. [His] Majesty spoke (?) to him [...]:

"Who [...] your mother? Who has guided you? Who has guided you? Who, then, has guided you? Who has guided you [so that you have abandoned] the path of life? Has heaven then rained with arrows? I was [content] when Southerners bowed down and Northerners (said): 'Place us within your shade!' Was it bad that the King (?) [of Hermopolis came (?)] bearing his offerings? The heart is a rudder, which capsizes its owner by what issues from the wrath of god, when he has seen flame in the cool waters in (?) the heart. [...] / There is no adult who is seen with his father, for your nomes are filled (only) with children."

Then he threw himself on his belly in the presence of His Majesty: "[Peace be with you,] Horus, Lord of the palace! It is your wrath which has done this against me. I am one of the King's servants who pays taxes to the treasury as daily offerings. Make a reckoning of their taxes. I have provided for you far more than they."

Then he presented silver, gold, lapis lazuli, turquoise, copper, and every sort of gemstone in great quantity.

8. "She of the One of Lower Egypt"; reading following Rougé, Kitchen, and sense. The reading "Nestent" ("She of the One of") adopted by Breasted, Lichtheim, and Grimal is senseless and does not account for the final signs.

Then the treasury was filled with this tribute, and he brought a horse with his right hand and a sistrum in his left—a sistrum of gold and lapis lazuli.

Then His Majesty appeared in splendor from his palace, proceeding to the temple of Thoth, Lord of Hermopolis, and he sacrificed long-horned cattle, short-horned cattle, and fowl for his father Thoth, Lord of Her-

60 mopolis, and the Ogdoad in the temple of the / Ogdoad.

The troops of the Hare nome proceeded to shout and sing, saying:

> "How beautiful is Horus, appeased in his city,
> The Son of Re, Piye!
> May you celebrate for us a jubilee,
> As you protect the Hare nome!"

His Majesty then proceeded to the house of King Namlot, and he went into every chamber of the palace, his treasury and his storehouses. He caused that there be presented to him the royal wives and the royal daughters. They proceeded to hail His Majesty with feminine wiles, but His Majesty did not pay attention to them. His Majesty then proceeded to the stable of the horses and the quarters of the foals. When he saw [that]

65 / they were starved, he said: "As I live, as Re loves me, as my nose is rejuvenated with life, how much more painful it is in my heart that my horses have been starved than any other crime that you have committed at your discretion. Your neighbor's fear of you is testimony for me. Are you unaware that the shadow of god is over me, and that my deeds have not failed because of him? If only another had done it to me, whom I did not know, whom I had not rebuked because of it! I am one fashioned in the womb and created in the egg of god, with the seed of god within me! As his *ka*-spirit endures, I have not acted in ignorance of him! He is the one who commanded me to act!"

70 Then his property was assigned to the treasury / and his granary to the endowment of Amon in Karnak.

The ruler of Heracleopolis, Peftchauauibast, then came bearing tribute to Pharaoh: gold, silver, every sort of gemstone, and the pick of the horses of the stable. He threw himself upon his belly in the presence of His Majesty, saying:

> "Hail to you, Horus, mighty King, bull who attacks bulls!
> The netherworld has seized me, and I am deep in darkness!

O you who give me the enlightenment of your face,
I cannot find a friend on a day of distress,[9]
who will stand up on a day of fighting,
except for you, O mighty King!
From me you have stripped away the darkness.
I shall be a servant together with my property, while
Heracleopolis is levied with taxes / for your domain.
You are indeed Horachty, chief of the imperishable stars!
As he exists, so do you exist as king.
He will not perish, nor will you perish,
O King of Upper and Lower Egypt, Piye, living forever!"

His Majesty then sailed northward to the opening of the canal beside Ill-ahun, and he found Per-Sekhemkhepere with its ramparts heightened, its fortress closed, and filled with every valiant warrior of Lower Egypt.

Then His Majesty sent word to them saying:

> "O living dead! O living dead!
> O miserable wretches! O living dead!
> If the moment passes without opening to me,
> behold, you belong to the tally of the fallen!
> Such is the one subjected to royal punishment.
> Do not bar the gates of your life so as to confront the
> slaughter block of this day!
> Do not desire death so as to hate life!
> [Choose (?)] life in the presence of the entire land!"

Then they sent word to His Majesty, saying:

> "Behold, the shadow of god is upon you.
> The son of Nut, may he give to you his arms,
> then your wish will come to pass directly
> like what issues from the mouth of the god.
> Behold, you are born of god,
> because we see (it) by the actions of your arms.
> Behold, as for your city and its fortifications,

9. A conscious paraphrase of a passage from the classical Middle Kingdom literary text "The Instructions of Amonemhat I," see A. Gardiner, "The Earliest Manuscripts of the Instruction of Amenemmes I," *Mélanges Maspero* I/2, MIFAO 66/2, Cairo, 1935–38, 482.

80         / [do what pleases] you with them.
        May entrants enter and goers go;
        may His Majesty do what he will."

Then they came out with a son of the Chief of the Ma, Tefnakht. The troops of His Majesty then entered into it, without his slaying anyone among all the people whom he found [there. ...] men and treasurers to seal his possessions, while his treasuries were assigned to the treasury, and his granaries to the endowment of his father Amon-Re, Lord of the Thrones of the Two Lands. His Majesty then went sailing northward and he found that in Meidum, the House of Sokar, Lord of Illumination, had been closed, not having been attacked, and had intent to fight. [...] seized them; fear [overpowered(?)] them; awe sealed their mouths.

Then His Majesty sent word to them, saying:

        "Behold, two ways are before you; choose as you wish.
        Open, you will live; close, you will die.
        My Majesty will not pass by a closed city!"

Then they opened to him directly, and His Majesty entered within this city and he presented a [great] offering [to] Imenhy, foremost of Illumination. Its treasury and granaries were assigned to the endowment of Amon in Karnak. His Majesty then sailed north to Lisht, and he found the stronghold closed and the walls filled with valiant troops of Lower Egypt.

Then they opened the fortifications and they threw themselves on their bellies in the presence of [His Majesty, and they said to] His Majesty:

        "Your father has entrusted to you his legacy.
        Yours are the Two Lands, and yours those in them.
        You are the Lord of what is upon earth."

His Majesty then proceeded to have a great offering presented to the gods who are in this city, consisting of long-horned cattle, short-horned cattle, fowl, and everything good and pure.

Then its treasury was assigned to the treasury and its granaries to the
85   endowment of / his father Amon-[Re, Lord of the Thrones of the Two Lands. His Majesty then sailed northward to] Memphis.

Then he sent word to them, saying: "Do not close; do not fight, O residence of Shu from the primordial time! The entrant—let him enter; the goer—let him go! No traveler will be hindered. I shall offer an oblation to

Ptah and the gods who are in the Memphite nome; I shall make offering to Sokar in his sanctuary; I shall behold (Ptah) South-of-His-Wall; and I shall sail northward in peace, [while the people] of Memphis are safe and sound, and children are not mourned. Look, then, to the nomes of the South. None among them has been slain except for the rebels who blasphemed god, so that a slaughter was made among the traitors."

Then they closed their fortification and they sent out troops against some of the troops of His Majesty, who were but craftsmen, architects and sailors who had come [... to] the harbor of Memphis. Now that Chief of Sais arrived in Memphis at night, ordering his soldiers, his sailors, all the elite of his army, a total of 8,000 men, ordering them firmly:

"Behold, Memphis is filled with troops comprising all the elite of Lower Egypt, with barley, emmer, every sort of grain, with the granaries overflowing, and with every sort of weapon [of war. It is protected(?) by a] stronghold; a great battlement has been built as a work of skillful crafts-manship; the river encircles its East, and fighting will not be found there. The stables here are filled with oxen, the treasuries supplied with every-thing: silver, gold, copper, clothing, incense, honey, and oil. I shall go that I might give things to the Chiefs of Lower Egypt, that I might open for them their nomes,[10] and that I might become [...] days until I return."

He then mounted upon his horse, as he did not trust his chariot. He then went northward in fear of His Majesty. As the land lightened and the morning dawned, His Majesty arrived at Memphis. When he moored on its north, he found the water risen to the ramparts, with ships moored at 90 / [the houses of] Memphis.

Then His Majesty saw that it was strong, the enclosure walls high with new construction, and the battlements supplied in strength. No way of attacking it was found. Every man proceeded to state his opinion among the troops of His Majesty, entailing every tactic of fighting, with every man saying: "Let us lay siege [to Memphis.] Behold, its army is numerous," while others were saying: "Make a ramp against it so that we elevate the ground to its ramparts. Let us put together a (siege) platform, erecting masts and using sails as walls for it. Let us divide it by this means on every side of it, with talus and [...] on its north, to elevate the ground to its rampart so that we might find a path for our feet."

10. Tefnakht vows to restore northern towns to their local rulers in return for defensive assistance against Piye.

Then His Majesty raged against it like a panther, saying:

"As I live, as Re loves me, as my father Amon favors me, I have discovered that this has happened for it by the command of Amon. This is what [all] men [of Lower Egypt] and the nomes of the South say: 'Let them open to him from afar! They do not place Amon in their hearts, nor do they know what he has commanded. He has done it expressly to give evidence of his wrath and to cause that his grandeur be seen.' I shall seize it like a cloudburst; [my father Amon] has commanded me."

Then he sent his ships and his troops to assault the harbor of Memphis, and they brought away for him every boat, every ferry, every pleasure boat, as many ships as were moored at the harbor of Memphis with prow rope 95 fastened among its houses. / [There was not] a common soldier who wept among the entire army of His Majesty. His Majesty himself went to arrange the battle formation of the ships, as many as they were. His Majesty commanded his army:

"Forward against it! Mount the ramparts! Enter the houses atop the river! If one among you enters over the rampart, no one will stand in his way, [...] no troops will repel you. It would be vile, then, that we should seal Upper Egypt, moor at Lower Egypt, and yet sit in siege at "The Balance of the Two Lands.""

Then Memphis was taken like a cloudburst, with numerous people slain within it, in addition to those brought as prisoners to the place where His Majesty was. Now [after the land] lightened and a second day occurred, His Majesty sent men into it, protecting the temples of the god for him, consecrating the shrines of the gods, offering cool water to the divine tribunal of Hikuptah, purifying Memphis with natron and incense, and putting priests in their assigned places. His Majesty proceeded to the estate of [Ptah], his purification was performed in the robing room, and there was performed for him every ritual which is performed for a king. He entered into the temple. A great offering was made to his father Ptah, South-of-His-Wall, consisting of long-horned cattle, short-horned cattle, fowl and everything good. His Majesty then returned to his house.

Then every nome that was in the region of Memphis heard (it): Heripademi, Peninaiua, The Fort of Biu, and The Oasis of Bit, opening their fortifications and fleeing in flight, and no one knew where they went.

King Iuput then came together with the Chief of the Ma, Akanosh, 100 and the Hereditary Prince, Padiese, / and all the counts of Lower Egypt, bearing their tribute in order to behold the beauty of His Majesty.

Then the treasuries and granaries of Memphis were assigned, made over to the endowments of Amon, of Ptah and of the Ennead which is in Hikuptah.

As the land lightened and the morning dawned, His Majesty proceeded to the East. An offering to Atum was made in Babylon (Old Cairo), to the Ennead in the Estate of the Ennead, and to the cavern and the gods within it, consisting of long-horned cattle, short-horned cattle, and fowl, so that they might give life, prosperity, and health to the King of Upper and Lower Egypt, Piye, living forever.

His Majesty proceeded to Heliopolis over that mountain of Babylon on the road of the god Sepa[11] to Babylon. His Majesty proceeded to the camp which is on the west of Ity, his purification was performed, he was purified in the midst of the Lake of Cool Water, and his face was washed in the river of Nun where Re washed his face.

Proceeding to the High Sand in Heliopolis. Making a great offering on the High Sand in Heliopolis in the sight of Re at his rising, consisting of white oxen, milk, myrrh, incense, and every sort of sweet-smelling perfume pellets. Coming in procession to the Estate of Re. Entering into the temple in great acclamation, with lector priests adoring god and ritually repelling enemies from the king. Performing the rites of the robing room. Tying on the *sedeb*-garment. Purifying him with incense and cool water. Presenting to him bouquets of the Mansion of the *Benben*-mound. Bringing to him amulets of life. Mounting the stairway to the great window to behold Re in the Mansion of the *Benben*-mound, while the king himself stood alone. Breaking the seals of the doorbolts. Opening the doors. Seeing his father Re in the Mansion of the *Benben*-mound. Consecrating the morning-bark for Re and the evening-bark for Atum. Bringing the doors back into position. Applying the clay. Sealing / with the king's own seal. Giving orders to the priests: "I myself have inspected the seal. No other can enter into it, among all the kings who may arise." Before His Majesty they placed themselves on their bellies, saying: "(It is) to be established and enduring without fail, O Horus, beloved of Heliopolis!" Coming and entering the Estate of Atum. Presenting myrrh to the image of his father Atum-Khepri, the great one of Heliopolis. King Osorkon (IV) came expressly to behold the beauty of His Majesty.

105

11. On the deity's mythological journey from Heliopolis, see R. K. Ritner, "Horus Cippus 'Text C' and the 'Business of Sepa,' " *Varia Aegyptiaca* 6/3 (1990): 167–68.

As the land lightened and the morning dawned, His Majesty proceeded to the harbor at the head of his ships and crossed over to the harbor of the nome of Athribis, and the camp of His Majesty was made on the south of Kaheny, on the east of the nome of Athribis. Then there came these kings and counts of Lower Egypt, all the plume-wearing chiefs, all viziers, all chiefs, all royal confidants, from the West, from the East, and from the islands in between, to behold the beauty of His Majesty. Then the Hereditary Prince Padiese threw himself upon his belly in the presence of His Majesty, saying:

"Come to Athribis, that you might behold the god Khentykhety, that the goddess Khuyt might protect you,[12] that you might present an offering to Horus in his temple, consisting of long-horned cattle, short-horned cattle, and fowl. May you enter into my house, for my treasury is open to you. I shall gratify you with my ancestral property, and I shall give you gold to the limits of your desire, turquoise heaped up before you, and many horses from the best of the stable, the foremost of the stall."

His Majesty then proceeded to the Estate of Horus Khentykhety to have long-horned cattle, short-horned cattle, and fowl presented to his father Horus Khentykhety, Lord of Athribis. His Majesty proceeded to the house of Hereditary Prince Padiese, who presented him with silver, gold, 110 / lapis lazuli, turquoise, a great heap of everything, clothing of royal linen of every thread count, couches spread with fine linen, myrrh, unguent in jars, and horses both male and female, being all the foremost of his stable. He purified himself by a divine oath even in the sight of these kings and great chiefs of Lower Egypt:

"Any one here who conceals his horses or who hides for himself his worth, he shall die the death of his father! I have said this just so that you might testify for me, your humble servant, in all that you know that I possess. You should say whether I have hidden from His Majesty anything of my father's house: gold ingots, gemstones, every sort of vase, armlets, gold bracelets, necklaces, collars inlaid with gemstones, amulets of every limb, garland crowns for the head, rings for the ears, every royal adornment, all the vessels of the king's purification in gold and every sort of gemstone. All of these I have presented in the royal presence, and clothing of royal linen by the thousands, being all the best of my weaving workshop.

12. In contrast to Piye's exalted addresses in classic Middle Egyptian, the speech of his Libyan foes reflects common, contemporary grammar.

I know that you will be satisfied with it. Proceed to the stall, choose what you wish among all the horses that you desire."

Then His Majesty did likewise. These kings and counts said before His Majesty: "Send us to our towns that we might open our treasuries, that we might choose in accordance with what your heart desires, and that we might bring to you the best of our stalls, the foremost of our horses." Then His Majesty did likewise.

The list of them:

King Osorkon (IV) in Bubastis and the district of Ranefer,
King Iuput (II) in Leontopolis (Tell Moqdam) and Taan,
115 Count Djedamoniuefankh / in Mendes and The Granary of Re,
His eldest son, the general in Hermopolis Parva, Ankhhor,
Count Akanosh in Sebennytos, in Iseopolis (Behbeit el-Hagar), and Diospolis Inferior,
Count and Chief of the Ma, Patchenefy in Saft el-Henneh and in the Granary of Memphis,
Count and Chief of the Ma, Pamai in Busiris,
Count and Chief of the Ma, Nesnaiu in Hesebu,
Count and Chief of the Ma, Nakhthornashenu in Pergerer,
Chief of the Ma, Pentaweret,
Chief of the Ma, Pentabekhnet,
Prophet of Horus, Lord of Letopolis (Ausim), Padihorsomtus,
Count Horbes in the Estate of Sakhmet, Lady of Eset, and the Estate of Sakhmet, Lady of Rahesu,
Count Djedkhiu in Khentnefer,
Count Pabasa in Babylon (Old Cairo) and in Atar el-Nabi, bearing all their good tribute [...] of gold, silver, [...] couches spread
120 [with fine] linen, myrrh in jars, [...] of good value, horses / [both male and female, being all the foremost of his stable ...]

[Now after]wards, one came to say to [His] Majesty [...] army(?) [...] him [his] walls [through fear (?)] of you, while he has set fire to his treasury [and to his ships on] the river. He has reinforced Mosdai with soldiers even while he [...].

Then His Majesty sent his army to see what had happened there among the troops of the Hereditary Prince Padiese. They returned to report /
125 to His Majesty, saying: "We slew every man whom we found there." Then His Majesty gave it as a gift to the Hereditary Prince Padiese.

Then the Chief of the Ma Tefnakht heard it and sent a messenger in fawning supplication to the place where His Majesty was, saying:

"Peace be with you! I cannot look upon your face in days of shame. I cannot stand before your fiery blast, for I am terrified of your grandeur. Indeed, you are the Ombite (Seth), Lord of Upper Egypt, Montu, the strong-armed bull! To whatever city you might turn your attention, you cannot not find me, your humble servant, until I have reached the islands
130 of the sea, / for I am fearful of your wrath, saying: 'His flame is hostile to me.' Is not the heart of Your Majesty cooled by these things that you have done to me? I am indeed one justly reproached, but you did not smite me commensurably with my crime. Weigh with the balance, ascertain with the weights! May you multiply them for me in triplicate, (but) leave the seed that you may harvest it in season. Do not tear out the grove to its roots! As your *ka*-spirit endures, terror of you is in my body, fear of you is within my bones! I cannot sit in the beer hall, nor has the harp been played for
135 me. For I have eaten bread in hunger, I have drunk[13] water in / thirst, since that day when you heard my name! Bitterness is in my bones, my head is balding, my clothing rags, until Neith is appeased toward me! Long is the course that you have brought upon me, and your face is against me yet. It is a year for purging my soul. Cleanse the servant of his fault! Let my property be received into the treasury: gold and every sort of gemstone, even the foremost of the horses, repayments in every kind.[14] Send to me a messenger in haste, that he might dispel fear from my heart! Then I shall go to the
140 temple in his sight to cleanse myself by a divine / oath.

When His Majesty sent the chief lector priest Padiamon(neb)nesut-tawy and the general Pawerem, he (Tefnakht) presented him with silver, gold, clothing, and every sort of precious gemstone. When he went into the temple, he praised god and cleansed himself by a divine oath, saying:

"I shall not transgress the royal command. I shall not thrust aside that which His Majesty says. I shall not do wrong to a count without your knowledge. I shall act in accordance with what the king has said. I shall not transgress what he has commanded."

Then His Majesty was satisfied concerning it.

145 One came to say / to His Majesty: "Crocodilopolis has opened its fortress and Aphroditopolis is placed upon its belly. There is no nome

---

13. Like the other Libyan dynasts, Tefnakht uses common Late Egyptian constructions.
14. Or, following an early suggestion of Griffith, "horses, adorned with everything."

sealed against His Majesty among the nomes of the South and North, while the West, the East and the islands in between are upon their bellies through fear of him, having their property sent to the place where His Majesty is, like servants of the palace."

As the land lightened and the morning dawned, these two rulers of Upper Egypt and two rulers of Lower Egypt, those entitled to royal uraei, came to kiss the ground because of the wrathful power of His Majesty. Now, however, these kings and counts of Lower Egypt who came to behold

150   the beauty of His Majesty, their legs / were like the legs of women.[15] They could not enter into the palace since they were uncircumcised and eaters of fish—such is an abomination of the palace. However, king Namlot entered into the palace since he was pure and did not eat fish. Three stood in their positions while one entered the palace.

Then the ships were loaded with silver, gold, copper, clothing, and everything of Lower Egypt, every product of Syria, every incense pellet

155   of god's land. / His Majesty then sailed southward with his heart gladdened and all those on both sides of him shouting. The West and East took up the announcement, shouting round about His Majesty.

The chant of jubilation which they said:

> "O mighty ruler, O mighty ruler! Piye, O mighty ruler!
> You return having conquered Lower Egypt;
> making bulls into women!
> Happy is the heart of the mother who bore you,
> and of the male whose seed is within you!
> Those in the Nile valley praise her,
> the cow who gave birth to a bull!
> You are eternal, your victory enduring,
> O ruler beloved of Thebes!"

15. Trembling in fear.

# THE FAMINE STELA

L ightly carved on a granite boulder on Sehel Island near the first cataract, this description of "seven lean years in Egypt" was surely composed and copied in the Ptolemaic period, though set in the Third Dynasty reign of Djoser, some 2,500 years earlier. The text provides the priesthood of Khnum at Elephantine with a "historical" claim to all revenue of the territory known as the Dodecaschoinus (twelve schoinoi, or some eighty miles), extending southward from Aswan into Lower Nubia. The late date is indicated by vocabulary, grammar, orthography, and the divine filiation accorded Djoser's famous deified architect, Imhotep. It is possible, however, that the text reflects a late rendition of earlier documents or legends. As noted by Miriam Lichtheim, the claim was probably motivated by the encroaching demands of the younger, but increasingly prestigious temple of Isis at Philae, located just south of Elephantine and thus directly adjacent to the wealthy territory in question. Above the rectangular stela is a depiction of Djoser offering to the primary deities of Elephantine: Khnum-Re, Satis, and Anukis. The text, discovered by the American Egyptologist Charles Wilbour in 1889, preserves the earliest explicit link between the "Horus Netcherkhet," builder of the Saqqara Step Pyramid, and the "King Djoser" known from an early ivory plaque and formal king lists. For the historical background of the text, see Gertrud Dietze, "Philae und die Dodekaschoinos in ptolemäischer Zeit," Ancient Society 25 (1994): 94–97.

R.K.R.

Regnal year 18 of the Horus: Netcherkhet, the King of Upper and Lower Egypt: Netcherkhet, the Horus of Gold: Djoser, under the authority of the count, hereditary prince and ruler of southern estates, overseer of Nubians in Elephantine, Mesir. This royal decree was brought to him to inform you:

"I was despondent upon my throne, and those in the palace were in grief. My heart was extremely sad since the Inundation had not come on time for a period of seven years. Grain was scarce, the kernels dried out, everything edible in short supply. Every man was so restrained by his taxation that they went inside so as not to go out. The child was in tears, the youth astray, and the elderly—their hearts were miserable, their legs drawn together, squatting on the ground with their arms held inward. The courtiers were in ruin, the temples sealed up, the chapels dusty, everything found wanting. I directed my thoughts back to the past, and I consulted a member of the staff of the Ibis, the chief lector priest Imhotep,[1] son of Ptah South-of-His-Wall:

'Where is the place that the Inundation is born? What town is the undulating one in? What god is resident that he might join / with me?'

He arose: 'I shall proceed to the sanctuary of Thoth at Hermopolis,[2] being wary for the confidence of everyone regarding what they should do. I shall enter into the House of Life, I shall spread out the "Souls of Re,"[3] and I shall be guided by them.'

So he departed and he returned to me directly. He informed me about the flow of the Inundation, [its regions] and everything with which they are provided. He revealed to me the hidden wonders to which the ancestors, without equal among the kings since the very beginning, had made their way. He declared to me:

'There is a city in the midst of the flood waters. The Inundation surrounds it. Elephantine is its name. It is the first of the first. It is the first nome adjacent to Wawat.[4] Earthly mound and celestial height, it is the seat of Re when he calculates casting life before everyone. "Sweetness of Life" is the name of its sanctuary, "Twin Caverns" the name of the water. They are the breasts that nourish everything. It is the bedchamber of the Inundation, [in which] he rejuvenates himself in [his] time. [It is the place from which]

5

---

1. Barguet, followed by Lichtheim, inserts an unnecessary genitive: "the chief lector priest of Imhotep."
2. Lit. "The Mansion of the Net."
3. Sacred scriptures.
4. Lower Nubia.

he [seizes(?)] the shore, fecundating by mounting as a male, a bull to a female, renewing his virility, providing for his desire, surging at twenty-eight cubits and passing Sema-behdet[5] at seven.

Khnum is the deity there, [...] his sandals placed on the flood, holding the doorbolt in his hand, opening the (flood)gates as he wishes. He is eternal there as Shu. Master of largess,[6] overseer of fields, so he will be named when he has reckoned the land of Upper and Lower Egypt / to grant allotments to every god. It is he who has regulated barley, [emmer], fowl, fish, and everything by which they live. The cord is there with the scribal palette; the sighting stick is there with his royal[7] level for his plumb bob, he being master of largess because of it, in accordance with what Shu, son of Re, has placed in heaven.

His temple is open to the southeast, just so that Re rises opposite it each day. Its waters rage at its southern side by a *schoenus,* a wall separating the Nubians daily.[8] A range of mountains are its foundation on the east, with all sorts of precious stones and hard quarry stones, and everything that is sought to build every temple of Upper and Lower Egypt, together with the stalls of the sacred animals, and the royal tombs, and every statue that stands within temple and sanctuary.

Their products are gathered before Khnum and round about him, and similarly the tall plants and every sort of flower that exists starting from Elephantine and ending in Bigeh, present there on the east and on the west. There is in the midst of the river, covered by water at its yearly season, its place of relaxation for every man who works these stones on its banks. There exists in the river, in sight of[9] this city of Elephantine itself, a central outcrop, difficult in its form, called the snare[10] of Elephantine.

---

5. Tell el-Balamun (Diospolis Inferior) in the Delta. From Elephantine to the Delta, the flood is said to drop twenty-one cubits, about thirty-six feet.
6. For the term, see D. Inconnu-Bocquillon, "Les titres ẖry idb et ẖry wḏb dans les inscriptions des temples gréco-romains," *RdE* 40 (1989): 65–89.
7. Barguet identifies the word as a phonetic spelling of "plank." Lichtheim does not translate the passage, which specifies Khnum's role as surveyor and distributor of lands after the annual flood.
8. A reference to the first cataract at Aswan, an effective buffer against southern riverine attack.
9. The term *snk* is written for *stw.t* (cf. *Wb.* IV, 332).
10. Coptic κροϥ· The two outcrops correspond to Mophi and Crophi, mentioned in Herodotus II.28.

Learn the names of the gods who are prominent in the temple of Khnum: Satis,[11] Anukis, Hapy, Shu, Geb, Nut, Osiris, Horus, Isis, and Nephthys.

15     Learn the names / of the stones that are there, lying in the midst of the district, present in the east and west, present [on the banks of the] canal of Elephantine, present in Elephantine, present in the midst of the east and west, and present in the midst of the river: greywacke, granite, *mḫtbtb, r'gs,* and *wtšy* prominent in the east, *prḏn* in the west, *tšy* in the west and present in the river. The names of the precious stones of the quarries which are in the area above these, present among them for a distance of four *schoenoi:* gold, silver, copper, iron, lapis lazuli, turquoise, green-stone, red jasper, *g'y,* quartz, beryl, and rock crystal(?). In addition to these, green feldspar, red ochre, garnet, *ibḥt,* haematite, malachite, galena, carnelian, *shrt, mimi,* and ochre are within this township.'

I heard what was in it, and my heart brooded.[12] When I had listened about the flood, the sealed scrolls were opened. I made a purification, I made a procession of the secret ones, and I made a complete offering consisting of bread, beer, fowl, oxen, and every good thing for the gods and goddesses in Elephantine whose names are invoked. I slept in peace,[13] and I found a god standing facing me. I propitiated him by adoration; I prayed to him in his presence. He revealed himself to me with radiant face,[14] and he spoke:

'I am Khnum, your fashioner. My arms are behind you to shelter your body, to make healthy your limbs. I have dispatched to you gemstones upon gemstones, [that had not been found] previously and with which no work had been done to build temples, to renew ruins, or to inlay both parts of a statue's eyes.[15] For I am the lord of fashioning, I am the one who fashioned himself, the very great Abyss, who came into being at the first, the Inunda-

20 tion who courses / as he wills, who crafts mankind, who guides every man in his (critical) hour, Tatenen, the father of the gods, Shu the great, the chief of heaven.

11. Written as Sothis.
12. Reading *w3* as carved. Barguet emended the text and translated "rejoiced." Lichtheim suggested "was guided" with hesitation.
13. Lit. "in life and dominion."
14. The expression may also have the figurative meaning of "joyous" (Second Kamose Stela, l. 32).
15. A reference to the inlay of white and black stones for the sclera and pupil.

There are two sockets[16] for the naos that bears me. The wellspring, I have released it. I know the Inundation will embrace the fields with an embrace that joins life to every nostril, even as embracing the field will rejuvenate it. Thus I shall have the Inundation flow forth for you, with no year of want or sluggishness for any land. The fields will grow, bowed down beneath the growth of their meal. Renenutet will preside over everything, with everything readied in millions.

I shall cause that your kindred be filled, so that they might take possession together with you. Gone will be the hunger years that begot borrowing from their granaries. The land of Egypt will come at a clip, the banks will glisten, the flood will be excellent, and their hearts will be happier than they had ever been previously.'

So I awakened while my mind raced, now separated from my fatigue, and I made this decree beside my father Khnum.

A royal offering to Re-Khnum, lord of the cataract region, preeminent in Nubia: 'In return for these things that you have done for me, I shall offer to you your western border in Manu, your eastern border in Bakhu, from Elephantine down to Takhompso, comprising twelve *schoenoi* on the east and west, consisting of fields and canals, of river and of every place within the alloted *schoenoi*. Let every man who cultivates the fields and those who revive the slain by irrigating the banks and all new lands that are within the alloted *schoenoi* deliver[17] their harvests to your magazine, / in addition to your share that is in Hermopolis.[18] All fishermen and of all hunters who catch fish or trap birds and any sort of game, who trap any lions on the desert—I shall tax them one-tenth[19] of the take of all these, and all the calves born of the herds within the alloted *schoenoi* in [their entirety]. I shall give the branded animals for every burnt offering and all daily offerings of every day, and I shall give one-tenth of gold, ivory, ebony, carob wood, ochre, carnelian, *shrt, diw*-plants, *nfw*-plants, wood of every sort of tree, and

25

16. *Kr.ty;* see *Wb.* V, 58/2. The term refers both to architectural features and to the supposed twin sources of the Nile beneath Elephantine.
17. Lit. "Let, (with regard to) every man who cultivates . . . that their harvests be delivered . . . "
18. Reading *'Ibt.t* with Barguet; Lichtheim read *'Ibw* "Elephantine."
19. For this donation, see M. Lichtheim, "The Naucratis Stela Once Again," *Studies in Honor of George R. Hughes,* SAOC 39 (Chicago, 1976), 142–44.

everything that the Nubians of Lower Nubia[20] bring to Egypt, and every man who goes under the supervision of those among them.

No administrative staff are to give orders in these places or to exact anything from among them, for the property is protected with respect to my grant for your sanctuary.[21] I shall offer to you this domain containing stones and good arable land, without anybody therein [subtracting] anything from it. The residents, your scribes, the agents of the South and the archivists will document everything that the gardeners, and the smiths, and the master craftsmen, and the goldsmiths, and the reckoners of herdsmen,[22] and the Nubians, and the gang of crewmen[23] and all the corvée labor who act to finish these stones, will give in gold, silver, copper, lead, baskets of [...], firewood, the things that every man working with them should give in payment, / comprising one-tenth of all these. And I shall give one-tenth of the gemstones and quarry stones brought from the upper area and the stones on the east. And there is to be an overseer who measures the quantity of gold, silver, copper, true gemstones, and the things that the sculptors will mark for the house of gold[24] to fashion sacred images or to erect statues that have fallen into disrepair, together with any necessity not present. Everything is to be placed in a storehouse until they are refashioned, with everything that was lacking in your temple ascertained, that it might be as it was in ancient times.

Publish this decree in writing on a stela in a sacred place, because it happened as said, and on a tablet so that the divine words concerning it might exist in the temples twice over. He who spits upon it unjustly is destined for punishment. The overseers of priests and the overseer of everyone of the temple will make my name remain in the temple of Khnum-Re, lord of Elephantine, mighty forever."

30

---

20. Khenty-hen-nefer, "South of the good boundary," a Nubian region south of the second cataract.
21. Reading $r$ (= $iw$) $nb$ $h.wt$ $r$ $di$ =($i$) ($n$) $r$-$pr$=$k$.
22. Reading $hsb.w$-$nr$.
23. *Wb.* I, 181/6. Or read "Hapiru," foreign workers often linked to the ethnic designation "Hebrew"; see R. Giveon, "Hapiru," *LÄ* II, (1977), cols. 952–55.
24. A designation of the official sculptural workshop and associated magazines.

# THE SATRAP STELA
# (CAIRO JdE 22182)

I n November 311 B.C., while Egypt was officially ruled by Alexander the
Great's infant son (Alexander II of Egypt, IV of Macedon), real authority
was exercised by the satrap Ptolemy (I), former general and founder of the
Ptolemaic dynasty that would rule until the suicide of Cleopatra the Great.
After victories in 312/11 secured the extension of Ptolemy's control into Syria-
Palestine, the ambitious satrap celebrated a thanksgiving festival that culmi-
nated in a royal donation decree to the native gods of Pe and Dep, precincts of
the sacred city of Buto. The text of this donation, known as the Satrap Stela,
maintains the fiction of Alexander's kingship, while according Ptolemy unprece-
dented praise, even adapting the narrative "Königsnovelle" format. The text
preserves the most extensive information concerning the brief reign of Khababash between the Persian occupations and typifies late ideology of kingship,
with dire consequences for rulers who abandon divine law.[1]

Within the quoted dialogue, references to "His Majesty" are ambiguous,
referring either to the yet uncrowned Ptolemy, as assumed by the first editor,
Brugsch, or to Khababash, as suggested by Wilcken and followed by subsequent
translators. While Ptolemy certainly uses nonroyal expressions for himself, it is
less certain that the priesthood would hesitate to flatter the de facto ruler with

---

1. See Ritner, "Khababash and the Satrap Stela—A Grammatical Rejoinder," *ZÄS* 107
(1980): 136–37.

*the titles of "Sovereign" and "Majesty." Ambiguity is perhaps intentional, for in the upper lunette, a king in traditional royal regalia, but with blank cartouches, offers land and products in flanking scenes to Horus and Edjo, local deities of Buto and patrons of kingship.*                                                R.K.R.

1    Regnal year 7, first month of Inundation season, under the Majesty of the Horus: "The youthful one, great of strength"; The Two Ladies: "The beloved of the gods, to whom was given the office of his father"; The Horus of Gold: "The ruler in the entire land"; the King of Upper and Lower Egypt, Lord of the Two Lands, Haaibre-Setepenamon,[2] the Son of Re, Alexander (II), living forever, beloved of the gods of Pe and Dep. He is king in the Two Lands and the foreign countries. His Majesty is in the midst of the Asiatics, while a great Prince is in Egypt, whose name is Ptolemy.

He is a youthful man, strong in his two arms, effective in plans, with mighty armies, stout hearted, firm footed, who attacks the powerful without turning his back, who strikes the face of his opponents when they fight, with precise hand, who grasps to himself the bow without shooting astray, who fights with his sword in the midst of battle, with none who can stand in his vicinity, a champion whose arms are not repulsed, with no reversal of what issues from his mouth, who has no equal in the Two Lands or the foreign countries.

As he brought back the sacred images of the gods which were found within Asia, together with all the ritual implements and all the sacred scrolls of the temples of Upper and Lower Egypt, so he restored them in their proper places. As he made his residence, named the Fortress of the King of Upper and Lower Egypt Merikaamon-Setepenre,[3] the Son of Re, Alexander, whose former name was Rakotis, on the shore of the great green

5    sea of the Greeks, so he assembled many Greeks with / their horses and many ships with their troops. He then went with his armies to the land of the Syrians, with the result that they fought with him and he entered among them with his heart strong like a raptor in pursuit of small birds, seizing them in a single instant. To Egypt he brought away their princes, their horses, their ships, and all their wonders.

Afterward, he made an expedition to the territory of Irem,[4] seizing

2. "The heart of Re rejoices, Chosen of Amon."
3. "Beloved of the *ka*-spirit of Amon, Chosen of Re."
4. Beginning with Brugsch in 1871, the place name has been read *Mr-mr-tỉ* and identified with Marmarica because of a known campaign by Ptolemy against the Libyan

them in a single moment. In retaliation for what they had done against Egypt, he brought away their people, both male and female, together with their gods. He then returned to Egypt with his heart happy at these things that he had done.

As he was celebrating a holiday, so this great Prince was seeking bene-factions for the gods of Upper and Lower Egypt, with the result that those who were beside him together with the grandees of Lower Egypt said to him:

"The northern marshland, whose name is The Land of Edjo, the King of Upper and Lower Egypt Senenenptah-setepentenen,[5] the Son of Re, Khababash, living forever, gave it to the gods of Pe and Dep after His Majesty proceeded to Pe and Dep, making a circuit of the marshland that is in its entire territory, going into the interior of the swamps and examining each Nile branch that goes to the sea, in order to repel the ships of Asia from Egypt."

Then His Majesty[6] said to those who were beside him: "This marsh-land, inform me (about it)!," so that they said before His Majesty: "The northern marshland, whose name is The Land of Edjo, it formerly belonged to the gods of Pe and Dep, before the enemy Xerxes revoked it. He did not make offerings from it to the gods of Pe and Dep."

Then His Majesty said: "Let the priests and high dignitaries of Pe and

---

Cyrenaica (Sethe, 15; Bouché-Leclerq, 106, n. 2; Mahaffy, 39; Bevan, 30). As recog-nized by *Wb.*I/116, however, the spelling corresponds to the Nubian site of Irem, attested from the New Kingdom and localized in the Sudanese Butana near Shendi by David O'Connor, "The Location of Irem," *JEA* 73 (1987): 99–136. This location corresponds to the site of Meroe in Ptolemaic times, so Ptolemy's campaign was against "Meroitic territory" in its broadest sense, most probably in Lower Nubia. See further P. M. Fraser, *Ptolemaic Alexandria* (Oxford, 1972), vol. 2, 12, n. 28.

5. "The image of Ptah, Chosen of (Ptah)-Tenen."

6. Here punctuated, with some hesitation, as Ptolemy. Wilcken's suggestion of Khaba-bash requires that the king's questioning of "those who were beside him" in l.8 cannot be the logical response to the statement of "those who were beside him" in the preceding line. The priests' historical narration (of Khababash's conversation) would continue from ll. 7 to 12, with an abrupt and unmarked change of address from Khababash to Ptolemy in l. 12, and no mention of how Khababash's donation after Xerxes was reversed. With the Brugsch interpretation, conversation alternates be-tween the king and his courtiers, Khababash is noted as the initial donor, Xerxes the subsequent disturber, and Ptolemy the restorer, who alone can be said to have given the land "a second time" (l. 12).

Dep be brought!," so that they were brought to him in haste. Then His
Majesty said: "Inform me of the wrath of the gods of Pe and Dep, how
they dealt with the enemy / because of the evil deed that he had done!
Behold, they say that the enemy Xerxes did an evil deed against Pe and
Dep, having seized its property," so that they said before His Majesty:

"Sovereign, our lord! Horus the son of Isis, the son of Osiris, ruler of
rulers, the ideal Upper Egyptian King, the ideal Lower Egyptian King, the
protector of his father, the Lord of Pe, the foremost of the gods who came
into existence afterward, after whom there is no king, expelled the enemy
Xerxes[7] from his (Egyptian) palace together with his eldest son; thus it is
perceived in Sais of Neith today beside the God's Mother."

Then His Majesty said: "This god, champion among the gods, after
whom there is no king, let me be placed upon the path of His Majesty on
which a King lives!"[8]

Then the priests and high dignitaries of Pe and Dep said: "Let Your
Majesty command to give back the northern marshland, whose name is The
Land of Edjo, to the gods of Pe and Dep, including its bread, beer, oxen,
fowl and every good thing.[9] Let its renewal be heralded in your name
regarding its donation to the gods of Pe and Dep a second time in exchange
for making your deeds successful."[10]

Then this great Prince said: "Let a written command be made at the
record office of the royal accounting scribe saying:

'(By order of) Ptolemy the Satrap. The Land of Edjo, I shall give it to

7. For Artaxerxes, as noted by Spiegelberg, 1907, 5–6. The notary of a Demotic
document of year 1 of Khababash also notarized a document of year 9 of Alexander
the Great (324 b.c.), so that the reign of Khababash could precede that of Artaxerxes (342–339), but not that of Xerxes (486–465). Briant, 1044, has suggested that
Egyptians used Xerxes as a generic name.

8. Or, "Let me be placed upon the path of His Majesty so that I might live on it." "His
Majesty" here refers to Horus as true king. For the common notion of a personal
"path of life," cf. The Eloquent Peasant, Papyrus Insinger, and the discussion in
Ritner, "Khababash and the Satrap Stela—A Grammatical Rejoinder," *ZÄS* 107
(1980): 136–37.

9. The land is given primarily for its produce, the source of income for the temple.
Thus, in the lunette scene, the offering of land is balanced by an offering of the
derived produce. Wilcken's interpretation makes this the conclusion of the narration, with the following mention of "your name" addressed to Ptolemy.

10. Ptolemy's successful military invasion is here credited to the intervention of the
gods.

Horus, the protector of his father, Lord of Pe, and to Edjo, Lady of Pe and Dep, from today forever, together with all its towns, all its villages, all its inhabitants, all its acreage, all its water, all its cattle, all its flocks, all its herds[11] and everything that derives from it and which has been part of it previously, together with whatever is added to it, together with the donation made by the King of Upper and Lower Egypt, Lord of the Two Lands, Khababash, living forever,

15
> its south: the district of the town of Buto / and northern Hermopolis up to the doors of Nilopolis,
> north: the dunes[12] at the shore of the sea,
> west: the doors of the canal[13] of the rudder [...] divine waters to the dunes,
> east: the district of Sebennytos.

Its short-horned cattle shall be destined for the great sacred falcons, its long-horned cattle for the dromos of the Lady of the Two Lands, its oxen for the living falcons, its milk for the noble child, its birds for the one residing in Khemmis,[14] who lives on blood, with everything that derives from its arable land being on the offering table of Horus himself, the Lord of Pe, and Edjo, the serpent who is on the brow of Re-Horachty, forever.

All of this the King of Upper and Lower Egypt, Lord of the Two Lands, Senenenptah-setepentenen, the Son of Re, Khababash, living forever, donated to the gods of Pe and Dep forever, and this great ruler of Egypt, Ptolemy, has renewed the donations to the gods of Pe and Dep forever, with the reward for this that he has done being the giving to him of valor and victory in happiness, while fear of him pervades the foreign lands to their full extent.[15]

11. Further specified by hieroglyphic determinatives of cattle, ram, ibex, pig, and donkey.
12. Lit. "ground" *Wb.* III, 423.
13. *Wb.* III, 332/5.
14. Carved as "Inundation season," probably a Ptolemaic substitution of one swamp hieroglyph for another (cf. *Wb.* I, 13/2–4). The resident of Khemmis is Horus, whose sacred animal the falcon does live on the blood of small birds, cf. the royal encomium in line 5 of this text.
15. The phraseology parallels the conclusion of traditional royal donation texts; cf. Kawa stelae 3, 4, and 8 in M. F. Laming Macadam, *The Temples of Kawa*, vol. 1 (London, 1949). For the final curses, a feature common to both royal and private

The Land of Edjo, the one who will inventory[16] it or who will disturb it so as to seize property from it, he is in the bonds of Those who are in Pe; he is in the fury of Those who are in Dep, while he shall be in the fiery blast of the goddess Weptawi on the day of her raging. Neither his son nor daughter will give him water.' "

---

donations, see H. Sottas, *La préservation de la propriété funéraire dans l'ancienne Égypte* (Paris, 1913), 136–38.

16. For the term, see Ritner, *CdE* 63, no. 126, (1989): 279–80, contra E. Bresciani, "Registraziane catastale . . . ," *Egitto e Vicino Oriente* 6 (1983): 28 (l. 14).

# VII

AUTOBIOGRAPHIES

# THREE AUTOBIOGRAPHIES OF THE OLD KINGDOM

I t is curious and significant that three of the most interesting private (as opposed to royal) texts from Dynasty 6 come from sites in the south, away from the royal capital at Memphis and the pyramid cemeteries at Giza, Saqqara, and Abusir. Weni's text, along with various elements of his tomb, comes from Abydos in Upper Egypt Nome VIII, Harkhuf's text from the facade of his rock-cut tomb on the west side of the Nile at Aswan in Upper Egypt Nome I, and Qar's text from the false door of his tomb chapel at Edfu in Upper Egypt Nome II. Weni's extraordinary career began under Teti, the first ruler of Dynasty 6, and continued under kings Pepy I and Merenre. Qar also started his career under Teti and continued under Pepy I and Merenre. Harkhuf's career began under Merenre and continued into the early years of the young ruler Pepy II. Most of the many texts from the mastaba and rock tombs of the Old Kingdom are replete with the owner's titles, the often-repeated offering formulae, and the frequent address to the living who will pass by the tomb. Few have as interesting "autobiographical" elements as the following three.

W.K.S.

## WENI THE ELDER

*Weni's career is the subject of this long inscription from his tomb at the Middle Cemetery at Abydos. The false door and other elements of the tomb mentioned in the text are preserved in the Egyptian Museum, Cairo. The sarcophagus of Merenre, which he had quarried and brought back from Nubia, according to the text, is still in the burial chamber of the king's pyramid. In his analysis of the career, Eyre sums up Weni's personality: "His entire career was spent in close personal contact with the king in a period of real political tension. By the end of the reign of Pepy I, Weni should have been the archetypal Egyptian gerontocrat, aged at least 60, and by his death under Merenre probably over 70. From his own account he fitted the Egyptian ideal of the selfless, self-effacing, effective royal servant . . . reality is likely to have involved a degree of ruthless opportunism." The hieroglyphic text is presented in K. Sethe,* Urkunden des alten Reichs *I, 2nd ed. (Leipzig, 1932), 98–110. In the following translation the numbering refers to the paragraphing according to subject in Sethe's edition. For discussions, see bibliography under Weni the Elder, particularly Eyre 1994. Weni's mastaba at Abydos was relocated with some fragments of text by an expedition in 1999.*

(1) [The count and overseer of the southland], he who is in the palace, the custodian of Nekhen, the chief Nekhebite, sole companion, venerated before Osiris-Foremost-of-the-Westerners, Weni [the Elder. He says]:

(2) [I was a youth (*ḥwn*)] who tied on the headband[1] under the Majesty of Teti, my office being that of overseer of the storehouse. When I served as assistant supervisor of the officials of the palace, and ... elder lector priest of the robing room under the Majesty of Pepy [I], His Majesty placed me in the office of companion and assistant supervisor of the priests of his pyramid town, although my office was (only) that of ...

(3) His [Majesty placed me] as senior warden of Nekhen, his heart being filled with me more than that of any servant of his, when I judged cases by myself together with the vizier in all confidence and [all matters] connected with the reputation of the king, with the Privy Palace, and with the Six Great Estates, because the heart of His Majesty was filled with me more than that of any official of his, any noble of his, and any servant of his.

---

1. This is a ritual of passage, cited also in the text of Qar (below). It possibly refers to the age of about eighteen or the beginning of manhood. See Edward J. Brovarski, "Varia," *Serapis* 3 (1975–76): 1–8.

(4) I requested from the Majesty of my lord that there be brought for me a sarcophagus of limestone from Tura,[2] and His Majesty had a god's treasurer cross over together with a detachment of sailors under his charge to fetch for me this sarcophagus from Tura. It (the sarcophagus) returned with him in a great cargo boat of the (royal) Residence, together with its lid, a false door, a lintel, two door jambs, and one offering table.[3] Never had the like been done for any servant of his, for I was excellent in the heart of His Majesty, because I was firmly rooted in the heart of His Majesty, and because the heart of His Majesty was filled with me, although my office was (only) that of senior warden of Nekhen.

(5) His Majesty appointed me as sole companion and overseer of the officials of the palace, and four officials of the palace who were there were dispossessed.[4] I acted so that His Majesty praised me in carrying out body-guard service, in preparing the royal road, and in carrying out the (royal) stations. I acted to perfection, so that His Majesty praised me because of it more than anything.

(6) When proceedings were instigated in the Privy Palace against the queen,[5] "great of scepter," in private, His Majesty had me go down to judge, my being singled out, there not being any vizier or any official there except for me, because of my excellence, because of my being rooted in the estimation of His Majesty, and because of His Majesty's heart being filled with me. It was I who put it into writing alone together with a single senior warden of Nekhen, while my office was (only that of) overseer of the officials of the palace. Never before had the like been heard in a private matter of the Privy Palace, except for His Majesty's having me judge, because of my excellence in the estimation of His Majesty more than any official of his, more than any noble of his, and more than any servant of his.

2. Tura was the site to the east of modern Cairo from which the finest limestone was quarried. The casing stone for the pyramids was transported across the river from Tura. Weni boasts that the king provided him with this fine limestone, which had to be shipped upstream (against the current) for quite a distance from Tura and then overland to the cemetery at Abydos.
3. Several of these elements were actually excavated at Weni's tomb, as was the text of his autobiography, and are now registered in the Egyptian Museum Cairo.
4. There is some question as to the meaning of this "replacement" of four officials.
5. On the "harem conspiracy" and trial of the queen, designated by her title and not her real name, see Hans Goedicke, "An Approximate Date for the Harem Investigation under Pepi I," *JAOS* 74 (1954): 32–34.

(7) It was after he had formed an army of many ten thousands of the southland in its entirety that His Majesty took action against the sand-dwellers of the Aamu,[6] southwards at Elephantine and northwards at Medjenit,[7] from the northland (Delta), from the two halves (of the Delta) in their entirety, from Sedjer, from the interior of Sedjeru,[8] from the Nubians of Jrtjet, from the Nubians of Medja, from the Nubians of Iam, from the Nubians of Wawat, from the Nubians of Kaau, and from the Libyan of the land of Temehu.[9]

(8) His Majesty sent me at the head of this army, there being counts, there being royal sealbearers, there being sole companions of the Great Estate, there being chieftains and estate rulers of the southland and northland, companions, overseers of foreign tongue speakers, overseers of priests of the southland and northland, and overseers of the work centers at the head of the troop of the southland and northland and the estates and towns which they governed, (as well as) the Nubians of these foreign lands. I used to effectuate (military) plans for them, my office being (only) that of overseer of the officials of the palace, through the rectitude of my position, so that not one of them struck his fellow, so that not one of them took away a loaf of bread or a pair of sandals from a wayfarer, so that not one of them seized a bolt of cloth from any town, so that not one of them took away a goat from anyone. I led them from the northern island, the gateway of I(m)hotep, the plateau of Hor-neb-Maat,[10] this office of mine being (only) that of . . . everything. I inspected (?) these troops of mine. Never (before) had they been inspected by any (such) servant.

(9) Having hacked up the land of the sand-dwellers,
    this army (of mine) returned safely.
Having trounced the land of the sand-dwellers,
    this army (of mine) returned safely.

6. The term "Aamu" refers to the Asiatic people of the time.
7. Medjenit is a nome at the extreme north of "Upper Egypt," just south of the Memphite region, hence the entire area of Upper Egypt.
8. Sedjer and Khen-Sedjeru are thought to be parts of the Delta but are otherwise not known.
9. Temehu is one of the designations of the lands to the west of Egypt generally designated as Libya.
10. The gateway of Imhotep and the district of Hor-neb-Maat lie at the northeast corner of the Delta and serve as the "entry" to Palestine.

Having overturned its walled settlements,
> this army (of mine) returned safely.

Having cut down its figs and its vines,
> this army (of mine) returned safely.

Having set fire to (the crops) of all its people,
> this army (of mine) returned safely.

Having slain the troops therein by many ten thousands,
> this army (of mine) returned safely.

[Having brought back the troops] therein very greatly as captives,
> this army (of mine) returned safely.

[With the result that] His Majesty praised me on account of it more than anything.

(10) His Majesty sent me to lead [this army of mine] on five occasions to crush the land of the sand-dwellers each time they rebelled, with these troops of mine. I acted so that His Majesty [praised me on account of it more than anything].

(11) I was told that there were rebels because of a dispute among these foreigners at Sheret-Tep-Wendju (Nose-of-the-head-of the goat).[11] I crossed over with rafts together with these troops of mine. While half of this army of mine was (still) on the upper way, it was to the north of the land of the sand-dwellers that I put to land at the rear of the heights of the ridge. It was (only) after I had captured them in their entirety and (only) after I had slain every rebel among them that I returned.

(12) When I was a tutor of the Great Estate and sandal-bearer, the King of Upper and Lower Egypt Merenre, my lord, living forever, placed me as count and overseer of the southland, southward at Elephantine and northward at Medjenyt, for I was excellent in the estimation of His Majesty, for I was rooted in the heart of His Majesty, for His Majesty filled his heart with me. When I was tutor and sandal-bearer, His Majesty praised me for my vigilance, for the escort duty which I performed in the service of attendance more than any official of his, more than any courtier of his, and more than any servant of his. Never had this office been carried out by any (such)

---

11. The geographical designation, previously read as Gazelle Nose, is controversial. It is usually considered to be the promontory of Mount Carmel, but claims have been made that the ridge lies farther south within Egypt itself. See Hans Goedicke, "The Alleged Military Campaign in Southern Palestine in the Reign of Pepi I (VIth Dynasty)," *RSO* 38 (1963): 187–97.

servant previously. I acted for him (the king) as overseer of the southland to satisfaction, so that no man in it struck [his] fellow, I having carried out all works, I having counted everything countable to the (royal) Residence in this (part of the) southland on two occasions, and all corvée duty due to the Residence in this (part of the) southland on two occasions, I having performed my official duty, performing excellently in this (part of the) southland. Never had the like been done in this (part of the) southland previously. I performed outstandingly so that His Majesty would praise me for it.

(13) His Majesty sent me to Ibhat[12] to fetch a lord of life (sarcophagus),[13] a chest of life, together with its lid and together with a costly and august pyramidion for Kha-nefer-Merenre (the king's pyramid), my mistress. His Majesty sent me to Elephantine to fetch a false door of granite together with its offering table, door jambs, and lintels of granite and to fetch portals of granite, and offering tables for the upper chamber of Kha-nefer-Merenre, my mistress. It was on a single riverine expedition that (they) fared northward in my charge to Kha-nefer-Merenre in six broad barges, three towboats, and three eight-ribbers. Never had (both) Ibhat and Elephantine been visited by a single riverine expedition since the time of all the kings. It has been in accordance with all that His Majesty ordered that everything that His Majesty ordered came to pass outstandingly.

(14) His Majesty sent me to Hatnub to fetch a great offering table of travertine of Hatnub.[14] I had this offering table go down within seventeen days, being quarried in Hatnub, it being made to travel north on this broad cargo boat, for I had hewed for it (the offering table) a broad cargo boat in acacia sixty cubits long by thirty cubits wide, assembled in seventeen days in the third month of Shomu, while there was no water on the sandbanks, it being (subsequently) moored at Kha-nefer-Merenre safely. It was according to the utterance of the Majesty of my lord that it came to pass through my charge outstandingly.

12. Ibhat is a quarry site in Nubia.
13. The sarcophagus of the king is still in his pyramid. See Myriam Wissa, "Le sarcophage de Merenre et l'éxpedition à Ibhat (I)," in Catherine Berger, Gisèle Clerc, and Nicolas Grimal, eds., *Hommages à Jean Leclant* I (Cairo, IFAOC, 1994), 379–87.
14. Hatnub is the well-known quarry on the east of the Nile in Upper Egyptian Nome XV, the nome wherein the Middle Kingdom site of Bersheh and the later Tell el Amarna are situated. It was the site for quarrying Egyptian alabaster, a kind of calcite now generally termed travertine.

(15) His Majesty sent me to excavate five canals in the southland and to fashion three barges and four towboats of acacia-wood of Wawat (Nubia) while the chieftains of Jrtjet, Wawat, Iam, and Medja were felling wood for them.[15] I carried it out entirely in a single year, they being launched and laden with granite very greatly destined for Kha-nefer-Merenre. Now an (economic) saving (or shortening of the distance?) was made for the Palace with these five watercourses in their entirety through the worthiness, through the renown, and through the awe of the might of the King of Upper and Lower Egypt, Merenre, living forever, more than that of any gods. It was according to the utterance of the command of his *Ka* that everything comes to pass.

(16) I was one indeed beloved of his father, praised of his mother, and favored by his brothers. The count, true overseer of the southland, venerated before Osiris, Weni [the Elder].

## HARKHUF

*The facade of the rock-cut tomb of Harkhuf is inscribed with his autobiographical text. Several tombs of the late Old Kingdom and Dynasty 12 were cut into the rock overlooking the river on the west side of the Nile, some with steep causeways connecting the tombs to the river. These nomarchs occupied an advantageous situation on the border with Nubia to the south and controlled the Nubian and even more southerly trade for the royal house. On the island of Elephantine, chapels were set up for their cult, and temples were later built for the deities of the nome, Khnum, Satis, and Anukis, as well as for a venerated official of the Old Kingdom named Heqaib. The hieroglyphic text is presented in K. Sethe,* Urkunden des alten Reichs I, *2nd ed. (Leipzig, 1932), 120–31, with the numbering in the translation following that of Sethe's edition. See bibliography under Harkhuf.*

### A. Above the Entrance

(1) A gift which the king grants and a gift which Anubis upon his mound, foremost of the shrine, he who is in the place of bandaging, lord of the necropolis grants (namely) that he (Harkhuf) be buried in the western necropolis of the western desert, having grown very gracefully old, one

15. The Nubian chieftains were thus made responsible for having the timber cut down.

venerated before the great god ... the great god. The count, overseer of the southland, royal sealbearer, sole companion, lector priest, overseer of foreigners, venerated before Ptah-Sokar, Harkhuf.

(2) A gift which the king grants and a gift which Osiris, Lord of Busiris, grants (namely) that he travel in peace upon the sacred roads of the West upon which the venerated ones travel, and (namely) that he ascend to the God, Lord of the Sky, as one venerated before .... [Count, counselor], guardian of Nekhen, chief Nekhebite, sole companion, lector priest, venerated before Osiris, Harkhuf.

(3) A gift which the king grants (namely) that an invocation offering come forth for him in the necropolis and that he be made a well-equipped spirit (*akh*) by the lector priest on every festival of the Opening of the Year, on the Thoth festival, on the festival of the [First] of the Year, on the *Wag* festival, on the festival of Sokar, on the [Great] Festival, [on every festival of every day.] ... for the king's sealer, the sole companion, the lector priest, overseer of foreigners Harkhuf.

(4) It was after having built my tomb, its doors having been set up, and after having dug a pool, sycamores having been planted, and after the king had praised me and my father had made a transfer deed of property for me, that I came forth today from my town and that I went down from my nome. I was an excellent one, ... [beloved] of my father, praised by his (my) mother and beloved of all his (my) brothers.

(5) I gave bread to the hungry and I clothed the naked. I brought to land the one who had no rowboat. O living ones and those upon the earth [who shall pass by this tomb] faring north or south, and who shall utter a thousand loaves of bread and a thousand jars of beer (6) for the owner of this tomb, I shall intercede for them in the necropolis. I am an excellent and well-equipped spirit (*akh*), a lector priest who knows his spells. (But) as for any man who shall enter into [this] tomb [in his impurity], [I shall wring] his [neck] like a bird. He shall be judged for it by the great god.

(7) I am one who speaks what is good and repeats what is desired. Never would I say anything malicious to a superior against any men, for I desired that it be well for me with the great god. Never would I [judge a brother of two brothers] ... on an occasion of my depriving a son of the property of a father.

(8) A gift which the king grants and a gift which Anubis upon his mound, foremost of the shrine grants, (namely) that an invocation offering

come forth for him in the western necropolis, for the one venerated before Anubis, who is upon his mound, foremost of the shrine ... the count and lector priest ... the sole companion, lector priest, overseer of foreigners, the venerated Harkhuf.

## B. To the Right of the Entrance

(1) The count, sole companion, lector priest, counsellor, guardian of Nekhen, chief Nekhebite, royal sealbearer, sole companion, lector priest, overseer of foreigners, confidant of all the affairs of the Head of the South, one who is in the heart of his lord, Harkhuf.

(2) Royal sealbearer, sole [companion], lector priest, overseer of foreigners, who brings the produce of all foreign lands to his lord, who brings tribute for the king's regalia, overseer of all foreign lands of the Head of the South, who sets the fear (3) of Horus in the foreign lands, who executes what is praised of his lord, royal sealbearer, sole companion, lector priest, overseer of foreigners, venerated before Ptah-Sokar, Harkhuf. He says:

(4) The Majesty of Merenre, my lord, sent me together with my father, the sole companion and lector priest Jry to Iam[1] to open the road to this foreign land. I reached it in seven months, bringing all tribute therein, precious and rare. I was rewarded very greatly for it.

(5–6) It was by myself that His Majesty sent me a second time, and it was on the Elephantine road that I set forth. It was in the space of eight months that I returned from Jrtjet, Mekher, and Terres within Jrtjetje.[2] It was in bringing produce from this foreign land very greatly that I returned. Never had the like been brought to this land previously. It was from the region of the domain of the ruler of Satju and Irertjet[3] that I returned, (9) having opened up these foreign lands. Never had I found that any sole companion and overseer of foreigners had done (it), having gone forth to Iam formerly.

(10) Now His Majesty sent me a third time to Iam, and it was on the

---

1. The location of Iam (Yam) has been much discussed, some placing it in Nubia and others far to the south in the Sudan at or near Kerma. See David B. O'Connor, "The Locations of Yam and Kush and Their Historical Implications," *JARCE* 23 (1986): 27–50; D. M. Dixon, "The Land of Yam," *JEA* 44 (1958): 40–55.
2. Sites in Nubia.
3. Sites in Nubia, apparently adjacent and ruled at this time by a single chieftain.

Thinite road of the Oasis that I set forth.[4] I found the ruler of Iam having gone to the land of the Tjemeh (Libyan) to strike the Tjemeh at the western bend of the sky. I set forth after him to the land of the Tjemeh, and it was in order that he would thank all the gods for the Sovereign that I appeased him.

## C. Left of the Entrance, Continuing B

(1) [I sent ...] and the Iam[ite] of the following of [Horus] to inform the Majesty of Merenre, my lord, (2) [that I had come forth to the land of the Tjemeh] after the ruler of Iam, after I had appeased that ruler of Iam. [I returned from ...] on the south of Jrtjet and the north of Satju, when I found the ruler of Jrtjet, Satju, and Wawat (4) [united in] one cause. It was with 300 donkeys laden with incense, ebony, oil, aromatics, panther skins, ivory carvings, boomerangs, and all good products that I returned. Then the ruler of Jrtjet, Satju, and Wawat observed how strong and numerous were the troops of Iam which had returned with me toward the Residence with the expeditionary force sent with me. (7) This [ruler] accompanied me and gave me cattle and goats / sheep in leading me [on] the roads of the hillsides of Jrtjet, because of my capabilities and the watchfulness which I exercised, more than any companion and overseer of foreigners who were sent to Iam previously. Now when this servant fared north toward the (royal) Residence, one had the [count], sole companion, and overseer of the double cooling house Khuni come to meet me with barges laden with date wine, cakes, bread, and beer. (10) The [count], royal sealer, sole companion, lector priest, god's sealbearer, confidant of decrees, the venerated Harkhuf.

## D. To the Extreme Right of the Entrance (B)

(1) The king's own seal. Regnal Year 2, month 3 of Akhet, day 15.

(2) The decree of the king (to) the sole companion, lector priest, overseer of foreigners Harkhuf.

(3) The matter of this letter of yours, which you directed to the king at the chamber, has been (duly) noted, to inform me that you have returned (4) safely from Iam with the expeditionary force which is with you. What

---

4. This time the route taken seems to start near Abydos into the Western Desert.

you have said [in] this letter of yours was that you are bringing back (5) all great and fine tribute which Hathor, mistress of Imaaw[5] has given (6) to the *Ka* of the King of Upper and Lower Egypt Neferkare (Pepy II), living eternally and forever. What you have said in this letter of yours is that you are bringing back a pigmy[6] (7) of the god's dancers from the land of the spirits, the like of the pigmy which (8) the god's sealbearer Wer-djed-ba brought back from Punt in the time of (King) Isesi. What you have said to My Majesty is that (9) his like has never been brought back by any other who reached Iam previously. Indeed, how knowledgeable you are (10–11) in how to do everything your lord desires and rewards. It is in taking care of doing everything My Majesty desires, rewards, and orders that you spend the day and you spend the night. His (My) Majesty will fulfill your wishes (12) abundantly and excellently so as to benefit the son of your son forever, so that all men will say, (13) when they hear what My Majesty will do for you, "Was anything like this done for the sole companion Harkhuf (14) when he went down to Iam—because of the vigilance which he maintained to carry out what (15) his lord desired, rewarded, and ordered?"

Come northward to the (royal) Residence at once. Hurry! Bring back (16) this pigmy with you, which you have brought from the land of the Horizon-dwellers, living, sound, and healthy, (17) for the dances of the god, to distract the heart and to thrill the heart of the King of Upper and Lower Neferkare, living forever.

(18) When he goes down with you to the boat, get capable persons who will be around him (19) on both sides of the boat. Take care lest he fall in the water! When he sleeps by night, get (20) capable persons sleeping around him in his cabin. Inspect ten times during the night, (21) for My Majesty desires to see this pigmy more than the produce of the mining country of (22) Punt. If you arrive at the (royal) Residence, this pigmy being with you, (23) living, sound, and healthy, My Majesty will do for you something greater than that which was done for the god's sealbearer Wer-djed-ba (24) in the time of (King) Isesi, according to the determination of My Majesty to see this pigmy.

(25) Dispatches have been brought to the chiefs of the new towns,

5. Imaaw is not otherwise known, but it is an area in Nubia where a cult of Hathor was apparently observed.
6. See David P. Silverman, "Pygmies and Dwarfs in the Old Kingdom," *Serapis* 1 (1969): 53–62.

companions, and overseers of the priests to order the requisitioning of foodstuffs (26) in their charge from every estate of the storehouse administration and from every temple. No exemption will be made therein.

## QAR

*Although most texts included in this anthology are translated in their complete state, except for several of which the latter sections are very destroyed, only the last part of this text is represented, since the first, lengthy section is mainly a list of titles. Qar was one of the nomarchs of Edfu at the end of the Old Kingdom, the next to southernmost nome, just north of Elephantine (Aswan) from which the text of Harkhuf derives. In his recent study, J. C. Moreno Garcìa (1998) stresses several relatively new ideas represented: the individual initiative of the official to insure prosperity for the royal house, ameliorating the effects of famine, etc., the excessive demands for taxes from the rulers, the conscription of men for royal projects, as well as casting the nomarch as a beneficent governor who can forgive the debtor by repaying a loan. As with texts from the following periods, much is made of the pride of the local nomes, with a corresponding lack of emphasis on the royal house. The hieroglyphic text is presented in K. Sethe,* Urkunden des alten Reichs I, 2nd ed. (Leipzig, 1932), 253–55. *See bibliography under Qar.*

## Section D

(3) I was a youth who tied on the headband in the time of (King) Teti.[1] I was brought to (King) Pepy (Pepy I) for education among the children of magistrates and I was appointed as sole companion and as overseer of the officials of the palace under (King) Pepy. The Majesty of (King) Merenre had me fare southward to Westjet-Hor (Edfu) as overseer of southern grain and overseer of priests, (4) by virtue of my excellence and my worthiness in His Majesty's estimation.

It was at the head of every nomarch(?) of the southland in its entirety that I came to my town. It was I who opened the southland in its entirety. I caused the oxen of this nome be foremost among oxen (and) my cattle stables (to be) at the head of the southland in its entirety. It was not indeed something which I found done by a nomarch of this nome previously, (5) by

1. See n. 1 to the text of Weni the Elder, above.

virtue of my watchfulness and because my management was effective for the (royal) Residence. It was I who was privy to the confidences in every matter which was brought at the gateway of Elephantine (?) and the southern lands.

I gave bread to the hungry and clothing to the naked of those I found in my nome, I gave jugs of milk. I measured out southern grain from my own estate for the hungry whom I found in this nome. (6) As for every man whom I found in this nome with a loan against him by another, it was I who repaid it to its owner from my (own) estate. It was I who buried every man of this nome, who did not have a son, with cloth from my property of my estate. I pacified all desert lands for the Residence, because my watchfulness was effective therein, and I was rewarded by my lord. I rescued a poor man from one more powerful than he. I judged two brothers so that they were satisfied. (7) I was beloved by his father, praised by his mother, and loved by his brothers.

O living ones, those who are upon the earth, who will pass by this tomb, those beloved of the king, may you invoke a thousand breads, a thousand beer jars, and a thousand cattle offerings for the sole companion Meryre-nefer (Qar).

# THE STELA OF TJETJI

T he Stela of Tjetji (British Museum 614) dates from the First Intermediate Period and provides an excellent example of the classic tomb autobiography. In a horizontal inscription of fourteen lines, Tjetji gives the
titulary of the Theban king Intef II, a self-laudatory inscription, and the details
of his successful career under the reigns of Intef II and Intef III. The lower
section of the stela consists of a vertical inscription of five columns containing
the prayer for offerings and for a successful journey to the Western Land.
Several publications of the text exist: Hieroglyphic Texts from Egyptian Stelae,
etc., in the British Museum, vol. 1 (London, 1911), pl. 49f.; E. A. W. Budge,
Egyptian Sculptures in the British Museum, 1914, pl. viii; and A. M. Blackman, JEA 17 (1931): 55–61. Other translations of the text may be found in M.
Lichtheim, Ancient Egyptian Literature, vol. 1 (Berkeley, 1973), 90–93, and
in M. Lichtheim, Ancient Egyptian Autobiographies Chiefly of the Middle
Kingdom: A Study and Anthology (1988), 46–49.

V.A.T.

THE STELA OF TJETJI

## HORIZONTAL INSCRIPTION

1 The Horus Wah-Ankh,[1] King of Upper and Lower Egypt, Son of Re, Intef, born of Nefru, he who lives eternally like Re: His faithful servant who was loyal to his wishes, foremost of rank in the palace of his lord, a magnanimous nobleman who knew the concerns of his lord's heart, who followed him in his every venture, unique of His Majesty's affection in very truth, foremost of the notables of the royal house, supervisor of the treasury in the secret place which his lord kept private even from the nobles, one who gladdened the heart of Horus with what he loved,[2] one who was in the

3 confidence of his lord, his favorite, overseer of the treasure which was in / the secret place loved by his lord, the overseer of the treasure, the king's chamberlain, the venerated one, Tjetji, says:

"I am one whom his lord loved, one whom he commended during the course of every day. I passed a lifetime of many years under the Majesty of My lord, the Horus Wah-Ankh, King of Upper and Lower Egypt, the Son of Re, Intef. Lo, this land was under his rule southwards as far as Yebu[3] and reaching as far (northward) as Abydos, while I was his body-servant, his loyal chamberlain.

He made me important, promoted my rank, and appointed me to a
5 position / of his favor in the private suite of his palace. The treasury was in my keeping and under my seal, and it was the choicest of every good thing which had been brought to his majesty my lord from Upper Egypt and from Lower Egypt, everything pleasant which gladdens the heart, (which had been brought to him) as the tribute of this entire land because of the fear of him throughout this land, and what had been brought to his majesty my lord by the rulers who control the Red Land[4] because of the fear of him throughout the hill countries. He in turn entrusted these things to me, because he knew that my efficiency was excellent, and I reported back to
7 him concerning them. Never was there found in me any fault / deserving of disapproval because of my proficiency.

1. Wah-Ankh: "Enduring of Life."
2. I.e., who fulfilled his every wish.
3. Yebu was the Egyptian name of the site known to the Greeks as Elephantine (modern Aswan), situated at the first cataract of the Nile, the traditional southern boundary of Egypt.
4. The term "Red Land" (Eg. *Dšrt*) refers to the infertile desert lands outside the boundaries of Egypt which was normally known as Kemet, the "Black Land."

I was indeed a trustworthy favorite of my lord, an official great of heart and quiet of temper in the palace of his lord, one who bowed down in respect among the nobles. I did not seek after the evil on account of which men are hateful. I am one who loved good and hated evil, one who was loved in the palace of his lord, one who performed every duty in obedience to the will of his lord. Indeed, as for every task which he commanded me

9    to undertake, / either dealing justly with a petitioner or attending to the request of a poor man, I performed it rightly and justly. Never did I disobey the orders he gave me; never did I substitute one thing for another. I was not haughty by reason of my power; I did not take a bribe in return for doing a favor. Moreover, as for every responsibility of the royal palace which the majesty of my lord committed to me, and for which he caused me to perform some task, I did it for him in accordance with everything which

11   his *ka* desired. I made all their procedures more efficient, and never / was there found in me any fault because of my proficiency.

I constructed a boat for the city, a vessel for every function (such as) the financial accounting with the nobles and every occasion of (official) business or missions.

I became wealthy, I became great. I supported myself by my own possessions which the majesty of my lord had given to me because of his favor toward me, the Horus Wah-Ankh, King of Upper and Lower Egypt, Son of Re, Intef, he who lives eternally like Re, until he journeyed in peace to his horizon.

13   Then upon his son's succession to his throne, / the Horus Nakht-Neb-Tep-Nefer, King of Upper and Lower Egypt, Son of Re, Intef, born of Nefru, he who lives eternally like Re, I followed him to all his good places which gladden the heart. Never did he find fault with me because of my efficiency. He gave to me every duty which had been under my authority during the time of his father to continue it under his majesty, and no fault of mine occurred in it. I spent all my time on earth as the body-servant of the king. I became powerful, I became great under his majesty. I am one who proved his (good) character, one who was commended by his lord during the course of every day."

## VERTICAL INSCRIPTION

15   An offering given by the king and by Osiris, the Lord of Busiris, the Ruler of those who are in the West, the Lord of Abydos, on all his thrones: An

offering of a thousand of bread and beer, a thousand of oxen and fowl, a thousand of unguent jars and clothing, a thousand of everything good and pure, the offerings of the funerary meal, the provisions of the Lord of Abydos, the pure bread of the temple of Montu, libations and offerings of the provisions from which the spirits love to eat, for the overseer of the treasure, the chamberlain of the king, the revered one, Tjetji.

17  May he traverse the heavens and cross the sky,
    May he ascend to the Great God and arrive in peace at the beautiful West.
    May the desert open to him its arms and the West offer its hands to him.
    May he reach the council of the gods,
    May there be said to him "Welcome in peace" by the great ones of Abydos.
    May assistance be given to him in the *neshmet*-barque on the roads of the West,
19  May he journey well and in peace to the horizon, / to the place where Osiris is.
    May he open the ways he desires to the portals of the sacred land.[5]
    May they who have abundantly give to him their hands
    On the desert plateau which provides offerings,
    While his *ka* is with him, and his offerings are in his presence,
    The revered one, Tjetji.

5. "Sacred Land": the necropolis.

# AMENEMHET AND KHNUMHOTEP II AT
# BENI HASAN

T he *"autobiographies" of these two nomarchs of the Oryx Nome (Upper Egyptian XVI) in Middle Egypt from the first reigns of Dynasty 12 reveal a considerable amount about their reasons for building their tombs and their desire for eternal recognition, wishes which have indeed been rewarded by readers today, almost four thousand years after their deaths. The texts are published by Percy E. Newberry,* Beni Hasan Part I, Archaeological Survey of Egypt 1 *(London, 1893); K. Sethe,* Historisch-biographische Inschriften des Mittleren Reiches: Urk. VII (Leipzig, 1935), 14–40. *The text of Amenemhet is translated in Miriam Lichtheim,* Ancient Egyptian Autobiographies Chiefly of the Middle Kingdom (Freiburg/Göttingen, 1988), 135–41. *The text of Khnumhotep II is presented in A. de Buck,* Egyptian Reading Book, vol. 1: Exercises and Middle Egyptian Texts (Leiden, 1948), 67–72, *and in a detailed study by Alan B. Lloyd, "The Great Inscription of Khnumhotpe II at Beni Hasan," in Alan B. Lloyd, ed.,* Studies in Pharaonic Religion and Society in Honour of J. Gwyn Griffiths (London, 1992), 21–36, *to which add Karl Jansen-Winkeln, "Der Schluβsatz der Biographie des Chnumhotep in Beni Hassan,"* GM 180 (2001): 77–80. See also Janice Kamrin, *The Cosmos of Khnumhotep II at Beni Hasan (London, 1998).

W.K.S.

## AMENEMHET

Regnal Year 43 under the Majesty of the Horus Ankh-Mesut, King of Upper and Lower Egypt Kheper-ka-Re, living forever, He of the Two Ladies Ankh-mesut, Falcon of Gold Ankh-Mesut, Son of Re Senwosret (I), living forever and ever, corresponding to Year (=counting) 25 in the Oryx Nome as (?) hereditary noble, count, gracious of arm, Ameny, the vindicated, Regnal Year 43, month 2 of Akhet, day 14.

O you who love life and hate death, say a thousand bread loaves and jugs of beer, a thousand cattle and fowl for the *Ka* of the hereditary lord, count, gracious of arm, chief administrator (nomarch) of the Oryx Nome, he who is in the office, shepherd of Nekhen, chief Nekhebite, overseer of priests, A[men]y, the vindicated.

I followed my lord when he sailed south to overthrow his enemies among the foreigners, for it was as the son of the count, royal sealbearer, great overseer of the army of the Oryx Nome, as a man replacing my aged father, that I sailed south, through the favors of the royal house and the love of him in the palace.

I passed through Kush, sailing southward, having reached the ends of the earth, having brought the tribute of my lord, and praise of me reached the sky.

Then his Majesty proceeded in peace, having overthrown his enemies in miserable Kush, and it was as one having gained experience that I returned in his following, no loss having taken place in my army. I had sailed south to bring back gold ore for the Majesty of the King of Upper and Lower Egypt Kheper-ka-Re (Senwosret I), living forever and ever.

It was with the hereditary prince, count, king's eldest son Ameny,[1] l.p.h., that I sailed south, having sailed with 400 enlisted men from all the best of my army, returning safely without any loss to them, I having brought back the gold assigned to me. I was praised for it in the royal house, and the king's son thanked god for me.

Then I sailed (back) to deliver the mineral products to the wharf of Koptos, together with the hereditary lord, count, overseer of the city, the vizier Senwosret.

I sailed with 600 enlistees of all my best of the Oryx Nome. I returned

---

1. Evidently the future king Amenemhet II. For the chronological implications, see William K. Simpson, "Studies in the Twelfth Egyptian Dynasty III: Year 25 in the Era of the Oryx Nome and the Famine Years in Early Dynasty 12," *JARCE* 38 (2001): 7–8.

safely, my expeditionary force intact, having accomplished everything that was said to me.

I am a possessor of grace, enduring of love, a ruler whom his city loves, having spent years as ruler of the Oryx Nome. All the imposts of the royal house came through me. Then the overseer of the gangs of the administrative districts of the custodians of the Oryx Nome gave me 3,000 bulls with their yoke oxen, and I was praised for it in the royal house every year of the cattle tax, and I delivered all their imposts to the royal house. There were no arrears against me in any of its offices. I worked the entire Oryx Nome with enduring zeal.

There was no daughter of a citizen whom I violated.

There was no widow whom I forced.

There was no farmer whom I punished.

There was no shepherd whom I confined.

There was no overseer of a gang of five whose men I took away for labor.

There was no one poor in my vicinity.

There was no one hungry in my time.

Now years of hunger came to pass. I ploughed all the fields of the Oryx Nome up to its southern and northern border, nourishing its inhabitants, acquiring its food. There was no hungry person in it. I gave to the widow just as to the one who had a husband. I did not distinguish between great and small in everything which I gave. Then high Niles came to pass, having barley and emmer and having everything, and I did not exact the arrears for the land taxes.

## KHNUMHOTEP II

The hereditary lord and count, royal acquaintance, one beloved of his god, overseer of the eastern desert lands Nehri's son Khnumhotep, the vindicated, born to the daughter of a count, the house-mistress Baqet, vindicated. As his memorial did he make (it).

His first deed consisted of making his township effective, as he caused his name to endure for eternity and made it effective forever in his tomb in the cemetery (as well as) making the name(s) of his council endure, they (likewise) being made effective according to their offices, (namely) the efficient ones within his household whom he distinguished from among his associates, every office which he administered, and every craft as it is undertaken.

His mouth, it says: The Majesty of the Horus Heken-em-Maat, He of the Two Ladies Heken-em-Maat, the Falcon of Gold "Vindicated," the King of Upper and Lower Egypt Nub-kau-Re, the Son of Re Amenemhet (II), given life, stability, dominion like Re forever, placed me as hereditary lord and count, overseer of the eastern desert lands, rober of Horus and Pakhet,[1] to the inheritance of the father of my mother in Menat-Khufu,[2] as he (the king) established for me a southern boundary stela and made effective the northern (one) like the sky (permanently), and divided the great river on its back (just) as was done for the father of my mother by the decree which came forth from the mouth of the Majesty of the Horus, Wehem-Mesut, He of the Two Ladies, Wehem-Mesut, the Falcon of Gold [Wehem]-Mesut, King of Upper and Lower Egypt Sehetepibre, the Son of Re Amenemhet (I), given life, stability, dominion like Re forever, as he appointed him (the father of my mother) to be hereditary lord and count, overseer of the eastern desert lands in Menat-Khufu, as he established for him a southern boundary stela, making effective a northern (one) like the sky, and dividing for him the great river on its back, its eastern side to the Horus-Mountain as far as the eastern desert lands, when His Majesty returned (after) suppressing evil and appearing as Atum himself, he having brought back into order that which he found laid waste and that which a town had appropriated from its neighbor, a town (now) knowing its boundary with a town, bringing into order their boundary stelae like the sky, their waters being recognized according to that which was in writing and assessed according to that which was of old, inasmuch as he loved Maat.

Then he placed him (Khnumhotep I) as hereditary lord and count, favored one, great chief (nomarch) of the Oryx Nome (Upper Egyptian Nome XVI), he having established the southern boundary stelae as his border with the Hare Nome (Upper Egyptian Nome XV) and his northern as far as the Cynopolite Nome (Upper Egyptian Nome XVII), dividing for him(?) the great river on its back, his waters, his fields, his trees, and his sandy lands as far as the western desert lands. He placed his eldest son Nakht, the vindicated, the possessor of an honored state, to rule his

1. A lioness goddess of the district.
2. An area within or adjacent to Upper Egyptian Nome XVI.

inheritance in Menat-Khufu, by the great favor on the part of the king, by the decree which came forth from the mouth of the Majesty of the Horus, Ankh Mesut, He of the Two Ladies, Ankh Mesut, Falcon of Gold, Ankh Mesut, King of Upper and Lower Egypt Kheper-ka-re, the Son of Re Senwosret (I), given life, stability, and dominion like Re forever.

My (own) first distinction pertaining to my birth was when my mother proceeded to (the office of) hereditary lady and countess as daughter of the ruler of the Oryx Nome at the Estate of Sehetepibre, given life, stability, and dominion like Re forever, and to be the wife of the hereditary lord and count, ruler of the new towns, one proclaimed by the King of Upper Egypt, fosterling of the King of Lower Egypt, in his dignity as overseer of the Residence Town, Nehri, the vindicated, possessor of an honored state.

The King of Upper and Lower Egypt Nub-kau-re (Amenemhet II), given life, stability, and dominion like Re forever, brought me as son of the count to the inheritance of the rulership of the father of my mother inasmuch as he loved Maat. He is Atum himself, Nub-kau-Re, given life, stability, dominion, and joy, like Re forever, and it was in (his) Regnal Year 19 that he placed me as count in Menat-Khufu. Then I made it effective, its wealth having become great. I caused the name(s) of my father(s) to endure, and I brought into order their *ka*-chapels, I following my statues to the temple and offering them their loaves, bread, beer, libations, presents, and meat offerings allotted to my *ka*-priest. I endowed him with fields and serfs.

An invocation offering of bread, beer, cattle, and fowl was ordered for me on every festival of the cemetery on the first of the year, the opening of the year, the great yearly festival, the lesser yearly festival, the end of the year festival, the great festival, on the great burning festival, on the lesser burning festival, on the festival(s) of the five epagomenal days, on the *shedet-sha,* on the twelve monthly and twelve half-monthly festivals and every festival of one on the earth and one well on the mountain.

Moreover, as for a *ka*-priest or any men who would destroy it, he will no longer exist and his son will not be upon his seat. Greater was my favor in the palace than that of any sole companion, for it was before his nobles that he distinguished me, I being placed in front of those who were in front of me. The council of the palace united to present praises accordingly, and I was appointed according to the favors which took place in the presence of the utterance of the king himself. The like had never happened for servants whom their lord had praised, for he recognized my eloquence and the youthful vigor of my character. I was an esteemed one before the king and my praise was before his courtiers, while my graciousness was in the presence of his companions, (namely) the hereditary lord and count, Nehri's son Khnumhotep, possessor of an honored state.

Another favor which was done for me: my eldest son, Nakht, born to Khety, was appointed to be ruler of the Cynopolite Nome (Upper Egyptian Nome XVII), to the inheritance of the father of his mother, he being elevated as a sole companion and set at the head of Upper Egypt. He was granted a number of distinctions by the Majesty of the Horus Seshemutowy, He of the Two Ladies Sekha-Maat, Falcon of Gold Netjeru-hetepu, King of Upper and Lower Egypt Kha-kheper-re, the Son of Re Senwosret (II), given life, stability, and dominion, like Re forever. It was in the Cynopolite Nome that he made his memorials in bringing into order that which he found laid waste, what one town had seized from its neighbor, he being caused to know his border according to the land register and assessed according to what was of old. A boundary stela was placed at his southern border, and his northern one was brought into order like the sky, they being established on the fields of the low-lying lands, a total of fifteen boundary stelae, they being established at his northern fields with his border as far as the Oxyrhyncus Nome (Upper Egyptian Nome XIX). The great river was divided for him on its back, its western side belonging to the Cynopolite Nome as far as the western deserts according to the petition of the hereditary lord and count Khnumhotep's son Nehri, the vindicated, possessor of an honored state, when he said: I do not know my waters.

A great favor on the part of the king: another official was appointed as sole companion, greatest among the companions, one great in respect to tribute in the palace, a sole companion without equal, one to whom the judges hearken, a sole speaker who eliminates (other) speakers, one who brings that which is beneficial to its lord, the gateway of the desert lands, Nehri's son Khnumhotep's son Khnumhotep born to the mistress of the house Khety.

I made the names of my fathers to live which I found destroyed upon the gateways, being known through written signs, exact for reading, not placing one (individual or hieroglyphic sign?) in place of another. Indeed, he is an excellent son who perpetuates the names of (his) ancestors, (namely) Nehri's son Khnumhotep, the vindicated, the possessor of an honored state.

My primary distinction consisted of making for myself (this) rock-cut tomb chapel, for a man emulates that which his father has done, as my father made for himself a *ka*-chapel in Mer-nefret of fine (lime)stone of Tura, so as to cause his (own) name to endure for eternity, causing it to last forever, his name living in the speech of men and lasting in the speech of the living in his tomb in the necropolis (namely) in his effective house of eternity, his place of everlastingness, through the favor of the king and the love of him in the palace, he having governed his town as a child, not yet having been circumcised, having carried out the business of the king. His two feathers danced (while he was) a youth because of his character (?), for the king recognized his eloquence and the youthfulness of his station, Sobek-ankhu's son Nehri, the vindicated, possessor of an honored state, whom he distinguished over his nobles to govern his town.

That which took place through the count Khnumhotep: I made my memorial within my town. I built a columned hall which I found in ruin, having erected it with columns anew (or: of granite), inscribed with my own name. I perpetuated the name of my father, having inscribed(?) what I did upon every memorial which I made. A door of 6 cubits of cedar of Negau for the first portal of the tomb, a double door of 5 cubits and 2 palms for the chapel of the august chamber which is inside this tomb, mortuary requirements and invocation offerings ⟨inscribed⟩ on every monument which I made. I filled a pool. I built its ..., giving air to this columned hall. Greater was (my) memorial within this town than those of my fathers, the offspring of this town, more excellent its monuments of its desert region than those of the predecessors who came before me.

I was noble as to memorials. In order that my name might be effective on every memorial which I made, they being established for me, I taught all the crafts which had disappeared within this town. No payment arrears were outstanding in that I had to have the ⟨goods⟩ of a ship of another man to come. The hereditary noble and count Nehri's son Khnumhotep, born to Baqet, the vindicated, possessor of an honored state.

The administrator of the tomb, overseer of the seal, Baqet.

# THE STELA OF IYKHERNOFRET

T his seriously abraded limestone stela, thirty-nine inches high, presents one of the most interesting texts of the Middle Kingdom (Berlin 1204, acquired from the Drovetti Collection in 1837/38). Iykhernofret describes his mission on behalf of King Senwosret III from the court in the north to Abydos, probably in the king's nineteenth regnal year on the basis of a stela in Geneva, to refurbish the god's statue, the statues of the associated gods, and the related ritual equipment, and to conduct the major processions carried out as part of the ritual drama at the site. Compare the text of the Neferhotep Stela in the section on Royal Stelae.

The round top stela is surmounted by a winged sun disk identified as the Behdetite and with the royal titulary. On the upper part of the frame on each side are two columns of text with the royal titulary and Abydene epithets. Below on each side are two columns of text with an expanded titulary and epithets of Iykhernofret himself. Several stelae related to his family derive from Abydos, and it is likely that they were all placed at his memorial chapel (cenotaph) or in small chapels added to it. See bibliography under Iykhernofret Stela.

W.K.S.

1    *Main text:* Live the Horus Divine of Transformations, He of the Two Ladies Divine of Manifestations, Falcon of Gold Transformations, King of

Upper and Lower Egypt Kha-kau-Re, Son of Re Senwosret (III), granted life like Re forever.

Royal decree to the hereditary lord, governor ..., king's sealbearer, sole companion, overseer of the double house of gold, overseer of the double house of silver, overseer of sealbearers, Iykhernofret, possessor of an honored state:

Now my Majesty has decreed that you proceed southward to Abydos in the Thinite Nome to make a monument for my father, Osiris-Foremost-of-the-Westerners, and to make effective his mysterious [image] of the fine gold which He had my Majesty bring back from Nubia in victory and in triumph. You shall do this in a proper manner / in carrying out such a task, thereby satisfying my father Osiris, since my Majesty is sending you, my heart confidant that you may carry out everything in order to fill (?) the heart of my Majesty and since, indeed, you were brought up as a student of my Majesty, you having grown up as a foster child of my Majesty, a sole student of my palace. My Majesty made you a companion (?) when you were a young man of twenty-six years. Because my Majesty considered you as one excellent of counsel, eloquent, one who had come forth from the womb as one already wise, my Majesty did this. Now my Majesty sends you to carry this out because my Majesty perceives that there is none who can do all of this except you. Go quickly and return (?) after you have done everything my Majesty has ordered.

/ I acted according to everything His Majesty commanded in making effective what my lord commanded for his father, Osiris-Foremost-of-the-Westerners, lord of Abydos, the great powerful one within the Thinite Nome. I performed (the duty of) "his beloved son" for Osiris-Foremost-of-the-Westerners, I making effective (for him?) the great (barque?), eternal and enduring. For him I made the transport sled, which carries the beauty of Foremost-of-the-Westerners, of gold, silver, lapis lazuli, copper, *sesnedjem*-wood, and cedar. The (statues of the) gods who were in his Ennead were fashioned, and their shrines were made anew. I assigned the hourly priests of the temples to carry out their duties and I had them know the rituals of each day and the festivals of the beginnings of the year. I directed the work on the *neshmet*-barque.[1] I fashioned the barque-shrine.

/ I embellished the breast of the lord of Abydos with lapis lazuli and with turquoise, fine gold, and all precious stones which are the ornaments

1. The *neshmet*-boat was a ritual vessel used in the theatrical religious drama at Abydos.

of the god's body, and I clothed the god with his ornaments in my function as one versed in the mysteries and my duty as stolist (ritual rober). I was pure of hand in decorating the god, a *sem*-priest clean of fingers.

I conducted the procession of Wep-wawet when he proceeds to avenge his Father. I repelled the rebels from the *neshmet*-barque and I felled the enemies of Osiris. I conducted the great procession following the god at his footsteps. I caused the god's barque to sail on, with Thoth leading the voyage. I equipped the barque "The lord of Abydos arises in Maat" with a shrine, / his fine regalia being set in place as he proceeded to Poqer in the Thinite nome.[2] I cleared the god's paths to his cenotaph tomb in front of Poqer. I avenged Wen-nofer on that day of the great fighting, and I felled all his enemies on the sand-banks of Nedit.[3]

And I had him proceed within the Great Barque and it carried his beauty, gladdening the eastern deserts and [creating] joy in the heart of the western deserts when they saw the beauties of the *neshmet*-barque as it put to land at Abydos and as it brought back [Osiris-Foremost-of-the-Westerners, lord of] Abydos to his palace.

And I followed the god into his temple, his purification done, his throne widened. I untied the knot within the temple [as he came to rest among] his ... and among his entourage.

*Below the main text the owner is represented seated, facing right toward two registers of offerings and attendants. He is captioned* "Overseer of seal-bearers, Iykhernofret, possessor of an honored state, born to Sit-Khonsu." *In the upper subregister a seated man before an offering table faces toward him and is identifed as* "his brother, his beloved, the deputy of the overseer of sealbearers Ameny, possessor of an honored state." *In the lower subregister are two small seated figures facing the owner identified as* "his son, his beloved, Iykhernofret" *and* "his son, his beloved, Si-Satet." *Following them is a larger figure bearing a mirror and a stone offering vessel, captioned* "the assistant of the overseer of sealbearers Min-hotep" *followed by a seated figure before an offering tray captioned* "his brother, his beloved, the royal acquaintance Si-Satet." *Min-hotep was probably an (adoptive or honorific) son of Iykhernofret and indicated on his own stela (now in the British Museum) that it was placed by his father's orders in his father's memorial chapel.*

2. Poqer is the name of the area of the tombs of the rulers of Dynasty 1 and 2 at Abydos, where the tomb of Osiris was later thought to be situated.

3. Nedit is a region at Abydos, the site where the god Osiris was murdered.

# VIII

SCRIBAL TRADITIONS

# THE SATIRE ON THE TRADES: THE INSTRUCTION OF DUA-KHETY

*T*he theme of the superiority of the scribe's lot is a popular element in the *Ramesside "miscellany literature," but it received its standard treat-ment at an earlier date in The Instruction of Dua-Khety, also known as The Satire on the Trades. Composed in the Middle Kingdom, it is extant in papyri, writing boards, and numerous ostraca. The most complete text is that of Papyrus Sallier II, which in many parts is almost incomprehensible. As a general rule, the transmission of Egyptian texts is one of scribal copying: one scribe copies from an earlier manuscript, and the mistakes, which are multiplied, reflect the misunderstanding or careless copying of what he sees in the text before him.*

*The latest edition with translation and commentary is Wolfgang Helck,* Die Lehre des Dwȝ-Ḫtjj, 2 parts *(Wiesbaden, 1970). Helck has managed to reconstruct many of the obscure passages on the assumption that the scribal transmission of the text reflects a different type of error: the scribe wrote from dictation and his errors derive from misinterpreting what he heard (words which sound alike, etc.). In our translation some of these reconstructed readings by Helck have been adopted, if not with complete conviction. The study of the text has also been advanced through the contribution of Peter Seibert,* Die Charakteristik *(Wiesbaden, 1967). For reference to earlier studies and editions, see Erman,* The Ancient Egyptians, *p. xxvii, and particularly the comments made on the text by Posener. I have benefited from James E. Hoch, "The*

431

*Teaching of Dua-Kheti: A New Look at the Satire of the Trades," JSSEA 21–22*
*(1991–92, pub. 1994): 88–100. See also John L. Foster, "Some Comments on*
*'Satire on the Trades,'" in: Emily Teeter and John A. Larson, eds.,* Gold of
Praise: Studies Presented in Honor of Edward F. Wente, SAOC 20 *(Chicago,*
*2000), 121–29.*

*In the introduction to the Instruction the father sets out to instruct his son*
*while taking him from their home to the Residence. After describing the sorry*
*lot of the professions other than the scribe's, he continues (beginning with*
*chapter 22) with more general advice on the lines of earlier instruction litera-*
*ture. The characterization of the instruction as a satire is perhaps not correct, but*
*there are clearly satirical elements in the description of the sorry lot of the other*
*professions.*

W.K.S.

1. The beginning of the teaching which the man of Tjel[1] named Dua-
Khety[2] made for his son named Pepy, while he sailed southwards to the
Residence to place him in the school of writings[3] among the children of the
magistrates, the most eminent men of the Residence.

2. Thereupon he spoke to him: Since I have seen those who have been
beaten, it is to writings that you must set your mind. See for yourself, it
saves one from work.[4] Behold, there is nothing that surpasses writings!
They are like [a boat] upon the water. Read then at the end of the Book of
Kemyet[5] and you will find this statement in it saying: As for a scribe in any
office in the Residence, he will not suffer want in it.

3. When he fulfills the bidding of another, he does not come forth
satisfied. I do not see an office to be compared with it, to which this maxim
could relate. I shall make you love books more than your mother, and I shall

1. Tjel is Sile in the northeast Delta on the borders of Egypt. Thus the man and his son
are characterized as citizens of an outlying district far from the cultural and political
center of Memphis.
2. The reading of the name has been determined beyond reasonable doubt by Seibert.
Earlier translations have rendered it as Khety son of Duauf.
3. The father, ambitious for his son's advancement, takes him away to school at the
Residence.
4. The order of the following phrases seems illogical, although the manuscripts agree.
5. Part of this composition is preserved elsewhere, including this phrase. Citations of
other works are not uncommon. See Brunner, "Lehren" and "Zitate aus Lebenslehren" in the general bibliography.

place their excellence before you. It[6] is indeed greater than any office. There is nothing like it on earth. When he began to become sturdy but was still a child, he was greeted (respectfully). When he was sent to carry out a task, before he returned he was ⌐dressed in adult garments⌐.

4. I do not see a stoneworker on an (important) errand or a goldsmith in a place to which he has been sent,[7] but I have seen a coppersmith at his work at the mouth of his furnace. His fingers were like the claws of the crocodile, and he stank more than fish eggs.

5. Every carpenter who bears the adze is wearier than a laborer. His field is his wood, his hoe is the axe. It is the night that will rescue him, for he must labor excessively in (his) activity. But at nighttime he (still) must light (his lamp).

6. The jeweler pierces (stone) in stringing beads in all kinds of hard stone. When he has completed the inlaying of the eye amulets, his strength vanishes and he is tired out. He sits until ⌐the arrival of the sun⌐, his knees and his back bent at (the place called) Aku-Re.[8]

7. The barber shaves until the end of the evening. ⌐But he must be up early, crying out, his bowl upon his arm⌐. He takes himself from street to street to seek out someone to shave. He wears out his arms to fill his belly, like bees who eat (only) according to their work.

8. The arrowmaker goes north to the Delta to fetch himself arrows. He must work excessively in (his) activity. When the gnats sting him and the sand fleas bite him as well, then he is judged.

9. The potter is covered with earth, although his lifetime is still among the living.[9] He burrows in the field more than swine to bake his cooking vessels. His clothes being stiff with mud, his headcloth consists (only) of rags, so that the air which comes forth from his burning furnace enters his nose. He operates a pestle with his feet, ⌐with which he himself is pounded⌐, penetrating the courtyard of every house and driving (earth) into (every) open place.

10. I shall also describe to you the like of the mason-bricklayer. His kidneys are painful.[10] When he must be outside in the wind, he lays bricks

6. The office of scribe.
7. Opportunities for travel do not exist for the craftsmen, or they must remain confined indoors.
8. Perhaps, "the entering of the sun."
9. He is under the earth and yet alive.
10. Or, "what he experiences is painful."

without a loin cloth. His belt is a cord for his back, a string for his buttocks. His strength has vanished through fatigue and stiffness, kneading all his excrement. He eats bread with his fingers, although he washes himself but once a day.

11. It is miserable for the carpenter when he planes the roofbeam. It is ⟨the roof of⟩ a chamber 10 by 6 cubits. A month goes by in laying the beams and spreading the matting. All the work is accomplished. But as for the food which should be given to his household (while he is away), there is no one who provides for his children.

12. The vintner hauls his shoulder-yoke. Each of his shoulders is burdened with age. A swelling is on his neck, and it festers. He spends the morning in watering leeks and the evening (with) corianders, ⌜after he has spent the midday in the palm grove⌝. So it happens that he sinks down (at last) and dies ⌜through his deliveries⌝, more than one of any (other) profession.

13. The field hand cries out forever. His voice is louder than the ⌜raven's⌝. His fingers have become ⌜ulcerous⌝ with an excess of stench. He is tired out in Delta labor, he is in tatters. He is well among lions but his experience is painful. The forced labor then is tripled. If he comes back from the marshes there, he reaches his house worn out, for the forced labor has ruined him.

14. The weaver inside the weaving house is more wretched than a woman. His knees are drawn up against his belly. He cannot breathe the air. If he wastes a (single) day without weaving, he is beaten with fifty whip lashes. He has to give food to the doorkeeper to allow him to come out to the daylight.

15. The weapon maker, completely worn out, goes into the desert. Greater (than his own pay) is what he has to spend for his she-ass for its work afterwards. Great is also what he has to give to the fieldhand to set him on the (right) road (to the flint source). When he reaches his house in the evening, the journey has ruined him.

16. The ⌜courier⌝[11] goes abroad after handing over his property to his children, being fearful of the lions and the Asiatics. He only knows himself (again) when he is (back) in Egypt. He reaches his household by evening, but the journey has ruined him. But his house (by then) is only ⌜a garment and a paved [road]⌝. ⌜There is no happy homecoming⌝.

---

11. Perhaps a trader.

17. The ˹furnace-tender˺, his fingers are foul, the smell thereof is as corpses. His eyes are inflamed because of the heaviness of the smoke. He cannot get rid of his dirt, although he spends the day cutting reeds. Clothes are an abomination to him.

18. The sandalmaker is utterly wretched carrying his tubs forever. His stores are provided with carcasses, and what he bites is hides.

19. The washerman launders at the riverbank in the vicinity of the crocodile. I shall go away, father, from the flowing water, said his son and his daughter, to a more satisfactory profession, one more distinguished than any (other) profession. His food is mixed with filth, and there is no part of him which is clean. He cleans the clothes of a woman in menstruation. He weeps when he spends all day with a beating stick and a stone there. One says to him, dirty laundry, come to me, the brim overflows.

20. The fowler is utterly afflicted while searching out for the denizens of the sky. If the flock passes by above him, then he says: would that I might have nets. But God will not let this come to pass for him, for He is opposed to his activity.

21. I mention to you also the fisherman. He is more miserable than (one of) any (other) profession, one who is at his work in a river infested with crocodiles. When the totaling of his account is subtracted for him, then he will lament. One did not tell him that a crocodile was standing there, and fear has (now) blinded him. When he comes to the flowing water, so he ˹falls˺ (as) through the might of God. See, there is no office free from supervisors, except the scribe's. He is the supervisor![12]

22. But if you understand writings, then it will be better for you than the professions which I have set before you. Behold the official and the dependent pertaining to him. The tenant farmer of a man cannot say to him: Do not keep watching (me). What I have done in journeying southward to the Residence is what I have done through love of you. A day at school is advantageous to you. ˹Its work of mountains is forever,˺ while the workmen I have caused you to know hurry on and I cause the recalcitrant to hasten.

23. I will also tell you another matter to teach you what you should know at the station of your ˹debating˺. ˹Do not come close to where there is a dispute.˺ If a man reproves you, and you do not know how to oppose his anger, make your reply cautiously in the presence of listeners.[13]

12. Here ends the catalogue of professions. There follows more usual advice in the nature of traditional wisdom literature.

13. See Ptahhotep Maxims 2–4.

24. If you walk to the rear of officials, approach from a distance behind the last. If you enter while the master of the house is at home, and his hands are extended to another in front of you, sit with your hand to your mouth. Do not ask for anything in his presence. But do as he says to you. Beware of approaching the table.[14]

25. Be serious, and great as to (your) worth. Do not speak secret matters. For he who hides his innermost thoughts is one who makes a shield for himself. Do not utter thoughtless words when you sit down with an angry man.

26. When you come forth from school after midday recess has been announced to you, go into the courtyard and discuss the last part of your ⌈lesson book⌉.

27. When an official sends you on a mission, then say what he said. Neither take away nor add to it.[15] The impatient man falls into oblivion, his name will not endure. He who is wise in all his ways, nothing will be hidden from him, and he ⌈will not be rebuffed from⌉ any station of his.

28. Do not say anything false about your mother. This is an abomination to the officials. The offspring who does useful things, his condition is equal to the one of yesterday. Do not indulge with an undisciplined man, for it is bad after it is heard about you. When you have eaten three loaves of bread and swallowed two jugs of beer, and the body has not yet had enough, fight against it. But if another is satiated, do not stand around, take care not to approach the table.

29. See, it is good if you write frequently. Obey the words of the officials. Then you may assume the characteristics of the children of men, and you may walk in their footsteps. One values a scribe for (his) understanding, for understanding transforms an eager person. Beware of words against it. Your feet shall not hurry when you walk. Do not approach (only) a trusted man, but associate with one more distinguished than you. But let your friend be a man of your generation.

30. See, I have placed you on the path of God. The fate of a man is on his shoulders on the day he is born. He comes to the judgment hall and the court of magistrates made for the people. See, there is no scribe lacking sustenance, the provisions of the royal house l.p.h. It is Meskhenet[16] who is

14. For advice on table manners, see Kagemni, I, 5–10 and Ptahhotep Maxim 7.
15. Compare Ptahhotep Maxim 8.
16. See King Cheops, n. 16.

turned toward the scribe who presents himself before the court of magistrates. Honor (your) father and mother who have placed you on the path of the living. Mark this, which I have placed before your eyes, and the children of your children.

It has come to an end in peace.

# THE SCRIBAL TRADITIONS IN
# THE SCHOOLS

*I n the Ramesside era apprentice scribes were set by their masters to copy several of the literary works of the past and short compositions on the lot of the scribe as contrasted with that of other professions. Among the set-pieces are also hymns of praise to the Ramesside Residence and complicated compositions listing parts of chariots and the names of foreign towns. The papyri have been edited by Alan H. Gardiner in* Late-Egyptian Miscellanies, *(Brussels, 1937), and translated with extensive commentary by Ricardo Caminos,* Late-Egyptian Miscellanies, *(London, 1954). The selections translated below correspond respectively to Papyrus Sallier I, 6, 1–9 (Caminos, 315–17), Papyrus Anastasi V, 8, 1–9, 1 (Caminos, 231–32), Papyrus Anastasi V, 9, 2–10, 2 (Caminos, 232–34), Papyrus Anastasi IV, 10, 1–5 (Caminos, 170–74), and Papyrus Anastasi IV, 9, 4–10, 1 (Caminos, 168–70). See bibliography under* Miscellanies.

W.K.S.

## REMINDER OF THE SCRIBE'S SUPERIOR STATUS
### (P. SALLIER I, 6, 1–9)

The overseer of the record-keepers of the treasury of Pharaoh, l.p.h., Amunemone speaks to the scribe Pentawere. This letter is brought to you saying: I have been told that you have abandoned writing and that you reel about in pleasures, that you have given your attention to work in the fields, and that you have turned your back on hieroglyphs. Do you not remember the condition of the field hand in the face of the registration of the harvest-tax, the snake having taken away half of the grain and the hippopotamus having eaten the remainder? The mice are numerous in the field, the locust descends, and the cattle eat. The sparrows bring want to the field hand. The remainder which is ⟨on⟩ the threshing floor is finished, and it is for the thieves. Its ⌜value in copper⌝ is lost, and the yoke of oxen is dead from threshing and ploughing. The scribe has moored ⟨at⟩ the riverbank. He reckons the tax, with the attendants bearing staffs and the Nubians rods of palm. They [say]: Give the grain! There is none. They beat [him] vig-orously. He is bound and cast into the well. They beat [him], drowning [him] head first, while his wife is bound in his presence. His children are manacled; his neighbors have abandoned them and fled. Their grain is gathered. But a scribe, he is the taskmaster of everyone. There is ⟨no⟩ taxing of the work of the scribe. He does not have dues. So take note of this.

## ADVICE TO THE YOUTHFUL SCRIBE
### (P. ANASTASI V, 8, 1–9, 1)

O scribe, do not be idle, do not be idle, or you shall be curbed straight-way. Do not give your heart to pleasures, or you shall fail. Write with your hand, recite with your mouth, and converse with those more knowledge-able than you. Exercise the office of magistrate, and then you will find it [advantageous] in old age. Fortunate is a scribe skilled in his office, the possessor of (a good) upbringing. Persevere in action daily, and you will gain mastery over them. Do not spend a day of idleness or you shall be beaten. The youth has a back and he hearkens to the beating of him. Pay attention. Hearken to what I have said. You will find it advantageous. One teaches apes ⟨to⟩ dance, and one tames horses. One can place a kite in a nest, and a falcon can be caught by the wings. Persevere in conversation. Do not be idle. Write. Do not feel distaste.

## PRAYER TO THOT FOR SKILL IN WRITING
### (P. ANASTASI V, 9, 2–10, 2)

Come to me, Thot, O noble Ibis, O god who longs for Khmun, O dispatch-writer of the Ennead, the great one of Unu.[1] Come to me that you may give advice and make me skillful in your office. Better is your profession than all professions. It makes (men) great. He who is skilled in it is found (fit) to exercise (the office of) magistrate. I have ʼseenʼ many for whom you have acted, and they are in the Council of the Thirty, they being strong and powerful through what you have done. You are the one who has given advice. You are the one who has given advice to the motherless man. Shay and Renenwetet are with you.[2] Come to me that you may advise me. I am the servant of your house. Let me relate your prowess in whatever land I am. Then the multitude of men shall say: How great are the things that Thot has done. Then they shall come with their children to brand[3] them with your profession, a calling good to the lord of victory. Joyful is the one who has exercised it.

## PRAYER TO AMUN IN A YEAR OF NEED
### (P. ANASTASI IV, 10, 1–5)

Come to me, Amun, save me in a year of need. The sun comes, but it does not rise. Winter is come in summer, the months come turned backward, and the hours are in disarray. The great ones call out to you, Amun, and the young seek you out. Those who are in the arms of their nurses [say]: Give breath, Amun. Perhaps Amun will come in peace, the sweet breeze before him. May he cause me to become the wing of a vulture, like an equipped *mesti*-boat,[4] so say the herdsmen in the field, the washermen on the riverbank, the Madjoy who come from the district,[5] and the gazelles on the desert.

1. Khmun and Unu are centers of the cult of Thot in Upper Egyptian Nome XV. The Ennead is the group of Nine Gods for whom Thot acts as a letter writer.
2. Destiny and Fortune.
3. Probably used metaphorically, as pointed out by Caminos, p. 234.
4. Caminos, p. 173, notes a suggestion made by Glanville that the passage compares the feathering of the vulture's wing to the banks of oars of a boat.
5. The Madjoy are a Nubian people of the desert who served as police and soldiers in Egypt of the New Kingdom.

## THE HARDSHIPS OF THE SOLDIER'S LIFE
### (P. ANASTASI IV, 9, 4–10,1)

What is it that you say they relate, that the soldier's is more pleasant than the scribe's (profession)? Come, let me tell you the condition of the soldier, that much castigated one. He is brought while a child to be confined in the camp. A ⌐searing⌐ beating is given his body, an open wound inflicted on his eyebrows. His head is split open with a wound. He is laid down and he is beaten like papyrus. He is struck with torments. Come, ⟨let me relate⟩ to you his journey to Khor[6] and his marching upon the hills. His rations and his water are upon his shoulder like the load of an ass, while his neck has been made a backbone like that of an ass. The vertebrae of his back are broken, while he drinks of foul water. He stops work (only) to keep watch. He reaches the battle, and he is like a plucked fowl. He proceeds to return to Egypt, and he is like a stick which the worm has devoured. He is sick, prostration overtakes him. He is brought back upon an ass, his clothes taken away by theft, his henchman fled. Scribe Inena,[7] turn back from the saying that the soldier's is more pleasant than the scribe's (profession).

6. Syria-Palestine.
7. To the scribe Inena we are indebted for several manuscripts including that of The Tale of the Two Brothers. The present text was written in the reign of Seti II of Dynasty 19 around 1210 B.C., but the set piece on the soldier's lot is probably earlier and not of his own composing. Inena was the apprentice of the scribe of the treasury Kageb.

# IX

## DEMOTIC LITERATURE

# THE PROPHECY OF THE LAMB
## (P. VIENNA D. 10,000)

I n surviving fragments of the Egyptian historian Manetho, the brief entry
for Pharaoh Bakenrenef ("Bocchoris"), sole ruler of the Twenty-fourth
Dynasty, notes: "in his reign a lamb spoke." A reference to this oracular
lamb appears also as an explanation for a portentous Alexandrian proverb "The
lamb has spoken to you."[1] Papyrus Vienna D 10,000, copied in 7–8 B.C. under
Augustus Caesar, preserves what remains of the original prophetic text. The
lamb, an emissary of the god Khnum, foretells the imminent overthrow of the
king and a prolonged period of foreign domination and disaster under Assyrians, Medes (Persians), and Greeks. A false savior will appear for two years
before the rise of a national "founder" who will reign for fifty-five years (half the
Egyptian ideal age of 110) under the control of the ram himself, now transformed into the "uraeus upon the head of Pharaoh." The specificity of the regnal
years 2 and 55 probably refers to known historical figures, and both modern and
ancient scholars have offered varying suggestions. Quotations from the "Prophecy of the Lamb" reappear in variant recensions of the Greco-Egyptian "Potter's
Prophecy" of 129 and 116 B.C., perhaps alluding to the reigns of the rebel king
Harsiese (two years) and Ptolemy Euergetes II (only fifty-four years).

Surviving sections of the prophecy evoke traditional Egyptian imagery: a

---

1. "Pseudo-Plutarch," De proverbiis Alexandrinorum, no. 21; see W. G. Waddell, Manetho (Cambridge, Mass., 1940), 164–65.

*river of blood, gods and symbols of rulership withdrawn, and social reversals. The lamb's poetic chant of "woe and abomination" recalls biblical oracles against Egypt (Ezekiel 30:13–19 and Isaiah 19:11–14). In contrast, the savior will return justice to Egypt and restore the shrines plundered by Assyrians and Medes, an important benefaction first stressed in the Satrap Stela for Ptolemy I and commonly repeated for later members of his dynasty.*

R.K.R.

1/1  [... Pasaenhor read the] book of the days that [happened in Egypt together with those that] will happen regarding a [... He said to me the punishments that will happen in the town,] the field and the [entire] district. [I said to him: "Shut] your mouth!" I spoke previously about the [...].

Pasaenhor [discovered] the fate [of the children who] will be born to us. We did not [know what we should do(?) ... The] great water of Egypt will become [blood(?) ... Afterwards, there occurred for her] the hour of birth, [and she bore two children], but she was unable to cast the [children into the water(?)² ...] he was better than him [... the fate] that would [not]

1/10  be diverted from them. [...] preparation (?) against [...] capture / [...] drink a [...] we [...] it because of [...] against him, as they lacked a child. These [...] sword against his [...].

[And it will] happen in the time in question that the rich man will

1/15  become a [poor] man. [...] / [... The] man who was served will perform their labors. [... Falsehood will thrive] in Egypt. Men will not speak the truth. [...] Many [evils(?) will be] in Egypt, inflicting injury upon [...] against their standing men.³ They were unable to speak against the people of Egypt. [... Evil will happen to the] temples. The gods will not be able

1/20  to take for themselves the [offerings(?) ...] / [... Such are the punishments that] Pre will create in Egypt. After these things, [... will happen] in Egypt for some few days. Their fighting(?) [...] years. However, the Medes will come to [Egypt ...] judgment will [happen] to them when they place Egypt [...] give birth [...] brazier, the heat, the inflammation [...]

2/1  / [...] the Greeks in a fire of papyrus. They will lead him to a stake. [...] They will bring him down in the third month of Winter and the fourth

2. Following the restoration of Zauzich, but this is based on his interpretation of col. 2/7, reread in this translation.

3. Perhaps a term for servants or armies.

month of Winter. They will plow a quantity of barley; they will not [harvest it(?) ...] They will remove the White Crowns [of the kings(?)] from Egypt. They will be sought; they will not be found. A small [...] will [...] as a curse, [being] great in the heart of the gods, being insignificant in the heart of men, being [...] / [...] ... a sovereign ... he of the two (years), who is not ours. It is he of the fifty-five (years) who is our founder.[4]

Many abominations will happen in Egypt. The birds of the sky and [the fish of] the sea will eat their blood and their flesh, living with respect to[5] them. A man will go[6] to the water [...] him upward. He will not be able to drink [or eat] in accordance with the book and what is in it. The humble man will bring [...]. He will seize the [...] of the great men while he is present (though) they did not question him. / A man will go before [his companions]; he will say to them what is [...], it being in his heart, saying: 'Who is it?' A man will go before them to the [place] of judgment with his companion; they will receive property from the one stronger than them because of the path(?).[7]

Woe and abomination for the youth, small in age! They will take him away to the land of Syria before his father and mother.

Woe and abomination for the [women] who will give birth to the youths small in age! They will be taken away to the land of Syria before them.

Woe to Egypt! [It will weep because] of the curses that are numerous within it.

Weep, / Heliopolis, while the west and east are under attack [...]!

Weep, Bubastis! Weep, Nilopolis!

They shall make the streets of Sebennytos into grape orchards, with the

---

4. The cryptic remarks concerning the rulers lasting 2 and 55 years reappear in the Greek copies of the Egyptian "Prophecy of the Potter," though it is uncertain to which rulers these designations apply; see Zauzich, p. 170, and L. Koenen, "A Supplementary Note on the Date of the Oracle of the Potter," *ZPE* 54 (1984): 9–13. The term here translated "founder" corresponds to Greek "initiator" (uparxon) and should be read *Pa-tꜣ-snty.t* (lit. "he of the foundation").

5. Or "more than."

6. Throughout the text, Zauzich reads *ḫꜣꜥ* "to cast" in place of *r rmt šm* "a man will go," but cf. col. 2/21 *r nꜣ rmt.w Kmy šm* "the people of Egypt will go."

7. A reference to the path of life? Zauzich reads *mw.t=f* "his likeness," but that would require *pꜣy=f mỉ.ty.*

pool of The Temple of Hatmehyt (Mendes) become bushes, palms and cucumbers.[8]

Weep, O great trees of Upoke![9]

Weep, Memphis, the city of Apis!

Weep, Thebes, the city of Amon!

Weep, Letopolis, the city of Shu, which has experienced fear and suffering!"

2/20   The lamb concluded all the curses regarding them. Pasaenhor said to him: "Will these happen only without our having seen them?" He said to him: "These will happen only when I am the uraeus upon the head of Pharaoh, which will happen at the completion of 900 years, when I control Egypt after the occurrence of the Mede."

He turned his attention to Egypt, abandoning the foreign powers:[10] "Truth will be manifest. Falsehood will perish.[11] Law and judgment will occur within Egypt. The shrines of the Egyptian gods will be recognized[12] for them at Nineveh in the district of Syria.[13] When it [happens] that the people of Egypt go to the land of Syria, they will control its districts and 3/1   they will find / the shrines of the Egyptian gods. Because of the good fortune that will happen in Egypt they will be speechless. The one abominable to god will fare badly. The one beneficent to god will receive beneficence from god also when he is buried. The barren woman will sigh; the one who gives birth will rejoice because of the good things that will happen in Egypt.[14] The small number of people who will be in Egypt will say: 'If only

---

8. The sacred pool of the fish goddess will become an overgrown garden, the current fate of the sacred lake at Dendera.

9. The burial precinct of Osiris at Abydos, noted for its sacred grove. See M. Smith, *Enchoria* 16 (1988): 68–69, and idem, *The Liturgy of Opening the Mouth for Breathing* (Oxford, 1993), 68–69.

10. *Gmgm.w* with foreign land determinative. The narrator's comment serves to introduce the lamb's prophecies for a reinvigorated and independent Egypt.

11. The disputed text reads *r mt.t-mȝˁ.t r pr r [mt.t]-ˁd r ˁq.*

12. Reading *iw=w š[p]-swn.*

13. Amur (*'Imˁr*) commonly conflated with Assyria; see Richard Steiner, "Why the Aramaic Script Was Called 'Assyrian' in Hebrew, Greek and Demotic," *Or* 62 (1993): 80–82.

14. Conditions are so wonderful that the barren regret that they have no children to experience them. This is in contrast to the oppressive period of the earlier prophecy when "woe and abomination" confronted pregnant women.

my father and the father of my father were here with me in the good time /

that has occurred!' "

The lamb concluded absolutely all of the matters to be said, and he died.[15] Pasaenhor had him taken up upon a new boat. He did not delay in going to the place where Pharaoh Bakenrenef was. They read the papyrus scroll before Pharaoh. Pharaoh said to them: "These evils, will they all happen in Egypt?" Pasaenhor said: "Before you have died they will happen." Pharaoh said to Pasaenhor: "Look after the lamb! Let him be placed in a [golden] shrine! Let him be buried in the manner of a god! Let it happen on earth in accordance with the custom that prevails for /

sovereign!" Afterwards, Pharaoh caused that he be buried in accordance with the sacred writings.

This is the conclusion of the papyrus scroll. Written in year 33 of Caesar, month 4 of Summer, day 8. Written by Khetba son of Herieu the younger, the name of whose mother is Khetba the elder. Behold here the curse that Pre made against Egypt from the sixth regnal year of Pharaoh Bakenrenef.

15. Lit. "His purification occurred."

# THE TALE OF AMASIS AND THE SKIPPER

D espite official claims of divine status, Egyptian pharaohs were often the subject of satirical tales. The sulking of Senefru and the cunning of Khufu motivate episodes of Papyrus Westcar, the sexual exploits of Pepy II are the focus of "Pepy and His General Sasenet," and Tuthmosis III is abused in "The Adventures of Setna and Si-Osire" (Setna II). In the present tale, the protagonist is Amasis, the last major ruler of the Saite Twenty-sixth Dynasty, who obtained the throne during an army revolt. The new ruler's common origins proved a source of amusement for later writers, and native legends regarding Amasis and his drinking are preserved in Herodotus II, 172–74. In the Demotic tale, the hangover of Amasis is implicitly compared to the self-induced sickness of a young skipper. Diodorus I, 60 and 95 offer conflicting accounts of the severity of the king's rule, but most accounts stress the broad popular support for his reign. As the good-natured satire of Senefru does not indicate a devaluation of kingship in the Old Kingdom, so the stories of Amasis are not, in themselves, evidence of an inferior royal status in Saite times.[1]

The text of the Amasis tale forms the first column on the verso of the oracular "Demotic Chronicle" (Papyrus 215 of the Bibliothèque Nationale in Paris). The story ends abruptly and is presumably incomplete. Like the "Chronicle," the Amasis story was copied in the early Ptolemaic period. Subsequent

---

1. A point stressed in the tale preserved in Herodotus II, 172.

*columns comprise a miscellany written by various scribes: priestly regulations, the codification of Egyptian law under Darius, temple finance under Cambyses, and animal fables.*

R.K.R.

A day occurred in the reign of Pharaoh Amasis when Pharaoh said to his great men: "I want to drink a vat[2] of Egyptian wine!" They said: "Our great lord, drinking a vat of Egyptian wine is overpowering." He said to them: "Do not oppose what I shall say!" They said: "Our great lord! The wish of Pharaoh, may he do it." Pharaoh said: "Let them set off for the sea shore!" They acted in accordance with what Pharaoh had commanded.

Pharaoh washed himself for a meal[3] together with his wives, with no other wine before them at all except a vat of Egyptian wine, so that the faces of Pharaoh and his wives were cheerful. / He drank an extremely large quantity of wine because of the craving that Pharaoh had for a vat of Egyptian wine. Pharaoh lay down at the sea shore on that same night. He slept beneath a grapevine toward the north.[4] Morning came, and Pharaoh was unable to raise himself because of the hangover[5] that he had. The time drew near and he was unable to raise himself. The council lamented, saying: "Is it a thing that can happen? It's happened that Pharaoh has a terrible hangover!" No one on earth was able to go to speak to Pharaoh. The council went to the place where Pharaoh was. / They said: "Our [great] lord! What is the sickness that Pharaoh is in?" Pharaoh said: "I have a terrible hangover. It isn't [in my] power[6] to do any work at all. However, look, is there a man among you who is able to recite a story to me, so that I can derive some amusement because of it?"

There was a priest of Neith among the council, whose name was

---

2. A *qlby*-jug measure of approximately twelve liters, see K. Th. Zauzich, "Wie maß-voll war Amasis?," *Enchoria* 16 (1988): 139–40.

3. Lit. "Pharaoh purified himself"; for the present nuance, see Günter Vittmann, *Der demotische Papyrus 9. Teil II. Kommentare und Indizes*, ÄUAT 38 (Wiesbaden, 1998), 430 and 461.

4. Amasis lies facing the cooling north wind.

5. Literally, "beating"; the term signifies the stupifying effects of a hangover.

6. Reading: *bn-iw=[s] ꜥ.wy=[i r] ir wp.t.* F. Hoffmann, "Einige Bemerkungen zur Geschichte von König Amasis und dem Schiffer," *Enchoria* 19/20 (1992–93): 16–17, restores *bn-iw [P]r-ꜥꜣ [rḫ]*, but the Amasis text writes only *bn-iw rḫ* + noun; cf. ll. 7 and 9.

Panetti,[7] [and who] was a [very] wise man. He came into the center in the presence of Pharaoh, and he said: "My great lord! Has Pharaoh not heard[8] [of the things] that happened to a young skipper called Hormaakheru, son of Osor[kon]?[9] He lived in the reign of Pharaoh [...], / and he had his wife whose name was Shepmeret, and she was called Ankhet as another name. As for the name of the skipper, she would call [him] Patiese. She loved him, and he loved her also.

A day occurred when Pharaoh sent him to Daphnae.[10] He [returned][11] on the next day, with a bad storm before him, after Pharaoh had commanded, saying: "It is a rushed cargo delivery. You shall go to Daphnae today. You shall return tomorrow." He got a terrible sickness from not being able to disregard the commissions that Pharaoh had given to him, saying that it was his affair (?) that he had been made to undertake in the presence of Pharaoh.[12] He went to his / house. He washed himself for a meal with his wife; he was unable to drink in his normal manner. The time came for the two of them to lie down; he was unable to touch her to have sex with her because of the severity of the sickness in which he was. She said to him: "O may he be cured from the fear of the river!"

7. Spiegelberg read Pet-sotem(?).
8. Lit. "Is it beyond the hearing of Pharaoh?"
9. For the reading of the names, see F. Hoffmann, pp. 17–18.
10. The garrison city named "Those of the Asiatic and the Nubian," cf. 'Onchsheshonqy col. 4/6, 9, and 18.
11. This obvious restoration is dictated by the traces and context and is noted also in F. Hoffmann, 20–21. Spiegelberg translated "arose" with hesitation.
12. Reading: $\underline{d}=f$ $t\dot{s}y=f$ $mt.t(?)$ $t\dot{s}y$-$t\dot{i}=w$ $\check{s}m=f$ $n$-$\dot{i}m=s$ $m$-$b\dot{s}\underline{h}$ $Pr$-$\degree$. Cf. the idiom $\check{s}m$ $n$ $mt.t$ (Lit. "go into a thing") meaning "to attempt/undertake something" in 'Onchsheshonqy col. 12/21.

# THE ROMANCE OF SETNA KHAEMUAS
# AND THE MUMMIES
# (SETNA I)

D uring Egypt's Late Period, the fourth son of the legendary Ramesses
II became the central focus of one or more cycles of tales, somewhat
reminiscent of the Arthurian cycles of medieval Western literature.
In the Egyptian tales, Prince Khaemuas is designated by his priestly title Setna
(older Setem), and it is his interest in ancient religious texts and magic that
motivate the plot. This characterization has a firm basis in history, since the real
Khaemuas served as High Priest or Setem of the Memphite god Ptah and justly
may be termed the first known Egyptologist. His zeal for the investigation and
restoration of ancient monuments is documented by his inscriptions throughout
the Memphite necropolis, where he was buried beside the sacred bulls of Ptah.
Such public texts undoubtedly inspired the Demotic romances of later authors.
By Ptolemaic times, Khaemuas appears even in the "Book of the Dead," where
he is credited with discovering ancient magical writings beneath the head of an
entombed mummy, a scenario closely related to the following romance.[1]

Tales of magicians are a traditional genre of Egyptian literature, extending
back to Papyrus Westcar set in the Old Kingdom. The Setna tales, however, cast
the central figure as an intelligent but "flawed" hero who brings misfortune
upon himself. Such a character type is also traditional, as evidenced by Sinuhe,

---

1. Spells Pleyte 167–69; see T. G. Allen, *The Book of the Dead,* SAOC 37 (Chicago,
1974), 216.

*Wenamon, and the pivotal Naneferkaptah in the following tale. Told within a series of interlocking narratives nested like the chests enclosing the critical scroll of Thoth, the tale employs sophisticated symbolism, symmetry, and word play. The importance of this and similar Egyptian romances for the development of the later Alexandrian "novel" has been much debated, but there can be little doubt that these Egyptian tales reached a Greek audience. One tale of Setna is even recorded by Herodotus (II, 141). The Setna story has proved influential in modern popular culture as well. The tale was recast into English verse by Gilbert Murray in 1911 (as* Nefrekepta), *provided the model for the seductress in Mika Waltari's* The Egyptian *in 1949 (filmed in 1954), and is the source of the "scroll of Thoth," central to the 1932 Universal film* The Mummy *and its many sequels. Boris Karloff's transformation into an aged Egyptian who leads excavators to the hidden tomb of his ancient love is borrowed directly from the final page of Setna I. In 1990, the ancient novel was in turn "novelized" as* Mirage *by Pauline Gedge.*

*The manuscript of the first Setna tale, P. Cairo 30646, lacks the initial two columns, as indicated by the surviving pagination numbers. The Demotic handwriting is of excellent quality and dates to the early Ptolemaic period. In the lost beginning, Setna and his foster brother Inaros have entered the Memphite burial chamber of a long deceased Prince Naneferkaptah in search of the magical scroll of Thoth, the divine scribe and patron of science and magic. There they confront the mummy of Naneferkaptah as well as the disembodied ghost (akh) of his wife and sister, Ihweret, and that of her child, Merib. Ihweret relates their family history to a disinterested Setna, explaining that in her love for her brother, she sent a steward to entreat her father to allow them to marry. Pharaoh is irritated by the request, and when questioned by the steward, he replies with the words that begin column 3.*

R.K.R.

3/1[2]    [...]

"You are the one who irritates me. If it happens that I have but two children, is it the custom to cause that they dwell with each other? I shall cause Naneferkaptah to dwell with the daughter of a general, [and I shall cause] Ihweret [to dwell] with the son of another general. May it happen that our family will multiply!"

2. Labeled "the third (page)."

The time came for setting up the festival in the presence of Pharaoh. They came for me, and they took me to the festival, [though my heart was] exceedingly sad, nor did I have my demeanor of yesterday. Pharaoh said to me: "Ihweret, is it you who had them come to me regarding these foolish words, saying: 'Let me dwell with [Naneferkaptah, my] elder [brother]'?"

I said to him: "Let me dwell with the son of a general. Let him dwell with the daughter of another general for his part. May it happen that our family will multiply!" I laughed and Pharaoh laughed.[3]

3/5      / [The palace steward came,] and Pharaoh [said to him]: "Palace steward, let Ihweret be taken to the house of Naneferkaptah tonight. Let everything that is beautiful be taken with her, omitting nothing." They took me as wife to the house of Naneferkaptah [on that night, and Pharaoh] caused that they bring to me a gift of silver and gold. The entire household of Pharaoh had themselves brought to me. Naneferkaptah celebrated with me, and he received the entire household of Pharaoh. He slept with me that very night. He found me [very pleasing, and he slept] with me again and again. Each one of us loved the other.

My menstrual cycle came, and I did not menstruate.[4] It was reported in the presence of Pharaoh, and his heart became exceedingly happy. Pharaoh caused that many things be taken [from the treasury of Pharaoh]. He caused that they bring to me a gift of silver, gold, and royal byssus, all of which was exceedingly beautiful. My time of giving birth came, and I bore this youth who is before you, named Merib. He was taught to write letters in the House of Life.[5]

[It happened that] Naneferkaptah, my brother, had no occupation on earth except to walk on the *gebel* of Memphis reading the writings that were in the tombs of the Pharaohs and the stelae of the scribes of the House

3/10   of Life and the writings that were on / [the other monuments, for] exceedingly [great was his zeal] about writings. After these things, there occurred

3. The literary device of "borrowed speech" is used to less comic effect by the devious wife in The Tale of the Two Brothers (col. 5/2–3).

4. Lit. "My time of making natron happened and I did not make natron again." Natron, a naturally occurring bicarbonate of soda, was used as a cleanser for medical and ceremonial purposes.

5. The sentence indicates that Merib was taught "letter writing" (the common term for Demotic) in the temple scriptorium, in contrast to Ihweret, who does not write (col. 4/3). The traditional translation assumes the existence of a birth registry ("They caused that he be inscribed in the documents of the House of Life").

a processional festival pertaining to Ptah. Naneferkaptah went into the temple to worship. It happened that he was walking behind the procession, reading the writings that were on the shrines of the gods. [An] old [priest looked] at him, and he laughed. Naneferkaptah said to him: "Why are you laughing at me?"

He said: "I am not laughing at you. I am laughing just because you are reading some writings that have no [value at all.] If you wish to read writing, come to me that I might take you to the place where this scroll is, since it was Thoth who wrote it with his own hand when he was going down following the gods. There are two written formulas that are on it. If you [read the first formula, you will] enchant heaven, the earth, the underworld, the mountains, and the seas. You will find out what all the birds of the heaven and all the reptiles will say. You will behold the fish of the deep, though there are [twenty-one divine cubits[6] of water] above them. If you read the second formula, whether it is the case that you are in the West or you are in your earthly form either, you will behold Pre appearing in heaven with his Ennead together with the moon in its manner of rising."[7]

3/15     / [Naneferkaptah said: "My good lord,] O may he live! Let me be told a favor that you desire so that I might do it for you, and you send me to the place where this scroll is." The priest said to Naneferkaptah: "If it happens that you wish [me to] send you [to the place where this scroll] is, you will give to me 100 *deben* of real silver toward my burial, and you will have my two brothers made priests tax free." Naneferkaptah called to a servant. He had the 100 *deben* of silver given to the priest. He caused that the wishes [for his] two [brothers] be done. He had them made [priests tax free.]

[The priest said to] Naneferkaptah: "As for the scroll in question, it is in the midst of the sea of Coptos within a chest of iron, with the chest of iron within a chest [of bronze, with the chest of] bronze within a chest of Aleppo pinewood, with the chest of Aleppo pinewood within a chest of ivory and ebony, with the chest of ivory and ebony within a [chest of silver, with the chest of] silver within a chest of gold, with the scroll within it, with

6. 11.025 m. or almost 36 feet. The reading here and in cols. 3/37 and 4/3 was established simultaneously by Frank T. Miosi, " 'Wassergeist'(?)," *SSEA Newsletter* 2/2 (1971): 6–9; and K. Th. Zauzich, "Gottesellen statt Gotteskraft," *Enchoria* 1 (1971): 83–86.

7. For such magical techniques, see R. K. Ritner, *The Mechanics of Ancient Egyptian Magical Practice*, SAOC 54 (Chicago, 1993), 63–64.

one [*schoinos*]⁸ of snakes, scorpions, and all manner of reptiles about
3/20  the perimeter of the chest in which the scroll is, and with / [an eternal snake
about the perimeter] of this same chest."⁹

At the very moment when the priest recounted [this before] Naneferkaptah, he did not know where on earth he was. He came out from within
the temple, and he related [to me everything that the priest said to him] in
its entirety. He [said] to me: "I shall go to Coptos. I shall bring back this
scroll, [without having] delayed in coming north again." It happened that I
accused the priest, saying: "May Neith curse you, O priest! You have already related before him these [dreadful things. You have brought] me
conflict; you have brought me strife. As for the Thebaid, I have found it
[abhorrent." I did] all that I could with Naneferkaptah to prevent him from
going to Coptos. He did not listen to me. He went before [Pharaoh, and he
related before] Pharaoh everything that the priest said to him in its entirety.

Pharaoh said to him: "What is it that [you wish?"] He said to him: "Let
the royal yacht be given to me together with its equipment. I shall take
Ihweret [and Merib, her] child, to the south with me. I shall bring back this
scroll, without having delayed." The royal yacht was given to him together
with its equipment. We went up on board it. We sailed, and we reached /
3/25  [Coptos. Report was made] of it before the priests of Isis of Coptos and the
chief inspector of Isis. They came down before us. They did not delay in
going before Naneferkaptah. Their wives came down before me, myself.
[We went up from the shore, and we went into the] temple of Isis and
Harpocrates. Naneferkaptah caused that there be brought beef, fowl, and
wine. He made a burnt offering and a libation before Isis of Coptos and
Harpocrates. They took us to a house which was exceedingly beautiful,
[filled with all good things].

Naneferkaptah spent four days celebrating with the priests of Isis of
Coptos, while the wives of the priests of Isis celebrated with me, myself.
The morning of our fifth day occurred, and Naneferkaptah had pure [wax
brought] before him. He made a boat filled with its rowers and its sailors.
He recited a spell to them. He caused them to live. He gave them breath.

8. Approximately 10.5 km.
9. The ouroboros imagery corresponds to that found on protective stelae; see R. K.
   Ritner, "A Uterine Amulet in the Oriental Institute Collection," *JNES* 43/3 (1984):
   219–21.

He cast them into the sea. He filled the pleasure boat of Pharaoh with sand, [and he tied it to the other boat.] He went up on board, and I myself sat above the sea of Coptos, saying: "I shall find out what will happen to him."

He said to the rowers: "Row bearing me up to the place where this 3/30 scroll / [is." They rowed by night] as by day. In three days he reached it. He cast sand before him, and a gap formed in the river. About the perimeter [of the chest] where the scroll was he found a *schoinos* of snakes, scorpions, and all manner of reptiles. About the perimeter of the same chest he found an eternal snake. He recited a spell to the *schoinos* of snakes, scorpions and all manner of reptiles that were about the perimeter of the chest. He prevented them from flying up. [He went to the place where the] eternal snake was. He fought with it. He killed it. It returned to life. He did the same thing again. He fought with it again for a second time. He killed it. It returned to life again. He [fought with it again for a] third time. He cut it into two pieces. He placed sand between one piece and the other. [It died.] It did not resume its form ever again.

Naneferkaptah went to the place where the chest was. [He found that] it was a chest of iron. He opened it. He found a chest of bronze. He opened it. He found a chest of Aleppo pinewood. He opened it. He found a 3/35 chest of ivory and ebony. / [He opened it. He found a chest of] silver. He opened it. He found a chest of gold. He opened it. He found the scroll within it. He brought up the scroll from within the chest of gold. He recited a written formula from it. [He enchanted heaven, the earth, the underworld, the] mountains and the seas. He found out what all the birds of heaven, the fish of the deep, and the herds of the desert were saying. He recited the other written formula. He beheld [Pre appearing in heaven with his Ennead] together with the rising moon and the stars in their arrangement. He beheld the fish of the deep, though there were twenty-one divine cubits of water atop them.

He recited a spell to the [water. He caused it to resume its form. He went up on] board. He said to the rowers: "Row bearing me up to the place [from which] you [came]."[10] They rowed bearing him by night as by day. He reached the place where I [was, even as I was sitting] above the sea of Coptos without having drunk or eaten, without having done anything at

---

10. Or, "[from which] you [took me]," which would also fit the space and traces, but cf. F. Hoffmann, "Einige Bemerkungen zur Ersten Setnegeschichte (P. Kairo CG 30646)," *Enchoria* 23 (1996): 54–55.

all, looking like a person who has reached the Good House.[11] I said to
3/40  Naneferkaptah: / ["Welcome back.] Let me look at this scroll for which we
have taken these [great] pains." He put the scroll in my hand. I recited a
4/1  written formula from it. I enchanted heaven,[12] / the earth, the underworld,
the mountains, and the seas. I found out what all the birds of heaven, all the
fish of the deep, and all the herds were saying. I recited another written
formula. I beheld Pre appearing in heaven with his Ennead. I beheld the
rising moon and all the stars of heaven and their arrangement.[13] I beheld
the fish of the deep, though there were twenty-one divine cubits of water
above them, even though I can't write,—I was speaking with regard to
Naneferkaptah, my elder brother, who is a good scribe and a very wise man.
He caused that a new sheet of papyrus be brought before him. He wrote
down every word that was on the papyrus before him, completely. He had it
burned with fire; he dissolved it in water. He recognized that it had dissolved; he drank it and he knew that which was in it.[14]

4/5  / We returned to Coptos on that very day. We celebrated before Isis of
Coptos and Harpocrates. We went up on board, we sailed downstream,
and we reached the north of Coptos by one *schoinos*.[15]

However, Thoth had already found out everything that had happened
to Naneferkaptah concerning the scroll. Thoth did not delay in going to
report it before Pre, saying: "Ascertain my legal rights and my judgment
with Naneferkaptah, the son of Pharaoh Mernebptah.[16] He went to my
treasury, and he plundered it. He took my chest containing my legal document. He killed my guardian who was watching over it."

They said to him: "He is at your disposal together with absolutely every
person belonging to him." They sent a slaughtering demon down from

---

11. Euphemistic designation of the embalmers' workshop.
12. The page begins "The fourth" and repeats by dittography: "I enchanted heaven."
13. The constellations.
14. For this magical procedure and its association with funerary spells, see Ritner, *The Mechanics of Ancient Egyptian Magical Practice*, 102–10, esp. 107–8.
15. Setna can go no farther than one river measure from the base at Coptos, a restricted perimeter corresponding to the one *schoinos* circuit of the eternal snake about Thoth's scroll. In both cases, there are "chests" (coffers/coffins) surrounded by one *schoinos* of divine force.
16. The name of this ancient royal ancestor is a garbled form of Merneptah, the younger brother of Khaemuas who succeeded Ramesses II.

heaven, saying: "Do not allow Naneferkaptah to reach Memphis safely, nor any person belonging to him at all!"

But a moment later,[17] Merib the youth came out from under the canopy of the royal yacht.[18] He fell into the river, and he became a "praised one"[19] of Pre. Absolutely every man who was on board uttered a loud cry. Naneferkaptah came out from under his canopy. He recited a spell to him, 4/10 and he caused that he fly up, though there were / twenty-one divine cubits of water atop him. He recited a spell to him, and he caused that he relate before him everything that had happened to him in its entirety, together with the nature of the complaint that Thoth had made before Pre. We returned to Coptos with him. We caused that he be taken to the Good House, we caused that they attend to him, and we caused that he be embalmed like a wealthy aristocrat. We caused that he rest in his stone chest[20] on the *gebel* of Coptos. Naneferkaptah my brother said: "Let us sail downstream. Let us not delay, lest Pharaoh hear the things that happened to us and his heart become sad because of it." We went up on board, we sailed downstream, and we did not delay in going to the north of Coptos by one *schoinos*, the place where Merib the youth fell into the river.

I came out from under the canopy of the royal yacht. I fell into the river. I became a "praised one" of Pre. Absolutely every man who was on board uttered a loud cry. They told it to Naneferkaptah. He came out from under the canopy of the royal yacht. He recited a spell to me, and he caused 4/15 that I fly up, though there were twenty-one divine cubits / of water atop me. He caused that I be brought up, he recited a spell to me, and he caused that I relate before him everything that had happened to me in its entirety,

---

17. Lit. "It was a moment that happened."

18. The members of Setna's party fall victim to Pre's vengeance only when they are exposed to the rays—and thus the power—of the sun. For similar reasons, magical potions are either exposed to or hidden from sunlight, and Akhenaton's solar temples were unroofed.

19. An expression for the deified "drowned." For the idiom and Setna's consultation of his deceased wife and son, see the discussion in R. Ritner, "Necromancy in Ancient Egypt," in Leda Ciraolo and Jonathan Seidel, eds., *Magic and Divination in the Ancient World* (Leiden, 2002), 89–96; and idem, "Des preuves de l'existence d'une nécromancie dans l'Egypte ancienne," in Yvon Koenig, ed. (Paris: 2002), 285–304. *La magie en Egypte: à la recherche d'une définition.*

20. The term for the "chest" of Merib is the same word used for the various chests that enclosed the scroll of Thoth. For plundering the set of divine chests, Setna's family now fills a series of funerary chests.

together with the nature of the complaint that Thoth had made before Pre. He returned to Coptos with me. He caused that I be taken to the Good House, he caused that they attend to me, and he caused that I be embalmed like a very wealthy aristocrat. He caused that I rest in the tomb where Merib the youth rested. He went up on board, he sailed downstream, and he did not delay in going to the north of Coptos by one *schoinos*, to the place where we fell into the river. He spoke with his heart, saying: "Shall I be able to go to Coptos and dwell there, or were it to happen that I went to Memphis at once, and Pharaoh asks me about his children, what is it that I shall say to him? Shall I be able to say to him: 'I took your children to the Thebaid, I killed them, though I am alive, and I have returned to Memphis, though I am yet alive?'"

He had them bring before him a strip of sheer royal linen that he possessed. He made it into a linen bandage.[21] He bound the scroll, he 4/20 placed it on his body, / and he made it tight. Naneferkaptah came out from under the canopy of the royal yacht. He fell into the river. He became a "praised one" of Pre. Absolutely every man who was on board uttered a loud cry, saying: "Great woe! Vile woe! Has he withdrawn himself, the good scribe, the wise man, like whom no other has existed?"

The royal yacht sailed downstream without anyone on earth knowing the place where Naneferkaptah was. They reached Memphis, and it was reported before Pharaoh. Pharaoh came down before the royal yacht wearing mourning linen, while all the population of Memphis wore mourning linen as did the priests of Ptah, the chief inspector of Ptah, the councilors of Pharaoh, and all the household of Pharaoh. They beheld Naneferkaptah, even as he was grasping the rudders of the royal yacht by means of his skill as a good scribe. They brought him up, and they beheld the scroll on his body. Pharaoh said: "Let them remove this scroll that is on his body."

Then the councilors of Pharaoh together with the priests of Ptah and the chief inspector of Ptah said before Pharaoh: "Our great lord, O may he attain the lifetime of Pre! Naneferkaptah was a good scribe and a very 4/25 wise man." / Pharaoh caused that he be given entry to the Good House for sixteen days, with a wrapping of thirty-five, for an embalming of seventy days. He was caused to rest in his stone chest in his resting place.

Such are the evil matters that happened to us because of this scroll of

---

21. For this passage, see R. K. Ritner, "Two Demotic Notes," *Enchoria* 13 (1985): 213–14.

which you say: 'Let it be given to me!' You have nothing to do with it, whereas because of it our life on earth was taken!"

Setna said: "Ihweret, let me be given this scroll that I have seen between you and Naneferkaptah, or I shall take it by force!" Naneferkaptah raised himself from upon the bier. He said: "Are you Setna before whom this woman is saying these woeful matters, without your having taken them in at all? As for the scroll in question, will you be able to take it by means of the strength of a good scribe or by contest through playing a game against me? Let us adopt the procedure of playing for it, just us two." Setna said: "I'm ready."

The game board was brought before them together with its pieces.[22] The two men played. Naneferkaptah took one game from Setna. He recited a spell to him. He gave a blow to his head with the gaming board that was before him. He caused that he go into the ground up to his feet. He did the same in the second game. He took it / from Setna. He caused that he go into the ground up to his penis. He did the same in the third game. He caused that he go into the ground up to his ears.

4/30

After that, Setna was in great difficulty at the hands of Naneferkaptah. Setna called out to Inaros, his foster brother, saying: "Don't delay in going up to the surface and relate everything that has happened to me before Pharaoh and bring back to me the amulets of Ptah, my father, together with my scrolls of taking security."[23] He did not delay in going up to the surface. He related before Pharaoh everything that had happened to Setna. Pharaoh said: "Take to him the amulets of Ptah, his father, together with his scrolls of taking security."

Inaros did not delay in going down into the tomb. He put the amulets on the body of Setna, and he flew upwards at that very instant. Setna stretched out his hand after the scroll, and he took it. It happened that Setna was coming up from within the tomb as the light went before him and the darkness went after him, while Ihweret wept behind him, saying: "Hail, O darkness! Farewell,[24] O light! Everything that was / in the tomb has gone away in its entirety." Naneferkaptah said to Ihweret: "Don't be sad hearted!

4/35

22. Lit. "dogs," a term generalized from the popular game of "hounds and hares."
23. Setna's magical books. For the term, see Ritner, *The Mechanics of Ancient Egyptian Magical Practice*, 68–69.
24. Lit. "Horus be your protection!" The scroll radiates illumination; cf. col. 6/2, below.

I shall cause that he bring this scroll back here, with a forked stick in his hand and a brazier of fire on his head."[25]

Setna came up from within the tomb, and he secured it in its proper fashion. Setna went into the presence of Pharaoh. He related before him everything that had happened to him on account of the scroll. Pharaoh said to Setna: "Take this scroll back to the tomb of Naneferkaptah like a wise man, or he will cause that you take it back with a forked stick in your hand and a brazier of fire on your head." Setna did not listen to him. It transpired that Setna had no occupation on earth except to spread out the scroll and read aloud from it before everyone.

After that, a day occurred when Setna was strolling on the dromos of Ptah. He beheld a woman who was exceedingly beautiful, no woman having existed with her look. She was beautiful, with some works of gold in great quantity upon her, some female servants walking behind her, and with two men of the household assigned to her.

5/1    / At the very moment that Setna beheld her, he did not know where on earth he was.[26] Setna called out to his attending servant, saying: "Don't delay in going to the place where this woman is. Learn what is happening with her affairs." The attending servant did not delay in going to the place where the woman was. He called out to the maidservant who was walking behind her. He asked her, saying: "What sort of person is she?" She said to him: "She is Tabubu,[27] the daughter of the prophet of Bastet, the Lady of Ankhtawy. She has come here specifically to worship before Ptah, the great god."

The servant returned to Setna. He related before him everything that she had said to him in its entirety. Setna said to the servant: "Go! Say to the

---

25. This penitential posture reflects the hieroglyphic symbol for a defeated enemy, bound to a forked stake. The brazier shooting fire is a reinterpretation of the blood trail or axe depicted atop the head of this hieroglyph. See Ed Meltzer, *SSEA Newsletter* 7/1 (1976): 10–11.

26. The column is labeled "The fifth." For this idiom of lovesickness, cf. the reaction of Naneferkaptah regarding the scroll of Thoth (col. 3/20) and R. K. Ritner, *JNES* 45 (1986): 244, n. 3. The phrase is translated into Greek in the love charm PGM LXI; see H. D. Betz, ed., *The Greek Magical Papyri in Translation, Including the Demotic Spells* (Chicago, 1986), 291.

27. "She of The Radiant One," probably a reference to Bastet or Hathor, goddesses of love.

maidservant that it is Setna Khaemuas, the son of Pharaoh Usermaatre,[28] who has sent me, saying: 'I shall give you 10 *deben* of gold. Spend an hour with me! Or, should you / have an accusation of rape, I shall have it done to you. I shall have you taken to a hidden place where no man on earth will find you.' "

The servant returned to the place where Tabubu was. He called out to her maidservant. He spoke with her. She made a cackling noise as if it were blasphemy that he had said. Tabubu said to the servant: "Stop speaking with this stinking girl! Come and speak with me!" The servant hurried to the place where Tabubu was. He said to her: "I shall give 10 *deben* of silver. Spend an hour with Setna Khaemuas, the son of Pharaoh Usermaatre. Or, should you have an accusation of rape, he will have it done, too. He will take you to a hidden place where no man on earth will find you."

Tabubu said: "Go! Say to Setna that I am pure; I am not a lowly person. If it happens that you wish to do what you desire with me, you will come to the estate of Bastet to my house. All manner of supplies are within it. You will do what you desire with me only while no man on earth has / discovered me, and while I have not acted as a common woman in the street either."

The servant returned to Setna. He related before him everything that she had said to him in its entirety. He said: "It is agreeable." Woe to every man who was in the vicinity of Setna![29] Setna caused that a ship be brought for him. He mounted up on board it. He did not delay in going to the estate of Bastet. He came to the west of the cultivation.[30] He found a house that was extremely tall, with a wall surrounding it, with a garden on its north and with a bench before its gate. Setna inquired, saying: "This house, whose house is it?" They told him: "It is the house of Tabubu." Setna went inside the wall. He turned his attention directly to the guardhouse of the garden, and it was reported to Tabubu. She came down, and she grasped the hand of Setna, saying: "By the fortune of the house of the prophet of Bastet, the Lady of Ankhtawy, which you have penetrated,[31] it will please me greatly! Sail yourself on up with me."

28. The throne name of Ramesses II, preserved in Greek as Ozymandias.
29. A direct intrusion of the narrator, rare in Egyptian literature.
30. Lit. "the (land of) Egypt." For this passage, see J. C. Darnell, "Articular *Km.t/Kmy* and Partitive ⲕⲏⲙⲉ (Including an Isis of Memphis and Syria, and the *Kmy* of Setne I 5,11 West of Which Lived Ta-Bubu)," *Enchoria* 17 (1990): 69–81.
31. The verb "to reach/penetrate/attain orgasm" is employed throughout the text for a series of erotic word play.

5/15    Setna went up / upon the staircase of the house with Tabubu. He found
the upper story of the house swept, decorated,[32] with its floor decorated with
real lapis lazuli and real turquoise, with many beds in it spread with sheer
royal linen, and with some gold cups in great quantity on the dining table.[33]
A gold cup was filled with wine, and it was placed in the hand of Setna. She
said to him: "Let it be so, that you will eat as you please." He said to her:
"There is nothing that I shall be able to do."[34] Incense was placed upon the
brazier. Unguents were brought before him of the quality of royal provisions. Setna celebrated with Tabubu, never having seen her like, ever!

Setna said to Tabubu: "Let us accomplish that for which we came
here!" She said to him: "You will reach your house, the one in which you
are. I am pure; I am not a lowly person. If it happens that you wish to do
what you desire with me, you will make for me a deed of financial support,
5/20    together with a / document of sale regarding everything and all movable
property belonging to you in its entirety." He said to her: "Let the scribe of
the school be brought." He was brought immediately. He caused that there
be made for her a deed of financial support and a document of sale regarding everything and all movable property belonging to him in its entirety.

It was but a moment that transpired, and it was reported before Setna
that: "Your children are below." He said: "Let them be brought up." Tabubu arose. She put on a dress of sheer royal linen. Setna beheld all her
limbs within it. His desire surged even in excess of what he had been in
previously. Setna said: "Tabubu, let me accomplish that for which I came
here!"[35] She said to him: "You will reach your house, the one in which you
are. I am pure; I am not a lowly person. If it happens that you wish to do
what you desire with me, you will cause that your children subscribe my
document. Do not leave them to contest with my children for your property." He caused that his children be brought. He had them subscribe the
document.

5/25    Setna said to Tabubu: "Let me accomplish / that for which I came
here!" She said to him: "You will reach your house, the one in which you

32. Lit. "sprinkled." Perhaps a reference to mosaic inlay of lapis and turquoise.
33. "The pure place," a term used also of the embalming table, an appropriate word play
    here.
34. Setna's inability to eat or drink corresponds to the standard threats of Egyptian love
    magic, which render the "lovesick" victim an abject slave of the magician, unable to
    eat, sleep or think properly.
35. In his excitement, Setna changes his demand from "let us" to "let me."

are. I am pure; I am not a lowly person. If it happens that you wish to do what you desire with me, you will cause that your children be killed. Do not leave them to contest with my children for your property." Setna said: "Let there be done to them the abomination that has reached your heart." She had his children killed before him. She cast them down out of the window before the dogs and cats. They ate their flesh while he listened to them, drinking with Tabubu.

Setna said to Tabubu: "Let us accomplish that for which we came here![36] Everything that you have said, I have already done it for you in its entirety." She said to him: "Sail yourself over to this treasury." Setna went to the treasury. He lay down on a bed of ivory and ebony whose value was worth gold.[37] Tabubu lay down beside Setna. He stretched out his hand 5/30 to touch her. She opened her mouth to / the ground in a great cry.

Setna awoke in a heated state, with his penis inside a chamber pot(?)[38] and without any clothing on him at all. It was but a moment that transpired, and Setna beheld a noble mounted upon a palanquin, who had many men running beneath his feet and who was in the guise of Pharaoh. Setna started to raise himself, but he was unable to raise himself because of the shame that he had no clothing on him. Pharaoh said: "Setna, what is with you in this condition that you are in?" He said: "It is Naneferkaptah who has done it all to me." Pharaoh said: "Go to Memphis! As for your children, they are seeking for you. They are standing in their ranks in the presence of Pharaoh."[39]

36. The only discernable reaction of the enchanted Setna to the death and mutilation of his children is the switch back to "let us" from the self-absorbed "let me." The local cats and dogs may be a sly reference to the sacred animals of the nearby Bubasteion and Anubeion. Being exposed to animals is the ultimate disgrace, entailing the destruction of body and spirit; cf. the fate of the evil wife in The Tale of the Two Brothers (col. 8/8).

37. Lichtheim translates: "his wish about to be fulfilled," lit. "his wish receiving gold." The gender is incorrect for the word "wish/desire," however, and the term is here taken as a feminine abstract "desirability."

38. The uncertain word, attested uniquely here, is determined by two signs indicating dung and either water or a pot. Maspero (1915, 140, n.2, and 1880, 16 and 17, n. 2) translated the term as a jar. Compare early Western symbolic associations between chamber pots and promiscuous women in Mary Ellin D'Agostino, "Privy Business: Chamber Pots and Sexpots in Colonial Life," *Archaeology* 53/4 (2000): 33–37.

39. The aristocrat "in the form of Pharaoh" is either Naneferkaptah or the god Ptah, Setna's divine protector (cf. 5/39).

Setna said in the presence of Pharaoh: "My great lord, O may he attain the lifetime of Pre! How shall I be able to go to Memphis with no clothing at all on me?" Pharaoh called out to a servant who was standing by. He had him give clothing to Setna. Pharaoh said: "Setna, go to Memphis! As for your children, they are alive. They are standing in their ranks in the presence of Pharaoh."

Setna returned to Memphis. He embraced his children when he found them alive. Pharaoh said: "Was is drunkenness that you were in previously?" Setna related everything that had happened to him with Tabubu and Naneferkaptah in its entirety. Pharaoh said: "Setna, I did all that I could with you previously, saying: 'They will kill you if you don't take this scroll back to the place from which you brought it away.' You have not listened to me up to this moment, either. Let this scroll be taken to Naneferkaptah while there is a forked stick in your hand and a brazier of fire on your head."

Setna came away from the presence of Pharaoh with a forked stick in his hand and a brazier of fire on his head. He went down to the tomb in which Naneferkaptah was. Ihweret said to him: "Setna, it was Ptah, the

6/1  great god, who brought you back safely." Naneferkaptah laughed, / saying: "It is what I said to you previously."[40] Setna greeted Naneferkaptah. He found that one would say that it was the sun which was in the whole tomb.[41] Ihweret and Naneferkaptah greeted Setna enthusiastically.

Setna said: "Naneferkaptah, is there a matter which is a problem?" Naneferkaptah said: "Setna, you know that Ihweret and Merib her child are in Coptos. It is only by the craft of an excellent scribe that they are here in this tomb. Let it be your obligation,[42] and take the trouble and go to

6/5  Coptos and bring them back / here."

Setna came out from within the tomb. He went into the presence of Pharaoh. He related before Pharaoh everything which Naneferkaptah had said to him in its entirety. Pharaoh said: "Setna, go to Coptos! Bring back Ihweret and Merib her child!" He said before Pharaoh: "Let me be given the royal yacht together with its equipment." He was given the royal yacht

40. The column is labeled "The sixth" and repeats: " 'It was Ptah, the great god, who brought you back safely.' Naneferkaptah laughed."

41. The return of the scroll fills the tomb with light, evoking imagery of the sun god's passage through the underworld as described in the Amduat texts.

42. Lit. "Let it be commanded before you."

together with its equipment. He mounted up on board. He sailed, he did not delay, and he reached Coptos.

It was reported before the priests of Isis of Coptos and the chief inspector of Isis. They came down before him and they conducted him to the banks. He went up among them. He reached the temple of Isis of Coptos and Harpocrates. He had oxen, fowl, and wine brought, and he made a burnt offering and a libation in the presence of Isis of Coptos and Harpocrates. He went to the *gebel* of Coptos together with the priests of Isis and the chief inspector of Isis. They spent three days and three nights seeking in all the tombs that were on the *gebel* of Coptos, turning over the stelae of the scribes of the House of Life and reading the texts that were on them.

6/10   They did not find the resting / places in which Ihweret and Merib her child were.

Naneferkaptah discovered that they had not found the resting places of Ihweret and Merib her child. He arose as an elder priest who was extremely aged. He came before Setna, and Setna looked at him. Setna said to the old man: "You have the appearance of a man who is old. Do you know the resting places in which Ihweret and Merib her child are?" The old man said to Setna: "The father of the father of my father said before the father of my father: 'The father (of the father) of my father said before the father of my father that it is beside the southern corner of the house of the chief of police [Harsiese(?)] that the resting places of Ihweret and Merib her child are.' "[43]

Setna said to the old man: "Perhaps there is an injury which the chief of police has done to you, and you are going to have his house brought down because of it." The old man said to Setna: "Let them watch over me,

6/15   and let them / destroy the house of the police chief. If it happens that they have not found Ihweret and Merib her child under the southern corner of his house, let me be punished."

They watched over the old priest, and they found the resting place of Ihweret and Merib her child under the southern corner of the house of the chief of police. Setna gave a processional entrance to the nobles onto the royal yacht. He had them rebuild the house of the chief of police in accordance with its former condition. Naneferkaptah caused that Setna discover

43. Or, "My great-grandfather said before my grandfather that his great-grandfather said before his grandfather..." The scribe has omitted a generation in copying from col. 6/12 to 6/13. The priest's great-grandfather relates a story of his own great-grandfather, thus six generations before the priest impersonated by Naneferkaptah. The passage is unduly truncated in Lichtheim's translation.

the fact that it was he who had come to Coptos to cause them to find the resting place in which Ihweret and Merib were.

Setna mounted up on board the royal yacht. He sailed, he did not delay, and he reached Memphis with the whole group that was with him. It was reported before Pharaoh. He came down before the royal yacht. He gave a processional entrance to the nobles into the tomb in which Naneferkaptah was. He caused that they be sealed / over all together.

6/20

It is the complete text, the narrative of Setna Khaemuas and Naneferkaptah and Ihweret his wife and Merib her child. This hand copy was written by Pasher[...] in regnal year 15, the first month of Winter.

# THE ADVENTURES OF SETNA
# AND SI-OSIRE
# (SETNA II)

P urchased in Aswan in 1895, the second tale of Setna (P. British Museum
604) is written on the verso of two reused Greek account papyri, joined
to produce a scroll. The Greek texts contain official land registers dated
to year 7 of Emperor Claudius (A.D. 46–47) in regard to fields at Crocodilopolis
near Gebelein, and this copy of the Demotic tale probably derives from the same
region and century. One or more pages at the beginning of the tale are lost, as is
much of the first of the seven preserved columns. In comparison with the first
Setna tale, the manuscript of Setna II is far less carefully written, with obvious
omissions, phonetic renderings, and a few scribal corrections. Beyond the initial
publication, however, the text has received scant philological study and little
modification in subsequent translations. The current translation contains a
number of lexical and grammatical revisions, of which only the most important
are referenced in the notes.

The British Museum scroll contains three distinct tales, in each of which
Setna's son Si-Osire is the pivotal character: Si-Osire's miraculous birth, Si-
Osire's visit with Setna to the underworld, and Si-Osire's magical duel with a
Nubian shaman. As the final episode makes Si-Osire the reincarnation of yet
another magician, Setna II links the cycles of three magician heroes: Setna, Si-

*Osire, and Hor son of Punesh ("The Wolf"), whose adventures are known from both Demotic and Aramaic versions.[1]*

*The existence of an Aramaic translation of a magician's tale is evidence of the international appeal of these stock characters of Egyptian literature, prominent also in the nascent Alexandrian Greek novel. Cultural influence was hardly unidirectional, and two adaptations of Greek myth are clearly recognizable in Setna's "harrowing of hell," during which he views individuals punished with futile labors: plaiting ropes invariably gnawed by donkeys or attempting to reach food suspended overhead while the ground gives way beneath. The former torment is that of Oknos, the Greek personification of delay, and the latter a variant of that administered to Tantalus, a son of Zeus, who stole the food of the gods for mankind. In the Setna tale, however, the basic Greek imagery has been recast for Egyptian cultural values. These damned are not single mythic figures, but common people whose earthly misdeeds and misfortunes are reenacted in the underworld, maintaining the longstanding Egyptian view of the afterlife as a repetition of life (wḥm ꜥnḫ), contingent upon a weighing of the heart. The equation of the voracious donkeys with ill-fated men's wives who "rob them behind their backs" echoes contemporary Demotic wisdom literature, as in ꜥOnchsheshonqy, col. 12/13–14.*

*Traditional Egyptian motifs include incubation for pregnancy, as in the stela of Taimhotep (British Museum 147); the damned as a doorsocket, found in architecture and netherworld descriptions; and the visit to the netherworld itself, long a feature of funerary spells and central to Papyrus Vandier, a tale of the magician Meryre copied in the late sixth century B.C. Suggestions of an Orphic inspiration for this underworld visit may be safely disregarded. An Egyptian origin has also been noted for the "Dives and Lazarus" motif of the rich and poor man, later found in Luke 16: 19–31 and medieval sources. No less traditional is the overt hostility to Nubia, its food and magicians,[2] here set in the reigns of Thutmose III and Ramses II, both prominently memorialized in conquered Nubian territory.*

R.K.R.

1. See B. Porten and A. Yardeni, *Textbook of Aramaic Documents from Ancient Egypt,* vol. 3 (Jerusalem, 1993), 23 and 54–57. Dating to the fifth century B.C., the Aramaic translation of "Hor Bar Punesh" is the earliest Aramaic literary text known from Egypt.
2. See S. Sauneron, "L'avis des Egyptiens sur la cuisine soudanaise," *Kush* 7 (1959): 63–69; and R. K. Ritner, *The Mechanics of Ancient Egyptian Magical Practice,* SAOC 54 (Chicago, 1993), 140.

[Setna and his wife Meheweskhe desire a child so she sleeps in a temple and there sees ... a] dream, while they spoke with her, [saying: "Are] you Meheweskhe, [the wife] of Setna, who sleeps here [in the temple] to gain a remedy? [... When] tomorrow [morning] has come, go to the entrance [of the] cistern of Setna, your husband. There you will find a melon vine[3] growing. [...] to them. Break it with its gourds, and grind it. [Make it] into a remedy and put [it in water and drink it. ... You will conceive in a fluid of conception] from him on that very night.

Meheweskhe awoke [from] the dream, with these being the things that she had seen. She acted in accordance with [every]thing / [that she had been told in the dream. She lay down] beside [Setna] her husband. She conceived in a fluid of conception from him. Her [menstrual cycle] came, [and she showed] evidence [of a woman who has conceived. It was announced to Setna, and] his heart was very [happy] on account of it. [He] bound [on her an] amulet, and he recited for her a spell.

Setna slept one night [and dreamed that they] spoke with him, saying: "Meheweskhe, your wife, [has] received [conception in the night.] The child who will be born [should be named] Si-Osire. Many [are the wonders that he will do in the land of Egypt.] Setna [awoke] from the dream, with these being the things that he had seen, [and his heart was] very [happy.] Her months of pregnancy were apportioned, while she was in [... Her time of bearing came,] and she bore a male child. Setna was informed of it, [and he named him] Si-Osire in accordance with what had been said in the dream. [He was put] at the breast, / [... they] cradled [him] and nurtured him.

It happened that when the child [Si-Osire was one year old], people would say that he was two years old, and when he was two years old, people would say that he was three years old. [Setna did not spend an hour] failing to look at the child Si-Osire, so very great was the love [that he had for him.] He became big and strong. He was put in school, [and soon] he surpassed the scribe who had been assigned to give him instruction. It happened that the child [Si-Osire] began to recite writings with the scribes of the House of Life in [the temple of Ptah. All who heard were] earthshaken in wonder by him. Setna was desirous [to have them] bring him to

3. Suggested to be a persea tree in F. Hoffmann, "Einige Bemerkungen zur Zweiten Setnegeschichte," *Enchoria* 19/20 (1992/93): 11–12.

the festival before Pharaoh, and that [Pharaoh ask him many questions], and that he give him an answer to all of them.[4]

1/15    [Afterward, a day occurred when] Setna was purified for the festival in accordance with [the custom of] his home, / [...] and the child [Si-Osire was to go to the] festival with [him also.] At that very [moment], Setna heard the sound of a wailing [...] He looked [down from the window] of his home, [and he saw the coffin of a rich man] who was being carried out to the necropolis, while the wailing was [very great ...] and great were the honors [...] He looked [again]; he [looked toward his] feet, and he saw [the corpse of a poor man being carried out of Memphis] wrapped [in] a mat, while there was [silence(?)], with no [one] walking behind [him.]

Setna [said]: "By [Ptah, the great god, how much happier is the rich man who is honored with] the sound [of wailing] than the poor man whom they carry to the necropolis [...]."

1/20    / [Si-Osire said to his father: "May there be done to you in the West] like [that which] will be done to this poor man in the West. [There shall not be done to you what will be done to this rich man in the West. ...] the place(?) [...] you will [go(?)] in the West [...]"

[When he had heard the words of Si-Osire,] the heart of Setna was very [grieved on account of] it. [... He said: "Do I] hear the voice of [my son?"] The child [Si-Osire] said: ["If you wish I will show you the fate of the poor man who was not mourned and that of the rich man who was taken] to his

1/25    [tomb with] mourning. / [Setna] asked [him: "How can you do this?"[5] ...]

Afterward, [he did not] know [where on earth he was.[6] ... Si-Osire had] Setna go to a place [... , saying: "...] in [the West]. You will [see ...

1/30    Osiris and the council of(?)] his nobles [...] / [...] which is on the [necropolis(?) ...] life [...] like [...] his [...] there. [...] give [...]. They made [...]

[They went into the fourth hall. Setna saw some people who were plaiting ropes, while donkeys were gnawing on them ], and there were some

2/1    others whose[7] / provision of water and bread was suspended above them,

4. Restoration following Hoffmann, ibid., 12–13.
5. Restorations of ll. 24–25 conjectural, following Lichtheim and Bresciani (see bibliography).
6. Lit. "Afterwards, [he could not] find [any place on earth in which he was]." The conjectural restoration, indicating Setna's obsession and disorientation, follows Setna I, 3/20 and 5/1, and Setna II, 2/32 and 3/3–4 and 7–8.
7. Column 2 begins with dittography, repeating: "and there were some others whose."

and as they raced to bring them down, some others dug pits under their feet to prevent them from reaching it.

They went into the fifth hall. Setna saw the noble spirits standing in their ranks. Those who had accusations of violence were standing at the door pleading, and the pivot of the door of the fifth hall was fixed in the right eye of a man who was pleading and crying out loudly.[8]

They went inside the sixth hall. Setna saw the gods of the [council] of the inhabitants of the West standing in their ranks, while the servants of the West stood giving reports.

They went inside the seventh hall. Setna saw the secret form of Osiris, the great god, / seated upon his throne of fine gold and crowned with the *atef*-crown, with Anubis, the great god, on his left, the great god Thoth on his right and the gods of the council of the inhabitants of the West standing to the left and right of him, the balance being set up in the center before them while they measured the faults against the good deeds and Thoth, the great god, wrote while Anubis gave information to his colleague. And the one who will be found with his faults more numerous than his good deeds will be given to the Devourer belonging to the Lord of the West, while his *ba*-spirit and corpse are destroyed, nor does she let him breathe ever again. But the one whom they will find that his good deeds are more numerous than his faults, they will bring him in among the gods of the council of the Lord of the West, while his *ba*-spirit goes to heaven with the noble spirits. And the one whom they will find that his good deeds are equal to his faults, they will bring him in among the excellent spirits who serve Sokar-Osiris.

Setna saw a rich man who was wrapped[9] in a garment of royal linen and who was near the place where Osiris was, being of very high rank. Setna was earthshaken in wonder by what he had seen in the West. Si-Osire walked out before him. He said to him: "My father Setna, don't you see / this rich man who is wrapped in a garment of royal linen and who is near the place where Osiris is? He is that poor man whom you saw as they were bringing him out from Memphis with no one walking behind him and who was wrapped in a mat. They brought him to the underworld. They mea-

2/5

2/10

8. For the image and its Egyptian antecedents, see Ritner, *The Mechanics of Ancient Egyptian Magical Practice*, 117–19.

9. The text entails a play on words between the "mat" (*tm*) in which the poor man was once placed and his current "wrapping" (*tm*) in royal linen.

sured his faults against his good deeds that he had done on earth. They found his good deeds more numerous than his faults in proportion to his span of life that Thoth wrote for him to be given to him and in proportion to his luck on earth. It was commanded before Osiris to transfer the burial equipment of that wealthy man whom you saw as they were bringing him out from Memphis and for whom the honors made were great, to that same poor man, and that he be brought in among the noble spirits as a man of god who serves Sokar-Osiris and who is near to the place where Osiris is. That wealthy man whom you saw, they brought him to the underworld. They measured [his] faults against his good deeds. They found that his faults were more numerous than his good deeds that he had done on earth. It was commanded to punish him in the West. He is [the man whom you] saw with the pivot of the door of the West fixed in his right eye, so that they shut and open out (the doors) on his eye while his mouth is open in a loud cry. By Osiris, the great god, Lord of the West, I said to you on earth: ['May there be done] / to you according to what will be done to this poor man. There shall not be done to you according to what will be done [to] this rich man,' since I knew the outcome that had happened to him."

2/15

Setna said: "My son Si-Osire, many are the wonders that I have seen in the West. However, let me discover [what is happening] to these people who are plaiting ropes while the donkeys gnaw at them, with some others whose provision of water and bread is suspended above them, and as they race to bring them down, some others dig pits under their feet to prevent them from reaching them."

Si-Osire said: "It is true, my father Setne. These people whom you saw who are plaiting ropes while the donkeys gnaw them, they are the counter-part of the people who are on earth and who are under the curse of god, working by night and day for their livelihood, while their women rob them behind their backs, and they find no bread to eat. They have come to the West also. Their faults were found to be more numerous than their good deeds. They found [that what] had happened to them on earth happens to them there in the West; and similarly those other people whom you saw, whose provision of water and bread is suspended above them, and as they race to bring them down, some / others dig pits under their feet to prevent them from reaching them: the counterpart of the people who are on earth and whose life is before them, but god digs a pit beneath their feet to prevent them from discovering it. They have come to the West [also]. It

2/20

has been set down that what had happened to them on earth happens to them [in the West] also when their *ba*-spirits have been received into the underworld.

Take it to heart, my father Setna, that the one who is beneficent on earth, they are beneficent to him in the West, while the one who is evil, they are evil to him. This is established [and will not be changed] ever. The things that you have seen in the underworld of Memphis, they occur in these forty-two nomes in which [reside the judges] of Osiris, the great god. See, then, [...] Abydos, the place of promenade, the houses of the hereditary princes [in(?)] Philae."

(Si)-Osire finished these words spoken before Setna, [his father, and] he proceeded up onto the necropolis of Memphis, [with his father Setna] embracing him, his hand in his hand. Setna asked [him]: "My son, Si-Osire, is the place by which we went down different / [from] the place by which we came up?" Si-[Osire] did not answer Setna in any manner whatsoever. Setna marveled at the situation he was in, thinking: "He will be able to be a noble spirit, a man of god, [while I] go with him, saying: 'He is my son!'" Setna recited [a protective spell from] the "Scroll of Exorcising Spirits," while yet earthshaken in wonder from what he had seen in the West, and what he had seen weighed [upon] him heavily, since he was unable to reveal [them to any] man [on earth.] The child Si-Osire [attained] twelve years of age, and it happened that there was no [good scribe or wise man who could] surpass him in Memphis in the recitation of protective spells.[10]

[Afterwards,] a day occurred when Pharaoh User [maatre[11] went] to the court of the palace in Memphis, [while the council] of the nobles, of the generals and of the great men of Egypt were standing [in their] ranks in the court. Then came [a messenger, saying:] "There is a report that a shaman[12]

2/25

10. Lit. "writings which take protection," cf. Setna I, 4/31–32.
11. The throne name of Ramses II, preserved in Greek as Ozymandias.
12. Determined as a foreign word, the term *ꜣte* has often been considered a variant of the Egyptian *ity* "sovereign" (Wolja Erichsen, *Demotisches Glossar* [Copenhagen, 1954], p. 46), but as early as 1918 Griffith and Gardiner linked the term with the Nubian rebel "Aata" noted in the campaigns of Ahmose (*Wb.* I, 2/7 = Urk. IV, 5). For more recent discussion, see C. Vandersleyen, *Les guerres d'Amois* (Brussels, 1971), 76–77; M. Smith, *The Mortuary Texts of Papyrus BM 10507* (London, 1987), 61, n.d., and cf. the possible Meroitic title *ate-qere* "royal ate" in B. Trigger, *Meroitic*

2/30 of Cush has made, [who is sealed] on his body with a letter." He was reported / [before] Pharaoh. He was brought to the court. He gave salutation [and said: "Is there anyone who] will read this letter that I have brought to Egypt before Pharaoh without removing its seal, and who will read the writings that are on it without opening it?[13] If it happens that [there is no good scribe or wise man] in Egypt who will be able to read it without opening it, I shall take the humiliation of Egypt to the land of Nubia, my country."

At the moment when Pharaoh [and the nobles] heard these words, [they did not know where on] earth they were, so that they said: "By Ptah, [the great god,] is it in the power of a good scribe or a wise man to read writings [at whose] edge he has looked, or yet to read a letter [without opening it?] Pharaoh [said]: "Let them summon to me Setna [Khaemu]as, my son!" They ran; they brought him back at that moment. He bowed

3/1 himself[14] / to the ground, he adored [Pharaoh,] he [raised] himself, and he stood on his feet performing the salutations of the adoration of Pharaoh.

Pharaoh said to him: "My [son] Setna, have you heard the words that this shaman [of Cush] has said before me, saying: 'Is there a good scribe or wise man in Egypt who will be able to read this letter which [I possess] without removing its seal and who will discover what is written on it without opening it?' "

At the moment when Setna heard the words, he did not know where [on earth] he was, so that he said: "My good lord, who will be able to read a document without opening it? However, let me be given ten days further,

3/5 so that I might see what I can / do [to] prevent the humiliation of Egypt from being taken to the land of Nubia, the country of gum eaters." Pharaoh said: "They are given to my son Setna."

---

*Funerary Inscriptions from Arminna West* (New Haven, 1970), 13 and 46 (Text 3a, l. 15). A further Demotic example appears in an unpublished Copenhagen tale; see A. Volten, *Archiv Orientální* 19 (1951): 72. As the role of these individuals regularly concerns Nubian magic, the title is here translated "shaman."

13. Egyptian spells for this purpose are noted in R. K. Ritner, "Egyptian Magical Practice under the Roman Empire: The Demotic Spells and Their Religious Context," in Wolfgang Haase, ed., *Aufstieg und Niedergang der römischen Welt* II.18.5 (Berlin, 1995), 3344–45.

14. The third column begins with dittography, repeating: "they brought him back at that moment. He bowed himself."

Rooms for relaxation were given to the Cushite. They made for him swill[15] in the Cushite manner. Pharaoh arose in the court, with his heart very grieved. He lay down without drinking or eating. Setna went off to his home without knowing where on earth he was going. He bundled himself in his clothing from his head to his feet. He lay down without knowing where on earth he was.

Meheweskhe his wife was informed of it, and she came to the place where Setna was. She extended her hand inside his clothing. She found no warmth. He lay listless in his clothing. She said to him: "My brother, Setna, there is no warmth in the breast. A change for the worse is in the flesh. Illness and grief are in the heart."

3/10 / He said to her: "Leave me alone, my sister Meheweskhe. The matter about which my heart grieves, it is not a matter fit to reveal to a woman." The child Si-Osire came inside. He stood above Setna his father. He said to him: "My father, why are you lying down with your heart grieving? The matters that are enclosed in your heart, tell them to me so that I might heal them.[16] He said: "Leave me alone, my son Si-Osire. As for the matters that are in my heart, you are too young and have not yet gained mastery over yourself."[17] Si-Osire said: "Tell them to me so that I might comfort your heart regarding them."

Setna said: "My son Si-Osire, there is a shaman of Cush who has come up to Egypt sealed on his body with a letter, saying: 'Is there anyone who will [be able] to read it without opening it? If it happens that there is
3/15 no good scribe or wise man in Egypt / who will be able to read it, I shall take the humiliation of Egypt to the land of Nubia, my country.' It is because my heart is grieved on account of it that I am lying down, my son Si-Osire."

At the moment that Si-Osire heard these words, he laughed for a long time. Setna said to him: "Why are you laughing?" He said: "I am laughing because it is on account of this trivial matter that you are lying down with your heart grieved. Raise yourself, my father Setna! I shall be able to read the letter that was brought to Egypt without opening it, and I shall discover what is written on it without removing its seal."

At the moment that Setna heard these words, he raised himself at once, saying: "What is the proof of the words that you have said, my son Si-

15. Lit. something "sinful/injurious."
16. Lit. "cause that they cease." For the medical nuance, cf. Coptic ⲧⲁⲗϭⲟ (CD 411b).
17. The previously misunderstood passage reads: *iw b-ir.t=k mḥ r-ḥr=k.*

3/20 Osire?" He said to him: "My father Setna, go to the ground-floor rooms of your home. Every scroll that you will lift up / from inside the chest, I shall say to you what sort of scroll it is. I shall read it without looking at it while I stay above you in your ground-floor rooms."

Setna raised himself. He stood on his feet. Everything that Si-Osire had said to him, he acted completely in accordance with it. Si-Osire read every scroll that Setna his father lifted up opposite him without opening them. Setna came up from within the ground-floor rooms of his home, being in utmost joy. He did not delay in going to the place where Pharaoh was. He related before him all the words that the child Si-Osire had said to him. His heart was very happy on account of it. Pharaoh purified himself for a festival at the same time together with Setna. He had Si-Osire brought to the festival before him. They drank and celebrated.

3/25 The morning for the next day occurred, / and Pharaoh appeared at the court among his great men. Pharaoh sent for the shaman of Cush. He was brought to the court sealed on his body with the letter. He stood in the center of the court. The child Si-Osire came to the center. He stood before the shaman of Cush. He spoke opposite him, saying: "Woe, O villain of Cush, at whom Amon, his god, rages! You who have come up to Egypt, the beautiful garden of Osiris, the footstool of Re-Horachty, the beautiful horizon of Fate, saying: 'I shall take [its] humiliation to the land of Nubia.' The possessive wrath of Amon, your god, is cast upon you! The words that I shall utter, which are those that are written in the letter, do not tell a lie about them before Pharaoh, your lord!"

3/30 At the moment when the shaman / of Cush saw the child Si-Osire standing in the court, he lowered his head. He spoke, saying: "Everything that you will say, I shall not tell a lie about them."

The beginning of the narration that Si-Osire told, narrating before Pharaoh and his nobles, while the throngs of Egypt listened to his voice as he said: "Such are the things that are written in the letter of the shaman of Cush who is standing in our midst, stating: A time occurred in the reign of
4/1 Pharaoh Menkheperre Si-Amon, who was[18] / an excellent king of the entire land, with Egypt overflowing with all good things in his reign, since he was generous in granting expenditures and work in the great temples of Egypt.

18. The fourth column begins with dittography, repeating: "Menkheperre Si-Amon, who was." The royal name is a phonetic rendering of the throne name of Thutmose III of Dynasty 18.

A day occurred when the chieftain[19] of the land of Nubia was resting(?) in the forests of the domain of Amon.

He heard the voices of three shamans of Cush [in the] latrine,[20] while one of them spoke with a loud voice saying: 'But that Amon not find fault with me and the chieftain of Egypt have [me punished], I would cast my magic up against Egypt / and I would cause the masses of Egypt to spend three days and three nights, [having] seen [no] light but only darkness.'

The other among them said: 'But that Amon not find fault with me and the chieftain of Egypt have me punished, I would cast my magic up against Egypt, and I would have Pharaoh brought from Egypt to the land of Nubia, and I would have him beaten with 500 blows of the whip in public[21] before the chieftain, and I would cause that they return him back [up] to Egypt before six hours have elapsed.'[22]

{The third said: 'But that Amon not find fault with me and the chieftain of Egypt have me punished, I would cast my magic up within Egypt, and I would not allow the fields to be productive for three years.'}[23]

At the moment when the chieftain heard the words voiced by the three shamans of Cush, he had them brought before him. He said to them: 'Who is it among you who said: I shall cast / my magic up against Egypt. I shall not let [them] see the light for three days and three nights.' They said: 'It is Horus-son-of-the-Sow.'

He said: 'Who is it who said: I shall cast my magic up against Egypt. I shall bring Pharaoh to the land of Nubia. I shall have him beaten with 500 blows of the whip in public before the chieftain. I shall cause that they return him back up to Egypt before six hours have elapsed.' {They} said: 'It is Horus-the-son-of-the-Nubian-woman.'

He said: 'Who is it who said: I shall cast my magic up within Egypt. I shall not allow the fields to be productive for three years.' They said: 'It is Horus-the-son-of-[the]-Princess.'

The chieftain said (to Horus-the-son-of-the-Nubian-woman): 'Do it,

19. Written *kwr*, for the Meroitic title qere "king," here translated "chieftain" from the ethnocentric Egyptian perspective.
20. Lit. "the place of the buttocks."
21. Lit. "in the center."
22. The previously misunderstood text reads: *ẖn wnw.t 6 ỉw b-ỉr.t=w mnq* "in six hours when they have not yet finished."
23. Deleted in error by the scribe and restored on the basis of lines 13–14.

4/15    your spell[24] of magical / writing! By Amon the bull of Meroe, my god, if your hand provides satisfaction, I shall provide for you many good things.'

Horus-the-son-of-the-Nubian-woman made a litter of wax with four footmen. He recited a spell to them; he gave them the breath of hardiness; he caused them to live. He commanded them, saying: 'You shall go up to Egypt, and you shall bring Pharaoh from Egypt up to the place where the chieftain is. He shall be beaten with 500 blows of the whip in public before the chieftain. You shall return him back up to Egypt in six hours. They said: 'Fine, we shall not overlook anything.'

The sorceries of the Cushite flew up to Egypt. They became masters of

4/20    the night; they became masters of Pharaoh / Menkheperre Si-Amon. They took him to the land of Nubia to the place where the chieftain was. They beat him with 500 blows of the whip in public before the chieftain. They returned him back up to Egypt before six hours had elapsed."

As for these narratives, it was Si-Osire who was narrating them in public in the presence of Pharaoh and his nobles while the throngs of Egypt listened to his voice as he said: "The possessive wrath of Amon, your god, is cast upon you! The words that I am [saying], are they what is written according to the letter that you possess?" The shaman of the Cushites said: "Read on beyond what you have read. As for every word that you are saying, they are all true."

Si-Osire said in the presence of Pharaoh: "When these things had

4/25    happened, they returned Pharaoh / Si-Amon back up to Egypt with his buttocks badly beaten with severe blows. He lay down in the resting place of the palace of Horus with his buttocks badly beaten. The morning for the next day occurred, and Pharaoh said to the councilors: 'What is it that has taken control[25] of Egypt up to the point that I am removed from it?' Shameful were the things in the hearts of the councilors as they thought: 'Perhaps Pharaoh's mind has gone.' They said: 'You are well; you are well, O Pharaoh, our great lord! Isis the great goddess will put an end to your afflictions! What is the meaning of the words that you have just said before us, O Pharaoh, our great lord? It is in the resting place of the [palace of] Horus that you sleep; the gods guard you.'

24. For this term, "deed of written magic," see Ritner, *The Mechanics of Ancient Egyptian Magical Practice*, 68–69.
25. The verb *gm* in the sense of "control"; cf. Coptic ϭⲟⲙ "strength/power" (*CD* 815b).

4/30      Pharaoh raised himself. / He had the councilors look at his back that was badly beaten with severe [blows], and he said: 'By Ptah, the great

5/1    god,²⁶ / I was taken to the land of Nubia this night, and I was beaten with 500 blows of the whip in public before the chieftain, and {I} was returned to Egypt before six hours had elapsed.' At the moment of looking at Pharaoh's buttocks badly beaten with severe blows, they opened their mouths in a loud cry.

Menkheperre Si-Amon had a magician²⁷ named Horus-the-son-of-the-Wolf.²⁸ He was a very wise man. He came to the place where he was; he cried out loudly, saying: 'My [great lord], they are sorceries of the Cushites! By your rear end,²⁹ I shall make them end up at your [...] and slaughter.' [Pharaoh] said [to him]: 'Hurry to me! Do not let me be taken to the

5/5    land of Nubia / on yet another night!'

The magician [Horus-the-son-of]-the-Wolf returned immediately. He took his scrolls and his amulets [to the place where Pharaoh] was. He recited for him a spell. He bound on him an amulet to prevent the sorceries of the Cushites from gaining control over him. He [came] out from before Pharaoh. He took his burnt offerings and libations. He went on board a boat. He did not delay in going to Hermopolis. He went off into the temple of Hermopolis. He [performed his] burnt offerings and libations before Thoth the [eight times] great,³⁰ the lord of Hermopolis, the great god. He prayed before him, saying: 'Give your attention to me, my lord Thoth! Do

26. The fifth column begins with dittography, repeating: "and he said: 'By Ptah, the great god.'"

27. Lit. "Chief (lector priest)"; for the equation of this title with "magician," see Ritner, *The Mechanics of Ancient Egyptian Magical Practice,* 220–22.

28. Written as Horus-son-of-Paneshy, the name might be interpreted as "Horus, son of the Expeller (*nš Wb.* II, 337/12–14)," an appropriate designation for the exorcist hero. However, the pun in 6/13 shows that the writing *Pȝ-nšy* is a contraction for *Pȝ-wnšy* "The Wolf," a suspicion confirmed by Demotic and Aramaic versions of further adventures of this Egyptian magician, see Ritner, *The Mechanics of Ancient Egyptian Magical Practice,* 70–71, n. 320.

29. The damaged signs suggest *pḥ.w(y)* "rear" (Erichsen, *Demotisches Glossar,* 138), forming a pun on the hero's threat to have the villains reach/end up at (*pḥ*) royal punishment. Oaths to kings are sworn on royal body parts, cf. 6/34.

30. For such epithets of Thoth, see R. K. Ritner, "Hermes Pentamegistos," *GM* 49 (1981): 73–75, and idem, "Additional Notes to Hermes Pentamegistos," *GM* 50 (1981): 67–68.

not let the Cushites take the humiliation of Egypt to the land of Nubia! You are the one who [created] magical writings. You are the one who suspended the heaven as he established the earth and the underworld, placing the gods and the [spirits]. Let me learn the way to save Pharaoh [from the sorceries of the] Cushites!'

5/10     Horus-the-son-of-the-Wolf lay down / in the temple. That same night he beheld himself in a dream, while the secret form of the great god Thoth spoke with him, saying: 'Are you Horus-the-son-of-the-Wolf, the magician of Pharaoh Menkheperre Si-Amon? When the morning for the next day occurs, you should go into the library of the temple of Hermopolis. You will discover a locked and sealed chamber. Open it. You will discover a chest in the same chamber with a papyrus book in it, the one that I wrote with my own hand. Pick it up, take a copy of it, and set it down in its place again. Its name is the Book of Magic. It has protected me from the enemies, and it is what will protect Pharaoh and save him from the sorceries of the Cushites.'

Horus-the-son-of-the-Wolf awoke from the dream, with these being 5/15 the things that he had seen. / He discovered the fact that they were divine revelations. He acted in accordance with everything that was told to him by dream. He did not delay in going to the place in which Pharaoh was. He made amuletic protection[31] for him against the sorceries by the writings.

The second day occurred, and the sorceries of Horus-the-son-of-the-Nubian-woman returned back up to Egypt at night to the place where Pharaoh was. They returned to the place where the chieftain was at the very same moment, since they were unable to gain control over Pharaoh because of the amulets and the magical spells that the magician Horus-the-son-of-the-Wolf had bound to him.

The morning for the next day occurred, and Pharaoh related before the magician Horus-the-son-of-the-Wolf everything that he had seen at night and the manner in which the sorceries of the Cushites were turned away, since they were unable to gain control over him. Horus-the-son-of-the-Wolf had a great amount of pure wax brought to him. He made a litter 5/20 with four footmen. He recited / a spell to them; he gave them the breath of hardiness; he caused them to live. He commanded them, saying: 'You shall go to the land of Nubia tonight, and you shall bring the chieftain up to

31. This term for protection also signified "amulets," and phylacteries are here intended; see Ritner, *The Mechanics of Ancient Egyptian Magical Practice,* 49–51 and 216.

Egypt to the place where Pharaoh is. He shall be beaten with 500 blows of the whip in public in the presence of[32] Pharaoh. You shall return him to the land of Nubia again before six hours have elapsed. They said: 'Fine, we shall not overlook anything.'

The sorceries of Horus-the-son-of-the-Wolf flew below the clouds of the sky. They did not delay in going to the land of Nubia by night. They became masters of the chieftain. They brought him up to Egypt. They beat him with 500 blows of the whip in public in the presence of Pharaoh. They returned him to the land of Nubia before six hours had elapsed."

5/25   As for these narratives, it was Si-Osire who was narrating them in public in the presence of Pharaoh / and his nobles while the throngs of Egypt listened to his voice as he said: "The possessive wrath of Amon, your god, is cast upon you, O villain of the Cushites! The words that I am saying, are they what is written in this letter?" The shaman spoke with his head lowered, saying: "Read on beyond what you have read. As for every word that you are saying, they are what is written in this letter."

Si-Osire said: "When these things had happened, after they returned the chieftain to the land of Nubia before six hours had elapsed, they left him in his place. He slept; he rose in the morning badly beaten with the blows that he had been given up in Egypt. {He said to his nobles: 'I was taken up to the land of Egypt}, and I was beaten with 500 blows of the whip in public in the presence of Pharaoh of Egypt, and {I} was returned to the land of Nubia again.' He turned his back to the nobles; they opened their mouths in a loud cry.

5/30   The chieftain sent them after Horus-the-son-of-the-Nubian-woman. He said: 'May Amon / the bull of Meroe, my god, curse you! It is you who went against the people of Egypt. Set me at rest to see the method that you will use to save me from the hand of Horus-the-son-of-the-Wolf.' He made his sorceries. He bound them to the chieftain in order to protect him from the sorceries of Horus-the-son-of-the-Wolf.

The night of the second day occurred, and the sorceries of Horus-the-son-of-the Wolf flew to the land of Nubia. They brought the chieftain up to Egypt. They beat him with 500 blows of the whip in public in the presence

32. The scribe has corrected the simple preposition "before," used in parallel passages for the Nubian chieftain (4/18 and 21), to the preposition "in the presence of" reserved for Egyptian royalty and gods.

of Pharaoh. They returned him to the land of Nubia before six hours had elapsed. This pattern happened to the chieftain for three days, for the sorceries of the Cushites were unable to save the chieftain from the hand of Horus-the-son-of-the-Wolf.

The chieftain was sorely troubled. He had Horus-the-son-of-the-Nubian-woman brought before him. He said to him: 'Woe, O villain of 5/35 the Cushites! You have caused that I suffer at the hands of / the people of Egypt! You have not been able to save me from their hand! By Amon the bull [of] Meroe, my god, if it happens that you won't be able to cause me [to be safe] from the assaults[33] of the people of Egypt, I shall have you put to a miserable and prolonged death.'

He said: 'O my lord the chieftain, have me sent up to Egypt, so that I might see the one who performs magic among them, that I might be victorious against him, and that I might cause him to discover the scorn that opposes[34] his hand.'

Horus-the-son-of-the-Nubian-woman was sent away from before the chieftain. He came to the place where the Nubian woman, his mother, was. 6/1 / {He told her what had happened to him, and she said to him: 'Do not go to the place where Horus-the-son-of-the-Wolf} is! If you go up to Egypt to perform magic in it, guard yourself against the people of Egypt. You will not be able to contend with them. Do not suffer at their hands and so not return to the land of Nubia ever!'

He said: 'There is nothing to them, the words that you say. I shall not be able to avoid going up to Egypt and casting my magic up within it.' The Nubian woman, his mother, said to him: 'When it has happened that you have gone up to Egypt, leave some signs between me and you, so that if it happens that you are suffering, I shall come to you and see if I can save you.' He said to her: 'If it happens that I am suffering, may it happen regarding drinking [or eating], that the meat and water will become the color of blood before you, the food before you will become the color of 6/5 meat, / and the sky will become the color of blood before you.'

Horus-the-son-of-the-Nubian-woman made signs between [himself]

33. Formerly misunderstood as "aerial cars" (Griffith) or "sky-boats" (Lichtheim), the term signifies "semen" or "injury" (Erichsen, *Demotisches Glossar,* pp. 103 and 106 "Verderben") comparable to earlier Egyptian *mtw.t* "semen/poison."

34. The previously unread word is *mtr* "to be opposite" (Erichsen, *Demotisches Glossar,* 191).

and his mother; he flew up to Egypt engorged[35] with magic. He inspected from what Amon had made[36] up to Memphis to the place where Pharaoh was, sniffing after [the] one who made magical spells in Egypt. He came to the court in the presence of Pharaoh. He spoke with a loud voice, saying: 'Woe, O he who performs magic against me in the court, in the place where Pharaoh is, with the throngs of Egypt looking at him, whether it be two scribes of the House of Life or one scribe of the House of Life who performs magic against the chieftain, bringing him up to Egypt in spite of me!'

And as he said these very words, Horus-the-son-of-the-Wolf was standing in the court in the presence of Pharaoh, saying: 'Woe, O villain of Cush! Are you not Horus-the-son-of-the-Nubian-woman, whom I saved in the

6/10 gardens of Pre when your companion / from Cush was with you, and you were both fallen into the water, cast down from the mountain on the east of Heliopolis? Didn't you give thought to the freedom of Pharaoh, your lord, when you had his buttocks beaten in the place where the chieftain was, and when you came up to Egypt, saying: Is there someone performing magic against me? By Atum, the lord of Heliopolis, the gods of Egypt have brought you back to repay you in their country! You are met! I am coming to you!'

At the moment when Horus-the-son-of-the-Wolf said these words, Horus-the-son-of-the-Nubian-woman answered him, saying: 'Is it the one whom I had instructed in the language of wolves[37] who now performs magic against me?' The shaman of Cush made a spell of magical writing. He caused fire to break out in the court. Pharaoh and the nobles of Egypt cried out loudly, saying: 'Hurry to us, O magician Horus-the-son-of-the-Wolf!'

6/15 Horus-the-son-of-the-Wolf made / a magical formula.[38] He caused the sky to make an Upper Egyptian rainstorm[39] above the fire, so that it was extinguished immediately.

35. The term "swallow" also signifies "to know" and is used for puns in magical contexts where, as here, food serves as a magical signal; see Ritner, *The Mechanics of Ancient Egyptian Magical Practice,* 105–6.

36. A designation of Nubia.

37. Like the events of ll. 9–10 regarding the gardens of Pre, this seems a reference to a lost episode of the cycle, though here the Nubian shaman puns upon his opponent's name Paneshy as Pa-(we)neshy "The Wolf."

38. For this term "a pattern of writing," see Ritner, *The Mechanics of Ancient Egyptian Magical Practice,* 70–71.

39. The term refers to the infrequent but sudden and drenching downpours found in Upper Egypt.

The Cushite made another spell of magical writing.[40] He created a great mist over the court, while no one among them was able to see his brother or his colleague. Horus-the-son-of-the-Wolf recited a spell to the sky. He caused it to stop being foul from the vile wind in which it had been. Horus-the-son-of-the-Nubian-woman made another spell of magical writing. He created a great vault of stone, amounting to 200 cubits in height by 50 cubits in width above Pharaoh and his nobles, so that it was about to make Egypt devoid of a king and the land lacking a lord. Pharaoh looked at the sky, he saw the stone vault above him, and he opened his mouth in 6/20 a loud cry together with the throng who were in the court. / Horus-the-son-of-the-Wolf recited a magical formula. He created a papyrus bark. He caused that it carry away the vault of stone. It halted with it beside the Great Lake,[41] the large water of Egypt.

The shaman of Cush realized that he would not be able to contend with [the Egyptian]. He made a spell of magical writing to prevent his seeing him in the court, as well as the way that he would have himself go to the land of Nubia and his city. Horus-the-son-of-the-Wolf recited a spell to him. He caused that the sorceries of the Cushite be revealed. He caused Pharaoh and the throngs of Egypt who were standing in the court to see him in the form of an evil bird[42] that was about to get away. Horus-the-son-of-the-Wolf recited a spell to him. He caused {him} to turn over on his back, while a fowler stood above him with his sharp knife in his hand, about to punish him.

When all these things happened, the signs that Horus-the-son-of-the- 6/25 Nubian-woman had left / between himself and his mother happened before her in their entirety, so that she did not delay in going up to Egypt in the shape of a goose. She stood above the palace crying out in her voice to her son as he was in the form of an evil bird with the fowler standing above him. Horus-the-son-of-the-Wolf looked at the sky; he saw the Nubian woman in the form in which she was. He recognized that she was the Nubian woman, the Cushite. He recited a spell to her. He caused her to be turned over on her back, while a fowler stood above her with his sword about to kill her. She ceased being in the shape in which she was. She made her form into a

40. The sentence is repeated by dittography at the beginning of l. 16.
41. Presumably a reference to the Faiyum, known as the "Great Water."
42. For this form adopted by the Nubian and his mother, see Ritner, *The Mechanics of Ancient Egyptian Magical Practice,* 160–61; and Hoffmann, *Enchoria* 19/20 (1992/93): 13–14.

Nubian woman as she pleaded, saying: 'Do not destroy us, O Horus-the-son-of-the-Wolf! Forgive us this misdeed! If it happens that you might give us a bark, we shall not return to Egypt ever again!'

6/30 Horus-the-son-of-the-Wolf made an oath of Pharaoh and of the gods / of Egypt, saying: 'I shall not withdraw myself with respect to the spell of magical writing[43] until you have made for me an oath not to return back up to Egypt on another occasion.' The Nubian woman raised her hand, so as not to come up to Egypt forever and ever. Horus-the-son-of-the-Nubian-woman made an oath, saying: 'I shall not come up to Egypt for 1500 years!' Horus-the-son-of-the-Wolf withdrew his hand from his spell of magical writing. He gave a bark to Horus-the-son-of-the-Nubian-woman and the Nubian woman his mother. They flew off to the land of Nubia and their city."

As for these narratives, it was Si-Osire who was making them in the presence of Pharaoh, while the throngs of Egypt listened to his voice, Setna his father saw everything, and the head of the shaman of Cush was lowered, as he said: "By your face, my great lord, this one who is before you, he is Horus-the-son-of-the-Nubian-woman, this one whose story I am narrating, and who has not given thought to what he has done previously! He has
6/35 come up to / Egypt at the end of 1500 years in order to cast magic into it. By Osiris, the great god and lord of the West owing to whom I rest, I myself am Horus-the-son-of-the-Wolf who stands in the presence of Pharaoh! What I did in the West was to discover that the villain of Cush was going to cast his magic into it, when there was no good scribe or wise man in Egypt at
7/1 the time who would be able to contend / with him. I made a request in the presence of Osiris in the West to let me go out to the earth once more to prevent his taking the humiliation of Egypt to the land of Nubia. It was commanded before Osiris to send me to the earth. I awoke. I settled in a skull[44] [to] find Setna, the son of Pharaoh, on the necropolis of Heliopolis

43. Reading the inserted correction above the line as *ḏ bn-ỉw=ỉ r tỉ wy.t=ỉ* followed by *n-rn pỉ sp n ḥyq sš.*
44. Written *wỉḥ=ỉ r swḥ.t-ḏỉḏỉ*, cf. *CD* 505b (a soul leaves the body and settles on the hand of an archangel), and 374a ("egg of the head"). It would seem that in the lost beginning, the magician's spirit temporarily occupied a skull in two cemeteries. Previous interpretations have combined an unetimological spelling with an unattested idiom to produce: "I flew up to find Setna."

and on the necropolis of Memphis, with the result I grew as that melon vine, which was the way to return to the body again so that I might be born on earth to perform magic against this villain of Cush who stands in the court."

Horus-the-son-of-the-Wolf made a spell of magical writing, while yet in the shape of Si-Osire, against the shaman of Cush. He caused fire to 7/5 surround him. It consumed him in the midst of the court / as Pharaoh watched him, together with the nobles and the throngs of Egypt. Si-Osire passed away as a shadow from the presence of Pharaoh and Setna, his father, without their having seen him. Pharaoh was earthshaken in wonder together with his great men at the things that they had seen in the court, as they said: "There is no good scribe or wise man like Horus-the-son-of-the-Wolf! No other will come into existence after him ever again!"[45] Setna opened his mouth in a loud cry when Si-Osire passed away as a shadow without his having seen him.

Pharaoh arose in the court, fainthearted at the things that he had seen. Pharaoh commanded to have preparation made before Setna in order to receive him because of Si-Osire, his son, so as to comfort his heart. Evening came. Setna went to his home with his heart very grieved. Meheweskhe 7/10 lay down at his side. / She conceived in a fluid of conception from him that same night, nor did she delay in giving birth to a male child. His given name was Usermaatre.[46] It happened that Setna never failed to make burnt offerings and libations before the spirit of Horus-the-son-of-the-Wolf at all times.

It is the conclusion of the scroll. WRITTEN.

45. Written *bn-iw-n* *g* [*r*] *ḫpr m-s*=*f* '*n sp-2*. For the form of the negative future, cf. J. Johnson, *The Demotic Verbal System,* SAOC 38 (Chicago, 1976), 174. The description recalls that of Naneferkaptah in Setna I, 4/20–21: "the good scribe, the wise man, like whom no other has existed."

46. Previously misread, the name is written phonetically as *Wsy-mn-R*ʿ, corresponding to the Greek rendering Zmanres; cf. E. Lüddeckens et al., *Demotisches Namenbuch,* I/2 (Wiesbaden, 1981), 128 (no. 23).

# THE CHILDHOOD OF SI-OSIRE
## (JUG STRASSBURG)

A variant of the fragmentary beginning of Setna II was copied as a Demotic writing exercise on a jug preserved in Strassburg—a counterpart to the Berlin jug inscribed with the tales of Hihor and the Swallow and the Sea. Inserted within a model petition, the brief and damaged narrative recorded the birth and early school misadventures of Setna's remarkable son. While fairly negligible in its surviving content, the text does attest to the continuing popularity of the Setna cycle in the Roman era (first to second century A.D.) and the dissemination of such literature in the form of school exercises.

R.K.R.

The petition of Nesmetu, [...] before his superior as a greeting: "O may Pre lengthen his lifetime! Bear witness [... the story(?)] of my father and a [...] today: He did that which these superiors said, which is with[in] this writing that Khonsu [wrote(?) ...]. My mother went while she was [...] very young. My father found a wife [...] She was a [priestess] of the goddess. She was very beautiful. Her name was Meheweskhe. Her menstrual cycle came, [and she did not menstruate,[1] and her heart was very happy that she

---

1. Lit. "Her time of making natron happened [and she did not make natron again.]," restored from Setna I, col. 3/7–8.

5  would] / give birth. [There came her time of] giving birth, and she bore a male child[2] who was of pure form, in the manner of a great noble. [... He was named Si-Osire.] He was nurtured, he was cradled, and he became strong. He attained school age and he was given over to instruction to-gether with [... Mehe]weskhe there. He found that he was very good. She made her way to his schoolteacher, saying: 'Is my son foolish?' [...] he whom you will seize after the beating of my limbs by the blows of a whip, while I was writing. I have not forgiven an absence for you. We(?) have not [... Mehewe]skhe(?)." WRITTEN

2. For this and the following passages, cf. Setna II, col. 1/9–11.

# THE MAGICIAN HIHOR
## (JUG BERLIN 12845)

C opied as a writing exercise and framed as a model letter, the story of
Hihor preserves but a single episode from an adventure tale otherwise
lost. Nonetheless, the brief Demotic narrative illustrates the continuing popularity within Egyptian fiction of stories recounting the exploits of
magicians. Indicative of the late dominance of the genre are both the Setna cycle
and the many comparable tales that yet await publication in the Demotic collection of the University of Copenhagen. The pivotal role of the magician is a
common feature of early Greek romance as well, and scholars remain divided
over whether Greek use of Egyptian settings and magicians reflects direct borrowing. One "Greek" magician's tale, "The Romance of Nectanebo," was certainly translated from Demotic, as four copies of the Egyptian original have now
been identified among the Copenhagen collection.[1] The little-known narrative
of Hihor is the first of several tales inscribed on a jug once preserved in the
Berlin Museum but destroyed during the Second World War. A further tale from
this lost jug is The Swallow and the Sea, translated elsewhere in this volume.

R.K.R.

1. See Kim Ryholt, "A Demotic Version of Nectanebo's Dream (P. Carlsberg 562)," *ZPE*
122 (1998): 197–200. Additional copies include P. Carlsberg 424, 499, and 559. All
are from the Tebtunis temple library.

1    Hihor the Magician. Hereafter is the petition of Hihor the magician of the royal palace:

[The petition of Hihor the magician] before Pharaoh: "My [great] lord! If it happens that it is granted, I shall present him: The brother of Taneith[2] and his birds and everything pertaining to him and Pharaoh in its entirety." There[after, Hi]hor the magician, the chief scribe [...]. He presented the brother of Taneith and his birds and everything pertaining to him and Pharaoh in its entirety.

It happened that [Hihor the] magician was imprisoned in the prisons
5    of Pharaoh at Elephantine. / Thereafter occurred the time when the birds of heaven fly up to Egypt. The duck and the hen flew up to Egypt. They inquired after the movements of Hihor the magician, and they learned that he was imprisoned in the prisons of Pharaoh near Elephantine. They flew south to Elephantine, and they alighted beside the prisons of Pharaoh at Elephantine. They spoke inside, saying: "O Hihor the magician, we are the two bird eggs that you have brought to life. We request if it pleases, that it be ordered that your words be written down on two petitions, so that we might carry them and cast them into the columned hall before Pharaoh." He was given the writing materials and he wrote his words on two petitions. He gave one copy to the duck and another copy to the hen. Another copy was placed with them, and they cast them into the columned hall before Pharaoh.

2. Previous translators have read "Sentanub" as an otherwise unattested personal name. For Taneith, see E. Lüddeckens et al., eds., *Demotisches Namenbuch,* vol. I/16 (Wiesbaden, 1999), p. 1193.

# THE FABLE OF THE SWALLOW AND
# THE SEA

T his cautionary tale was the last of four Demotic writing exercises composed as model letters on a jug formerly in the Berlin Museum (no.
12845) but destroyed in the Second World War. Dating to the Roman
era (first to second centuries A.D.) and probably deriving from Mit Rahina,
the epistolary narrative has traditional antecedents in both form and content.
Model letters are a feature of Egyptian education and literature from the Middle
Kingdom onward.[1] As a satirical letter, this Demotic example continues the
genre best typified by the taunting letter of Hori preserved in Papyrus Anastasi I. Here, however, it is the theoretically unassailable Pharaoh himself who is
satirized, corresponding to the depiction of tyrannical Khufu in Papyrus Westcar, the unnamed, but ineffectual, Pharaoh in "The Admonitions of Ipuwer" or
drunken Amasis in Papyrus Paris Bibliothèque Nationale 215, vo. The central
imagery of the tale, the immensity of the desert and sea in terms of usual
measurements, appears as early as the Amarna hymn of Ay that anticipates the
wording of Isaiah 40:12.[2]

The animal fable that forms the core of the letter is a traditional literary
device as well. Attested on figured ostraca and in narratives, such fables are best

1. See E. Wente, *Letters from Ancient Egypt* (Atlanta, 1990), 6 and 66–67 (no. 77); and
R. Caminos, "Briefe," *LÄ* 1 (1975): 858.
2. See B. Couroyer, "Isaïe XL, 12," *Revue Biblique* 73 (1966): 186–96.

*exemplified by the collection in the "Myth of the Solar Eye" that influenced the later Greek tales popularly attributed to Aesop. The Berlin Demotic fable, in which the futility of Pharaoh's threat to destroy Arabia is compared to that of a swallow's attempt to destroy the sea, also reveals cross-cultural influence. Later versions of the tale appear in rabbinical literature of the fourth century and, more fully, in the Indian Panchatantra attested from the sixth century.³ Although these parallels were first noted in the textual edition of 1912, the coherence of all three versions has become evident only in 1999 through revisions in the Demotic text presented by Phillipe Collombert, who is preparing a new critical edition. Despite its importance, the fable is rarely anthologized.*

R.K.R.

The [petition of] Ausky, the chief of the land of Arabia, before Pharaoh: "Hear the goodness of Pre [regarding(?) the] chiefs of the land [of Arabia]. Great is my lord! O may he celebrate millions of jubilees! What does it mean that Pharaoh, my great lord, has said: 'I shall devastate⁴ the land of Arabia'? Come, may Pharaoh, my great (lord), hear the tale of what happened to the swallow when it was giving birth beside the sea. When she was coming and going out to seek food for her young, she said: 'O sea, watch over my young until I come back in.' It happened that this was her custom daily. Now afterwards, a day occurred when the swallow happened to be coming and going out to seek food for her young. She said: 'O sea, watch over the young for me until I come back in, in accordance with my custom that transpires with me daily.' But it happened that the sea came up raging; it took the young of the swallow away before it. With her mouth full, her eyes wide,⁵ and her heart very happy, the swallow was coming back in. But she could not find her young there before her. She said: 'O sea, hand over the young whom I entrusted to you! Should it happen that you haven't given back my young whom I entrusted to you, I shall scoop you out on that day. I shall carry you away. I shall bail with my beak. I shall carry you to the sand of the surrounding area and carry the sand of the surrounding area to you.' It happened that this was the custom of the swallow daily [ . . .] the

3. See W. Spiegelberg, 8–11. The ultimate origin of the Panchatantra has been dated as early as the second century B.C.
4. Lit. "cut out/away." This expression, used to describe Pharaoh's attempt to destroy Arabia in line 2, is consciously selected in Ausky's rejoinder in line 8.
5. An Egyptian idiom signifying happiness or good fortune.

habit which she did. The swallow began to go, filling her mouth with the sand of the surrounding area and pouring it out in the sea. She filled her mouth with the water of the sea; she poured it out on the sand of the surrounding area. It happens that here then is the daily custom of the swallow before Pharaoh, my great lord. Should it happen that the swallow does scoop out the sea, then it[6] will devastate the happy heart from the land of Arabia."

WRITTEN

6. So Spiegelberg thought his handcopy suggests "I shall."

# THE INSTRUCTION OF
# 'ONCHSHESHONQY
# (P. BRITISH MUSEUM 10508)

T he ancient genre of wisdom literature continues without interruption into the Late Period. Of the various hieratic and Demotic examples, the most colorful is this Demotic composition that combines a narrative frame story with a lamentation on divine retribution and twenty-three columns of individual maxims. Although derided by its original editor as mere "practical wisdom" for the "peasant farmer," The Instruction of 'Onchsheshonqy has subsequently been compared to the works of Hesiod and the Greek Stoics, the Hebrew wisdom of Ben Sira and Qoheleth (Ecclesiastes), and the Syriac tale of Ahiqar. By virtue of its length, complexity, and paleographical clarity, it now serves as the textual basis for the standard introductory grammar of Demotic Egyptian.

Parallels between the Instruction and foreign works have been considered evidence of strong international influence on the Egyptian author, but the themes and imagery of 'Onchsheshonqy are overwhelmingly traditional.[1] The most common topics include the contrast between the wise man and his counterparts (fool, incompetent, or troublemaker), the untrustworthiness of women (except for one's own mother), the symbolic rapacity of the crocodile, and the

---

1. A Yale University dissertation on the topics in Demotic wisdom literature has now been completed by Jennifer Houser-Wegner, "Cultural and Literary Continuity in the Demotic Instructions" (New Haven, 2001).

*primacy of god as the source of fate and fortune. Agricultural matters constitute approximately a tenth of the Instruction, in keeping with conventional wisdom texts of earlier periods and the agricultural nature of the society. Cows and fields formed the economic base for much of the upper and middle classes and not just the "peasant farmer." New topics and attitudes reflect internal developments. Political, social, and ethnic fragmentation probably accounts for the expressed distrust of masters, outsiders, and venal merchants. Other "international maxims" in the Instruction may result from common experience and converging philosophies.*

*As is evident from personal and geographic names, the tale is set in the Saite, or Twenty-sixth, Dynasty. The priest ʿOnchsheshonqy is informed of a plot against Pharaoh but does not report it. The conspirators are discovered and executed, and ʿOnchsheshonqy is left to languish in prison, where he daily inscribes his wisdom on the sherds of his broken wine jars. This tale of an imprisoned sage owes nothing to the Aramaic Ahiqar, for its true antecedent is "The Eloquent Peasant" of the Middle Kingdom. The hero's punishment is in accord with native judicial practice, comparable to the fate of "criminals" in the harem conspiracy against Ramses III who similarly had heard conspirators and failed to report them. The frame story's date of composition is disputed, with suggestions ranging from the third to the late first century B.C. The problem is yet more acute for the collection of maxims, which likely was assembled from sources of differing dates.*

*In most cases, these maxims are presented as single sentences, or "monostichs," written on separate lines. Whether intentional or not, this format reinforces the tale's premise that they were written sequentially on small sherds of pottery. Despite their appearance as "one-liners," many of these pithy remarks are part of larger groupings linked by topic, word choice, or grammar, with couplets being particularly common. Contrary to previous editions, the following translation indicates the most obvious of these sections by interlinear spacing. Collectively, the maxims are termed both an "instruction" and a "teaching" for the author's young son,[2] following the standard motivation for Egyptian wisdom literature. The sayings themselves range from humorous to morose and pious to cynical, with several stock pronouncements that may be considered current "proverbs." Of these, the most common is the admonition not to sleep with another man's wife, the first advice offered on a Demotic ostracon from*

---

2. For the terminology of "instruction" and "teaching," see R. K. Ritner, *BiOr* 44 (1987): 641–43.

*Deir el-Bahari to "a child who is very, very young."³ The true meaning of proverbs are often culturally bound, with a significance not readily apparent from the literal wording. The non-American would be perplexed that the saying "The apple doesn't fall far from the tree" is not a statement of families living contiguously, but of offspring physically resembling parents. Similarly, only the Egyptians may have understood fully the implications of a donkey shaking a palm tree (col. 11/18) or a crocodile putting on a wig (col. 24/8).⁴*

*The primary manuscript (P. British Museum 10508) is late Ptolemaic in date and derives from the burial of a priest at Akhmim. Parallels to the instructions in the British Museum text are found in the brief composition P. Louvre E 2414 (second century B.C.), the fragmentary P. inv. Sorbonne 1260 (second century B.C.) and P. Cairo 30682 (first to second century B.C.), and the unpublished P. Berlin 15658. A late-second-century A.D. version of the frame story alone survives from the library of the Sobek temple at Tebtunis. The revised beginning of the frame story makes use of rearrangements and parallels indicted by Thissen and Ryholt.*

R.K.R.

[...] It happened that they had sprinkled [... two priest]s(?) of P[re.(?)] The one among [them was called Tchaine]fer son of 'Onch[sheshonqy, and] the other was called [Ramose son of ..., amounting to] two persons. There occurred to each of them a male child. [...] The child [of Tchainefer] was called ['Onch]sheshonqy by name, and the child [of Ra]mose [son of ... was called Har]si[ese by name. They were given to] / the nurses. They were nourished and [they] grew strong. [... They were made students at the school.⁵ It happened that] there was not a youth among the priests of Pre ... [so that 'Onchsheshonqy became a priest of Pre, and Harsiese became a physician.]

1/5

3. Cf. cols. 8/12, 17/3, 21/18–19, 23/6–7, and the instruction "Do not have sex with a woman who is not yours," in Ronald J. Williams, "Some Fragmentary Demotic Wisdom Texts," in J. H. Johnson and E. F. Wente, eds., *Studies in Honor of George R. Hughes,* SAOC 39 (Chicago, 1976), 270–71.

4. Both the crocodile and donkey are symbolic animals for the Egyptians (for greed and licentiousness, respectively), and like "swine" in English, the names may be used to characterize people.

5. Cf. the Tebtunis parallel in Kim Ryholt, "A New Version of the Introduction to the Teachings of 'Onch-Sheshonqy," in P. J. Frandsen and K. Ryholt, eds., *A Miscellany of Demotic Texts and Studies* (Copenhagen, 2000), 121, n.37.

Afterwards, a day happened when Pharaoh sent word [to bring a wise] youth [to the] house of the physicians. [They brought Harsiese],[6] son of Ramose to the house of the physicians. [The physicians examined] him, and he was good with his prescriptions. [They took him] before the chief physician. [The chief physician] asked him [many questions. He told him] the answer to all of them. [The chief] physician [discovered] / the fact that he was knowledgeable [... They brought Harsiese before] Pharaoh. Pharaoh asked him many [things]. He told him the answer to all [of them]. Pharaoh was very [pleased]. It happened that he was the one [who made prescrip]tions for the houses of the chief physician, while the chief physician did not do anything except for something on which he had consulted Harsiese son of Ramose.

A few days later it happened that [the] chief physician departed to his fathers. Harsiese son of Ramose was made chief physician, he was given everything that belonged to the chief physician / entirely, and his brothers were made priests without a fee. It happened that Pharaoh did not do anything except for something on which he had consulted Harsiese son of Ramose, the chief physician.

Afterwards, a day occurred when 'Onchsheshonqy son of Tchainefer became very ill in the interior of his home. He mused in his heart, saying: "What suits my heart is to go to Memphis and stay with Harsiese son of Ramose. I have been told that he has been made chief physician, [that he has been given] everything that belonged to the chief physician / entirely, and that his brothers were made priests without a fee. Perhaps god will put it [into his heart] to do for me what is suitable." He came out from Heliopolis without having let anyone at all discover his movements. He found a boat that was sailing [...] / [... Harsiese son of Ramose received 'Onchsheshon]qy [son of Tchainefer.] He [said: "I shall inquire about] your [freedom from duty before Phar]aoh. Stay here in Memphis with me / [and] my mid-wife. You [can go to] Heliopolis [to] your people three times a month." It happened that 'Onchsheshonqy [son of Tchainefer stayed in Memphis with] Har[si]ese son of Ramose. It happened that he[7] was the one [who in]quired about his freedom from duty, [and so he went to] Heliopolis to his people three times a month.

1/10

1/15

1/20

2/1

2/5

6. Mistakenly copied as ['Onchssheshon]qy.
7. Harsiese inquires for 'Onchsheshonqy.

Afterwards, a day occurred when the [members of the palace] made an evil pact to cast salt on the wound(?) [of Pharaoh, and they] consulted Harsiese son of Ramose, the chief physician. Harsiese son of [Ramose consult]ed 'Onchsheshonqy son of Tchainefer about it. 'Onchshesh[onqy son of Tchainefer] said to him: ["Take care] for yourself! Your life's breath,

2/10    may it be safe! Pharaoh [is] the image of Pre! / [It is] the gods [who watch over you![8] Why have you] agreed to the misfortune of Pharaoh? Pharaoh has done for you many good things, [more than for] all [the great men of the] palace. When you had no property on earth you were brought to the palace. He caused that you be made chief physician. He caused that there be given to you everything that belonged to the chief physician entirely. He caused that your brothers be made priests without a fee. Can it be that what you will do to him in return for it is to allow him to be killed?" He said:

2/15    "Leave me alone, 'Onchsheshonqy son of Tchainefer! There is nothing to them, the words that you are saying! The guards, the generals, / and the great men of the palace are all in agreement upon it in order to do it."

It happened that, as for every word which Harsiese son of Ramose was saying to 'Onchsheshonqy son of Tchainefer and those which 'Onchshe-shonqy son of Tchainefer said to him in return, there was a man of the household inside a place listening to the voices of the two men, and he was called Wahibre-mekhy son of Ptahertais by name. That very man, it was

2/20    [his] evening for spending the night in the portico of / the resting place in which Pharaoh was. [Evening] came, and he spent the night in the portico of the resting place in which Pharaoh was. The [time] of the eighth hour of night occurred, and Pharaoh awoke. He uncovered his face, and he called out, saying: "Who is outside?" Wahibre-mekhy son of Ptahertais answered him. Pharaoh said to him: "Woe [at] his [hand!] Woe at the hand of Pre

3/1    and the gods who / [are with him!]" ... Pharaoh said: "Is there any man on] earth [who will be able to save] me?" He said before [Pharaoh: "My great lord,] it is at the [feet of your god] that Pharaoh should ask."

At the moment that he said it, [the face of Pharaoh] brightened, as he swore by Him who is Great of Strength, saying: "Do I have salvation, do [I have] salvation, Wahibre-mekhy son of Ptahertais? Do I have salvation?"

---

8. The passage is restored following the Tebtunis variant, col. V, 1.6 and Fragment A, 1. 1, see Kim Ryholt, "A New Version of the Introduction to the Teachings of 'Onch-Sheshonqy," 124, 128, 131, and 133.

He said: "You will be saved through the hand of Pre and the gods who are with him, and Neith the great, the god's mother, [the] great goddess, will

3/5 place all the foreign countries of the / whole earth under the feet of Pharaoh." He related before Pharaoh every word that he had heard the voice of Harsiese son of Ramose saying to 'Onchsheshonqy son of Tchainefer together with those that 'Onchsheshonqy son of Tchainefer said to him in return, without a word among them being changed. Pharaoh was unable to sleep until morning.

The morning for the next day occurred, and Pharaoh sat in the court of the palace in Memphis. The guards stood [in] their ranks and the generals

3/10 in their places of attendance. Pharaoh looked toward the station / of Harsiese son of Ramose. Pharaoh said to him: "Harsiese son of Ramose, it was when you had no property on earth that you were brought to the palace. I caused that you be made chief physician. I caused that there be given to you everything that belonged to the chief physician entirely. I caused that your brothers be made priests without a fee. What is it that you have done, being in agreement against me to have me killed?"

He said before Pharaoh: "My great lord, on the day when Pre ordained for me that which is favorable, he placed the best interest of Pharaoh in my heart. On the day when Pre ordained for me that which is unfavorable,

3/15 he placed the misfortune of / Pharaoh in my heart."

Pharaoh said to him: "The words, when they were told to you, did you say them before any man on earth?" He said: "I said them before 'Onchsheshonqy son of Tchainefer, a priest of Pre who is here in Memphis with me." Pharaoh said to him: " 'Onchsheshonqy son of Tchainefer, what sort of man is he to you?" He said: "His father was the companion of my father. His

3/20 heart was very attached to him."[9] Pharaoh said: "Have / 'Onchsheshonqy son of Tchainefer brought." They ran after ('Onchsheshonqy son of)[10] Tchainefer. They ran and, bringing him before Pharaoh immediately, they returned. Pharaoh said to him: " 'Onchsheshonqy son of Tchainefer, have

---

9. The text repeats in error: "Pharaoh said to him: ' 'Onchsheshonqy son of Tchainefer, what sort of man is he to you?' He said: 'His father was the companion of my father. His heart was very attached to him.' " The dittography was later enclosed by the scribe in long brackets. The phrase "attached to" seems literally to mean "be firm/solid with."

10. The scribe has accidentally omitted the name, confusing identical signs for "after" and "son of."

502

you eaten my bread and heard evil against me without having come to let me discover it by saying: 'They are conspiring against you in order to kill you'?"

4/1     / [... 'Onchsheshonqy son of Tchainefer said to Pharaoh: "My great lord, I said to him: 'Take care for yourself! Your life's breath, may it be safe! Pharaoh is the image of Pre! It is the gods who watch over you! Why have you agreed to the misfortune of Pharaoh? Pharaoh has done for you many good things, more than for all the great men of the palace. When you had no property on earth you were brought to the palace. He caused that you be made chief physician. He caused that there be given to you everything that belonged to the chief physician entirely. He caused that your brothers be

4/x+1 made priests without a fee.[11] And it is you who have acted so as] / to cause that I reach [the position that you are in] together with absolutely every person who belongs to [you]. Can it be that what you will do to him in return for it is to allow him to be killed?' By your face, my great lord, I did all that I could against him. He did not tell me an answer. I was aware that they were matters that would not be hidden from Pharaoh."

At the moment he had said it, Pharaoh caused an earthen altar to be built at the door of the palace. He caused that Harsiese son of Ramose be

4/x+5 placed / on the brazier with absolutely every person who belonged to him and with every person who had agreed to the misfortune of Pharaoh.[12] He caused that 'Onchsheshonqy son of Tchainefer be taken to the houses of detention at Daphnae. A deputy and a staff-bearer, a man of the royal household, was assigned to him. It happened that his food was brought out from the palace daily.

Afterwards, there occurred the accession day of Pharaoh. Pharaoh released every man who was in the prisons of Daphnae except 'Onchshe-

4/ shonqy son of Tchainefer. His heart despaired / because of it. He said to the

x+10 staff-bearer who was assigned to him: "Let there be done for me this favor before you. Let a palette and a papyrus scroll be [brought] to me because of the fact that I have a young boy and I have not reached him to instruct him. Let me write for him an instruction so that I may have it taken to him in Heliopolis to instruct him by means of it." The staff-bearer said: "I shall report it before Pharaoh first." The staff-bearer reported a report about it before Pharaoh first. Pharaoh commanded, saying: "Let a palette be taken

11. Restored from col. 2/8–13.

12. For incineration of prisoners in cult and state executions, see R. K. Ritner, *The Mechanics of Ancient Egyptian Magical Practice*, SAOC 54 (Chicago, 1993), 157–59.

4/     to him. Do not have taken to him / a papyrus scroll." A palette was taken to

x+15   him. A papyrus scroll was not taken to him. He wrote on the sherds of the pots the words by which he would be able to instruct his son. WRITTEN[13]

Here is the instruction which the god's-father 'Onchsheshonqy son of Tchainefer, whose mother is Satnebu,[14] wrote for his son on the sherds of the pots which they would take in to him containing mixed wine, while he was imprisoned in the houses of detention of Daphnae, saying: "Oppression and misery, my great lord, O Pre! It is imprisonment and oppression that has been done to me because of the fact that I did not kill a man! It is your abomination, my great lord, O Pre! Is it the way in which Pre will display anger at a land? O people who will find the sherds of the pots, listen to me concerning the way in which Pre will display anger at a land!

5/     [If Pre is angry at a] land, he will cause [...]; he does not [...] it.

x+1    [If P]re is angry at a land, its ruler will abandon the law.

If Pre is angry at a land, he will cause the laws to cease within it.

If Pre is angry at a land, he will cause purity to cease within it.

5/     If Pre is angry at a land, he will cause truth to cease within it.

x+5    If Pre is angry at a land, he will cause value to be minimal within it.

If Pre is angry at a land, he does not allow trust to be [within] it.

If Pre is angry at a land, he does not allow positions of status [...] to be taken within it.

If Pre is angry at a land, he will elevate its humble men, and he will humble its great men.

5/     If Pre is angry at a land, he will cause the fools to be rulers of the educated.

x+10  If Pre is angry at a land, he will command its ruler to make its people fare badly.

If Pre is angry at a land, he will make its bureaucrat[15] to be the authority over it.

If Pre is angry at a land, he will make its washerman to be chief of police."

13. For discussion of these section dividers in 4/x+16, 5/19, and 28/11, see K.-Th. Zauzich, "Anchscheschonqi—eine Lehre für den Schreiber?" in M. Schade-Busch, ed., *Weg öffnen* (Wiesbaden, 1996), 376–80.

14. Understood as "Satnecho" by Heinz J. Thissen, *Die Lehre des Anchscheschonqi (P. BM 10508), Einleitung, Übersetzung, Indices* (Bonn, 1984), 42–43. The name employs a hieratic writing of *nb* "lord," found also in "Mernebptah" (from Merneptah) in Setna I, col. 4/6.

15. Lit. "scribe."

Hereafter, the words which 'Onchsheshonqy son of Tchainefer wrote on
5/    / the sherds of the pots which they would take in to him containing mixed
x+15  wine in order to give it as a teaching for his son, while they reported them
before Pharaoh and his great men daily. 'Onchsheshonqy son of Tchainefer
discovered the fact that he was lingering while imprisoned, since he had not
been released. He wrote on the sherds of the pots the words by which he
would be able to instruct his son. WRITTEN

6/1   Serve [your] brother, that he may make protection for you.
Serve your brothers, that you may acquire good repute.
Serve a wise man, that he may perform your service.
Serve the one who will serve you.
6/5   Serve any man, that you may find worth.
Serve your father and your mother, that you may go and prosper.

Inquire about any matter, that you may understand them.

Be small in wrath and stout-hearted, that your heart may be pleasing.

It is only after the acquisition of character that any teaching comes to
fruition.

6/10  Do not set your heart upon the property of another, saying: "I shall live by
means of it." Acquire for yourself your own.

Do not oppress when you fare well, lest you fare badly.

Do not send a lowly woman on your business. It is on her own that she will go.
Do not send a wise man on a small matter when there awaits an important
matter.
Do not send a fool on an important matter when there is a wise man whom
you can send.
6/15  Do not send to a town in which you will find loss.

Do not long for your house when you are sent.
Do not long for your house to drink beer in it at midday.

Do not pamper your flesh, lest you be weak.
Do not pamper yourself when you are young, lest you be weak when you
are old.

6/20  Do not hate a man at the mere sight of him when you do not know anything
about him.

Do not become distressed so long as you possess something.
Do not worry yourself so long as you possess something.
Do not become distressed over a matter.
Do not become distressed over your occupation.

7/1 [...].
Compel [your] son; do not compel him more than your servant.
Do not spare your son work when you are able to make him do it.

Do not instruct a fool, lest he hate you.
7/5 Do not instruct one who will not listen to you.

Do not set your heart on a fool.
Do not set your heart on the property of an incompetent.[16]

Do not go into hiding[17] and then let yourself be found.
Do not go into hiding when you have no food.
7/10 The one who goes into hiding when he has no food is in the situation of someone who seeks it.
Do not go off and then return of your own accord.
Do not go off after having been beaten, lest your punishment be doubled.

Do not act overly familiar with the one who is greater than you.

Do not hesitate to serve your god.
7/15 Do not hesitate to serve your master.
Do not hesitate to serve the one who will serve you.
Do not hesitate to acquire for yourself a male and female servant when you are able to do it.

A servant who is not beaten, great is the cursing in his heart.
A lesser man whose wrath is great, his stench is copious.
7/20 A great man whose wrath is small, his praise is copious.

Do not say "boy" to one who has grown old.
Do not belittle in your heart one who has grown old.

Do not be hasty when you speak, lest you offend.
Do not say at once that which comes from your heart.

16. A legal category that includes both the mentally disabled and immature children.
17. Hiding as a fugitive from duties and taxes became increasingly common in the Greco-Roman eras, leading to temple asylum and, later, to anchoritic communities.

8/1   Do not […] yourself […].

Learning and incompetence exist among those of [your] town. Exalt in your heart those of your town.

Do not say: "I am educated." Set yourself to learn.

Do not do something about which you have not first inquired.

8/5   Your best interest is in inquiring.

You should inquire of three wise men about an individual matter if it is important enough for an oracular petition[18] of the great god.

Do good for your body during your good days.

There is no one who does not die.

Do not withdraw yourself from a scribe when he is taken to the houses of detention.

8/10   You should withdraw yourself from a scribe when he is taken to his mansion of eternity.

Do not go to court with one who is greater than you when you do not have protection.

Do not take to yourself a woman whose husband is living, lest he become an enemy to you.

Whether times are constrained or times are joyful, property multiplies by spreading it.

May your fate not be the fate of the one who begs and is given.

8/15   If you perform field work, do not pamper your body.

Do not say: "Here is the plot of my brother." It is at your own that you should look.

The blessing of a town is in a ruler who exercises judgment.[19]

The blessing of a temple is in a sanctuary.

The blessing of a plot is in its time of being worked.

18. For the term *pḥ-nṯr*, see Ritner, *The Mechanics of Ancient Egyptian Magical Practice*, 214–20.

19. Reading *rnn.t n tmy (n) ḥry*. The good fortune/blessing of a town resides in/derives from a ruler. Traditionally, cols. 8/17–9/4 (and 11/11–12) have been considered defectively written nominal expressions: "The good fortune/blessing of a town (is) a ruler."

8/20    The blessing of a storehouse is in stocking it.
The blessing of a treasury is in a single hand.
The blessing of property is in a wise woman.
The blessing of a wise man is in his mouth.

9/1    The blessing of [...].
The blessing of an army is in a [general.]
The blessing of a town is in not taking sides.
The blessing of a craftsman is in his equipment.

Do not despise a document that has a claim on you.
Do not despise a remedy that you regularly use.
Do not despise a matter of Pharaoh.
Do not despise a matter that pertains to a cow.
The one who frequently despises a thing, it is from it that he dies.

9/10    Do not quarrel over a matter in which you are wrong.

Do not say: "My field is growing." Do not fail to inspect it.

Do not dwell in a house with your in-laws.
Do not be a neighbor to your master.

Do not say: "I have plowed the farmland, but there has been no return."
Plow again; it is good to plow.

9/15    More beautiful is the face of the one who has come up from the farmland than that of the one who has spent the day in the town.

Do not say: "It is summer." It is accompanied by winter.
The one who does not gather wood in summer cannot heat himself in winter.

Do not dwell in a place in which affairs of property will not reach you.
Do not entrust your property in a place excessively.

9/20    Do not put your property in a single place.
Do not put your property in a town to which you must send.

Property seizes its owner.
It is the owner of a cow who ends up running.

Do not incur expense when you have not established your storehouse.

9/25    You should incur expense in accordance with what you have.

10/1  Do not say: ["I am] beautiful(?) at writing and you [...].
Do not say: "I am good at writing" and not be able [to write] your [name.]

A scribe in a shipyard—a craftsman at the harbor.[20]

If a crocodile shows itself, the respect of it will be measured.
10/5  A crocodile does not die of gladness, it is of hunger that it dies.

"It is an insult to me that will be done," so says the fool when he is instructed.

You may stumble with your foot in the house of a great man; you should not stumble with your tongue.

If you are thrown out of the house of your master, become his door-keeper.
10/10  If it happens that your master is sitting beside the river, do not / moisten your hands in his presence.

Would that my brother were the groom of the horses, mounting mine in valor![21]
Would that my companion speak with the knowledge of Thoth!
Would that he not die, the one for whom I would rend my clothing!
Would that it were the "elder brother"[22] of the town who was assigned to it!
10/15  Would that it were the charitable brother of the family who acted as "elder brother" for it!
Would that I possessed and that my brother possessed, that I might eat my own without having cast down my eyes!
Would that the floodwater not fail to come!
Would that the farmland not fail to grow green!
Would that it were the bad field of the farmland that grew herbage in excess!

20. The expected position of both professionals is reversed. The scribe belongs at harborside recording shipments, not at the shipyard with the carpenters. Comparable expressions in English include "a bull in a china shop" and "a fish out of water." An alternative reading of the final phrase "a craftsman with a fixed deadline" is proposed in Zauzich, "Anchscheschonqi—eine Lehre für den Schreiber?" 380–81.
21. Reading $iw=f$ ts $n\dot{s}y=\dot{\imath}$ $(n)$ qny.
22. In this and the following line, the term "elder brother" is a legal designation meaning "trustee/administrator."

10/20 Would that the vagina receive its male![23]
Would that the son were more honored than his father!
Would that it were the master's son who became master!
Would that my mother were my hairdresser, that she might do for me what is pleasant!
Would that the moon succeed the sun, without failing to appear!
Would that existence always succeed death!

11/1 Would that I might cast the [...]!
Would that I might extend my hand to my enemy [...] were received!
Would that I knew my neighbor, that I might give to him my property!
Would that I knew my brother, that I might open my heart to him!

11/5 Do not often be a hindrance, lest you be cursed.
Do not often get drunk, lest you go mad.

Take for yourself a wife when you are twenty years old, that you may have a son when you are young.

Do not kill a snake and leave its tail.

Do not cast a lance when you are unable to control its end.

11/10 The one who spits at heaven, it is on his face that it falls.

The character of a man is in his family.[24]
The character of a man is in his association.
The character of a man is on his face.
The character of a man is one of his limbs.

11/15 Without knowing that it is god who sends to every place, the fisherman casts into the water.[25]

Do not reach evening on the road, saying: "I am sure of the houses." You do not know the hearts of their inhabitants.

A guard robs, his son is a poor man.

Do not let your donkey kick against the date palm, lest he shake it.

23. Lit. "bull," see Ritner, *BiOr* 44 (1987): 645.
24. *ꜣmy.t (n) rmt (n) tꜣy=f mḥw.t;* cf. col. 21/25. Family and associations are the source of character.
25. For the fisherman as a symbol of uncertainty and fate, see cols. 645–46 and col. 18/25, and Ritner, *BiOr* 44 (1987): 645–46.

Do not laugh at your son in the presence of his mother, lest you learn the significance of his father.

11/20 It is not from a male[26] that a male is born.

Do not say: "The enemy of god is living today." It is at the end that you should look.
You will say: "A good fate" at the end of old age.
Put your affairs in the hands of god.

12/1 Do not [...].

Do not create your amusement(?) [...] being distressed.
A man does not know his days of misery.

Do not entrust your people to one who has not experienced distress.

12/5 Do not delay in creating for yourself a tomb on the *gebel*. You do not know the length of your life.

Do not do evil to a man so as to cause that another do it to you.[27]

Do not be disheartened regarding the one whom you will be able to ask.
Happy is the heart of the one who has exercised judgment in the presence of a wise man.
A wise master who asks, his house is established forever.

12/10 Disdain ruins the great man.
It is the great crime, when it begins, that is raged against.

The work of a fool does not come to fruition in a place where there is a wise man.

Let your wife look at your property. Do not trust her with it.
Do not trust her with her food and clothing allowance for a single year.

12/15 My brother was not ashamed to steal; I was not ashamed to bind him.

Do not seek revenge. Do not cause revenge to be sought against you.

Let your good deed reach the one who has need of it.
Do not be stingy. Property does not provide security.

26. Lit. "bull."
27. The Egyptian version of the "Golden Rule," employing a negative construction, a device preferred also in the "Negative Confession" of Book of the Dead 125.

A philanthropic master even kills for contentment.

12/20 A wise killer has not been killed.

Do not undertake a matter that you will not be able to do.
Do not speak in a forceful voice to a man when you will not be able to intimidate him by it.

Loud is the voice of the one who acted when he has been commanded.
Do not say a thing when it is not its proper time.

13/1 Do not [...].

It is the wise man who seeks [a friend. It is the fool who] seeks an enemy.

A man for whom a good deed has been done previously will not be able to repay it.

Bad is the fate of the poor man ...

13/5 Do not give your son to the wetnurse so as to cause that she cast out hers.

The companion of a fool is a fool. The companion of a wise man is a wise man.
The companion of an incompetent is an incompetent.
It is the mother who gives birth. It is the road (of life) that gives a companion.

Every man acquires property. It is the wise man who knows how to secure it.

13/10 Do not give your property into the hand of your younger brother so as to cause that he act the elder brother to you by means of it.

Do not prefer one to another of your children. You do not know the one who will be charitable to you among them.

If you find your wife with her lover, take for yourself a bride on the basis of worthiness.

Do not acquire an attendant for your wife when you do not have a servant.
Do not acquire for yourself two voices.

13/15 Speak truth to every man. Let it be inherent in your speech.

Do not open your heart to your wife. What you have said to her belongs to the street.

Do not open your heart to your wife or to your servant.

You may open it to your mother. She is a female container.[28]

As for a woman, it is just her business that she knows.

13/20 The teaching of a woman is like a sack of sand with its side split open.

Her savings are stolen property.

What she will do with her husband today, she does with another man tomorrow.

Do not dwell beside one greater than you.

Do not take for yourself a youth as a companion.

14/1 [...].

It is in [his] stench and with the condemnation of god after him also that he causes him to give it.

Do not take for yourself a thief for a companion, [lest] he cause that you be killed.

A man who has even a small matter, it is what takes hold of him.

14/5 Shut up a house and from it it will die.

The one who is stouthearted in a bad matter does not discover its harm.

The one who robs the property of another does not discover its profit.

If you should be the companion of a wise man whose heart you do not know, do not open your heart to him.

If you do a good deed for 100 men and one of them recognizes it, one portion has not perished.

14/10 Make burnt offering and libation in the presence of god. Let fear of him be great in your heart.

At night a thief steals; at midday he is found.

Do not multiply your words.

It is to the one who has property in his hand that a house is open.

He who is bitten by the bite of a snake is afraid of a coil of rope.

14/15 A man who looks in front of himself does not stumble and fall.

28. Lit. "basket."

Do not abandon a woman of your house when she does not become pregnant or give birth.

Good fortune turns aside destruction by a great god.

Exalt your man(servant),[29] that your intent may come to fruition and that you may acquire another.
Do not let your serving boy experience want regarding his wages.

14/20    Do not cast an eye at the property of another, lest you become poor.
Do not trespass on the territory of another.

Do not put a house on farmland.

Do not cause a man to lodge a complaint against you.

15/1    Do not [...] ... [...].

Do not [fail to do] the thing that your master has commanded specifically to you.

There is no [...] which reaches the sky.
There is no [...] which fails to cry.

15/5    Do not say: "[I did] this good deed for this man. He did not acknowledge it to me."
There is no good deed except a good deed that you have done for him who has need of it.

If you have attained maturity and acquired much property, let your brothers be great with you.

Need, should word of it become known in the street, as disgrace it is reckoned.

A young man who is educated, it is on the error of what he has done that he thinks thoughts.

15/10    A man who has acquired his first money, its expenditure consists of drinking it and eating it.

29. Following Glanville and the sense of the following line in this couplet. Lichtheim and Thissen translate "(fellow) man." See the bibliography.

A man who smells of myrrh, his wife is a cat in his presence.
A man who is in distress, his wife is a lioness in his presence.

Do not be afraid to do that in which you are in the right.
Do not steal. It will be discovered to your debt.

15/15 Do not allow your son to take a wife from another town, lest he be taken from you.

More pleasing is dumbness than hastiness of the tongue.
More pleasing is sitting than doing a trivial errand.

Do not say: "I undertook this matter," when you did not undertake it.

Anger should not command you.
15/20 Gluttony will not give you the goose.

If you are sent after chaff and find wheat, do not buy [it].
If you are a merchant of straw when it is wanted, you should not make the rounds with wheat.

Do not do what you hate to a man so as to cause another to do it to you.

Do not associate with a man who is disheartened and says: "It is just one moment of distress that I have."
One hundred men are killed because of one moment of distress.

16/1 Do not [... and you] be poor forever.
Do not [...] and you agree.

Do not send your son for instruction at the door of the storehouse in a lean year.

Do not go to your brother when you are distressed. You should go to your friend.
16/5 Do not drink water in the house of a merchant. He will charge you for it.

Do not deliver a servant into the hand of his master.
Do not say: "My master hates me. I will not serve him."
Zealous service repels hatred.

Borrow money at interest and put it into farmland.
16/10 Borrow money at interest and take for yourself a wife.

Borrow money at interest and celebrate your birthday.
Do not borrow money at interest to live in grand style by means of it.

Do not swear falsely when you are in distress, lest you fare worse than your current condition.

Do not inquire on your own behalf before god and pass over what he has said.

16/15 Do not laugh at a cat.

Do not speak of a state matter during beer.

Do not make a judgment in which you are wrong.
Do not be fainthearted in a bad matter.

Do not conceal yourself from a stranger who has come from abroad.
16/20 If it happens that there is nothing in your hand, there may be in his.

Do not lend money at interest without security in your hand.
Do not be too trusting, lest you become a poor man.

Do not hate him who will say to you: "I am your brother; small is the share in the house of my father. It will not increase."

16/25 Do not despise a small document, a small flame, or a small soldier.[30]

17/1 [...] ... you will not [...].

[Do not place(?)] your property under seal [...] crime of another.

[Do not] take liberties with a woman when her husband is listening to your voice.

[Do not be ashamed] to do the work by which you will be able to live.

17/5 [Do not] acquire property when you do not have a storehouse.
Do not accept a gift when you will not make a contract.

Do not say: "My illness has gone away. I shall not use a remedy."

Do not often go away, lest you be hated.
Do not give a weary look toward the door bolt.

30. The word "small" indicates a "minor" document or "subordinate" soldier.

17/10 Do not be hasty when you speak before your master.
Do not run too fast, lest you wait.

Do not often wash yourself with water alone.
Water wears down stone.

Do not go on the road without a stick in your hand.

17/15 Do not be circumspect regarding a man in the presence of his opponent during the trial.

Do not walk alone at night.

Do not scorn your master before a lesser man.

If you associate with a man and you are on good terms with him, if he fares badly, do not abandon him.
Let him attain his mansion of eternity.
17/20 He who comes after him will ensure that you live.

A woman who is loved, when she is abandoned, she *is* abandoned.

Inventory your house each and every hour that you may find its thief.

Teach your son to write, to plow, to fish, and to trap because of a year of withdrawn inundation, and he will find the profit in what he has done.

Take dung, take manure, but do not make an occupation of scavenging.

17/25 Do not often relate matters in the presence of your master.

Be small in wrath and your respect will be great in the hearts of all men.

18/1 [...] know regarding you, do not (?) [...].

[If a] gardener acts as a fisherman, his [trees] will perish.

[If] you have acquired 100 [...], give one of them for protection.

[If you do] farmwork, do not be dishonest.

18/5 Better is noble failure than half success.

If you are powerful, throw your documents into the river. If you are weak, throw them also.

When a lesser man says: "I will kill you," he will truly kill you.
When a great man says: "I will kill you," lay your head on his doorstep.

Give 100 pieces of silver to a wise woman. Do not accept 200 pieces of silver from a foolish one.

18/10 He who is in the battlefield together with those of his town is in the celebration with them.

The children of the fool wander in the street, those of the wise man are beside him.

He who hides behind his master will acquire 100 masters.

A man who has no town, his character serves as his family.
A man who has no property, his wife acts as his divisional partner.

18/15 Do not rejoice over the beauty of your wife, her heart is set just on her sexual gratification.

Do not say: "I have this property. I will not serve god and I will not serve man either."
Property ceases; it is serving god that generates.

Do not send word about a matter to one whom you do not know.

He who loves his house so as to dwell in it warms it to its beams.
18/20 He who hates it builds it and then mortgages it.

Do not be despondent when you are ill, lest your mooring[31] be made.

Do not say: "I shall give this property to this man," when you will not give it to him.

Take a great man to your home; take a lesser man to your boat.

When the inundation comes it makes allotments for everyone.

18/25 Being sent to the one who will eat it, a fish is brought up from the depths.

19/1 They said to you [...] have sex with the [...].
You said to me [...] you are dead. You said to me [...] you are alive.

31. Docking at the underworld, a common euphemism for "death."

Sweeter is the water of the one who has given it than the wine of the [one who has received] it.

In the country a cow is stolen; in the town its owner is fought.

19/5 If your enemy entreats you, do not hide from him.

If a bird takes off from one place to that of another, a feather will fall from it.[32]

There is no son of Pharaoh at night.

If an incompetent man repents, he will become a wise man.

A man does not love the one who hates him.

19/10 Do a good deed and throw it into the flood. When it subsides you will find it.

If two brothers quarrel, do not come between them.
He who comes between two brothers when they quarrel is placed between them when they are at peace.

If it were the daughter of the farmer who ate, a daughter of the stonemason would be her opposite.[33]
If it were a master's son who acted as master, men would not worship god.[34]

19/15 Do not be fainthearted when you are ill and so beg for death.
He who lives, his herbage grows.
There is no poor man except him who has died.

A thousand servants are in the house of the merchant. The merchant is one of them.

If your master says to you something wise, it is respect for him that you should feel.

32. Probably meaning that a bird loses feathers in a fight over another's nest and not simply that a bird leaves evidence of its passing.
33. A stonemason's daughter would have but stones to eat if only the farmer's family had access to food. For discussion and a varying interpretation of this passage, see Zauzich, "Anchscheschonqi—eine Lehre für den Schreiber?" 382–84.
34. Compare 10/22. If inheritance and stability were assured, prayer would be unnecessary.

19/20   It is a wise man who understands what passes before him.

Give your voice with your property, that it may make two gifts.

Beer matures only on its mash.
Wine matures only so long as it has not been opened.
A remedy is good only in the hand of its physician.

19/25   If it is for incompetence you are given bread, let learning be an abomination to you.

20/1   [...] him.
If he is sick, [...] his wife.
If he is weak, the [...] his heart.

End by planting any tree, begin by planting a sycamore.

20/5   The warp is no stranger to the woof.

In the hands of god is all good fortune.

One plowing makes no ...
One ... is not accurate.

More important are the hissings of the snake than the brayings of the donkey.

20/10   There is running to which sitting is preferable.
There is sitting to which standing is preferable.

Do not dwell in a house that is sick.[35] Death does not say: "I have come."

A serpent that is eating has no venom.

A window with a large opening, its heat gusts outnumber its cooling breezes.

20/15   All manner of beasts are welcome in a house. A thief is not welcome.

The approach of the fool means fleeing from him.

If you harness a big team, lie down in its shade.

35. Perhaps meaning a house in which there is sickness or a decayed or haunted house. Cf. col. 22/14.

Exalt in your heart the men who are elders, that you may be exalted in the hearts of all men.

It is in accordance with the character of her husband that a woman allows herself to be seduced.

20/20 A man does not eat what is under his eyes.

A treasury filled with kidney beans, all manner of worth is found within it.

The waste of a house is in not dwelling in it.
The waste of a woman is in not knowing her carnally.
The waste of a donkey is in carrying bricks.
20/25 The waste of a boat is in carrying straw.

21/1 There is no [...] who says: "They will find [...]."
There is no [...] who loves to do work.
There is no [...] who is buried.
There is no tooth that breaks and stabilizes another.
21/5 There is no Nubian who can change his skin.
There is no friend who passes away alone.
There is no wise man who finds loss.
There is no fool who finds profit.
There is no one who insults his superior who is not himself the one insulted.
21/10 There is no one who abandons his traveling companion against whom god does not reckon it.
There is no one who employs deceit who is not deceived.
There is no one who fails who regularly goes and prospers.

Do not hasten and petition a guard and then draw back from him.

He who is ashamed to have sex with his wife, no children are borne to him.

21/15 Do not be greedy, lest you be insulted.
Do not be stingy, lest you be hated.

Do not steal copper or cloth from the house of your master.

Do not violate a woman who has a husband.
He who violates on a bed a woman who has a husband, it is on the ground that his wife is violated.

21/20 Better a statue of stone than a foolish son.
Better to have none than a brother who is a failure.
Better death than want.

If you are thirsty at night, let your mother give you something to drink.

Do not be in a town in which you have no people.
21/25 If you should be in a town in which you have no people, your character serves as your family.[36]

22/1 [...] weak(?) ... [...].

Do not raise your hand when [you will not] be able to [...].
Do not set a fire when you will [not] be able to extinguish it.

Give your daughter as a wife to the gold merchant. Do not give [your son to] his daughter.

22/5 The one who shakes the stone, it is on his foot that it falls.

He who loves a woman of the street, the side of his purse is split open.

One does not load a beam on a donkey.

If a woman loves a crocodile, she takes on its character.
A woman at night, a saint at midday.
22/10 Do not speak ill of a beloved woman.
Do not speak praise of a hated woman.

For a fool to go about with a wise man is for a goose to go about with its butcher knife.
A fool in a house is like clothing in a storehouse for wine.

A house that is sick[37] does not seize the stranger.
22/15 A crocodile does not seize a townsman.[38]

If you are hungry, eat what you abominate. If you are stated, abominate it.

36. Cf. col. 11/11.
37. Cf. col. 20/12.
38. This couplet clearly contrasts the fate of stranger and locals, contra the interpretation of A. Botta and S. Vinson, "The Cowardly Crocodile in 'Onchsheshonqy 22/15 and Merikareʿ P. 97–98," *Enchoria* 23 (1996): 177–78.

He who does not have his eye on the river, let him give his attention to the needs of the waterpots.

If you are about to say something before your master, count on your hand up to ten.

Give one loaf to your laborer; take two by means of his strong arms.

22/20 Give one loaf to the one who does the labor, give two to the one who gives commands.

Do not insult a common man.
If insult occurs, beating will occur.
If beating occurs, killing will occur.
Killing does not occur without god knowing.

22/25 Nothing occurs except what god will ordain.

23/1 A man is able to reckon(?)[39] [...].

[It is] the character [of a man] that [...].

The great team in its stable [...].

Silence hides incompetence.

23/5 It is from the [...] that sunlight is taken; it is [by] the north wind that it is [...].

Do not desire a woman who has a husband.
He who desires a woman who has a husband, it is on her doorstep that he is killed.

It is better to dwell in your own small house than to dwell in the great house of another.
Small property intact is better than large property despoiled.

23/10 A slip of the tongue in the palace is a slip of the rudder at sea.

A male ox does not cry out to the calf. A great stable is not destroyed.

The path of god is before all men. The troublemaker does not find it.

"Did I ever live?"—so says the one who has died.

39. Reading *i-ir rmt r[ḫ i]p* [ . . .].

Every hand is extended to god. He accepts the hand only of his beloved.

23/15 A cat who loves fruit hates the one who eats it.

"My voice is as your voice," so says the weakling.

Do not be energetic in every sort of work and so be lazy in your work.
He who is not lazy for his father, he[40] will be energetic for him.

It is the builders who build the houses. It is the dancers who perform the dedication.

23/20 It is the frogs who praise the Inundation. It is the mice who eat the emmer. It is the oxen who bring about the barley and emmer. It is the donkeys who eat them.

Do not put a poor man in the presence of a rich man.

Do not drink water from a well and then throw the pitcher into it.

Body of a woman, mind of a horse.

24/1 [...].

[...] lifetime [...].

[...] bend down to [every]one [...].

If you acquire much property, [...] your [...].

24/5 [...] be early to your [...], you will die.

Do not make an unhappy woman your wife.

If a donkey walks with a horse, it performs its motions.
If a crocodile loves a donkey, it puts on a wig.
A horse is found to go after a lion; a donkey is not found to conduct it.

24/10 Man is better than a donkey at copulating; it is his purse that restrains him.

Because of inspecting, rations are given to an inspector. If he doesn't inspect, they are cut off.
No drunkenness of yesterday halts the thirst of today.

40. The father.

Better to scavenge[41] in hunger than to die in need.
Do not be ashamed to do your [...] without scorning it.

24/15 If you are infuriated with your master, do not say to him the full extent of your heart.

When a town is in the process of beginning,[42] [...] go into it.
When a town is in the process of destruction, [... leave] from it.

He who does not carry the wheat of his father [...] will carry chaff to their storehouses.

Do not take control of a matter whose ending you will not be able to control.

24/20 A woman is a stone quarry. It is the big block that works her.[43] A good woman of high character is as sustenance come forth during hunger.

There is no profit in my son whom I shall not find fit to reward.
There is no profit in my servant who will not do my work.
There is no profit in my brother who will not care for me.

25/1 [...].

Do not [...] poor man.
Do not [...] before the [...] to him.

Far more numerous are the [...] of god in the [...] than the festival processions of Pre in the great hall.

25/5 If a [woman is at] peace [with] her husband, it is the influence of god.

Do not sell your house and your endowment in exchange for one day, and so be a poor man forever.

Do not seize a common man from the property of Pharaoh, lest he destroy you and your family.

---

41. Reading *twtw*.
42. Lit. "coming to take off/begin" (*iy r gp*), cf. Coptic ϭⲱⲡⲉ (CD 826–27).
43. The saying employs quarry imagery for bodily parts. A woman is a "body of stone" and the term "work" (*bȝk*) puns on the word for "impregnate" (*bkȝ*). The term "big block" is considered not anatomical, but "blockhead" in Zauzich, "Anchscheschonqi—eine Lehre für den Schreiber?" 381–82.

Do not take a woman's [words] to your heart.

A woman is a blight, who does not quit the tree without having destroyed it.

25/10 Learn the manner of sending word to the palace.

Learn the manner of sitting in the presence of Pharaoh.

Learn the ways[44] of heaven.

Learn the ways of earth.

Would that the heart of a woman and the heart of her husband were far from anger.

25/15 Choose a wise husband for your daughter. Do not choose for her a rich husband.

Spend one year consuming the property that you have on hand, so that you spend three years [...] the bank.

Do not take an impious woman as your wife, lest she give impious instruction to your children.

If a woman is at peace with her husband, they do not ever fare badly.

If a woman whispers about her husband, [they do not] ever fare well.

25/20 If a woman does not desire the property of her husband, another man is in her heart.

A lowly woman has no life.

A bad woman has no husband.

The wife of a fool beats her [...] while they say: "My [...]."

I have no [...] I have no [...].

26/1 [...] it.

[...] while it is bitter to drink it.

[There is a ... for] sending a man out.

[There is] a stick for bringing him inside.

26/5 There is imprisonment for granting life.

There is release for killing.

There is one who hoards who does not control.

They are all in the hand of fate and god.

44. Lit. "custom"; cf. ⲤⲰⲚⲦ (CD, 346a).

All sickness is painful. It is the wise man who knows how to be sick.

26/10 It is to the one who has done it that a thing happens.
It is to the heart that god looks.[45]

It is in battle that [a man finds] for himself a brother.
It is on the road that a man finds for himself a companion.

The plans of god are one thing, the thoughts [of men] are another.
26/15 The plans of the fisherman are one thing, [the will of god(?)] is different from them.

If a merchant finds a merchant, he will [...].

There is one who plows, who does not [reap].
There is one who reaps, who does not [eat].

The one who has sickness in his wheat, do not [...].

26/20 The one who bears scorn [...].
The one who digs a pit [is the one who falls] into [it].

I love my friend [...] outside.

There is no great strength [...].

27/1 [...].

Reckon the extent of [...] his house daily.

A troublemaker who does not know [...].

Do not cause another to fare well [... and] you fare badly yourself.

If [...] it is on the ground.

It is [...] that they [...].

If a woman is of more exalted birth than her husband, let him give way to her.

You have caused [...] say to him: "Do not!," he will say: "I will!"

---

45. These sentences seem to form a couplet, linking retribution and reward with divine oversight.

If you are commanded [...], it is your body that made its bad condition.

27/10 The instruction of another does not enter into the heart of a fool. What is in his heart is in his heart.

Do not say [...] disdain.

Instruction [...] because of god.

A man who fights with those of his town is a poor man forever.

Do not dwell in a house [that] is cursed by god, lest his destruction turn against you.

27/15 Do not cause [...] against you.

If a wise man is abandoned [...] he perishes.

If I do [...] I find my justice.
If I fear [...].

If you do not [...], to whom should you cry out concerning the bitterness?

27/20 Do not [...] your enemy [...].

If you are troubled, [...] god.

Do not call [... before] your master, when he is not with you.

[...] a jug measure [...] upward [...] kind.

28/1 [Do not ...]

Do not say: "I am rich in property," and so belittle[46] the one greater than you.

Speak in a pleasant voice [to] your servants [...].

Do not take a merchant as your friend. He lives by taking a cut.

28/5 Do not let [...] linger, without having inquired about it.

Let [...] reach [...] cause that god succeed to her [...].

---

46. Reading *[ti] sbk.*

Do not often speak your anger to a common man, lest you be scorned.

Do not often speak [...] to a common man, lest he be destroyed by accusation.

Do not [...], lest he discover what you will do.

28/10 Do not be weary of calling to god. He has his hour for listening to the scribe.[47]

*WRITTEN*

47. This translation follows the traditional interpretation, by which the final line provides an apt conclusion to the frame story of the imprisoned scribe 'Onchsheshonqy. The word for "scribe" is considered a sectional marker ("written") in Zauzich, "Anchscheschonqi—eine Lehre für den Schreiber?" 376–80, but this seems unnecessarily redundant with the following marker in l. 11.

# BIBLIOGRAPHY

T his bibliography is selective, with emphasis on "recent" publications. For additional items, consult the bibliographies in Lichtheim's Ancient Egyptian Literature, vols. 1–3, and Parkinson's The Tale of Sinuhe. For the individual texts, the main hieroglyphic text is cited first, followed by the entry in LÄ (W. Helck et al., eds., Lexikon der Ägyptologie), and for the Demotic texts, the listing in Marc Depauw's A Companion to Demotic Studies. More attention is accorded to strictly literary texts, such as Sinuhe and The Tale of the Two Brothers. Texts which are primarily historical or religious are treated summarily or omitted, since an extensive treatment would increase the size of the bibliography substantially.

W.K.S.

## GENERAL

Anthes, Rudolph, "Egyptian Theology in the Third Millennium B.C.," JNES 18, 1959, 169–212.

Assmann, Aleida, "The History of the Text Before the Era of Literature: Three Comments," in G. Moers, ed., Lingua Aegyptia: Studia monographica 2: Definitely: Egyptian Literature, Göttingen, 1999, 83–90.

Assmann, Jan, "Der literarische Text im alten Ägypten: Versuch einer Begriffsbestimmung," *OLZ* 69, 1974, 117–26.

——, "Weisheit, Loyalismus und Frömmigkeit," in Erik Hornung and Othmar Keel, eds., *Studien zu Altägyptischen Lebenslehren,* OBO 28, Freiburg/Göttingen, 1979, 11–72.

——, "Schrift, Tod und Identität. Das Grab als Vorschule der Literatur in alten Ägypten," in Aleida Assmann, Jan Assmann, and Christof Hardmeier, eds., *Beiträge zur Archäologie der literarischen Kommunikation,* Munich, 1983, 64–93.

——, "Gibt es eine 'Klassik' in der ägyptischen Literaturgeschichte? Ein Beitrag zur Geistesgeschichte der Ramessidenzeit," *ZDMG* supp. 6, 1985, 35–52.

——, "Sepulkrale Selbstthematisierung im Alten Ägypten," in Alois Hahn and Volker Kapp, eds., *Selbstthematisierung und Selbstzeugnis: Bekenntnis und Geständnis,* Frankfurt, 1987, 208–32.

——, in Otto Kaiser, ed., TUAT II/6: *Lieder und Gebete* II, 1991.

——, "Egyptian Literature," in D. N. Friedman, ed., *The Anchor Bible Dictionary* II, New York, 1992, 378–90.

——, "Grundformen hymnischer Rede im Alten Ägypten," in A. Loprieno, ed., *Ancient Egyptian Literature: History and Forms,* Leiden, 1996, 335–47.

——, "Kulturelle und literarische Texte," in A. Loprieno, ed., *Ancient Egyptian Literature: History and Forms,* Leiden, 1996, 59–82.

——, "Der literarische Aspekt des ägyptischen Grabes und seine Funktion im Rahmen des 'monumentalen Diskurses,'" in A. Loprieno, ed., *Ancient Egyptian Literature: History and Forms,* Leiden, 1996, 97–104.

——, "Cultural and Literary Texts," in G. Moers, ed., *Lingua Aegyptia: Studia monographica 2: Definitely: Egyptian Literature,* Göttingen, 1999, 1–15.

——, "Literatur zwischen Kult und Politik: zur Geschichte des Textes vor dem Zeitalter der Literatur, in Jan Assmann and Elke Blumenthal, eds., *Literatur und Politik im pharaonischen Ägypten,* IFAO, BdE 127, Cairo, 1999, 3–22.

Assmann, Jan, and Elke Blumenthal, eds., *Literatur und Politik im pharaonischen Ägypten,* IFAO, BdE 127, Cairo, 1999.

Assmann, Jan, Erika Feucht, and Reinhard Grieshammer, eds., *Fragen an die altägyptische Literatur: Studien zum Gedenken an Eberhard Otto,* Wiesbaden, 1977.

Baines, John, "Classicism and Modernism in the Literature of the New Kingdom," in A. Loprieno, ed., *Ancient Egyptian Literature: History and Forms,* Leiden, 1996, 157–74.

——, "Myth and Literature," in A. Loprieno, ed., *Ancient Egyptian Literature: History and Forms,* Leiden, 1996, 361–77.

——, "Prehistories of Literature: Performance, Fiction, Myth," in G. Moers, ed., *Lingua Aegyptia: Studia monographica 2: Definitely: Egyptian Literature,* Göttingen, 1999, 17–41.

——, "Research on Egyptian Literature: Background, Definitions, Prospects," Eighth International Congress of Egyptologists, Cairo, forthcoming.

Beinlich-Seeber, Christine, *Bibliographie Altägypten 1822–1946, ÄAbh* 61, 3 vols., Wiesbaden, 1998.

Bleiberg, E., "Economic Man and the Truly Silent One: Cultural Conditioning and the Economy in Ancient Egypt," *JSSEA* 24, 1994 (pub. 1998), 4–16. Considerations of the wisdom literature of various periods in respect to the goals advanced, the audiences targeted, and the changes over time.

Blumenthal, Elke, "Die literarische Verarbeitung der Übergangszeit zwischen Altem und Mittleren Reich," in A. Loprieno, ed., *Ancient Egyptian Literature: History and Forms,* Leiden, 1996, 105–35.

——, "Prolegomena zu einer Klassifizierung der Ägyptischen Literatur," in C. J. Eyre, ed., *Proceedings of the Seventh International Congress of Egyptologists,* OLA 82, 1998, 173–83.

Bresciani, Edda, *Letteratura e Poesia dell'Antico Egitto,* Turin, 1969.

Brunner, Hellmut, "Die 'Weisen,' ihre 'Lehren' und 'Prophezeiungen' in altägyptischen Sicht," *ZÄS* 93, 1966, 29–35.

——, *Grundzüge einer Geschichte der altägyptischen Literatur,* Darmstadt, 1966.

——, "Lehren," *LÄ* III, 1979, 964–68.

——. "Zitate aus Lebenslehren," in Erik Hornung and Othmar Keel, eds., *Studien zu Altägyptischen Lebenslehren,* OBO 28, Freiburg/ Göttingen, 1979, 105–71.

——, *Altägyptische Weisheit,* 2d ed., Zurich, 1991.

——, "Vorbild und Gegenbild in Biographien, Lehren und Anweisungen," in Alan B. Lloyd, ed., *Studies in Pharaonic Religion and Society in Honour of J. Gwyn Griffiths,* London, 1992, 164–68.

Brunner-Traut, Emma, *Altägyptische Märchen,* 8th ed. Munich, 1989.

Burkard, Günter, *Textkritische Untersuchungen zu ägyptischen Weisheitslehren des alten und mittleren Reiches,* ÄAbh 34, Wiesbaden, 1977.

——, "Der Formale Aufbau altägyptische Literaturwerke: Zur Problematik der Erschliessung seiner Grundstruktur," *SÄK* 10, 1983, 79–118. With particular emphasis on "metrics," including bibliography on the subject.

——, "Metrik, Prosodie und formaler Aufbau ägyptischer literarischer Texte," in A. Loprieno, ed., *Ancient Egyptian Literature: History and Forms,* Leiden, 1996, 447–63.

Cannuyer, Christian, "Variations sur le thème de ville dans les maximes sapientiales de l'ancienne Egypte," *CdE* 64, 1989, 44–54. Mainly demotic situation, but earlier also. Village as xenophobic/egocentric. Not open city concept.

Chappaz, Jean-Luc, "Quelques reflexions sur les conteurs dans la littérature égyptienne ancienne," in A. Guillaumont, ed., *Hommages à François Daumas* I, Montpellier, 1986, 103–8. On audience, plural *mtn* as well as *mk.*

Collier, Mark, "The Language of Literature: On Grammar and Texture," in A. Loprieno, ed., *Ancient Egyptian Literature: History and Forms,* Leiden, 1996, 531–53.

Coulon, Laurent, "La rhétorique et ses fictions: Pouvoirs et duplicité du discours à travers la littérature égyptienne du Moyen et du Nouvel Empire," *BIFAO* 99, 1999, 103–32.

Demidchik, A. E., "The 'Region of the Northern Residence' in Middle Kingdom Literature," in C. J. Eyre, ed., *Proceedings of the Seventh International Congress of Egyptologists,* OLA 82, 1998, 325–30.

Derchain, Philippe, "Allusion, citation, intertextualité," in M. Minas and J. Zeidler, eds., *Aspekte spätägyptischer Kultur. Festschrift . . . Winter,* Aegyptiaca Treverensia 7, Mainz, 1994, 69–76.

——, "Auteur et société," in A. Loprieno, ed., *Ancient Egyptian Literature: History and Forms,* Leiden, 1996, 83–94.

——, "Théologie et littérature," in A. Loprieno, ed., *Ancient Egyptian Literature: History and Forms,* Leiden, 1996, 351–60.

Erman, A. ed., *The Ancient Egyptians: A Sourcebook of Their Writings,* trans. Aylward M. Blackman, introduction to the Torchbook edition by William Kelly Simpson, New York, 1966.

Eyre, Christopher J., "Fate, Crocodiles, and the Judgment of the Dead," *SÄK* 4, 1976, 103–14.

——, "Is Egyptian Historical Literature 'Historical' or 'Literary'?" in A. Loprieno, ed., *Ancient Egyptian Literature: History and Forms,* Leiden, 1996, 415–33.

Faulkner, R. O., *The Ancient Egyptian Pyramid Texts,* Oxford, 1969.

——, *The Ancient Egyptian Coffin Texts,* 3 vols., Warminster, 1973, 1977, 1978.

——, *The Egyptian Book of the Dead: The Book of Coming Forth by Day,* with contributions by O. Goelet et al., Cairo, 1998.

Fecht, G., "Die Wiedergewinnung der altägyptischen Verskunst," *MDAIK* 19, 1963, 54–96.

——, "Die Form der altägyptischen Literatur: Metrische und stilistische Analyse," *ZÄS* 91, 1964, 11–63; *ZÄS* 92, 1965, 10–32.

——, *Literarische Zeugnisse zur 'Persönlichen Frömmigkeit' in Ägypten,* Abhandlungen der Heidelberger Akademie der Wissenschaften, Phil-hist. Klasse 1965, 1. Abh., Heidelberg, 1965.

——, "The Structural Principle of Ancient Egyptian Elevated Language," in J. C. de Moor and W. G. E. Watson, eds., *Verse in Ancient Near Eastern Prose,* Wiesbaden, 1993, 69–94.

Fermat, André, and Michel Lapidus, *Les prophéties de l'Egypte ancienne, Textes traduits et commentés,* Paris, 1999.

Fischer-Elfert, Hans-W., "Die Arbeit am Text: Altägyptischer Literaturwerke aus philologischer Perspektive," in A. Loprieno, ed., *Ancient Egyptian Literature: History and Forms,* Leiden, 1996, 499–513.

Foster, John L., *Echoes of Egyptian Voices: An Anthology of Ancient Egyptian Poetry.* Norman, 1992.

——, *Hymns, Prayers and Songs: An Anthology of Ancient Egyptian Lyric Poetry,* Atlanta, 1995.

——, *Ancient Egyptian Literature: An Anthology,* Austin, 2001.

Foti, L., "The History in the Prophecies of Noferti: Relation between the Egyptian Wisdom and Prophecy Literatures," *StudAeg* 2, 1976, 3–18.

Fox, Michael, "Two Decades of Research in Egyptian Wisdom Literature," *ZÄS* 107, 1980, 120–35.

Görg, M., "Komparatistische Untersuchungen an ägyptischer und israelitischer Literatur," in Jan Assmann, Erika Feucht, Reinhard Grieshammer, eds., *Fragen an die altägyptische Literatur: Studien zum Gedenken an Eberhard Otto,* Wiesbaden, 1977, 197–216.

Grandet, Pierre, *Contes de l'Egypte ancienne,* Paris, 1998.

Grapow, Hermann, "Beiträge zur Untersuchung des Stils ägyptischer Lieder," *ZÄS* 79, 1954, 17–27.

Guglielmi, Waltraud, "Probleme bei der Anwendung der Begriffe 'Komik,' 'Ironie,' und 'Humor' auf die altägyptische Literatur," *GM* 36, 1979, 69–85.

——, "Zu einigen literarischen Funktionen des Wortspiels," in F. Junge, ed., *Studien zur Sprache und Religions Ägyptens zu Ehren von Wolfhart Westendorf* I, Göttingen, 1984, 491–506.

——, "Der Gerbrauch rhetorische Stilmittel in der ägyptischen Literatur," in A. Loprieno, ed., *Ancient Egyptian Literature: History and Forms,* Leiden, 1996, 465–97.

Guksch, Heike, "Sehnsucht nach der Heimatstadt: ein ramessidische Thema?" *MDAIK* 50, 1994, 101–6.

Gumbrecht, H. U., "Does Egyptology Need a Theory of Literature," in A. Loprieno, ed., *Ancient Egyptian Literature: History and Forms,* Leiden, 1996, 3–18.

Helck, W., "Zur Frage der Entstehung der ägyptischen Literatur," *WZKM* 63/64, 1972, 6–26.

Helck, W., E. Otto, and W. Westendorf, eds., *Lexikon der Ägyptologie* I– VII, Wiesbaden, 1972–92.

Herrmann, Siegfried, *Untersuchungen zur Überlieferungsgestalt mittelägyptischer Literaturwerke,* Berlin, 1957.

Hollis, Susan Tower, "Tales of Magic and Wonder from Ancient Egypt," in Jack Sasson, ed., *Civilizations of the Ancient Near East* IV, New York, 1995, 2255–64.

Hornung, Erik, *Altägyptische Dichtung,* Stuttgart, 1996.

Hornung, Erik, and Othmar Keel, eds., *Studien zu Altägyptischen Lebenslehren,* OBO 28, Freiburg/Göttingen, 1979.

Israelit-Groll, Sarah, ed., *Studies in Egyptology Presented to Miriam Lichtheim,* 2 vols., Jerusalem, 1990.

Janssen, Jozef M. A.; Heerma Van Voss, M. S. H. G.; Zonhoven, L. M. J.; and Hovestreydt, W., *Annual Egyptological Bibliography, 1947–1999,* Leiden and Warminster, 1947–99.

Junge, Friedrich, "Die Welt der Klagen," in Jan Assmann, Erika Feucht, and Reinhard Grieshammer, eds., *Fragen an die altägyptische Literatur: Studien zum Gedenken an Eberhard Otto,* Wiesbaden, 1977, 275–84.

Kaiser, Otto, ed., *Texte aus dem Umwelt des Alten Testaments* I/1–6; II/1–6; III/1–6 + Ergänzungslieferung, Gütersloh, 1982–2001.

Kaplony, Peter, "Die Definition der schönen Literatur in alten Ägypten," in Jan Assmann, Erika Feucht, Reinhard Grieshammer, eds., *Fragen an die altägyptische Literatur: Studien zum Gedenken an Eberhard Otto,* Wiesbaden, 1977, 289–314.

Kitchen, K. A., "Proverbs and Wisdom Books of the Ancient Near East: The Factual History of a Literary Form," *Tyndale Bulletin* 28, 1977, 69–114.

——, *Poetry of Ancient Egypt,* Jonsered, 1999. Extensive review by Robyn Gillam in *CdE* 76, 2001, 100–115.

Korostovtsev, A., "A propos du genre "historique" dans la littérature de l'ancienne Egypte," in Jan Assmann, Erika Feucht, and Reinhard Grieshammer, eds., *Fragen an die altägyptische Literatur: Studien zum Gedenken an Eberhard Otto,* Wiesbaden, 1977, 315–24.

Lalouette, Claire, *Textes sacrés et textes profanes de l'ancienne Egypte,* I: *Des Pharaons et des hommes,* Paris, 1984; II: *Mythes, contes et poésie,* Paris, 1987.

Leclant, J., ed. *Les Sagesses du Proche-Orient Ancien,* Paris, 1963. With articles by J. Leclant, H. Cazelles, J. Nougayrol, P. Montet, S. Morenz, A. Volten, H. Brunner, W. Zimmerli, H. Gaese, G. Posener, J. Sainte Fare Garnot, J. Vergote, and B. van de Walle.

Lefebvre, G., *Romans et contes égyptiens de l'époque pharaonique,* Paris, 1949.

Lesko, Leonard H., "Some Comments on Ancient Egyptian Literacy and Literati," in S. I. Groll, ed., *Studies in Honour of Miriam Lichtheim* II, Jerusalem, 1990, 656–67.

Lichtheim, Miriam, "Have the Principles of Ancient Egyptian Metrics Been Discovered?" *JARCE* 9, 1971, 103–10.

——, *Ancient Egyptian Literature:* I *The Old and Middle Kingdoms;* II *The New Kingdom;* III *The Late Period,* Berkeley, 1973, 1976, 1980.

——, "Some Corrections to My *Ancient Egyptian Literature* I–III," *GM* 41, 1980, 67–74.

——, *Ancient Egyptian Autobiographies Chiefly of the Middle Kingdom,* OBO 84, Freiburg/Göttingen, 1988.

——, "Didactic Literature," in A. Loprieno, ed., *Ancient Egyptian Literature: History and Forms,* Leiden, 1996, 243–62.

——, *Moral Values in Ancient Egypt,* OBO 155, Göttingen, 1997.

Loprieno, A., *Topos und Mimesis: zum Bild des Ausländers in der ägyptischen Literatur,* ÄAbh 48, 1988.

——, "Defining Egyptian Literature: Ancient Texts and Modern Literary Theory," in Jerold S. Cooper and Glenn M. Schwartz, eds., *The Study of the Ancient Near East in the Twenty-First Century: The William Foxwell Albright Centennial Conference,* Winona Lake, Ind., 1996, 209–32.

——, "Defining Egyptian Literature: Ancient Texts and Modern Theories," in A. Loprieno, ed., *Ancient Egyptian Literature: History and Forms,* Probleme der Ägyptologie 10, Leiden, 1996, 39–58.

——, "The 'King's Novel,' " in A. Loprieno, ed., *Ancient Egyptian Literature: History and Forms,* Leiden, 1996, 277–95.

——, "Linguistic Variety and Egyptian Literature," in A. Loprieno, ed., *Ancient Egyptian Literature: History and Forms,* Leiden, 1996, 515–29.

Loprieno, A., ed., *Ancient Egyptian Literature: History and Forms,* Leiden, 1996.

Manuelian, Peter Der, ed., *Studies in Honor of William Kelly Simpson,* 2 vols., Boston, 1996.

McDowell, A. G., *Village Life in Ancient Egypt: Laundry Lists and Love Songs,* New York, 1999.

Moers, Gerald, "Fiktionalität und Intertextualität als Parameter ägyptologischer Literaturwissenschaft. Perspektiven und Grenzen der Anwendung zeitgenössischer Literaturtheorie," in Jan Assmann and Elke Blumenthal, eds., *Literatur und Politik im pharaonischen Ägypten,* IFAO, BdE 127, Cairo, 1999, 37–52.

——, *Fingierte Welten in der ägyptischen Literatur des 2. Jahrtausends v. Chr.: Grenzüberschreitung, Reisemotiv und Fiktionalität,* Leiden, 2001.

——, "Travel as Narrative in Egyptian Literature," in G. Moers, ed., *Lingua Aegyptia: Studia monographica 2: Definitely: Egyptian Literature,* Göttingen, 1999, 43–61.

Moers, Gerald, ed., *Lingua Aegyptia: Studia monographica 2: Definitely: Egyptian Literature,* Göttingen, 1999.

Morenz, Ludwig D., *Beiträge zur Schriftlichkeitskultur im Mittleren Reich und in der 2. Zwischenzeit,* ÄUAT 29, 1996.

Patané, Massimo, "Existe-t-il dans l'Egypte ancienne une littérature licencieuse?" *BSEG* 15, 1991, 91–94.

Parkinson, R. B., *Voices from Ancient Egypt: An Anthology of Middle Kingdom Writings* London, 1991.

——, "Teachings, Discourses and Tales from the Middle Kingdom," in S. Quirke, ed., *Middle Kingdom Studies,* New Malden, 1991, 91–122.

——, "Individual and Society in Middle Kingdom literature," in A. Loprieno, ed., *Ancient Egyptian Literature: History and Forms,* Leiden, 1996, 137–55.

——, "Types of Literature in the Middle Kingdom," in A. Loprieno, ed., *Ancient Egyptian Literature: History and Forms,* Leiden, 1996, 297–312.

——, *The Tale of Sinuhe and Other Ancient Egyptian Poems, 1940–1640 BC,* Oxford, 1997.

——, "The Dream and the Knot: Contextualizing Middle Kingdom Literature," in G. Moers, ed., *Lingua Aegyptia: Studia monographica* 2: *Definitely: Egyptian Literature,* Göttingen, 1999, 63–82.

——, *Poetry and Culture in Middle Kingdom Egypt: A Dark Side to Perfection,* London and New York, 2002.

Peet, T. Eric, *A Comparative Study of the Literatures of Egypt, Palestine, and Mesopotamia: Egypt's Contribution to the Literature of the Ancient World,* London, 1929.

Perdu, Olivier, "Ancient Egyptian Autobiographies," in Jack Sasson, ed., *Civilizations of the Ancient Near East* IV, New York, 1995, 2243–54.

Pestman, P. W., "Who Were the Owners, in the 'Community of Workmen,' of the Chester Beatty Papyri?" in R. J. Demarée and Jac. J. Janssen, eds., *Gleanings from Deir el-Medina,* Leiden, 1982, 157–72.

Piccato, Aldo, "The Berlin Leather Roll and the Egyptian Sense of History," *Lingua Aegyptia* 5, 1997, 137–59. General considerations on the idea of history in literature with respect also to the Prophecy of Neferty and Middle Kingdom literature, the Kamose texts, and the "historicity of foreign people."

Posener, Georges, "Les Richesses inconnues de la littérature égyptienne (Recherches littéraires I)," *RdE* 6, 1951, 27–48; "Section finale d'une sagesse inconnue (Recherches littéraires, II), *RdE* 7, 1950, 71–84; "Ostraca inédits du Musée de Turin (Recherches littéraires, III)," *RdE* 8, 1951, 171–89.

——, *Littérature et politique dans l'Egypte de la XIIe Dynastie,* Paris, 1956.

——, *Literature,* chap. 9 in J. R. Harris, ed., *The Legacy of Egypt,* Oxford, 1971, 220–56.

Quirke, Stephen, "Frontier or Border? The North-west Delta in Middle Kingdom Texts," in *Proceedings of Colloquium: The Archaeology, Geography, and History of the Egyptian Delta in Pharaonic Times, DE,* Special Number 1, Oxford, 1989, 261–75. With special attention to Middle Kingdom literary texts.

——, "Archive," in A. Loprieno, ed., *Ancient Egyptian Literature: History and Forms,* Leiden, 1996, 379–401.

——, "Narrative literature," in A. Loprieno, ed., *Ancient Egyptian Literature: History and Forms,* Leiden, 1996, 263–76.

Redford, Donald B., "Ancient Egyptian Literature: An Overview," in Jack Sasson, ed., *Civilizations of the Ancient Near East* IV, New York, 1995, 2223–41.

Redford, Donald B., ed., *The Oxford Encyclopedia of Ancient Egypt,* 3 vols., New York, 2000. Contains articles on almost all of the texts in the present anthology.

Roccati, Alessandro, "Magia e letteratura nell'Egitto del II millennio A.C.," in *Mélanges Adolphe Gutbub,* Montpellier, 1984, 201–10.

——, *Sapienza egizia: La letteratura educativa in Egitto durante il II millennio a. C.,* Brescia, 1994. Translations with excellent up-to-date bibliography of Hardedef, Kagemni, Ptahhotep, Merikare, Amenemhet I, Khety, Loyalist Instruction, Man to His Son, Ani, Amenemope, Amennakht.

Roeder, Günther, *Altägyptischen Erzählungen und Märchen,* Jena, 1927.

Sasson, Jack, ed., *Civilization of the Ancient Near East* I–IV, 1995, 1751–61. Many essays of interest, of which only a few are noted here.

Schenkel, Wolfgang, "Zur Relevanz der altägyptischen 'Metrik,'" *MDAIK* 28, 1972, 103–7.

——, "Sonst—Jetzt: Variationen eines literarischen Formelelements," *WdO* 15, 1984, 51–61. Passus such as he who was (once) rich is (now) poor. etc. Bad/Good; Good/Bad in Admonitions, Neferty, Instruction of a Man. Peasant: He who (should do) . . . (now) does.

——, "Ägyptische Literatur und ägyptologische Forschung: eine wissenschaftsgeschichtliche Einleitung," in A. Loprieno, ed., *Ancient Egyptian Literature: History and Forms,* Leiden, 1996, 21–38.

——, "Littérature et politique: Fragstellung oder Antwort? Zwei Diskussionsbeiträge," in Jan Assmann and Elke Blumenthal, eds.,

*Literatur und Politik im pharaonischen Ägypten,* IFAO, BdE 127, Cairo, 1999, 63–74.

Schlichting, R., "Prophetie," *LA* IV, 1982, 1122–25.

Shirun, Irene, "Parallelismus Membrorum und Vers," in Jan Assmann, Erika Feucht, and Reinhard Grieshammer, *Fragen an die altägyptische Literatur: Studien zum Gedenken an Eberhard Otto,* Wiesbaden, 1977, 463–92.

Shirun-Grumach, Irene, "Bemerkungen zu Rythmus, Form und Inhalt in der Weisheit," in Erik Hornung and Othmar Keel, eds., *Studien zu Altägyptischen Lebenslehren,* OBO 28, Freiburg/Göttingen, 1979, 317–52.

Shupak, Nili, "Stylistic and Terminological Traits Common to Biblical and Egyptian Literature," *WdO* 14, 1983, 216–30.

——, "Egyptian 'Prophecy' and Biblical Prophecy: Did the Phenomenon of Prophecy, in the Biblical Sense, Exist in Ancient Egypt?" *JEOL* 31, 1989–90, x–xx.

——, *Where Can Wisdom Be Found? The Sage's Language in the Bible and Ancient Egyptian Literature,* OBO 130, Freiburg, 1993.

——, " 'Canon' and 'Canonization' in Ancient Egypt," *BiOr* 58, 2001, 536–47.

Simpson, William K., "*Belles lettres* and propaganda," in A. Loprieno, ed., *Ancient Egyptian Literature: History and Forms,* Leiden, 1996, 435–43.

Spalinger, A., Review of Lichtheim, *Ancient Egyptian Literature,* vol. 2, *OLZ* 74, 1979, 525–27. With an important analysis and designation of the literary genres.

Suhr, Claudia, "Zum fiktiven Erzähler in der ägyptischen Literatur," in G. Moers, ed., *Lingua Aegyptia: Studia monographica 2: Definitely: Egyptian Literature,* Göttingen, 1999, 91–129.

Tobin, V. A., "Myth and Politics in the Old Kingdom of Egypt," *BiOr* 59, 1991, 605–36.

van der Walle, B., *La transmission des textes littéraires égyptiens,* Brussels, 1948.

——, *L'Humour dans la littérature et dans l'art de l'Ancienne Egypte,* Leiden, 1969.

——, "Humor," *LÄ* III, 1977, 73–77.

Verhoeven, Ursula, "Von hieratischen Literaturwerke in der Spätzeit," in Jan Assmann and Elke Blumenthal, eds., *Literatur und Politik im pharaonischen Ägypten,* IFAO, BdE 127, Cairo, 1999, 255–65.

Vernus, Pascal, "Langue littéraire et diglossie," in A. Loprieno, ed., *Ancient Egyptian Literature: History and Forms,* Leiden, 1996, 555–64.

——, *Sagesses de l'Egypte pharaonique,* Imprimerie Nationale, 2001. A major study with introductions, translations, and extensive notes to all pharaonic wisdom texts and instructions. References to this study are not indicated in the translations in the present anthology, since Vernus's work appeared too late for inclusion.

Vittmann, Günter, *Altägyptische Wegmetaphorik,* Beiträge zur Ägyptologie 15, Vienna, 1999.

Wessetsky, V., "An die Grenze von Literatur und Geschichte," in Jan Assmann, Erika Feucht, and Reinhard Grieshammer, eds., *Fragen an die altägyptische Literatur: Studien zum Gedenken an Eberhard Otto,* Wiesbaden, 1977, 499–502.

Williams, R. J., "Scribal Training in Ancient Egypt," *JAOS* 92, 1972, 214–21.

——, "The Sages of Ancient Egypt in the Light of Recent Scholarship," *JAOS* 101, 1981, 1–14.

Yoyotte, Jean, "A propos d'un monument copié par G. Daressy (Contribution à l'histoire littéraire), *BSFE* 11, 1952, 67–72.

## DEMOTIC LITERATURE, GENERAL BIBLIOGRAPHY

Depauw, Mark, *A Companion to Demotic Studies,* Brussels, 1997.

Tait, W. John, "Demotic Literature and Egyptian Society," in Janet H. Johnson, ed., *Life in a Multi-Cultural Society: Egypt from Cambyses to Constantine and Beyond,* SAOC 51, Chicago, 1992, 303–10.

——, "Egyptian Fiction in Demotic and Greek," in J. R. Morgan and R. Stoneman, eds., *Greek Fiction: The Greek Novel in Context,* London, 1994, 203–22.

——, "Demotic Literature: Forms and Genres," in A. Loprieno, ed., *Ancient Egyptian Literature: History and Forms,* Leiden, 1996, 175–87.

## INDIVIDUAL READINGS

### Admonitions

Gardiner, Alan H., *The Admonitions of an Egyptian Sage, from a Hieratic Papyrus in Leiden,* Leipzig, 1909, 1–95; Helck, Wolfgang, *Die*

*"Admonitions" Pap. Leiden I 344 recto,* Kleine Ägyptische Texte 11, Wiesbaden, 1995.

Spiegel, J., "Admonitions," *LÄ* I, 1975, 65–66.

Barta, Winfried, "Das Gespräch des Ipuwer mit dem Schöpfergott," *SÄK* 1, 1974, 19–33. Agrees with Otto and Fecht that the reproach is addressed to the creator god, a composition of the 1st Intermediate Period incorporated into the similar times of Dynasty 13 by the author.

Faulkner, R. O., "Notes on 'The Admonitions of an Egyptian Sage,' " *JEA* 50, 1964, 24–36.

Fecht, G., *Der Vorwurf on Gott in den 'Mahnwörter des Ipu-wer,'* Abhandlungen der Heidelberger Akademie der Wissenschaften, Phil.-hist. Klasse 1972, I, Heidelberg, 1972.

——, "Ägyptische Zweifel am Sinn des Opfers: Admonitions 5, 7–9," *ZÄS* 100, 1973, 6–16.

Fischer-Elfert, Hans-W., "Kinder des Nackens' oder 'Wunschkinder' in Admonitions 4, 3–4 resp. 5, 6: Ein rein textkritisches Problem?" *ZÄS* 128, 2001, 87–88.

Gilula, M., "Does God Exist?" in D. W. Young, ed., *Studies Presented to Hans Jakob Polotsky,* Boston, 1981, 390–400.

Hermann, S., "Die Auseinandersetzung mit dem Schöpfergott," in Jan Assmann, Erika Feucht, and Reinhard Grieshammer, eds., *Fragen an die altägyptische Literatur: Studien zum Gedenken an Eberhard Otto,* Wiesbaden, 1977, 257–74.

Morenz, Ludwig D., *Beiträge zur Schriftlichtkeitskultur im Mittleren Reich und in der 2. Zwischenzeit,* ÄUAT 29, 1996, 78–106.

——, "Geschichte als Literatur. Reflexe der Ersten Zwischenzeit in den *Mahnworten,*" in Jan Assmann and Elke Blumenthal, eds., *Literatur und Politik im pharaonischen Ägypten,* IFAO, BdE 127, Cairo, 1999, 111–38.

Otto, E., *Der Vorwurf an Gott: zur Entstehung der ägyptischen Auseinandersetzungsliteratur,* Hildesheim, 1951.

Posener, G., "Admonitions 3, 14," *RdE* 5, 1946, 254–55.

Renaud, Odette, "Ipouer le mal-aimé," *BSEG* 12, 1988, 71–75. Distinguishes the text as a theatrical kind of raving, a discourse of exasperation, a railing against the weakness of royal power, a work of real political philosophy, the author an ideologue, the text close to wisdom literature, on a different level from the other "pessimism" texts: Lebensmüder, Neferty (a competent public relations author who wrote an elegant propaganda clip), Khakheperresonbe.

Schott, E., "Admonitions 9, 3," *GM* 13, 1974, 29–30.


## Amasis and the Skipper

Spiegelberg, Wilhelm, *Die sogenannte Demotische Chronik des Pap. 215 der Bibliothèque Nationale zu Paris,* Leipzig, 1914, 26–28, and pls. VI–VIa.

Depauw, Mark, *A Companion to Demotic Studies,* Brussels, 1997, 89–90.

Bresciani, Edda, *Letteratura e Poesia dell'Antico Egitto,* Turin, 1969, 613–14.

Brunner-Traut, Emma, *Altägyptische Märchen,* Düsseldorf and Cologne, 8th ed., 1989, 194–7 and 328–30.

Hoffmann, Friedhelm, "Einige Bemerkungen zur Geschichte von König Amasis und dem Schiffer," *Enchoria* 19/20, 1992–93, 15–21.

Zauzich, Karl-Theodor, "Wie maβ-voll war Amasis?" *Enchoria* 16, 1988, 139–40.


## Amenemhet, Instruction of

Helck, W., *Der Text der 'Lehre Amenemhets I. für seinen Sohn,'* Kleine Ägyptische Texte 1, Wiesbaden, 1969.

Blumenthal, E., "Lehre Amenemhets I," *LÄ* III, 1980, 968–71.

Anthes, R., "Zur Echtheit der Lehre des Amenemhet," in Jan Assmann, Erika Feucht, and Reinhard Grieshammer, eds., *Fragen an die altägyptische Literatur: Studien zum Gedenken an Eberhard Otto,* Wiesbaden, 1977, 41–54.

——, "The Instruction of Amenemhet," JNES 16, 1957, 146–917.

Beckerath, J. v., "Zur Begründung der 12. Dynastie durch Ammenemes I," *ZÄS* 92, 1965, 4–10.

Blumenthal, E., "Die erste Koregenz der 12. Dynastie," *ZÄS* 110, 1983, 104–21.

——, "Die Lehre des Königs Amenemhet," *ZÄS* 111, 1984, 85–107; 112, 1985, 104–15.

Burkard, G., " 'Als Gott erschienen spricht er,' Die Lehre des Amenemhet als postumes Vermächtnis," in Jan Assmann and Elke Blumenthal, eds., *Literatur und Politik im pharaonischen Ägypten,* IFAO, BdE 127, Cairo, 1999, 153–73. Favors the assumption of a successful assassination in Year 30 of Amenemhet I with no coregency.

Egberts, A., "Python or Worm? Some Aspects of the Rite of Driving the Calves," *GM* 111, 1989, 33–45. sꜣ–tꜣ = worm (grain-eating).

Faulkner, R. O., "Some Notes on the 'Teaching of Amenemmes I to His Son,'" in *Studies Presented to F. Ll. Griffith,* London, 1932, 69–73.

Fischer-Elfert, H.-W., "Textkritische Kleinigkeiten zur 'Lehre des Amenemhet,'" *GM* 70, 1984, 89–90.

Foster, J. L., "The Conclusion to the *Testament of Ammenemes, King of Egypt,*" *JEA* 67, 1981, 36–47.

Goedicke, Hans, *"The Beginning of the Instruction of King Amenemhet,"* *JARCE* 7, 1968, 15–21.

——, *Studies in the Instructions of King Amenemhet I for His Son, VA,* supp. 2, fasc. 1 and 2, 1988, with extensive bibliography.

Grimal, Nicolas, "Le sage, l'eau et le roi," in Bernadette Menu, ed., *Les problèmes institutionnels de l'Eau en Egypte ancienne et dans l'Antiquité méditerranénne,* IFAO, BdE 110, Cairo, 1994, 195–203.

——, "Corégence et association au trone: L'enseignement d'Amenemhat Ier," *BIFAO* 95, 1995, 273–80.

Jansen-Winkeln, Karl, "Das Attentat auf Amenemhet I: Und die erste ägyptische Koregentschaft," *SÄK* 18, 1991, 241–64.

Konrad, K., "Wortverzeichnis und lexikostastische Untersuchung der Lehre Amenemhets," *GM* 169, 1999, 87–100.

Obsomer, C., *Sésostris Ier: Etude chronologique et historique du règne,* Brussels, 1995, 112–33.

Parkinson, R. B., *"The Teaching of Amenemhat I* at el-Amarna: BM EA 57458 and 57479," in: Anthony Leahy and John Tait, eds., *Studies on Ancient Egypt in Honour of H. S. Smith,* London, 1999, 221–226.

Schaefer, A., "Zur Entstehung der Mitregentschaft als Legitimationsprinzip von Herrschaft," *ZÄS* 113, 1986, 44–55.

Thériault, Carolyn A., *"The Instruction of Amenemhet* as Propaganda," *JARCE* 30, 1993, 151–60.

Volten, Aksel, *Zwei Altägyptische Politische Schriften: Die Lehre für König Merikare (Pap. Carlsberg VI) und Die Lehre des König Amenemhet,* Analecta Aegyptiaca IV, Copenhagen, 1945.

Westendorf, W., "Die Menschen als Ebenbilder Pharaos: Bemerkungen zur 'Lehre des Amenemhet' (Abschnitt V)," *GM* 46, 1981, 33–42.

Amenemope

Budge, E. A. Wallis, *Hieratic Papyri in the British Museum,* 2d ser., London, 1923, pls. 1–14; Lange, H. O., *Das Weissheitsbuch des Amenemope aus dem Papyrus 10,474 des British Museum,* Copenhagen, 1925.

Shirun-Grumach, I., "Lehre des Amenemope," *LÄ* III, 1979, 971–74.

Alt, Albrecht, "Zur literarischen Analyse der Weisheit des Amenemope," in *Wisdom in Israel and in the Ancient Near East* = Supplements to *Vetus Testamentum* III, Leiden, 1955, 16–25.

Altenmüller, H., "Bemerkungen zu Kapitel 13 der Lehre des Amenemope (Am. 15, 19–16, 14)," in M. Görg, ed., *Fontes atque Pontes: Eine Festgabe für Hellmut Brunner,* ÄUAT 5, Wiesbaden, 1983, 1–17.

Drioton, E., "Sur la Sagesse d'Aménémope," in H. Cazelles, ed., *Mélanges bibliques rédigés en l'honneur de André Robert,* Paris, 1957, 254–80.

——, "Le Livre des Proverbes et la Sagesse d'Aménémope," in J. Coppens, A. Descamps, and E. Massaux, eds., *Sacra Pagina: Miscellanea biblica congressus internationalis Catholici de re biblica* I, Paris, 1959, 229–41.

Fischer-Elfert, Hans W., "Dein Heisser in pAnastasi V 7, 5–8, 1 und seine Beziehung zur Lehre des Amenemope Kap 2–4," *WdO* 14, 1983, 83–90.

——, "Vermischtes: Amenemope und der Spucknapf ('Spitoon')," *GM* 127, 1992, 33–47.

Goedicke, Hans, "The Teaching of Amenemope, Chapter XX," *RdE* 46, 1995, 99–106.

Griffith, F. Ll., "The Teaching of Amenophis the Son of Kanakht, Papyrus B.M. 10474," *JEA* 12, 1926, 191–231.

Grumach, Irene, *Untersuchungen zur Lebenslehre des Amenope,* MÄS 23, Munich, 1972.

Hannig, Rainer H. G., "Amenemope—5. Kapitel. Ein Textprofil," in Dieter Kessler and Regine Schulz, eds., *Gedenkschrift für Winfried Barta,* MÄU 4, Munich, 1995, 179–98.

Israeli, Shlomit, "Chapter Four of the Wisdom Book of Amenemope," in Sarah Israelit-Groll, ed., *Studies in Egyptology Presented to Miriam Lichtheim* I, Jerusalem, 1990, 464–84.

Iversen, E., "Amenemope: Some Suggestions," *ZÄS* 123, 1996, 41–45.

Kaiser, M., "Agathon und Amenemope," *ZÄS* 92, 1966, 102–5.

Petersen, B. J., "A New Fragment of the Wisdom of Amenemope," *JEA* 52, 1966, 120–28.

——, "A Note on the Wisdom of Amenemope 3.9–4.10," *StudAeg* 1, Budapest, 1974, 323–28.

Posener, Georges, "Amenemope 22, 9–10 et l'infirmité du crocodile," in Wofgang Helck, ed., *Festschrift für Siegfried Schott zu seinem 70. Geburtstag am 20, August 1967,* Wiesbaden, 1968, 106–11.

——, "Le chapitre IV d'Aménémope," *ZÄS* 99, 1973, 129–35.

Ruffle, John, "The Teaching of Amenemope and Its Connection with the Book of Proverbs," *Tyndale Bulletin* 28, 1977, 29–68.

Shirun-Grumach, Irene, in Otto Kaiser, ed., TUAT III/2: *Weisheitstexte* II, 1991, 222–50.

Shupak, Nili, *Where Can Wisdom Be Found: The Sage's Language in the Bible and in Ancient Egyptian Literature,* OBO 130, Göttingen, 1993.

Simpson, D. C. "The Hebrew Book of Proverbs and the Teaching of Amenophis," *JEA* 12, 1926, 232–39.

Vernus, Pascal, *Essai sur la conscience de l'Histoire dans l'Egypte pharaonique,* Paris, 1995, 24–33. On chap. 5.

Washington, Harold C., *Wealth and Poverty in the Instruction of Amenemope and the Hebrew Proverbs,* SBL Dissertation Series, Atlanta, 1994.

Williams, R. J. "The Alleged Semitic Original of the *Wisdom of Amenemope,*" *JEA* 47, 1961, 100–106.

Amunnakhte, Instruction of

Bickel, Susanne, and Bernard Mathieu, "L'Ecrivain Amennakht et son *Enseignement,*" *BIFAO* 93, 1993, 31–51.

Helck, W., "Lehren, verschiedene," *LÄ* III, 1979, 991–92.

von Beckerath, Jürge, "Ostrakon München ÄS 393," *SAK* 10, 1983, 63–69.

Williams, R. J., "Scribal Training in Ancient Egypt," *JAOS* 92, 1972, 214–21.

Apophis and Seknenre

Gardiner, Alan H., *Late-Egyptian Stories,* Bibliotheca Aegyptiaca 1, Brussels, 1932, xiii, 85–89.

Brunner, H., "Apophis und Seqenenre," *LÄ* I, 1973, 353–54.

Goedicke, Hans, *The Quarrel of Apophis and Seqenenre,* San Antonio, 1986.

Hofmann, Inge, "Der rechtmässige Herrscher als Nilpferdjäger," *GM* 45, 1981, 19.

Störk, L., "Was störte den Hyksos am Gebrüll der thebanischen Nilpferde?" *GM* 43, 1981, 67–68.


Astarte Text

Gardiner, Alan H., *Late-Egyptian Stories,* Bibliotheca Aegyptiaca 1, Brussels, 1932, xii, 76–81.

Stadelmann, Rainer, "Astartepapyrus," *LÄ* I, 1975, 509–11.

Collombert, Philippe, and Laurent Coulon, "Les dieux contre la mer: Le début du 'papyrus d'Astarte' (pBN 202)," *BIFAO* 100, 2001, 193–242.

Gardiner, Alan H., "The Astarte Papyrus," in *Studies Presented to F. Ll. Griffith,* London, 1932, 74–85.

Posener, Georges, "La légende égyptienne de la mer insatiable," *Annuaire de l'Institut de Philologie et d'Histoire Orientales et Slaves* 13, 1953, 461–78.

Redford, Donald B., "The Sea and the Goddess," in S. I. Groll, ed., *Studies in Honour of Miriam Lichtheim* II, Jerusalem, 1990, 824–35.

Ritner, Robert K., "The Legend of Astarte and the Tribute of the Sea," in William W. Hallo, ed., *The Context of Scripture,* vol. 1: *Canonical Compositions from the Biblical World,* Leiden, 1997, 35–36.


Aten Hymn

Davies, N. de Garis, *The Rock Tombs of El Amarna,* pt. 6, London, 1908, 29–31, pls. 27, 41.

Assmann, Jan, "Aton," *LÄ* I, 1973, 526–49.

Assmann, Jan, in Otto Kaiser, ed., TUAT II/6: *Hymnen und Gebete* II, 1991, 846–53.

——, *Ägyptische Hymnen und Gebete,* Zurich, 1975, 215–21, 557–58.

——, "Zwei Sonnenhymnen der späten XVIII: Dynastie in thebanischen Gräbern der Saitenzeit," *MDAIK* 27, 1971, 1–33.

Foster, John, "The Hymn to Aten: Akhenaten Worships the Sole God," in Jack Sasson, ed., *Civilization of the Ancient Near East,* 1995, III, 1751–61.

Grandet, Pierre, *Hymnes de la religion d'Aton (Hymnes du XIVe siècle avant J.-C.),* Paris, 1995.

Lorton, D. "God's Beneficient Creation: Coffin Texts Spell 1130, the Instruction for Merikare, and the Great Hymn to the Aton," *SAK* 20, 1993, 125–58.

Murnane, William J., *Texts from the Amarna Period in Egypt,* Atlanta, 1995, 112–16.

## Autobiographies

Clère, J. J., "Autobiographie d'un général gouverneur de la Haute Egypte à l'époque saite," *BIFAO* 83, 1983, 85–100.

Coulon, Laurent, "Véracité et rhétorique dans les autobiographies égyptiennes de la Première Période Intermédiare," *BIFAO* 97, 1997, 109–38.

Gnirs, A. M., "Die ägyptische Autobiographie," in A. Loprieno, ed., *Ancient Egyptian Literature, History and Forms,* Leiden, 1996, 191–241.

Kahl, Jochem, *Siut-Theben: Zur Wertschätzung von Traditionen im alten Ägypten,* Probleme der Ägyptologie 13, Leiden, 1999, 206–39.

Klothe, Nicole, *Die (auto-)biographischen Inschriften des ägyptischen Alten Reiches: Untersuchungen zu Phraseologie und Entwicklung, SAK Beiheft* 8, Hamburg, 2002.

Lichtheim, Miriam, *Ancient Egyptian Autobiographies Chiefly of the Middle Kingdom: A Study and an Anthology,* OBO 84, Freiburg/Göttingen, 1988.

——, "Autobiography as Self Exploration," in *Atti del Sesto Congresso Internazionale di Egittologia* I, Turin, 1992, 409–14.

——, *Maat in Egyptian Autobiographies and Related Studies,* OBO 120, Freiburg/Göttingen, 1992.

Moreno García, Juan Carlos, "De l'Ancien Empire à la première période intermédiaire: L'Autobiographie de *Q3r* d'Edfou, entre tradition et innovation," *RdE* 49, 1998, 151–60.

——, *Etudes sur l'administration, le pouvoir et l'idéologie en Egypte, de l'Ancien au Moyen Empire,* Aegyptiaca Leodiensia 4, Liège, 1997.

Perdu, O., "Ancient Egyptian Autobiographies," in Jack Sasson, ed., *Civilizations of the Ancient Near East* IV, 1995, 2243–54.

Roccati, A., "Note lessicali sulle biografie egiziane," *RSO* 47, 149–59.


Bentresh Stela

Broze, Michèle, *La princesse de Bakhtan,* Monographies Reine Elisabeth 6, Brussels, 1989. Reviews by Kitchen, *OLZ* 86/4, 1991, 368–69, and Winand, *BiOr* 48/3–4, 1991, 456–59. Kenneth Kitchen, *Ramesside Inscriptions,* vol. 2, Oxford, 1979, 284–87. Adriaan de Buck, *Egyptian Readingbook,* Leiden, 1948, 106–09.

Westendorf, W., "Bentresch-Stele," *LÄ* I, 1975, 698–700.

Bell, Lanny, "The Epigraphic Survey," *Oriental Institute Annual Report 1978/79,* Chicago, 1979, 25; *1980/81,* Chicago, 1981, 17.

Bresciani, Edda, *Letteratura e Poesia dell'antico Egitto,* Turin, 1969, 533–36.

Brunner-Traut, Emma, *Altägyptischen Märchen,* 8th ed., Munich, 1989, 163–67.

Coenen, Marc, "A propos de la stèle de Bakhtan," *GM* 142, 1994, 57–59.

Devauchelle, Didier, "Notes sur la stèle de Bentresh," *RdE* 37, 1986, 149–50.

Donadoni, Sergio, "Per la data della Stele di Bentres," *MDAIK* 15, 1957, 47–50.

Lefebvre, Gustave, *Romans et Contes de l'Epoque Pharaonique,* Paris, 1949, 221–32, with extensive bibliography.

Lichtheim, Miriam, *AEL* III, 90–94.

Morschauser, Scott. "Using History: Reflections on the Bentresh Stela," *SAK* 15, 1988, 203–23.

Posener, Georges, "A propos de la stèle de Bentresh," *BIFAO* 34, 1933, 75–81.

Spalinger, Anthony, "On the Bentresh Stela and Related Problems," *JSSEA* 8/1, 1977, 11–18.

Wilson, John, "The Legend of the Possessed Princess," *ANET,* 29–31.

For additional early references, see Ida B. Pratt, *Ancient Egypt,* New York Public Library, New York, 1925, 358–59; and *Supplement,* 1942, 249.


Book of the Dead, Chapter 125

Maystre, Charles, *Les déclarations d'innocence (Livre des Morts, chapitre 125),* IFAO, Cairo, 1937; Naville, Edouard, *Das aegyptische*

*Todtenbuch der XVIII. bis XX. Dynastie,* Berlin, 1886, 275–335, pls. 133–39.

Faulkner, Raymond O., *The Egyptian Book of the Dead: The Book of Coming Forth by Day,* Cairo, 1998, pls. 31–32.

## Cheops and the Magicians

Blackman, A. M., *The Story of King Kheops and the Magicians, Transcribed from Papyrus Westcar (Berlin Papyrus 3033),* ed. W. V. Davies, Reading, Eng., 1988.

Simpson, W. K., "Pap. Westcar," *LÄ* IV, 1982, 744–46.

Altenmüller, Hartwig, "Die Stellung der Königsmutter Chentkaus beim Übergang von der 4. zur 5. Dynastie," *CdE* 45, 1970, 223–35.

Barocas, C., "Les Contes du Papyrus Westcar," *SAK Beiheft* 3, 1988, 121–29.

Borghouts, J. F., "The Enigmatic Chests," *JEOL* 7, no. 23 (1973–74), 1975, 358–64.

Brunner-Traut, Emma, "Die Geburtsgeschichte der Evangelien im Lichte ägyptologischer Forschungen," *Zeitschrift für Religions- und Geistesgeschichte* 12, 1960, 97–111.

——, "Pharao und Jesus als Söhne Gottes," *Antaios* 2, 1960–61, 266–84.

Derchain, P., "Snéferou et les rameuses," *RdE* 21, 1969, 19–25.

——, "Deux notules à propos de Papyrus Westcar," *GM* 89, 1986, 15–21.

El-Aguizy, Ola, "The Particle *k3* and Other Related Problematic Passages in Papyrus Westcar," *BIFAO* 97, 1997, 157–63.

El-Hamrawi, Mahmoud, "Bemerkungen zu pWestcar 5, 1–7 und Sinuhe B 147," *Lingua Aegyptia* 7, 2000, 141–52.

Eyre, C. J., "Fates, Crocodiles and the Judgment of the Dead: Some Mythological Allusions in Egyptian Litterature," *SAK* 4, 1976, 103–14.

——, "Yet Again the Wax Crocodile: P. Westcar 3, 12ff.," *JEA* 78, 1992, 280–81.

Fischer, H. G., "Some Iconographic and Literary Comparisons: 3. The Servants of Djedi (Papyrus Westcar VII, 15–16); 4. Boats Manned with Women (Westcar V, 1ff.)," in Jan Assmann, Erika Feucht, and Reinhard Grieshammer, eds., *Fragen an die altägyptische Literatur: Studien zum Gedenken an Eberhard Otto,* Wiesbaden, 1977, 160–65.

Gilula, Mordechai, "*Pyr.* 604 *c-d* and Westcar 7/17–19," *JEA* 64, 1978, 45–51.

Goedicke, Hans, "Rudjedet's Delivery," *VA* 1, 1985, 19–26. Based on social customs of the times.

——, "Gentlemen's Salutations," *VA* 2, 1986, 161–70.

——, "Thoughts about the Papyrus Westcar," *ZÄS* 120, 1993, 23–36. Perhaps Rudjetet is Ahhotep and the future kings are Kamose and Ahmose. Importance of Re after Hyksos, *jpwt* is perhaps allotted fate designed at birth but unknown to its bearer.

Goyon, Georges, "Est-ce enfin Sakhebou?" in *Hommages à Serge Sauneron,* vol. 1: *Egypte Pharaonique,* IFAO, BdE 81, Cairo, 1979, 43–50.

Graefe, Erhart, "Die Gute Reputation des Königs 'Snofru' " in Sarah Israelit-Groll, ed., *Studies in Egyptology Presented to Miriam Lichtheim* I, Jerusalem, 1990, 257–63.

Grapow, Hermann, "Zu zwei Stellen des Westcar," *ZÄS* 77, 1941–42, 21–23.

Hays, H. M., "The Historicity of Papyrus Westcar," *ZÄS* 129, 2002, 20–30.

Helck, Wolfgang, "Heliopolis und die Sonnenheiligtümern," in *Sundries in Honour of Torgny Säve-Söderbergh,* Boreas 13, Uppsala, 1984, 67–72. Translates "the measurements of the strongroom of Thot" for Cheops pyramid.

Hornung, E., "Die 'Kammern' des Thot-Heiligtumes," *ZÄS* 100, 1974, 33–35.

Jenni, Hanna, "Der Papyrus Westcar," *SAK* 25, 1998, 113–41.

Knigge, Carsten, "Die Bekleidung der Ruderinnen in der Geschichte des Papyrus Westcar," *GM* 61, 1997, 103–5.

Manniche, Lise, *How Djadjaemankh Saved the Day: A Tale from Ancient Egypt,* New York, 1977.

Mathieu, Bernard, "Les contes du Papyrus Westcar: une interprétation," *Egypte Afrique and Orient* 15, 1999, 29–40.

Meltzer, Edmund S., "The Art of the Storyteller in Papyrus Westcar: An Egyptian Mark Twain?" in Betsy M. Bryan and David Lorton, eds., *Essays in Egyptology in Honor of Hans Goedicke,* San Antonio, 1994, 169–75.

Morenz, L. D., *Beiträge zur Schriftlichtkeitskultur im Mittleren Reich und in der 2. Zwischenzeit,* ÄUAT 29, 1996, 107–23.

Sauneron, Serge, "La ville de S3ḫbw," *Kemi* 11, 1950, 63–72.

Staehelin, E., "Bindung und Entbindung: Erwägungen zu Papyrus Westcar 10,2," *ZÄS* 96, 1970, 125–39.

## Coffin Texts

de Buck, Adriaan, *The Egyptian Coffin Texts* II, Oriental Institute Publications 49, Chicago, 1938, 209–26 (Spell 148), 389–405 (Spell 162).

van Voss, M. H., "Sargtexte," *LÄ* V, 1983, 468–71.

Barguet, Paul, *Les textes des sarcophages égyptiens du Moyen Empire,* Paris, 1986, 434–36 (Spell 148), 268–69 (Spell 162).

Faulkner, R. O., *The Ancient Egyptian Coffin Texts,* vol. 1: *Spells 1–354,* Warminster, 1973, 125–27 (Spell 148), 140–41 (Spell 162).

Foster, John L., *Echoes of Egyptian Voices: An Anthology of Ancient Egyptian Poetry,* Norman, 1992, 33–35 (Spell 162).

Gilula, Mordechai, "Coffin Texts Spell 148," *JEA* 57, 1971, 14–19.

Lalouette, Claire, *Textes sacrés et textes profanes de l'ancienne Egypte: Mythe, contes et poésie. Traductions et commentaires,* Paris, 1987, 90–92 (Spell 148), 147–48 (Spell 162).

O'Connell, Robert H., "The Emergence of Horus: An Analysis of Coffin Text Spell 148," *JEA* 69, 1983, 66–87.

## Doomed Prince

Gardiner, Alan H., *Late Egyptian Stories,* Bibliotheca Aegyptiaca 1, Brussels, 1932, ix, 1–9.

Brunner-Traut, E., "Prinzenmärchen," *LÄ* IV, 1982, 1107–12.

Cruz-Uribe, E., "Late Egyptian Varia," *ZÄS* 113, 1986, 18–19.

Gosline, S. L., "Orthographic Notes on the 'Tale of the Doomed Prince,'" *ZÄS* 126, 1999, 111–16.

Helck, W., "Die Erzählung vom Verwunschenen Prinzen," in Jürgen Osing and Günter Dreyer, eds., *Form und Mass: Beiträge zur Literatur, Sprache und Kunst des alten Ägypten. Festschrift für Gerhard Fecht,* ÄUAT 12, 1987, 218–25.

Hubai, Péter, "Eine literarische Quelle der ägyptischen Religions-philosophie? Das Märchen vom Prinzen, die drei Gefahren zu überstehen hatte," in Ulrich Luft, ed., *The Intellectual Heritage of Egypt: Studies Presented to László Kákosy,* Studia Aegyptiaca 14, Budapest, 1992, 277–300.

Manniche, Lise, *The Prince Who Knew His Fate: An Ancient Egyptian Tale Translated from Hieroglyphs and Illustrated,* New York, 1981.

Peet, T. Eric, "The Legend of the Capture of Joppa and the Story of the Foredoomed Prince," *JEA* 11, 1925, 225–29.

Posener, Georges, "On the Tale of the Doomed Prince," *JEA* 39, 1953, 107.

Spiegelberg, W., "Die Schlusszeilen der Erzählung vom verwunschenen Prinzen," *ZÄS* 64, 1929, 86–87.


Eloquent Peasant

Parkinson, R. B., *The Tale of the Eloquent Peasant,* Oxford, Griffith Institute, 1991.

Fecht, G., "Bauerngeschichte," *LÄ* I, 1975, 638–51.

Ayad, Mariam, "Nemty-Nahkt's Warning to the Peasant," *GM* 152, 1996, 9–10.

Allam, Schafik, "Social and Legal Aspects Regarding the Trader from the Oasis," *Lingua Aegyptia* 8, 2000, 83–92.

Arnold, Felix, "The High Stewards of the Early Middle Kingdom," *GM* 122, 1991, 7–14.

Berlev, Oleg, "The Date of the Eloquent Peasant," in Jürgen Osing and Günter Dreyer, eds., *Form und Mass: Beiträge zur Literatur, Sprache und Kunst des alten Ägypten. Festschrift für Gerhard Fecht,* ÄUAT 12, 1987, 78–83.

Bontty, Monica, "Conflict Management in Ancient Egypt: Law as a Social Phenomenon," Michigan: UMI Dissertation Services, 1998.

——, "Images of Law and the Disputing Process in the Tale of the Eloquent Peasant," *Lingua Aegyptia* 8, 2000, 93–107.

Coulon, Laurent, "La rhétorique et ses fictions: Pouvoirs et duplicité du discours à travers la littérature égyptienne du Moyen et du Nouvel Empire," *BIFAO* 99, 1999, 103–32.

Dakin, A. N., "Of the Untranslatability of Maat and Some Questions about the *Tale of the Eloquent Peasant,*" in C. J. Eyre, ed., *Proceedings of the Seventh International Congress of Egyptologists,* OLA 82, 1998, 295–301.

Devauchelle, Didier, "Le *Paysan* déraciné," *CdE* 70, 1995, 34–40.

Eyre, J. Christopher, "The Performance of the Peasant," *Lingua Aegyptia* 8, 2000, 9–25.

Fecht, G., "Der beredete Bauer: Die Zweite Klage," in P. D. Manuelian, ed., *Studies in Honor of William Kelly Simpson,* Boston, 1996, 227–66.

Fischer, H. G. "Some Iconographic and Literary Comparisons: 2. The staff of Old Age (Peasant B 1, 22, 278)," in Jan Assmann, Erika Feucht, and Reinhard Grieshammer, eds., *Fragen an die altägyptische Literatur: Studien zum Gedenken an Eberhard Otto,* Wiesbaden, 1977, 158–60.

Foster, John, "Word Play in the Eloquent Peasant: The Eighth Complaint," *BES* 10 1989–90, 61–76.

Gilula, Mordechai, "Peasant B 141–45," *JEA* 64, 1978, 129–30: "and builds the destroyed mounds."

Gnirs, Andrea, "The Language of Corruption: On Rich and Poor in the Eloquent Peasant," *Lingua Aegyptia* 8, 2000, 125–55.

Goedicke, Hans, "Comments Concerning the 'Story of the Eloquent Peasant,'" *ZÄS* 125, 1998, 109–25.

Hare, Tom, "The Supplementarity of Agency in the Eloquent Peasant," *Lingua Aegyptia* 8, 2000, 1–7.

Junge, Friedrich, "Die Rahmenerzählung des Beredtenbauern: Innenansichten einer Gesellschaft," *Lingua Aegyptia* 8, 2000, 157–81.

Herrmann, S., "Die Auseinandersetzung mit dem Schöpfergott," in Jan Assmann, Erika Feucht, and Reinhard Grieshammer, eds., *Fragen an die altägyptische Literatur: Studien zum Gedenken an Eberhard Otto,* Wiesbaden, 1977, 257–73.

Kuhlmann, Klaus, "Bauernweisheiten," in Ingrid Gamer-Wallert and Wolfgang Helck, eds., *Gegengabe: Festschrift für Emma Brunner-Traut,* Tübingen, 1992, 191–209.

Leprohon, R. J., "The Wages of the Eloquent Peasant," *JARCE* 12, 1975, 97–98.

Light, Matthew A., "The Power of Law: Procedure as Justice in the Eloquent Peasant," *Lingua Aegyptia* 8, 2000, 109–24.

Le Guilloux, Patrice, *Le Conte du Paysan éloquent: Texte hiéroglyphique, translitération et traduction commentée,* Angers, 2002.

Loprieno, Antonio, "Literature as Mirror of Social Institutions: The Case of the Eloquent Peasant," *Lingua Aegyptia* 8, 2000, 183–98.

Miosi, F. Terry, "A Possible Reference to the Non-Calendar Week," *ZÄS* 101, 1974, 150–52.

Morenz, Ludwig D., "Sa-mut/*kyky* und Menna, zwei reale Leser/Hörer des *Oasenmannes* aus dem Neuen Reich?" *GM* 165, 1998, 73–81.

——, "Zum Oasenmann—'Entspanntes Feld,' Erzählung und Geschichtes," *Lingua Aegyptia* 8, 2000, 53–82.

Pamminger, Peter, "Gottesworte und Zahlensymbole in den 'Klagen des Bauern," *SAK* 20, 1993, 207–22. Stresses lowly condition of protagonist, good bibliography.

Parkinson, R. B., "The Tale of the Eloquent Peasant: A Commentary." Ph.D. diss. Oxford University, n.d.

——, "The Date of the Eloquent Peasant," *RdE* 42, 1991, 171–81.

——, "Literary Form and the 'Tale of the Eloquent Peasant,'" *JEA* 78, 1992, 163–78.

——, "Imposing Words: The Entrapment of Language in the Tale of the Eloquent Peasant," *Lingua Aegyptia* 8, 2000, 27–51.

Roccati, Alessandro, "Plaidoyer pour le paysan plaideur," in Christian Cannuyer and Jean-Marie Kruchten, eds., *Individu, Société et Spiritualité dans l'Egypte Pharaonique et Copte (Mélanges égyptologiques offerts au Professeur Aristide Théodoridès),* Ath-Bruxelles-Mons, 1993, 253–56. Suggested date early Dynasty 12, Sesostris I (?), with bibliography.

Shupak, Nili, "A New Source for the Study of the Judiciary and Law of Ancient Egypt: The Tale of the Eloquent Peasant," *JNES* 51, 1992, 1–18.

Simpson, William K., "Allusions to the Shipwrecked Sailor and the Eloquent Peasant in a Ramesside Text," *JAOS* 78, 1958, 50–51.

——, "The Political Background of the Eloquent Peasant," *GM* 120, 1991, 95–99.

van den Boorn, G. P. F., "Wḏꜥ-ryt and Justice at the Gate," *JNES* 44, 1985, 1–26.

Vernus, Pascal, "La date du Paysan Eloquent," in Sarah Israelit-Groll, ed., *Studies in Egyptology Presented to Miriam Lichtheim* II, Jerusalem, 1990, 1033–47.

VerSteeg, Russ, "Law in Ancient Egyptian Fiction," *Georgia Journal of International and Comparative Law* 24, 1994, 37–97.

Wente, Edward F., "A Note on the 'Eloquent Peasant,' B I, 13–15," *JNES* 24, 1965, 105–9: "My course is good. Only one (wisp) has been destroyed. It is for its (i.e., the wisp's price) that I will buy back my donkey if you seize possession of it for a (mere) filling of its mouth with a wisp of Upper Egyptian barley."

Westendorf, W., "Das strandende Schiff. Zur Lesung und Übersetzung von Bauer B 1,58 = R 101," in Jan Assmann, Erika Feucht, and Reinhard Grieshammer, eds., *Fragen an die altägyptische Literatur: Studien zum Gedenken an Eberhard Otto,* Wiesbaden, 1977, 503–10.

## Famine Stela

Barguet, Paul, *La stèle de la famine, à Sehel,* BdE 34, Cairo, 1953.
Zibelius, Karol, "Hungersnotstele," *LÄ* III, 1980, col. 84.

Goedicke, Hans, *Comments on the "Famine Stela,"* VA supp. 5, 1994.
Lichtheim, Miriam, *AEL* III, 94–103, with extensive bibliography.
Wilson, John, "The Tradition of Seven Lean Years in Egypt," *ANET,* 31–32.

## Ghost Story

Alan H. Gardiner, *Late Egyptian Stories,* Bibliotheca Aegyptiaca 1, Brussels, 1932, 89–94.
Brunner-Traut, E., "Chonsuemheb und der Geist," *LÄ* I, 1974, 963–64.

von Beckerath, Jürgen, "Zur Gechichte von Chonsemhab und dem Geist," *ZÄS* 119, 1992, 90–107.

## Hardjedef (Djedefhor), Instruction of

Helck, Wolfgang, *Die Lehre des Djedefhor und Die Lehre eines Vaters an seinen Sohn,* Kleine Ägyptische Texte 8, Wiesbaden, 1984. Important review by Roccati, *BiOr* 43, 1986, 398–99.
Posener, G., "Lehre des Djedefhor," *LÄ* III, 1980, 978–80.
von Beckerath, Jürgen, "Djedefhor," *LÄ* I, 1974, 1099.

Posener, G., "Le début de L'enseignement de Hardjedef (Recherches littéraires, IV. Compléments aux Richerches inconnues), *RdE* 9, 1952, 109–20.

Ritter, Vanessa, "Hordjédef ou le Glorieux Destin d'un Prince Oublié," *Egypte Afrique et Orient* 15, 1999, 41–50.

Roccati, Alessandro, "Su un passo di Hardjedef," *JEA* 68, 1982, 16–19.


## Harkhuf

Sethe, K., *Urkunden des alten Reichs,* Urk. I, 2d ed., Leipzig, 1932, 120–31.

Doret, Eric, *The Narrative Verbal System of Old and Middle Egyptian,* Geneva, 1986. Virtually the entire text is translated and commented upon in the examples of verbal forms cited. See index thereto.

Edel, Elmar, "Inschriften des Alten Reiches. V. Die Reiseberichte *Ḥrw-ḫwjf* (Herchuf)," in O. Firchow, ed., *Ägyptologische Studien,* Berlin, 1955, 51–75.

——, "Die Ländernamen und die Ausbreitung der C-Gruppe nach den Reiseberichten des *Ḥrw-ḫwjf,*" *Orientalia* 36, 1967, 133–58.

Fecht, G., "Die Berichte *Ḥrw-ḫwj.f* über seine Reise nach Jȝm," in Manfred Görg and Edgar Pusch, eds., *Festschrift Elmar Edel,* Bamberg, 1979, ÄUAT 1, 1979, 105–34.

Goedicke, Hans, "Harkhuf's Travels," *JNES* 40, 1981, 1–20.

Kendall, Timothy, "Ethnoarchaeology in Meroitic Studies," Studia Meroitica 1984, *Meroitica* 10, 1989, 625–745, esp. 697–703.

Roccati, A., *La Littérature historique sous l'ancien Empire égyptien,* Paris, 1982, 200–207, with extensive bibliography with many items not listed here.

Silverman, David P., "Pygmies and Dwarfs in the Old Kingdom," *Serapis* 1, 1969, 53–62.

See also entries under Autobiographies above.


## Harper Songs

For the bibliography of the harper's songs, see the list by Michael V. Fox, below, under sources, pp. 302–5. Budge, E. A. W., *Facsimiles of Egyptian Hieratic Papyri in the British Museum,* 1st ser., London, 1910.

Assmann, Jan, "Harfnerlieder," *LÄ* II, 1977, 972–82.

Altenmüller, H., "Zur Bedeutung der Harfnerlieder des alten Reiches," *SAK* 6, 1976, 16–28.

Assmann, Jan, "Fest des Augenblicks-Verheißung der Dauer. Die

Kontroverse der ägyptischen Harfnerlieder," in Jan Assmann, Erika Feucht, and Reinhard Grieshammer, eds., *Fragen an die altägyptische Literatur: Studien zum Gedenken an Eberhard Otto,* Wiesbaden, 1977, 55–84.

——, in Otto Kaiser, ed. TUAT II/6: *Lieder und Gebete* II, 1991, 905–8.

Barucq, André, "Quelques reflexions à propos du Psaume 49 et des 'Chantes du Harpiste,' " in A. Guillaumont, ed., *Hommages à François Daumas* II, Montpellier, 1986, 67–73.

Bochi, P., "Gender and Genre in Ancient Egyptian Poetry: The Rhetoric of Performance in the Harper's Song," *JARCE* 35, 1998, 89–95.

Brunner, H., "Wiederum die ägyptischen 'Make Merry' Lieder," *JNES* 25, 1966, 130–31.

Buchberger, Hannes, "Das Harfnerlied vom Grab des *K3(=j)-m-ʿnḫ* oder *'Die riten des sn-nṯrw,'* " in Dieter Kessler and Regine Schulz, eds., *Gedenkschrift für Winfried Barta,* MÄU 4, 1995, 93–123.

Fox, Michael V., "The Entertainment Song Genre in Egyptian Literature," *Egyptological Studies: Scripta Hierosolymitana* 28, 1982, 268–316.

Gilbert, P., "Les chants du Harpiste," *CdE* 29, 1940, 38–44.

Goedicke, Hans, "The Date of the Antef Song," in Jan Assmann, Erika Feucht, and Reinhard Grieshammer, eds., *Fragen an die altägyptische Literatur: Studien zum Gedenken an Eberhard Otto,* Wiesbaden, 1977, 185–96.

Kákosy, L., and Z. I. Fabian, "Harper's Song in the Tomb of Djehutimes (TT 32), *SAK* 22, 1995, 211–25.

Lichtheim, Miriam, "The Songs of the Harpers," *JNES* 4, 1945, 178–212, pls. 1–7.

Osing, Jürgen, "Les Chants du Harpiste au Nouvel Empire," in *Aspects de la Culture Pharaonique,* Paris, 1992, 11–24, with additional bibliography.

Patané, Massimo, "A propos du Chant du Harpiste d'Antef," *BSEG* 11, 1987, 99–105 (NK redaction or original?), with bibliography.

Simpson, W. K., "A Short Harper's Song of the Late New Kingdom in the Yale University Art Gallery," *JARCE* 8, 1970, 49–50.

Varille, Alexandre, "Trois nouveaux chantes de Harpistes," *BIFAO* 35, 1935, 153–60.

Wente, Edward F., "The Egyptian 'Make Merry' Songs Reconsidered," *JNES* 21, 1962, 118–28, pls. 16–19.

Heavenly Cow

Hornung, Erik, *Der ägyptische Mythos von der Himmelskuh: Eine Ätiologie des Unvollkommenen,* OBO 46, Frieburg/Göttingen, 1982; Maystre, Charles, "Le Livre de la Vache du Ciel dans les tombeaux de la Vallée des Rois," *BIFAO* 40, 1941, 53–115; Pleyte, W., and F. Rossi, *Papyrus de Turin,* 2 vols., Leiden, 1869–76, plate vol., pl. 84.

Hornung, Erik, "Kuhbuch," *LÄ* III, 1979, 837–38.

Guilhou, Nadine, *La vieillesse des dieux,* Montpellier, 1989.

——, "Un nouveau fragment du Livre de la Vache céleste," *BIFAO* 98, 1998, 197–214.

Lorton, David, Review of Erik Hornung, *Der ägyptische Mythos von der Himmelskuh: Eine Ätiologie des Unvollkommenen,* OBO 46, Freiburg/Göttingen, 1982, in *BiOr* 40, 1983, 609–16.

Piankoff, Alexandre, *The Shrines of Tut-Ankh-Amon,* New York, 1955, 1962, 27–34.

Roccati, Alessandro, "Les papyrus de Turin," *BSFE* 99, 1984, 23.

Spalinger, A., "The Destruction of Mankind: A Transitional Literary Text," *SAK* 28, 2000, 257–82.

Sternberg-el-Hotabi, Heike, "Der Mythus von der Vernichtung des Menschengeschlechtes," in Otto Kaiser, ed., TUAT III/5, *Mythen und Epen* III, Gütersloh, 1995, 1018–37.

Yoyotte, Jean, "Les origines de la subversion et la retraite de Re d'après le 'Livre de la Vache du Ciel,'" in Ecole Pratique des Hautes Etudes, Ve section 79, 1971–72, 162–64.

Hihor, the Magician

Spiegelberg, Wilhelm, *Demotische Texte auf Krügen,* Demotische Studien 5, Leipzig, 1912, 8, 14–15, 48–49, and pls. 1, 3, and 4 (repr. Milan, 1977).

Depauw, Mark, *A Companion to Demotic Studies,* Brussels, 1997, 90–91.

Brunner-Traut, Emma, *Altägyptischen Märchen,* Düsseldorf and Cologne, 1963 (2d ed., 1965), 215–16 and 300–301.

Roeder, Günther, *Altägyptischen Erzählungen und Märchen,* Jena, 1927, 312–13.

## Horus and Seth

Gardiner, Alan H., *Late Egyptian Stories,* Bibliotheca Aegyptiaca 1, Brussels, 1932, x, 37–60; idem, *The Library of A. Chester Beatty: Description of a Hieratic Papyrus with a Mythological Story, Love-Songs, and Other Miscellaneous Texts,* London, 1931.

Schlichting, Robert, " 'Streit des Horus und Seth,' " *LÄ* VI, 1986, 84–86; te Velde, Herman, "Horus und Seth," *LÄ* III, 1977, 25–27.

Allam, S., "Legal Aspects in the 'Contendings of Horus and Seth,' " in Alan B. Lloyd, ed. *Studies in Pharaonic Religion and Society in Honour of J. Gwyn Griffiths,* Egypt Exploration Society, London, 1992, 137–45.

Barta, Winfried, "Zur Reziprozität der homosexuellen Beziehung zwischen Horus und Seth," *GM* 129, 1992, 33–38.

Broze, Michèle, *Mythe et roman en Egypte ancienne: Les Aventures d'Horus et Seth dans le Papyrus Chester Beatty I,* OLA 76, Brussels, 1996.

Chappaz, Jean-Luc, "Que diable allaient-ils faire dans cette galère? Recherche sur le thème de la navigation dans quelques contes égyptiens," *BSEG* 3, 1980, 3–7.

Goedicke, Hans, "Two Notes on Recent Articles," *JSSEA* 10, no. 1, 1979, 59–61.

Griffiths, J. G., *The Conflict of Horus and Seth from Egyptian and Classical Sources,* Liverpool, 1960.

Junge, Friedrich, "Mythos und Literarizität: Die Geschichte vom Streit der Götter Horus und Seth," in Heike Behlmer, ed., . . . *Quaerentes Scientiam: Festgabe für Wolfhart Westendorf zu seinem 70. Geburtstag,* Göttingen, 1994, 83–101.

——, "Die Erzählung vom Streit der Götter Horus und Seth um die Herrschaft," in Otto Kaiser, ed., TUAT III/5, Mythen und Epen III, Gütersloh, 1995, 930–50.

Lesko, Leonard H., "Three Late Egyptian Stories Reconsidered," in Leonard H. Lesko, ed., *Egyptological Studies in Honor of Richard A. Parker,* Hanover, N.H., 1986, 98–103.

Miosi, F. T., "Horus as a Trickster," *JSSEA* 9, no. 2, 1979, 75–78.

Patané, Massimo, "Essai d'interprétation d'un récit mythique 'Le Conte d'Horus et de Seth,' " *BSEG* 7, 1982, 83–89.

Spiegel, Joachim, *Die Erzählung vom Streite des Horus und Seth in Pap. Beatty I als Literaturwerk,* Leipzig Ägyptologische Studien 9, Glückstadt, 1937.

Théodoridès, Aristide, "Harpocrate dans les 'Dém^ elés d'Horus et Seth,'" in Christian Cannuyer and Jean-Marie Kruchten, eds., *Individu, Société et Spiritualité dans l'Égypte pharaonique et copte,* Ath-Bruxelles-Mons, 1993, 1–22.

te Velde, Herman, *Seth, God of Confusion: A Study of His Role in Egyptian Mythology and Religion,* Probleme der Ägyptologie 6, rev. ed., Leiden, 1967.

## Israel Stela

Kitchen, K. A., *Ramesside Inscriptions: Historical and Biographical* IV, Oxford, 1968, 12–19.

Ebach, Jürgen, "Israel, Israelstele," *LÄ* III, 1978, 205.

Ahlström, G. W., and D. Edelman, "Merneptah's Israel," *JNES* 44, 1985, 59–61.

Davies, Benedict G., *Egyptian Historical Inscriptions of the Nineteenth Dynasty,* Documenta Mundi, Aegyptiaca 2, Jonsered, 1997, 173–88.

Engel, Helmut, "Die Siegesstele des Merenptah: Kritischer Überblick über die verschiedenen Versuche historischer Auswertung des Schluβabschnitts," *Biblica* 60, 1979, 373–99.

Fecht, Gerhard, "Die Israelstele, Gestalt und Aussage," in Manfred Görg, ed., *Fontes atque Pontes: Eine Festgabe für Hellmut Brunner,* ÄUAT 5, Wiesbaden, 1983, 106–38.

Garthoff, B. W. B., "Merenptah's Israel Stele. A Curious Case of Rites de Passage?" in J. H. Kamstra, H. Milde, and K. Wagtendonk, eds., *Funerary Symbols and Religion: Essays Dedicated to Professor M. S. H. G. Heerma van Voss,* Kampen, 1988, 23–33.

Hasel, Michael G., *Domination and Resistance: Egyptian Military Activity in the Southern Levant, 1300–1185 BC,* Probleme der Ägyptologie 11, Leiden, 1998, 257–71.

Hornung, Erik, "Die Israelstele des Merenptah," in Manfred Görg, ed., *Fontes atque Pontes: Eine Festgabe für Hellmut Brunner,* ÄUAT 5, Wiesbaden, 1983, 224–33.

Kaplony-Heckel, Ursula, "Die Israel-Stele des Mer-en-Ptah, 1208 v. Chr.," in Otto Kaiser, ed., TUAT I/6, Historisch-chronologische Texte III, Gütersloh, 1985, 544–52.

Kitchen, K. A., "The Physical Text of Merenptah's Victory Hymn (The 'Israel' Stela)," *JSSEA* 24, 1994 (pub. 1998), 71–76.

Kruchten, Jean-Marie, "Quelques passages difficiles de la Stèle d'Israël," *GM* 140, 1994, 37–48.

Rainey, Anson F., in "Scholars Disagree: Can You Name the Panel with the Israelites?" *Biblical Archaeology Review* 17, no. 6, 1991, 56–60, 93.

Redford, Donald B., "The Ashkelon Relief at Karnak and the Israel Stela," *Israel Exploration Journal* 36, 1986, 188–200.

Stager, Lawrence E., "Merenptah, Israel and Sea Peoples. New Light on an Old Relief," *Eretz-Israel* 18, 1985, 56*–64*.

Stein, H. Emily, "The Israel Stele," in *Papers for Discussion: Presented by the Department of Egyptology, Hebrew University, Jerusalem* I, 1981–82, 156–65.

von der Way, Thomas, *Göttergericht und "Heiliger" Krieg im Alten Ägypten. Die Inschriften des Merenptah zum Libyerkrieg des Jahres 5,* SAGA 4, Heidelberg, 1992.

Yurco, Frank J. "Merenptah's Canaanite Campaign," *JARCE* 23, 1986, 189–215.

——, "3,200-Year-Old Picture of Israelites Found in Egypt," *Biblical Archaeology Review* 16, no. 5, 1990, 20–38.

——, in "Scholars Disagree: Can You Name the Panel with the Israelites?" *Biblical Archaeology Review* 17, no. 6, 1991, 61.

Iykhernofret Stela

Schäfer, Heinrich, "Die Mysterien des Osiris in Abydos unter König Sesostris III," UGAÄ 4, 1903–5, repr. 1964, 1–42.

Helck, Wolfgang, "Ichernofret," *LÄ* III, 1977, 122.

Anthes, Rudolf, "Die Berichte des Neferhotep und des Ichernofret über das Osirisfest in Abydos," in *Festschrift zum 150 Jährigen Bestehen des Berliner Ägyptischen Museum,* Berlin, 1974, 15–49.

Simpson, W. K., *The Terrace of the Great God: The Offering Chapels of Dynasties 12 and 13,* Publications of the Pennsylvania-Yale Expedition to Egypt 5, New Haven and Philadelphia, 1974, 17, pl. 1.

## Joppa, Capture of

Gardiner, Alan H., *Late Egyptian Stories,* Bibliotheca Aegyptiaca 1, Brussels, 1932, xii, 82–85; E. A. Wallis Budge, *Facsimilies of Egyptian Hieratic Papyri in the British Museum,* 2d ser., London 1923, 24–25, pl. XLVII.
Helck, Wolfgang, "Joppe," *LÄ* III, 1978, 269–70.

Goedicke, Hans, "The Capture of Joppa," *CdE* 43, 1968, 219–33.
Peet, T. Eric, "The Legend of the Capture of Joppa and the Story of the Foredoomed Prince," *JEA* 11, 1925, 225–29.

## Kagemni, Instruction for

Gardiner, Alan H., "The Instruction Addressed to Kagemni and His Brethren," *JEA* 32, 1946, 71–74.
Barta, Winfried, "Lehre für Kagemni," *LÄ* III, 1979, 980–82.

Gunn, Battiscombe, *The Instruction of Ptah-hotep and the Instruction of Ka'gemni: The Oldest Books in the World,* London, 1918, 62–64.
Morschauser, Scott, "The Opening Lines of *K3.gm.n.i* (P. Prisse I, 1–3a)," in Betsy M. Bryan and David Lorton, eds., *Essays in Egyptology in Honor of Hans Goedicke,* San Antonio, 1994, 177–85.
Yoyotte, Jean, "A propos d'un monument copié par G. Daressy (Contribution à l'histoire littéraire), *BSFE* 11, 1952, 67–72.

## Kamose Stelae

Habachi, Labib, *The Second Stela of Kamose and His Struggle against the Hyksos Ruler and His Capital,* Abhandlungen DAIK 8, Glückstadt, 1972; Helck, Wolfgang, *Historisch-Biographische Texte der 2. Zwischenzeit und Neue Texte der 18. Dynastie,* 2. überarbeitete Auflage, Kleine Ägyptische Texte 6, Wiesbaden, 1983.
Vandersleyen, Claude, "Kamose," *LÄ* III, 1978, 306–8.

Darnell, J. C., "Two Sieges in the Æthiopic Stelae," in D. Mendel and U. Claudi, eds., *Ägypten in Afro-Orientalischen Kontext: Gedenkschrift Peter Behrens,* Cologne, 1991, 73–93.
Smith, H. S., and Alexandrina Smith, "A Reconsideration of the Kamose Texts," *ZÄS* 103, 1976, 48–76.

Spalinger, Anthony, "*Nsw-mnḫ* and the Beginning of the Kamose Stele," *Nineteenth International Congress of Orientalists—Abstracts of Papers,* sections 1–5, Paris, 1973, 23.

## Khakheperres-onbe

Gardiner, Alan H., *The Admonitions of an Egyptian Sage, from a Hieratic Papyrus in Leiden,* Leipzig, 1909, 95–110; Parkinson, R. B., "The Text of Khakheperreseneb: New Readings of EA 5645, and an Unpublished Ostracon," *JEA* 83, 1997, 55–68.

Helck, W., "Lehre des Cha-cheper-Re-seneb," *LÄ* III, 1980, 977.

Otto, E., "Chacheperreseneb," *LÄ* I, 1975, 896–97.

Chappaz, Jean-Luc, "Un manifeste littéraire du Moyen Empire—Les lamentations de Kha-khéper-ré-séneb, *BSEG* 2, 1979, 3–12.

Colin, Gérard, "Khakheperreseneb et la conscience de l'histoire," *GM* 150, 1996, 43–46.

Herrmann, S., *Untersuchungen zur Überlieferungsgestalt mittelägyptischer Literaturwerke,* Berlin, 1957, 48–54.

Junge, F., "Die Welt der Klagen," in Jan Assmann, Erika Feucht, and Reinhard Grieshammer, eds., *Fragen an die altägyptische Literatur: Studien zum Gedenken an Eberhard Otto,* Wiesbaden, 1977, 289–314.

Kadish, Gerald E., "British Museum Writing Board 5645: The Complaints of Kha-kheper-Ré-senebu," *JEA* 59, 1973, 77–90.

Moers, Gerald, "The Interplay of Reenactment and Memory in the *Complaints of Khakheperreseneb,*" *Lingua Aegyptia* 10, 2002, 293–308.

Self-Fashioning Identity: The Interplay of Reiteration and Remembrance in the 'Complaints of Khakheperreseneb,' " *Forty-ninth Annual Meeting of the American Research Center in Egypt, Los Angeles, April 24–26, 1998, Program and Abstracts,* 46.

Ockinga, B., "The Burden of Khakheperreseneb," *JEA* 69, 1983, 88–95.

Parkinson, R. B., "*Khakheperreseneb* and Traditional Belles Lettres," in P. D. Manuelian, ed., *Studies in Honor of William Kelly Simpson,* vol. 2, Boston, 1996, 647–54.

Vernus, Pascal, *Essai sur la conscience de l'Histoire dans l'Egypte pharaonique,* Paris, 1995, 1–33, with extensive bibliography.

## Lamb, Prophecy of the

Zauzich, Karl-Theodor, "Das Lamm des Bokchoris," *Papyrus Erzherzog Rainer (P. Rainer Cent.),* Vienna, 1983, 165–74 and pl. 2; Janssen, Jozef M., "Over Farao Bocchoris," *Varia Historica aangeboden aan Professor Doctor A. W. Byvanck,* Assen (Netherlands), 1954, 17–29.

Zauzich, Karl-Theodor, "Lamm des Bokchoris," *LÄ* III, 1980, 912–13.

Depauw, Mark, *A Companion to Demotic Studies,* Brussels, 1997, 98.

Bresciani, Edda, *Letteratura e Poesia dell' Antico Egitto,* Turin, 1969, 561–62.

Kákosy, L., "Prophecies of Ram Gods," *Acta Orientalia Hungarica* 19 (1966), 341–58.

——, "King Bocchoris and the Uraeus Serpent," *Acta Classica Universitatis Scientiarum Debreceniensis,* vol. 28, Debrecini, 1993, 3–5.

Krall, Jakob, "Vom König Bokchoris. Nach einem demotischen Papyrus der Sammlung Erzherzog Rainer," *Festgaben zu Ehren Max Büdinger,* Innsbruck, 1898, 3–11.

Zauzich, Karl-Theodor, "Der Schreiber der Weissagung des Lammes," *Enchoria* 6, 1976, 127–28.

## Love Songs

Mathieu, Bernard, *La Poésie Amoureuse de l'Egypte Ancienne: Recherches sur un genre littéraire au Nouvel Empire,* IFAO, BdE 115, Cairo, 1996. Review by W. Brunsch, *BiOr* 55, 1998, 37–400.

Meeks, Dimitri, "Liebeslieder," *LÄ* III, 1979, 1048–52.

Assmann, Jan, in Otto Kaiser, ed., TUAT II/6: *Lieder und Gebete* II, 1991, 900–904.

Cuenca, Esteban Llagostera, and Xesus Rabade Paredes, *La Poesía Erótico-Amorosa en el Egipto Faraónico,* Ferrol, Esquio, 1995.

Donadoni, Sergio, "Al seguito di Mehy," in A. Giuillaumont, ed., *Hommages à François Daumas* I, Montpellier, 1986, 207–12. Draws the parallel to religious piety in following Amun or another god.

Foster, J. *Love Songs of the New Kingdom,* Austin, 1992.

Fowler, Barbara Hughes, *Love Lyrics of Ancient Egypt,* Chapel Hill, 1994.

Fox, Michael V., *The Song of Songs and the Ancient Egyptian Love Songs,* Madison, Wisc., 1985.

Gardiner, A. H., *The Library of A. Chester Beatty: The Chester Beatty Papyri I,* London, 1931.

Gilbert, Pierre, "Le grande poème d'amour du Papyrus Chester-Beatty I," *CdE* 17, 1942, 194–97.

Gillam, Robyn A., "The Mehy Papers: Text and Lifestyle in Translation," *CdE* 75, 2000, 207–16.

Griffiths, John Gwyn, "Love as a Disease," in Sarah Israelit-Groll, ed., *Studies in Honour of Miriam Lichtheim* I, Jerusalem, 1990, 349–64.

Guglielmi Waltraud, "Die ägyptische Liebespoesie," in A. Loprieno, ed., *Ancient Egyptian Literature: History and Forms,* Leiden, 1996, 335–47.

Hermann, Alfred, "Beiträge zur Erklärung der ägyptischen Liebesdichtung," in O. Firchow, ed., *Ägyptologische Studien,* Berlin, 1955, 118–39.

——, *Altägyptische Liebesdichtung,* Wiesbaden, 1959.

Hoenn, Karl, and Siegfried Schott, eds., *Altägyptische Liebeslieder,* 2d ed., Zurich, 1950.

Jasnow, Richard, "Remarks on Continuity in Egyptian Literary Tradition," in Emily Teeter and John A. Larson, eds., *Gold of Praise: Studies on Ancient Egypt in Honor of Edward F. Wente,* SAOC 58, Chicago, 2000, 193–210.

Kitchen, K. A., *Poetry of Ancient Egypt,* Documenta Mundi Aegyptiaca 1, Jonsered, 1999, 317–420.

Mathieu, Bernard, "Etudes de métrique égyptienne I: Le distique heptamétrique dans les chants d'amour," *RdE* 39, 1988, 63–82.

Schott, S., *Altägyptische Liebeslieder,* Zurich, 1950.

Schott, Siegfried, and Paule Krièger, *Chants d'Amour de l'Egypte antique,* Paris, 1996.

Smither, Paul C., "Prince Mehy of the Love Songs," *JEA* 34, 1948, 116.

Suys, E., "Les chants d'amour du Papyrus Chester Beatty I," *Biblia* 13, 1932, 210–15.

Vernus, Pascal, *Chants d'amour de l'Egypte antique,* Paris, 1992.

## Loyalist Instruction

Posener, Georges, *L'enseignement loyaliste: Sagesse égyptienne du Moyen Empire,* Geneva, 1976.

Posener, Georges, "Lehre, loyalistiche," *LÄ* III, 1980, 982–84.

Chappaz, J.-L., "Un nouvel ostracon de *L'enseignement loyaliste,*" *BSEG* 7, 1982, 3–9.

Fischer-Elfert, H.-W., "Vermischtes III: Loyalistische Lehre und Totenbrief (*Cairo Bowl*) im Vergleich," *GM* 143, 1994, 41–44.

Loprieno, A., "Loyalty to the King, to God, to Oneself," P. D. Manuelian, ed., *Studies in Honor of William Kelly Simpson* II, Boston, 1996, 533–52.

——, "Loyalistic Instructions," in A. Loprieno, ed., *Ancient Egyptian Literature: History and Forms,* Leiden, 1996, 403–14.

## Man Who Was Weary of Life

Faulkner, R. O., "The Man Who Was Tired of Life," *JEA* 42, 1956, 21–40.

Osing, J., "Gespräch des Lebensmüden," *LÄ* II, 1977, 571–73.

Barta, W., *Das Gespräch eines Mannes mit seinem BA* (papyrus Berlin 3024), MÄS 18, Berlin, 1969.

Brunner-Traut, E., "Der Lebensmüder und sein Ba," *ZÄS* 94, 1967, 6–15.

Cannuyer, Christian, and Gilles Delpech, "La dernière demeure du Désespéré: Note de traduction (P. Berlin 3024), l. 153–54)," *GM* 172, 1999, 11–16.

Derchain, Ph., "Le Dialogue du Désespéré: A propos d'un livre récent ⟨Renaud⟩," *GM* 125, 1991, 17–20.

Fecht, G., "Die Belehrung des *ba* und der 'Lebensmüder,'" *MDAIK* 47, 1991, 113–26.

Fox, M. V., "A Study of Antef," *Or* 46, 1977, 393–423.

Hannig, R., "Die erste Parabel des 'Lebensmüden' (LM 68–80)," *Journal of Ancient Civilizations* 6, 1991, 23–31.

Leahy, A., "Death by Fire in Ancient Egypt," *JESHO* 27, 1984, 199–206.

Letellier, Bernadette, "De la vanité des biens de ce monde: L'évocation d'un personnage de fable dans le 'Désespéré,' P. Berlin 3024, col. 30–39," in *Mélanges Jacques Jean Clère,* Cahier de Recherches de l'Institut de Papyrologie at d'Egyptologie de Lille 13, 1991, 99–106.

Lohmann, Katherina, "Das Gespräch eines Mannes mit seinem Ba," *SAK* 25, 1998, 207–36.

Mathieu, B., "Le souvenir de l'Occident (Sḫ3 Jmnt.t): Une expression de la piété religieuse au Moyen Empire," *RdE* 42, 1991, 262–63.

Parkinson, R. B., "The lost start of the Dialogue of a Man and His

Soul and the History of the Berlin Library," *ZÄS* 30, 2003, forth-coming.

Renaud, Odette, *Le Dialogue du Désespéré avec son Ame: Une interpretation Littéraire,* Cahier de la Société Egyptologique Genève 1, Geneva, 1991.

Scharff, Alexander, *Das Bericht über das Streitgespräch eines Lebensmüden mit seiner Seele, SPAW Phil.-hist. Klasse* 9, Munich, 1937.

Thausing, Gertrud, "Betrachtungen zum 'Lebensmüden,' " *MDAIK* 15, 1957, 262–67.

Tobin, Vincent Arieh, "A Re-Assessment of the *Lebensmüde," BiOr* 48, 1991, 342–63.

——, review of Renaud, in *BiOr* 50, 1993, 122–25.

Welch, E. Douglas, "The Lebensmüde and Its Setting in the Intellectual History of Egypt," Ph.D. diss., Brandeis University, 1978.

Williams, R. J., "Reflections on the Lebensmüde," *JEA* 48, 1962, 49–56.

## Man for His Son, Instruction of a

Helck, Wolfgang, *Die Lehre des Djedefhor und Die Lehre eines Vaters an seinen Sohn,* Kleine Ägyptische Texte 8, Wiesbaden, 1984, 25–72; Fischer-Elfert, Hans-W., *Die Lehre eines Mannes für seinen Sohn— Eine Etappe auf dem 'Gottesweg' des loyalen und solidarischen Beamten der frühen 12. Dynastie,* ÄAbh 60, Wiesbaden, 1998. Extensive review of latter by J. F. Quack in *BiOr* 57, 2000, 534–41.

Posener, Georges, "Lehre eines Mannes an seinen Sohn," *LÄ* III, 1979, 984–86.

Blumenthal, Elke, "Eine neue Handschrift der Lehre eines Mannes für seinen Sohn (P. Berlin 14374), in *Festschrift zum 150 Jährigen Bestehen des Berliner Ägyptischen Museums,* Berlin, 1974, 55–66.

Burkard, G., *Textkritische Untersuchungen zu altägyptischen Weisheitslehren des Alten und Mittleren Reiches,* ÄAbh 34, Wiesbaden, 1977.

Fecht, Gerhard, "Schicksalsgöttinnen und König in der 'Lehre eines Mannes für seinen Sohn,' " *ZÄS* 105, 1978, 14–42.

Fischer-Elfert, Hans-W., "Neue Fragmente zur *Lehre eines Mannes für seinen Sohn* (P. BM EA 10775 und P. BM EA 10778)," *JEA* 84, 1998, 85–92.

Foster, John L., "Texts of the Egyptian Composition 'The Instruction of a Man for His Son' in the Oriental Institute Museum," *JNES* 45, 1986, 197–211.

Gaal, E., "Eines Neues Ostracon zur 'Lehre eines Mannes für seinen Sohn,'" *MDAIK* 40, 1984, 13–25.

Hoffmann, Friedhelm, "Einige Bemerkungen zur Lehre eines Mannes für seinem Sohn," *GM* 182, 2001, 7–8.

Posener, Georges, "L'enseignement d'un homme à son fils," in Erik Hornung and Othmar Keel, eds., *Studien zu Altägyptischen Lebenslehren,* OBO 28, Freiburg/Göttingen, 1979, 307–16.

——, "Pour la reconstruction de L'enseignement d'un homme à son fils," *RdE* 36, 1985, 115–19.

——, "L'enseignement d'un homme a son fils: Cinq nouveaux ostraca," in J. Osing and G. Dreyer, eds., *Form und Mass: Beiträge zur Literatur, Sprache und Kunst des alten Ägypten, Festschrift für Gerhard Fecht,* ÄUAT 12, 1987, 361–67.

Roccati, Alessandro, *Sapienza egizia: La letteratura educativa in Egitto durante il II millennio a.C.,* Brescia, 1994, 97–103.

## Merikare

Quack, Joachim Friedrich, *Studien zur Lehre für Merikare,* Göttinger Orientforschungen I, IV. Reihe: Ägypten, 23, Wiesbaden, 1992. Review by H. Goedicke, *BiOr* 53, 1996, 53–58, agrees with later dating. Review by H. W. Fischer-Elfert *Lingua Aegyptia* 7, 2000, 261–67. Helck, W., *Die Lehre für König Merikare,* Kleine Ägyptische Texte 5, Wiesbaden, 1977.

Posener, G., "Lehre für Merikare," *LÄ* III, 1980, 986–89.

Assmann, Jan, "Aus der Lehre für Merikare," in Otto Kaiser, ed., TUAT II/6: *Lieder und Gebete* II, 1991, 835–36.

Blumenthal, E., "Die Lehre für König Merikare," *ZÄS* 107, 1980, 5–41.

Darnell, John Coleman, "The Message of King Wahankh Antef II to Khety, Ruler of Heracleopolis," *ZÄS* 124, 1997, 101–8.

Demidchik, A., "A Note to #141 of Sir A. H. Gardiner's 'Egyptian Grammar,'" *GM* 134, 1993, 29–30. "Lo, the vile Asiatic is the dreary place (itself), in which he is (dwelling)." *qsn pw nj bw ntj.f jm.*

——, "The 'Region of the Northern Residence' in Middle Kingdom

Literature," in C. J. Eyre, ed., *Proceedings of the Seventh International Congress of Egyptologists,* OLA 82, Leuven, 1998, 325–330.

——, "The Reign of Merikare Khety," *GM* 192, 2003, 25–36.

Derchain, Philippe, "Eloquence et Politique: L'Opinion d'Akhtoy," *RdE* 40, 1989, 37–47.

Donadoni, S., "A propos de l'histoire du text de 'Merikare,' " in *Cultura del'antico Egitto: Scritti di Sergio F. Donadoni,* Rome, 1986, 129–36.

Goedicke, Hans, "Merikare E 106–115," *ZÄS* 129, 2002, 115–121.

Kammerzell, F., "Merikare E 30–31: Ein Fall van indirekter Rede mit Einaktantenanpassung im Mittelägyptische," *GM* 161, 1997, 97–101.

Lopez, J., "L'Auteur de l'enseignement pour Mérikarê," *RdE* 25, 1973, 178–91.

Lorton, D., "The Instruction for Merikare and Amarna Ideology," *GM* 134, 1993, 69–83. Influence of one on the other. Ref. Assmann, *SAK* 8, 1980, 1–32. *GM* 134, 1993, 69 (Lorton): "a comparison between the situation in Amarna and that of the beginning of Dyn. XII, in both of which there was a need to employ propaganda to help assure the loyalty of the administrative class."

——, "God's Beneficient Creation: Coffin Texts Spell 1130, the Instruction for Merikare, and the Great Hymn to the Aton," *SAK* 20, 1993, 125–58.

Morenz, L. D., "Ein Wortspiel mit dem Namen Chetys, des Assertors der *Lehre für Meri-ka-re?* (Meri-ka-re, E 143f.)," *GM* 159, 1997, 75–81.

Nowak, Edyta, "On the Passage of Merikare E 88–90," *GM* 183, 2001, 83–86.

Oréal, Elsa, "Une Relecture de *Mérikare,* E 109–15," *RdE* 51, 2000, 141–52.

Posener, G., "Trois passages de L'enseignement à Mérikarê," *RdE* 7, 1950, 176–80.

——, *"Enseignement pour le roi Mérikarê"* [summary of course], Annuaire du Collège de France 62, 1962, 290–95; 63, 1963, 303–5; 64, 1964, 305–7; 65, 1965, 343–46; 66, 1966, 342–45.

Quack, Joachim Friedrich, "Zwei Ostraka-Identifizierung," *GM* 115, 1990, 83–84.

Rathke-Konrad, K., "Wortverezeichnis und lexikostatische Untersuchung der Lehre für König Merikare," *GM* 160, 1997, 85–107.

Rowinska, R. K. W., "Staatsausdehnung (P 67–68) und Massnahmen zur

Verstärkerung der Nordgrenze (P 106–109) in der Lehre für König Merikare," *ZÄS* 119, 1992, 22–37.

Shoufu, Jin, "Drei Gruppenbezeichnungen für Beamten in der *Lehre für Merikare,*" *GM* 180, 2001, 89–95.

Vinson, Steve, and Alejandro Botta, "The Cowardly Crocodile in 'Onchsheshonqy 22/15 and Merikare' P. 97–98," *Enchoria* 23, 1996, 177–78.

Volten, Aksel, *Zwei Altägyptische Politische Schriften: Die Lehre für König Merikare (Pap. Carlsberg VI) und Die Lehre des König Amenemhet,* Analecta Aegyptiaca IV, Copenhagen, 1945.


Miscellanies—Scribal Traditions

Gardiner, Alan H., *Late Egyptian Miscellanies,* Bibliotheca Aegyptiaca 7, Brussels, 1937; Caminos, Ricardo, *Late-Egyptian Miscellanies,* London, 1954.

Brunner, H., "Schülerhandschriften," *LÄ* V, 1984, 737–39.

Assmann, Jan, in Otto Kaiser, ed., TUAT II/6: *Lieder und Gebete* II, Gütersloh, 1991, 827–928.

Erman, A., *Die ägyptische Schülerhandschiften,* ADAW 2, Berlin, 1925.

Fecht, Gerhard, *Literarische Zeugnisse zur "Persönlichen Frömmigkeit" in Ägypten: Analyse der Beispiele aus den ramessidischen Schulpapyri,* Abh. der Heidelberger Akad. der Wiss. Phil.-hist. Klass 1965, 1. Abh. Heidelberg, 1965.

Fischer-Elfert, Hans-W., "Textkritische und Lexicographische Notizen zu den *Late Egyptian Miscellanies,*" *SAK* 10, 1983, 141–49.

Guglielmi, W., "Berufsatiren in der Tradition des Cheti," in Manfred Bietak et al., eds., *Zwischen den Beiden Ewigkeiten: Festschrift Gertrud Thausing,* Vienna, 1994, 44–72.

Iversen, E., "Anastasi IV, 2.4–2.9 = Koller, 2.2–2.3 = Anastasi V, 5.1," in Gertie Englund and Paul John Frandsen, eds., *Crossroad,* CNI Publications 1, Copenhagen, 1986, 181–87.

Katary, Sally L. D., "Cultivator, Scribe, Stablemaster, Soldier: The Late Egyptian Miscellanies in the Light of Papyrus Wilbour," *Ancient World* 6, 1983, 71–94.

Tacke, Nikolaus, *Verspunkte als Gliederungsmittel in ramessidischen Schülerhandschriften,* SAGA 22, Heidelberg, 2001.

## Neferhotep Stela

Helck, Wolfgang, *Historisch-Biographische Texte der 2. Zwischenzeit und Neue Texte der 18. Dynastie,* 2, überarbeitete Auflage, Kleine Ägyptische Texte 6, no. 32, Wiesbaden, 1983, 21–29.

Pieper, Max, *Die Grosse Inschrift des Königs Neferhotep in Abydos: Ein Beitrag zur ägyptischen Religions- und Literaturgeschichte,* Mitteilungen der Vorderasiatisch-Aegyptischen Gesellschaft (E.V.) Band 32, Heft 2, 1929.

Stracmans, Maurice, "La grande inscription du Roi Neferhotep Ier (XIIIe dynastie égyptienne) (1)," *Phoibos* 5, 1949, 173–81.

——. "Les Lignes 36–38 de la Grande Inscription du roi Neferhotep de la XIIIe dynastie," *CdE* 25, 1950, 27–30.

## Neferty

Helck, Wolfgang, *Die Prophezeiung des Nfr.tj,* 2d ed., Kleine Ägyptische Texte 2, Wiesbaden, 1992.

Blumenthal, E., "Neferti, Prophezeiung des," *LÄ* IV, 1982, 380–81.

Blumenthal, E., "Die Prophezeiung des Neferti," *ZÄS* 109, 1982, 1–27.

Demidchik, A. E., "The 'Region of the Northern Residence' in Middle Kingdom Literature," in C. J. Eyre, ed., *Proceedings of the Seventh International Congress of Egyptologists,* OLA 82, Leuven, 1998, 325–30.

Eyre, C. J., "Why Was Egyptian Literature?" in *Sesto Congresso Internazionale di Egittologia: Atti II,* Turin, 1993, 115–27.

Foti, L., "The History in the Prophecies of Noferti: Relation between the Egyptian Wisdom and Prophecy Literatures," *StudAeg* 2, 1976, 3–18.

Graefe, E., "Die gute Reputation des Königs Snofru," in Sarah Israelit-Groll, ed., *Studies in Egyptology Presented to Miriam Lichtheim* I, Jerusalem, 1990, 257–63.

Kammerzell, F., "Die Prophezeihung des Neferti," in Otto Kaiser, ed., TUAT II/1, 1986, 102–10.

Quack, J. F., "Beiträge zur Textkritik der Prophezeihung des Neferti," *GM* 135, 1993, 77–79. E 25, 34, 46, 57, with bibliography.

## 'Onchsheshonqy, Instruction of

Glanville, S. R. K., *The Instructions of 'Onchsheshonqy (British Museum Papyrus 10508),* (Catalogue of Demotic Papyri in the British Museum

2), London 1955; Smith, H. S., "The Story of 'Onchsheshonqy,'" *Serapis* 6, 1980, 133–57 (for frame story); Thissen, Heinz J., *Die Lehre des Anchscheschonqi (P. BM 10508) Einleitung, Übersetzung, Indices,* Bonn, 1984 (with revised reconstruction of frame story, 14).

Thissen, Heinz J., "Die Lehre des Anch-Scheschonqi," *LÄ* III, 1980, 974–75.

Depauw, Mark, *A Companion to Demotic Studies,* Brussels, 1997, 100–101.

Bresciani, Edda, *Letteratura e Poesia dell'Antico Egitto,* Turin, 1969, 563–84.

Botta, Alejandro, and Steve Vinson, "The Cowardly Crocodile in 'Onchsheshonqy 22/15 and Merikarie' P. 97–98," *Enchoria* 23, 1996, 177–78.

Brunsch, Wolfgang, "Anchscheschonqi und die Frauen," *GM* 161, 1997, 37–49.

Burkes, Shannon, *Death in Qoheleth and Egyptian Biographies of the Late Period,* Atlanta, 1999, 221–34.

Depuydt, Leo, " 'Onksheshonqy' 2,13 and 4,1–2: A Philological Note," in S. I. Groll, ed., *Studies in Honor of Miriam Lichtheim* I, Jerusalem, 1990, 116–21.

Gemser, Berend, "The Instructions of 'Onchsheshonqy and Biblical Wisdom Literature," in James L. Crenshaw, ed., *Studies in Ancient Israelite Wisdom,* New York, 1976, 134–60.

Johnson, Janet H., *Thus Wrote 'Onchsheshonqy: An Introductory Grammar of Demotic,* SAOC 45, Chicago, 1986 (2d rev. ed., 1991).

Lichtheim, Miriam, *AEL* III, 159–84.

——, *Late Egyptian Wisdom Literature. A Study of Demotic Instructions,* OBO 52, Freiburg, 1983.

——, Review of Heinz Thissen, *Die Lehre des Anchscheschonqi (P. BM 10508), WdO* 15, 1984, 205–6.

Ritner, Robert K., Review of M. Lichtheim, *AEL* III, *JNES* 45, 1986, 243–44.

——, Review of Heinz Thissen, *Die Lehre des Anchscheschonqi (P. BM 10508), BiOr* 44, 1987, 641–46.

Ryholt, Kim, "A New Version of the Introduction to the Teachings of 'Onch-Sheshonqy," in P. J. Frandsen and K. Ryholt, eds., *A Miscellany of Demotic Texts and Studies,* Copenhagen, 2000, 113–40.

Sanders, Jack T., *Ben Sira and Demotic Wisdom,* Chico, Calif., 1983, 103–5.

Stricker, B. H., "De wijsheid von Anchsjesjonq," *OMRO* 39, 1958, 56–79.

Thissen, Heinz J., "Die Lehre des Anchscheschonqi," in G. Burkhard et al., eds., *Weisheitstexte II,* TUAT, 1991, 251–77.

Zauzich, Karl-Theodor, "Anchscheschonqi—eine Lehre für den Schreiber?" in M. Schade-Busch, ed., *Weg öffnen,* Wiesbaden, 1996, 376–80.


## Penitential Hymns

Kitchen, K. A., *Ramesside Inscriptions: Historical and Biographical* III, Oxford, 1980, 653–55 (Berlin 20377), 772–73 (Turin N 50058), 771–72 (British Museum 589).

Assmann, Jan. *Ägyptische Hymnen und Gebete,* Zurich, 1975, 351–56.

——, "Ägyptische Hymnen und Gebete," in Otto Kaiser, ed., TUAT II/6: *Lieder und Gebete* II, Gütersloh, 1991, 872–75 (Berlin 20377), 876–77 (Turin N 50058).

Barucq, André, and François Daumas, *Hymnes et prières de l'Égypte ancienne,* Paris, 1980, 236–39 (Berlin 23077), 468–69 (Turin N 50058), 408–9 (British Museum 589).

Erman, Adolf, "Denksteine aus der thebanischen Gräberstadt," *SBAW, phil.-hist. Klasse* 49, Berlin, 1911, 1086–1110.

Gunn, Battiscombe, "The Religion of the Poor," *JEA* 3, 1916, 81–94.

Wilson, John A., "Egyptian Hymns and Prayers," *ANET,* 380–81 (Berlin 20377, Turin N 50058).


## Piye Stela

Grimal, N.-C., *La stèle triomphale de Pi('ankh)y au Musée du Caire,* Cairo, 1981.

Leclant, Jean, "Pi(anchi)," *LÄ* IV, 1982, cols. 1045–52.

Gardiner, Alan H., "Piankhy's Instructions to His Army," *JEA* 21, 1935, 219–23.

Gomaà, Farouk, *Die libyschen Fürstentümer des Deltas,* Wiesbaden, 1974.

Lichtheim, Miriam, *AEL* III, 66–84.

Spalinger, Anthony, "The Military Background of the Campaign of Piye (Piankhy)," *SAK* 7, 1979, 273–301.

——, "Notes on the Military in Egypt during the XXVth Dynasty," *JSSEA* 11, 1981, 37–58.


Ptahhotep

Zába, Zybněk, *Les Maximes de Ptahhotep,* Prague, 1956; Jéquier, G., *Le papyrus Prisse et ses variantes . . . ,* Paris, 1911; Dévaud, E., *Les Maximes de Ptahhotep d'après le Papyrus Prisse, les Papyrus 10371 et 10509 du British Museum et la Tablette Carnarvon, Texte,* Fribourg, 1916; Caminos, R., *Literary Fragments in the Hieratic Script,* Oxford, 1956, 52–53, pls. 28–30.

Brunner, H., "Lehre des Ptahhotep," *LÄ* III, 1980, 989–91.

Barns, John W. B., "Some Readings and Interpretations in Sundry Egyptian Texts," *JEA* 58, 1972, 159–66.

Blumenthal, Elke, "Ptahhotep und das Stab des Alters," in J. Osing and G. Dreyer, eds., *Form und Mass: Beiträge zur Literatur, Sprache und Kunst des alten Ägypten-Festschrift für Gerhard Fecht,* ÄUAT 12, 1987, 84–97.

Burkard, Günter, "Ptahhotep und das Alter," *ZÄS* 115, 1988, 19–30. Extensive treatment of section on old age: verses 8–27.

——, in Otto Kaiser, ed., TUAT III/2, *Weisheitstexte* II 1991, 195–221.

Cannuyer, C., "L'obèse de Ptahhotep et de Samuel," *ZÄS* 113, 1986, 92–103.

Eichler, Eckhard, "Zur Datierung und Interpretation der Lehre des Ptahhotep," *ZÄS* 128, 2001, 97–107.

Faulkner, R. O., "Ptahhotep and the Disputants," in O. Firchow, ed., *Ägyptologische Studien,* Berlin, 1955, 81–84.

Fecht, G., *Der Habgierige und Die Maat in der Lehre des Ptahhotep (5. und 19. Maxime)* Abhandlungen des Deutschen Archaologögischen Institutes Kairo, I, Glückstadt, 1958.

——, "Ptahhotep und die Disputierer (Lehre des Ptahhotep nach Papyrus Prisse, Max. 2–4; Dév. 60–83)," *MDAIK* 37, 1981, 143–50; errata sheet *MDAIK* 38, 1982.

——, "*Cruces Interpretum* in der Lehre des Ptahhotep (Maximen 7, 9, 13, 14) und das Alter der Lehre," in A. Guillaumont, ed., *Hommages à François Daumas* I, Montpellier, 1986, 227–51. Dates original to Old Kingdom but regards it as revised to Middle Kingdom metrics and language.

Federn, Walter, "Notes on the Instruction to Kagemni and His Brethren,"
    *JEA* 36, 1950, 48–50.

Fischer-Elfert, H.-W., "Vermischtes III: Zwei neue Ptahhotep-Spuren,"
    *GM* 143, 1994, 45–47.

Foster, John L., *Thought Couplets and Clause Sequences in a Literary Text:
    The Maxims of Ptah-hotep,* SSEA Publications, vol. 5, Toronto, 1977.

Gardiner, Alan, "Kagemni Once Again," *JEA* 37, 1951, 109–10.

Goedicke, H., "Unrecognized Sportings," *JARCE* 6, 1967, 97–102.

Gunn, Battiscombe, *The Instruction of Ptah-hotep and the Instruction of
    Ka'gemni: The Oldest Books in the World,* London, 1918, 11–61.

Jacq, C., *L'enseignement du sage égyptien Ptahhotep, le plus ancien livre du
    monde,* Paris, 1999.

Kurth, Dieter, *Altägyptische Maximen für Manager: Die Lehre des
    Ptahhotep,* Darmstadt, 1999.

Lacombe-Unal, Françoise, "Le prologue de Ptahhotep: Interrogations et
    propositions," *BIFAO* 99, 1999, 283–97.

Lexa, F., "Quelques corrections, compléments et remarques sur ma
    traduction de L'enseignement de Ptahhotep," in *Studies Presented to
    F. Ll. Griffith,* London, 1932, 111–18.

Troy, L., "Good and Bad Women: Maxim 18/284–288 of the Instructions
    of Ptahhotep," *GM* 80, 1984, 77–81.

Vernus, P., "L'Intertextualité dans la culture pharaonique: L'enseignement
    de Ptahhotep et le grafitto d'*Imny* (Ouâdi Hammâmât n. 3042)," *GM*
    147, 1995, 103–9.

——, "Le début de L'enseignement de Ptahhotep: Un nouveau
    manuscript," *CRIPEL* 18, 1996, 119–40.

——, "Le vizir et le balancier: A propos de L'enseignement de Ptahhotep,"
    in Catherine Berger and Bernard Mathieu, eds., *Etudes sur l'Ancien
    Empire et la nécropole de Saqqara dédiées à Jean-Philippe Lauer.* Tome
    2, Montpellier, 1997, 437–43.

——, "Le discours politique dans l'*Enseignement de Ptahhotep,*" in Jan
    Assmann and Elke Blumenthal, eds., *Literatur und Politik im
    pharaonischen Ägypten,* IFAO, BdE 127, Cairo, 1999, 139–52.

## Qar

Sethe, Kurt, *Urkunden des Alten Reichs,* Urk. I, 2d ed., Leipzig, 1932,
    253–55.

Doret, Eric, *The Narrative Verbal System of Old and Middle Egyptian,* Geneva, 1986. Virtually the entite text is translated and commented upon in the examples of verbal forms cited. See index.

El-Khadragy, Mahmoud, "The Edfu Offering Niche of Qar in the Cairo Museum," *SAK* 30, 2002, 203–28.

Moreno García, J. C., "De l'Ancien Empire à la première période intermédiaire: L'Autobiographie de *Q3r* d'Edfou, entre tradition et innovation," *RdE* 49, 1998, 151–60.

Roccati, Alessandro, *La Littérature historique sous l'ancien empire égyptien,* Paris, 1982, 179–80.


Satire on the Trades

Helck, Wolfgang, *Die Lehres des Dw3-Htjj, Textzusammenstellung* Teile 1–2, Kleine Ägyptische Texte 3, Wiesbaden, 1970.
Brunner, H., "Lehre des Cheti," *LÄ* III, 1980, 977–78.

Beckerath, J. von, "Ostracon München ÄS 396," *SAK* 10, 1983, 63–69.
Brunner, Hellmut, *Die Lehre des Cheti, Sohnes des Duauf,* ÄF 13, Glückstadt, 1944.
——, *Altägyptische Weisheit: Lehren für das Leben,* Zurich, 1988.
Curto, Silvio, *La Satira nell'Antico Egitto,* Turin, n.d.
Foster, John L., "Some Comments on Khety's Instruction for Little Pepi on His Way to School (Satire on the Trades)," in Emily Teeter and John A. Larson, eds., *Gold of Praise: Studies on Ancient Egypt in Honor of Edward F. Wente,* SAOC 20, Chicago, 2000, 121–29.
Guglielmi, Waltraud, "Berufssatiren in der Tradition des Cheti," in Manfred Bietak et al., eds., *Zwischen die Beiden Ewigkeiten: Festschrift Gertrud Tausing,* Vienna, 1994, 44–72. Discussion in detail of four passages in the Miscellany literature and pChester Beatty IV, V, and the later development of the themes of the satire on the professions. With remarks on the concept of satire in general and references to satire from Ben Sira through the Middle Ages.
Hoch, James, "The Teaching of Dua-Khety: A New Look at the Satire of the Trades," *JSSEA* 21–22, 1991–92 (issued 1995), 88–100.
Mathieu, Bernard, "La Satire des Metiers indications bibliographiques," *Grafma Newsletter* 1999, 37–40.
Parkinson, R. B., "Two or Three Literary Artefacts: British Museum EA

41650/47896, and 22878–9," in W. V. Davies, ed., *Studies in Egyptian Antiquities: A Tribute to T. G. H. James,* British Museum Occasional Paper 123, London, 1999, 49–57.

Posener, Georges, "L'auteur de la Satire des Métiers," in J. Vercoutter, ed., *Livre du Centenaire de l'IFAO (1880–1980),* Cairo, 1980, 55–59.

Quack, J. F., "Zwei Ostraka-Identifizierungen," *GM* 115, 1990, 83–84.

Roccati, A., *Sapienza egizia: La letteratura educativa in Egitto durante il II millennio a.C.,* Brescia, 1994, 79–87. Translation incorporating an unpublished papyrus in Museo Egizio, Turin.

——, "Réflexions sur la Satire des Métiers," *BSFE* 148, 2000, 5–17.

Seibert, P., *Die Charakteristik: Untersuchung zu einer altägyptischen Sprechsitte und ihren Ausprägungen in Folklore und Literatur,* Teil I: *Philologische Bearbeitung der Bezeugungen,* ÄAbh 17, Wiesbaden, 1967.

Théodoridès, A., "La 'Satire des Métiers' et les marchands," *Annuaire de l'Institute de Philologie et d'Histoire Orientales et Slaves* 15, 1958–60, 39–69.

van der Walle, B., "Le thème de la Satire des Métiers dans la littérature égyptienne,' *CdE* 22, 1947, 55–72.

Westendorf, W., "Eine Formel des Totenbuches als Schreibfehler in der 'Lehre des (Dua-)Cheti,' " *GM* 5, 1973, 43–45.

## Satrap Stela

Kamal, Ahmed Bey, *Stèles ptolémaiques et romaines,* Cairo, 1905, 168–71 and pl. LVI (with further early bibliography); Sethe, Kurt, *Hieroglyphische Urkunden der griechisch-römischen Zeit,* Urk. II, Leipzig, 1904–16, 11–22, no. 9; Mariette, Auguste, *Monuments divers recueillis en Égypte et en Nubie,* Paris, 1872, § 3, pl. XIV (plate reversed).

Bianchi, Robert S., "Satrapenstele," *LÄ* V, 1983, cols. 492–93.

Bevan, Edwin, *A History of Egypt under the Ptolemaic Dynasty,* London, 1927, 28–32.

Bouché-Leclercq, A., *Histoire des Lagides,* vol. 1, Paris, 1903, 104–8, and vol. 4, 303.

Briant, Pierre, *Histoire de l'Empire Perse,* Paris, 1996, 738, 877–81, and 1043–45.

Brugsch, Heinrich, "Ein Decret Ptolemaios' des Sohnes Lagi, des Satrapen," *ZÄS* 9, 1871, 1–13.

Huss, W., "Der rätselhäfte Pharao Chababasch," *Studi epigrafici e linguistici sul Vicino Oriente Antico* 11, 1994, 97–112 (with further recent bibliography).

Ritner, Robert K., "Khababash and the Satrap Stela—A Grammatical Rejoinder," *ZÄS* 107, 1980, 135–37.

Spalinger, A., "The Reign of King Chabbash: An Interpretation," *ZÄS* 105, 1978, 142–54.

Spiegelberg, Wilhelm, *Papyrus Libbey: An Egyptian Marriage Contract,* Toledo, 1907, 2–6.

Wilcken, Ulrich, "Zur Satrapenstele," *ZÄS* 35, 1897, 81–87.

## Senwosret III Hymns

Griffith, F. Ll, *Hieratic Papyri from Kahun and Gurob,* London, 1898, text, 1–3; pls. 1–3.

Sethe, K., *Ägyptische Lesestücke,* Leipzig, 1924, 65–67; G. Möller, *Hieratische Lesestücke* I, 1909, pls. 4–5.

Assmann, Jan, *Ägyptische Hymnen und Gebete,* Zurich, 1975, 476–80.

Derchain, Philippe, "Magie et politique: A propos de l'hymne à Sesostris III," *CdE* 62, 1987, 21–29. Includes recent bibliography of text. Discussion of first Hymn, magic is a weapon of king. Translates *tsw.f* as "ses sortileges."

Patané, Massimo, "Le structure de l'hymne à Sésostris III," *BSEG* 8, 1983, 61–65.

Peet, T. E., *A Comparative Study of the Literatures of Egypt, Palestine, and Mesopotamia,* 1931, 66–69.

## Semna Stela

Sethe, Kurt, *Ägyptische Lesestücke: Texte des Mittleren Reiches,* Leipzig, 1924, 83–84.

Helck, Wolfgang, "Grenzsteine," *LÄ* II, 1976, 897.

Barta, Winfried, "Der Terminus *twt* auf den Grenzstelen Sesostris' III. in Nubien," in *Festschrift zum 150 Jährigen Bestehen des Berliner*

*Ägyptischen Museum,* Berlin, 1974, 51–54, with photographic plate (Tafel 1).

Eyre, Christopher J., "The Semna Stelae: Quotation, Genre, and Functions of Literature," in Sarah Israelit-Groll, ed., *Studies in Egyptology Presented to Miriam Lichtheim* I, Jerusalem, 1990, 134–65.

Leclant, Jean, in D. Wildung, ed., *Sudan Ancient Kingdoms of the Nile,* Paris, 1997, no. 81, 78–79.

Obsomer, Claude, *Les campagnes de Sésostris dans Hérodote: Essai d'interprétation du texte grec à la lumière des réalités égyptiennes,* Brussels, 1989.

Seidlmayer, Stephan Johannes, "Zu Fundort und Aufstellungskontext der großen Semna-Stele Sesostris' III," *SAK* 28, 2000, 233–42.

Théodoridès, Aristide, "Les relations d'Egypte pharaonique avec ses voisins," *Revue internationale des droits de l'antiquité,* 3d ser., 22, 1975, 87–140.

Setna and Si-Osire, Adventures of (Setna II)

Griffith, F. Ll., *Stories of the High Priests of Memphis,* Oxford, 1900 (repr. Osnabrück, 1985); Erichsen, Wolja, *Demotische Lesestücke,* Leipzig, 1937, 41–49 (hand copy).

Bresciani, Edda, "Chaemwese-Erzählungen," *LÄ* I, 1975, 899–901.

Depauw, Mark, *A Companion to Demotic Studies,* Brussels, 1997, 87–88.

Bresciani, Edda, *Letteratura e Poesia dell'Antico Egitto,* Turin, 1969, 627–41.

Brunner, Hellmut, "Die religiöse Wertung der Armut im Alten Ägypten," *Saeculum* 12, 1961, 336–39.

Brunner-Traut, Emma, *Altägyptische Märchen,* Düsseldorf and Cologne, 1963 (2d ed., 1965), 192–214 and 299–300.

Donadoni, Sergio, *Storia della letteratura egiziana antica,* Milan, 1957, 319–25.

Gressmann, Hugo, "Vom reichen Mann und armen Lazarus, mit ägyptologischen Beiträgen von G. Möller," *Abhandlungen der Berliner Akademie der Wissenschaften, Philosophisch-historische Klasse* 7, Berlin, 1918 (trans. Möller, 62–68).

Grimal, Nicolas, "Le Roi et la Sorcière," in *Homages à Jean Leclant,* BdE
106/4, Cairo, 1994, 97–108.

Hoffmann, Friedhelm, "Einige Bemerkungen zur Zweiten
Setnegeschichte," *Enchoria* 19/20, 1992/93, 11–14.

Lichtheim, Miriam, *AEL* III, Berkeley, 1980, 138–51.

Maspero, Gaston, *Popular Stories of Ancient Egypt,* Cambridge, 1915
(repr. New York, 1967; English trans. by A. S. Johns, from *Les contes
populaires de l'Egypte ancienne,* 1882), 144–70.

Pieper, M., "Zum Setna-Roman," *ZÄS* 67, 1931, 71–74.

Ritner, Robert K., *The Mechanics of Ancient Egyptian Magical Practice,*
SAOC 54, Chicago, 1993 (citations gathered in index, 321).

For additional early references, see Ida B. Pratt, *Ancient Egypt,* New York
Public Library, New York, 1925, 358–59; and *Supplement,* 1942, 249.

Setna Khaemuas and the Mummies, Romance of (Setna I)

Griffith, F. Ll., *Stories of the High Priests of Memphis,* Oxford, 1900 (repr.
Osnabrück, 1985); Spiegelberg, Wilhelm, *Die demotischen
Denkmäler,* vol. 2: *Die demotischen Papyrus,* Catalogue général . . . du
musée du Caire, Leipzig, 1908, 88 and pls. 44–47 (for text photos);
Erichsen, Wolja, *Demotische Lesestücke,* Leipzig, 1937, 1–40 (hand
copy).

Bresciani, Edda, "Chaemwese-Erzählungen," *LÄ* I, 1975, 899–901.

Depauw, Mark, *A Companion to Demotic Studies,* Brussels, 1997, 87–88.

Barns, John W. B., "Some Readings in Sundry Egyptian Texts," *JEA* 58,
1972, 165–66.

——, "Egypt and the Greek Romance," in H. Gerstinger, ed., *Akten VIII.
Internationalen Kongresses für Papyrologie,* Mitteilungen aus der
Papyrussammlung der Nationalbibliothek in Wien, new series 5,
Vienna, 1956, 29–36.

Bresciani, Edda, *Letteratura e Poesia dell'Antico Egitto,* Turin, 1969, 615–
26.

Brunner-Traut, Emma, *Altägyptischen Märchen,* Düsseldorf and Cologne,
1963 (2d ed., 1965), 171–92 and 295–98.

Darnell, John C. "Articular *Km.t/Kmy* and Partitive ⲕⲏⲙⲉ (Including an
Isis of Memphis and Syria, and the *Kmy* of Setne I 5, 11 West of
Which Lived Ta-Bubu)," *Enchoria* 17, 1990, 69–81.

Donadoni, Sergio, *Storia della letteratura egiziana antica,* Milan, 1957, 315–18.

Gedge, Pauline, *Mirage,* New York, 1990 (repr. of *Scroll of Saqqara,* 1990; modern novelization).

Gilula, Mordechai, "Setna 6/4," *Enchoria* 6, 1976, 125.

Gunn, B., in Bernard Lewis, ed., *Land of Enchanters,* London, 1948, 67–83.

Hoffmann, Friedhelm, "Einige Bemerkungen zur Ersten Setnegeschichte (P. Kairo CG 30646)," *Enchoria* 23, 1996, 54–55.

Lichtheim, Miriam, *AEL* III, 125–38.

Maspero, Gaston, *Popular Stories of Ancient Egypt,* Cambridge, 1915 (repr. New York, 1967; English trans. by A. S. Johns, from *Les contes populaires de l'Egypte ancienne,* 1882), 115–44.

——, "Une page du Roman de Satni transcrite en hiéroglyphes," *ZÄS* 18, 1880, 15–22 and pl. 1.

Meltzer, Edmund S., "With a Forked Stick in His Hand and a Fiery Censer upon His Head," *SSEA Newsletter* 7/1, 1976, 10–11.

Miosi, Frank T., " 'Wassergeist'(?)," *SSEA Newsletter* 2/1, 1971, 6–9.

Murray, Gilbert, *Nefrekepta,* Oxford, 1911 (rendered into verse).

Piccione, Peter A., "The Gaming Episode in the *Tale of Setne Khamwas* as Religious Metaphor," in David Silverman, ed., *For His Ka: Essays Offered in Memory of Klaus Baer,* SAOC 55, Chicago, 1994, 197–204.

Ritner, Robert K., "Two Demotic Notes," *Enchoria* 13, 1985, 213–14.

——, Review of Lichtheim, *AEL* III, *JNES* 45, 1986, 243–44.

——, *The Mechanics of Ancient Egyptian Magical Practice,* SAOC 54, Chicago, 1993 (citations gathered in index, 321).

Rutherford, Ian. "Kalasiris and Setne Khamwas: A Greek Novel and Some Egyptian Models," *ZPE* 117, 1997, 203–9.

Tait, W. John, "P. Carlsberg 207: Two Columns of a Setna-Text," in P. J. Frandsen, ed., *Demotic Texts from the Collection,* The Carlsberg Papyri I, Copenhagen, 1991, 19–46 and pls. 1–3.

Vikentiev, Vladimir, "La première histoire de Setné Khamouas et quelques contes apparentés," *BIE* 29, 1948, 301–18.

West, Stephanie, "P. Mich. 3378: A Voice from the Grave?" *ZPE* 51, 1983, 55–58.

Zauzich, Karl-Theodor, "Gottesellen statt Gotteskraft," *Enchoria* 1, 1971, 83–86.

——, "Die schlimme Geschichte von dem Mann der Gottesmutter, der ein Gespenst war," *Enchoria* 6, 1976, 79–82.

For additional early references, see Ida B. Pratt, *Ancient Egypt,* New York Public Library, New York, 1925, 358–59; and *Supplement,* 1942, 249.


Shipwrecked Sailor

Blackman, A. M., *Middle Egyptian Stories,* Bibliotheca Aegyptiaca 2, Brussels, 1932, 41–48; De Buck, Adriaan, *Egyptian Readingbook, Exercises and Middle Egyptian Texts,* Leiden, 1948, 100–106.

Simpson, W. K., "Schiffbrüchiger," *LÄ* V, 1983, 619–22.


Altenmüller, Hartwig, "Die 'Geschichte des Schiffbrüchigen'—Ein Aufruf zum Loyalismus?" in H. Altenmüller and R. Germer, eds., *Miscellanea Aegyptologica Wolfgang Helck zum 75. Geburtstag,* Hamburg, 1989, 7–21.

Baines, John, "Interpreting the Story of the Shipwrecked Sailor," *JEA* 76, 1990, 55–72, with bibliography.

Bagnani, G., "Il Nafragio del 'Naufrago' e il valore del geroglifico," *Aegyptus* 12, 1932, 357–64.

Berg, David, "Syntax, Semantics and Physics: The Shipwrecked Sailor's Fire," *JEA* 76, 1990, 168–70. "Removing the fire drill when I had ignited the fire, I made a holocaust to the gods."

Bolshakov, Andrey O., "Some *De Visu* Observations on P. Hermitage 1115," *JEA* 79, 1993, 254–59. Indicates that a page was probably missing at the beginning.

Bomhard, A. S. von, "Le conte du Naufragé et le Papyrus Prisse," *RdE* 50, 1999, 61–65.

Bradbury, Lisa, "Reflections on Travelling to 'God's Land,' and Punt in the Middle Kingdom," *JARCE* 25, 1988, 127–56.

Bryan, Betsy, "The Hero of the 'Shipwrecked Sailor,'" *Serapis* 5, 1979, 3–13.

Burkard, Günter, *Überlegungen zur Form der ägyptischen Literatur, die Geschichte des Schiffbrüchigen als literarisches Kunstwerk,* ÄUAT 22, Wiesbaden, 1993.

Cannuyer, Christian, "Encore le naufrage du Naufragé," *BSEG* 14, 1990, 15–21.

Derchain in Merikare article (see above) cites Shipwrecked Sailor as possible subversive tale in presenting a ruler more interested in the profit of his expedition than the life of his messenger!

Derchain-Urtel, Maria-Theresia, "Die Schlange des Schiffbrüchigen," *SAK* 1, 1974, 83–104.

Devauchelle, Didier: "Naufragé 184–186," *GM* 101, 1988, 21–25.

Dévaud, E., "Le Conte du naufragé: Remarques grammatiques, lexicographiques, paléographiques, etc.," *Recueil de Travaux* 38, 1916–17, 188–210.

Dochniak, C. C., "A Note on the Shipwrecked Sailor 135–138," *GM* 142, 1994, 69–71.

Donadoni, Sergio, "Il naufragio del 'Naufrago,'" *BSEG* 9–10, 1984–85, 87–88. Contrasts competence of crew in foretelling storm and then being wrecked.

Fischer, H. G., "Some Iconographic and Literary Comparisons: 1. A Human-Headed Serpent (Shipwrecked Sailor, 62–66)" in Jan Assmann, Erika Feucht, and Reinhard Grieshammer, eds., *Fragen an die altägyptische Literatur: Studien zum Gedenken on Eberhard Otto,* Wiesbaden, 1977, 155–58.

——, "Two Replies 1. The Serpent of the Shipwrecked Sailor," *GM* 49, 1981, 25–27.

Foster, John L., "The Shipwrecked Sailor: Prose or Verse (Postponing Clauses and Tense-neutral Clauses)," *SAK* 15, 1988, 69–109.

——, *The Shipwrecked Sailor: A Tale from Ancient Egypt,* Cairo, 1998. With amusing and excellent illustrations by Lyla Pinch Brock.

Gilula, M., "Shipwrecked Sailor, Lines 184–85," in J. Johnson and E. F. Wente, eds., *Studies Done in Honor of George R. Hughes,* SAOC 39, Chicago, 1977, 75–82.

Goedicke, Hans, *Die Geschichte des Schiffbrüchigen,* ÄAbh 30, Wiesbaden, 1974.

——, "The Snake in the Story of the Shipwrecked Sailor," *GM* 30, 1980, 27–31.

Helck, Wolfgang, "Die 'Geschichte des Schiffbrüchigen'—Eine Stimme der Opposition?" in J. Osing and E. R. Nielsen, eds., *The Heritage of Ancient Egypt, Studies in Honor of Erik Iversen,* 1992, 73–76.

Ignatov, S., "Some Notes on the Story of the Shipwrecked Sailor," *JEA* 80, 1994, 195–98.

Kurth, Dieter, "Zur Interpretationen der Geschichte des Schiffbrüchigen," *SAK* 14, 1987, 167–79. Detailed review of literature, new ideas. Literature of pessimism, skepticism, dated to First Intermediate Period.

Lanzckowski, G., "Die Geschichte des Schiffbrüchigen: Versuch einer religionsgeschichtlichen Interpretation," *ZDMG* 103 (N.F. 28), 1953, 360–71.

Lapidus, Michel, *La quête de l'île merveilleuse (le conte du naufragé),* Paris, 1995.

Le Guilloux, Patrice, *Le conte du naufragé (papyrus Ermitage 1115),* Angers, 1996.

Loprieno, A., "The Sign of Literature in the Shipwrecked Sailor," in U. Verhoeven and E. Graefe, eds., *Religion und Philosophie* (Fs. Derchain), OLA 39, Leuven, 1991, 209–17.

Manuelian, Peter Der, "Interpreting 'The Shipwrecked Sailor,' " in Ingrid Gamer-Wallert and Wolfgang Helck, eds., *Gegengabe: Festschrift für Emma Brunner-Traut,* Tübingen, 1991, 223–33.

Meltzer, E., "The Setting of the Shipwrecked Sailor," *GM* 22, 1976, 47–50.

Mode, Markus, "Das Gleichnis des schiffbrüchigen Gefolgsmannes (Bemerkungen zu Papyrus 1115 der Stattlichen Ermitage in Leningrad)," *Hallesche Beiträge zur Orientwissenschaft* 2, 1980, 5–57.

Morenz, L. "Gottesunmittelbarkeit und skandalöses Suffixpronomen— Zum 13. Kapitel des Schiffbrüchigen," *GM* 141, 1994, 77–80.

Nibbi, A., "The Shipwrecked Sailor," *GM* 24, 1977, 53–55.

Otto, E., "Die Geschichten des Sinuhe und des Schiffbrüchigen als 'Lehrhafte Stücke,' " *ZÄS* 93, 1966, 100–111.

Radomska, Barbara, "Die Insel des Schiffbrüchigen—eine Halbinsel?" *GM* 99, 1987, 27–30. Answer by Westendorf in negative below.

Redford, Donald B., "The Shipwrecked Sailor's Snake," *SSEA Newsletter* 6, no. 2, 1975, 13–16.

——, "A Note on *Shipwrecked Sailor* 147–8," *JEA* 81, 1981, 174–75.

Rendsburg, Gary A., "Literary Devices in the Story of the Shipwrecked Sailor," *JAOS* 120, 2000, 13–23.

Simpson, W. K., "Allusions to the Shipwrecked Sailor and the Eloquent Peasant in a Ramesside Text," *JAOS* 78, 1958, 50–51.

——, "Amor dei: *nṯr mrr rmt m tȝ wȝ* (Sh. Sai. 147–148) and the Embrace," in Jan Assmann, Erika Feucht, and Reinhard Grieshammer, eds., *Fragen an die altägyptische Literatur: Studien zum Gedenken an Eberhard Otto,* Wiesbaden, 1977, 493–98.

Spalinger, A., "An Alarming Parallel to the End of Shipwrecked Sailor,'"
GM 73, 1984, 91–95.

Vandersleyen, Claude, "En relisant le Naufragé," in Sarah Israelit-Groll,
ed., *Studies in Egyptology Presented to Miriam Lichtheim* II,
Jerusalem, 1990, 1019–24.

——, *Wadj our: Un autre aspect de la vallée du Nil,* Connaissance de
l'Egypte Ancienne, Etude 7, Brussels, 1999. Cf. review by K. A.
Kitchen in *DE* 46, 2000, 123–38; reply by Vandersleyen in *DE* 47,
2000, 95–109.

Vergote, J. "Une nouvelle Interprétation de deux Passages du Naufragé
(132b–136 et 167b–169)," *MDAIK* 15, 1957, 132–36. "If you are
strong, control your heart."

Vittmann, G., "Zum Verständnis vom Schiffbrüchingen 129f.," *GM* 29,
1978, 149–52.

Vycichl, W., "Notes on the Story of the Shipwrecked Sailor," *Kush* 5, 1957,
70–72.

Westendorf, W., "Die Insel des Schiffbrüchigen-keine Halbinsel!'" in
Sarah Israelit-Groll, ed., *Studies in Egyptology presented to Miriam
Lichtheim* II, Jerusalem, 1990, 1056–64.

## Sinuhe

Koch, Roland, *Die Erzählung des Sinuhe,* Bibliotheca Aegyptiaca 17,
Brussels, 1990. Autographed text of all papyri and ostraca.

Simpson, W. K., "Sinuhe," *LÄ* V, 1984, 950–55.

Allam, S., "Sinuhe's Foreign Wife Reconsidered," *DE* 4, 1986, 15–16.
Adoptive daughter.

Altenmüller, Hartwig, "Die Zeit 'diesseits und jenseits der Todesschwelle'
in Brief Sesostris' I. an Sinuhe," *GM* 188, 2002, 9–14.

Assmann, J., "Die Rubren in der Überlieferung der Sinuhe-Erzählung," in
M. Görg, ed., *Fontes atque Pontes: Eine Festgabe für Hellmut Brunner,*
ÄUAT 5, Wiesbaden, 1983, 18–41.

Baines, J., "Interpreting *Sinuhe,*" *JEA* 68, 1982, 31–44. A major study.

Barns, J. W. B., "Sinuhe's Message to the King: A Reply to a Recent
Article," *JEA* 53, 1967, 6–14.

——, "Some Readings and Interpretations in Sundry Egyptian Texts," *JEA*
58, 1972, 159–66, esp. 160–61.

Barta, Miroslav, *Sinuhet's Flight from Egypt: Egypt, Syria and Palestine during the Time of Abraham,* Prague, 1999, in Czech (forthcoming in English in 2003).

Barta, Winfried, "Der 'Vorwurf an Gott' in der Lebensgeschichte des Sinuhe," in B. Schmitz and A. Eggebrecht, eds., *Festschrift Jürgen von Beckerath: zum 70 Geburtstag am 19. Februar 1990,* HÄB 30, Hildesheim, 1990, 21–27.

Behrens, P., "Sinuhe B 134 ff oder die Psychologie eines Zweikampfes," *GM* 44, 1981, 7–11. On interpretation of weapons' fall(?).

Berg, D., "Notes on Sinuhe B 5–7," *GM* 79, 1984, 11–13.

Blumenthal, Elke, *Altägyptische Reiseerzählungen: Die Lebensgeschichte des Sinuhe; Der Reisebericht des Wen-Amun,* Leipzig, 1982.

——, "Zu Sinuhes Zweikampf mit dem Starken von Retjenu," in M. Görg, ed., *Fontes atque Pontes: Eine Festgabe für Hellmut Brunner,* ÄUAT 5, Wiesbaden, 1983, 42–46.

——, "Die Erzählung des Sinuhe," in Otto Kaiser, ed., *Mythen und Epen* TUAT III/5, Gütersloh, 1995, 884–911, translation with notes and references.

Brunner, H., "Das Besänftigungslied im Sinuhe (B 269–279)," *ZÄS* 80, 1955, 45–53.

——, "Zu Sin. B 115f.," *ZÄS* 91, 1964, 139–40.

Cannuyer, C., "Note à propos de *Sinouhé* B 133–134," *GM* 88, 1985, 11–13.

Colin, Gérard, "Dans une proximité lointaine ou En allant et venant? (Sinouhé B 2 [R25])," *RdE* 46, 1995, 203–4.

Davies, W. V., "Readings in the Story of Sinuhe and Other Egyptian Texts," *JEA* 61, 1975, 45–53.

Defossez, M., "Note lexicographique sur le mot *ḫwtf,*" *RdE* 38, 1987, 187–90.

Depuydt, Leo, *Conjunction, Contiguity, Contingency,* Oxford, 1993, 178–85.

Derchain, P., "La réception de Sinouhé à la cour de Sésostris Ier," *RdE* 22, 1970, 79–83.

——, "Sinouhé et Ammounech," *GM* 87, 1985, 7–13.

Donadoni, S. F., "L'ispirazione divina di Sinuhe," in *Cultura del'antico Egitto: Scritti di Sergio Donadoni,* Rome, 1986, 289–91.

Donner, B., " 'Zum Streitlustigen' in Sinuhe B 110," *ZÄS* 81, 1956, 61–62.

El-Hamrawi, Mahmoud, "Bemerkungen zu pWestcar 5, 1–7 und Sinuhe B 147," *Lingua Aegyptia* 7, 2000, 141–52.

Fecht, Gerhard, "Sinuhes Zweikampf als Handelskern des dritten Kapitels des Sinuhe-'Romans,'" in F. Junge, ed., *Studien zu Sprache und Religion Ägyptens zu Ehren von Wolfhart Westendorf,* Band I: Sprache, Göttingen, 1984, 465–84.

Foster, John, "*Sinuhe:* The Ancient Egyptian Genre of Narrative Verse," *JNES* 39, 1980, 89–117.

——, "Cleaning Up Sinuhe," *JSSEA* 12, no. 2, 1982, 81–85.

——, "The *sḏm.f* and *sḏm.n.f* forms in The Tale of Sinuhe," *RdE* 34, 1982–83, 27–52.

——. *Thought Couplets in the Story of Sinuhe,* MÄU 3, Munich, 1993.

Galán, José M., "Two Passages of *Sinuhe* Reconsidered," *SAK* 25, 1998, 71–81. On B 97–99 and B 161–162.

Gardiner, A. H., *Notes on the Story of Sinuhe,* Paris, 1916.

Goedicke, Hans, "The Riddle of Sinuhe's Flight," *RdE* 35, 1984, 95–103.

——, "Sinuhe's Reply to the King's Letter," *JEA* 51, 1965, 29–47.

——, "Sinuhe's Duel," *JARCE* 21, 1984, 197–201.

——, "Sinuhe's Foreign Wife," *BSEG* 9–10 (1984–85), 103–7. Senior daughter, given without bride price because of Amuneshi's regard for Sinuhe.

——, "The Encomium of Sesostris I," *SAK* 12, 1985, 5–28.

——, "Three Passages in the Story of Sinuhe: I. The King's Passing R 5–8; II. What Was Sinuhe's Lie?; III. Sinuhe's Good Life in Retjenu," *JARCE* 23, 1986, 167–74.

——, "Readings V: Sinuhe B 10," *VA* 4, 1988, 201–6.

——, "Sinuhe's Self-Realization (Sinuhe B 113–127)," *ZÄS* 117, 1990, 129–39.

——. "Where Did Sinuhe Stay in Asia (Sinuhe B 29–31)?" *CdE* 67, 1992, 28–40.

——, "The Song of the Princesses (*Sinuhe* B 269–279)," *BSEG* 22, 1998, 29–36.

——. "Sinuhe B 147–9," *GM* 181, 2001, 39–41.

Görg, Manfred, "Das Land J33 (Sin B 81.238)," in Jürgen Osing and Günter Dreyer, eds., *Form und Mass: Beiträge zur Literatur, Sprache und Kunst des alten Ägypten, Festschrift für Gerhard Fecht,* ÄUAT 12, 1987, 142–53. Perhaps J33 is "plant-land," Kulturland, but also a southern locality based on terms known from Ugaritic, Amarna, and Ramesside texts, essentially the hinterland of Byblos.

Gordon, Cyrus, "The Marriage and Death of Sinuhe," in John A. Marks and Robert M. Good, eds., *Love and Death in the Ancient Near East: Essays in Honor of Marvin H. Pope,* Guilford, Conn., 1987, 43–44. Cites Nuzi parallel adoption/marriage text indicating that son-in-law renounces rights and property if marriage is terminated: thus Sinuhe leaves his wife, children, and property when he decides to return to Egypt.

Grapow, H., *Der stilistische Bau der Geschichte des Sinuhe, Untersuchungen zur ägyptischen Stilistik I,* Berlin, 1952.

Green, M., "The Syrian and Lebanese Topographical Data in the Story of Sinuhe," *CdE* 58, 1983, 38–59.

——, "The Word *ngꜣw* in Sinuhe B 13," *GM* 70, 1984, 27–29. Inteprets as "deserted quay."

Greig, Gary S., "The *sḏm=f* and *sḏm.n=f* in the Story of Sinuhe and the Theory of the Nominal (Emphatic) Verbs," in Sarah Israelit-Groll, ed., *Studies in Honour of Miriam Lichtheim* I, Jerusalem, 1990, 264–348. An extensive treatment.

Harris, J. R., "A Note on the Ramesside Text of 'Sinuhe,'" *GM* 11, 1974, 25–28. Suggests that the Ramesside text of Sinuhe was composed in the Amarna Period.

Hermann, A., "Sinuhe—ein ägyptische Schelmenroman," *OLZ* 48, 1953, 101–9.

Hornung, Erik, *Gesänge vom Nil: Dichtung am Hofe der Pharaonen,* Zurich, 1990, 31–51.

Iversen, Erik, "The Story of Sinuhe—Some Suggestions on the Translation," *Lingua Aegyptia* 9, 2001, 139–42.

Kahl, J., "Es ist vom Anfang bis zum Ende gekommen, wie es in der Schrift geworden war: zu Überlieferung der Erzählung des Sinuhe," in M. Dietrich and I. Kottspier, eds., *Und Moses schrieb dieses Lieder auf: Studien zum Altes Testament und zum Alten Orient. Festschrift für Oswald Loretz zur Vollendung seines 70. Lebensjahres,* Münster, 1998, 383–400.

Kitchen, Kenneth A., "Sinuhe's Foreign Friends and Papyri (Coptic) Greenhill 1–4," in C. J. Eyre, Anthony Leahy, and Lisa Montagno Leahy, eds., *The Unbroken Reed: Studies in the Culture and Heritage of Ancient Egypt in Honour of A. F. Shore,* Egypt Exploration Society, Occasional Papers 11, London 1994, 161–69.

——, *Poetry of Ancient Egypt,* Jonsered, 1999, 91–96, 151–58.

Knauf, E. A., "Zum 'Einzelkämpfer' Sinuhe B 110," *GM* 33, 1979, 33.

Koyama, M., "Essai de réconstitution de la composition de l'Histoire de Sinouhé," *Orient* (Tokyo) 18, 1982, 41–64.

Lanczkowski, G., "Die Geschichte vom Riesen Goliath und der Kampf Sinuhes mit dem Starken von Retenu," *MDAIK* 16, 1958, 214–18.

Loprieno, Antonio, "Sinuhe als Asiat," chap. 5 of *Topos und Mimesis,* ÄAbh 48, 1988, 41–59.

Lorton, David, "The Treatment of Criminals in Ancient Egypt through the New Kingdom," *JESHO* 22, 1977, 2–64.

Luino, Philippe, *La véritable histoire de Sinouhé,* Paris, 1998.

Malaise, M., "La traduction de Sinouhe B 160," *GM* 10, 1974, 29–34.

Meltzer, Edmund S., review of John Foster's *Thought Couplets in the Story of Sinuhe, JARCE* 32, 1995, 271–73.

——, "*Sḏm.f, Sḏm.n.f* and Verbs of Motion in *Sinuhe:* Some Reflections," *JARCE* 28, 1991, 133–38.

Morschauser, Scott, "What Made Sinuhe Run: Sinuhe's Reasoned Flight," *JARCE* 37, 2000, 187–98.

Obsomer, Claude, "Sinouhé l'Egyptien et les raisons de sa fuite," *Le Muséon* 112, 1999, 207–71.

Otto, E., "Die Geschichten des Sinuhe und des Schiffbrüchigen als 'Lehrhafte Stücke,'" *ZÄS* 93, 1966, 100–111.

Parant, Robert, *L'Affaire Sinouhé: Tentative d'approche de la justice répressive égyptienne au début du II millénaire av, J.C.,* Aurillac, 1982. Review by Elke Blumenthal in *BiOr* 84, 1989, 149–51.

Parkinson, R. B., "Individual and Society in Middle Kingdom Literature," in A. Loprieno, ed., *Ancient Egyptian Literature: History and Forms,* 1996, 137–55.

——, *The Tale of Sinuhe and Other Ancient Egyptian Poems, 1940–1640 BC,* Oxford, 1997, 21–53.

Patané, Massimo, "Quelques remarques sur Sinouhé," *BSEG* 13, 1989, 131–33.

Purdy, S., "Sinuhe and the Question of Literary Types," *ZÄS* 104, 1977, 12–37.

Sander-Hansen, C. E., "Bemerkungen zu der Sinuhe-Erzählung, *Acta Orientalia* 22, 1957, 142–49.

Schenkel, W., *Grundformen mitteläg: Sätze anhand der Sinuhe-Erzählung,* MÄS 7, Munich, 1965.

Schneider, Thomas, "Sinuhe's Notiz über die Könige; Syrisch-Anatolische Herrschertitel in Ägyptischer Überlieferung," *Aegypten und Levante* 12, 2002, 257–272.

Shirin-Grumach, Irene, "Sinuhe R 24—Wer rief?" in F. Junge, ed., *Studien zu Sprache und Religion Ägyptens: zu Ehren Wolfhart Westendorf,* Band I: Sprache, Göttingen, 1984, 621–29. *njs.n.tw* (*tw* = Ses. I). Note references, esp. to Dechain, *RdE* 22, 1970, 79–83, Westendorf, *SAK* 5, 1977, 293–304, on Besänftigungslied.

Spalinger, Anthony, "Orientations on *Sinuhe,*" *SAK* 25, 1998, 311–39.

Théodoridès, A., "L'Amnistie et la raison d'état dans 'Les Aventures de Sinouhé' (début du IIe millénaire acv J.-C.)," *Revue internationale des droits de l'antiquité,* 3d ser., 31, 1984, 75–144.

Tobin, Vincent A., "The Secret of Sinuhe," *JARCE* 32, 1995, 161–78.

Vandersleyen, Claude, "Sinouhé B 221," *RdE* 26, 1974, 117–21.

Wessetzky, Vlimos, "Sinuhe's Flucht," *ZÄS* 90, 1963, 124–27. Indicates that the flight was motivated by Sinuhe's unwillingness to tell the reason for Amenemhet's death, which he had overheard.

Westendorf, Wolfhart, "Sinuhe B 160," in W. Helck, ed., *Festschrift für Siegfried Schott zu seinem 70. Geburtstag,* Wiesbaden, 1968, 125–31.

——, "Noch einmal: Die 'Wiedergeburt' des heimgekehrten Sinuhe," *SAK* 5, 1977, 293–304.

Yoyotte, J., "A propos du panthéon de Sinouhé (B 205–212)," *Kêmi* 17, 1964, 69–73.

Zivie, A. P., "Les carrières et la butte de Yak," *RdE* 30, 1978, 151–62.

Zonhoven, L., "Polotsky, Sinuhe, and the sḏm.n.f," *JEOL* 33, 1993–94, 39–108.

## Si-Osire, Childhood of

Spiegelberg, Wilhelm, *Demotische Texte auf Krügen,* Demotische Studien 5, Leipzig, 1912, 1, 19, 51–52, 57, and pls. 5–6 (repr. Milan, 1977).

Depauw, Mark, *A Companion to Demotic Studies,* Brussels, 1997, 88, 90–91.

Brunner-Traut, Emma, *Altägyptische Märchen,* Düsseldorf and Cologne, 8th ed., Munich, 1989, 264–5 and 345–6.

Roeder, Günther, *Altägyptische Erzählungen und Märchen,* Jena, 1927, 180.

## Swallow and the Sea

Spiegelberg, Wilhelm, *Demotische Texte auf Krügen,* Demotische Studien 5, Leipzig, 1912, 8–11, 16–17, 50–51 (Jug A, text 4, mistakenly labeled "third letter"), and pls. 2–4 (repr. Milan, 1977).

Depauw, Mark, *A Companion to Demotic Studies,* Brussels, 1997, 90–91.

Brunner-Traut, Emma, *Altägyptische Märchen,* 8th ed., Munich, 1989, 161–2 and 317–18.

Collombert, Phillipe, "Une nouvelle lecture du conte de l'hirondelle et la mer," lecture given at the Seventh International Conference of Demotic Studies, Copenhagen, August 24, 1999.

## Tjetji

Scott-Moncrieff, P. D., *Hieroglyphic Texts from Egyptian Stelae &C.,* part 1, London, 1911, 16, pls. 49–50; Clère, J. J., and J. Vandier, *Textes de la Première Période Intermédiaire et de la XIème Dynastie,* 1er Fascicule, Bibliotheca Aegyptiaca 10, Brussels, 1948, no. 20, 15–17.

Blackman, A. M., "The Stele of Thethi, Brit. Mus. No. 614," *JEA* 17, 1931, 55–61.

Schenkel, Wolfgang, *Memphis. Herakleopolis. Theben: Die Epigraphischen Zeugnisse der 7.–11.Dynastie Ägyptens,* ÄAbh 12, Wiesbaden, 1965, 103–7.

## Thutmose III Stela, Poetical Stela

Kurt Sethe, *Urkunden der 18. Dynastie,* Urk. IV, Leipzig, 1927/30, 610–19.

Osing, Jürgen, "Zur 'Poetischen Stele' Thutmosis' III," in Jan Assmann and Elke Blumenthal, eds., *Literatur und Politik im pharaonischen Ägypten,* IFAO, BdE 127, Cairo, 1999, 75–86.

Kitchen, K. A., *Poetry of Ancient Egypt,* Jonsered, 1999, 165–76, with extensive bibliography.

## Truth and Falsehood

Gardiner, Alan H., *Late-Egyptian Stories,* Bibliotheca Aegyptiaca 1, Brussels, 1932, x, 30–36; idem, *Hieratic Papyri in the British Museum,* 3d ser., London, 1935, I, 2–6, II, 14.

Griffiths, J. Gwyn, "Wahrheit und Lüge," *LÄ* VI, 1986, 1140–42.

Coulon, Laurent, "La rhétorique et ses fictions: Pouvoirs et duplicité du discours à travers la littérature égyptienne du Moyen et du Nouvel Empire," *BIFAO* 99, 1999, 103–32.

Lesko, Leonard H., "Three Late Egyptian Stories Reconsidered," in Leonard H. Lesko, ed., *Egyptological Studies in Honor of Richard A. Parker,* Hanover, N.H., 1986, 98–103.

Mathieu, Bernard, "*Vérité et Mensonge,* Un conte égyptien du temps des Ramsès," *Égypte Afrique et Orient* 11, 1998, 27–36.

Spies, Otto, "Eine altägyptische Quelle zum Märchen 'Die Beiden Wanderer' der Brüder Grimm," in Manfred Görg and Edgar Pusch, eds., *Festschrift Elmar Edel,* ÄUAT 1, Bamberg, 1979, 397–408.

## Two Brothers

Gardiner, Alan H., *Late-Egyptian Stories,* Bibliotheca Aegyptiaca 1, Brussels, 1932, ix–x, 9–30.

Brunner-Traut, Emma, "Papyrus D'Orbiney," LÄ IV, 1982, 697–704.

Assmann, Jan, "Das ägyptische Zweibrüdermärchen (Papyrus d'Orbiney): Eine Textanalyse auf drei Ebenen am Leitfaden der Einheitsfrage," *ZÄS* 104, 1977, 1–25.

Blumenthal, Elke, "Die Erzählung des Papyrus d'Orbiney als Literaturwerk," *ZÄS* 99, 1972, 1–17.

Derchain, Philippe, "Le perruque et le cristal," *SAK* 2, 1975, 55–74.

Hollis, Susan Tower, *The Ancient Egyptian "Tale of the Two Brothers": The Oldest Fairy Tale in the World,* Norman, Okla., 1990.

——. "Anubis's Mortuary Functions in the 'Tale of Two Brothers,' " in Terence DuQuesne, ed., *Hermes Aegyptiacus: Egyptological Studies for B. H. Stricker, DE* special no. 2, Oxford, 1995, 87–100.

Katary, Sally L. D., "*The Two Brothers* as Folktale: Constructing the Social Context, *JSSEA* 24, 1994 (pub. 1998), 39–70.

Lesko, Leonard H., "Three Late Egyptian Stories Reconsidered," in Leonard H. Lesko, ed., *Egyptological Studies in Honor of Richard A. Parker,* Hanover, N.H., 1986, 98–103.

Manniche, Lise, "The Wife of Bata," *GM* 18, 1975, 33–38.

Posener, Georges, "La légende de la tresse d'Hathor," in Leonard H.

Lesko, ed., *Egyptological Studies in Honor of Richard A. Parker,* Hanover, N.H., 1986, 111–17.

Rowinska, E., and J. K. Winnicki, "Zur Interpretation von Pap. d'Orbiney 4,10: Die Bedeutung von *bsj,*" *GM* 134, 1993, 85–89.

Schuler, François, *Conte des deux frères suivi de Le mari trompé,* Mayenne, 1999.

Westendorf, Wolfhart, "Pap. d'Orbiney 4,6: Die angeblich wundgeprügelte Frau und das angebliche Fremdwort *pdr* 'Fett,'" *BSEG* 5, 1981, 57–60.

——, "... und durch Liebe (pD'Orbiney 7,8 frei nach Schiller)," in Betsy M. Bryan and David Lorton, eds., *Essays in Egyptology in Honor of Hans Goedicke,* San Antonio, 1994, 349–352.

Wettengel, Wolfgang, "Zur Rubrengliederung der Erzählung von den zwei Brüdern," *GM* 126, 1992, 97–106.


Wenamon

Gardiner, Alan H., *Late-Egyptian Stories,* Bibliotheca Aegyptiaca 1, Brussels, 1932, xi–xii, 61–76; Korostovtsev, M. A., *Puteshestviye Un-Amuna v Bibl. Egipetskiy iyeraticheskiy papirus no 120 Gosudarstvennogo muzeya izobrazitel'nykh iskusstv im. A. S. Pushkina v Moskve,* Moscow, 1960.

Helck, Wolfgang, "Wenamun," *LÄ* VI, 1986, 1215–16.


Baines, John, "On *Wenamun* as a Literary Text," in Jan Assmann and Elke Blumenthal, eds., *Literatur und Politik im pharaonischen Ägypten,* IFAO, BdE 127, Cairo, 1999, 209–33.

Blumenthal, Elke, *Altägyptische Reiseerzählungen: Die Lebensgeschichte des Sinuhe. Der Reisebericht des Wen-Amun,* Leipzig, 1982.

Bunnens, Guy, "La Mission d'Ounamoun en Phénicie: Point de vue d'un non-égyptologue," *Rivista di Studi Fenici* 6, Rome, 1978, 1–16.

——, *L'expansion phénicienne en Méditerranée: Essai d'interprétation fondé sur une analyse des traditions littéraires,* Brussels, 1979, chap. 2.

Cody, Aelred, "The Phoenician Ecstatic in Wenamun: A Professional Oracular Medium," *JEA* 65, 1979, 99–106.

Ebach, Jürgen H., and Udo Rüterswörden, "Der byblitische Ekstatiker im Bericht des *Wn-Imn* und die Seher in der Inschrift des *ZKR* von Hamath," *GM* 20, 1976, 17–22.

Egberts, Arno, "The Chronology of *The Report of Wenamun*," *JEA* 77, 1991, 57–67.

——, "Hard Times: The Chronology of 'The Report of Wenamun' Revised," *ZÄS* 125, 1998, 93–108.

——, "Double Dutch in *The Report of Wenamun*, *GM* 172, 1999, 17–22. A response to Satzinger's article (see below).

Eyre, Christopher J., "Irony in the Story of Wenamun: The Politics of Religion in the 21st Dynasty," in Jan Assmann and Elke Blumenthal, eds., *Literatur und Politik im pharaonischen Ägypten,* IFAO, BdE 127, Cairo, 1999, 235–52.

Haller, Friedrich, "Miszelle: Widerlegung der allgemeinen Annahme, der Bericht des Wenamun (Papyrus Moskau, nr. 120) breche gegen Ende unvermittelt ab und der Schuß sei veloren," *GM* 173, 1999, 9.

Gardiner, Sir Alan, *Egypt of the Pharaohs,* Oxford, 1961, 306–13.

Goedicke, Hans, *The Report of Wenamun,* Baltimore, 1975.

Görg, Manfred, "Der Ekstatiker von Byblos," *GM* 23, 1977, 31–33.

Graefe, Erhart, "Die letzte Zeile des 'Wenamun,'" *GM* 188, 2002, 73–75.

Green, Michael, "Wenamun's Demand for Compensation," *ZÄS* 106, 1979, 116–20.

——, "*m-k-m-r* und *w-r-k-t-r* in der Wenamun-Geschichte," *ZÄS* 113, 1986, 115–19.

Hornung, Erik, "Sinuhe und Wenamun—zwei ägyptische Wanderer," *Eranos,* N.F. 3, 1995, 55–65.

Jackson, Howard M., " 'The Shadow of Pharaoh, Your Lord, Falls upon You': Once Again *Wenamun* 2.46," *JNES* 54, 1995, 273–86.

Meltzer, E. S., "Wenamun 2, 46," *JSSEA* 17, 1987, 86–88.

Moers, Gerald, "Die Reiseerzählung des Wenamun," in Otto Kaiser, ed., TUAT III/5, Mythen und Epen III, Gütersloh, 1995, 912–21.

Morschauser, Scott N., " 'Crying to the Lebanon': A Note on Wenamun 2,13–14," *SAK* 18, 1991, 317–30.

Nibbi, Allesandra, "The City of Dor and Wenamun," *DE* 35, 1996, 77–95.

——, "Wenamun without Cyprus," *DE* 53, 2002, 71–74.

Nims, Charles F., "Second Tenses in Wenamun," *JEA* 54, 1968, 161–64.

Posener, Georges, "L'extatique d'Ounamon, 1 38–40," *RdE* 21, 1969, 147.

——, "À propos d'Ounamon 2, 21–22," in Sarah Israelit-Groll, ed., *Studies in Egyptology Presented to Miriam Lichtheim* II, Jerusalem, 1990, 773–75.

Satzinger, Helmut, "How Good Was Tjeker-Ba'l's Egyptian?" *Lingua Aegyptia* 5, 1997, 171–76.

Scheepers, Anne, "Anthroponymes et toponymes du récit d'Ounamon," in E. Lipiński, ed., *Phoenicia and the Bible,* OLA 44, 1991, 17–83.

——, "Le voyage d'Ounamon: un texte 'littéraire' ou 'non-littéraire'?" in Claude Obsomer and Ann-Laure Oosthoek, eds., *Amosiadès: Mélanges offerts au Professeur Claude Vandersleyen par ses anciens étudiants,* Louvain-la-Neuve, 1992, 355–65.

Spens, Renaud de, "Droit international et commerce au début de la XXIe dynastie: Analyse juridique du rapport d'Ounamon," in Nicolas Grimal and Bernadette Menu, eds., *Le commerce en Egypte ancienne,* IFAO, BdE 121, 1998, 105–26.

Winand, Jean, "Derechef Ounamon 2,13–14," *GM* 139, 1994, 95–108.

——, *Le Voyage d'Ounamoun: Index verborum, Concordance, Relevés grammaticaux,* Aegyptiaca Leodiensia 1, Liège, 1987.

## Weni the Elder

Sethe, K., *Urkunden des alten Reichs,* Urk. I, 2d ed., Leipzig, 1932, 98–110.

Roccati, A., "Uni," *LÄ* VI, 1985, 851–52.

Breasted, J. H., BAR I, 1906, 143–44.

Doret, Eric, *The Narrative Verbal System of Old and Middle Egyptian,* Geneva, 1986. Virtually the entire text is translated and commented upon in the examples of verbal forms cited. See index on p. 191.

Edel, Elmar, "Inschriften des alten Reiches. XI," *ZÄS* 85, 1959, 18–23.

El-Khadragy, Mahmoud, "Some Palaeographical Features of Weni's Biography," *GM* 188, 2002, 61–72.

Eyre, C. J., "Weni's Career and Old Kingdom Historiography," in C. J. Eyre, Anthony Leahy, and Lisa Montagno Leahy, eds., *The Unbroken Reed: Studies in the Culture and Heritage of Ancient Egypt in Honour of A. F. Shore,* London, 1994, 106–24.

Hofmann, Tobias, "Die Autobiographie des Uni von Abydos," *Lingua Aegyptia* 10, 2002, 225–237.

Klothe, Nicole, "Beobachtungen zu den biographischen Inschriften des alten Reiches," *SAK* 25, 1998, 189–205.

Osing, Jürgen, "Zur Syntax der Biographie der *Wnj*," *Orientalia* 46, 1977, 165–82.

Piacentini, P. *L'autobiografie di Uni, principe e governatore dell alto Egitto,* Pisa, 1990.

Richards, Janet, "Quest for Weni the Elder," *Archaeology* 54, no. 3, 2001, 48–49.

Roccati, A., "I tempi narrativi nella biografia di *Wnj*," *RSO* 37, 1962, 33–38.

——, *La Littérature historique sous l'ancien Empire égyptien,* Paris, 1982, 187–97. See also entries under Autobiographies, above.